Men's Lives

Men's Lives

Tenth Edition

Michael S. Kimmel
*State University of
New York–Stony Brook*

Michael A. Messner
*University of
Southern California*

New York   Oxford
OXFORD UNIVERSITY PRESS

Oxford University Press is a department of the University of Oxford.
It furthers the University's objective of excellence in research, scholarship,
and education by publishing worldwide. Oxford is a registered trade mark of
Oxford University Press in the UK and certain other countries.

Published in the United States of America by Oxford University Press
198 Madison Avenue, New York, NY 10016, United States of America.

© 2019 by Oxford University Press
© 2013, 2010, 2007, 2004, 2001 by Pearson Education, Inc.

This book was previously published by: Pearson Education, Inc.

For titles covered by Section 112 of the US Higher Education
Opportunity Act, please visit www.oup.com/us/he for the latest
information about pricing and alternate formats.

Cataloging-in-Publication data is on file at the Library of Congress
ISBN 9780190698232

9 8 7 6 5 4 3 2 1
Printed by LSC Communications, United States of America

CONTENTS

* Indicates new to this edition.

For more than three decades, we have taught courses on men's lives that have reflected both our own education and a growing body of research by feminist scholars and profeminist men in the United States and, increasingly, around the world. (By profeminist men, we mean active supporters of women's efforts against men's violence and claims for equal opportunity, political participation, sexual autonomy, family reform, and equal education.) Gender, scholars have demonstrated, is a central feature of social life—one of the chief organizing principles around which our lives revolve. Gender shapes our identities, our relationships, and the institutions in which we find ourselves. Since the early 1970s, women's studies programs and courses have explored the meaning of gender in women's lives. But what does it mean to be a man today?

This anthology is organized around specific themes that define masculinity and the issues men confront over the course of their lives. We deploy a social constructionist perspective that examines how men actively construct masculinity within social and historical contexts. Our examination also highlights the ways in which social class, race, sexuality, or national origin intersects with gender to shape different masculinities.

We begin Part I with issues and questions that unravel the *masculine mystique* and reveal various dimensions of men's position in society and their relationships with women and with other men. The subsequent sections of the book examine a range of issues that emerge for boys and men at different times of their lives. We touch on central moments related to boyhood, adolescence, sports, occupations, religion, families, and fatherhood. We explore men's emotional and sexual relationships with women and with other men and the ways in which masculinities are shaped and portrayed in mass media and popular culture. We also include a section on violence and masculinities, because violence remains the single behavior, attitude, or trait for which there are overwhelming, significant, and seemingly intractable gender differences. The final two sections of the book examine politics and social change, ending with a timely focus on how increasing numbers of men are joining with women to move our relationships, institutions, nation, and world in more peaceful and egalitarian directions.

Although a major component of the dominant definition of masculinity is independence, we are pleased to acknowledge those whose criticism and support have been a constant help throughout our work on the many iterations of *Men's Lives*. Colleagues at the State University of New York at Stony Brook, the Center for the Study of Men and Masculinities, and the University of Southern California have been supportive of this project. Sherith Pankratz and Grace Li, our editorial directors at Oxford University Press, inherited this project and have embraced it as their own, facilitating our work at every turn. For this edition, Sophia Boutelier provided judicious editing of the selections. Chris Cardone and Bruce Nichols, our original editors, and later Karen Hanson and Jeff Lasser, were supportive through the first nine editions of this book. Many other scholars whose past or current work on masculinities, including Maxine Baca Zinn, Bob Blauner, Robert Brannon, Tristan Bridges, Harry Brod, Rocco Capraro, Raewyn Connell, James Harrison, Adia Harvey Wingfield, Jeff Hearn, Michael Kaufman, Jim McKay, Patricia Yancey Martin, Jim Messerschmidt, Rob Okun, C. J. Pascoe, Joe Pleck, Tony Rotundo, Don Sabo, and Peter Stein, have contributed to a supportive intellectual community in which to work. We dedicate this tenth edition of *Men's Lives* to our friend Harry Brod, a pioneer in the study of men and masculinities who passed away in 2017. Harry inspired us with his profeminist activism and deepened our thinking with his sophisticated writings on masculinities.

Our families, friends, and colleagues have provided a rare atmosphere that combines intellectual challenge and emotional support. We want especially to acknowledge our fathers and mothers for providing such important models of being adults capable of career competence, emotional warmth, and nurturance (which should be considered neither masculine nor feminine traits).

Thanks to all of the people who reviewed this text: John Bartkowski, University of Texas at San Antonio; Dana Berkowitz, Louisiana State University; Adriane Brown, Augsburg College; Gordon Fellman, Brandeis University; Todd Migliaccio, California State University—Sacramento; Harmony Newman, University of Northern Colorado; Robert Strikwerda, Saint Louis University; Charlene Tung, Sonoma State University; Lisa Udel, Illinois College; and Anthony Vega, Washington State University.

Finally, we thank Amy Aronson and Pierrette Hondagneu-Sotelo, who have chosen to share our lives, and our sons, who didn't have much choice in it. Together, they fill our lives with so much joy.

M. S. K.
M. A. M.

This is a book about men. But unlike other books about men, which line countless library shelves, this is a book about men as men. It is a book in which men's experiences are not taken for granted as we explore the "real" and significant accomplishments of men, but a book in which those experiences are treated as significant and important in themselves.

MEN AS GENDERED BEINGS

But what does it mean to examine men *as men*? Most courses in a college curriculum are about men, aren't they? But these courses routinely deal with men only in their public roles, so we come to know and understand men as scientists, politicians, military figures, writers, and philosophers. Rarely, if ever, are men understood through the prism of gender.

But listen to some male voices from some of these "ungendered" courses. Take, for example, composer Charles Ives, debunking sissy types of music; he said he used traditional tough-guy themes and concerns in his drive to build new sounds and structures out of the popular musical idiom (cf. Wilkinson 1986, 103). Or architect Louis Sullivan, describing his ambition to create "masculine forms": strong, solid, commanding respect. Or novelist Ernest Hemingway, retaliating against literary enemies by portraying them as impotent or homosexual.

Consider also political figures, such as Cardinal Richelieu, the seventeenth-century French first minister to Louis XIII, who insisted that it was "necessary to have masculine virtue and do everything by reason" (cited in Elliott 1984, 20). Closer to home, recall President Lyndon Baines Johnson's dismissal of a political adversary: "Oh him. He has to squat to piss!" Or President Johnson's boast that during the Tet Offensive in the Vietnam War, he "didn't just screw Ho Chi Minh. I cut his pecker off!"

Democrats have no monopoly on unexamined gender coloring their political rhetoric. Indeed, recent political campaigns have revolved, in part, around gender issues, as each candidate attempted to demonstrate that he was not a wimp but a "real man." (Female politicians face the double task of convincing the electorate that they are not the "weak-willed wimps" that their gender implies in the public mind while simultaneously demonstrating that they are "real women.")

These are just a few examples of what we might call gendered speech, language that uses gender terms to make its case. And these are just a few of the thousands of examples one could find in every academic discipline of how men's lives are organized around gender issues and how gender remains one of the organizing principles of social life. We come to know ourselves and our world through the prism of gender—but we act as if we didn't know it.

Fortunately, in recent years, the pioneering work of feminist scholars, both in traditional disciplines and in women's studies, and that of feminist women in the political arena has made us aware of the centrality of gender in our lives. In the social sciences, gender has now taken its place alongside class and race as one of the three central mechanisms by which power and resources are distributed in our society and the three central themes from which we fashion the meanings of our lives.

We certainly understand how this works for women. Through women's studies courses and also in courses about women in traditional disciplines, students have explored the complexity of women's lives, the hidden history of exemplary women, and the daily experiences of women in the routines of their lives. For women, we know how gender works as one of the formative elements out of which social life is organized.

THE INVISIBILITY OF GENDER: A SOCIOLOGICAL EXPLANATION

Too often, however, we treat men as if they had no gender, as if only their public personae were of interest to us as students and scholars, as if their interior experience of gender was of no significance. This became evident when one of us was in a graduate seminar on feminist theory several years ago. A discussion between a white woman and a black woman revolved around the question of whether their similarities as women were greater than their racial differences as black and white. The white woman asserted that the fact that they were both women bonded them, despite their racial differences. The black woman disagreed.

"When you wake up in the morning and look in the mirror, what do you see?" she asked.

"I see a woman," replied the white woman.

"That's precisely the issue," replied the black woman. "I see a black woman. For me, race is visible every day, because it is how I am not privileged in this culture. Race is invisible to you, which is why our alliance will always seem somewhat false to me."

Witnessing this exchange, Michael Kimmel was startled. When he looked in the mirror in the morning, he saw, as he put it, "a human being: universally generalizable. The generic person." What had been concealed—that he possessed both race and gender—had become strikingly visible. As a white man, he was able not to think about the ways in which gender and race had affected his experiences.

There is a sociological explanation for this blind spot in our thinking: the mechanisms that afford us privilege are often invisible to us. What makes us marginal (unempowered, oppressed) are the mechanisms that we understand, because those are the ones that are most painful in daily life. Thus, white people rarely think of themselves as *raced* people and rarely think of race as a central element in their experience. But people of color are marginalized by race, and so the centrality of race both is painfully obvious and needs study urgently. Similarly, middle-class people do not acknowledge the importance of social class as an organizing principle of social life, largely because, for them, class is an invisible force that makes everyone look pretty much the same. Working-class people, in contrast, are often painfully aware of the centrality of class in their lives. (Interestingly, upper-class people are often more aware of class dynamics than are middle-class people. In part, this may be the result of the emphasis on status within the upper class, as lineage, breeding, and family honor take center stage. In part, it may also be the result of a peculiar marginalization of the upper class in our society, as in the overwhelming number of television shows and movies that are ostensibly about just plain [i.e., middle-class] folks.)

In this same way, men often think of themselves as genderless, as if gender did not matter in the daily experiences of our lives. Certainly, we can see the biological sex of individuals, but we rarely understand the ways in which *gender*—that complex of social meanings that is attached to biological sex—is enacted in our daily lives. For example, we treat male scientists as if their being men had nothing to do with the organization of their experiments, the logic of scientific inquiry, or the questions posed by science itself. We treat male political figures as if masculinity were not even remotely in their consciousness as they do battle in the political arena. This book takes a position directly opposed to such genderlessness for men. We believe that men are also *gendered* and that this gendering process, the transformation of biological males into socially interacting men, is a central experience for men. That we are unaware of it only helps to perpetuate the inequalities based on gender in our society. In this book, we examine the various ways in which men are gendered. We have gathered together some of the most interesting, engaging, and convincing materials from the past decade that have been written about men. We believe that *Men's Lives* will allow readers to explore the meanings of masculinity in contemporary US culture in a new way.

EARLIER EFFORTS TO STUDY MEN

Certainly, researchers have been examining masculinity for a long time. Historically, three general models have governed social scientific research on men and masculinity. *Biological models* have focused on the ways in which innate biological differences between males and females program different social behaviors. *Anthropological models* have examined masculinity cross-culturally, stressing the variations in the behaviors and attributes associated with being a man. And earlier *sociological models* have stressed how socialization of boys and girls includes accommodation to a *sex role* specific to one's biological sex. Although each of these perspectives helps us to understand the meaning of masculinity and femininity, each is also limited in its ability to explain fully how gender operates in any culture.

Relying on differences in reproductive biology, some scholars have argued that the physiological organization of males and females makes inevitable the differences we observe in psychological temperament and social behaviors. One perspective holds that differences in endocrine functioning are the cause of gender difference, that testosterone predisposes males toward aggression, competition, and violence, whereas estrogen predisposes females toward passivity, tenderness, and exaggerated emotionality. Others insist that these observed behavioral variances derive from the differences between the size or number of sperm and eggs. Since a male can produce one hundred million sperm with each ejaculation, whereas a female can produce fewer than two hundred eggs capable of producing healthy offspring over the course of her life, these authors suggest that men's "investment" in their offspring is significantly less than that of women. Other authors arrive at the same conclusion by suggesting that the different size of egg and sperm, and the fact that the egg is the source of the food supply, impels temperamental differences. Reproductive "success" to males means the insemination of as many females as possible; to females, reproductive success means carefully choosing one male to mate with and insisting that he remain present to care for and support their offspring. Still other authors argue that male and female behavior is governed by different halves of the brain: males are ruled by the left hemisphere, which controls rationality and abstract thought, whereas females are governed by the right hemisphere, which controls emotional affect and creativity. (For examples of these works, see Trivers 1972; Goldberg 1975; Wilson 1976; and Goldberg 1986.)

Observed normative temperamental differences between women and men that are assumed to be of biological origin are easily translated into political prescriptions. In this ideological sleight of hand, what is normative (i.e., what is prescribed) is translated into what is normal, and the mechanisms of this transformation are the assumed biological imperative. George Gilder, for example, assembles the putative biological differences between women and men into a call for a return to traditional gender roles. Gilder believes that male sexuality is, by nature, wild and lusty, insistent and incessant, careening out of control and threatening anarchic disorder, unless it can be controlled and constrained. This is the task of women. When women refuse to apply the brakes to male sexuality—by asserting their own or by choosing to pursue a life outside the domestic sphere—they abandon their "natural" function for illusory social gains. Sex education, abortion, and birth control are all condemned as facilitating women's escape from biological necessity. Similarly, Gilder argues against women's employment, since the "unemployed man can contribute little to the community and will often disrupt it, but the woman may even do more good without a job than with one" (Gilder 1986, 86).

The biological argument has been challenged by many scholars on several grounds. The implied causation between two observed sets of differences (biological differences and different behaviors) is misleading, since there is no logical reason to assume that one caused the other or that the line of causation moves only from the biological to the social. The selection of biological evidence is partial, and generalizations from lower animal species to human beings are always suspect. One sociologist asks, if these differences are natural, why must their enforcement be coercive, and why must males and females be forced to assume the rules that they are naturally supposed to play (see Epstein 1986, 8)? And one primatologist argues that the evidence adduced to support the current status quo might also lead to precisely the opposite conclusions, that biological differences would impel female promiscuity and male fragility (see Hrdy 1981). Biological differences between males and females would appear to set some parameters for differences in social behavior, but would not dictate the temperaments of men and women in any one culture. These psychological and social differences would appear to be the result far more of the ways in which cultures interpret, shape, and modify these biological inheritances. We may be born males or females, but we become men and women in a cultural context.

Anthropologists have entered the debate at this point, but with different positions. For example, some anthropologists have suggested that the universality of gender differences comes from specific cultural adaptations to the environment, whereas others describe the cultural variations of gender roles, seeking to demonstrate the fluidity of gender and the primacy of cultural organization. Lionel Tiger and Robin Fox argue that the sexual division of labor is universal because of the different nature of bonding for males and females. "Nature," they argue, "intended mother and child to be together" because she is the source of emotional security and food; thus, cultures have prescribed various behaviors for women that emphasize nurturance and emotional connection (Tiger and Fox 1984, 304). The bond between men is forged through the necessity of *competitive cooperation* in hunting; men must cooperate with members of their own tribe in the hunt and yet compete for scarce resources with men in other tribes. Such bonds predispose men toward the organization of the modern corporation or governmental bureaucracy.

Such anthropological arguments omit as much as they include, and many scholars have pointed out problems with the model. Why didn't intelligence become sex linked, as this model (and the biological model) would imply? Such positions also reveal a marked conservatism: the differences between women and men are the differences that nature or cultural evolution intended and are therefore not to be tampered with.

Perhaps the best-known challenge to this anthropological argument is the work of Margaret Mead. Mead insisted that the variations among cultures in their prescriptions of gender roles required the conclusion that culture was the more decisive cause of these differences. In her classic study *Sex and Temperament in Three Primitive Societies* (1935), Mead observed such wide variability among gender role prescriptions—and such marked differences from our own—that any universality implied by biological or anthropological models had to be rejected. And although the empirical accuracy of Mead's work has been challenged in its specific arguments, the general theoretical arguments remain convincing.

Psychological theories have also contributed to the discussion of gender roles, as psychologists have specified the developmental sequences for both males and females. Earlier theorists observed psychological distancing from the mother as the precondition for independence and autonomy or suggested a sequence that placed the capacity for abstract reason as the developmental stage beyond relational reasoning. Because it is normative for males to exhibit independence and the capacity for abstract reason, it was argued that males are more successful at negotiating these psychological passages and implied that women somehow lagged behind men on the ladder of developmental success. (Such arguments may be found in the work of Freud, Erikson, and Kohlberg.)

But these models, too, have been challenged by sociologist Nancy Chodorow (1978), who argued that women's ability to connect contains a more fundamentally human trait than the male's need to distance, and by psychologist Carol Gilligan (1982), who claimed that women's predisposition toward relational reasoning may contain a more humane strategy of thought than recourse to abstract principles. Regardless of our assessment of these arguments, Chodorow and Gilligan rightly point out that the highly ideological assumptions that make masculinity the normative standard against which the psychological development of both males and females was measured would inevitably make femininity problematic and less fully developed. Moreover, Chodorow explicitly insists that these "essential" differences between women and men are socially constructed and therefore subject to change.

Sociologists of the 1960s and 1970s attempted to synthesize these three perspectives into a systematic explanation of *sex roles*. These roles are the collection of attitudes, attributes, and behaviors that is seen as appropriate for males and appropriate for females. Thus, masculinity is associated with technical mastery, aggression, competitiveness, and cognitive abstraction, whereas femininity is associated with emotional nurturance, connectedness, and passivity. Sex role theory informed a wide variety of prescriptive literature (self-help books) that instructed parents on what to do if they wanted their child to grow up as a healthy boy or girl.

The strongest challenge to all these perspectives, as we have seen, has come from feminist scholars, who have specified the ways in which the assumptions about maturity, development, and health all made masculinity the norm against which both genders were measured. In all the social sciences, these feminist scholars have stripped these early studies of their academic facades to reveal the unexamined ideological assumptions contained within them. By the early 1970s, women's studies programs began to articulate a new paradigm for the study of gender, one that assumed nothing about men or women beforehand and that made no assumptions about which gender was more highly developed. And by the mid-1970s, the first group of texts about men appeared that had been inspired by these pioneering efforts by feminist scholars.

THINKING ABOUT MEN: THE FIRST GENERATION

In the mid-1970s, the first group of works on men and masculinity appeared that was directly influenced by these feminist critiques of the traditional explanations for gender differences. Some books underscored the costs to men of traditional gender role prescriptions, exploring how some aspects of men's lives and experiences are constrained and underdeveloped by the relentless pressure to exhibit other behaviors associated with masculinity. Books such as Marc Feigen-Fasteau's *The Male Machine* (1974) and Warren Farrell's *The Liberated Man* (1975) discussed the costs to men's health—both physical and psychological—and to the quality of relationships with women, other men, and their children of the traditional male sex role.

Several anthologies explored the meanings of masculinity in the United States by adopting a feminist-inspired prism through which to view men and masculinity. For example, Deborah David and Robert Brannon's *The Forty-Nine Percent Majority* (1976) and Joseph Pleck and Jack Sawyer's *Men and Masculinity* (1974) presented panoramic views of men's lives from within a framework that accepted the feminist critique of traditional gender arrangements. Elizabeth Pleck and Joseph Pleck's *The American Man* (1980) suggested a historical evolution of contemporary themes. These works explored both the costs and the privileges of being a man in modem US society.

Perhaps the single most important book to criticize the normative organization of the male sex role was Joseph Pleck's *The Myth of Masculinity* (1981). Pleck carefully deconstructed the constituent elements of the male sex role and reviewed the empirical literature for each component part. After demonstrating that the empirical literature did not support these normative features, Pleck argued that the male sex role model was incapable of describing men's experiences. In its place, he posited a male *sex role strain* model that specified the contemporary sex role as problematic, historically specific, and also an unattainable ideal.

Building on Pleck's work, a critique of the sex role model began to emerge. Sex roles had been cast as the static containers of behaviors and attitudes, and biological males and females were required to fit themselves into these containers, regardless of how ill-fitting the clusters of behaviors and attitudes felt. Such a model was ahistorical and suggested a false cultural universalism, and therefore it was ill-equipped to help us understand the ways in which sex roles change and the ways in which individuals modify those roles through the enactments of gender expectations. Most telling, however, was how the sex role model ignored the ways in which definitions of masculinity and femininity were based on, and reproduced, relationships of power. Not only do men as a group exert power over women as a group, but also the definitions of masculinity and femininity reproduce those power relations. Power dynamics are an essential element in both the definition and the enactments of gender.

This first generation of research on masculinity was extremely valuable, particularly since it challenged the unexamined ideology that made masculinity the gender norm against which both men and women were measured. The old models of sex roles had reproduced the domination of men over women by insisting on the dominance of masculine traits over feminine traits. These new studies argued against both the definitions of either sex and the social institutions in which those differences were embedded. Shapers of the new model looked at "gender relations" and understood how the definition of either masculinity or femininity was relational, that is, how the definition of one gender depended, in part, on the understanding of the definition of the other.

In the early 1980s, the research on women again surged ahead of the research on men and masculinity. This time, however, the focus was not on the ways in which sex roles reproduce the power relations in society, but rather on the ways in which femininity is experienced differently by women in various social groups. Gradually, the notion of a single femininity—which was based on the white middle-class Victorian notion of female passivity, languorous beauty, and emotional responsiveness—was replaced by an examination of the ways in which women differ in their gender role expectations by race, class, age, sexual orientation, ethnicity, region, and nationality.

The research on men and masculinity is now entering a new stage, in which the variations among men are seen as central to the understanding of men's lives. The unexamined assumption in earlier studies had been that one version of masculinity—white, middle-aged, middle-class, heterosexual—was the sex role into which all men were struggling to fit in our society. Thus, working-class men, men of color, gay men, and younger and older men were all observed as departing in significant ways from the traditional definitions of masculinity. Therefore, it was easy to see these men as enacting "problematic" or "deviant" versions of masculinity. Such theoretical assertions, however, reproduce precisely the power relationships that keep these men in subordinate positions in our society. Not only does middle-class, middle-aged, heterosexual white masculinity become the standard against which all men are measured, but also this definition, itself, is used against those who do not fit as a way to keep them down. The normative definition of masculinity is not the "right" one, but it is the one that is dominant.

The challenge to the hegemonic definition of masculinity came from men whose masculinity was cast as deviant: men of color, gay men, and ethnic men. We understand now that we cannot speak of *masculinity* as a singular term, but must examine *masculinities*: the ways in which different men construct different versions of masculinity. Such a perspective emerged in several works of the late 1980s, such as Harry Brod's *The Making of Masculinities* (1987), Michael Kimmel's *Changing Men: New Directions in Research on Men and Masculinity* (1987), and Tim Carrigan, R. W. Connell, and John Lee's "Toward a New Sociology of Masculinity" (1985). Raewyn Connell's *Gender and Power* (1987) and Jeff Hearn's *The Gender of Oppression* (1987). Connell argues that the oppression of women is a chief mechanism that links the various masculinities and that the marginalization of certain masculinities is an important component of the reproduction of male power over women. This critique of the hegemonic definition of masculinity as a perspective on men's lives is one of the organizing principles of our book, the first edition of which (in 1989) was the first college-level text in this second generation of work on men and masculinities. Now that we have reviewed some of the traditional explanations for gender relations and have situated this book within the research on gender in general, and men in particular, let us briefly outline exactly the theoretical perspective we have employed in the book.

THE SOCIAL CONSTRUCTION OF MASCULINITIES

Men are not born, growing from infants through boyhood to manhood, to follow a predetermined biological imperative encoded in their physical organization. To be a man is to participate in social life as a man, as a gendered being. Men are not born; they are made. And men make themselves, actively constructing their masculinities within a social and historical context.

This book is about how men are made and how men make themselves in contemporary US society. It is about what masculinity means, about how different masculinities are organized, and about the social institutions that sustain and elaborate them. It is a book in which we will trace what it means to be a man, for a range of boys and men, over the course of their lives.

Men's Lives revolves around three important themes that are part of a social scientific perspective. First, we have adopted a social constructionist perspective. By this, we mean that the important fact of men's lives is not that they are biological males, but that they become men. Our sex may be male, but our identity as men is developed through a complex process of interaction with the culture in which we both learn the gender scripts appropriate to our culture and attempt to modify those scripts to make them more palatable. The second axis around which the book is organized follows from our social constructionist perspective. As we have argued, the experience of masculinity is not uniform and universally generalizable to all men in our society. Masculinity differs dramatically in our society, and we have organized the book to illustrate the variations among men in the construction of masculinity. Third, we have adopted a life-course perspective, to chart the construction of these various masculinities in men's lives and to examine pivotal developmental moments or institutional locations during a man's life in which the meanings of masculinity are articulated. Social constructionism, variations among men, and the life-course perspective define the organization of this book and the criteria we have used to select the articles included.

The Social Constructionist Model

A social constructionist perspective argues that the meaning of masculinity is neither transhistorical nor culturally universal, but rather varies from culture to culture and within any one culture over time. Thus, males become men in the United States in the early twenty-first century in a way that is very different from men in Southeast Asia, or Kenya, or Sri Lanka.

Men's lives also vary within any one culture over time. The experience of masculinity in the contemporary United States is very different from the experience 150 years ago. Who would argue that what it meant to be a real man in seventeenth-century France (at least among the upper classes)—high-heeled patent leather shoes, red velvet jackets covering frilly white lace shirts, lots of rouge and white powder makeup, and a taste for the elegant refinement of ornate furniture—bears much resemblance to the meaning of masculinity among a similar class of French men today?

A perspective that emphasizes the social construction of gender is, therefore, both historical and comparative. It allows us to explore the ways in which the meanings of gender vary from culture to culture, how they change within any one culture over historical time, and even over the course of an individual's life, as we are learning from the experiences of transgender and gender-non-conforming people.

Variations Among Men

Masculinity also varies within any one society according to the various types of cultural groups that compose it. Subcultures are organized around other poles, which are the primary way in which people organize themselves and by which resources are distributed. And men's experiences differ from one another according to what social scientists have identified as the chief structural mechanisms along which power and resources are distributed. We cannot speak of masculinity in the United States as if it were a single, easily identifiable commodity. To do so is to risk positing one version of masculinity as normative and thus rendering all other masculinities problematic.

In the contemporary United States, masculinity is constructed differently by class culture, by race and ethnicity, and by age. And each of these axes of masculinity modifies the others. Black masculinities differ from white masculinities, and are also further modified by class and age. A thirty-year-old middle-class black man will have some things in common with a thirty-year-old middle-class white man that he might not share with a sixty-year-old working-class black man, although he is also likely to share with the latter man elements of masculinity that are different from those of the white man of his same class and age. The resulting matrix of masculinities is complicated by cross-cutting elements; without understanding this, we risk collapsing all masculinities into one hegemonic version. Our inquiries into men's lives must therefore be *intersectional*: we must be cognizant of the ways in which race or class or sexuality or age or religion or region—or a host of other axes around which we construct our identities— each modifies and shapes our experience of masculinity. And, at the same time, we must be cognizant of the ways that masculinities also shape our experiences of race and class and the like.

The challenge to a singular definition of masculinity as the normative definition is the second axis around which the readings in this book revolve.

The Life-Course Perspective

The meaning of masculinity is not constant over the course of any man's life but will change as he grows and matures. The issues confronting a man about proving himself and feeling successful and the social institutions in which he will attempt to enact his definitions of masculinity will change throughout his life. Therefore, we have adopted a life-course perspective to discuss the ways in which different issues will emerge for men at different times of their lives and the ways in which men's lives, themselves, change over time. The life-course perspective that we have employed will examine men's lives at various pivotal moments in their development from young boys to adults. As in a slide show, these points will freeze the action for a short while, to afford us the opportunity to examine in more detail the ways in which different men in our culture experience masculinity at any one time.

The book's organization reflects these three concerns. Part I sets the context through which we shall examine men's lives. Parts II through IX follow those lives through their full course, examining central moments experienced by men in the United States today. Specifically, Part II touches on boyhood and adolescence, discussing some of the institutions organized to embody and reproduce masculinities in the United States, such as fraternities, the Boy Scouts, and sports groups. Part III, "Men and Work," explores the ways in which masculinities are constructed in relation to men's occupations. Part IV, "Men and Health: Body and Mind," deals with heart attacks, stress, AIDS, and other health problems among men. Part V, "Men, Sex, and Relationships," describes men's emotional and sexual relationships. We deal with heterosexuality and homosexuality, mindful of the ways in which variations are based on specific lines (class, race, ethnicity). Part VI, "Men in Families," concentrates on masculinities within the family and the role of men as husbands, fathers, and senior citizens. Part VII, "Masculinities in Religion," explores several different approaches to thinking about the relationship between masculinity and religion. Part VIII, "Masculinities in the Media and Popular Culture," explores the different ways the media present modes of masculinity. Part IX, "Violence and Masculinities," looks at violence as the most obdurate, intractable behavioral gender difference. Part X, "Politics of Masculinities," explores men's actions in gender-based social movements and electoral politics. Part XI, "What Can Men Do?," examines some of the ways in which men are changing and points to some directions in which men might continue to change.

Our perspective, stressing the social construction of masculinities over the life course, will, we believe, allow a more comprehensive understanding of men's lives in the United States today.

New to This Edition

- Twenty-eight new articles.
- Expanded focus on gender-nonconforming children, transgender people, and "hybrid" masculinities.
- Expanded focus on violence, including articles on rape, mass shootings, and Internet-based gender violence.
- New section "Politics of Masculinities," illuminating men's anti-feminist backlash and U.S. policies that target immigrant men in the age of Donald Trump.
- New section "What Can Men Do?" focuses on men's actions as individuals and as members of organizations to end violence and in support of equality in the United States and in the world.

References

Brod, Harry, ed. 1987. *The Making of Masculinities*. Boston: Unwin, Hyman.

Carrigan, Tim, Bob Connell, and John Lee. 1985. "Toward a New Sociology of Masculinity." *Theory and Society* 14(5): 551–604.

Chodorow, Nancy. 1978. *The Reproduction of Mothering*. Berkeley: University of California Press.

Connell, Raewyn 1987. *Gender and Power*. Stanford, CA: Stanford University Press.

David, Deborah, and Robert Brannon, eds. 1976. *The Forty-Nine Percent Majority*. Reading, MA: Addison–Wesley.

Elliott, J. H. 1984. *Richelieu and Olivares*. New York: Cambridge University Press.

Epstein, Cynthia Fuchs. 1986. "Inevitabilities of Prejudice." *Society* 23(6): 7–15.

Farrell, Warren. 1975. *The Liberated Man*. New York: Random House.

Feigen-Fasteau, Marc. 1974. *The Male Machine*. New York: McGraw–Hill.

Gilder, George. 1986. *Men and Marriage*. Gretna, LA: Pelican.

Gilligan, Carol. 1982. *In a Different Voice*. Cambridge, MA: Harvard University Press.

Goldberg, Steven. 1975. *The Inevitability of Patriarchy*. New York: William Morrow.

Goldberg, Steven. 1986. "Reaffirming the Obvious." *Society* 23(6): 4–7.

Hearn, Jeff. 1987. *The Gender of Oppression*. New York: St. Martin's Press.

Hrdy, Sandra Blaffer. 1981. *The Woman That Never Evolved*. Cambridge, MA: Harvard University Press.

Kimmel, Michael S., ed. 1987. *Changing Men: New Directions in Research on Men and Masculinity*. Newbury Park, CA: Sage.

Mead, Margaret. 1935. *Sex and Temperament in Three Primitive Societies*. New York: McGraw–Hill.

Pleck, Elizabeth, and Joseph Pleck, eds. 1980. *The American Man*. Englewood Cliffs, NJ: Prentice Hall.

Pleck, Joseph. 1981. *The Myth of Masculinity*. Cambridge, MA: MIT Press.

Pleck, Joseph, and Jack Sawyer, eds. 1974. *Men and Masculinity*. Englewood Cliffs, NJ: Prentice Hall.

Tiger, Lionel, and Robin Fox. 1984. *The Imperial Animal*. New York: Holt, Rinehart & Winston.

Trivers, Robert. 1972. "Parental Investment and Sexual Selection." In *Sexual Selection and the Descent of Man*, edited by B. Campbell. Chicago: Aldine.

Wilkinson, Rupert. 1986. *American Tough: The Tough Guy Tradition and American Character*. New York: Harper & Row.

Wilson, E. O. 1976. *Sociobiology: The New Synthesis*. Cambridge, MA: Harvard University Press.

Masculinities

A quick glance at any magazine rack or television talk show is enough to make you aware that these days, men are confused. What does it mean to be a "real man"? How are men supposed to behave? What are men supposed to feel? How are men to express their feelings? Who are we supposed to be like: Eminem or Boyz Il Men? Jimmy Kimmel or Carson Kressley? Derek Jeter or Kobe Bryant? Rhett Butler or Ashley Wilkes?

We are bombarded daily with images and handy rules to help us negotiate our way through a world in which all the rules seem to have suddenly vanished or changed. Some tell us to reassert traditional masculinity against all contemporary challenges. But a strength that is built only on the weakness of others hardly feels like strength at all. Others tell us that men are in power, the oppressor. But if men are in power as a group, why do individual men often feel so powerless? Can men change?

These questions will return throughout this book. The articles in Part I begin to unravel the "masculine mystique" and suggest various dimensions of men's position in society: their power, their powerlessness, and their confusion.

But we cannot speak of "masculinity" as some universal category that is experienced in the same ways by each man. "All men are alike" runs a popular saying. But are they really? Are gay men's experiences with work, relationships, love, and politics similar to those of heterosexual men? Do black and Chicano men face the same problems and conflicts in their daily lives that white men face? Do middle-class men have the same political interests as blue-collar men? The answers to these questions, as the articles in this part suggest, are not simple.

Although earlier studies of men and masculinity focused on the apparently universal norms of masculinity, recent works have attempted to demonstrate how different the worlds of various men are. Men are divided along the same lines that divide any other group: race, class, sexual orientation, ethnicity, age, and geographic region. Men's lives vary in crucial ways, and understanding these variations will take us a long way toward understanding men's experiences.

Earlier studies that suggested a single universal norm of masculinity reproduced some of the problems they were trying to solve. To be sure, *all* men benefit from the inequality between women and men; for example, think of how male-exclusive sports culture or rape jokes provide contexts for the bonding of men across class, race, and ethnic lines while denying full public participation to women.

But the single, seemingly universal masculinity obscured ways in which some men hold and maintain power over other men in our society, hiding the fact that men do not all share equally in the fruits of gender inequality.

Here is how sociologist Erving Goffman put it in his important book *Stigma* (New York: Doubleday, 1963, p. 128):

> In an important sense there is only one complete unblushing male in America: a young, married, white, urban, northern, heterosexual Protestant father of college education, fully employed, of good complexion, weight, and height, and a recent record in sports. Every American male tends to look out upon the world from this perspective, this constituting one sense in which one can speak of a common value system in America. Any male who fails to qualify in any one of these ways is likely to view himself—during moments at least—as unworthy, incomplete, and inferior.

As Goffman suggests, middle-class, white, heterosexual masculinity is used as the marker against which other masculinities are measured, and by which standard men may be found wanting. What is *normative* (prescribed) becomes translated into what is *normal*. In this way, heterosexual men maintain their status by the oppression of gay men; middle-aged men can maintain their dominance over older and younger men; upper-class men can exploit working-class men; and white men can enjoy privileges at the expense of men of color.

"*Actually, Lou, I think it was more than just my being in the right place at the right time. I think it was my being the right race, the right religion, the right sex, the right socioeconomic group, having the right accent, the right clothes, going to the right schools . . .*"

Source: Warren Miller/The New Yorker Collection/www.cartoonbank.com

The articles in this part explore this idea of masculinities as plural. Edward Flores and Hernan Ramirez, and Yen Le Espiritu each focus on the different ways in which different groups of men (Latino and Asian American) experience masculinity. They suggest that an understanding of class differences and ethnic and racial minorities requires an understanding of how political, legal, and economic factors shape and constrain the employment possibilities as well as the personal lifestyle choices of different groups of men. Calls for "changing masculinities," which the articles in this part suggest, must involve an emphasis on *institutional* transformations. Bethany Coston and Michael Kimmel examine the lives of other men, marginalized by class, sexuality, or disability status.

And yet despite these differences, don't all men share some common experiences? Martha McCaughey shows how the new "science" of evolutionary psychology supports a resurgent public belief of biologically based male superiority.

Paul Kivel suggests that there is a widely accepted definition of manhood that includes the promise of male privilege for boys and men who conform with what's inside the "be a man box."

PART I DISCUSSION QUESTIONS

1. How do masculinities vary between groups of men? What kinds of resources are available to some men and not others?
2. How do masculinities simultaneously empower and hinder men and boys?
3. Paul Kivel shows the social structures and sanctions that keep men in the "man box." What are some examples of these forces from your own experience? For men who are (or want to be) outside of the box, what kind of social changes might be necessary?
4. Is masculinity ever a liability? How and for whom does this play out?
5. What is the evidence that masculinities are changing with society? Where are the sticking points that resist change?
6. Evolutionary theories are presented as timeless explanations for human behavior, but Martha McCaughey argues that caveman masculinity is specific to social and historical context. What evidence does she provide to support her argument?

Caveman Masculinity: Finding an Ethnicity in Evolutionary Science

MARTHA MCCAUGHEY

The Caveman as Retrosexuality

Most of us can call up some image of prehistoric man and his treatment of women. He's a shaggy, well-muscled caveman, whose name is Thor, and we might picture him, club in hand, approaching a scrawny but curvaceous woman, whom he bangs over the head and drags by the hair into a cave to mate. I'm sure the majority of readers recognize this imagery. Indeed, today an image of modern men as guided by such prehistoric tendencies is even celebrated on T-shirts sold to American men on websites that allow people to post and sell their own designs. One such image for sale on the cafepress website features a version of Thor, wearing a fur pelt and holding a club, accompanied by the slogan "ME FIND WOMAN!" Another image available for T-shirts, boxer shorts, baseball caps, and coffee mugs features a man dressed in a one-shoulder fur pelt, with his club, smiling behind a cavewoman who is wearing a fur bikini outfit and cooking a skinned animal on a spit, with the saying "MEN'S PRIORITYS [sic]: 10,000 YEARS LATER AND STILL ON THE HUNT FOR FOOD AND SEX!" Another image features only the club, with the saying, "caveman: primitive pimpin."

Everywhere we look we can find applications of an increasingly fashionable academic exercise—the invocation of evolutionary theory to explain human male behaviors, particularly deplorable behaviors such as sexual harassment, rape, and aggression more generally. The familiar portrayals of sex differences based in evolution popularize and legitimize an academic version of evolutionary thought known increasingly as evolutionary psychology, a field referred to as the "science of the mind."[1] The combination of scholarly and popular attention to evolution and human male sexuality has increasingly lodged American manhood in an evolutionary logic. The discourse of evolutionary science has become part of popular consciousness, a sort of cultural consensus about who men are.

The evolutionary theory is that our human male ancestors were in constant competition with one another for sexual access to fertile women, who were picky about their mate choices given the high level of parental investment required of the human female for reproduction—months of gestation, giving birth, and then years of lactation and care for a dependent child. The human male's low level of parental investment required for reproduction, we are told, resulted in the unique boorishness of the hairier sex: He is sexually promiscuous; he places an enormous emphasis on women's youth and beauty, which he ogles every chance he gets; he either cheats on his wife or wants to; and he can be sexually aggressive to the point of criminality.

We find references to man's evolutionary heritage not only on T-shirts but in new science textbooks, pop psychology books on relationships, men's magazine, and Broadway shows. There are caveman fitness plans and caveman diets. *Saturday Night Live*'s hilarious "Unfrozen Caveman Lawyer" and the affronted caveman of the Geico car insurance ads joke about the ubiquity of caveman narratives. More disturbingly, the Darwinian discourse also crops up when men need an excuse for antisocial behavior. One man, who was caught on amateur video participating in the Central Park group sexual assaults in the summer of 2000, can be heard on video telling his sobbing victim, "Welcome back to the caveman times." How does a man come to think of himself as a caveman when he attacks a woman? What made so many American men decide that it's the DNA, rather than the devil, that makes them do it?

Using the late sociologist Pierre Bourdieu's theory of habitus, or the account of how cultural ideas are taken up in the form of bodily habits and tastes that reinforce behavioral norms and social inequality, I suggest that scientific theories find their way into both popular culture and men's corporeal habits and attitudes. Evolution has become popular culture, where popular culture is more than just media representations but refers to the institutions of everyday life: family, marriage, school, work—all sites where gender and racial knowledges are performed according to images people have available to them in actionable repertoires, scripts, and narratives. As popular culture, evolutionary narratives offer men a way to embody male sexuality.

That an evolutionary account of heterosexual male desire has captured the popular imagination is obvious from *Muscle & Fitness* magazine's article "Man the visual animal," which explains why men leer at women. Using a theory of the evolved difference between human male and female sexual psychologies developed by leading evolutionary psychologist Donald Symons, the article offers the following explanation under the subheading "Evolution Happens":

Not much has changed in human sexuality since the Pleistocene. In his landmark book *The Evolution of Human Sexuality* (Oxford University Press, 1979), Symons hypothesizes that the male's sexual response to visual cues has been so rewarded by evolution that it's become innate.[2]

Such stories provide a means by which heterosexual male readers can experience their sexuality as acultural, primal[3]: "The desire to ogle is your biological destiny."

Evolution may happen (or may have happened), but these stories do not just happen. Their appeal seems to lie precisely in the sense of security provided by the imagined inevitability of heterosexual manhood. In a marketplace of masculine identities, the caveman ethos is served up as Viagra for the masculine soul. Just as the 1950s women suffering what Betty Friedan famously called the "feminine mystique" were supposed to seek satisfaction in their Tupperware collections and their feminine figures, men today have been offered a way to think of their masculinity as powerful, productive, even aggressive—in a new economic and political climate where real opportunities to be rewarded for such traits have slipped away.[4]

It's hardly that most men today find themselves raising children at home while female partners bring home the bacon. But, like the fifties housewife, more men must now find satisfaction despite working below their potential (given that their job skills have lost their position to technology or other labor sources) in a postindustrial service economy that is less rewarding both materially and morally. As Susan Faludi puts it in her book *Stiffed*: "The fifties housewife, stripped of her connections to a wider world and invited to fill the void with shopping and the ornamental display of her ultra-femininity, could be said to have morphed into the nineties man, stripped of his connections to a wider world and invited to fill the void with consumption and a gym-bred display of his ultra-masculinity."[5]

On top of the economic changes affecting men, during the 1990s a growing anti-rape movement also challenged men, taking them to task for the problem of violence against women. More state and federal dollars supported efforts to stop such violence, and men increasingly feared complaints and repercussions for those complaints. The rape trials of Mike Tyson and William Kennedy Smith, Jr., the increasingly common school shootings (executed overwhelmingly by boys), the sexual harassment of women by men at the Citadel, the media attention given to the notorious Spurr Posse (a gang of guys who sought sex for "points" at almost all costs), the local sexual assault trials of countless high school and college athletic stars, the sexual harassment allegations against Supreme Court Justice nominee Clarence Thomas, and the White House sex scandals involving Bill Clinton meant more lost ground. Indeed, the 1990s saw relentless—though not necessarily ill-founded—criticism of men's sexual violence and other forms of aggression.

Right-wing leaders were as upset with men as feminists and other progressives. Those opposing abortion rights argued that sexual intercourse without procreation was undermining male responsibility, and those opposing women's equal-rights legislation argued that women's liberation would only allow men to relinquish their economic obligations to their families, sending women and children into divorce-induced poverty. Considering that critics of men came from the political right and left, and from among men as well as women, it seems fair to say that in turn-of-the-century America, moral disdain for men, whatever their age, race, or economic rank, had reached an all-time high.

For some men, the response was to cultivate a rude-dude attitude—popularized by Howard Stern, *The Man Show*, and MTV's endless shows about college spring break vacations. For some others, the response was to face, with a sense of responsibility and urgency, men's animal natures and either accept or reform their caveman ways. While some men were embracing the role of consumers and becoming creatures of ornamentation—the "metrosexuals"—other men revolted against metrosexuality, embracing a can-do virility that Sara Stewart in *The New York Post* referred to as "retrosexuality," or that "cringe-inducing backlash of beers and leers."[6] Caveman masculinity, with its focus on men's irrepressible heterosexuality and natural vigor, is a scientifically authorized form of retrosexuality.

The Caveman as Popular Scientific Story

Popular culture is a political Petri dish for Darwinian ideas about sex. Average American guys don't read academic evolutionary science, but many do read about science in popular magazines and in bestselling books about the significance of the latest scientific ideas. As such, it is worth examining—even when magazine writers and television producers intentionally "dumb down" relatively sophisticated academic claims. In this section, I look at the way some popular texts make sense of evolutionary claims about men. Later I suggest that the caveman ideology, much of which centers on men's aggressive heterosexuality, gets embodied and thereby reproduced.[7]

In September of 1999, *Men's Health* magazine featured a caveman fitness program. Readers are shown an exercise routine that corresponds to the physical movements their ancestors would have engaged in: throwing a spear, hauling an animal carcass, honing a stone. A nice looking clean-shaven young man is shown exercising, his physical posture mirrored by a scruffy animal skin–clad caveman behind him in the photo. Each day of the week-long routine is labeled according to the caveman mystique: building the cave home; the hunt; the chase; the kill; the long trek home; preparing for the feast; and rest. That an exercise plan is modeled after man-as-caveman reveals the common assumption that being a caveman is good for a man, a healthy existence.

Another issue of *Men's Health* magazine explains "the sex science facts" to male readers interested in "the biology of attraction." We follow the steps of a mating dance, but don't quite understand that's what we're doing. Indeed, we must learn the evolutionary history of sex to see why men feel the way they do when they notice a beautiful woman walking down the street:

Of course, out there in the street, you have no thoughts about genetic compatibility or child-bearing. Probably the farthest thing from your mind is having a child with that beautiful woman. But that doesn't matter. What you think counts for almost nothing. In the environment that crafted your brain and body, an environment in which you might be dead within minutes of spotting this beauty, the only thing that counted was that your clever neocortex—your seat of higher reason—be turned off so that you could quickly select a suitable mate, impregnate her, and succeed in passing on your genes to the next generation.[8]

The article proceeds to identify the signals of fertility that attract men: youth, beauty, big breasts, and a small waistline. Focusing on the desire for youth in women, the article tells men that "the reason men of any age continue to like young girls is that we were designed to get them pregnant and dominate their fertile years by keeping them that way. . . . When your first wife has lost the overt signals of reproductive viability, you desire a younger woman who still has them all."[9] And, of course, male readers are reminded that "your genes don't care about your wife or girlfriend or what the neighbors will say."[10]

Amy Alkon's *Winston-Salem Journal* advice column, "The Advice Goddess," uses an evolutionary theory of men's innate loutishness to comfort poor "Feeling Cheated On," who sent a letter complaining that her boyfriend fantasizes about other women during their lovemaking. The Advice Goddess cited a study by Bruce J. Ellis and Donald Symons (whose work was also mentioned in *Muscle & Fitness*) to conclude that "male sexuality is all about variety. Men are hard-wired to want you, the entire girls' dorm next door, and the entire girls' dorm next to that."[11]

Popular magazines tell men that they have a biological propensity to favor women with the faces of 11½ year-old girls (where the eyes and chin are close together) and a waist-to-hip ratio of .7 (where the waist measures 70% that of the hips). Men are told that their sexist double standard concerning appearance is evolutionary. Some of this research

is very speculative—for instance, in some studies, men are simply shown photos of women with specific waist-to-hip ratios and then asked, "Would you like to spend the rest of your life with this woman?"—as though such staged answers reveal something about the individuals' real-life choices (or genes). But the results of this research make great copy.

Men's Health magazine in 1999 offers an article called "The Mysteries of Sex . . . Explained!" and relies on evolutionary theory, quoting several professors in the field, to explain "why most women won't sleep with you." The article elucidates:

> Stop blaming your wife. The fault lies with Mother Nature, the pit boss of procreation. Neil M. Malamuth, Ph.D., professor of psychology at UCLA, explains. "You're in Las Vegas with 10 grand. Your gambling strategy will depend on which form your money takes. With 10 chips worth $1,000 each, you'd weigh each decision cautiously. With 10,000 $1 chips, you'd throw them around." That's reproductive strategy in a nutshell.[12]

Popular magazine articles like this follow a standard formula. They quote the scientists, reporting on the evolutionary theorists' research, and offer funny anecdotes about male sexuality to illustrate the research findings. This *Men's Health* article continues to account for men's having fetishes: "Men are highly sexed creatures, less interested in relationship but highly hooked on visuals, says David Givens, Ph.D., an anthropologist. 'Because sex carries fewer consequences for men, it's easier for us to use objects as surrogate sexual partners.' Me? I've got my eye on a Zenith, model 39990."[13]

It's not just these popular and often humorous accounts of men that are based in some version of evolutionary theory. Even serious academic arguments rely on evolutionary theories of human behavior. For example, Steven Rhoads, a member of the University of Virginia faculty in public policy, has written *Taking Sex Differences Seriously* (2004), a book telling us why gender equity in the home and the workplace is a feminist pipedream. Rhoads argues that women are wrong to expect men to take better care of children, do more housework, and make a place for them as equals at work because, he states, "men and women still have different natures and, generally speaking, different preferences, talents and interests."[14] He substantiates much of his argument about the divergent psychological pre-dispositions in men and women with countless references to studies done by evolutionary scholars.

News magazines and television programs have also spent quite a bit of time popularizing evolutionary science and its implications for understanding human sex differences. The ABC news program *Day One* reported in 1995 on evolutionary psychologist David Buss's new book, *The Evolution of Desire*.[15] Buss appeared on the show, which elaborated his theory by presenting us with super model Cindy Crawford and Barbie (the doll), presumably as representations of what men are wired to find desirable. As Buss explained in the interview, our evolutionary fore-brothers who did not prefer women with high cheekbones, big eyes, lustrous hair, and full lips did not reproduce. As Buss puts it, those men who happened to like someone who was older, sicker, or infertile "are not our ancestors. We are all the descendants of those men who preferred young healthy women and so as offspring, as descendants of those men, we carry with us their desires."[16] On that same television show, *Penthouse* magazine publisher Bob Guccioni was interviewed and explained that men are simply biologically designed to enjoy looking at sexy women: "This may be very politically incorrect but that's the way it is. . . . It's all part of our ancestral conditioning."[17] Evolutionary narratives clearly work for publishers of pornography marketed to men.

Newsweek's 1996 cover story, "The Biology of Beauty: What Science has Discovered about Sex Appeal," argues that the beautylust humans exhibit "is often better suited to the Stone Age than to the Information Age; the qualities we find alluring may be powerful emblems of health, fertility and resistance to disease. . . ."[18] Though "beauty isn't all that matters in life," the article asserts, "our weakness for 'biological quality' is the cause of endless pain and injustice."[19]

Sometimes the magazines and TV shows covering the biological basis of sexual desire give a nod to the critics. The aforementioned *Newsweek* article, for instance, quotes feminist writer Katha Pollitt, who insists that "human beings cannot be reduced to DNA packets."[20] And then, as if to affirm Pollitt's claim, homosexuality is invoked as an example of the countless non-adaptive delights we desire: "Homosexuality is hard to explain as a biological adaptation. So is stamp collecting. . . . We pursue countless passions that have no direct bearing on survival."[21] So when there is a nod to ways humans are not hardwired, homosexual desires are framed as oddities having no basis in nature, while heterosexual attraction along the lines of stereotypical heterosexual male fantasy is framed as biological. Heterosexual desire enjoys a *biologically correct* status.

Zoologist Desmond Morris explains how evolutionary theory applies to humans in his 1999 six-part television series, *Desmond Morris The Human Animal: A Personal View of the Human Species*.[22] The first show in the series draws from his book, *The Naked Ape*, explaining that humans are relatively hairless with little to protect themselves besides their big brains.[23] This is stated as we watch two naked people, one male and one female, walk through a public place where everyone else is dressed in modern-day clothing. Both are white, both are probably 25 to 30 years old, both look like models (the man with well-chiseled muscles, a suntan, and no chest hair, the woman thin, yet shapely with larger than average breasts, shaved legs, and a manicured pubic region). This presentation of man and woman in today's aesthetically ideal form as the image of what all of us were once like is *de rigueur* for any popular representation of evolutionary theory applied to human sexuality. No woman is flabby, flat chested, or has body hair, no man has pimples or back hair. These culturally mandated ideal body types are presented as the image of what our human ancestors naturally looked like. In this way and others, such shows posit modern aesthetic standards as states of nature.

Time magazine's 1994 cover story on "Our Cheating Hearts" reports that "the emerging field known as evolutionary psychology" gives us "fresh detail about the feelings and thoughts that draw us into marriage—or push us out."[24] After explaining the basics about men being less discriminating about their sexual partners than women, the article moves on to discuss why people divorce, anticipating resistance to the evolutionary explanation:

> Objections to this sort of analysis are predictable: "But people leave marriages for emotional reasons. They don't add up their offspring and pull out their calculators." But emotions are just evolution's executioners. Beneath the thoughts and feelings and temperamental differences marriage counselors spend their time sensitively assessing are the stratagems of the genes—cold, hard equations composed of simple variables: social status, age of spouse, number of children, their ages, outside romantic opportunities, and so on. Is the wife really duller and more nagging than she was 20 years ago? Maybe, but maybe the husband's tolerance for nagging has dropped now that she is 45 and has no reproductive future.[25]

In case *Time* readers react to the new evolutionary psychology as part of a plot to destroy the cherished nuclear family, they are told that "progress will also depend on people using the explosive insight of evolutionary psychology in a morally responsible way. . . . We are potentially moral animals—which is more than any other animal can say—but we are not naturally moral animals. The first step to being moral is to realize how thoroughly we aren't."[26]

While many accounts of evolution's significance for male sexuality seem simply to rationalize sexist double standards and wallow in men's loutishness, a number of pop-Darwinist claims have the moral purpose of liberating men from being controlled by their caveman natures. Their message: Men can become enlightened cavemen. These popular versions of man as caveman make an attempt to liberate men by getting them to see themselves differently. They tell men that they are cavemen with potential. They either make fun of men's putatively natural shortcomings or encourage them to cage the caveman within through a kind of scientific consciousness-raising.

Rob Becker's one-man show, *Defending the Caveman*, played Broadway and elsewhere from 1993 to 2005. This performance piece poking fun at sex differences is the longest running solo play in Broadway history. It relies on a longstanding man-the-hunter and woman-the-gatherer framework, from which modern sex differences follow. Cavemen hunted and focused on their prey until killing it. Cavewomen gathered things to use in the cave home. Men are thus strong silent types while women are into communication and togetherness. More significantly, *Defending the Caveman*'s creator and performer believes men have a bad rap. Becker points out that women say "men are all assholes" with a kind of feminist cultural authority men no longer enjoy when they make derogatory remarks about women. Rob Becker thus echoes the common sentiment among American men today that men are in the untenable position of being both hated and ignorant. They may want to try but they are unable to succeed. The show validates many people's observations of the behavior patterns and sex battles in their daily lives, and seems to poke fun at men's shortcomings—all the while affirming a vision of men as being as similar as peas in a primordial pea soup.

Evolution as Ideology

A critical examination of evolutionary science in its popular cultural manifestations over the past 15 to 20 years—the way most men come to know of the theory about their sexuality—allows us to ask how men come to know what they know about themselves. This type of analysis assumes that evolution is an ideology—which is not to suggest that humans got here via God's creation or some means other than evolution by natural selection. Positioning evolutionary arguments about human nature as an ideology is to understand that people think and act in ways that take evolutionary theory, however they construe it, as a self-evident truth. Furthermore, positioning evolutionary theory applied to humans as an ideology allows us to examine the way evolutionary ideas about male sexuality circulate in our culture. It is on this basis that I challenge the convenient innocence with which men invoke science to explain their bodies and their actions.

The caveman is certainly not the only form of masculine identity in our times. But the emergence of a caveman masculinity tells us much about the authority of science, the flow of scientific ideas in our culture, and the embodiment of those ideas. In *Science, Culture and Society* Mark Erickson explains the connection between science and society in our times:

> We live with science: science surrounds us, invades our lives, and alters our perspective on the world. We see things from a scientific perspective, in that we use science to help us make sense of the world—regardless of whether or not that is an appropriate thing to do—and to legitimize the picture of the world that results from such investigations.[27]

In a culture so attached to scientific authority and explication, it is worth examining the popular appeal of evolutionary theory and its impact on masculine embodiment. The popularity of the scientific story of men's evolved desires—however watered down or distorted the science becomes as enthusiasts popularize it—can tell us something about the appeal and influence of that story.

The Caveman as Embodied Ethos

If the evolutionary stories appeal to many men, and it seems they do indeed, it's because they ring true. Many men feel like their bodies are aggressive. They feel urges, at a physical level, in line with evolutionary theoretical predictions. With a naive understanding of experience, men can see affect as having an authenticity and empirical validity to it. In other words, the men who feel like cavemen do not see their identity as a fiction; it is their bodily reality and is backed by scientific study.

Certainly, evolutionary scholars would argue that the actual evolved psychologies make men feel like cavemen, or at least make those feelings emerge or affect behavior in particular environments. I argue that this explanation too simplistically separates men's bodies from discourse.

The work of Pierre Bourdieu provides a tool for understanding how power is organized at the level of unconscious embodiment of cultural forces. I suggest that popular manifestations of scientific evolutionary narratives about men's sexuality have a real material effect on many men. Bourdieu's theory of practice develops the concepts of *habitus* and *field* to describe a reciprocally constitutive relationship between bodily dispositions and dominant power structures. Bourdieu concerned himself primarily with the ways in which socioeconomic class is incorporated at the level of the body, including class-based ways of speaking, postures, lifestyles, attitudes, and tastes.

Significant for Bourdieu is that people acquire tastes that mark them as members of particular social groups and particular social levels.[28] Membership in a particular social class produces and reproduces a class sensibility, what Bourdieu (1990) called "practical sense."[29] Habitus is "a somatized social relationship, a social law converted into an embodied law."[30] The process of becoming competent in the everyday life of a society or group constitutes habitus. Bourdieu's notion of embodiment can be extended to suggest that habitus, as embodied field, amounts to "the pleasurable and ultimately erotic constitution of [the individual's] social imaginary."[31]

Concerning the circulation of evolutionary narratives, we can see men taking erotic pleasure in the formation of male identity and the performance of accepted norms of heterosexual masculinity using precisely these tools of popular evolutionary science. Put differently, pop-Darwinism is a discourse that finds its way into men's bones and boners. The caveman story can become a man's practical sense of who he is and what he desires. This is so because masculinity is a dimension of embodied and performative practical sensibility—because men carry themselves with a bodily comportment suggestive of their position as the dominant gender, and they invest themselves in particular lifestyle practices, consumption patterns, attire, and bodily comportment. Evolutionary narratives thus enter the so-called habitus, and an aestheticized discourse and image of the caveman circulates through popular culture becoming part of natural perception, and consequently is reproduced by those embodying it.

In his study of the overwhelmingly white and male workspace of the Options Exchange floor, sociologist Richard Widick uses Bourdieu's theory to explain the traders' physical and psychical engagement with their work. Widick holds that "the traders' inhabitation and practical mastery of the trading floor achieves the bio-physical psychosocial state of a natural identity."[32] Hence the traders describe their manner as a "trading instinct." In a similar way, American men with what we might call a caveman instinct can be said to have acquired a "pre-reflexive practical sense" of themselves as heterosexually driven.[33]

Bourdieu gives the name "symbolic violence" to that process by which we come to accept and embody power relations without ever accepting them in the conscious sense of knowing them and choosing them. We hold beliefs that don't need to be thought—the effects of which can be "durably and deeply embedded in the body in the form of dispositions."[34] From this perspective, the durable dispositions of evolutionary discourse are apparent in our rape culture, for example, when a member of the group sexual assault in New York tells the woman he's attacking, "Welcome back to the caveman times." Embodying the ideology of irrepressible heterosexual desire makes such aggression appear to be natural.

Bourdieu's theory allows us to see that both cultural and material forces reveal themselves in the lived reality of social relations.[35] We can see on men's bodies the effects of their struggle with slipping economic privilege and a sense of entitlement to superiority over women. If men live out power struggles in their everyday experiences, then caveman masculinity can be seen as an imagined compensation for men's growing sense of powerlessness.[36] To be sure, some men have more social

and economic capital than others. Those with less might invest even more in their bodies and appearances.[37]

Sociologist R. W. Connell discusses the significance of naturalizing male power. He states:

> The physical sense of maleness is not a simple thing. It involves size and shape, habits of posture and movement, particular physical skills and the lack of others, the image of one's own body, the way it is presented to other people and the ways they respond to it, the way it operates at work and in sexual relations. In no sense is all this a consequence of XY chromosomes, or even of the possession on which discussions of masculinity have so lovingly dwelt, the penis. The physical sense of maleness grows through a personal history of social practice, a life-history-in-society.[38]

We see and believe that men's power over women is the order of nature because "power is translated not only into mental body-images and fantasies, but into muscle tensions, posture, the feel and texture of the body"[39] Scientific discourse constitutes the field for some men in the constructed figure of the caveman, enabling those men to internalize such an identity. The caveman thus becomes an imaginative projection that is experienced and lived as real biological truth.

In his book, *Cultural Boundaries of Science*, Thomas Gieryn comments on the cultural authority of science, suggesting that "if 'science' says so, we are more often than not inclined to believe it or act on it—and to prefer it to claims lacking this epistemic seal of approval."[40] To his observation I would add that we are also more likely to *live* it. Ideas that count as scientific, regardless of their truth value, become lived ideologies. It's how modern American men have become cavemen and how the caveman ethos enjoys reproductive success.

Cultural anthropologist Paul Rabinow gives the name "biosociality" to the formation of new group and individual identities and practices that emerge from the scientific study of human life.[41] Rabinow offers the example of neurofibromatosis groups whose members have formed to discuss their experiences, educate their children, lobby for their disease, and "understand" their fate. And in the future, he points out, "... [i]t is not hard to imagine groups formed around the chromosome 17, locus 16,256, site 654,376 allele variant with a guanine substitution."[42] Rabinow's concept of biosociality is instructive here; for the discourse of the caveman offers this form of biosociality. The caveman constitutes an identity based on new scientific "facts" about one's biology.

Of course, evolutionary psychologists would have us think that men's desires are, in some final instance, biological properties of an internal psyche or sexual psychology. I am suggesting, in line with Bourdieu, that men's desires are always performed in relation to the dominant discourses in circulation within their cultural lifeworlds, either for or against the representations that permeate those lifeworlds. We can see that a significant number of men are putting the pop-Darwinian rhetoric to good use in social interactions. The scientific discourse of the caveman (however unscientific we might regard it by the time it gets to everyday guys reading magazines and watching TV) is corporealized, quite literally incorporated into living identities, deeply shaping these men's experience of being a man.

The Caveman as Ethnicity

I recognize the lure of the caveman narrative. After all, it provides an explanation for patterns we do see and for how men do feel in contemporary society, tells men that they are beings who are the way they are for a specific reason, offers them an answer about what motivates them, and carries the authority of scientific investigation about their biological makeup. Evolutionary theory offers an origin story. Plus, it's fun: thinking of the reasons you might feel a certain way because such feelings might have been necessary for your ancestors to survive a hostile environment back in the Pleistocene can be a satisfying intellectual exercise.

In telling men a story about who they are, naturally, pop-Darwinism has the normalizing, disciplinary effect of forging a common, biological

identity among men. Embodying ideology allows men to feel morally exonerated while they reproduce that very ideology. The discourse of male biological unity suppresses many significant differences among men, and of course many ways in which men would otherwise identify with women's tastes and behaviors. The evolutionary explanation of men's sexual behavior is an all-encompassing narrative enabling men to frame their own thoughts and experiences through it. As such it's a *grand narrative*, a totalizing theory explaining men's experiences as though all men act and feel the same ways, and as though the ideas of Western science provide a universal truth about those actions and feelings.

I'm skeptical of this kind of totalizing narrative about male sexuality because evolution applied to human beings does not offer that sort of truth. The application of evolutionary theory to human behavior is not as straightforwardly scientific as it might seem, even for those of us who believe in the theory of evolution by natural selection. It is a partial, political discourse that authorizes certain prevalent masculine behaviors and a problematic acceptance of those behaviors. I think there are better—less totalizing, and differently consequential—discourses out there that describe and explain those same behaviors. I'm also skeptical of men's use of the evolutionary narrative because, at its best, it can only create "soft patriarchs"—kinder, gentler cavemen who resist the putative urges of which evolutionary science makes them aware.[43]

Caveman masculinity has become an "ethnic option," a way of identifying and living one's manhood. Mary C. Waters explains that ethnic identity is "far from the automatic labeling of a primordial characteristic"[44] but instead is a complex, socially created identity. As an ethnicity, caveman masculinity is seen as not only impossible but also undesirable to change.[45] The caveman as an ethnicity reveals an embrace of biology as a reaction to social constructionist understandings of masculinity, feminist demands on men, and the changing roles of men at work and in families.

To repeat: My quarrel is not limited to evolutionary theorists alone. Darwinian ideas are often spread by enthusiasts—secondary school teachers, science editors of various newspapers and magazines, and educational television show producers—who take up evolutionary theorists' ideas and convey them to mass audiences. Evolutionary thinking has become popular in part because it speaks to a publicly recognized predicament of men. Changing economic patterns have propelled men's flight from marriage and bread-winning, in conjunction with women's increased (albeit significantly less prosperous) independence. If a man today wants multiple partners with as little commitment as possible, evolutionary rhetoric answers why this is so.

Evolutionary science doesn't tell a flattering story about men. But more significantly, many people don't understand that it's *a story*. Evolution has become not only a grand narrative but also a lived ideology. Maleness and femaleness, like heterosexuality and homosexuality, are not simply identities but *systems of knowledge*.[46] And those systems of knowledge inform thinking and acting. Bourdieu's concept of habitus explains the ways in which culture and knowledge, including evolutionary knowledge, implant themselves at the level of the body, becoming a set of attitudes, tastes, perceptions, actions, and reactions. The status of science as objective, neutral knowledge helps make evolution a lived ideology because it feels truthful, natural, real.

Taking the historical and cultural changes affecting men seriously and embracing the diversity among men demand new understandings of masculinity, identity, and science. In gaining such a sociological perspective, men might resist making gender a new ethnicity and instead take a great leap forward to become new kinds of men.

Notes

1. For defenses of the study of the popularization of scientific discourse, and exemplary studies of the popularization of Darwinian discourse in different eras, see Alfred Kelly, *The Descent of Darwin: The Popularization of Darwinism in Germany, 1860–1914* (Chapel Hill: University of North Carolina Press, 1981) and Alvar Ellegård, *Darwin and the General Reader: The Reception of Darwin s Theory of Evolution in the British Press, 1859–1872* (Chicago: University of Chicago Press, 1990).

2. Mary Ellen Strote, "Man the Visual Animal," *Muscle & Fitness* (February 1994): 166.

3. Ibid., 166.

4. Betty Friedan, *The Feminine Mystique* (New York: Dell Publishing Company, 1963).

5. Susan Faludi, *Stiffed: The Betrayal of the American Man* (New York: HarperCollins, 1999), 40.

6. Sara Stewart, "Beasty Boys—'Retrosexuals' Call for Return of Manly Men; Retrosexuals Rising," *The New York Post*, July 18, 2006.

7. My argument here parallels a study of the pervasive iconography of the gene in popular culture. In *The DNA Mystique: The Gene As a Cultural Icon*, Dorothy Nelkin and M. Susan Lindee (New York: W. H. Freeman and Company, 1995, 11) explain that popular culture provides "narratives of meaning." Those narratives filter complex ideas, provide guidance, and influence how people see themselves and evaluate other people, ideas, and policies. In this way, Nelkin and Lindee argue, DNA works as an ideology to justify boundaries of identity and legal rights, as well as to explain criminality, addiction, and personality. Of course addict genes and criminal genes are misnomers—the definitions of what counts as an addict and what counts as a crime have shifted throughout history. Understanding DNA stories as ideological clarifies why, for example, people made sense of Elvis's talents and shortcomings by referring to his genetic stock (Ibid., 79–80). To call narratives of DNA ideological, then, is *not* to resist the scientific argument that deoxyribonucleic acid is a double-helix structure carrying information forming living cells and tissues, but to look at the way people make sense of DNA and use DNA to make sense of people and events in their daily lives.

8. Laurence Gonzales, "The Biology of Attraction," *Men's Health* 20.7 (2005): 186–93.

9. Ibid., 192.

10. Ibid., 193.

11. Amy Alkon, "Many Men Fantasize During Sex, But It Isn't a Talking Point," *Winston-Salem Journal*, 29 September 2005, p. 34.

12. Greg Gutfeld, "The Mysteries of Sex . . . Explained!," *Men's Health* April: 1999, 76.

13. Ibid., 76.

14. Steven E. Rhoads, *Taking Sex Differences Seriously* (San Francisco: Encounter Books, 2004), 4.

15. David M. Buss, *The Evolution of Desire: Strategies of Human Mating* (New York: Basic Books, 1994).

16. *Day One* reported in 1995. ABC News.

17. Ibid.

18. Geoffrey Cowley, "The Biology of Beauty," *Newsweek* 127 (1996): 62.

19. Ibid., 64.

20. Ibid., 66.

21. Ibid.

22. *Desmond Morris The Human Animal: A Personal View of the Human Species* ["Beyond Survival"]. Clive Bromhall, dir. (Discovery Communication/TLC Video, 1999).

23. Desmond Morris, *The Naked Ape* (New York: Dell Publishing, 1967).

24. Robert Wright, *The Moral Animal: Evolutionary Psychology and Everyday Life* (New York: Pantheon Books, 1994), 45.

25. Ibid., 50.

26. Ibid., 52.

27. Mark Erickson, *Science, Culture and Society* (Cambridge: Polity Press, 2005), 224.

28. Pierre Bourdieu, *Distinction: A Social Critique of the Judgment of Taste* (Cambridge: Harvard University Press, 1984).

29. Pierre Bourdieu, *The Logic of Practice* (Stanford: Stanford University Press, 1990).

30. Pierre Bourdieu, *Masculine Domination* (Stanford: Stanford University Press, 2001).

31. Richard Widick, "Flesh and the Free Market: (On Taking Bourdieu to the Options Exchange)," *Theory and Society* 32 (2003): 679–723, 716.

32. Widick, 701.

33. Ibid.

34. Bourdieu, *Masculine*, 39.

35. Lois McNay, "Agency and Experience: Gender As a Lived Relation," in *Feminism After Bourdieu*, ed. Lisa Adkins and Bev Skeggs (Oxford: Blackwell, 2004), 177.

36. See McNay 175–90 for a discussion of emotional compensation and lived experience.

37. See Beverley Skeggs, *Formations of Class and Gender: Becoming Respectable* (London: Sage, 1997) for a study pointing this out about working class women.

38. R. W. Connell, *Gender and Power: Society, the Person and Sexual Politics* (Cambridge: Polity Press, 1987), 84.

39. Ibid., 85.

40. Thomas F. Gieryn, *Cultural Boundaries of Science: Credibility on the Line* (Chicago: University of Chicago Press, 1999), 1.

41. Paul Rabinow, *Making PCR, A Story of Biotechnology* (Chicago: University of Chicago Press, 1996), 101–102.

42. Ibid., 102.

43. I am appropriating W. Bradford Wilcox's term, from his book *Soft Patriarchs, New Men: How Christianity Shapes Fathers and Husbands* (Chicago: University of Chicago Press, 2004). Wilcox argues that the Christian men's movement known as the Promise Keepers encourages men to spend more time with their wives and children without ever challenging the fundamental patriarchal family structure that places men at the top.

44. Mary C. Waters, *Ethnic Options: Choosing Identities in America*, (Berkeley: University of California Press, 1990), 16.

45. See Michael S. Kimmel, *Manhood in America: A Cultural History* (New York: Free Press, 1996), 127–137.

46. Steven Seidman, *Difference Troubles: Queering Social Theory and Sexual Politics* (Cambridge, UK: Cambridge University Press, 1997), 93.

The Act-Like-a-Man Box

PAUL KIVEL

How are boys trained in the United States? What is the predominant image of masculinity that boys must deal with while growing up?

From a very early age, boys are told to "Act Like a Man." Even though they have all the normal human feelings of love, excitement, sadness, confusion, anger, curiosity, pain, frustration, humiliation, shame, grief, resentment, loneliness, low self-worth, and self-doubt, they are taught to hide the feelings and appear to be tough and in control. They are told to be aggressive, not to back down, not to make mistakes, and to take charge, have lots of sex, make lots of money, and be responsible. Most of all, they are told not to cry.

My colleagues and I have come to call this rigid set of expectations the "Act-Like-a-Man" box because it feels like a box, a 24-hour-a-day, seven-day-a-week box that society tells boys they must fit themselves into. One reason we know it's a box is because every time a boy tries to step out he's pushed back in with names like wimp, sissy, mama's boy, girl, fag, nerd, punk, mark, bitch, and others even more graphic. Behind those names is the threat of violence.

These words are little slaps, everyday reminders designed to keep us in the box. They are also fighting words. If someone calls a boy a "wimp" or a "fag," he is supposed to fight to prove that he is not. Almost every adult man will admit that as a kid, he had to fight at least once to prove he was in the box.

The columns on either side of the box show the expectations our society holds for men. The abuse, pressure, and training boys receive to meet these expectations and stay in the box produce a lot of feelings. Yet they have to cover over those feelings and try to act like a man because one of the strictures of being a man is not to show your feelings.

Notice that many of the words we get called refer to being gay or feminine. This feeds into two things we're taught to fear: (1) that we are not manly enough and (2) that we might be gay. Homophobia, the fear of gays or of being taken for gay, is an incredibly strong fear we learn as boys and carry with us throughout our lives. Much too often we try to relieve our fears of being gay or effeminate by attacking others.

There is other training that keeps us in the box. Besides getting into fights, we are ostracized and teased, and girls don't seem to like us when we step out of the box. Many adults keep pushing us to be tough, and that process begins early. They seem convinced that if they "coddle" us, we will be weak and vulnerable. Somehow, withdrawal of affection is supposed to toughen us and prepare us for the "real" world. Withdrawal of affection is emotional abuse. And that's bad enough. But it often does not stop there. One out of every six of us is sexually abused as a child. Often, the verbal, physical, and sexual abuse continues throughout our childhood.

There are many cultural variations of this theme, but its prevalence in Western cultures is striking.

Paul Kivel , "The Act-Like-a-Man Box," adapted from *Men's Work and Boys Will Be Men*, copyright 1984. www.paulkivel.com.

"Act-Like-a-Man" Box

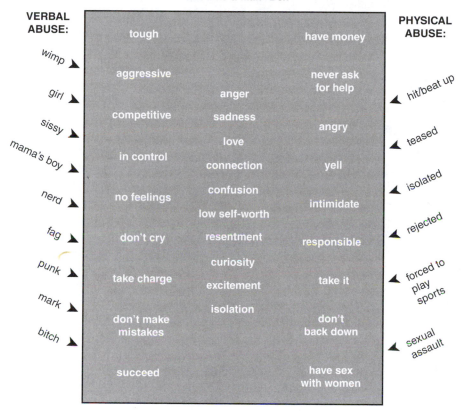

VERBAL ABUSE:

wimp
girl
sissy
mama's boy
nerd
fag
punk
mark
bitch

PHYSICAL ABUSE:

hit/beat up
teased
isolated
rejected
forced to play sports
sexual assault

tough · have money · aggressive · never ask for help · anger · competitive · sadness · angry · love · in control · connection · yell · no feelings · confusion · low self-worth · intimidate · don't cry · resentment · responsible · curiosity · take charge · excitement · take it · isolation · don't make mistakes · don't back down · succeed · have sex with women

All boys have different strategies for trying to survive in the box. Some might even sneak out of it at times, but the scars from living within the walls of the box are long-lasting and painful.

If we pay attention we can easily see the box's effects on boys. Just watch a group of them together. They are constantly challenging each other, putting each other down, hitting each other, testing to see who is in the box. They are never at ease, always on guard. At an early age they start to hide their feelings, toughen up, and will make a huge emotional effort not to cry. They stop wearing colorful clothing or participating in activities that they think might make them vulnerable to being labeled gay. They walk more stiffly, talk more guardedly, move more aggressively. Behind this bravura they are often confused, scared, angry, and wanting

closeness with others. But being in the box precludes closeness and makes intimacy unlikely.

The key to staying in the box is control. Boys are taught to control their bodies, control their feelings, control their relationships—to protect themselves from being vulnerable. Although the box is a metaphor for the pressures all boys must respond to, the possibility that a boy will have control over the conditions of his life varies depending on his race, class, and culture.

Being in control is not the same as being violent. In Western societies hitting people is frowned upon except in particular sports or military settings. It is deemed much more refined to retain control by using verbal, emotional, or psychological means rather than physical force. Financial manipulation, coercion and intimidation, and sexual pressure are also condoned as long as no one is physically injured.

Clearly, the more money, education, and connections a man has, the easier it is for him to buy or manipulate what he wants. Wealthy and upper- or middle-class white men are generally promoted and celebrated for being in control and getting what they want. Poor or working-class men and men of color are usually punished for these same behaviors, especially, but not only, if they use physical force.

Why are boys trained to be in control? Most boys will end up with one of three roles in society—to be workers, consumers, or enforcers. A small percentage of boys are trained to give orders—to be bosses, managers, or officers. The box trains boys for the roles they will play, whether they will make decisions governing the lives of others or carry out the decisions made by those at the top. The box prepares boys to be police officers, security cops, deans, administrators, soldiers, heads of families, probation officers, prison guards—the roles that men, primarily white men, are being trained to fill. Men of color, along with women and young people, are the people more often being controlled.

Many men are under the illusion that being in the box is like being in an exclusive club. No girls allowed. All men are equal. For working- and middle-class white men and for those men of color who aspire to be accepted by them, the box creates a false feeling of solidarity with men in power and misleads many of them into thinking they have more in common with the corporate executives, political and religious leaders, generals, and bosses than they have with women.

Nobody is born in the Act-Like-a-Man box. It takes years and years of enforcement, name-calling, fights, threats, abuse, and fear to turn us into men who live in this box. By adolescence we believe that there are only two choices—we can be a man or a boy, a winner or a loser, a bully or a wimp, a champ or a chump.

Nobody wants to live in a box. It feels closed in; much of us is left out. It was a revelation to realize how I had been forced into the box. It was a relief to understand how it had been accomplished and to know it didn't have to be that way. Today, it inspires me to see adult men choose to live outside the box. It is a choice each of us can, and must make—to step outside the box and back into our families and communities.

Seeing Privilege Where It Isn't

Marginalized Masculinities and the Intersectionality of Privilege

BETHANY M. COSTON AND MICHAEL KIMMEL

When discussing privilege, we often consider it a zero-sum quantity, one either has it or one does not. Since privilege is distributed along a range of axes, we consider three sites in which male privilege is compromised by marginalization by other statuses: disability status, sexuality, and class. Employing a Symbolic Interactionist approach, derived from Erving Goffman's Stigma *(1963), we observe strategies employed by disabled men, gay men and working class men to reduce, neutralize, or resist the problematization of masculinity as a constitutive element of their marginalization by class, sexuality, or disability.*

The idea that "privilege is invisible to those who have it" has become a touchstone epigram for work on the "super-ordinate"—in this case, White people, men, heterosexuals, and the middle class (Privilege: A reader, 2010). When one is privileged by class, or race or gender or sexuality, one rarely sees exactly how the dynamics of privilege work. Thus, efforts to make privilege visible, such as McIntosh's (1988) "invisible knapsack" and the "Male Privilege Checklist" or the "heterosexual questionnaire" have become staples in college classes.

Yet unlike McIntosh's autobiographical work, some overly-simple pedagogical tools like the "heterosexual questionnaire" or "Male Privilege checklist" posit a universal and dichotomous understanding of privilege: one either has it or one does not. It's as if all heterosexuals are white; all "males" are straight. The notion of intersectionality complicates this binary understanding.

We propose to investigate sites of inequality within an overall structure of privilege. Specifically, we look at three groups of men—disabled men, gay men, and working class men—to explore the dynamics of having privilege in one sphere but being unprivileged in another arena. . . .

This is especially important, we argue, because, for men, the dynamics of removing privilege involve assumptions of emasculation—exclusion from that category that would confer privilege. Gender is the mechanism by which the marginalized are marginalized. That is, gay, working class, or disabled men are seen as "not-men" in the popular discourse of their marginalization. It is their masculinity—the site of privilege—that is specifically targeted as the grounds for exclusion from privilege. Thus, though men, they often see themselves as reaping few, if any, of the benefits of their privileged status as men (Pratto & Stewart, 2012). . . .

Doing Gender and the Matrix of Oppression

In the United States, there is a set of idealized standards for men. These standards include being brave, dependable, and strong, emotionally stable, as well as critical, logical, and rational. The ideal male is supposed to be not only wealthy, but also in a position of power over others. Two words sum up the expectations for men: hegemonic masculinity (cf. Connell, 1995). That is, the predominant, over-powering concept of what it is to be a "real man."

The idealized notion of masculinity operates as both an ideology and a set of normative constraints. . . . One of the more popular ways to see gender is as an accomplishment; an everyday, interactional activity that reinforces itself via our activities and relationships. "Doing gender involves a complex of socially guided perceptual, interactional, and micropolitical activities that cast particular pursuits as expressions of masculine and feminine 'natures'" (West & Zimmerman, 1987).

These "natures," or social *norms* for a particular gender, are largely internalized by the men and women who live in a society, consciously and otherwise. In other words, these social norms become personal identities. Moreover, it is through the intimate and intricate process of daily interaction with others that we fully achieve our gender, and are seen as valid and appropriate gendered beings. . . .

. . . While the men we discuss below may operate within oppression in one aspect of their lives, they have access to alternate sites of privilege via the rest of their demographics (e.g., race, physical ability, sexual orientation, gender, sex, age, social class, religion). A working class man, for example, may also be White and have access to white privilege and male privilege. What is interesting is how these men choose to navigate and access their privilege within the confines of a particular social role that limits, devalues, and often stigmatizes them as not-men. . . .

It is important to realize that masculinity is extremely diverse, not homogenous, unchanging, fixed, or undifferentiated. Different versions of masculinities coexist at any given historical period and can coexist within different groups. However, it is this diversity and coexistence that creates a space for marginalization. "The dominant group needs a way to justify its dominance—that difference is inferior" (Cheng, 2008).

Dynamics of Marginalization and Stigma

Marginalization is both gendered and dynamic. How do marginalized men respond to the problematization of their masculinity as they are marginalized by class, sexuality or disability status? . . . Stigma is a stain, a mark, and "spoiled identity," Goffman (1963) writes, an attribute that changes you "from a whole and usual person to a tainted and discounted one." People with stigmatized attributes are constantly practicing various strategies to ensure minimal damage. . . .

Goffman identified three strategies to neutralize stigma and revive a spoiled identity. He listed them in order of increased social power—the more power you have, the more you can try and redefine the situation (these terms reflect the era in which he was writing, since he obviously uses the Civil Rights Movement as the reference). They are:

1. *Minstrelization*: If you're virtually alone and have very little power, you can over-conform to the stereotypes that others have about you . . . to *exaggerate* the differences between the stigmatized and the dominant group. Thus, for example, did African Americans over-act as happy-go-lucky entertainers when they had no other recourse. Contemporary examples might be . . . gay men who really "camp it up" like Carson Kressley on "Queer Eye for the Straight Guy." Minstrels exaggerate difference in the face of those with more power; when they are with other stigmatized people, they may laugh about the fact that the powerful "actually think we're like this!" That's often the only sort of power that they feel they have.

2. *Normification*: If you have even a small amount of power, you might try to minimize the differences between the stigmatized groups. "Look," you'll say, "we're the same as you are, so there is no difference to discriminate against us." Normification is the

strategy that the stigmatized use to enter institutions formerly closed to them, like when women entered the military or when Black people ran for public office. . . . Normification involves exaggerating the similarities and downplaying the differences.

3. *Militant Chauvinism*: When your group's level of power and organization is highest, you may decide to again *maximize* differences with the dominant group. But militant chauvinists don't just say "we're different," they say "we're also better." For example, there are groups of African-Americans ("Afrocentrists" or some of the Nation of Islam) who proclaim Black superiority. Some feminist women proclaim that women's ways are better than the dominant "male" way. These trends try to turn the tables on the dominant group. . . .

These three responses depend on the size and strength of the stigmatized group. . . . However, we might see these three strategic responses to stigma through a somewhat different lens. The over-conformity of normification accepts the criteria that the dominant group uses to maintain its power; normifiers simply want to be included. By contrast, both minstrelizers and militant chauvinists resist their marginalization by rejecting the criteria by which they are marginalized. . . .

Disabled Men

Discrimination against men with disabilities is pervasive in American society, and issues of power, dominance, and hegemonic masculinity are the basis. . . . Disabled men do not meet the unquestioned and idealized standards of appearance, behavior, and emotion for men. The values of capitalist societies based on male dominance are dedicated to warrior values, and a frantic able-bodiedness represented through aggressive sports and risk-taking activities, which do not make room for those with disabilities.

For example, one man interviewed by Robertson (2011) tells the story of his confrontations with those who discriminate against him. Frank says,

If somebody doesn't want to speak to me 'cause I'm in a chair, or they shout at me 'cause I'm in a chair, I wanna know why, why they feel they have

to shout. I'm not deaf you know. If they did it once and I told them and they didn't do it again, that'd be fair enough. But if they keep doing it then that would annoy me and if they didn't know that I could stand up then I'd put me brakes on and I'd stand up and I'd tell them face-to-face. If they won't listen, then I'll intimidate them, so they will listen, because it's important. (p. 12)

. . . Men with physical disabilities have to find ways to express themselves within the role of "disabled." Emotional expression is not compatible with the aforementioned traits because it signifies vulnerability; in this way, men, especially disabled men, must avoid emotional expression. If they fail in stoicism, discrimination in the form of pejorative words ("cripple," "wimp," "retard") are sometimes used to suppress or condemn the outward expressions of vulnerability.

But, men with disabilities don't need verbal reminders of their "not-men" status. Even without words, their social position, their lack of power over themselves (let alone others), leads them to understand more fully their lacking masculinity. One man, Vernon, detailed these feelings specifically,

Yeah, 'cause though you know you're still a man, I've ended up in a chair, and I don't feel like a red-blooded man. I don't feel I can handle 10 pints and get a woman and just do the business with them and forget it, like most young people do. You feel compromised and still sort of feeling like "will I be able to satisfy my partner." Not just sexually, other ways, like DIY, jobs round the house and all sorts. (Robertson, 2011, pp. 8–9)

. . . When reformulating ideas of masculinity, these men usually focus on personal strengths and abilities, regardless of the ideal standards. This can include maneuvering an electric wheelchair or driving a specially equipped vehicle, tasks that would be very difficult for other people. Men who rely on hegemonic ideals are typically very aware of other's opinions of masculinity. These men internalized ideals such as physical and sexual prowess, and athleticism, though it can be nearly impossible for them to meet these standards. Then there are men who reject hegemonic masculinity. These men believe that masculine norms are wrong; they sometimes form their own standards for masculinity, which often go against what society thinks is right for men. Some men [tried] devaluing masculinity's importance altogether. The operative word is *try* because despite men's best efforts to reformulate or reject hegemonic masculinity, the expectations and ideals for men are far more pervasive than can be controlled. Many men trying to reformulate and reject masculine standards often end up "doing" gender appropriately in one aspect of life or another.

Indeed, some men find that hypermasculinity is the best strategy. Wedgwood (2011) interviewed disabled men and Carlos was certainly one who appreciated gender conformity:

> The thrill you get out of doing it because I'm an adrenaline junkie! [laughs]. Contact for me, gets your adrenaline going, gets your blood going and it's a rush . . . if I have a really hard match and I'm getting bruised and getting smashed in there and I'm still trying to go for the ball and I keep getting hit—that's what I love about contact sports—I keep getting hit and everything and still getting up. (p. 14)

. . . However, as Erving Goffman (1963) writes, "The stigmatized individual tends to hold the same beliefs about identity that we do. . . . His deepest feelings about what he is may be his sense of being a 'normal person,' a human being like anyone else" (p. 116). Failing to maintain the hegemonic norms for masculinity has a direct, sometimes negative psychological effect. People tend to judge themselves and measure their worth based upon an intersubjective, sometimes impossible reality. Goffman (1963) later continues, any man that fails to meet the social standards for masculinity is "likely to view himself—during moments at least—as unworthy, incomplete, and inferior" (p. 128). Identity, self-worth, and confidence depend on whether or not he accepts, conforms to, or relies on the social norms.

Men with disabilities are no strangers to accepting and relying upon social norms of masculinity. Despite their sometimes stigmatized status, they do have access to sites of privilege. . . .

. . . For example, a 2008 documentary, "Real Life: For One Night Only," aired on Channel 4 in the United Kingdom and SBS in Australia, is described in an Australian newspaper review as a "charming documentary on the sexuality of disabled people" (Jeffreys, 2008). Here, a disabled man is taken on a trip to Spain by his parents to access prostituted women in a special brothel for 'people with various disabilities' (Schwartz, 2008). In this way, he claims male privilege—the ability to use economic resources to gain access to women's bodies—and we, the viewers, see his masculinity—his sexual needs, rights, and entitlements—as validated. . . .

The desire to maintain a disabled man's masculinity does not just stem from within that man, however. The model of rehabilitation of people with disabilities, the medical model of disability, has a male body and male sexuality in mind. "Rehabilitation programs seek to cultivate 'competitive attitudes' and address 'concerns about male sexuality'" (Jeffreys, 2008). They are about "enabling men to aspire to dominant notions of masculinity" (Begum, 1992).

Robert David Hall is an actor on the hit American television show *CSI* (Crime Scene Investigation) and walks on two artificial legs due to having both of his legs amputated in 1978 after an 18-wheeler crushed his car. His character is not defined by his disability. "I used to hate the word 'disability,'" he said. "But I've come to embrace the fact that I'm one of more than 58 million Americans with some kind of physical or learning disability" (p. 1). "After the accident, I realized I had more strength than I knew," Hall says. "I was forced to face up to reality, but facing such a reality helped me face any fears I had of taking risks" (Skrhak, 2008).

In today's world, men with disabilities fight an uphill battle against hegemonic masculinity—their position in the social order—and its many enforcers. Men with disabilities seem to scream, "I AM STILL A MAN!" They try to make up for their shortcoming by overexaggerating the masculine qualities they still have, and society accommodates this via their support of disabled men's sexual rights and the sexist nature of medical rehabilitation programs and standards.

Gay Men

. . . Today in the United States, gay men continue to be marginalized by gender—that is, their masculinity is seen as problematic. In a survey of over 3,000 American adults (Levitt & Klassen, 1976), 69% believed homosexuals acted like the opposite sex, and that homosexual men were suitable only to the "unmasculine" careers of artist, beautician, and florist, but not the "masculine" careers of judges, doctors, and ministers. Recent studies have found similar results, despite the changing nature of gay rights in America (Blashill & Powlishta, 2009; Wright & Canetto, 2009; Wylie, Corliss, Boulanger, Prokop, & Austin, 2010).

The popular belief that gay men are not real men is established by the links among sexism (the systematic devaluation of women and "the feminine"), homophobia (the deep-seated cultural discomfort and hatred felt towards same-sex sexuality); and compulsory heterosexuality. Since heterosexuality is integral to the way a society is organized, it becomes a naturalized, "learned" behavior. When a man decides he is gay (if this "deciding" even occurs), he is rejecting the *compulsion* toward a heterosexual lifestyle and orientation (Rich, 1980).

More than this, though, compulsory heterosexuality is a mandate; society demands heterosexuality; our informal and formal policies and laws all reflect this (Fingerhut, Riggle, & Rostosky, 2011). And, in response, men find that one of the key ways to prove masculinity is to demonstrate sexual prowess. Thus, a normifying process can be discerned among gay men of the pre-HIV, post-Stonewall era. . . .

Levine's classic ethnography of clone culture makes clear that, among gay men, hypermasculine display—clothing, affective styles, fashion, and, above all, sexual promiscuity—consisted of a large promissory note to the larger culture—a culture that was both heterosexist and sexist in its anti-gay sentiments (Levine, 1995). "We are real men!" that note read. "We not only perform masculinity successfully, but we embrace the criteria that denote and confer masculinity. And so we want you, the larger dominant culture, to confer masculinity on us."

Larger dominant culture has not, generally, conferred masculinity on gay men. Indeed, a recent study found that "the stereotype of gay men as more feminine and less masculine than other men appears robust" (Mitchell & Ellis, 2011). This research found that simply labeling a man gay, despite the man presenting as gender-typical, made the man more likely to be rated as effeminate. Gender-nonconforming gay men may often feel marginalized *within gay culture itself*, from other gay men, who are most likely to have experienced stigmatization and may have been effeminate earlier in their lives. Writing about gay men's feminine stereotype, Lehne (1989) noted that, "Effeminacy itself is highly stigmatized in the homosexual subculture" (p. 417). . . .

Sociologist Tim Edwards detailed this type of rejection and reliance: on one hand, there are the *effeminists* who express gender nonconformity and/or seek to denounce traditional masculinity because of their personal style or a commitment to feminism—in other words, they reject mass social norms and deny their importance or very foundation; on the other hand, there are the *masculinists* who are proponents of gay male "machismo" and seek to challenge the long-held effeminate stereotype of gay men—they rely heavily on the hegemonic ideals. . . .

The gay men who conform to hegemonic norms, secure their position in the power hierarchy by adopting the heterosexual masculine role and subordinating both women and effeminate gay men. Having noted that hypermasculine gay men have been accused of being "collaborators with patriarchy," Messner (1997) pointed out the prominence of hegemonic masculinity in gay culture: "it appears that the dominant tendency in gay culture eventually became an attempt to claim, eroticize, and display the dominant symbols of hegemonic masculinity" (p. 83).

Historically, camp and drag were associated with minstrelizers, those who exaggeratedly expressed stereotypic constructions of homosexual masculinity. The 1950s hairdresser, interior decorator and florist of classic cultural stereotype were embraced as lifestyle choices, if not yet a political position. Minstrelizers embraced the stereotypes; their effeminacy asked the question "who wants to be butch all the time anyway? It's too much work." . . .

The effeminists pointed to the possibilities for a liberated masculinity offered by feminism. Effeminism, they argued, is a positive political position, aligning anti-sexist gay men with women, instead of claiming male privilege by asserting their difference from women. Since, as Dansky et al. (1977) argued, male supremacy is the root of all other oppressions, the only politically defensible position was to renounce manhood itself, to refuse privilege. Dansky and his effeminist colleagues were as critical of mainstream gay male culture (and the denigration of effeminacy by the normifiers) as by the hegemomnic dominant culture. . . .

Working Class Men

Working class men are, perhaps, an interesting reference group when compared to disabled men and gay men. The way(s) in which they are discriminated against or stigmatized seem very different. These men, in fact, are often seen as incredibly masculine; strong, stoic, hard-workers, there is something particularly masculine about what they have to do day-in and day-out. Indeed, the masculine virtues of the working class are celebrated as the physical embodiment of what all men should embrace (Gagnon & Simon, 1973; Sanders & Mahalingam, 2012).

Working-class White males may work in a system of male privilege, but they are not the main beneficiaries; they are in fact expendable. The working class is set apart from the middle and upper classes in that the working class is defined by jobs that require less formal education, sometimes (not always) less skill, and often low pay. For men, these jobs often include manual labor such as construction, automotive work, or factory work. The jobs these men hold are typically men-dominant.

If the stereotypic construction of masculinity among the working class celebrates their physical virtues, it also problematizes their masculinity by imagining them as dumb brutes. . . . Minstrelizing

might be the sort of self-effacing comments such as "I'm just a working stiff." It can be a minstrelizing strategy of low-level resistance because these behaviors actually let the working class man off the hook when it comes to accountability or responsibility. . . .

We can also see this type of minstrelization in men who over-emphasize their adherence to strict gender roles—being rough, uncivilized, brave, or brutish. . . .

Of course, there also are elements of militant chauvinism in the proclamation of those stereotypes as well. For men in these positions, sexism and patriarchy are key features of their masculine dominance. When the work force is decidedly all or mostly male, relationships are often "built through a decidedly male idiom of physical jousting, sexual boasting, sports talk, and shared sexual activities" (Freeman, 1993). Here, what is key for men is how they can effectively "compensate" for being underlings in the eyes of the managers that rule over them and the families they go home to. Using physical endurance and tolerance of discomfort, required by their manual labor, they signify a truer masculinity than even their office-working bosses can embody. They somehow signify a truer masculinity than their effeminate, "yes-men," paper-pushing managers can lay claim to (Collinson, 1992).

Moreover, those in the working, or blue-collar, class form a network of relationships with other blue-collar workers that serve to support them and give them a sense of status and worth, regardless of actual status or worth in the outside world (Cohen & Hodges, 1963). In fact, because those in the working class cannot normally exercise a great amount of power in their jobs or in many other formal relationships, they tend to do so in their relationships with other working class members. "To a greater extent than other classes, [the lower-lower class] will tend to measure status by power, and to validate his own claim to status, where he feels entitled to it, by asserting a claim to power" (Cohen & Hodges, 1963).

However, for those who want to minimize the apparent differences between them and the more dominant masculine ideal, a site of normification could be the focus on all men's general relationship to women and the family. Those involved in the union movement, for example, stake claims to manhood and masculinity by organizing around the principle of men as breadwinners. The basic job that all "real men" should share is to provide for their wives and children. This would explain the initial opposition to women's entry into the workplace, and also now the opposition to gay men's and lesbian women's entrance. There is a type of White, male, working class solidarity vis-à-vis privilege that these men have constructed and maintained, that promotes and perpetuates racism, sexism, and homophobia—the nexus of beliefs that all men are supposed to value (Embrick, Walther, & Wickens, 2007).

. . . In the absence of legitimated hierarchical benefits and status, working class husbands and partners are more likely to "produce hypermasculinity by relying on blatant, brutal, and relentless power strategies in their marriages, including spousal abuse" (Pyke, 1996). However, violence can also extend outside the home. As Pyke (1996) points out, "The hypermasculinity found in certain lower-status male locales, such as on shop floors, in pool halls, motorcycle clubs, and urban gangs, can be understood as both a response to ascendant masculinity and its unintentional booster." . . .

Conclusion

Privilege is not monolithic; it is unevenly distributed and it exists worldwide in varying forms and contexts. Among members of one privileged class, other mechanisms of marginalization may mute or reduce privilege based on another status. . . . In this paper, we described these processes for three groups of men in the United States—men with disabilities, gay men, and working class men—who see their gender privilege reduced and their masculinity questioned, not confirmed, through their other marginalized status. We described strategies these men might use to restore, retrieve, or resist that loss. Using Goffman's discussion of stigma, we described three patterns of response. It is through these strategies—minsterlization, normification,

and militant chauvinism—that a person's attempt to access privilege can be viewed, and, we argue, that we can better see the standards, ideals, and norms by which any society measures a man and his masculinity, and the benefits or consequences of his adherence or deviance.

References

Begum, N. (1992). Disabled women and the feminist agenda. *Feminist Review*, *40*, 70–84.

Blashill, A. J., & Powlishta, K. K. (2009). The impact of sexual orientation and gender role on evaluations of men. *Psychology of Men & Masculinity*, *10*(2), 160. doi: 10.1037/a0014583.

Cheng, C. (2008). Marginalized masculinities and hegemonic masculinity: An introduction. *The Journal of Men's Studies*, *7*(3), 295–315.

Cohen, A. K., & Hodges Jr., H. M. (1963). Characteristics of the lower-blue-collar-class. *Social Problems*, *10*(4), 303–334.

Collinson, D. (1992). *Managing the shopfloor: Subjectivity, masculinity, and workplace culture*. New York, NY: Walter de Gruyter.

Connell, R. W. (1995). *Masculinities*. Berkeley: University of California Press.

Dansky, S., Knoebel, J., & Pitchford, K. (1977). The effeminist manifesto. In J. Snodgrass (Ed.), *A book of readings: For men against sexism* (pp. 116–120). Albion, CA: Times Change Press.

Embrick, D. G., Walther, C. S., & Wickens, C. M. (2007). Working class masculinity: Keeping gay men and lesbians out of the workplace. *Sex Roles*, *56*(11), 757–766.

Fingerhut, A. W., Riggle, E. D. B., & Rostosky, S. S. (2011). Same-sex marriage: The social and psychological implications of policy and debates. *Journal of Social Issues*, *67*(2), 225–241.

Freeman, J. B. (1993). Hardhats: Construction workers, manliness, and the 1970 pro-war demonstrations. *Journal of Social History*, *26*(4), 725–744. Retrieved from http://www.jstor.org.libproxy.cc.stonybrook.edu/stable/pdfplus/3788778.pdf.

Gagnon, J. H., & Simon, W. (1973). *Sexual conduct: The social origins of human sexuality*. Chicago, IL: Aldine.

Goffman, E. (1963). *Stigma*. Englewood Cliffs, NJ: Prentice-Hall.

Jeffreys, S. (2008). Disability and the male sex right. *Women's Studies International Forum, 31*(5), 327–335. doi: 10.1016/j.wsif.2008.08.001.

Lehne, G. K. (1989). Homophobia among men: Supporting and defining the male role. In M. Kimmel & M. Messner (Eds.), *Men's lives* (pp. 416–429). New York, NY: Macmillan.

Levine, M. (1995). *Gay Macho*. New York: New York University Press.

Levitt, E. E., & Klassen, A. D. (1976). Public attitudes toward homosexuality. *Journal of Homosexuality, 1*(1), 29–43. doi: 10.1300/J082v01n01_03.

Mcintosh, P. (1988). *White privilege and male privilege: A personal account of coming to see correspondences through work in women's studies*. Working Paper no. 189. Wellesley, MA: Wellesley College Center for Research on Women.

Messner, M. A. (1997). *Politics of masculinities: Men in movements*. New York, NY: Sage.

Mitchell, R. W., & Ellis, A. L. (2011). In the eye of the beholder: Knowledge that a man is gay promotes American college students' attributions of cross-gender characteristics. *Sexuality & Culture, 15*(1), 80–100.

Pratto, F., & Stewart, A. L. (2012). Group Dominance and the Half-Blindness of Privilege. *Journal of Social Issues, 68*(1), 28–45. doi: 10.1111/j.1540-4560.2011.01734.x.

Pyke, K. D. (1996). Class-based masculinities: The interdependence of gender, class, and interpersonal power. *Gender and Society, 10*(5), 527–549.

Rich, A. (1980). Compulsory heterosexuality and lesbian existence. *Signs, 5*(4), 631–660.

Sanders, M. R., & Mahalingam, R. (2012). Under the radar: The role of invisible discourse in understanding class-based privilege. *Journal of Social Issues, 68*(1), 112–127. doi: 10.1111/j.1540-4560.2011.01739.x.

Schwartz, L. (2008). *For one night only*. Melbourne: The Age.

Skrhak, K. S. (2008). CSI's Robert David Hall is still standing. *Success Magazine*. Retrieved from http://www.successmagazine.com/csi-robert-david-hall-is-still-standing/PARAMS/article/1134/channel/22 on October 11, 2011.

West, C., & Zimmerman, D. (1987). Doing gender. *Gender and Society, 1*(2), 125–151.

Wright, S. L., & Canetto, S. (2009). Stereotypes of older lesbians and gay men. *Educational Gerontology, 35*(5), 424–452. doi: 10.1080/03601270802505640.

Wylie, S. A., Corliss, H. L., Boulanger, V., Prokop, L. A., & Austin, S. B. (2010). Socially assigned gender nonconformity: A brief measure for use in surveillance and investigation of health disparities. *Sex Roles*, 1–13.

All Men Are *Not* Created Equal

Asian Men in U.S. History

YEN LE ESPIRITU

Today, virtually every major metropolitan market across the United States has at least one Asian American female newscaster. In contrast, there is a nearly total absence of Asian American men in anchor positions (Hamamoto, 1994, p. 245; Fong-Torres, 1995). This gender imbalance in television news broadcasting exemplifies the racialization of Asian American manhood: Historically, they have been depicted as either asexual or hypersexual; today, they are constructed to be less successful, assimilated, attractive, and desirable than their female counterparts (Espiritu, 1996, pp. 95–98). The exclusion of Asian men from Eurocentric notions of the masculine reminds us that not all men benefit—or benefit equally—from a patriarchal system designed to maintain the unequal relationship that exists between men and women. The feminist mandate for gender solidarity tends to ignore power differentials among men, among women, and between white women and men of color. This exclusive focus on gender bars traditional feminists from recognizing the oppression of men of color: the fact that there are men, and not only women, who have been "feminized" and the fact that some white middle-class women hold cultural power and class power over certain men of color (Cheung, 1990, pp. 245–246; Wiegman, 1991, p. 311). Presenting race and gender as relationally constructed, King-Kok Cheung (1990) exhorted white scholars to acknowledge that, like female voices, "the voices of many

men of color have been historically silenced or dismissed" (p. 246). Along the same line, black feminists have referred to "racial patriarchy"—a concept that calls attention to the white/patriarch master in U.S. history and his dominance over the black male as well as the black female (Gaines, 1990, p. 202).

Throughout their history in the United States, Asian American men, as immigrants and citizens of color, have faced a variety of economic, political, and ideological racism that have assaulted their manhood. During the pre–World War II period, racialized and gendered immigration policies and labor conditions emasculated Asian men, forcing them into womanless communities and into "feminized" jobs that had gone unfilled due to the absence of women. During World War II, the internment of Japanese Americans stripped *Issei* (first generation) men of their role as the family breadwinner, transferred some of their power and status to the U.S.-born children, and decreased male dominance over women. In the contemporary period, the patriarchal authority of Asian immigrant men, particularly those of the working class, has also been challenged due to the social and economic losses that they suffered in their transition to life in the United States. As detailed below, these three historically specific cases establish that the material existences of Asian American men have historically contradicted the Eurocentric, middle-class constructions of manhood.

Yen Le Espiritu, "All Men Are *Not* Created Equal: Asian Men in U.S. History." Reprinted by permission of the author.

Asian Men in Domestic Service

Feminist scholars have argued accurately that domestic service involves a three-way relationship between privileged white men, privileged white women, and poor women of color (Romero, 1992). But women have not been the only domestic workers. During the pre–World War II period, racialized and gendered immigration policies and labor conditions forced Asian men into "feminized" jobs such as domestic service, laundry work, and food preparation.[1] Due to their non-citizen status, the closed labor market, and the shortage of women, Asian immigrant men, first Chinese and later Japanese, substituted to some extent for female labor in the American West. David Katzman (1978) noted the peculiarities of the domestic labor situation in the West in this period: "In 1880, California and Washington were the only states in which a majority of domestic servants were men" (p. 55).

At the turn of the twentieth century, lacking other job alternatives, many Chinese men entered into domestic service in private homes, hotels, and rooming houses (Daniels, 1988, p. 74). Whites rarely objected to Chinese in domestic service. In fact, through the 1900s, the Chinese houseboy was the symbol of upper-class status in San Francisco (Glenn, 1986, p. 106). As late as 1920, close to 50 percent of the Chinese in the United States were still occupied as domestic servants (Light, 1972, p. 7). Large numbers of Chinese also became laundrymen, not because laundering was a traditional male occupation in China, but because there were very few women of any ethnic origin—and thus few washerwomen—in gold-rush California (Chan, 1991, pp. 33–34). Chinese laundrymen thus provided commercial services that replaced women's unpaid labor in the home. White consumers were prepared to patronize a Chinese laundryman because as such he "occupied a status which was in accordance with the social definition of the place in the economic hierarchy suitable for a member of an 'inferior race'" (cited in Siu, 1987, p. 21). In her autobiographical fiction *China Men*, Maxine Hong Kingston presents her father and his partners as engaged in their laundry business for long periods each day—a business

considered so low and debased that, in their songs, they associate it with the washing of menstrual blood (Goellnicht, 1992, p. 198). The existence of the Chinese houseboy and launderer—and their forced "bachelor" status—further bolstered the stereotype of the feminized and asexual or homosexual Asian man. Their feminization, in turn, confirmed their assignment to the state's labor force which performed "women's work."

Japanese men followed Chinese men into domestic service. By the end of the first decade of the twentieth century, the U.S. Immigration Commission estimated that 12,000 to 15,000 Japanese in the western United States earned a living in domestic service (Chan, 1991, pp. 39–40). Many Japanese men considered housework beneath them because in Japan only lower-class women worked as domestic servants (Ichioka, 1988, p. 24). Studies of Issei occupational histories indicate that a domestic job was the first occupation for many of the new arrivals, but unlike Chinese domestic workers, most Issei eventually moved on to agricultural or city trades (Glenn, 1986, p. 108). Filipino and Korean boys and men likewise relied on domestic service for their livelihood (Chan, 1991, p. 40). In his autobiography *East Goes West*, Korean immigrant writer Younghill Kang (1937) related that he worked as a domestic servant for a white family who treated him "like a cat or a dog" (p. 66).

Filipinos, as stewards in the U.S. Navy, also performed domestic duties for white U.S. naval officers. During the ninety-four years of U.S. military presence in the Philippines, U.S. bases served as recruiting stations for the U.S. armed forces, particularly the navy. Soon after the United States acquired the Philippines from Spain in 1898, its navy began actively recruiting Filipinos—but only as stewards and mess attendants. Barred from admissions to other ratings, Filipino enlistees performed the work of domestics, preparing and serving the officers' meals, and caring for the officers' galley, wardroom, and living spaces. Ashore, their duties ranged from ordinary housework to food services at the U.S. Naval Academy hall. Unofficially, Filipino stewards also have been ordered to perform menial chores such as walking the officers' dogs and acting as personal servants for the officers' wives (Espiritu, 1995, p. 16).

As domestic servants, Asian men became subordinates of not only privileged white men but also privileged white women. The following testimony from a Japanese house servant captures this unequal relationship:

> Immediately the ma'am demanded me to scrub the floor. I took one hour to finish. Then I had to wash windows. That was very difficult job for me. Three windows for another hour! . . . The ma'am taught me how to cook. . . . I was sitting on the kitchen chair and thinking what a change of life it was. The ma'am came into the kitchen and was so furious! It was such a hard work for me to wash up all dishes, pans, glasses, etc., after dinner. When I went into the dining room to put all silvers on sideboard, I saw the reflection of myself on the looking glass. In a white coat and apron! I could not control my feelings. The tears so freely flowed out from my eyes, and I buried my face with my both arms. (quoted in Ichioka, 1988, pp. 25–26)

The experiences of Asian male domestic service workers demonstrate that not all men benefit equally from patriarchy. Depending on their race and class, men experience gender differently. While male domination of women may tie all men together, men share unequally in the fruits of this domination. For Asian American male domestic workers, economic and social discriminations locked them into an unequal relationship with not only privileged white men but also privileged white women (Kim, 1990, p. 74).

The racist and classist devaluation of Asian men had gender implications. The available evidence indicates that immigrant men reasserted their lost patriarchal power in racist America by denigrating a weaker group: Asian women. In *China Men*, Kingston's immigrant father, having been forced into "feminine" subject positions, lapses into silence, breaking the silence only to utter curses against women (Goellnicht, 1992, pp. 200–201). Kingston (1980) traces her father's abuse of Chinese women

back to his feeling of emasculation in America: "We knew that it was to feed us you had to endure demons and physical labor" (p. 13). On the other hand, some men brought home the domestic skills they learned on the jobs. Anamaria Labao Cabato relates that her Filipino-born father, who spent twenty-eight years in the navy as a steward, is "one of the best cooks around" (Espiritu, 1995, p. 143). Leo Sicat, a retired U.S. Navy man, similarly reports that "we learned how to cook in the Navy, and we brought it home. The Filipino women are very fortunate because the husband does the cooking. In our household, I do the cooking, and my wife does the washing" (Espiritu, 1995, p. 108). Along the same line, in some instances, the domestic skills which men were forced to learn in their wives' absence were put to use when husbands and wives reunited in the United States. The history of Asian male domestic workers suggests that the denigration of women is only one response to the stripping of male privilege. The other is to institute a revised domestic division of labor and gender relations in the families.

Changing Gender Relations: The Wartime Internment of Japanese Americans

Immediately after the bombing of Pearl Harbor, the incarceration of Japanese Americans began. On the night of 7 December 1941, working on the principle of guilt by association, the Federal Bureau of Investigation (FBI) began taking into custody persons of Japanese ancestry who had connections to the Japanese government. On 19 February 1942, President Franklin Delano Roosevelt signed Executive Order 9066, arbitrarily suspending civil rights of U.S. citizens by authorizing the "evacuation" of 120,000 persons of Japanese ancestry into concentration camps, of whom approximately 50 percent were women and 60 percent were U.S.-born citizens (Matsumoto, 1989, p. 116).

The camp environment—with its lack of privacy, regimented routines, and new power hierarchy—inflicted serious and lasting wounds on Japanese American family life. In the cramped twenty-by-twenty-five-foot "apartment" units, tensions were high as men, women, and children struggled to recreate family life under very trying conditions. The internment also transformed the balance of power in families: husbands lost some of their power over wives, as did parents over children. Until the internment, the Issei man had been the undisputed authority over his wife and children: he was both the breadwinner and the decision maker for the entire family. Now "he had no rights, no home, no control over his own life" (Houston and Houston, 1973, p. 62). Most important, the internment reverted the economic roles—and thus the status and authority—of family members. With their means of livelihood cut off indefinitely, Issei men lost their role as breadwinners. Despondent over the loss of almost everything they had worked so hard to acquire, many Issei men felt useless and frustrated, particularly as their wives and children became less dependent on them. Daisuke Kitagawa (1967) reports that in the Tule Lake relocation center, "the [Issei] men looked as if they had suddenly aged ten years. They lost the capacity to plan for their own futures, let alone those of their sons and daughters" (p. 91).

Issei men responded to this emasculation in various ways. By the end of three years' internment, formerly enterprising, energetic Issei men had become immobilized with feelings of despair, hopelessness, and insecurity. Charles Kikuchi remembers his father—who "used to be a perfect terror and dictator"—spending all day lying on his cot: "He probably realizes that he no longer controls the family group and rarely exerts himself so that there is little family conflict as far as he is concerned" (Modell, 1973, p. 62). But others, like Jeanne Wakatsuki Houston's father, reasserted their patriarchal power by abusing their wives and children. Stripped of his roles as the protector and provider for his family, Houston's father "kept pursuing oblivion through drink, he kept abusing Mama, and there seemed to be no way out of it for anyone. You couldn't even run" (Houston and Houston, 1973, p. 61). The experiences of the Issei men underscore the intersections of racism and

sexism—the fact that men of color live in a society that creates sex-based norms and expectations (i.e., man as breadwinner) which racism operates simultaneously to deny (Crenshaw, 1989, p. 155).

Camp life also widened the distance and deepened the conflict between the Issei and their U.S.-born children. At the root of these tensions were growing cultural rifts between the generations as well as a decline in the power and authority of the Issei fathers. The cultural rifts reflected not only a general process of acculturation, but were accelerated by the degradation of everything Japanese and the simultaneous promotion of Americanization in the camps (Chan, 1991, p. 128; see also Okihiro, 1991, pp. 229–232). The younger *Nisei* also spent much more time away from their parents' supervision. As a consequence, Issei parents gradually lost their ability to discipline their children, whom they seldom saw during the day. Much to the chagrin of the conservative parents, young men and women began to spend more time with each other unchaperoned—at the sports events, the dances, and other school functions. Freed from some of the parental constraints, the Nisei women socialized more with their peers and also expected to choose their own husbands and to marry for "love"—a departure from the old customs of arranged marriage (Matsumoto, 1989, p. 117). Once this occurred, the prominent role that the father plays in marriage arrangements—and by extension in their children's lives—declined (Okihiro, 1991, p. 231).

Privileging U.S. citizenship and U.S. education, War Relocation Authority (WRA) policies regarding camp life further reverted the power hierarchy between the Japan-born Issei and their U.S.-born children. In the camps, only Nisei were eligible to vote and to hold office in the Community Council; Issei were excluded because of their alien status. Daisuke Kitagawa (1967) records the impact of this policy on parental authority: "In the eyes of young children, their parents were definitely inferior to their grown-up brothers and sisters, who as U.S. citizens could elect and be elected members of the Community Council. For all these reasons many youngsters lost confidence in, and respect for, their parents" (p. 88). Similarly, the WRA salary scales were based on English-speaking ability and on citizenship status. As a result, the Nisei youths and young adults could earn relatively higher wages than their fathers. This shift in earning abilities eroded the economic basis for parental authority (Matsumoto, 1989, p. 116).

At war's end in August 1945, Japanese Americans had lost much of the economic ground that they had gained in more than a generation. The majority of Issei women and men no longer had their farms, businesses, and financial savings; those who still owned property found their homes dilapidated and vandalized and their personal belongings stolen or destroyed (Broom and Riemer, 1949). The internment also ended Japanese American concentration in agriculture and small businesses. In their absence, other groups had taken over these ethnic niches. This loss further eroded the economic basis of parental authority since Issei men no longer had businesses to hand down to their Nisei sons (Broom and Riemer, 1949, p. 31). Historian Roger Daniels (1988) declared that by the end of World War II, "the generational struggle was over: the day of the Issei had passed" (286). Issei men, now in their sixties, no longer had the vigor to start over from scratch. Forced to find employment quickly after the war, many Issei couples who had owned small businesses before the war returned to the forms of manual labor in which they began a generation ago. Most men found work as janitors, gardeners, kitchen helpers, and handymen; their wives toiled as domestic servants, garment workers, and cannery workers (Yanagisako, 1987, p. 92).

Contemporary Asian America: The Disadvantaged

Relative to earlier historical periods, the economic pattern of contemporary Asian America is considerably more varied, a result of both the postwar restructured economy and the 1965 Immigration Act.[2] The dual goals of the 1965 Immigration Act—to facilitate family reunification and to admit educated workers needed by the U.S. economy—have produced two distinct chains of emigration from

Asia: one comprising the relatives of working-class Asians who had immigrated to the United States prior to 1965; the other of highly trained immigrants who entered during the late 1960s and early 1970s (Liu, Ong, and Rosenstein, 1991). Given their dissimilar backgrounds, Asian Americans "can be found throughout the income spectrum of this nation" (Ong, 1994, p. 4). In other words, today's Asian American men both join whites in the well-paid, educated, white collar sector of the workforce *and* join Latino immigrants in lower-paying secondary sector jobs (Ong and Hee, 1994). This economic diversity contradicts the model minority stereotype—the common belief that most Asian American men are college educated and in high-paying professional or technical jobs.

The contemporary Asian American community includes a sizable population with limited education, skills, and English-speaking ability. In 1990, 18 percent of Asian men and 26 percent of Asian women in the United States, age 25 and over, had less than a high school degree. Also, of the 4.1 million Asians 5 years and over, 56 percent did not speak English "very well" and 35 percent were linguistically isolated (U.S. Bureau of the Census, 1993, Table 2). The median income for those with limited English was $20,000 for males and $15,600 for females; for those with less than a high school degree, the figures were $18,000 and $15,000, respectively. Asian American men and women with both limited English-speaking ability and low levels of education fared the worst. For a large portion of this disadvantaged population, even working full-time, full-year brought in less than $10,000 in earnings (Ong and Hee, 1994, p. 45).

The disadvantaged population is largely a product of immigration: Nine tenths are immigrants (Ong and Hee, 1994). The majority enter as relatives of the pre-1956 working-class Asian immigrants. Because immigrants tend to have socioeconomic backgrounds similar to those of their sponsors, most family reunification immigrants represent a continuation of the unskilled and semiskilled Asian labor that emigrated before 1956 (Liu, Ong, and Rosenstein, 1991). Southeast Asian refugees, particularly the second-wave refugees who arrived after 1978, represent another largely disadvantaged group. This is partly so because refugees are less likely to have acquired readily transferable skills and are more likely to have made investments (in training and education) specific to the country of origin (Chiswick, 1979; Montero, 1980). For example, there are significant numbers of Southeast Asian military men with skills for which there is no longer a market in the United States. In 1990, the overall economic status of the Southeast Asian population was characterized by unstable, minimum-wage employment, welfare dependency, and participation in the informal economy (Gold and Kibria, 1993). These economic facts underscore the danger of lumping all Asian Americans together because many Asian men do not share in the relatively favorable socioeconomic outcomes attributed to the "average" Asian American.

Lacking the skills and education to catapult them into the primary sector of the economy, disadvantaged Asian American men and women work in the secondary labor market—the labor-intensive, low-capital service, and small manufacturing sectors. In this labor market, disadvantaged men generally have fewer employment options than women. This is due in part to the decline of male-occupied manufacturing jobs and the concurrent growth of female-intensive industries in the United States, particularly in service, microelectronics, and apparel manufacturing. The garment industry, microelectronics, and canning industries are top employers of immigrant women (Mazumdar, 1989, p. 19; Takaki, 1989, p. 427; Villones, 1989, p. 176; Hossfeld, 1994, pp. 71–72). In a study of Silicon Valley (California's famed high-tech industrial region), Karen Hossfeld (1994) reported that the employers interviewed preferred to hire immigrant women over immigrant men for entry-level, operative jobs (p. 74). The employers' "gender logic" was informed by the patriarchal and racist beliefs that women can afford to work for less, do not mind dead-end jobs, and are more suited physiologically to certain kinds of detailed and routine work. As Linda Lim (1983) observes, it is the "*comparative disadvantage* of women in the wage-labor market that gives them a comparative advantage vis-à-vis men in the occupations and industries where they are concentrated—so-called female ghettoes of employment" (p. 78). A white male production manager and hiring supervisor in a California Silicon Valley assembly shop discusses his formula for hiring:

> Just three things I look for in hiring [entry-level, high-tech manufacturing operatives]: small, foreign, and female. You find those three things and you're pretty much automatically guaranteed the right kind of work force. These little foreign gals are grateful to be hired—very, very grateful—no matter what. (Hossfeld, 1994, p. 65)

Refugee women have also been found to be more in demand than men in secretarial, clerical, and interpreter jobs in social service work. In a study of Cambodian refugees in Stockton, California, Shiori Ui (1991) found that social service agency executives preferred to hire Cambodian women over men when both had the same qualifications. One executive explained his preference, "It seems that some ethnic populations relate better to women than men. . . . Another thing is that the pay is so bad" (cited in Ui, 1991, p. 169). As a result, in the Cambodian communities in Stockton, it is often women—and not men—who have greater economic opportunities and who are the primary breadwinners in their families (Ui, 1991, p. 171).

Due to the significant decline in the economic contributions of Asian immigrant men, women's earnings comprise an equal or greater share of the family income. Because the wage each earns is low, only by pooling incomes can a husband and wife earn enough to support a family (Glenn, 1983, p. 42). These shifts in resources have challenged the patriarchal authority of Asian men. Men's loss of status and power—not only in the public but also in the domestic arena—places severe pressure on their sense of well-being. Responding to this pressure, some men accepted the new division of labor in the family (Ui, 1991, pp. 170–173); but many others resorted to spousal abuse and divorce (Luu, 1989, p. 68).

A Korean immigrant man describes his frustrations over changing gender roles and expectations:

> In Korea [my wife] used to have breakfast ready for me. . . . She didn't do it any more because she said she was too busy getting ready to go to work. If I complained she talked back at me, telling me to fix my own breakfast. . . . I was very frustrated about her, started fighting and hit her. (Yim, 1978, quoted in Mazumdar, 1989, p. 18)

Loss of status and power has similarly led to depression and anxieties in Hmong males. In particular, the women's ability—and the men's inability—to earn money for households "has undermined severely male omnipotence" (Irby and Pon, 1988, p. 112). Male unhappiness and helplessness can be detected in the following joke told at a family picnic, "When we get on the plane to go back to Laos, the first thing we will do is beat up the women!" The joke—which generated laughter by both men and women—drew upon a combination of "the men's unemployability, the sudden economic value placed on women's work, and men's fear of losing power in their families" (Donnelly, 1994, pp. 74–75). As such, it highlights the interconnections of race, class, and gender—the fact that in a racist and classist society, working-class men of color have limited access to economic opportunities and thus limited claim to patriarchal authority.

Conclusion

A central task in feminist scholarship is to expose and dismantle the stereotypes that traditionally have provided ideological justifications for women's subordination. But to conceptualize oppression only in terms of male dominance and female subordination is to obscure the centrality of classism, racism, and other forms of inequality in U.S. society (Stacey and Thorne, 1985, p. 311). The multiplicities of Asian men's lives indicate that ideologies of manhood and womanhood have as much to do with class and race as they have to do with sex. The intersections of race, gender, and class mean that there are also hierarchies among women and among men and that some women hold power over certain groups of men. The task for feminist scholars, then, is to develop paradigms that articulate the complicity among these categories of oppression, that strengthen the alliance between gender and ethnic studies, and that reach out not only to women, but also to men, of color.

Notes

1. One of the most noticeable characteristics of pre–World War II Asian America was a pronounced shortage of women. During this period, U.S. immigration policies barred the entry of most Asian women. America's capitalist economy also wanted Asian male workers but not their families. In most instances, families were seen as a threat to the efficiency and exploitability of the workforce and were actively prohibited.

2. The 1965 Immigration Act ended Asian exclusion and equalized immigration rights for all nationalities. No longer constrained by exclusion laws, Asian immigrants began arriving in much larger numbers than ever before. In the 1980s, Asia was the largest source of U.S. legal immigrants, accounting for 40 percent to 47 percent of the total influx (Min, 1995, p. 12).

References

Broom, Leonard and Ruth Riemer. 1949. *Removal and Return: The Socio-Economic Effects of the War on Japanese Americans*. Berkeley: University of California Press.

Chan, Sucheng. 1991. *Asian Americans: An Interpretive History*. Boston: Twayne.

Cheung, King-Kok. 1990. "The Woman Warrior Versus the Chinaman Pacific: Must a Chinese American Critic Choose Between Feminism and Heroism?" In *Conflicts in Feminism*, edited by Marianne Hirsch and Evelyn Fox Keller (pp. 234–251). New York and London: Routledge.

Chiswick, Barry. 1979. "The Economic Progress of Immigrants: Some Apparently Universal Patterns." In *Contemporary Economic Problems* edited by W. Fellner (pp. 357–399). Washington, DC: American Enterprise Institute.

Crenshaw, Kimberlee. 1989. "Demarginalizing the Intersection of Race and Sex: A Black Feminist Critique of Antidiscrimination Doctrine, Feminist Theory and Antiracist Politics." In *University of Chicago Legal Forum: Feminism in the Law: Theory, Practice, and Criticism* (pp. 139–167). Chicago: University of Chicago Press.

Daniels, Roger. 1988. *Asian America: Chinese and Japanese in the United States Since 1850*. Seattle: University of Washington Press.

Donnelly, Nancy D. 1994. *Changing Lives of Refugee Hmong Women*. Seattle: University of Washington Press.

Espiritu, Yen Le. 1995. *Filipino American Lives*. Philadelphia: Temple University Press.

Espiritu, Yen Le. 1996. *Asian American Women and Men: Labor, Laws, and Love*. Thousand Oaks, CA: Sage.

Fong-Torres, Ben. 1995. "Why Are There No Male Asian Anchormen on TV?" In *Men's Lives*, 3rd ed., edited by Michael S. Kimmel and Michael A. Messner (pp. 208–211). Boston: Allyn and Bacon.

Gaines, Jane. 1990. "White Privilege and Looking Relations: Race and Gender in Feminist Film Theory." In *Issues in Feminist Film Criticism*, edited by Patricia Erens (pp. 197–214). Bloomington: Indiana University Press.

Glenn, Evelyn Nakano. 1983. "Split Household, Small Producer and Dual Wage Earner: An Analysis of Chinese-American Family Strategies." *Journal of Marriage and the Family*, February: 35–46.

Glenn, Evelyn Nakano. 1986. *Issei, Nisei, War Bride: Three Generations of Japanese American Women at Domestic Service*. Philadelphia: Temple University Press.

Goellnicht, Donald C. 1992. "Tang Ao in America: Male Subject Positions in *China Men*." In *Reading the Literatures of Asian America*, edited by Shirley Geok-lin-Lim and Amy Ling (pp. 191–212). Philadelphia: Temple University Press.

Gold, Steve and Nazli Kibria. 1993. "Vietnamese Refugees and Blocked Mobility." *Asian and Pacific Migration Review* 2: 27–56.

Hamamoto, Darrell. 1994. *Monitored Peril: Asian Americans and the Politics of Representation*. Minneapolis: University of Minnesota Press.

Hossfeld, Karen J. 1994. "Hiring Immigrant Women: Silicon Valley's 'Simple Formula.'" In *Women of Color in U.S. Society*, edited by Maxine Baca Zinn and Bonnie Thornton Dill (pp. 65–93). Philadelphia: Temple University Press.

Houston, Jeanne Wakatsuki and James D. Houston. 1973. *Farewell to Manzanar*. San Francisco: Houghton Mifflin.

Ichioka, Yuji. 1988. *The Issei: The World of the First Generation Japanese Immigrants, 1885–1924*. New York: The Free Press.

Irby, Charles and Ernest M. Pon. 1988. "Confronting New Mountains: Mental Health Problems Among Male Hmong and Mien Refugees. *Amerasia Journal* 14: 109–118.

Kang, Younghill. 1937. *East Goes West*. New York: C. Scribner's Sons.

Katzman, David. 1978. "Domestic Service: Women's Work." In *Women Working: Theories and Facts in Perspective*, edited by Ann Stromberg and Shirley Harkess (pp. 377–391). Palo Alto, CA: Mayfield.

Kim, Elaine. 1990. " 'Such Opposite Creatures': Men and Women in Asian American Literature." *Michigan Quarterly Review*, 68–93.

Kingston, Maxine Hong. 1980. *China Men*. New York: Knopf.

Kitagawa, Daisuke. 1967. *Issei and Nisei: The Internment Years*. New York: Seabury Press.

Light, Ivan. 1972. *Ethnic Enterprise in America: Business and Welfare Among Chinese, Japanese, and Blacks*. Berkeley and Los Angeles: University of California Press.

Lim, Linda Y. C. 1983. "Capitalism, Imperialism, and Patriarchy: The Dilemma of Third-World Women Workers in Multinational Factories." In *Women, Men, and the International Division of Labor*, edited by June Nash and Maria Patricia Fernandez-Kelly (pp. 70–91). Albany: State University of New York.

Liu, John, Paul Ong, and Carolyn Rosenstein. 1991. "Dual Chain Migration: Post-1965 Filipino Immigration to the United States." *International Migration Review* 25(3): 487–513.

Luu, Van. 1989. "The Hardships of Escape for Vietnamese Women." In *Making Waves: An Anthology of Writings by and About Asian American Women*, edited by Asian Women United of California (pp. 60–72). Boston: Beacon Press.

Matsumoto, Valerie. 1989. "Nisei Women and Resettlement During World War II." In *Making Waves: An Anthology of Writings by and about Asian American Women*, edited by Asian Women United of California (pp. 115–126). Boston: Beacon Press.

Mazumdar, Sucheta. 1989. "General Introduction: A Woman-Centered Perspective on Asian American History." In *Making Waves: An Anthology by and about Asian American Women*, edited by Asian Women United of California (pp. 1–22). Boston: Beacon Press.

Min, Pyong Gap. 1995. "Korean Americans." In *Asian Americans: Contemporary Trends and Issues*, edited by Pyong Gap Min (pp. 199–231). Thousand Oaks, CA: Sage.

Modell, John, ed. 1973. *The Kikuchi Diary: Chronicle from an American Concentration Camp*. Urbana: University of Illinois Press.

Montero, Darrell. 1980. *Vietnamese Americans: Patterns of Settlement and Socioeconomic Adaptation in the United States*. Boulder, CO: Westview.

Okihiro, Gary Y. 1991. *Cane Fires: The Anti-Japanese Movement in Hawaii, 1865–1945*. Philadelphia: Temple University Press.

Ong, Paul. 1994. "Asian Pacific Americans and Public Policy." In *The State of Asian Pacific America: Economic Diversity, Issues, & Policies*, edited by Paul Ong (pp. 1–9). Los Angeles: LEAP Asian Pacific American Public Policy Institute and UCLA Asian American Studies Center.

Ong, Paul and Suzanne Hee. 1994. "Economic Diversity." In *The State of Asian Pacific America: Economic Diversity, Issues, & Policies*, edited by Paul Ong (pp. 31–56). Los Angeles: LEAP Asian Pacific American Public Policy Institute and UCLA Asian American Studies Center.

Romero, Mary. 1992. *Maid in the U.S.A.* New York: Routledge.

Siu, Paul. 1987. *The Chinese Laundryman: A Study in Social Isolation*. New York: New York University Press.

Stacey, Judith and Barrie Thorne. 1985. "The Missing Feminist Revolution in Sociology." *Social Problems* 32: 301–316.

Takaki, Ronald. 1989. *Strangers from a Different Shore: A History of Asian Americans*. Boston: Little, Brown.

Ui, Shiori. 1991. "'Unlikely Heroes': The Evolution of Female Leadership in a Cambodian Ethnic Enclave." In *Ethnography Unbound: Power and Resistance in the Modern Metropolis*, edited by Michael Burawoy et al. (pp. 161–177). Berkeley: University of California Press.

U.S. Bureau of the Census. 1993. *We the American Asians*. Washington, DC: U.S. Government Printing Office.

Villones, Rebecca. 1989. "Women in the Silicon Valley." In *Making Waves: An Anthology of Writings by and About Asian American Women*, edited by Asian Women United of California (pp. 172–176). Boston: Beacon Press.

Wiegman, Robyn. 1991. "Black Bodies/American Commodities: Gender, Race, and the Bourgeois Ideal in Contemporary Film." In *Unspeakable Images: Ethnicity and the American Cinema*, edited by Lester Friedman (pp. 308–328). Urbana and Chicago: University of Illinois Press.

Yanagisako, Sylvia Junko. 1987. "Mixed Metaphors: Native and Anthropological Models of Gender and Kinship Domains." In *Gender and Kinship: Essays Toward a Unified Analysis*, edited by Jane Fishburne Collier and Sylvia Junko Yanagisako (pp. 86–118). Palo Alto, CA: Stanford University Press.

Latino Masculinities in the Post-9/11 Era

HERNAN RAMIREZ AND EDWARD FLORES

American television, movies and magazines depict Latino[1] men in contradictory ways, as dangerous gun-toting hardened criminals and as family-oriented, low-wage laborers. The subordinate, "sleepy Mexican" still circulates in satirical form, as we saw in the 2009 film *Brüno*, which featured a talk show where Mexican gardeners kneel on all fours, substituting as chairs for the guests. Meanwhile, the image of Latino men as foreign, dangerous, and subversive appears more frequently in news reports of drug traffickers and gang members. The *Los Angeles Times* recently reported on military-style gang sweeps involving over one thousand law enforcement officials, assault rifles, and tanks. Readers posted racist comments online, such as, "They don't get deported and we taxpayers have to support them."

These two popular images of Latino men—as violently subversive foreign threats, or as docile low-wage workers—reflect sociologist Alfredo Mirande's (1997) analysis of Latino masculinity as rooted in dualistic cultural expressions of honor and dishonor. Over time, these dualistic images have had tremendous staying power. The mid-twentieth century movie image of Joaquin Murrieta's Mexican bandits marauding on horseback, killing lawmen, and stealing gold has morphed today into stereotypical portrayals of the violent urban Latino gang. The past image of the sleepy Mexican in a poncho and a sombrero has today become that of the docile Latino gardener. Mirande would argue that together, these two images have their origins in Mexican men's compensatory reactions to colonial subordination. The cultural meanings of "macho," Mirande emphasizes, are best understood not as an attempt by Latino men to dominate women, but rather, as Latino men's multifaceted attempts to forge a respected and honored position in a context of cultural subordination.

Alternatively, gender scholars have located Latino masculinities within shifting political–economic relations in the United States. Maxine Baca Zinn (1982) argues that "manhood takes on greater importance for those who do not have access to socially valued roles," and that "to be 'hombre' . . . may take on greater significance when other roles and sources of masculine identity are structurally blocked." This view emphasizes that Latino men's masculine expressions are a result of contemporary structural conditions. Blocked economic mobility, poor schools, and dangerous urban neighborhoods compromise Latinos' and Blacks' access to conventional masculine expressions (i.e., Smith 2006; Lopez 2003; Bourgois 1995; Anderson 1990; Ferguson 2000).

In this article we report on our in-depth ethnographic research with Latino men behind these two images, the gardener and the gangster. Hernan Ramirez's research highlights Mexican immigrant gardeners' experience with low-wage labor and economic mobility, and the masculinities that organize, and are organized by, such a precarious social position. Edward Flores's research focuses on recovering gang members' experiences with rehabilitation, and the way in which masculinity organizes such rehabilitation. Our research is based in Los Angeles, and highlights how nativist backlash and persisting structural obstacles shape Latino men's masculine expressions.

We begin by considering the larger political and economic conditions in which the masculinity of Latino gang members and gardeners is embedded and expressed. By understanding some of the structural conditions that funnel Chicano men into gang activity and Mexican immigrant men into suburban maintenance gardening, respectively, we can enlarge our inquiry into contemporary Latino men and masculinities beyond the cultural stereotype of machismo.

Context

In the 1970s and 1980s, the effects of economic restructuring and deindustrialization were evident in major cities throughout the United States, as stable, relatively well-paid manufacturing jobs disappeared while low-wage service sector jobs grew (Kasarda 1995). In global cities (Sassen 1991) such as New York and Los Angeles, this decline in manufacturing was accompanied by an expanding high-income professional and managerial class. Problems endemic to America's inner cities— including gangs, drugs, unemployment, and violent crime—were linked to the disappearance of blue-collar jobs in the wake of deindustrialization (Wilson 1987, 1996). Moreover, with changes to U.S. immigration law in 1965, large numbers of immigrants from Asia and Latin America began entering the United States. By the 1990s, these new immigrants were increasingly present in retail and service employment (Lamphere et al. 1994), as exploited workers in hotels and restaurants, and in other jobs where wages are low and career ladders are short (Bobo et al. 2000). These structural transformations, coupled with years of disinvestment in

our nation's public school systems, have left many young, urban Latino men at a marked economic disadvantage. Today, Mexican immigrant and Chicano men often find themselves on insecure economic ground, relying on casual work and a growing informal economy (i.e., one largely outside of formal regulations, union contracts, and guaranteed benefits) for their livelihoods.

Against this backdrop of swirling economic changes, the political climate faced by post-1965 Mexican immigrants has been ambivalent at best, and outright xenophobic at worst. For example, a 2001 *Time* magazine cover featured the word "Amexica," with colors from the national Mexican and American flags, and a statement about the vanishing border. Anthropologist Leo Chavez (2008) argues that by juxtaposing foreign images onto familiar American icons, media representations of Latinos suggest that post-1965 immigrants are unlike those of previous generations and will soon alter the nation's landscape. Similarly, the *Los Angeles Times* article on the gang sweep was presented in ways that meshed racist/sexist constructions of Latino males as foreigners and subversive.

The image of Latino men as foreign invaders has grown in the post-9/11 era. The USA PATRIOT Act of 2001 enhanced the discretion of law enforcement and immigration authorities in detaining and deporting immigrants suspected of terrorism-related acts, and it also added a looser definition of "domestic terrorism," now vague enough to apply not just to anti-American militia groups but urban gang members (Brotherton and Kretsedemas 2008). Although the FBI found no established link between gang members and international terrorism, these fears of urban gang members as foreign and subversive coalesced when the FBI investigated suspicions that Jose Padilla, an arrested Al-Qaeda operative, had gang ties in the United States (Brotherton and Kretsedemas 2008).

At the same time that this debate has unfolded, there has been an upswing in the number of right-wing pundits and politicians who characterize Latino immigrant men as a threat. Espousing a fear of immigrants as potential "terrorist" intruders, criminals, and threats to national security, radio and television hosts such as Lou Dobbs, Rush Limbaugh, and Glenn Beck rally support for restrictive immigration policies, increased federal funding for Border Patrol/ICE activities, and the building of a fence along the U.S.–Mexico border. The degree of virulent, xenophobic rhetoric leveled against Mexican immigrant men can be explained as an outgrowth of the post-9/11 fear of brown-skinned "outsiders" as well as a continuation of decades-old patterns of anti-Latino immigrant hysteria and discrimination. Since 9/11, cities across the United States have formulated anti-day laborer ordinances that have had the indirect—but intended—effect of excluding undocumented immigrants from their jurisdictions (Varsanyi 2008). One extreme right-wing nativist website claims that "some of the most violent murderers, rapists, and child molesters are illegal aliens who work as day laborers" (daylaborers.org), even though the social scientific literature indicates that most day laborers attend church regularly, and that nearly two-thirds of them have children (Valenzuela et al. 2006). These are certainly not characteristics one would expect to find among a population of men purportedly out to prey upon America's women and children.

In reality, the large concentrations of Latino immigrant men who work in the construction and home improvement trades, including roofers, painters, and dry-wall installers, as well as landscapers and gardeners, have become integral pistons in America's economic engine. Remarkably, one out of every eight Mexican immigrants in the United States currently works in the construction industry (Siniavskaia 2005). In New Orleans, post–Hurricane Katrina reconstruction efforts were spearheaded by thousands of immigrant men from Mexico and Central America (Quiñones 2006). This reliance on Mexican immigrant men to fill the nation's labor needs has historical precedence, as evidenced by the Bracero Program of the mid-twentieth century. Nevertheless, the link between images of Latino men, immigration, and crime has crystallized in the post-9/11 era. This has spurred a heightened fear of Latinos and has renewed interest in militarization of the border and the deportation of undocumented immigrants.

The political and economic transformations outlined have placed Chicano and Mexican immigrant men in a precarious situation vis-à-vis access to jobs and resources. Moreover, they have been subjected to discriminatory treatment and vilified as dangerous "outsiders" and potential criminal threats in the wake of 9/11. We can now take a closer look at a specific group of Latino men, *jardineros*—or Mexican immigrant gardeners—and think about how their masculinity is a response to structural inequality, exclusion, and discrimination.

Latino Masculinity at Work: *Jardinero* Masculinity

Gendered divisions of labor are well established and found throughout the economy. In fact, scholars of gender and work have long been concerned with understanding the ways in which gender itself is constructed on the job. While our knowledge of masculinity in blue-collar work settings has been growing (Ouellet 1994; Paap 2006; Desmond 2007), less is known about Latino immigrant men's work and how predominantly Latino immigrant workplaces serve as an arena for the construction and negotiation of Latino working-class masculinities. Although it was historically associated with the labor of Japanese American men in Pacific Coast cities (Tsuchida 1984; Tsukashima 1991), suburban maintenance gardening is today institutionalized as a Mexican man's job. Particularly large concentrations of Mexican immigrant men can be found working in the sunny climes of Los Angeles and Southern California more generally, mowing lawns, pruning trees, and maintaining the lush, leafy landscapes with which the region is so often associated.

As Smith (2003) notes, much of the literature on immigration is too quick to treat men as thoughtlessly embracing a traditional "ranchero" masculinity they may have been raised on in their rural villages of origin, one which legitimizes men's dominant and women's subordinate position. In reality, some migrant men pragmatically adapt to their new environment and engage in an ongoing critique of traditional masculinity (Smith 2006). Most *jardineros* come from ranches or rural villages in central-western Mexico, yet their displays of masculinity are influenced and shaped by their immigration experiences and by their structural position as low-wage laborers in the U.S. informal economy.

Jardinero masculinity refers to the distinctly working-class form of masculinity that Mexican immigrant men construct through their daily work activities in residential maintenance gardening, a male-dominated occupational niche, and in their daily on-the-job interactions with their fellow workers. This particular version of masculinity is unique in that it unfolds in the specific, working-class occupational and regional context of Southern Californian maintenance gardening and is deployed against a backdrop of racialized nativism and citizenship hierarchy in the United States. It finds its expression on the ground level, as *jardineros* engage in hard, dirty work on a daily basis to provide sustenance for their family members; as they engage in on-the-job conversations with their co-workers that can range from measured talk to friendly verbal banter; and as they put their bodies to the test in the course of their daily work routines.

Understanding *jardinero* masculinity requires sensitivity both to culture and to social structure. Moving beyond a sort of reiteration of a one-dimensional, cultural concept of "machismo," one culturally grounded in Mexico and simply re-articulated in the United States, *jardinero* masculinity stresses a more nuanced structural understanding of Mexican immigrant men's masculinity and how it is intertwined with their daily performance of masculinized "dirty" work in private residences. Yes, *jardineros* sometimes engage in on-the-job drinking and catcalling, traditionally "machista" modes of behavior. But the better part of these men's days is not spent in those activities, but rather with back-breaking, dangerous, physically hard manual work.

Like most men, *jardineros* derive their status primarily from their control of subsistence, through which they fulfill their primary cultural obligation, the economic support of their wives and children

(Stone and McKee 2002: 129). The ideal man, one who is truly "manly," will provide for all of his family's needs. In practice, though, this ideal of male behavior may be very difficult for Mexican immigrant *jardineros* to achieve in the public world. This is especially true for *ayudantes*, young, apprentice gardeners who—unlike more experienced, self-employed owners of gardening routes—tend to be recently arrived, undocumented immigrants. *Ayudantes* typically share crowded apartments with other undocumented *paisanos* who are in a similar situation. They must work long hours while making low wages and evading the gaze of the authorities. *Ayudantes* present us with one type of *jardinero* masculinity, in which men's ability to fulfill socially valued breadwinner roles is severely limited by an important structural barrier: undocumented status.

Mexican immigrant gardeners express their masculinity in subtle ways, through their words and actions. While on the job, they often use humor as a "male bonding" mechanism, playfully teasing each other in order to alleviate the tedium of working together for long hours under the sun. Their workplace is where the *jardineros* develop the strong bodies and weathered hands that are a hallmark of their masculinity. Although they are readily available, *jardineros* often prefer to work without protective gloves. This can be explained in part by one *jardinero*'s observation that it is better to develop a pair of rough and callused hands because they are "manos de hombre," or "man hands," an outward symbol of their working-class masculinity.

Through their hard work cleaning and maintaining other people's properties, Mexican immigrant gardeners are able to provide for their families, but they are also able to gain the respect and esteem of their co-workers, projecting a masculinity that is honored by their fellow working-class men. For instance, as Carlos, a very young, recently arrived *ayudante*, proclaimed that he had entered the United States in order "to work hard, not to be lazy"("a trabajar duro, no a estar de huevon"), his older co-workers nodded in approval.

The difficulties faced by undocumented *jardineros* who hope to better provide for their loved ones by becoming self-employed route owners are described by Jose, a *veteran jardinero* with more than 20 years of experience:

> Well, there are obstacles that make things more difficult, really, because if a guy doesn't have a driver's license nowadays, how can he start his business? Without "papeles" (legal papers), you can't get a license. What do you do? Nobody knows you. How do you charge your clients? They give you a check, where do you cash it? It's tough, it's really tough without a license, because how are you going to go ahead and invest money in a truck and in equipment and everything, if later they're going to take everything away? The police will catch you driving without a license and will take everything away from you. That's what happened to a guy that I know.

Once again we are reminded of the importance of understanding the structural constraints faced by Mexican immigrant men and how these impinge on their masculinity. Nationwide, many states have banned the issuance of driver's licenses to undocumented immigrants (Vock 2007; Seif 2003). This has had a deleterious effect on the livelihoods of undocumented Mexican immigrant men who work in gardening and landscaping, as well as in other jobs that require driving from jobsite to jobsite on a daily basis.

Many people believe that since Mexican immigrant gardeners wear dirty clothes, do dirty jobs, and have little formal education, they are necessarily drains on social services and the economy. Yet things are not as they appear to outsiders, as the maintenance gardening sector has allowed some *veteran jardineros* to achieve financial success and upward mobility (Ramirez and Hondagneu-Sotelo 2009). Most self-employed, independent owners of gardening routes entered the United States as undocumented immigrants some 20 or 30 years ago, speaking little or no English, but have since gone on to become legal residents or U.S. citizens, purchasing homes in the United States and even putting their children through college. Such men are *worker-entrepreneurs* who have worked hard day

in and day out alongside their *ayudantes*, but who have done quite well for themselves by building and looking after gardening routes that can generate six-figure incomes. These financially solvent, self-employed owners of gardening routes (or "rutas") present us with a second type of *jardinero* masculinity: as *worker-entrepreneurs*, gardening route owners enjoy a great deal of autonomy and are able to fulfill the masculine ideal of providing for their families.

While *ayudantes* might fit the public's conception of Mexican immigrant men as "docile" low-wage workers, gardening route owners are essentially small entrepreneurs who display a remarkable degree of business acumen. However, behind the potential for economic success and mobility that comes with running one's own business there lay some hidden costs. Gardening route owners typically work very long hours, six days a week. Consequently, the amount of "quality time" they are able to spend with their spouses and children is very limited. Miguel, a gardening route owner, poignantly describes his situation:

> I would want the best for my kids. That they wouldn't . . . well, that they wouldn't have to work like I've had to work. I'd want them to have a better life. Better for them. Less backbreaking. I also get home late. I get home late from work, tired. Sometimes, I can't describe what I feel—[My kids] even tell me, "You don't want to play with us, papi." "I tell them, "No, son, it's because I get back home really tired. You want me to start playing with you, to play, to run, to play basketball . . . Son, don't you know how tired I am when I return home from work? And you still want to keep playing . . ." [laughs]. I tell them, "No, it's because I can't."

Gardening route owners must thus grapple with work–family conflicts that can diminish their ability to be as present in the lives of their children and spouses as they would like to be. Unlike *ayudantes*, who are low-wage workers, gardening route owners are a hybrid form of worker and entrepreneur; as such, they must spend long days toiling under the sun while constantly strategizing and thinking about ways of keeping their businesses afloat, even if it detracts from the amount—and quality—of time they spend with their family members. The work takes a physical toll on them, but it also takes a toll on their ability to fulfill their masculine roles as husbands and fathers.

Having considered the case of masculinity among Mexican immigrant gardeners, encompassing the experiences of young *ayudantes* and veteran gardening route owners, let us turn now to an examination of masculinity among another group of Latino men in Los Angeles: recovering gang members.

Latino Masculinity in Recovery: Reformed Barrio Masculinity

In contrast to immigrant Latino men employed in the densely concentrated maintenance gardening sector, men who have spent the majority of their life in the United States express different types of masculinities. Male Latinos are exposed to a particular type of masculine socialization in the barrio that makes them vulnerable to join gangs (Vigil 1988; Moore 1991; Yablonski 1997; Smith 2006). Three activities form the core of male Latino gang life, or *deviant barrio masculinity*: substance abuse, gang violence, and extramarital affairs. These three activities are embodied in a gang member's clothes, speech, and swagger. As one man said, "My role model was a gang member, all tattoos, coming out of prison, being buff, having all kinds of women, that's what I wanted to grow up to be" (Flores 2009).

Nevertheless, some Chicano gang members do want to exit from gang lifestyle, and do so by reconstructing notions of what it means to be a man. Gang members in recovery have conventional aspirations, such as getting married and having children, working in the formal labor market, and owning a home (Flores 2009). The young man quoted above said he had converted to Christianity the night he attended a play in which a Pentecostal church performed a drama with ex-gang members, "So I seen all that in the play, I see nothing but homeys with big ole' whips, tattoos, in the play talking about God, and that they're not using drugs, and they're not in prison no more, and I say, 'ey, cool.'"

Masculinity is central to faith-based rehabilitation, as leaders facilitate the process of recovery by transforming gang members' gendered expressions from deviant barrio masculinity to *reformed barrio masculinity* (Brusco 1995). Pastors frequently chastise members for abusing substances, not holding down a job, or engaging in extramarital affairs. Recovering gang members, instead of desiring to be like the leaders of the gang hierarchy, desire to become more like the leaders in the organization facilitating rehabilitation. Yablonski (1997) corroborates this and finds that ex-gang members often find meaning by becoming counselors in a therapeutic community. In such communities men are instructed to make social and economic contributions to their household and to abstain from substance abuse, gang violence, and extramarital affairs.

At sites such as Victory Outreach, a highly spiritual Pentecostal church, and Homeboy Industries, a nondenominational nonprofit, leaders and members contest the notion that urban gang members are unable to change. The Latino men at these organizations approach this process in different ways. Spiritual worship plays an important role in the process of gendered recovery. At Homeboy Industries, Latino ex-gang members make use of Native American spiritual practices, such as sweat lodges, or Eastern spiritual practices, such as meditation and yoga, to symbolically expel cravings for drugs or violence. They get involved in 12-step programs, such as Alcoholics Anonymous, Substance Abuse, or Criminals and Gang Members Anonymous. The class moderators use the clinical language of therapeutic rehabilitation to encourage respect and honesty among class participants. They also juxtapose social critiques of the United States as an unequal society, such as the heightened sentencing handed out to gang members, with personal narratives that ask for redemption and seek personal change.

At Victory Outreach, a Latino pastor makes an altar call at the end of each sermon, proclaiming the opportunity for persons who are "serious" about "changing" or "rededicating" their life to God. Often, many members of the congregation gather in front of the pastor, worshipping in a tightly congested space, placing hands on each other, and speaking stream-of-thought prayers. During the regular sermon, a band plays loud, fast-paced Christian music that members clap and move to, and this alternates with soft music and prayer for roughly 45 minutes. A Victory Outreach pastor then allows men in recovery to "take the pulpit" and give announcements, recaps of important events, share testimonies, or even give a guest sermon. They also juxtapose biblical references of helping persons in need, such as that found in the Book of Mark, with their personal narratives of redemption and change. In these spiritually-based social interactions, men repeatedly frame the meaning of "being a man."

The patriarchal characteristics of reformed barrio masculinity motivate many Latino men to continue with recovery. Members at Victory Outreach often voice their ambition to be a "man of God," to one day get "launched out," or to "take a city" as the pastor of a new church.

Members aspire not only to recover from gang life, but to fulfill the ideals of the patriarchal American dream: to get married, hold a good job, and own a home. Several claim to have faith in God and to want to follow in the footsteps of their leaders because God "blessed" their pastor with a wife and children and a home. Members at Homeboy Industries talk about wanting to experience rehabilitation in order to provide for their mothers, partners, and children. Members that experienced close relationships with Father Greg, during the early years of a much smaller Homeboy Industries, say they aspire to be like Father Greg.

Unfortunately, the process of recovery is not a straight-line trajectory; many Latino gang members oscillate between recovery and sometimes the elements of gang lifestyle, such as smoking marijuana, drinking, or socializing with old acquaintances in the gang's neighborhood, that can spur a complete relapse. Several men became weary of placing themselves in situations that could escalate to a full relapse. Chris, a member of Victory Outreach who has been in recovery for four years, expressed a fear that he could easily engage in the same types of destructive social interactions by simply being around old gang members. As he put it, "I was really afraid to run into my old homies, because I know they were a big influence on me . . . it would just take a couple of hours for me to start drinking, or start getting high . . . you never know what could happen. You could get into a fight, you could get shot. [I]t doesn't take very long for you to go all the way back into your whole lifestyle." In order to prevent from engaging in gang behavior, Chris must now make his therapeutic community (Victory Outreach) his primary sphere of socialization. He hopes to become a leader, possibly even a pastor, within the Victory Outreach hierarchy.

Some men also admitted to relapsing into gang activity. Matthew, a 20-year-old member of Homeboy Industries, asked if I knew of any vocational programs that could lead to stable employment. He said he had recently called a well-known vocational school but that they were reluctant to answer his questions after they found out he had two felonies on his record. A week later, I read in the *Los Angeles Times* that Matthew was picked up in a major gang sweep. I scanned through the photos of the military-style operation and read that a police officer alleged he had been selling drugs; the evidence—FBI wiretaps linking Matthew's involvement to his gang—however was four to five years old, predating his entry into rehabilitation. For carrying a gun during drug deals several years ago, Matthew is now facing a third felony. Under California law, this carries a mandatory sentence of life in prison without the possibility of parole.

Conclusion

The true diversity and complexity of Latino masculinities in the post-9/11 era goes well beyond the images that circulate in American television, movies, and magazines. Two dominant media images of Latino men, that of the docile low-wage worker and the hyper-masculine, criminal gang member, reiterate Mirande's (1997) views of machismo: It is a strictly cultural response to colonization and European domination, wherein the docile worker is colonized and the gangster remains defiant. Our ethnographic research with the real men behind these two images reveals an array of masculinities that, taken together, highlight the deficiencies of thinking about Latino men strictly in terms of traditional machismo, or a rigid cult of masculinity. Instead, our approach follows the lead of Baca Zinn (1982), who calls on students of Latino masculinity to view it as a response to structural inequality, exclusion, and discrimination. Culture plays a role, but structural constraints that keep men from living up to dominant masculine ideals must also be taken into consideration. As we saw, recent political and economic transformations have placed Chicano and Mexican immigrant men in an especially difficult situation vis-à-vis access to jobs and resources. Moreover, they have been vilified as brown-skinned "outsiders" and potential criminal threats in the wake of the terrorist attacks of 9/11.

Against this structural context, *jardinero masculinity* has developed as a distinctly working-class form of masculinity that Mexican immigrant men construct through their daily work activities in residential maintenance gardening, a male occupational niche. Its very expression is linked to their daily performance of hard, dirty, manual labor. In addition, while young apprentice gardeners, or *ayudantes*, find their ability to fulfill traditional masculine roles blocked by their undocumented status, upwardly mobile owners of gardening routes face unique constraints on their ability to balance work and family life. With *jardineros* as with gang members, looks can be deceiving. Just as it may be difficult to tell an *ayudante* from a successful gardening route owner based strictly on their appearance, it may also be difficult to tell an active gang member from a recovering one. But by looking closely at recovering gang members in two faith-based outreach organizations, Homeboy Industries and Victory Outreach, we can see men leaving behind a life of substance abuse and gang violence, and actively embracing a *reformed barrio masculinity*, characterized by more conventional aspirations, such as getting married and starting a family. In the post-9/11 era, it is imperative that we continue to explore the structural conditions that are linked to multiplicities of Latino masculinities.

Note

1. Although this article is concerned with both native and foreign-born Latino men living in the United States, its primary emphasis is on first-generation Mexican immigrant men and Chicano, or Mexican American, men in the Los Angeles area.

References

Anderson, Elijah. 1990. *Streetwise: Race, Class, and Change in an Urban Community*. Chicago: University of Chicago Press.

Baca Zinn, Maxine. 1982. "Chicano Men and Masculinity." *Journal of Ethnic Studies* 10(2):29–144.

Bobo, Lawrence D., Melvin L. Oliver, James H. Johnson, Jr., and Abel Valenzuela, Jr. 2000. "Analyzing Inequality in Los Angeles." pp. 3–50 in *Prismatic Metropolis: Inequality in Los Angeles*. New York: Russell Sage Foundation.

Bourgois, Philippe. 1995. *In Search of Respect: Selling Crack in El Barrio*. Cambridge: Cambridge University Press.

Brotherton, David C., and Philip Kretsedemas (eds.). 2008. *Keeping Out the Other: A Critical Introduction to Immigration Enforcement Today*. New York: Columbia University Press.

Brusco, Elizabeth. 1995. *The Reformation of Machismo: Evangelical Conversion and Gender in Colombia*. Austin: University of Texas Press.

Chavez, Leo R. 2008. *The Latino Threat: Constructing Immigrants, Citizens, and the Nation*. Stanford, CA: Stanford University Press.

Desmond, Matthew. 2007. *On the Fireline: Living and Dying with Wildland Firefighters*. Chicago: University of Chicago Press.

Ferguson, Ann Arnett. 2000. *Bad Boys: Public Schools in the Making of Black Masculinity*. Ann Arbor: University of Michigan Press.

Flores, Edward. 2009. "I Am Somebody: Barrio Pentecostalism and Gendered Acculturation among Chicano Ex-Gang Members." *Ethnic and Racial Studies* 32:6.

Kasarda, John. 1995. "Industrial Restructuring and the Changing Location of Jobs." pp. 215–267 in *State of the Union: America in the 1990s*, edited by Reynolds Farley. New York: Russell Sage Foundation.

Lamphere, Louise, Alex Stepick, and Guillermo Grenier. 1994. *Newcomers in the Workplace: Immigrants and the Restructuring of the U.S. Economy*. Philadelphia: Temple University Press.

Lopez, Nancy. 2003. *Hopeful Girls, Troubled Boys: Race and Gender Disparity in Urban Education*. New York: Routledge.

Mirande, Alfredo. 1997. *Hombres y Machos: Masculinity and Latino Culture*. Boulder: Westview Press.

Moore, Joan. 1991. *Going Down to the Barrio: Homeboys and Homegirls in Change*. Philadelphia: Temple University Press.

Ouellet, Lawrence J. 1994. *Pedal to the Metal: The Work Lives of Truckers*. Philadelphia: Temple University Press.

Paap, Kris. 2006. *Working Construction: Why White Working-Class Men Put Themselves—and the Labor Movement—in Harm's Way*. Ithaca, NY: Cornell University Press.

Quiñones, Sam. 2006. "Migrants Find a Gold Rush in New Orleans." *Los Angeles Times*, April 4.

Ramirez, Hernan, and Pierrette Hondagneu-Sotelo. 2009. "Mexican Immigrant Gardeners: Entrepreneurs or Exploited Workers?" *Social Problems* 56(1):70–88.

Sassen, Saskia. 1991. *The Global City: New York, London, Tokyo*. Princeton: Princeton University Press.

Seif, Hinda. 2003. "'Estado de Oro'o 'Jaula de Oro'? Undocumented Mexican Immigrant Workers, the Driver's License, and Subnational legalization in California." UC San Diego, Working Papers, The Center for Comparative Immigration Studies.

Siniavskaia, Natalia. 2005. "Immigrant Workers in Construction." National Association of Home Builders. Available at: http://www.nahb.org/generic.aspx?genericContentID=49216 (accessed October 2009).

Smith, Robert C. 2003. "Gender Strategies, Settlement and Transnational Life." Paper presented at the 2003 Meetings of the American Sociological Association. Atlanta, GA.

———. 2006. *Mexican New York: Transnational Lives of New Immigrants*. Berkeley: University of California Press.

Stone, Linda, and Nancy P. McKee. 2002. *Gender and Culture in America*. 2nd edition. Upper Saddle River, NJ: Prentice Hall.

Tsuchida, Nobuya. 1984. "Japanese Gardeners in Southern California, 1900–1941." pp. 435–469 in *Labor Immigration Under Capitalism: Asian Workers in the United States Before World War II*, edited by Lucie Cheng and Edna Bonacich. Berkeley: University of California Press.

Tsukashima, Ronald Tadao. 1991. "Cultural Endowment, Disadvantaged Status and Economic Niche: The Development of an Ethnic Trade." *International Migration Review* 25(2):333–354.

Valenzuela, Abel, Nik Theodore, Edwin Melendez, and Ana Luz Gonzalez. 2006. "On the Corner: Day Labor in the United States." UCLA Center for the Study of Urban Poverty.

Varsanyi, Monica W. 2008. "Immigration Policing through the Backdoor: City Ordinances, the 'Right to the City,' and the Exclusion of Undocumented Day Laborers." *Urban Geography* 29(1):29–52.

Vigil, James Diego. 1988. *Barrio Gangs: Street Life and Identity in Southern California*. Austin: University of Texas Press.

Vock, Daniel C. 2007. "Tighter License Rules Hit Illegal Immigrants." *Stateline*. August 24. Available at: http://www.stateline.org/live/details/story?contentId=234828 (accessed October 2009).

Wilson, William Julius. 1987. *The Truly Disadvantaged*. Chicago: University of Chicago Press.

———. 1996. *When Work Disappears: The World of the New Urban Poor*. New York: Vintage Books.

Yablonski, Lewis. 1997. *Gangsters: Fifty Years of Madness, Drugs, and Death on the Streets of America*. New York: New York University Press.

Boyhood

"One is not born, but rather becomes, a woman," wrote the French feminist Simone de Beauvoir in her ground-breaking book *The Second Sex* (New York: Vintage, 1958). The same is true for men. And the social processes by which boys become men are complex and important. How does early childhood socialization differ for boys and girls? What specific traits are emphasized for boys that mark their socialization as different? What types of institutional arrangements reinforce those traits? How do the various institutions in which boys find themselves— school, family, and circles of friends—influence their development? What of the special institutions that promote "boys' life" or an adolescent male subculture?

During childhood and adolescence, masculinity becomes a central theme in a boy's life. *New York Times* editor A. M. Rosenthal put the dilemma this way: "So there I was, 13 years old, the smallest boy in my freshman class at DeWitt Clinton High School, smoking a White Owl cigar. I was not only little, but I did not have longies—long trousers—and was still in knickerbockers. Obviously, I had to do something to project my fierce sense of manhood" (*New York Times*, April 26, 1987). That the assertion of manhood is part of a boy's natural development is suggested by Roger Brown in his textbook *Social Psychology* (New York: Free Press, 1965, p. 161):

In the United States, a real boy climbs trees, disdains girls, dirties his knees, plays with soldiers, and takes blue for his favorite color. When they go to school, real boys prefer manual training, gym, and arithmetic. In college the boys smoke pipes, drink beer, and major in engineering or physics. The real boy matures into a "man's man" who plays poker, goes hunting, drinks brandy, and dies in the war.

The articles in this part address the question of how boys develop, focusing on the institutions that shape boys' lives. Ellen Jordan and Angela Cowan describe how professional-class ideas of masculinity shape and constrain the experiences of young boys, in the kindergarten classroom. Families are also powerful sites of gender construction. Ann Travers shows how gender nonconformity affects young people in sports, and Victoria Redel challenges readers to think carefully before offering parenting advice about gender conformity.

In schools too, one of the key policing mechanisms of masculinity is homophobia. C. J. Pascoe argues that "fag discourse"—a ubiquity of homophobic slurs in schools—places powerful constraints on boys, while helping to reinforce the higher status of (apparently) heterosexual boys. There's little softening of masculinity in the tough, ritual performances of masculine fighting that Jessica Pfaffendorf examines in a boarding school.

Together, these studies of boys suggest that institutional contexts—what kinds of schools, what kinds of families—matter greatly in how boys' identities and relationships are shaped and constrained.

PART II DISCUSSION QUESTIONS

1. What are the similarities and differences between manhood and boyhood? How are they maintained in wider society?
2. Referring to Jordan and Cowan's article, how does a classroom characterized by free choice become a gendered space? How do the children contribute to this process? How do the teacher and the physical space itself do so?
3. Sports can be a microcosm for gendered and racial protest in society at large. According to Ann Travers's piece, how does sports culture challenge or reproduce gender constructs? What are some contemporary protests visible in sports that reflect wider debates about race and gender?
4. Why is intersectionality important for studying boyhood? In Pfaffendorf's piece, what does a study of race and class alongside gender show when considering the reproduction of power for certain types of men?
5. Considering the arguments made by C. J. Pascoe, why do you think boys are so threatened by the "unmasculine" behaviors of other boys? Why and how does gender become a collective institution?
6. Boyhood both naturalizes and upsets biologically deterministic arguments for innate masculinity. How do the readings in this section relate to this tension?

Bedecked

VICTORIA REDEL

Tell me it's wrong the scarlet nails my son sports or the toy store rings he clusters
    four jewels to each finger.

He's bedecked. I see the other mothers looking at the star choker, the rhinestone
    strand he fastens over a sock.
Sometimes I help him find sparkle clip-ons when he says sticker earrings
    look too fake.

Tell me I should teach him it's wrong to love the glitter that a boy's only a boy
    who'd love a truck with a remote that revs,
battery slamming into corners or Hot Wheels loop-de-looping off tracks
    into the tub.

Then tell me it's fine—really—maybe even a good thing—a boy who's got some girl
    to him,
and I'm right for the days he wears a pink shirt on the seesaw in the park.

Tell me what you need to tell me but keep far away from my son who still loves
    a beautiful thing not for what it means—
this way or that—but for the way facets set off prisms and prisms spin up
    everywhere
and from his own jeweled body he's cast rainbows—made every shining true color.

Now try to tell me—man or woman—your heart was ever once that brave.

Warrior Narratives in the Kindergarten Classroom
Renegotiating the Social Contract?

ELLEN JORDAN AND ANGELA COWAN

Since the beginning of second wave feminism, the separation between the public (masculine) world of politics and the economy and the private (feminine) world of the family and personal life has been seen as highly significant in establishing gender difference and inequality (Eisenstein 1984). Twenty years of feminist research and speculation have refined our understanding of this divide and how it has been developed and reproduced. One particularly striking and influential account is that given by Carole Pateman in her book *The Sexual Contract* (1988).

Pateman's broad argument is that in the modem world, the world since the Enlightenment, a "civil society" has been established. In this civil society, patriarchy has been replaced by a fratriarchy, which is equally male and oppressive of women. Men now rule not as fathers but as brothers, able to compete with one another, but presenting a united front against those outside the group. It is the brothers who control the public world of the state, politics, and the economy. Women have been given token access to this world because the discourses of liberty and universalism made this difficult to refuse, but to take part they must conform to the rules established to suit the brothers.

This public world in which the brothers operate together is conceptualized as separate from the personal and emotional. One is a realm where there is little physicality—everything is done rationally, bureaucratically, according to contracts that the brothers accept as legitimate. Violence in this realm is severely controlled by agents of the state, except that the brothers are sometimes called upon for the supreme sacrifice of dying to preserve freedom. The social contract redefines the brawling and feuding long seen as essential characteristics of masculinity as deviant, even criminal, while the rest of physicality—sexuality, reproduction of the body, daily and intergenerationally—is left in the private sphere. Pateman quotes Robert Unger, "The dichotomy of the public and private life is still another corollary of the separation of understanding and desire. . . . When reasoning, [men] belong to a public world. . . . When desiring, however, men are private beings" (Pateman 1989, 48).

This is now widely accepted as the way men understand and experience their world. On the other hand, almost no attempt has been made to look at how it is that they take these views on board, or why the public/private divide is so much more deeply entrenched in their lived experience than in women's. This article looks at one strand in the complex web of experiences through which this is achieved. A major site where this occurs is the school, one of the institutions particularly characteristic of the civil society that emerged with the Enlightenment (Foucault 1980, 55–57). The school does not deliberately condition boys and not girls into this dichotomy, but it is, we believe, a site where what

Ellen Jordan and Angela Cowan, "Warrior Narratives in the Kindergarten Classroom: Renegotiating the Social Contract?" From *Gender & Society* 9(6): 727–743. Copyright 1995. Reprinted by permission of SAGE Publications, Inc.

Giddens (1984, 10–13) has called a cycle of practice introduces little boys to the public/private division.

The article is based on weekly observations in a kindergarten classroom. We examine what happens in the early days of school when the children encounter the expectations of the school with their already established conceptions of gender. The early months of school are a period when a great deal of negotiating between the children's personal agendas and the teacher's expectations has to take place, where a great deal of what Genovese (1972) has described as accommodation and resistance must be involved.

In this article, we focus on a particular contest, which, although never specifically stated, is central to the children's accommodation to school: little boys' determination to explore certain narratives of masculinity with which they are already familiar—guns, fighting, fast cars—and the teacher's attempts to outlaw their importation into the classroom setting. We argue that what occurs is a contest between two definitions of masculinity: what we have chosen to call "warrior narratives" and the discourses of civil society—rationality, responsibility, and decorum—that are the basis of school discipline.

By "warrior narratives," we mean narratives that assume that violence is legitimate and justified when it occurs within a struggle between good and evil. There is a tradition of such narratives, stretching from Hercules and Beowulf to Superman and Dirty Harry, where the male is depicted as the warrior, the knight-errant, the superhero, the good guy (usually called a "goody" by Australian children), often supported by brothers in arms, and always opposed to some evil figure, such as a monster, a giant, a villain, a criminal, or, very simply, in Australian parlance, a "baddy." There is also a connection, it is now often suggested, between these narratives and the activity that has come to epitomize the physical expression of masculinity in the modern era: sport (Duthie 1980, 91–94; Crosset 1990; Messner 1992, 15). It is as sport that the physicality and desire usually lived out in the private sphere are permitted a ritualized public presence. Even though the violence once characteristic

of the warrior has, in civil society and as part of the social contract, become the prerogative of the state, it can still be re-enacted symbolically in countless sporting encounters. The mantle of the warrior is inherited by the sportsman.

The school discipline that seeks to outlaw these narratives is, we would suggest, very much a product of modernity. Bowles and Gintis have argued that "the structure of social relations in education not only inures the student to the discipline of the work place, but develops the types of personal demeanor, modes of self-presentation, self-image, and social-class identifications which are the crucial ingredients of job adequacy" (1976, 131). The school is seeking to introduce the children to the behavior appropriate to the civil society of the modern world.

An accommodation does eventually take place, this article argues, through a recognition of the split between the public and the private. Most boys learn to accept that the way to power and respectability is through acceptance of the conventions of civil society. They also learn that warrior narratives are not a part of this world; they can only be experienced symbolically as fantasy or sport. The outcome, we will suggest, is that little boys learn that these narratives must be left behind in the private world of desire when they participate in the public world of reason.

The Study

The school where this study was conducted serves an old-established suburb in a country town in New South Wales, Australia. The children are predominantly Australian born and English speaking, but come from socioeconomic backgrounds ranging from professional to welfare recipient. We carried out this research in a classroom run by a teacher who is widely acknowledged as one of the finest and most successful kindergarten teachers in our region. She is an admired practitioner of free play, process writing, and creativity. There was no gender definition of games in her classroom. Groups composed of both girls and boys had turns at playing in the Doll Corner, in the Construction Area, and on the Car Mat.

The research method used was nonparticipant observation, the classic mode for the sociological study of children in schools (Burgess 1984; Thorne 1986; Goodenough 1987). The group of children described came to school for the first time in February 1993. The observation sessions began within a fortnight of the children entering school and were conducted during "free activity" time, a period lasting for about an hour. At first we observed twice a week, but then settled to a weekly visit, although there were some weeks when it was inconvenient for the teacher to accommodate an observer.

The observation was noninteractive. The observer stationed herself as unobtrusively as possible, usually seated on a kindergarten-sized chair, near one of the play stations. She made pencil notes of events, with particular attention to accurately recording the words spoken by the children, and wrote up detailed narratives from the notes, supplemented by memory, on reaching home. She discouraged attention from the children by rising and leaving the area if she was drawn by them into any interaction.

This project thus employed a methodology that was ethnographic and open-ended. It was nevertheless guided by certain theories, drawn from the work on gender of Jean Anyon, Barrie Thorne, and R. W. Connell, of the nature of social interaction and its part in creating personal identity and in reproducing the structures of a society.

Anyon has adapted the conceptions of accommodation and resistance developed by Genovese (1972) to understanding how women live with gender. Genovese argued that slaves in the American South accommodated to their contradictory situation by using certain of its aspects, for example, exposure to the Christian religion, to validate a sense of self-worth and dignity. Christian beliefs then allowed them to take a critical view of slavery, which in turn legitimated certain forms of resistance (Anyon 1983, 21). Anyon lists a variety of ways in which women accommodate to and resist prescriptions of appropriate feminine behavior, arguing for a significant level of choice and agency (Anyon 1983, 23–26).

Thorne argues that the processes of social life, the form and nature of the interactions, as well as the choices of the actors, should be the object of analysis. She writes, "In this book I begin not with individuals, although they certainly appear in the account, but with *group life*—with social relations, the organization and meanings of social situations, the collective practices through which children and adults create and recreate gender in their daily interactions" (1993, 4).

These daily interactions, Connell (1987, 139–141) has suggested, mesh to form what Giddens (1984, 10–13) has called "cyclical practices." Daily interactions are neither random nor specific to particular locations. They are repeated and recreated in similar settings throughout a society. Similar needs recur, similar discourses are available, and so similar solutions to problems are adopted; thus, actions performed and discourses adopted to achieve particular ends in particular situations have the unintended consequence of producing uniformities of gendered behavior in individuals.

In looking at the patterns of accommodation and resistance that emerge when the warrior narratives that little boys have adapted from television encounter the discipline of the classroom, we believe we have uncovered one of the cyclical practices of modernity that reveal the social contract to these boys.

Warrior Narratives in the Doll Corner

In the first weeks of the children's school experience, the Doll Corner was the area where the most elaborate acting out of warrior narratives was observed. The Doll Corner in this classroom was a small room with a door with a glass panel opening off the main area. Its furnishings—stove, sink, dolls' cots, and so on—were an attempt at a literal re-creation of a domestic setting, revealing the school's definition of children's play as a preparation for adult life. It was an area where the acting out of "pretend" games was acceptable.

Much of the boys' play in the area was domestic:

Jimmy and Tyler were jointly ironing a tablecloth. "Look at the sheet is burnt, I've burnt it," declared

Tyler, waving the toy iron above his head. "I'm telling Mrs. Sandison," said Jimmy worriedly. "No, I tricked you. It's not really burnt. See," explained Tyler, showing Jimmy the black pattern on the cloth. (February 23, 1993)

"Where is the baby, the baby boy?" Justin asked, as he helped Harvey and Malcolm settle some restless teddy babies. "Give them some potion." Justin pretended to force feed a teddy, asking "Do you want to drink this potion?" (March 4, 1993)

On the other hand, there were attempts from the beginning by some of the boys and one of the girls to use this area for nondomestic games and, in the case of the boys, for games based on warrior narratives, involving fighting, destruction, goodies, and baddies.

The play started off quietly, Winston cuddled a teddy bear, then settled it in a bed. Just as Winston tucked in his bear, Mac snatched the teddy out of bed and swung it around his head in circles. "Don't hurt him, give him back," pleaded Winston, trying vainly to retrieve the teddy. The two boys were circling the small table in the center of the room. As he ran, Mac started to karate chop the teddy on the arm, and then threw it on the floor and jumped on it. He then snatched up a plastic knife, "This is a sword. Ted is dead. They all are." He sliced the knife across the teddy's tummy, repeating the action on the bodies of two stuffed dogs. Winston grabbed the two dogs, and with a dog in each hand, staged a dog fight. "They are alive again." (February 10, 1993)

Three boys were busily stuffing teddies into the cupboard through the sink opening. "They're in jail. They can't escape," said Malcolm. "Let's pour water over them." "Don't do that. It'll hurt them," shouted Winston, rushing into the Doll Corner. "Go away, Winston. You're not in our group," said Malcolm. (February 12, 1993)

The boys even imported goodies and baddies into a classic ghost scenario initiated by one of the girls:

"I'm the father," Tyler declared. "I'm the mother," said Alanna. "Let's pretend it's a stormy night and I'm afraid. Let's pretend a ghost has come to steal the dog." Tyler nodded and placed the sheet over his head. Tyler moaned, "ooooOOOOOOOOAH-HHH!!!" and moved his outstretched arms toward Alanna. Jamie joined the game and grabbed a sheet from the doll's cradle, "I'm the goody ghost." "So am I," said Tyler. They giggled and wrestled each other to the floor. "No! you're the baddy ghost," said Jamie. Meanwhile, Alanna was making ghostly noises and moving around the boys. "Did you like the game? Let's play it again," she suggested. (February 23, 1993)

In the first two incidents, there was some conflict between the narratives being invoked by Winston and those used by the other boys. For Winston, the stuffed toys were the weak whom he must protect knight-errant style. For the other boys, they could be set up as the baddies whom it was legitimate for the hero to attack. Both were versions of a warrior narrative.

The gender difference in the use of these narratives has been noted by a number of observers (Paley 1984; Clark 1989, 250–252; Thorne 1993, 98–99). Whereas even the most timid, least physically aggressive boys—Winston in this study is typical—are drawn to identifying with the heroes of these narratives, girls show almost no interest in them at this early age. The strong-willed and assertive girls in our study, as in others (Clark 1990, 83–84; Walkerdine 1990, 10–12), sought power by commandeering the role of mother, teacher, or shopkeeper, while even the highly imaginative Alanna, although she enlivened the more mundane fantasies of the other children with ghosts, old widow women, and magical mirrors, seems not to have been attracted by warrior heroes.[1]

Warrior narratives, it would seem, have a powerful attraction for little boys, which they lack for little girls. Why and how this occurs remains unexplored in early childhood research, perhaps because data for such an explanation are not available to those doing research in institutional settings. Those undertaking ethnographic research in preschools find the warrior narratives already in possession in these sites (Paley 1984, 70–73, 116; Davies 1989, 91–92).

In this research, gender difference in the appeal of warrior narratives has to be taken as a given—the data gathered are not suitable for constructing theories of origins; thus, the task of determining an explanation would seem to lie within the province of those investigating and theorizing gender differentiation during infancy, and perhaps, specifically, of those working in the tradition of feminist psychoanalysis pioneered by Dinnerstein (1977) and Chodorow (1978). Nevertheless, even though the cause may remain obscure, there can be little argument that in the English-speaking world for at least the last hundred years—think of Tom Sawyer playing Robin Hood and the pirates and Indians in J. M. Barrie's *Peter Pan*—boys have built these narratives into their conceptions of the masculine.

Accommodation through *Bricolage*

The school classroom, even one as committed to freedom and self-actualization as this, makes little provision for the enactment of these narratives. The classroom equipment invites children to play house, farm, and shop, to construct cities and roads, and to journey through them with toy cars, but there is no overt invitation to explore warrior narratives.

In the first few weeks of school, the little boys un-self-consciously set about redressing this omission. The method they used was what is known as *bricolage*—the transformation of objects from one use to another for symbolic purposes (Hebdige 1979, 103). The first site was the Doll Corner. Our records for the early weeks contain a number of examples of boys rejecting the usages ascribed to the various Doll Corner objects by the teacher and by the makers of equipment and assigning a different meaning to them. This became evident very early with their use of the toy baby carriages (called "prams" in Australia). For the girls, the baby carriages were just that, but for many of the boys they very quickly became surrogate cars:

> Mac threw a doll into the largest pram in the Doll Corner. He walked the pram out past a group of his friends who were playing "crashes" on the Car Mat. Three of the five boys turned and watched him

wheeling the pram toward the classroom door. Mac performed a sharp three-point turn, raced his pram past the Car Mat group, striking one boy on the head with the pram wheel. (February 10, 1993)

> "Brrrrmmmmmm, brrrrrmmmmm," Tyler's revving engine noises grew louder as he rocked the pram back and forth with sharp jerking movements. The engine noise grew quieter as he left the Doll Corner and wheeled the pram around the classroom. He started to run with the pram when the teacher could not observe him. (March 23, 1993)

The boys transformed other objects into masculine appurtenances: knives and tongs became weapons, the dolls' beds became boats, and so on.

> Mac tried to engage Winston in a sword fight using Doll Corner plastic knives. Winston backed away, but Mac persisted. Winston took a knife but continued to back away from Mac. He then put down the knife, and ran away half-screaming (semi-seriously, unsure of the situation) for his teacher. (February 10, 1993)

In the literature on youth subcultures, bricolage is seen as a characteristic of modes of resistance. Hebdige writes:

> It is through the distinctive rituals of consumption, through style, that the subculture at once reveals its "secret" identity and communicates its forbidden meanings. It is predominantly the way commodities are used in subculture which mark the subculture off from more orthodox cultural formations. . . . The concept of *bricolage* can be used to explain how subcultural styles are constructed. (1979, 103)

In these early weeks, however, the boys did not appear to be aware that they were doing anything more than establishing an accommodation between their needs and the classroom environment.

This mode of accommodation was rejected by the teacher, however, who practiced a gentle, but steady, discouragement of such bricolage. Even though the objects in this space are not really irons, beds, and cooking pots, she made strong efforts to assert their cultural meaning, instructing the children in the "proper" use of the equipment and attempting to control their behavior by questions like "Would you do that with a tea towel in your house?" "Cats never climb up on the benches in *my* house." It was thus impressed upon the children that warrior narratives were inappropriate in this space.

The children, our observations suggest, accepted her guidance, and we found no importation of warrior narratives into the Doll Corner after the first few weeks. There were a number of elaborate and exciting narratives devised, but they were all to some degree related to the domestic environment. For example, on April 20, Justin and Nigel used one of the baby carriages as a four-wheel drive, packed it with equipment and went off for a camping trip, setting out a picnic with Doll Corner tablecloths, knives, forks, and plates when they arrived. On May 18, Matthew, Malcolm, Nigel, and Jonathan were dogs being fed in the Doll Corner. They then complained of the flies, and Jonathan picked up the toy telephone and said, "Flycatcher! Flycatcher! Come and catch some flies. They are everywhere." On June 1, the following was recorded:

> "We don't want our nappies [diapers] changed," Aaron informed Celia, the mum in the game. "I'm poohing all over your clothes mum," Mac declared, as he grunted and positioned himself over the dress-up box. Celia cast a despairing glance in Mac's direction, and went on dressing a doll. "I am too; poohing all over your clothes mum," said Aaron. "Now mum will have to clean it all up and change my nappy," he informed Mac, giggling. He turned to the dad [Nigel], and said in a baby voice, "Goo-goo, give him [Mac] the feather duster." "No! give him the feather duster, he did the longest one all over the clothes," Mac said to Nigel. (June 1, 1993)

Although exciting and imaginative games continued, the bricolage virtually disappeared from the Doll Corner. The intention of the designer of the Doll Corner equipment was increasingly respected. Food for the camping trip was bought from the shop the teacher had set up and consumed using the Doll Corner equipment. The space invaded by

flies was a domestic space, and appropriate means, calling in expert help by telephone, were used to deal with the problem. Chairs and tables were chairs and tables, clothes were clothes and could be fouled by appropriate inhabitants of a domestic space, babies. Only the baby carriages continued to have an ambiguous status, to maintain the ability to be transformed into vehicles of other kinds.

The warrior narratives—sword play, baddies in jail, pirates, and so on—did not vanish from the boys' imaginative world, but, as the later observations show, the site gradually moved from the Doll Corner to the Construction Area and the Car Mat. By the third week in March (that is, after about six weeks at school), the observer noticed the boys consistently using the construction toys to develop these narratives. The bricolage was now restricted to the more amorphously defined construction materials.

> Tyler was busy constructing an object out of five pieces of plastic straw (clever sticks). "This is a water pistol. Everyone's gonna get wet," he cried as he moved into the Doll Corner pretending to wet people. The game shifted to guns and bullets between Tyler and two other boys. "I've got a bigger gun," Roger said, showing off his square block object "Mine's more longer Ehehehehehehehe, got you," Winston yelled to Roger, brandishing a plastic straw gun. "I'll kill your gun," Mac said, pushing Winston's gun away. "No Mac You broke it. No," cried Winston. (March 23, 1993)

> Two of the boys picked up swords made out of blue- and red-colored plastic squares they had displayed on the cupboard. "This is my sword," Jamie explained to Tyler. "My jumper [sweater] holds it in. Whichever color is at the bottom, well that's the color it shoots out. Whoever is bad, we shoot with power out of it." "Come on Tyler," he went on. "Get your sword. Let's go get some baddies." (March 30, 1993)

The toy cars on the Car Mat were also pressed into the service of warrior narratives:

> Justin, Brendan, and Jonathan were busy on the Car Mat. The game involved police cars that were

chasing baddies who had drunk "too much beers." Justin explained to Jonathan why his car had the word "DOG" written on the front. "These are different police cars, for catching robbers taking money." (March 4, 1993)

Three boys, Harvey, Maurice, and Marshall, were on the Car Mat. "Here comes the baddies," Harvey shouted, spinning a toy car around the mat. "Crassssshhhhh everywhere." He crashed his car into the other boys' cars and they responded with laughter. "I killed a baddie everyone," said Maurice, crashing his cars into another group of cars. (May 24, 1993)

A new accommodation was being proposed by the boys, a new adaptation of classroom materials to the needs of their warrior narratives.

Classroom Rules and Resistance

Once again the teacher would not accept the accommodation proposed. Warrior narratives provoked what she considered inappropriate public behavior in the miniature civil society of her classroom. Her aim was to create a "free" environment where children could work independently, learn at their own pace, and explore their own interests, but creating such an environment involved its own form of social contract, its own version of the state's appropriation of violence. From the very first day, she began to establish a series of classroom rules that imposed constraints on violent or disruptive activity.

The belief underlying her practice was that firmly established classroom rules make genuine free play possible, rather than restricting the range of play opportunities. Her emphasis on "proper" use of equipment was intended to stop it being damaged and consequently withdrawn from use. She had rules of "no running" and "no shouting" that allowed children to work and play safely on the floor of the classroom, even though other children were using equipment or toys that demanded movement, and ensured that the noise level was low enough for children to talk at length to one another as part of their games.

One of the outcomes of these rules was the virtual outlawing of a whole series of games that groups of children usually want to initiate when they are playing together, games of speed and body contact, of gross motor self-expression and skill. This prohibition affected both girls and boys and was justified by setting up a version of public and private spaces: The classroom was not the proper place for such activities, they "belong" in the playground.[2] The combined experience of many teachers has shown that it is almost impossible for children to play games involving car crashes and guns without violating these rules; therefore, in this classroom, as in many others (Paley 1984, 71, 116), these games were in effect banned.

These rules were then policed by the children themselves, as the following interchange shows:

"Eeeeeeheeeeeeheeeeh!" Tyler leapt about the room. A couple of girls were saying, "Stop it Tyler" but he persisted. Jane warned, "You're not allowed to have guns." Tyler responded saying, "It's not a gun. It's a water pistol, and that's not a gun." "Not allowed to have water pistol guns," Tony reiterated to Tyler. "Yes, it's a water pistol," shouted Tyler. Jane informed the teacher, who responded stating, "NO GUNS, even if they are water pistols." Tyler made a spear out of Clever Sticks, straight after the banning of gun play. (March 23, 1993)

The boys, however, were not prepared to abandon their warrior narratives. Unlike gross motor activities such as wrestling and football, they were not prepared to see them relegated to the playground, but the limitations on their expression and the teacher disapproval they evoked led the boys to explore them surreptitiously; they found ways of introducing them that did not violate rules about running and shouting.

As time passed, the games became less visible. The warrior narratives were not so much acted out as talked through, using the toy cars and the construction materials as a prompt and a basis:

Tyler was showing his plastic straw construction to Luke. "This is a Samurai Man and this is his hat. A Samurai Man fights in Japan and they fight with the Ninja. The bad guys who use cannons and guns. My Samurai is captain of the Samurai and he is going to kill the sergeant of the bad guys. He is going to sneak up on him with a knife and kill him." (June 1, 1993)

Malcolm and Aaron had built boats with Lego blocks and were explaining the various components to Roger. "This ship can go faster," Malcolm explained. "He [a plastic man] is the boss of the ship. Mine is a goody boat. They are not baddies." "Mine's a steam shovel boat. It has wheels," said Aaron. "There it goes in the river and it has to go to a big shed where all the steam shovels are stopping." (June 11, 1993)

It also became apparent that there was something covert about this play. The cars were crashed quietly. The guns were being transformed into water pistols. Swords were concealed under jumpers and only used when the teacher's back was turned. When the constructed objects were displayed to the class, their potential as players in a fighting game was concealed under a more mundane description. For example:

> Prior to the free play, the children were taking turns to explain the Clever Stick and Lego Block constructions they had made the previous afternoon. I listened to Tyler describe his Lego robot to the class: "This is a transformer robot. It can do things and turn into everything." During free play, Tyler played with the same robot explaining its capacities to Winston: "This is a terminator ship. It can kill. It can turn into a robot and the top pops off." (March 23, 1993)

Children even protested to one another that they were not making weapons, "This isn't a gun, it's a lookout." "This isn't a place for bullets, it's for petrol."

The warrior narratives, it would seem, went underground and became part of a "deviant" masculine subculture with the characteristic "secret" identity and hidden meanings (Hebdige 1979, 103). The boys were no longer seeking accommodation but practicing hidden resistance. The classroom, they were learning, was not a place where it was acceptable to explore their gender identity through fantasy.

This, however, was a message that only the boys were receiving. The girls' gender-specific fantasies (Paley 1984, 106–108; Davies 1989, 118–122) of nurturing and self-display—mothers, nurses, brides, princesses—were accommodated easily within the classroom. They could be played out without contravening the rules of the miniature civil society. Although certain delightful activities—eating, running, hugging, and kissing (Best 1983, 110)—might be excluded from this public sphere, they were not ones by means of which their femininity, and thus their subjectivity, their conception of the self, was defined.

Masculinity, the School Regime, and the Social Contract

We suggest that this conflict between warrior narratives and school rules is likely to form part of the experience of most boys growing up in the industrialized world. The commitment to such narratives was not only nearly 100 percent among the boys we observed, but similar commitment is, as was argued above, common in other sites. On the other hand, the pressure to preserve a decorous classroom is strong in all teachers (with the possible exception of those teaching in "alternative" schools) and has been since the beginnings of compulsory education. Indeed, it is only in classrooms where there is the balance of freedom and constraint we observed that such narratives are likely to surface at all. In more formal situations, they would be defined as deviant and forced underground from the boys' first entry into school.

If this is a widely recurring pattern, the question then arises: Is it of little significance or is it what Giddens (1984, 10–3) would call one of the "cyclical practices" that reproduce the structures of our society? The answer really depends on how little boys "read" the outlawing of their warrior narratives. If they see it as simply one of the broad constraints of school against which they are continually negotiating, then perhaps it has no significance. If, on the other hand, it has in their minds a crucial connection to the definition of gender, to the creation of their own masculine identity, to where they position particular sites and practices on a masculine to feminine continuum, then the ostracism of warrior narratives may mean that they define the school environment as feminine.

There is considerable evidence that some primary school children do in fact make this categorization (Best 1983, 14–15; Brophy 1985, 118; Clark 1990, 36), and we suggest here that the outlawry of the masculine narrative contributes to this. Research by Willis (1977) and Walker (1988) in high schools has revealed a culture of resistance based on definitions of masculinity as antagonistic to the demands of the school, which are construed as feminine by the resisters. It might therefore seem plausible to see the underground perpetuation of the warrior narrative as an early expression of this resistance and one that gives some legitimacy to the resisters' claims that the school is feminine.

Is the school regime that outlaws the warrior narratives really feminine? We would argue, rather, that the regime being imposed is based on a male ideal, an outcome of the Enlightenment and compulsory schooling. Michel Foucault has pointed out that the development of this particular regime in schools coincided with the emergence of the prison, the hospital, the army barracks, and the factory (Foucault 1980, 55–57). Although teachers in the first years of school are predominantly female, the regime they impose is perpetuated by male teachers (Brophy 1985, 121), and this preference is endorsed by powerful and influential males in the society at large. The kind of demeanor and self-management that teachers are trying to inculcate in the early school years is the behavior expected in male-dominated public arenas like boardrooms, courtrooms, and union mass meetings.[3]

Connell (1989, 291) and Willis (1977, 76, 84) provide evidence that by adolescence, boys from all classes, particularly if they are ambitious, come to regard acquiescence in the school's demands as compatible with constructing a masculine identity. Connell writes:

> Some working class boys embrace a project of mobility in which they construct a masculinity organized around themes of rationality and responsibility. This is closely connected with the "certification" function of the upper levels of the education system and to a key form of masculinity among professionals. (1989, 291)

Rationality and responsibility are, as Weber argued long ago, the primary characteristics of the modern society theorized by the Enlightenment thinkers as based on a social contract. This prized rationality has been converted in practice into a bureaucratized legal system where "responsible" acceptance by the population of the rules of civil society obviates the need for individuals to use physical violence in gaming their ends or protecting their rights, and where, if such violence is necessary, it is exercised by the state (Weber 1978, 341–354). In civil society, the warrior is obsolete, his activities redefined bureaucratically and performed by the police and the military.

The teacher in whose classroom our observation was conducted demonstrated a strong commitment to rationality and responsibility. For example, she devoted a great deal of time to showing that there was a cause and effect link between the behavior forbidden by her classroom rules and classroom accidents. Each time an accident occurred, she asked the children to determine the cause of the accident, its result, and how it could have been prevented. The implication throughout was that children must take responsibility for the outcomes of their actions.

> Mac accidentally struck a boy who was lying on the floor, in the head with a pram wheel. He was screaming around with a pram, the victim was playing on the Car Mat and lying down to obtain a bird's eye view of a car crash. Mac rushed past the group and struck Justin on the side of the head. Tears and confusion ensued. The teacher's reaction was to see to Justin, then stop all play and gain children's attention, speaking first to Mac and Justin plus Justin's group:
>
> T. How did Justin get hurt?
> M. [No answer]

T. Mac, what happened?

M. I was wheeling the pram and Justin was in the way.

T. Were you running?

M. I was wheeling the pram.

The teacher now addresses the whole class:

T. Stop working everyone, eyes to me and listen. Someone has just been hurt because someone didn't remember the classroom rules. What are they, Harvey?

(Harvey was listening intently and she wanted someone who could answer the question at this point.)

H. No running in the classroom.

T. Why?

Other children offer an answer.

CHN. Because someone will get hurt.

T. Yes, and that is what happened. Mac was going too quickly with the pram and Justin was injured. Now how can we stop this happening next time?

CHN. No running in the classroom, only walk. (February 10, 1993)

Malcolm, walking, bumped Winston on the head with a construction toy. The teacher intervened:

T. [To Malcolm and Winston] What happened?

W. Malcolm hit me on the head.

M. But it was an accident I didn't mean it. I didn't really hurt him.

T. How did it happen?

M. It was an accident.

W. He [Malcolm] hit me.

T. Malcolm, I know you didn't mean to hurt Winston, so how did it happen?

M. I didn't mean it.

T. I know you didn't mean it, Malcolm, but why did Winston get hurt?

CHN. Malcolm was running.

M. No I wasn't.

T. See where everyone was sitting? There is hardly enough room for children to walk. Children working on the floor must remember to leave

a walking path so that other children can move safely around the room. Otherwise someone will be hurt, and that's what has happened today. (February 23, 1993)

This public-sphere masculinity of rationality and responsibility, of civil society, of the social contract is not the masculinity that the boys are bringing into the classroom through their warrior narratives. They are using a different, much older version—not the male as responsible citizen, the producer and consumer who keeps the capitalist system going, the breadwinner, and caring father of a family. Their earliest vision of masculinity is the male as warrior, the bonded male who goes out with his mates and meets the dangers of the world, the male who attacks and defeats other males characterized as baddies, the male who turns the natural products of the earth into weapons to carry out these purposes.

We would argue, nevertheless, that those boys who aspire to become one of the brothers who wield power in the public world of civil society ultimately realize that conformity to rationality and responsibility, to the demands of the school, is the price they must pay. They realize that although the girls can expect one day to become the brides and mothers of their pretend games, the boys will never, except perhaps in time of war, be allowed to act out the part of warrior hero in reality.

On the other hand, the school softens the transition for them by endorsing and encouraging the classic modern transformation and domestication of the warrior narrative, sport (Connell 1987, 177; Messner 1992, 10–12). In the school where this observation was conducted, large playground areas are set aside for lunchtime cricket, soccer, and basketball; by the age of seven, most boys are joining in these games. The message is conveyed to them that if they behave like citizens in the classroom, they can become warriors on the sports oval.

Gradually, we would suggest, little boys get the message that resistance is not the only way to live out warrior masculinity. If they accept a public/private division of life, it can be accommodated within the private sphere; thus, it becomes possible for those boys who aspire to respectability, figuring in civil society as one of the brothers, to accept that the school regime and its expectations are masculine and to reject the attempts of the "resisters" to define it (and them) as feminine. They adopt the masculinity of rationality and responsibility as that appropriate to the public sphere, while the earlier, deeply appealing masculinity of the warrior narratives can still be experienced through symbolic reenactment on the sports field.

Conclusion

We are not, of course, suggesting that this is the only way in which the public/private division becomes part of the lived awareness of little boys. We do, however, believe that we have teased out one strand of the manner in which they encounter it. We have suggested that the classroom is a major site where little boys are introduced to the masculinity of rationality and responsibility characteristic of the brothers in civil society; we have been looking at a "cycle of practice" where, in classroom after classroom, generation after generation, the mode of masculinity typified in the warrior narratives is first driven underground and then transferred to the sports field. We are, we would suggest, seeing renegotiated for each generation and in each boy's own life the conception of the "social contract" that is characteristic of the era of modernity, of the Enlightenment, of democracy, and of capitalism. We are watching reenacted the transformation of violence and power as exercised by body over body, to control through surveillance and rules (Foucault 1977, 9; 1984, 66–67), the move from domination by individual superiors to acquiescence in a public sphere of decorum and rationality (Pateman 1988).

Yet, this is a social *contract*, and there is another side to the bargain. Although they learn that they must give up their warrior narratives of masculinity in the public sphere, where rationality and responsibility hold sway, they also learn that in return they may preserve them in the private realm

of desire as fantasy, as bricolage, as a symbolic survival that is appropriate to the spaces of leisure and self-indulgence, the playground, the backyard, the television set, the sports field. Although this is too large an issue to be explored in detail here, there may even be a reenactment in the school setting of what Pateman (1988, 99–115) has defined as the sexual contract, the male right to dominate women in return for accepting the constraints of civil society. Is this, perhaps, established for both boys and girls by means of the endemic misogyny—invasion of girls' space (Thorne 1986, 172; 1993, 63–88), overt expressions of aversion and disgust (Goodenough 1987, 422; D'Arcy 1990, 81), disparaging sexual innuendo (Best 1983, 129; Goodenough 1987, 433; Clark 1990, 38–46)—noted by so many observers in the classrooms and playgrounds of modernity? Are girls being contained by the boys' actions within a more restricted, ultimately a private, sphere because, in the boys' eyes, they have not earned access to the public sphere by sharing their ordeal of repression, resistance, and ultimate symbolic accommodation of their gender-defining fantasies?

Author's Note

The research on which this article is based was funded by the Research Management Committee of the University of Newcastle. The observation was conducted at East Maitland Public School, and the authors would like to thank the principal, teachers, and children involved for making our observer so welcome.

Notes

1. Some ethnographic studies describe a "tom boy" who wants to join in the boys' games (Best 1983, 95–97; Davies 1989, 93, 123; Thorne 1993, 127–129), although in our experience, such girls are rare, rarer even than the boys who play by choice with girls. The girls' rejection of the warrior narratives does not appear to be simply the result of the fact that the characters are usually men. Bronwyn Davies, when she read the role-reversal story *Rita*

the Rescuer to preschoolers, found that many boys identified strongly with Rita ("they flex their muscles to show how strong they are and fall to wrestling each other on the floor to display their strength"), whereas for most girls, Rita remained "other" (Davies 1989, 57–58).

2. This would seem to reverse the usual parallel of outdoor/indoor with public/private. This further suggests that the everyday equation of "public" with "visible" may not be appropriate for the specialized use of the term in sociological discussions of the public/private division. Behavior in the street may be more visible than what goes on in a courtroom, but it is nevertheless acceptable for the street behavior to be, to a greater degree, personal, private, and driven by "desire."

3. There are some groups of men who continue to reject these modes of modernity throughout their lives. Andrew Metcalfe, in his study of an Australian mining community, has identified two broad categories of miner, the "respectable," and the "larrikin" (an Australian slang expression carrying implications of nonconformism, irreverence, and impudence). The first are committed to the procedural decorums of union meetings, sporting and hobby clubs, welfare groups, and so on; the others relate more strongly to the less disciplined masculinity of the pub, the brawl, and the racetrack (Metcalfe 1988, 73–125). This distinction is very similar to that noted by Paul Willis in England between the "ear'oles" and the "lads" in a working-class secondary school (Willis 1977). It needs to be noted that this is not a *class* difference and that demographically the groups are identical. What distinguishes them is, as Metcalfe points out, their relative commitment to the respectable modes of accommodation and resistance characteristic of civil society of larrikin modes with a much longer history, perhaps even their acceptance or rejection of the social contract.

References

Anyon, Jean. 1983. Intersections of gender and class: Accommodation and resistance by working-class and affluent females to contradictory sex-role ideologies. In *Gender, class and education*, edited by Stephen Walker and Len Barton. Barcombe, Sussex: Falmer.

Best, Raphaela. 1983. *We've all got scars: What girls and boys learn in elementary school*. Bloomington: Indiana University Press.

Bowles, Samuel, and Herbert Gintis. 1976. *Schooling in capitalist America: Educational reform and the contradictions of economic life*. London: Routledge and Kegan Paul.

Brophy, Jere E. 1985. Interactions of male and female students with male and female teachers. In *Gender influences in classroom interaction*, edited by L. C. Wilkinson and C. B. Marrett. New York: Academic Press.

Burgess, R. G., ed. 1984. *The research process in educational settings: Ten case studies*. Lewes: Falmer.

Chodorow, Nancy. 1978. *The reproduction of mothering: Psychoanalysis and the sociology of gender*. Berkeley: University of California Press.

Clark, Margaret. 1989. Anastasia is a normal developer because she is unique. *Oxford Review of Education* 15:243–255.

———. 1990. *The great divide: Gender in the primary school*. Melbourne: Curriculum Corporation.

Connell, R. W. 1987. *Gender and power: Society, the person and sexual politics*. Sydney: Allen and Unwin.

———. 1989. Cool guys, swots and wimps. The interplay of masculinity and education. *Oxford Review of Education* 15:291–303.

Crosset, Todd. 1990. Masculinity, sexuality, and the development of early modern sport. In *Sport, men and the gender order*, edited by Michael E. Messner and Donald F. Sabo. Champaign, IL: Human Kinetics Books.

D'Arcy, Sue. 1990. Towards a non-sexist primary classroom. In *Dolls and dungarees: Gender issues in the primary school curriculum*, edited by Eva Tutchell. Milton Keynes: Open University Press.

Davies, Bronwyn. 1989. *Frogs and snails and feminist tales: Preschool children and gender*. Sydney: Allen and Unwin.

Dinnerstein, Myra. 1977. *The mermaid and the minotaur: Sexual arrangements and human malaise.* New York: Harper and Row.

Duthie, J. H. 1980. Athletics: The ritual of a technological society? In *Play and culture*, edited by Helen B. Schwartzman. West Point, NY: Leisure.

Eisenstein, Hester. 1984. *Contemporary feminist thought*. London: Unwin Paperbacks.

Foucault, Michel. 1977. *Discipline and punish: The birth of the prison.* Translated by Alan Sheridan. New York: Pantheon.

———. 1980. Body/power. In *power/knowledge: Selected interviews and other writings 1972–1977*, edited by Colin Gordon. Brighton: Harvester.

———. 1984. Truth and power. In *The Foucault reader*, edited by P. Rabinow. New York: Pantheon.

Genovese, Eugene E. 1972. *Roll, Jordan, roll: The world the slaves made.* New York: Pantheon.

Giddens, Anthony. 1984. *The constitution of society: Outline of the theory of structuration.* Berkeley: University of California Press.

Goodenough, Ruth Gallagher. 1987. Small group culture and the emergence of sexist behaviour: A comparative study of four children's groups. In *Interpretive ethnography of education*, edited by G. Spindler and L. Spindler. Hillsdale, NJ: Lawrence Erlbaum.

Hebdige, Dick. 1979. *Subculture: The meaning of style.* London: Methuen.

Messner, Michael E. 1992. *Power at play: Sports and the problem of masculinity*. Boston: Beacon.

Metcalfe, Andrew. 1988. *For freedom and dignity: Historical agency and class structure in the coalfields of NSW*. Sydney: Allen and Unwin.

Paley, Vivian Gussin. 1984. *Boys and girls: Superheroes in the doll corner.* Chicago: University of Chicago Press.

Pateman, Carole. 1988. *The sexual contract.* Oxford: Polity.

———. 1989. The fraternal social contract. In *The disorder of women*. Cambridge: Polity.

Thorne, Barrie. 1986. Girls and boys together . . . but mostly apart: Gender arrangements in elementary schools. In *Relationships and development*, edited by W. W. Hartup and Z. Rubin. Hillsdale, NJ: Lawrence Erlbaum.

———. 1993 *Gender play: Girls and boys in school.* New Brunswick, NJ: Rutgers University Press.

Walker, J. C. 1988. *Louts and legends: Male youth culture in an inner-city school.* Sydney: Allen and Unwin.

Walkerdine, Valerie. 1990. *Schoolgirl fictions.* London: Verso.

Weber, Max. 1978. *Selections in translation.* Edited by W. G. Runciman and translated by Eric Matthews. Cambridge: Cambridge University Press.

Willis, Paul. 1977. *Learning to labour: How working class kids get working class jobs.* Farnborough: Saxon House.

Transgender and Gender-Nonconforming Kids and the Binary Requirements of Sport Participation in North America

ANN TRAVERS

Ray-Ray took off one time in a race—this was probably about grade five or six—and there was a guy standing on the edge of the field to tell the kids when they can cut in. He's one of the officials. He takes off running across the field yelling at the top of his lungs with the megaphone, "There's a girl on the track." And I was out there and I jogged beside him and I said, "That's a boy. He's my son. His name is Ray-Ray and he'll probably win." And I walked away. . . . That's how bad it was and he just went, he just persisted. But other kids I know who are gender-nonconforming would be horrified.

—Ray-Ray's mother

Since the 1950s, transgender and gender-nonconforming individuals have emerged as polemic and sensationalized figures in North American media accounts. Some of the controversy has centered on their participation in sex-divided sporting spaces—from Rene Richards's groundbreaking appearance on the Women's Tennis Association tour in 1977 (Birrell and Cole 1990) to more recent cases in amateur and professional sport. An increasing body of literature documents transgender and transsexual inclusion in sport (Birrell and McDonald 2000; Caudwell 2014; Karkazis et al. 2012; Martin and Martin 1995; Messner 1988; Pilgrim, Martin, and Binder 2002;

Spencer 2000; Tagg 2012; Travers 2006; Travers and Deri 2010). Literature in this field focuses almost exclusively on adult populations, however. This chapter illuminates how transgender and gender-nonconforming kids and their parents/guardians navigate social environments when attempting to access physical activity. I argue that sex-segregated facilities/locker rooms and sex-segregated or sex-differentiated sporting and physical recreation activities operate as points of crisis for transgender and gender-nonconforming kids. The barriers to participation they face are often catalysts to kids' binary and medical transition.

Trans Kids and Sport

Transgender and gender-nonconforming children are often invisible due to their tremendous efforts to avoid teasing, persecution, and scorn from peers, teachers, and family. Although limited, data currently shows that kids who "fail" to conform to or deliberately defy gender norms are disproportionately victims of "gendered harassment" (E. Meyer 2010) and bullying (Brill and Pepper 2008; Ehrensaft 2011; Hellen 2009; Kennedy 2008; E. Meyer 2008; Whittle et al. 2007) and experience "minority stress" (I. H. Meyer 2003). The intense social policing of gender identity among children makes it appear as if gender-nonconforming children are a rather tiny minority. However, the gender-censoring environment of most family, peer, school, sports, and religious settings reflects the circular reasoning of the Thomas Theorem: "Situations that are defined as real become real in their consequences" (Macionis and Gerber 2011, 332). The overwhelming practice of sorting children into boy and girl categories and teaching them to adhere to a racialized heteronormative gender order makes it appear as if these are natural lines of demarcation.

... By virtue of sex-segregated sporting spaces and grossly unequal cultural and economic spaces, sport in North America and much of the world is organized in terms of taken-for-granted racialized assumptions of binary and hierarchical sex difference. The underlying assumption of sex-segregated sporting spaces is that someone who is born male naturally has an "unfair advantage" when competing against women in sport (Sykes 2006). A number of scholars have refuted this assumption of athletic superiority (Cavanagh and Sykes 2006; Fausto-Sterling 2000; Kane 1995; McDonagh and Pappano 2008; Ring 2008; Sykes 2006) and is something I address substantially in several articles (Travers 2006, 2008, 2011, 2013; Travers and Deri 2010). More broadly, sport also normalizes the European diaspora morality of whiteness, heterosexual masculinity, and class privilege (Hall 2002; Lemert 2002; Lenskyj 2003; Love and Kelly 2011; McDonagh and Pappano 2008; Travers 2008, 2013)....

The pressure and constraint that kids feel to act in "gender appropriate" ways, depending on their racial and class location (Kumashiro 2002; Pascoe 2007), occur because gender is structured into institutions like families, sport, and school (Lorber 2005; Messner 2011).... As Elizabeth Meyer (2010, 9) observes, "Most traditional extracurricular activities have subtexts that subtly and overtly teach that certain forms of masculinity and femininity are valued over others."...

The study I present in this chapter critically examines key policies for transsexual and transgender inclusion in sport and focuses very specifically

on the experiences—as related mostly by their parents—of a sample of transgender and gender-nonconforming kids ages four to seventeen. My research is situated within the tradition of "reading sport critically" (McDonald and Birrell 1999), whereby cultural events relating to sport are read as texts that reveal relations of power and resistance. I apply this method to existing policy documents and high-profile reports relating to transsexual and transgender inclusion; the transcripts of "active" interviews (Holstein and Gubrium 1997) with parents of transgender and gender-nonconforming kids, with youth who speak for themselves; and the transcripts of interviews with three advocates for this population.

Sport Policy and Transgender People

... In 2004, the International Olympic Committee (IOC) developed the Stockholm Consensus ... [which] allows transsexual athletes who have obtained new medical–legal identities via full hormonal and surgical transition for at least two years and legal recognition of their new sex by their home governments to compete in elite amateur athletics. This policy has been roundly criticized by critical sport scholars (Cavanagh and Sykes 2006; Love 2014; Sykes 2006) as well as the Canadian Centre for Ethics in Sport (2012) for requiring genital surgeries that have no bearing on athletic performance. As Adam Love (2014, 379) argues, "While policies modeled on the one adopted by the IOC may provide a certain level of inclusion for some individuals, they do so in a way that is gender conforming rather than gender transforming."

Although many national and international sporting federations follow IOC protocol, youth and high school sports often adopt different standards. For example, Pat Griffin (Women's Sports Foundation) and Helen Carroll (National Council Lesbian Rights) deemed the Stockholm Consensus inappropriate for high school athletes altogether. In their influential 2010 report relating to the US context, "On the Team: Equal Opportunity for Transgender Student Athletes," they recommend that no hormonal or surgical treatment should be required for high school athletes. At least for this age group, they refute the discourse of unfair male advantage by acknowledging the considerable overlap in athletic ability across sex categories (Kane 1995). . . . The US Transgender Law and Policy Institute's "Guidelines for Creating Policies for Transgender Children in Recreational Sports" (2009) emphasizes the importance of students participating in sport based on their affirmed gender. Disputing assumptions of male athletic advantage among preadolescent children, the report argues that no "hormonally-based advantage or disadvantage between girls and boys exist" prior to adolescence, that "gender segregation in children's sports is purely social," and that "individual variation with respect to athletic ability *within* each gender is much more significant than any group differences between boys and girls" (2–3).

Similarly, in "Sport in Transition: Making Sport in Canada More Responsible for Gender Inclusivity," the Canadian Centre for Ethics in Sport (2012) speaks out against sex verification testing, acknowledging that the science of sex difference is flawed and therefore not a basis for organizing sport: "Where feasible, transitioning sport will aim for the widest and easiest possible inclusion by supporting integrated sport activities" (29). . . .

Human rights discourse has effectively changed policies in a handful of school districts that stipulate that binary-based transgender kids be treated according to their affirmed gender.[1] However, recommendations for transgender inclusion in high school at the national level in either the United States or Canada have yet to be adopted, and it is too soon to tell how recently introduced policies will work in practice. The interview data I collected clearly show how the binary organization of sport negatively impacts transgender and gender-nonconforming kids and that the desire to participate in sport plays a significant role in decisions relating to medicalized transition.

Gender Inclusion on the Ground

I interviewed thirteen parents of transgender or gender-nonconforming kids and two youth between July 2012 and September 2014. I found participants through word of mouth and snowball sampling and via two national US conferences for transgender kids and their families.[2] Participants' demographic information is presented in Table 8.1. Pseudonyms are used for all kids except a seventeen-year-old trans guy, Cory Oskam, who is a very public trans activist.

Barrie Thorne (1993) cautions against relying on parents' understandings of young people's experiences, and I acknowledge this limitation. Obtaining clearance to interview transgender or gender-nonconforming persons under the age of sixteen—as they are considered to be a vulnerable population by my university's research ethics board—would have prevented me from documenting immediate issues on the ground. The perspectives of parents, while not synonymous with those of their children, make important contributions because it is parents—especially mothers—who enroll and advocate for their children (Manning, forthcoming). The challenges they report thus shed light on institutionalized obstacles to participation in sport and physical recreation settings.

The sample I obtained has shortcomings in terms of diversity or representativeness. . . . Of the twelve children whose parent spoke with me, two are African American Canadian, one is Aboriginal Canadian, one is Asian American, and one is Asian Canadian. Only two of these children, however, have parents of color. Both of the youth I interviewed are white, as am I. My participants are distributed throughout North America. To the best of my knowledge, with the exception of one working-class family, my sample is uniformly middle-class. . . . One of the kids whose parent spoke with me is French Canadian, an identity that is important within the Canadian context where French-language rights and the preservation of French Canadian culture are key points of contention. Three of the kids are from single-parent (not lone-parent) families, and two have same-sex parents (one with two moms; one with two dads). At least three of the children have a visibly gender-nonconforming parent. I interviewed

Table 8.1 List of Interview Participants

Pseudonym	Gender Identity	Age/Interview Year	Regional Location
Cody	Gender nonconforming male; likes both superheroes and pretty things	5/2012	Oregon, USA
Dave	Male	17/2012	Manitoba, Canada
Bailey	Gender nonconforming, masculine identified	9/2012	Vermont, USA
Sydney	75% girl/25% boy	10/2012	Québec, Canada
Sean	Gender nonconforming girl	9/2013	British Columbia, Canada
River	Gender nonconforming boy	7/2013	Ontario, Canada
Wren	"I was born a boy but I like being a girl"	9/2014	British Columbia, Canada
Cory Oskam (real name)	Genderqueer/gender fluid/trans guy/"all of the above"	17/2014	Vancouver, Canada
Silver	"Just Silver"	9/2013	British Columbia, Canada
Ben	Boy	6/2014	British Columbia, Canada
Emily	Girl	4/2014	Newfoundland, Canada
Everest	Male	15/2012	New Jersey, USA
Ray-Ray	Genderqueer	15/2014	British Columbia, Canada
Shane	Masculine-identified, butch lesbian	11/2014	British Columbia, Canada
Madelaine	Girl	9/2013	British Columbia, Canada

eleven mothers and two fathers. All of the parents I interviewed, to varying but significant degrees, have deliberately created space from the outset for their children to defy gender stereotypes and assert nontraditional gender identities. . . .

Issues of Access (Sex-Segregated Sports, Programs, and Facilities)

Sex-segregated sporting facilities and programs are predicated on the assumption of fundamental differences between only two sexes and a corresponding belief in male athletic advantage. This creates a crisis situation for transgender and gender-nonconforming kids. All but one of the people I interviewed cited sex segregation and differentiation as the major obstacle to sport participation.

Dave (seventeen, male, white, Manitoba) participated in many sports when he was still presenting as a girl. Speaking on his own behalf, Dave said, "I pretty much stopped playing sports when I transitioned to male." As a boy, he described himself as too small to succeed in hockey, and he feels the competition in table tennis is much stiffer.

His participation is limited by the binary organization of sport. Shane's (eleven, masculine-identified, butch lesbian Asian Canadian, British Columbia) mom expressed similar concerns about the athletic superiority of boys of the same age: "His skill level cannot compete; it is getting to that point when all the boys start, you know, into puberty, right? So now their strength level [is much greater]."

. . . The difficulties faced by kids who want to identify outside the binary are extraordinary. According to her mom, Bailey (nine, gender-nonconforming, masculine-identified, potentially transgender boy, Asian American, Vermont) "will play sports with me in the yard but . . . she's not interested in joining a team." As an example, Bailey's mom explains that

there was this "girls on the run" after-school program that got promoted at the school last year when she was in third grade and it was all about redefining girlhood . . . and looking at the messages that come to you from the culture and . . . being able to choose to do sports and be athletic or . . . it was all about helping girls to think outside the box.

So I thought "Wow, this would be, this would be, so this could be such a great thing for her! Right?" Then I started talking to her about that she just looked at me sort of incredulous and said, "Are boys allowed to do it?" And I went "No, it's for girls. It's 'girls on the run.' Yeah, it would be great, wouldn't it, if it was a program for everybody but it is a program for girls," and she said, "Then I don't want to do it."

The sports teams in Bailey's school and wider community "are divided by sex. The soccer team is either a girls' soccer team or a boys' soccer team." Bailey's mom wonders, "Is it that she really doesn't want to play sports or is it that she wouldn't be able to play on the team that she would think of herself as wanting to be on?" Similarly, although she tried to sign River (seven, gender-nonconforming boy, white, Ontario) up for a dance program at their local community center, River's mom found it impossible to do so without specifying sex.

Shane has recently come out as a boy at school and asked for a name change and to be referred to using male pronouns. His mother reports that he does not want to take hormone blockers. He likes the way his body is changing through puberty and recently told his mother he sees himself more as a butch lesbian than a male. Last summer, Shane was always outside: playing with his friends and riding his bike around the neighborhood. Since he came out, the boys who were his friends have dropped him completely. But several of the girls in his class became staunch allies! Still, nobody comes to his house to play, and he rarely goes outside, playing video games alone in his bedroom. Once Shane's body started to develop he informed his mother that he no longer wanted to take swimming lessons because he felt uncomfortable in a bathing suit. He used to play floor hockey but now feels he doesn't belong on the girls' team because of his gender identity and he doesn't belong on the boys' team because of his body. His mother believes that the separation of girls' and boys' teams has made it impossible for her son to participate. He would like to participate in recreational activities and has looked online for summer camp options but experiences dismay when trying to imagine how he could fit in/navigate these normatively gendered spaces. And yet, his mother tells me, he is happy; after several years of being treated for a mood disorder, his family's support of his gender expression and his new name and pronoun at school have made the difference: "So now he's so happy these days. No play dates, and he's by himself, but still happy. I am so amazed that he's just happy. And a big smile like." Shane's mother admires his strength of character, that he would "rather have no friend" and be himself.

Sydney's (ten, 75 percent girl, 25 percent boy, French Canadian white, Québec) mom explains that swimming used to be a central family activity but is no longer an option, in part because of his gender nonconformity:[3] "I did enroll Sydney in September and I spoke to my husband I said, 'What the hell did I do?' And I cancelled actually because I told that, put him in a predicament of feeling uncomfortable because Sydney doesn't want to go swimming without girls' stuff anymore. So for Sydney it's important to have the girl swimming costume. Now in a swimming pool in a swimming lesson I can't enroll him in a girl's class with the girl's swimming costume without having any problems, you know what I mean? Because you see everything. It's difficult to hide the penis." Skiing continues to be a positive activity for Sydney and his family. As Sydney's mom explained, "He's really happy" to ski, in part because "nobody knows . . . what he's got in between his legs." Gender essentialism is clearly "harder" (Messner 2011) in some sports than others, as a result of the way certain sports are organized. . . .

Madelaine (girl, African Canadian, British Columbia) played soccer in a mixed league until the age of six, when she and her parents were surprised to discover the league was being divided along traditional gender lines. Although she identifies as a girl, Madelaine sees herself, according to her dad, as "one of the guys," and she is treated by them as "one of their people." Madelaine and another girl were permitted to stick with the boys they had been playing with but will have to play on a girls' team when they turn ten. Madelaine's dad foresees positive and negative effects: being one of the best on the girls' team could boost her confidence; he is concerned, however, because "it's really an interruption of what we've been building. Because what we've been building has been, you know, she's got a five-year connection with the coach, she's got a team that she's been on for five years, you know, acceleration of skills and all those other components.... Those points that are really important to her, that peer connection and all that would be really ripped out." ...

The "bathroom problem" (Halberstam 1998) is a clear and pervasive theme in queer and trans literature.... These issues are central to the general well-being of the population and are of obvious relevance to participation in sport and physical recreation, where sex-segregated locker/changing rooms are the norm....

For example, Silver's (nine, white and aboriginal, British Columbia) mom relayed the problems her gender-nonconforming child had accessing bathrooms. While Silver's mom uses a female pronoun to refer to her child, she resists all gender labels anyone might impose, insisting that Silver is "just Silver." Her mom explains that Silver is consistently read by people who don't know her as a boy and that Silver is comfortable with this—except when she needs to use a public bathroom.... Her mom reports that

> about halfway through grade one ... Silver told me, "this kid came in and she pointed at me in the bathroom and she said, 'You boy, out'" and Silver said, "No I'm a girl" and the kid repeated, "You boy, out" so what I think is that the kid was actually scared there was a big boy in the girls' bathroom.... So Silver left the bathroom and she went to the boys' bathroom and then a teacher found her so she still hasn't gone pee by this time and she's probably six years old in grade one.... So the teacher sent her to the principal's office because she was in the boys' bathroom which isn't allowed ... and so she peed her pants. So Silver no longer had anywhere to pee at the school.... So in grade one she started on a daily basis peeing her

> pants and [for] two weeks ... she peed her pants every day. She started bringing an extra shirt so she could tie it around her waist to cover up the pee so ... I started ... leaving work taking my lunch; I'm driving across town at lunch time and taking her pee and then leaving work so I could be there at quarter to three.... Obviously it wasn't sustainable ... [but] she was scared to go into the bathroom even with me.

After trying and failing to get the school principal to allow Silver to use a single-stall bathroom for staff, Silver's mom switched her to a different school where she was immediately accommodated. Silver now feels safe to use the bathroom at school. But she—like Wren (nine, "I was born a boy but like being a girl," African American Canadian, British Columbia)—does not feel safe going into public bathrooms without an adult accompanying her. According to Bailey's mom, Bailey regularly experiences a dilemma about choosing which bathroom to use:

> She chooses right now to use the girls' room and she wants to have and does have a peer from her class always with her because she experiences people who don't know her thinking she's a boy and that she's in the wrong bathroom and that is very upsetting to her. But she's not ready to/she only uses the boys' rooms when she can go in there with her dad and she uses girls' rooms in public when she can go with me and when it's a gender-neutral bathroom it's just not an issue.... They had to make hopes wishes and dreams for fourth grade and her hope for fourth grade is that her school would create a bathroom for both boys and girls.... But then she decided not to reveal that.

Bailey's mom thinks that her child would actually feel more comfortable in a boys' bathroom but is not willing to endure the process of coming out to her peers that this would entail.

Difficulties involved in using the bathroom or the changing room were referenced by all but one of my participants at some point, either in the past or in the present. According to her mom, when Wren was five "she said, 'Mommy, the bathrooms at church make me sad.' She didn't know which one to use but knew loss would accompany whichever one she picked." Cassandra (five, transgender girl, white, British Columbia) said to her mom upon seeing a sign with symbols indicating it was for people with disabilities/men/women, "I wish all bathrooms had that sign . . . then anybody could use any bathroom." Participating in sport and physical recreation often requires the use of a sex-segregated changing room and the "bathroom problem" becomes the "changing room problem." This is a significant barrier to physical recreation participation for transgender and gender-nonconforming kids.

Sex Differentiation within Sport/ Physical Activity

. . . While the formal sex segregation of sport has received much attention, sex-integrated activities remained problematic for children and youth in this study, albeit in more insidious ways. Within integrated sports, formal and informal rules differentiate different activities and uniforms for boys and girls. These rules pose problems for trans kids. In ballet or gymnastics, for example, boys and girls wear different uniforms and are required to train their bodies to perform in different ways that reflect and reassert widespread cultural beliefs in gender essentialism and male athletic superiority (Kane 1995). Consequently, sports that are ostensibly integrated continue to perpetuate binary gender differences.

. . . Sean (girl, white, British Columbia) is enrolled in gymnastics but prevented from doing the rings because they are designated as a "boys only" apparatus. As her dad explained, sex-differentiated programs in gymnastics have caused her both disappointment and disadvantage: "When she went in gymnastics she . . . had her heart set on doing the rings but the rings are not allowed to her . . . but she started gymnastics with a Brazilian coach who came and asked the girls . . . 'Can anybody do a chin-up?' But nobody could and then Sean came and just ripped off nine chin-ups and he was so excited he took her to all the other coaches but she

came back to me and said, 'I dunno what to do because I can't do the rings.'" Sean's dad observes that this has the effect of reinforcing assumptions about gendered strength. . . . Jo Kane (1995) notes the ways in which the "gender continuum" of overlapping sport performance is rendered invisible via such "gendered rules and practices and access to training," with the result that the natural basis of sex segregation and male "unfair advantage" goes unquestioned.

According to his mom, separate programs in gymnastics drove Sydney out of a sport he had loved participating in within a gender-integrated setting in another country:

> He did many, many gymnastics courses, was happy to do them. . . . He liked the gymnastics because you could wear leotard and stuff like that and so he really liked it. When we got to Canada we enrolled again in gymnastics and suddenly we found him liking it less because here it's gender-distinctive: Boys do program and girls do program. And I said, "Ah, c'mon, don't you have gender-neutral gymnastic classes?" And they said, "No, because at nine years . . . they develop differently, and they need to develop muscle, different muscle." And so . . . they put Sydney into the boys' class and obviously Sydney don't [makes noise showing distaste] so he stopped playing gymnastics.

Even in integrated community center dance classes, it is often impossible to register children without sharing information about their sex, something that made River's mom really mad. . . . Wren's mom describes the difficulties she encountered in attempting to find a dance class for her (at the time) gender-nonconforming son (Wren subsequently affirmed a female identity):

> When Wren was four and still identifying as a boy he took a ballet course through the community center and because he wanted the leotard and the tutu that the girls had—there were no other boys in the class—I got them for him and he basically blended in until my use of the male pronoun in a conversation with his teacher outed him as a boy. I asked the teacher to keep letting him dance as a

girl and it seemed to be going fine. Until the little performance at the end of the class. He was dancing in his pink leotard and tutu in the special performance in front of all the parents and friends of the dancers. When it ended, the teacher called out to him in front of everyone and instructed him to bow, not curtsy, that boys should bow, not curtsy. Everyone there looked very puzzled and Wren was mortified.

Like many parents when they encounter that first moment of overt discrimination against their child, Wren's mother marshaled her resources: "I was angry about it and did not sign him up there again. Instead I went through a long and arduous process to find a dance class where my son could dance as a girl without censure. I was surprised at how difficult it was. I did find one of the really serious programs that was fine with him doing it. But when I chatted with other parents before, during, and after the dance class I avoided using any pronouns to refer to Wren because I did not want to provoke any negative reactions or interfere with Wren's ability to fit in with the other kids. This felt really, really weird." . . .

Wren, Ben, and Cody (five, gender-nonconforming boy, white, Oregon) routinely get "mistaken" for girls. According to Cody's mom, he has long hair and a "mixed" wardrobe, and he likes superheroes, rough-and-tumble play, pretty things, and ballet. In his current ballet class they "dress the boys and girls in different clothes."

> He is supposed to wear a uniform. He's supposed to . . . wear black leggings and a white shirt and the girls are supposed to wear I think a black leotard and they can wear pink tights and they have pink ballet shoes. And he has black ballet shoes and I was so worried that he was going to flip his shit because he did not get to wear the pink ones [laughs] and the pink tights. It turned out not to be a problem and he's willing to go along with it. I mean it does visually distinguish him as like clearly he is one of the boys in the dance class with his really long blond hair that several weeks ago he wanted me to put up in a bun.

Issues of Climate/Informal Inequality

Ray-Ray (fifteen, genderqueer, white, British Columbia) has experienced regular gender policing for his failure to present convincingly "as a boy" from an early age. Ray-Ray has been competing in track since he was in third grade, and his mother reports that he is regularly marshaled away from the boys' competition and toward the girls.' "His name is Raymond Marvolo," his mother explains, but "they would move his name to the girls' marshaling list when they saw his long hair and then the guy marshaling the girls would stand there yelling his name until one of the kids who knew who he was from racing against him would say, 'He's not a girl, he's a boy.' And the guy still wouldn't get it. And I would often have to go to the marshaling tent. In fact, I almost always went to the marshaling tent to get him sorted and racing as a boy."

Ray-Ray's mother shares this and other examples to emphasize how crucial it has been for her to run interference at every track-and-field event he attends. . . . The importance of parental advocacy to facilitate their children's participation, a task that most often falls to mothers (Manning, forthcoming; Messner 2009) and that speaks to cultural capital and economic resources, is a key theme that emerges from the data. Kids who are marginalized require a great deal of parental support and advocacy work if they are to achieve some measure of social inclusion and self-esteem; the experiences of almost all of the kids in my study speak to this.

. . . Ray-Ray tried soccer a year ago but quit because the other boys never treated him as a team member and this was intolerable. His experience on his high school's mixed-sex Ultimate Frisbee team has been positive, however. Ultimate Frisbee requires that a certain number of girls/women be on the field at all times. Even though he now stands six foot two inches, Ray-Ray is often read by opponents as a girl. This is actually an advantage for his team because they are often short of girl players. His coach asked Ray-Ray if he would be okay to continue "playing as a girl," and he happily agreed. . . .

In group discussions or news interviews, it is not unusual to hear parents of trans kids talk about the importance of their child being able to bond with their teams in the locker room. Cory talked about the importance of team bonding and how necessary it was to use the same locker room as everyone else. When he was first transitioning, the school suggested he use a gender-neutral space, but he purposefully positioned himself as fundamentally male (rather than more authentically genderqueer) to enable himself to dress with the team. Despite being an important place for team bonding, male locker rooms are notorious for misogyny and homophobia (Curry 1991; Sabo 1999). Cory described his discomfort in a boys' hockey dressing room a few years ago, as one of his teammates make homophobic remarks to the group. He waited until they were alone to ask him, "Dude, why do you say those things?" . . . Dave, however, drew on the homophobic climate of the locker room to deflect attention away from his post-top-surgery chest. A boy asked him, "Why do your nipples look so weird?" Dave responded, "Dude, why are you looking at my nipples?" In contrast, Cory explained that the guys in his locker room used these terms to "really put down women," which he experienced as "really offensive because I do identify as like someone who was female at one point. And I do identify like as female once in a while. So it was not pleasant to hear." . . .

Informal Recreational Spaces

Interviews with several parents reminded me to broaden the focus of discussion around sport/physical recreation to include issues relating to unorganized recreational activity in playgrounds and parks. . . .

For example, Ben has been physically assaulted by children at local playgrounds because of his long hair. . . . "They've gotten physical with him . . . pushed him around. . . . We were at a playground here actually and there was kids that I knew that he wanted to play with them. They didn't want to play with him. And then they sort of lured him over to the other side of the playground—so I was

with [my younger child] on one side—they lured him over to the other side—he was littler at this point—and then spat in his hair." Although informal recreational spaces like playgrounds could provide an alternative to formal sport settings, they continue to be problematic, in part because of the way kids police gender when adults are not supervising their play, or often even when adult supervisors are complicit in gender policing.

Coping Strategies: Resistance/ Survival/Acquiescence

Transgender and gender-nonconforming kids and their parents in my study applied four strategies to negotiate these barriers preventing full participation: continuing to play, going stealth, undergoing medical treatment, and quitting altogether.

Continuing to participate is easier in some sports than others, such as how Sydney had an easier time continuing to ski versus swim. . . . As a result, the strategy of continuing to play requires significant amounts of class and race privilege. . . . Wren's mom's account of finding a dance class where her son could wear the pink outfit and dance "as a girl" exemplifies how parents must draw upon these privileges when negotiating physical recreation spaces. . . .

Children and adults who defy cisgender binary categorization tend to experience frequent gender policing from children and adults alike in the form of *the* most common question: "Are you a boy or girl?"[4] As a result, some trans kids who want to play sport go "stealth," meaning they present themselves as their affirmed rather than their birth sex. Going "stealth" works better for trans kids who embrace a binary identity and who are able to pass, either because they are younger or because they undergo medical treatment like Dave and Cory did. . . . Wren's mother reports that her participation in a swim and skate day camp program two years ago was the impetus for her transition from gender-nonconforming boy to a girl. She says that

> Wren got really clear about wanting to change her pronouns when . . . we put her in summer camp. . . . [My partner] asked her when we were in

the sign-up process, "Do you want to go to camp as a boy or a girl?" Which I thought was really, like, neat that she asked her, in spite of how annoyed I was that she had to tick one of two boxes on the intake form. Wren said, "A girl." And so [my partner] signed her up as a girl. She showed her how to change privately in the change room and Wren was totally successful and I think it gave her a lot of confidence. Two years later she's still doing it and she totally passes. We have grave concerns about the future, however, as she enters puberty.

. . . Wren's mothers are certainly prepared to provide their daughter with access to hormone blockers to delay the puberty that will make it more difficult to pass as female if necessary, but they do not want their daughter's choices to be limited to one of two binary-based choices. They are taking great care to follow their daughter's lead as much as possible. "It's a tricky balancing act," according to Wren's mother.

. . . According to Diane Ehrensaft, author of *Gender Born, Gender Made: Raising Healthy Gender-Nonconforming Children* and a psychologist with a clinical practice in the Bay Area specializing in children, youth, and gender (personal interview), the desire to participate in sport is a major factor driving kids who are more gender liminal to undergo binary transition. For example, . . . Cory, wanted to be able to undergo hormone therapy *and* continue to play on the girls' team. . . . Taking testosterone—considered a performance-enhancing drug in mainstream sport circles (Sykes 2006)—was really important for Cory because he did not want to develop breasts or have a period. He thus had to balance his desire to participate in girls' hockey with his need to shape his body in a manner consistent with his gender identity. Although Cory's former name was Annika and they had a very public gender-nonconforming identity of "just Annika" from age eight to thirteen, he decided to medically transition. Cory explained that his desire to take testosterone and still be able to play hockey ultimately was the difference maker in his decision to medically transition to a male identity. "Just Annika" just wasn't working anymore.

Finally, several kids in my study stopped participating in particular sports or stopped playing sports altogether when they transitioned. While this represents a loss for some kids, others are happy to quit. According to his mother, when Everest (fifteen, male, white, New Jersey) was given the option of dropping out of physical education, he jumped at it. He experienced his school's reluctance to allow him to participate fully as a boy as a blessing. His mom explained that "Everest hated PE and when the principal gave him the option of quitting [a course that was normally compulsory], he was thrilled." At the time of the interview (2011), Everest was happily participating in his school's marching band, where gender has not been an issue for him.

Conclusion: Sex-Segregated Sport as an Obstacle to or Catalyst for Binary Transition

This study has two major findings. First, sex-segregated facilities/locker rooms and sex-segregated or sex-differentiated sporting and physical recreation activities operate as points of crisis for transgender and gender-nonconforming kids. This is a major barrier to participation. And second, because of this, the desire to participate in sport is often a catalyst to kids' binary and medical transition.

Transgender children are likely to become marked as trans during puberty, thereby becoming incredibly vulnerable to violence or institutionally coerced medicalization. Although transgender children are not forced to take hormones against their will, the social context they find themselves in is so normatively gendered that hormone blockers and hormones are essential for their very survival. This is highly significant for at least two reasons. First, sex-segregated and sex-differentiated structures and programs in sport and physical recreation are often a catalyst for medical transition. And, second, the option of medical transition is a privilege disproportionately associated with whiteness and wealth. The solution is not to deny privileged kids hormone blockers and hormone therapy but to expand access to all kids who need such medical care. We also must take aim at oppressive gender systems and other vectors of vulnerability and security that disproportionately link transgender and gender-nonconforming kids with vulnerability and risk. I conjecture that most trans kids who lack access to parental support or appropriate health care either adapt to peer pressure or have their gender diversity driven underground, strategies that place kids disproportionately at risk of self-harm and suicide.

Advocacy and activism should target the organization of children by sex/gender and the structural inequalities that children encounter and are shaped by. According to trans activist and critical theorist Dean Spade (2011, 29), "We need to shift our focus from the individual rights framing of discrimination and 'hate violence' and think more broadly about how gender categories are enforced on all people in ways that cause particularly dangerous outcomes for trans people." . . . This places a target for correction squarely on the sport and physical recreation programs and spaces designed for kids that normalize the gender binary and female inferiority in conjunction with systems of privilege based on race and class.

If it were not for the totalizing pressure of gender categorization that children are subjected to (Berkowitz and Ryan 2011; Hellen 2009), if instead there was greater cultural flexibility concerning sex and gender identities, more kids would likely exhibit gender nonconformity. Currently, children from families with less cultural capital are disproportionately likely to remain invisible or "closeted," not because their families have less progressive views regarding gender, but because they lack the resources for successful child advocacy. . . . This strongly indicates that inclusion strategies, therefore, must be fundamentally intersectional by addressing the overlapping regimes of gender, sexuality, racialization, and class and focus on shaping environments in general as well as responding to the needs of a particular visible child or youth.

It is my hope that my findings will be useful in changing how sport and recreation institutions treat transgender and gender-nonconforming kids.

We must reduce how all kids are subjected to gender norms and gender policing. Because we know that most transgender and gender-nonconforming kids are invisible, sport programs must avoid passive solutions, such as "waiting for a transgender kid to show up" before adopting measures for inclusion (Travers 2014). We should certainly advocate for the kids who are able to be visible, but there is a need for a broader emphasis on undoing the structures of gender that, in tandem with racist and classist regimes, shape and regulate these institutions and spaces. . . .

And yet how do we increase transgender inclusion without completely eliminating spaces for girls and young women to develop confidence? In a previous work (Travers 2008), I argued that we need to eliminate male-only sport and physical recreation teams and spaces while maintaining optional segregated spaces for girls and women, so long as the latter have transinclusive boundaries, as an interim measure. This is an issue that needs a lot of thought and attention, lest we undo much of the progress that has been made in increasing the participation of girls and women in sport. There may be resistance to some short-term changes, but developing nonbinary sports institutions for kids with transgender inclusive policies are worthy rallying points for social activism and advocacy, not only on behalf of transgender and gender-nonconforming kids, but for all young people.

Acknowledgments

Funds in support of this research were provided by the Social Sciences and Humanities Research Council of Canada and the Faculty of Arts and Social Sciences, Simon Fraser University. I wish to thank three allies/advocates for these populations who allowed me to interview them—in 2013, Diane Ehrensaft, author of *Gender Born, Gender Made*, and in 2012, Asaf Orr, attorney with the National Council for Lesbian Rights (NCLR), and Helen Carroll, author of *An Equal Place on the Team*, also employed by the NCLR as director of their Sport Initiative. These interviews informed my understanding of relevant legal and policy issues.

The editors of this book, Michael Messner and Michela Musto, believed in my work from the outset and helped me to present it effectively. They were such a pleasure to work with, and I thank them for their hard work. Jennifer Thomas and Meagan Simon were both highly capable research assistants who helped with a variety of tasks that were essential to the completion of this project. A final thank-you to my kids—Langston, Kendry, and Hanna—and my precious partner and coparent—Gwen Bird—for making it all matter so much and not minding too much my occasional need to disappear for a weekend into my office.

Notes

1. For example, transgender eleven-year-old Tracey Wilson's parents launched a human rights complaint on her behalf against the Vancouver-area Catholic diocese and achieved the desired policy change to recognize transgender girls and boys as their affirmed sex (Canadian Press 2014). Similarly, Maine's highest court ruled in 2014 that a transgender student's rights were violated when her school forced her to use a staff bathroom rather than the girls' bathroom (Byrne 2014). The recent passage into law of AB 1266 in California, signed by the governor on August 12, 2013, allows children "to participate in sex-segregated programs, activities, and facilities" based on their affirmed gender rather than their birth sex. The law allows students to use bathrooms and locker rooms that correspond to their affirmed rather than assigned gender. Also see San Francisco Unified School District (2004); Toronto District School Board (2011); Edmonton Public Schools (2011); Vancouver School Board (Canadian Press 2014).

2. Gender Spectrum, Berkeley, CA, 2012; Gender Odyssey, Seattle, WA, August 2012.

3. Shortly after the interview Sydney switched pronouns from the masculine to the feminine. When she read a draft of this chapter, Sydney's mom found it very strange to see the use of the male pronoun for Sydney but agreed to leave it as is because it represented where things were at that point in Sydney's journey.

4. "Cisgender" refers to the sex/gender identity of people whose gender identity correlates with the reproductive organs that marked them as their birth sex (Aultman 2014).

References

Aultman, B. 2014. "Cisgender." *Transgender Studies Quarterly* 1.1–2: 61–62.

Berkowitz, Dana, and Maura Ryan. 2011. "Bathrooms, Baseball, and Bra Shopping: Lesbian and Gay Parents Talk about Engendering Their Children." *Sociological Perspectives* 54.3: 329–350.

Birrell, Susan, and C. L. Cole. 1990. "Double-Fault: Renee Richards and the Construction and Naturalization of Difference." *Sociology of Sport Journal* 7: 1–21.

Birrell, Susan, and Mary G. McDonald. 2000. "Reading Sport, Articulating Power Lines." In *Reading Sport: Critical Essays on Power and Representation*, edited by Susan Birrell and Mary G. McDonald, 3–13. Boston: Northeastern University Press.

Brill, Stephanie, and Rachel Pepper. 2008. *The Transgender Child*. San Francisco: Cleis Press.

Byrne, Matt. 2014. "Maine's Highest Court: Transgender Student's Rights Were Violated." *Press Herald*, January 30. http://www.pressherald.com/2014/01/30/maine_supreme_court_transgender_student_s_rights_were_violated/. Accessed August 29, 2014.

Canadian Centre for Ethics in Sport. 2012. "Sport in Transition: Making Sport in Canada More Responsible for Gender Inclusivity." Ottawa: Canadian Centre for Ethics in Sport.

Canadian Press. 2014. "Human Rights Complaint Prompts New Gender Policy in Vancouver Catholic Schools." CBC, July 14. http://www.cbc.ca/news/canada/british-columbia/human-rights-complaint-prompts-new-gender-policy-in-vancouver-catholic-schools-1.2709429. Accessed August 29, 2014.

Caudwell, Jane. 2014. "[Transgender] Young Men: Gendered Subjectivities and the Physically Active Body." *Sport, Education, and Society* 19.4: 398–414.

Cavanagh, Sheila, and Heather Sykes. 2006. "Transsexual Bodies at the Olympics: The International Olympic Committee's Policy on Transsexual Athletes at the 2004 Athens Summer Games." *Body and Society* 12: 75–102.

Curry, Timothy 1991. "Fraternal Bonding in the Locker Room: A Profeminist Analysis of Talk about Competition and Women." *Sociology of Sport Journal* 8: 119–135.

Edmonton Public Schools. 2011. "Sexual Orientation and Gender Identity Policy." http://www.epsb.ca/ourdistrict/policy/h/hfa-bp/.

Ehrensaft, Diane. 2011. *Gender Born, Gender Made: Raising Healthy Gender-Nonconforming Children.* New York: The Experiment.

Fausto-Sterling, Ann. 2000. *Sexing the Body: Gender Politics and the Construction of Sexuality.* New York: Basic Books.

Halberstam, Judith. 1998. *Female Masculinity.* Durham, NC: Duke University Press.

Hall, M. Ann. 2002. *The Girl and the Game.* Toronto: Broadview Press.

Hellen, Mark. 2009. "Transgender Children in Schools." *Liminalis* 3: 81–99.

Holstein, James A., and Jaber F. Gubrium. 1997. "Active Interviewing." In *Qualitative Research: Theory, Method, and Practice*, edited by David Silverman, 113–129. London: Sage.

Kane, Mary Jo. 1995. "Resistance/Transformation of the Oppositional Binary: Exposing Sport as a Continuum." *Journal of Sport and Social Issues* 19: 191–218.

Karkazis, Katrina, Rebecca Jordan-Young, Georgiann Davis, and Silvia Camporesi. 2012. "Out of Bounds? A Critique of the New Policies on Hyperandrogenism in Elite Female Athletes." *American Journal of Bioethics* 12.7: 3–16.

Kennedy, Natacha. 2008. "Transgendered Children in Schools: A Critical Review of Homophobic Bullying: Safe to Learn—Embedding Anti-Bullying Work in Schools." *Forum* 50.3: 383–396.

Kumashiro, Kevin. 2002. *Troubling Education: Queer Activism and Anti-oppressive Pedagogy.* New York: Routledge.

Lemert, Charles. 2002. *Dark Thoughts: Race and the Eclipse of Society.* New York: Routledge.

Lenskyj, Helen. 2003. *Out on the Field.* Toronto: Women's Press.

Lorber, Judith. 2005. *Breaking the Bowls: Degendering and Feminist Change.* New York: Norton.

Love, Adam. 2014. "Transgender Exclusion and Inclusion in Sport." In *Routledge Handbook of Sport, Gender, and Sexuality*, edited by Jennifer Hargreaves and Eric Anderson, 376–383. New York: Routledge.

Love, Adam, and Kimberly Kelly. 2011. "Equity or Essentialism? US Courts and the Legitimation of Girls' Teams in High School Sport." *Gender & Society* 25.2: 227–249.

Macionis, John, and Linda Gerber. 2011. *Sociology.* Toronto: Pearson.

Manning, Kimberley. Forthcoming. *Attachment Politics and the Rights of the Trans Child.*

Martin, Beth A., and James H. Martin. 1995. "Compared Perceived Sex Role Orientations of the Ideal Male and Female Athlete to the Ideal Male and Female Person." *Journal of Sport Behavior* 18.4: 286–302.

McDonagh, Eileen, and Laura Pappano. 2008. *Playing with the Boys.* New York: Oxford University Press.

McDonald, Mary, and Susan Birrell. 1999. "Reading Sport Critically: A Methodology for Interrogating Power." *Sociology of Sport Journal* 16: 283–300.

Messner, Michael A. 1988. "Sports and Male Domination: The Female Athlete as Contested Ideological Terrain." *Sociology of Sport Journal* 5.3: 197–211.

———. 2009. *It's All for the Kids: Gender, Families, and Youth Sports.* Berkeley: University of California Press.

———. 2011. "Gender Ideologies, Youth Sports, and the Production of Soft Essentialism." *Sociology of Sport Journal* 28: 151–170.

Meyer, Elizabeth. J. 2008. "Gendered Harassment in Secondary Schools: Understanding Teacher's (Non)interventions." *Gender and Education* 20.6: 555–572.

———. 2010. *Gender and Sexual Diversity in Schools.* New York: Springer.

Meyer, Ian H. 2003. "Prejudice, Social Stress, and Mental Health in Lesbian, Gay, and Bisexual Populations: Conceptual Issues and Research Evidence." *Psychological Bulletin* 129.5: 674.

Pascoe, C. J. 2007. *Dude, You're a Fag: Masculinity and Sexuality in High School.* Berkeley: University of California Press.

Pilgrim, Jill, David Martin, and Will Binder. 2002. "Far from the Finish Line: Transsexualism and Athletic Competition." *Fordham Intellectual Property, Media, and Entertainment Law Journal* 13.2: 495–549.

Ring, Jennifer. 2008. *Stolen Bases: Why American Girls Don't Play Baseball.* Chicago: University of Illinois Press.

Sabo, Don. 1999. "The Myth of the Sexual Athlete." In *Reconstructing Gender: A Multicultural*

Anthology, edited by Estelle Disch, 274–278. London: Mayfield.

San Francisco Unified School District Policy. 2004.

Spade, Dean. 2011. *Normal Life: Administrative Violence, Critical Trans Politics, and the Limits of Law.* Brooklyn, NY: South End Press.

Spencer, Nancy E. 2000. "Reading between the Lines: A Discursive Analysis of the Billie Jean King vs. Bobby Riggs 'Battle of the Sexes.'" *Sociology of Sport Journal* 17.4: 386–402.

Sykes, Heather. 2006. "Transsexual and Transgender Policies in Sport." *Women in Sport and Physical Activity Journal* 15.1: 3–13.

Tagg, Brendon. 2012. "Transgender Netballers: Ethical Issues and Lived Realities." *Sociology of Sport Journal* 29.2: 151–167.

Thorne, Barrie. 1993. *Gender Play: Girls and Boys in School.* New Brunswick, NJ: Rutgers University Press.

Toronto District School Board. 2011. "Toronto District School Board Guidelines for the Accommodation of Transgender and Gender Independent/Non-conforming Students and Staff." http://www.tdsb.on.ca/AboutUs/Innovation/GenderBasedViolencePrevention/AccommodationofTransgenderStudentsandStaff.aspx. Accessed August 29, 2014.

Travers, Ann. 2006. "Queering Sport: Lesbian Softball Leagues and the Transgender Challenge." *International Review for the Sociology of Sport* 41.3–4: 431–446.

———. 2008. "The Sport Nexus and Gender Injustice." *Studies in Social Justice Journal* 2.1: 79–101.

———. 2011. "Women's Ski Jumping, the 2010 Olympic Games, and the Deafening Silence of Sex Segregation, Whiteness, and Wealth." *Journal of Sport and Social Issues* 35.2: 126–145.

———. 2013. "Thinking the Unthinkable: Imagining an 'Un-American,' Girl Friendly, Women- and Trans-inclusive Alternative for Baseball." *Journal of Sport and Social Issues* 37.1: 78–96.

———. 2014. "Transformative Gender Justice as a Framework for Normalizing Gender Variance." In *Supporting Transgender and Gender Creative Youth: Schools, Families, and Communities in Action*, edited by E. Meyer and A. Pullen Sansfacom, 54–68. New York: Peter Lang.

Travers, Ann, and Jillian Deri. 2010. "Transgender Inclusion and the Changing Face of Lesbian Softball Leagues." *International Review for the Sociology of Sport* 46.4: 488–507.

US Transgender Law and Policy Institute. 2009. "Guidelines for Creating Policies for Transgender Children in Recreational Sports." US Transgender Law and Policy Institute.

Whittle, Stephen, Lewis Turner, Maryam Al-Alami, Em Rundall, and Ben Thom. 2007. *Engendered Penalties: Transgender and Transsexual People's Experiences of Inequality and Discrimination.* Wetherby: Communities and Local Government Publications.

Sensitive Cowboys

Privileged Young Men and the Mobilization of Hybrid Masculinities in a Therapeutic Boarding School

JESSICA PFAFFENDORF

Over the last 30 years, there has been a rapid expansion of a multi-billion-dollar industry for America's troubled upper-class youth. At the core of this industry are therapeutic boarding schools (TBS)[1]—new residential programs that mix therapy with elite education and activities. Most are private residential communities targeting various issues such as substance abuse, violence, depression, and anorexia by integrating tenets of 12-step programs[2] and other therapeutic models. Like traditional boarding schools, what these programs usually have in common is cost. Tuition is prohibitively expensive, ranging from $4,500 to $9,500 per month. The yearly cost of attending one of these programs is typically three to four times the approximate average of $40,000 per year at traditional boarding schools. This high-priced rehabilitation has become a go-to solution for some of the nation's wealthiest families with struggling teens. The number of TBS programs is rapidly approaching the total number of traditional boarding schools in the United States, increasing nearly three times over in the past two decades (National Association of Therapeutic Schools and Programs 2015).

Using interviews and ethnographic fieldwork, this article examines how privileged young men in a Western TBS program[3] for substance abuse, hereafter called The Canyon Foundation, construct hybrid masculinities (Bridges and Pascoe 2014) to navigate masculinity dilemmas (Wilkins 2009) that arise in the therapeutic context. The therapies that have become common in TBS programs—the 12-step program and equine-assisted therapy (EAT) in particular—promote qualities associated with femininities and subordinate masculinities[4] such as humility, commitment to service, and open emotional expression (Hochschild 1983; Moisio and Beruchashvili 2010; Wilkins 2009). These qualities conflict with dominant notions of masculinity, particularly those associated with upper-class masculinity: control, competition, and toughness (Poynting and Donaldson 2005). How do young privileged men in a TBS navigate these conflicting gender norms and expectations? While gender dilemmas have been identified among men in more typical rehabilitative contexts, there has been no research on these kinds of ruptures of masculinity among privileged youth.

I address this gap using a previously unexplored case to examine the role of privilege in the strategies used to reshape and reconstruct masculinity. Where previous scholarship shows that working-class men and men of color develop "compensatory manhood acts" or aggressive styles to (re)signify masculine selves in residential therapeutic communities (Ezzell 2012), contemporary studies of masculinities suggest that TBS students might be freer to incorporate qualities that seem out of sync with hegemonic styles of masculinity. Work on the hybridization of masculinity consistently illustrates the flexibility of identity afforded to privileged groups of men (Bridges and Pascoe 2014). Young, middle- to upper-class, white men are equipped with cultural advantages or "tools" (Swidler 1986)—dispositions, knowledge, interactional styles—that allow them to more successfully mobilize hybrid masculinities that incorporate gender identity elements coded as "feminine" or associated with subordinate masculinities in ways that reproduce power and inequality (Bridges 2014; Hughey 2012; Kleinman 1996; Messner 1993; Pascoe 2007; Thorne 1993; Wilkins 2009).

The TBS program offers a unique site to examine shifting styles of masculinity among privileged youth and how these styles operate to reproduce and conceal inequalities associated with gender, class, race, and age. In this case, hybrid masculine styles allow young men to distance themselves from configurations of hegemonic masculinity perceived as undesirable while simultaneously allowing them to assert themselves as leaders and as "better" men in contrast to various others. This article fills a gap in empirical work focused on gender issues among privileged young men. Despite a recent proliferation of research in elite contexts, studies of privileged men that interrogate intersecting dimensions of power and privilege remain limited, particularly with respect to youth.

Intersections, Hybridity, and Dilemmas of Masculinity

A growing body of literature examines changes in contemporary masculinities, but the meanings and effects of the different ways that men perform or "do" (West and Zimmerman 1987) gender are subject to debate. Especially contentious is whether new forms of masculinity are complicit in or resistant to systems of gender inequality and whether or not they support the reproduction of hegemonic masculinity—an idealized, privileged form of masculinity that supports the hierarchical dominance of certain men over women and other men (Connell 1995). A wide swath of the scholarship that addresses men's struggles to (re)define hegemonic masculinity focuses on how marginalized or subordinated men navigate dilemmas of asserting masculine identities (Ezzell 2012; Wilkins 2009). However, to fully unpack how hegemonic masculinity is either reworked or reproduced amid multiple and changing gender forms, it is essential to consider the experiences of privileged men as those who have perhaps the most power in shaping hegemonic masculinity (Connell and Messerschmidt 2005).

In addition to the experiences of privileged men, it is equally important to examine the elite spaces in which these privileges are embedded. These spaces—from traditional boarding schools to high-status occupations—are gendered; many remain "fundamentally . . . Anglo-Saxon and patriarchal" (Gaztambide-Fernández 2009, 160). Research on private preparatory schools where many TBS students spend formative adolescent years shows how privileged boys learn to construct "ruling class masculinities" premised on a "cool indifference" (Poynting and Donaldson 2005) and an "ease" of interaction (Khan 2011), in addition to toughness, control (particularly over emotions), self-reliance, certain types of violence, and competitive individualism (Cookson and Persell 1985; Poynting and Donaldson 2005). This context cultivates and rewards a detached, in-control masculine style, reproducing hegemonic masculinities among certain boys by subtly excluding a growing contingent of diverse youth who do not or cannot successfully embody it because of gender, race, and/or class differences (Gaztambide-Fernández 2009; Khan 2011).

Like other forms of masculinity, ruling-class masculinities are formed against a complex system of social arrangements involving gender, class, race, and age. The burgeoning "hybrid masculinities" framework is useful for examining how these arrangements play out when normative gender scripts and expectations come into conflict with gender norms in therapeutic settings. The term "hybrid masculinities" refers to the selective incorporation of qualities associated with subordinate or marginalized masculinities, and sometimes femininities, into men's gender performance (Bridges and Pascoe 2014). Hybrid masculinities have been primarily observed among young, white, middle-class, heterosexual men, which has been linked to the "flexibility of identity" afforded to privileged men (Bridges and Pascoe 2014). . . .

The potential flexibility that privileged young men have to construct and mobilize "hybrid masculinities" has important implications for the "masculinity dilemma" (Pascoe and Hollander 2015; Wilkins 2009) they confront in therapeutic contexts. Masculinity dilemmas refer to situations in which norms for masculine performance are challenged and have been documented in a variety of settings, including residential therapy. Research on hybrid masculinities, however, suggests that young men in TBS programs might use different strategies for reshaping what it means to be "men" in these contexts—particularly in contrast to working-class men and men of color who perform "compensatory manhood acts" (Ezzell 2012)—because of their ability to distance themselves from dominant forms of masculinity, "but not from the associated privileges" (Bridges 2014, 78). Important to note here is that although hybrid masculinities are implicated in the reproduction of privilege, this does not negate individual agency. The young men in this study use resources available to them creatively and strategically to make sense of who they are amid conflicting gendered meanings. However, much agentic work is reproductive of social structures (Hughey 2012).

Gender in Therapy and the Sites

Therapeutic contexts are gendered spaces largely because of the nature of the therapies they employ (Ezzell 2012). TBS programs use a variety of different therapeutic models for treating adolescent issues, but one of the most common for confronting substance abuse is the 12-step program (National Association of Therapeutic Schools and Programs 2015). This program originated in the archetypal support group of Alcoholics Anonymous (AA), offering a set of guiding principles for recovery from addiction that have become ubiquitous across treatment programs. The 12-step program employs a spiritual model of well-being (Moisio and Beruchashvili 2010) developed in consonance with Judeo-Christian religious beliefs rooted in surrender to a higher power, recognition of powerlessness, spiritual guidance, confession, and forgiveness (Travis 2009). . . . [T]he emphasis on powerlessness and the mandate to "quit playing God" can be taken as a condemnation of hegemonic masculinity (Travis 2009). The model also encourages modes of emotional expression more commonly associated with femininity (Hochschild 1983; Wilkins 2009). Equine Assisted Therapy (EAT) has also become a popular treatment in TBS programs. . . . Equine therapists maintain that establishing a trusting relationship with an animal requires expression of emotion and congruence between feeling and action. For this reason, EAT is deemed consonant with the relational and emotional nature of wellbeing among women. . . .

The Canyon Foundation encompasses two sites: The Canyon Ranch Academy and The Canyon House. The Canyon Ranch Academy is a Western boarding school and drug rehabilitation program for high school–aged boys located outside of a moderate-sized city. The site is structured as a total institution (Goffman 1961), removing students from outside life and arranging their daily activities in a rigid 7:00 A.M.–9:00 P.M. schedule. Upon enrollment, students begin therapy for substance abuse, which includes daily sessions with a therapist, 12-step treatment, and equine therapy. Outside of therapy and schoolwork, students participate in recreational activities such as horse treks, wilderness excursions, and competitive sports. The site contains a fully accredited high school, recreation and dining lodges, student housing facilities, a gym, and several sporting arenas—all on a working horse ranch. After graduating from the Ranch, students are encouraged to move on to Canyon House or "part two" of the program. The Canyon House is a transitional living facility located in the nearest city. The 12-step program is the core rehabilitation tool at this facility. In the first three months, residents must complete a "90 in 90" or 90 AA meetings in 90 days. They work closely with a sponsor (usually a Canyon alum or staff member) to move through the 12-steps. In addition, residents are required to work part-time or to enroll in college courses. However, residents must still comply with a rigid schedule that structures their interactions and activities. Students typically spend one year at each site, although this is dependent on individual progress. The total cost of participating in both parts of the program ranges between $175,000 and $200,000.

Methods

. . . Interviews were conducted at the Canyon House and ranged between one and three hours. The interview sample comprises most of the students in residence at the time ($n = 25$), staff members[5] ($n = 5$), and alumni of the program ($n = 4$). Except for one student who identified as "half-Black," all were white. The lowest reported family income was $180,000. However, family income was reported by students, many of whom did not know exactly how much their parents made, stating their parents were "well-off" or "worth in the 6-digits." Students were admitted for problems with substance abuse; thus, all are self-identified alcoholics or addicts. Many went through a treatment program before Canyon and attributed relapses to a lack of emphasis on the 12-steps. All students and alumni had at least one professional parent (business and medical professionals were most common). None of the students in the sample went to Canyon willingly; parents made the decision in all cases. The degree of resistance to attending Canyon and other characteristics of students and alumni are reported in Table 9.1.

The data are limited in that I was not able to conduct interviews or make systematic observations at the Canyon Ranch because of issues of researching children, many of whom were going through substance withdrawal and medical interventions that dramatically increased their vulnerability. In these physical and mental states, I judged it both

Table 9.1 Descriptive Characteristics of Canyon Students and Alumni

	n	%
Home region		
Northeast	14	49
California	6	21
South	4	14
Midwest	3	10
Pacific Northwest	1	3
Southwest	1	3
Previous school type		
Boarding school	16	55
Private preparatory school (nonboarding)	9	31
Public school	4	14
Age range, years		
18–20	21	72
21–23	8	28
Issues recognized/treated at Canyon other than substance abuse[a]		
Violence	17	59
Anxiety	7	24
Depression	4	14
Degree of resistance to attending Canyon		
Violent reaction (physically fought parents)	6	21
Volatile, but nonviolent reaction (screaming, barricading themselves in a room)	15	52
Nonviolent, nonvolatile reaction (attempted to negotiate with parents)	8	28
Additional characteristics		
Previous substance abuse treatment prior to Canyon	12	41
Self-described "loner"	2	7

[a] This category does not add to 100% because some students had more than one of these issues, and some did not have a co-occurring issue with substance abuse that was reported.

inappropriate and potentially counterproductive to recruit them for my research. Many Canyon House students told me that they "weren't all there" while in the Ranch program because of withdrawal, suggesting that interviews with these students may not have produced coherent results; the experience perhaps is better understood and articulated in retrospect. . . .

My awareness of how young men at Canyon embodied and talked about masculinity emerged inductively from initial visits and interviews. Moving forward, I developed a semi-structured interview guide to examine changes in gendered dispositions throughout the Canyon program. I asked questions about adolescent experiences commonly understood as gendered in previous school and family contexts. Students often discussed difficulties and resistance to the Canyon program on their own. Finally, I asked about personal transformations within the program and how they shaped interactions with others. I coded interviews and field notes in an iterative, inductive–deductive manner by constructing topic codes derived from theory and inductive codes based on emergent themes in the data.

The Dilemma: Boarding School Bros and Typical Dudes

Upon arriving at The Canyon Ranch Academy, students begin a transformation of self that has been found to be common in organizations structured as total institutions (Goffman 1961). This is not a top–down process, however, and to conceptualize the masculinity dilemma students negotiate in this context it is important to consider how students struggle with and reconcile previous styles of masculinity within Canyon's therapeutic environment. Students spoke at length about their pre-Canyon experiences, using particular terms and discourses that were markedly different from how they spoke about themselves in the present. Students described the transition into the TBS as chaotic. Wesley, a Canyon student, attributes this chaos to being "forced into the program and forced to act in ways that seemed completely insane to us." This issue—that students are forced into the program—is important in that students face pressure to act in accordance with expectations in the program. However, this does not mean that students cannot resist. Edward, a Canyon alum and staff member, contextualizes this clash by detailing

dominant styles of masculinity that undergirded his and other students' previous experiences:

> Boarding schools are all the same. The personalities are like "boarding school bro." . . . A lot of drugs, a lot of alcohol, sex, fights, and things like that. So, when guys get to the Ranch . . . it's like testosterone overload, these guys who, myself included, are like not having it, like "you're not the boss of me!" and inevitably someone starts a fight the first night, and . . . chaos.

Edward classifies himself and his previous classmates as "boarding school bros"—young men who engaged in excessive drinking, drug use, sex, and fighting. His account mirrors Kimmel's (2008) vivid descriptions of the modern world of "guys": a developmental stage and social space characterized by celebration of promiscuity, consumption, and irresponsibility. Evan provides another specific account of this chaotic transition, also noting how students' pre-Canyon identities led to issues like addiction and caused problems upon enrollment at Canyon:

> I was a typical dude. I loved sports and I started lacrosse in fourth grade and I was also into extreme sports. I loved downhill mountain biking, martial arts . . . the competitiveness at school kinda bred this like need to be more extreme. You can kinda see how the drug addiction came about. I wasn't allowed to do competitive sports [at Canyon] for a long time because they knew that it was an addiction for me . . . that was like the hardest part and why I hated it here at first.

Like Evan, who describes himself as the "typical dude," James invokes a similarly gendered concept of the "all-American" guy to describe his previous self:

> I was like the guy who had it all. All-American lacrosse player . . . lots of friends who was getting recruited for D1 schools . . . grades were good. And everything was good . . . but then my father died. I never talked about it . . . cause you can't talk about that stuff to those guys [at school]. I never even like looked at those feelings and I started

using heavily. They teach you here that trauma has effects . . . but I spent months at the Ranch saying I was fine, I wouldn't talk about anything, I'd pretend that my father hadn't died . . . it was ridiculous like total denial. Like an allergic reaction to admitting that I was hurting.

. . . Talk of sports, and particularly of being the best or most "extreme" in a certain sport, was prevalent and is consonant with literature describing the ultra-competitive nature of ruling-class masculinity (Poynting and Donaldson 2005) and athleticism among high-status boys in schools generally (Pascoe 2007; Thorne 1993). . . . Even within their narratives of transformation, students talked about sports intently with each other and with me, demonstrating their masculine histories as "that guy" (Pascoe 2007) who, as James says "had it all": athleticism, popularity, and good academic standing. Embedded in these discourses, however, is that the TBS environment precludes what it means to be "that guy": the competitive, unemotional, promiscuous, and sometimes violent behaviors that have come to shape the stage of life between adolescence and manhood (Kimmel 2008). Within Canyon's therapeutic environment, students begin to understand prior, perhaps normative (Kimmel 2008), masculine dispositions as pathological, marking a shift in how they understand themselves as young men. However, this process is gradual: a stark contrast in norms surrounding masculine performance at the beginning of the program erupting in chaos, fighting, and denial. It is a gender dilemma that James likens to an "allergic reaction."

Aside from two self-described "loners," students talked about themselves as popular kids who did well in school until drinking and drug use, partying, competitive behaviors, and sexual promiscuity caused problems. Although all students recognized these behaviors as problematic at the time they were interviewed, they report extreme resistance to thinking about them as such at the beginning of the program. Harrison recounts: "I refused to participate in stuff at the Ranch for months . . . I sat in my room and told them where they could shove

this emotional crap." The two "loner" students also recounted resistance to the therapeutic environment; one of them told me resolutely, "I wanted to kill myself when I got here . . . all these people prying into my shit." This gradual process of re-imagining what it means to be young men involves the construction of a competing discourse built on a hybrid masculine style that casts what it means to be a "typical dude" as contrary to what it means to be a "good guy." Students use AA and other therapeutic models to frame previous aspects of their gender identities as "defects"—incorporating humility, service, and emotionality into a reformulated masculine style to claim identities as "better" men (Weber 2012; Wilkins 2009).

The Qualities of "Good Guys"

The process of reshaping masculinity at Canyon begins with the strategies students develop to mobilize therapeutic discourse as a masculinity resource (Wilkins 2009). One of the central themes in conversations about the role of AA at Canyon was that it teaches "how to be a good guy." Caleb, for instance, explains the 12-steps as a guide for "living right." He said, "Here [the 12-steps are] mandatory and you have to actually show that you're living right. Like it goes beyond . . . treatment. It's like, 'here is how you live a good life.' Spelled out like that." . . . Liam, a student, elaborates on the meaning that AA takes on at Canyon:

I mean I recognize AA as a good program. I don't think it matters if you're an addict or not I think it just matters that in your life you are a generally good person. Like saying sorry when you're wrong and making up for your mistakes, help other people. It's all just . . . basic stuff that good people do, you know?

Put this way, the 12-steps become a life-practice that would be, as James, another student stated, "good for anyone." By re-framing the emotional qualities that underlie the 12-steps as qualities of good people, students understand the tenets of AA differently than the working-class men in Ezzell's (2012) study of residential treatment who perceive them as contradictions to manhood. Canyon students, by comparison, actively incorporate the 12-steps into their narratives of emotional growth to portray themselves as "good guys," thereby bolstering their masculinity relative to generalized notions of "other" young men (Weber 2012).

Indeed, students mobilize newfound un-entitled attitudes and humble dispositions as resources to signal the specific ways they were different from other young men. For instance, Caleb says:

> You know, here it's like . . . they're just really good guys . . . I go back home and you should see these guys. They just have these entitled attitudes, like "I can have whatever the hell I want." Whether it's money, women, whatever. They don't care about anyone but themselves, and like advancing their own shit.

Here, Caleb rejects the "culture of entitlement" that has become firmly affixed to the behaviors and cultural perceptions of contemporary guys (Kimmel 2008). David echoes Caleb's statement, using humility gained through the 12-steps as means of gendered distinction: "The 12-steps are just a basic practice of humility . . . but the guys I know are too selfish and entitled to ever admit they're wrong." Students like David and Caleb use their emotional transformations to claim masculinities that are "presumably more moral and desirable than the masculinities of other sorts of men" (Wilkins 2009, 260). By redefining dispositions that would previously have appeared "weak" or "suspicious" (Poynting and Donaldson 2005) as qualities of "good guys," students set themselves apart from other, "lesser" guys.

Canyon students also develop a service orientation, but one that functions to position them as leaders. David explains that service is important at Canyon "because the nature of addiction and alcoholism is pretty selfish and just like after having like taken from society for so long, we need to give back at this point." However, service takes on a unique and complex meaning at Canyon. When Braxton, an alum and staff member, discussed the importance of service to the AA community, through

sponsorship in particular, he notes that Canyon students were asked to be sponsors more frequently than other AA members:

> We have all these people who have really been in there and they really know their stuff, to the book. Like you go to an AA meeting and you hear people talk and their war stories and stuff, but all you really wanna listen to is these guys [Canyon students and staff], they're just hella good people. They even get other people to come in and ask them for sponsorship, it's just crazy!

Braxton suggests that Canyon students are leaders and experts in the AA community. Joshua, sounding much like Braxton, says, "I'm not sure that there are a lot of other people in AA who know the Big Book like we do, we really study the stuff. I think that's why we're called as sponsors more." Canyon students view sponsorship as service and as a way to "give back." However, sponsorship also operates as a way to assert leadership positions and expertise in the AA community. In Cookson and Persell's (1985) classic work on elite education, they note an inherent contradiction between being a "servant" and a "leader." Like other privileged youth, however, Canyon students resolve this contradiction by learning that to "serve" is to become decision makers in society (Cookson and Persell 1985; Gaztambide-Fernández 2009).

The ways Canyon students perform service relates to their positions as young, white, upper-class men in two major ways. The first is simply that students (via their families) have the resources to participate in a program that affords them abundant opportunities, including the time and guidance to "study," as Joshua says, therapeutic literature as if it were an academic subject, which contributes to the belief that they are the experts. Although four students recognized that they were "fortunate to be here" and that it was a function of their parents' wealth, others did not recognize this. The few who did made no connection between being the ones who "really know their stuff" in AA and their social class or differential resources—factors that enable the close guidance Canyon provides when working the 12-steps. Secondly, Canyon students confront men (they rarely spoke of women in AA) in AA meetings as "others." They do so explicitly in terms of class and age and implicitly in terms of race, developing a kind of "paternalistic savior" (Hughey 2012) mentality informed by negative beliefs associated with these categories. Wesley, a Canyon student, explains differences between Canyon students and other AA members in terms of sponsorship:

> I mean, there's a lot of different people in AA . . . lots of people here live in trailer parks, some are homeless. . . . If there is a fifty year old dude, with a long scruffy beard that can't dress right and he identifies himself as a recovering alcoholic . . . it's going to look a lot differently than me, an 18 year old upper-middle-class dude that looks pretty normal saying that I'm an alcoholic. I think that in and of itself leads people to seek us out as sponsors.

Wesley employs clear class and age distinctions—that upper-middle-class men look "normal" compared to old, working-class men—suggesting this is a reason "in and of itself" that Canyon students are better suited as sponsors. As being young and being white are often thought of as "natural" or "default" categories (Lewis 2004), age and whiteness are likely factors in his perception that he is normal compared to other men in AA in this Western locale, many of whom are Hispanic. In a different exchange, Liam erects another boundary between Canyon students and AA members. He said, "We're just in a different place, you know? Like if you look around here . . . we're not the typical people you'd meet at AA or outpatient. We can be there to help them . . . just not hang out with them cause it might not be good for us." Likely drawing on class differences and implicit negative cultural beliefs surrounding addicts and addiction, Liam differentiates Canyon students from "typical" alcoholics. He notes that as Canyon students, they are in a "different place," suggesting other AA members may have a polluting influence. He can be there as an adviser to instruct other AA members, but he is not one of them.

In AA meetings, Canyon students assumed leadership positions naturally. Students were facilitators (rotating discussion moderators designated by the group) in eight of the 11 meetings I attended. On one occasion, I arrived to an AA meeting a few minutes late with Chris, a Canyon alum and meeting facilitator. Before entering the room we heard shouts and a call of "There's our man!" Smiling and laughing, Chris sat down in a chair another man pulled out for him, greeting members by name and reaching over to pat them on the shoulder or shake hands. Amid the other members clad mostly in jeans and T-shirts, Chris stood out in a blue blazer paired artfully with a vintage button-up shirt over slacks. He moderated the discussion effortlessly, relating issues among other members to his own recovery, and suggesting solutions based on his experience while other members nodded and smiled in agreement. Throughout the meeting, Chris sat relaxed in his chair, one leg slung over the other while he casually flipped through the Big Book resting in his lap to call attention to relevant passages and interject advice as each of the members spoke in turn.

This ease of interaction that students displayed in all activities, but particularly in AA meetings, is related to what Khan (2011) calls the "ease" of privilege. One of the distinctive characteristics of the modern upper class is that success is no longer contingent on "building motes around culture . . . knowing particular things (like which is the salad fork)" (Khan 2011, 83). Instead, it is about embodying an ease that spans different cultural spaces—an expansive knowledge of how to act within a culturally varied world. For instance, Chris had no problem relating a spat with his younger brother to a long-standing issue between a 50-year-old AA member and his son, despite being half the man's age and not having children himself. He gave advice in a way that left no room but to believe he was the authority on any given subject, even when he rarely had direct experience with the issues the men brought up. He seemed a natural leader and authority figure in the meeting, something other members recognized as well. After the meeting, Chris introduced me to Ricky, a Hispanic man in his mid-thirties who he was sponsoring. As we walked out, Ricky told me—perhaps self-consciously given their age difference—"I still can't believe I'm taking advice from this 23 year old kid! They got something going on at [Canyon] though, tell you that." Ricky suggests that the boundaries students draw between themselves and other AA members are upheld outside of Canyon. He notes that there is something innately different about them, something that marks them as leaders and potential sponsors. The qualities that designate them as leaders—a corporal "ease" of interaction and an expertise in AA culture and literature—are anything but natural, however. They are products of repeated experiences in elite institutions (Khan 2011) and of the students' ability (via family resources) to attend a program like Canyon. That these differences are not attributed to status, but rather to differences of personality or something innate, operates to obscure the reproduction of privilege and hierarchy (Khan 2011).

In addition to AA, students also relate equine therapy to their personal and emotional transformations. Caleb talks about the role of EAT in his recovery: "Horses have been a big part of my recovery and transformation. . . . It makes you think about things outside of yourself and really care for something." As with service, however, the emotional proficiencies students attribute to EAT also function as tools to assert themselves as leaders. Daniel, a Canyon student, explains:

> My horse taught me how to lead. By showing my emotions, communicating my true self, I was able to guide her and we built an incredible relationship. We trust each other . . . she's helped me in so many ways . . . with this transformation into an honest, compassionate human being.

Daniel aligns "soft" emotional qualities with what it takes to be an effective leader. On one visit to the Canyon House, a group of students recognized the seeming inconsistency between these emotional qualities and the manly physicality of horseback riding and ranch work. Wesley—looking distinctly opposite of the rugged, weathered image of the American cowboy in his polo shirt, khaki shorts, and Sperry Topsider boat shoes—chuckles as he tells me:

> It's kinda funny. Like, if you look around the Ranch, it's like literally a Ranch. And you've got a bunch of boys walking around like a cheesy Western re-enactment riding horses and shoveling shit—like cowboys. I mean like how macho could you get? But then later in the day we're going to therapy, praying with a friend, talking about our *feelings*. [laughs] I guess we're pretty sensitive cowboys.

Wesley acknowledges the emotional aspects of Canyon's environment, and that they exist in opposition to the "macho" image of the cowboy. However, after he notes this contrast, he aligns the two, suggesting Canyon students embody a hybrid masculine construct as "sensitive cowboys."

Emotions and Intimacy-Talk

Canyon students employ emotion work (Hochschild 1983) and intimacy talk (Wilkins 2009) in line with this hybrid, "sensitive" style of masculinity, but in ways that tend to bolster masculinity. . . . Aware of contradictions in men expressing intimate feelings (Wilkins 2009), students often made light of their open emotionality. Thomas, for instance, says that at Canyon "they make us talk about our *feeeeeelings*." Thomas's response is consistent with how other students drew out the word "feelings," uttering the word in a mocking tone while laughing, or, as two students did, using air quotes. Despite discursively distancing themselves from an expressive practice usually coded as "feminine" (Bridges 2014), students drew on "intimacy-talk"—an emotional vocabulary that incorporates talk of vulnerability, trust, and intimacy—to restore family bonds and assume leadership roles in their families, and also to construct other men's aggressive and inexpressive demeanors as lesser, even vulgar (Weber 2012; Wilkins 2009). This initial discursive resistance is likely a function of the sharp disjuncture in feeling rules across Canyon and previous contexts—particularly families and schools.

The majority of students described their parents as emotionally distant and emphasized the role of the emotional growth they experienced in family therapy programs (phone conversations mediated by a therapist) at Canyon in restoring family bonds. Like Grant, a Canyon student, recounts:

> My family was the kind where you sit at the dinner table and nobody says a word, like no communication at all. If you have a bad day, deal with it. Go scream into a pillow . . . don't bring it up to us . . . Here you have to do these family workshops and phone sessions to talk about stuff that's wrong. Those really help to open the lines of communication with our families. You talk through resentments. . . . There are lots of tears, but it *works*. I have this incredible relationship with my family now.

Joshua describes family therapy at Canyon similarly, as a highly emotional encounter that involves emotion-talk to navigate difficult relationships and solve family problems:

> My parents were really unemotional and strict, and I think that's where the trust issues and emotional unavailability came from, but we dealt with it by putting it all out there in the family therapy here. Now I call my parents everyday, we talk about everything . . . we say "I love you" and it's really good.

Grant and Joshua's statements imply that expressing feelings to parents is something that "works" to enable communication and establish healthy relationships.

For alumni, the emotional coaching that occurs in family therapy was implicated in how they positioned themselves in their families and in their outcomes post-Canyon. Edward, an alum and staff member, explains how he interacts with his parents:

> I feel like when I go home I'm like the man of the house now. My parents have always had some issues and I'm the one who helps manage and talk through those at this point. The fact that I went through this program and can communicate between the two of them actually helps them with like whatever conflict is going on.

Edward asserts a "man of the house" role based on his ability to navigate conflict by facilitating communication. Similar to the ways students meld service and leadership, Edward's ability to resolve conflict by talking things through allows him to assert a dominant position relative to his parents. For Charles, working through emotional issues with his father re-opened routes to attainment in his father's digital marketing company:

> My dad and I used to have major trust issues . . . he used to threaten to kick me out, take me out of the will, all that. Now that we've worked through our issues and actually talk and trust each other with things, he's talking about putting me in charge of one of the divisions of his company after I get a degree.

The emotional tools students use to rebuild family relationships take on particular importance for students given their class positions. By establishing a trusting relationship with his father, Charles is reconsidered to carry on family business—as was the case with six other students in later stages of the program and two alums. As Khan (2011) notes, family bonds are important in the intergenerational transference of wealth and resources (networks, connections, etc.). Students repair these bonds via heightened communication with parents enabled by intimacy-talk.

The other significant disjuncture in feeling rules occurred across Canyon and previous schools. Previously, several students had attended military schools, which have historically served to reform "unruly" adolescent boys (Cookson and Persell 1985). The contrast in feeling-rules was evident in accounts of previous school experiences broadly, but military schools in particular, as Liam describes:

> It was pretty violent . . . and there was a certain stoic-ness about it. Like it was all drilling and training . . . kind of ridiculous, like talk about discipline and punishment just for the sake of discipline and punishment . . . totally different from [Canyon]. It's not fun. You don't smile a lot, a lot of the time you can't, like you will be punished for it. And to deal with stuff, you don't ever really *talk*. You deal with problems . . . by just doing

the routine . . . drills and training. . . . Here, like, [laughs] it's pretty normal to see a dude crying. Or saying he's struggling with guilt or whatever.

Although military schools exist as an extreme gendered space where masculine performances are heavily policed (Cookson and Persell 1985), research suggests that certain kinds of violence and control are "endemic" to ruling-class masculinity (Poynting and Donaldson 2005). Thomas, a Canyon student, describes the specific nature of the violence he engaged in while at school: "I got in fights all the time, but it was kind of sneaky and quiet. Me and my friends would like punish losers in the middle of the night. I was not a good guy." This "sneaky and quiet" style of violence was used to exert control and dominance over "losers"—presumably boys who performed subordinate masculinities. The few young men who had attended public high school prior to Canyon also recounted violent dispositions, but ones that lacked the "sneaky and quiet character" that Thomas describes. Harrison, a student who attended a Northeastern public high school, remarks, "I was pretty aggressive in school, fighting was just my reaction to everything. So, I was always in the office, usually trying to fight my way out [laughs]." However, as Liam indicates, emotional communication supplants violence as a solution to problems at Canyon where it is now normal to "see a dude crying."

Braxton touches on this reversal—from violent expression to emotional expression—mobilizing a "mature" emotional style to bolster his masculinity:

At seventeen I was more mature than most of the people that I knew and I would go back home and see people my own age and go back into the school setting and . . . Yeah, I would see kids and they would be like dumb and I would think, I actually hung out and acted like these people, this is ridiculous. Like why on earth would I possibly do this? But . . . I'm able to look at things in a different light . . . when something bad happens I'm not like, ". . . this is stupid" But I'm like, "Okay, you have your opinion." . . . I'm not going to act out and get all mad, punch a guy or whatever. I can tell you

how I feel and if you don't understand that, it's fine, I accept it. . . . It really helps . . . make that transition from boy to man quick.

Braxton explains that communicating feelings is a quality of true men, suggesting that aggression and violence is characteristic of immature, "dumb" kids. Like Braxton, Daniel feels that "you just can't communicate with guys our age. That's why [Canyon] is so influential for me . . . teaching me how to feel my feelings and how to communicate with other people and have better relationships all around."

Braxton and Daniel use intimacy-talk as a symbol of their depth, particularly in comparison to the immaturity linked with male youth (Weber 2012). Though intimacy-talk is seen as a feminine practice that might threaten manhood, students use it to bolster their masculinity. This finding is consistent with research that has found that men's use of emotional discourse can sometimes be used to maintain power in relationships. For instance, in Kleinman's (1996) research in an alternative health organization, men's emotional displays took on more value than women's since emotional disclosure was assumed to be more difficult for them (see also Weber 2012). . . . As emotionality is presumed lacking among men, especially young men (Kimmel 2008; Wilkins 2009), students' emotional displays take on greater significance. As Wilkins (2009) states, there is a belief that "men deserve more credit for their [emotional] efforts" (363). Emotional expression, then, becomes a valuable masculinity resource with respect to various others.

The Vulgarity of Masculinity

As students are required to work part-time or enroll in college classes during the final stages of their time at Canyon House, many students had interactions and friendships with people outside of the TBS and AA. When asked about these relationships, the overwhelming response was that they were difficult. Friendships with other young men were especially problematic. Some students, like Harrison, attribute difficulties in relationships to the fact that "most guys are into binge drinking and destructive patterns like that," engaging with what Kimmel (2008) finds a common cultural (mis)perception that all young men drink to excess. However, when prompted about peers who did not drink problematically, students still maintained these relationships were difficult. Wesley, a Canyon student, explains why:

> They might not be alcoholics . . . maybe some of them are, but the stuff they engage in, like just girl after girl, or like idiotic primal displays, like "oooh, oooh, oooh" [makes noises and hits chest imitating a monkey] . . . those are symptoms of this underlying disease . . . like the problems that lead to something like alcoholism.

Wesley identifies the behaviors of young men at large as causes of issues like alcoholism. Recounting an exchange with a student, Braxton, an alum and staff member, suggests that these behaviors are driven by purposelessness:

> I was talking [to a student] about the way we relieve ourselves of this depression is not for personal gain, it's to live a purposeful life . . . you could easily be out there with your high school friends, drinking and doing drugs, and casual sex, but where is the purpose in that? . . . There are not a lot of 18-year-olds that are doing service work and helping others, and that is the depth in our relationships.

Wesley and Braxton draw upon a "generic catch-all" category of the modern "guy" (Kimmel 2008), defined by excessive drinking, promiscuity, and aimlessness, to distinguish themselves from the average young man. They deem the masculine styles of "other" guys—styles they themselves embodied pre-Canyon—animalistic, purposeless, and symptomatic of a disease.

Edward, an alum and staff member, also draws on masculine stereotypes as he describes problems relating to peers:

> It's incredibly difficult, like I hang out with these guys, that not to be profane, but they are like, "Yo, I fucked this bitch last night!" . . . Like what is wrong with you? How old are you? And they say 22, and I'm like . . . that makes sense. And I hate

the frat life. There are not a lot of 23 year olds looking at where their abandonment issues come from. That are . . . looking at how can I help someone else today. . . . It does make interactions . . . difficult. It does put you in a unique position especially in the dating field you are different from the other guys so it makes it pretty easy for you.

Edward profanes the sexual promiscuity and derogation of women that he sees as characteristic of other guys. As a young man set upon self-reflection and helping others, he defines himself as "unique" against the backdrop of other, shallow, selfish men. . . . By similarly disavowing these configurations of masculinity in fields like dating, Canyon students claim higher relational worthiness vis-à-vis other men. Although students like Edward provided examples of how their transformations as men "worked" for them, I was able to observe this firsthand on a visit to the Canyon House. One afternoon, I ran into a girl named Emily who told me she was waiting for Daniel, a student in his final month of the program. I began talking with Emily, who had been casually dating Daniel for about two months, about the Canyon program and asked what she thought of it. She gushed about how inspiring it was to see so many young men who had "pulled a complete 180." On her relationship with Daniel, she smiled as she told me:

> I've never met anyone like him before! I've had two other real relationships with guys . . . you would call "emotionally unavailable" [laughs]. But Daniel is . . . the opposite . . . like we really talk, you know? . . . And that communication is important on my end too, so it's been really great. . . . I'm older so I was hesitant at first, but he's amazing!

For Emily, Daniel's emotional availability makes him a better partner than other men. Her hesitance at dating a younger man (21 to her 25) suggests that these distinctions are enabled by age. Although emotional inexpressiveness is a generalized quality of men, it is especially so among young men, making students like Daniel especially desirable compared to their counterparts in that they are rare (Wilkins 2009). This instance is illustrative of the ways hybrid masculinities operate in practice to help young men maintain privilege and reproduce relational hierarchies (Bridges and Pascoe 2014). Their co-optation of a more feminine style of emotionality allows them to maintain advantages in the dating field—making it "easy" for them to win women—and, as I discussed in other sections, to reassert leadership roles in varied contexts like AA and in families. Although these narratives of emotional transformation may seem to challenge ideals of hegemonic masculinity, they function to reinforce them by allowing young men new avenues of asserting dominance (Bridges 2014; Weber 2012; Wilkins 2009).

Conclusion

What are we to make of these "sensitive cowboys"? Scholarship on contemporary transformations of masculinities calls researchers to attend to the different configurations of masculinities in operation at various points in history to understand how gender is understood and enacted by individuals and in the larger culture (Bridges and Pascoe 2014; Messerschmidt 2016). It is particularly important to break down masculinity to understand the workings of privilege and power, not only between men and women but also within the category of "men." This article uses a previously unexamined case to illustrate how privileged young men navigate ruptures in hegemonic masculinity by constructing hybrid masculinities. In contrast to men of different social backgrounds in similar situations who cope with threats to masculinity using "compensatory manhood acts" (Ezzell 2012), the young men in this study draw from different cultural tools and strategies to construct hybrid masculinities that incorporate identity elements associated with femininity and subordinate masculinities.

. . . Using therapeutic discourse to frame themselves as sensitive and emotional young men committed to service, they are able to assert leadership roles and to distinguish themselves from other, "lesser" men (Weber 2012; Wilkins 2009). However, they continue to benefit from privileges associated with being young, white, upper-class, and male that make hybrid masculinities more available

as a resource (Bridges and Pascoe 2012). This sheds light on why there might be different strategies for resolving "masculinity dilemmas" in male therapeutic contexts depending on social status.

This article extends the line of theory and research showing that masculine styles that appear out of sync with hegemonic masculinity tend to reproduce and conceal systems of power in new ("softer") ways (Bridges 2014; Bridges and Pascoe 2014; Messner 1993; Wilkins 2009). It also contributes to research on contemporary transformations of masculinities among privileged youth—studies of whom remain limited. Also, recognition of the cultural resources and tools that inform how men of different social backgrounds respond to gender dilemmas in therapeutic contexts may aid therapeutic practitioners. This study was limited to observations of students in the later stages of one TBS program. Further research is needed to explore these processes across other programs and to discern how hybrid masculinities are implicated in outcomes post-TBS. Subsequent research must examine how well these hybrid masculine styles "stick" post-completion, particularly given that Canyon students, and likely other TBS students, do not enter these programs voluntarily and are under pressure to comply with norms and expectations. Although the few alums in this study fully embodied these emotional dispositions, they were those who remained closely involved with Canyon. Longitudinal research is necessary to explore further transformations in the masculinities of those who move out of the structure of the program and return home and to previous contexts and peer networks.

Notes

1. These programs are alternatively called "emotional growth academies" or "teen boot camps," but they are considered in the same general class of institutions by the National Association of Therapeutic Schools and Programs (2015).
2. The 12-step program originated in the support group of Alcoholics Anonymous (AA) and outlines 12 principles to overcome addiction.

3. The Canyon Foundation is a same-sex program. Although co-ed TBS programs exist, almost all are sex-segregated within facilities.

4. Men or women can exhibit the qualities discussed throughout this article. They are not essential features of femininity or masculinity but are culturally associated with one category more than the other (Hochschild 1983).

5. Of the five staff members interviewed, three were alums of the program. It is common for students who graduate the program to work at the facility soon after, usually for a brief period.

References

Connell, R. W. 1995. *Masculinities*. Berkeley: University of California Press.

Connell, R. W., and James Messerschmidt. 2005. Hegemonic masculinity: Rethinking the concept. *Gender & Society* 19 (6): 829–59.

Cookson, Peter W., and Caroline Hodges Persell. 1985. *Preparing for power: America's elite boarding schools*. New York: Basic Books.

Bridges, Tristan. 2014. A very "gay" straight? Hybrid masculinities, sexual aesthetics, and the changing relationship between masculinity and homophobia. *Gender & Society* 28 (1): 58–82.

Bridges, Tristan, and C. J. Pascoe. 2014. Hybrid masculinities: New directions in the sociology of men and masculinities. *Sociology Compass* 8 (3): 246–58.

Ezzell, Matthew. 2012. "I'm in control": Compensatory manhood in a therapeutic community. *Gender & Society* 26 (2): 190–215.

Gaztambide-Fernández, Ruben. 2009. *The best of the best: Becoming elite at an American boarding school*. Cambridge, MA: Harvard University Press.

Goffman, Erving. 1961. *Asylums*. Garden City, NY: Random House.

Hochschild, Arlie. 1983. *The managed heart: The commercialization of human feeling*. Berkeley: University of California Press.

Hughey, Matthew. 2012. *Whitebound*. Stanford: Stanford University Press.

Khan, Shamus Rahman. 2011. *Privilege: The making of an adolescent elite at St. Paul's School*. Princeton, NJ: Princeton University Press.

Kimmel, Michael. 2008. *Guyland*. New York: HarperCollins.

Kleinman, Sherryl. 1996. *Opposing ambitions: Gender and identity in an alternative organization*. Chicago: University of Chicago Press.

Lewis, Amanda. 2004. "What group?" Studying whites and whiteness in the era of "color-blindness." *Sociological Theory* 22 (4): 623–26.

Messerschmidt, James W. 2016. *Masculinities in the making: From the local to the global*. Lanham, MD: Rowman & Littlefield.

Messner, Michael. 1993. "Changing men" and feminist politics in the United States. *Theory and Society* 22 (5): 723–37.

Moisio, Risto, and Mariam Beruchashvili. 2010. Questing for well-being at weight watchers: The role of the spiritual–therapeutic model in a support group. *Journal of Consumer Research* 36 (6): 857–75.

National Association of Therapeutic Boarding Schools. https://natsap.org/ (accessed April 2015).

Pascoe, C. J. 2007. *Dude you're a fag: Masculinity and sexuality in high school*. Berkeley: University of California Press.

Pascoe, C. J., and Jocelyn A. Hollander. 2015. Good guys don't rape: Gender, domination, and mobilizing rape. *Gender & Society* 30 (1): 67–79.

Poynting, Scott, and Mike Donaldson. 2005. Snakes and leaders: Hegemonic masculinity in ruling-class boys' boarding schools. *Men and Masculinities* 7:325–25.

Swidler, Ann. 1986. Culture in action: Symbols and strategies. *American Sociological Review* 51 (2): 273–86.

Thorne, Barrie. 1993. *Gender play: Girls and boys in school*. New Brunswick, NJ: Rutgers University Press.

Travis, Trysh. 2009. "Handles to hang on to our sobriety": Commonplace books and surrendered masculinity in Alcoholics Anonymous. *Men and Masculinities* 12 (2): 175–200.

Weber, Jennifer. 2012. Becoming teen fathers: Stories of teen pregnancy, responsibility, and masculinity. *Gender & Society* 26 (6): 900–21.

West, Candace, and Don H. Zimmerman. 1987. "Doing gender." *Gender & Society* 1 (2): 125–51.

Wilkins, Amy C. 2009. Masculinity dilemmas: Sexuality and intimacy talk among Christians and Goths. *Journal of Women in Culture and Society* 34 (2): 343–68.

"Guys Are Just Homophobic"

Rethinking Adolescent Homophobia and Heterosexuality

C. J. PASCOE

Teenage Masculinity

Kevin, a high school student in suburban San Francisco, sits at an IHOP, short money for dinner. His friend, Craig, agrees to lend him money, but only on the following condition—that Kevin repeat a series of confessional phrases which Craig can videotape and place on YouTube. Kevin buries his head in his hands asking, "You're going to take a video of this and post it on YouTube aren't you?!" Craig ignores Kevin's plea saying, "Anyway, repeat after me. 'I Kevin James Wong.'"

> KEVIN: I, Kevin James Wong.
> CRAIG: 17 years old.
> KEVIN (who at this point starts to giggle embarrassedly): 17 years old.
> CRAIG: Senior at Valley High School.
> KEVIN: Senior at Valley High School.
> CRAIG: In Santa Clarita.
> KEVIN: In Santa Clarita.
> CRAIG: Am now confessing.
> KEVIN: Am now confessing.
> CRAIG: That I, Kevin Wong.
> KEVIN: That I, Kevin Wong.
> CRAIG: Am a homosexual male.
> KEVIN: Am a homosexual male.

They devolve into laughter as their friend Jesse jumps into the frame behind Kevin. Craig posted the video on YouTube and eagerly showed it to me as I interviewed him in a local Starbucks. He and his friends giggled as they continued to show me other YouTube videos, one of which featured them imitating men engaging in anal intercourse and then bursting into fits of laugher.

About two years before I watched Craig's video in that Santa Clarita coffee shop I found myself two hours away, at a high school in Riverton California, where a group of fifth graders had been bussed in for the day to participate in the local high school's performing arts day. As I looked around the outdoor quads decorated with student artwork and filled with choirs singing and bands playing, a student from River High, Brian, ran past me to the rear quad yelling to a group of the elementary school boys. He hollered at them, pointing frantically, "There's a faggot over there! There's a faggot over there! Come look!" The group of boys dashed after Brian as he ran down the hallway, towards the presumed "faggot." Peering down the hallway I saw Brian's friend, Dan, waiting for the boys. As the boys came into his view, Dan pursed his lips and began sashaying towards them. He swung his hips exaggeratedly and wildly waved his arms on the end of which his hands hung from limp wrists. To the boys Brian yelled, referring to Dan, "Look at the faggot! Watch out! He'll get you!" In response, the 10 year olds screamed in terror and raced back down the hallway. I watched Brian and Dan repeat this drama about the predatory faggot, each time with a new group of young boys.

Kevin, Craig, Brian and Dan enacted similar scenes containing similar messages: men or boys who do not conform to normative understandings of masculinity and sexuality should be mocked, humiliated and possibly feared. I have spent the better part of the last decade interviewing teens about and observing their behavior around definitions of masculinity and sexuality. Across a variety of geographic settings boys from a range of class and racial/ethnic backgrounds report sentiments much like those expressed by Kevin, Craig, Brian and Dan. Conversations with and observations of these boys indicate that homophobic taunts, jokes, teasing and harassment are central to the ways in which contemporary American boys come to think of themselves as men.

The homophobia articulated by Kevin, Craig, Brian and Dan seems representative of many American youth. Nationally, 93% of youth hear homophobic slurs at least occasionally and 51% hear them on a daily basis (National Mental Health Association 2002). Interestingly, in one state, 80% of youth who have been targeted with anti-gay harassment identify as heterosexual (Youth Risk Behavior Survey—Washington 1995). While this harassment is primarily directed at boys, girls suffer from sexualized harassment as well. The American Association of University Women documents that 83% of girls have been sexually harassed at school (2001). These cursory statistics point to an educational experience in adolescence characterized in part by sexualized and gendered aggression directed from boys at other boys *and* at girls.

This type of joking and teasing can have dire consequences. 90% of random school shootings have involved straight identified boys who have been relentlessly humiliated with homophobic remarks (Kimmel 2003). For instance, Michael Carneal and Andy Williams, both involved in rampage school shootings, had been harassed for being gay (Kimmel 2003; Newman et al. 2004). Michael Carneal's school newspaper actually published a report outing him as gay (though he did not self identify as such) (Newman et al. 2004). Eric Mohat, a 17 year old high school student in Ohio who enjoyed

theater and playing music, shot himself in 2007 after hearing homophobic taunts. Similarly, Carl Joseph Walker Hoover, an 11 year old middle school student in Massachusetts, suffered homophobic harassment from his classmates for performing well academically. He hung himself in a desperate response to the teasing. In 2008 Lawrence King, having been bullied relentlessly since third grade for his non-traditional gender presentation, was shot and killed by a fellow student whom he had asked to be his Valentine.

While certainly the sort of joking and minor humiliation exhibited in the two opening stories does not match the level of violence in these examples, a problematic intersection of gender and sexuality undergirds all of them. Practices that seem to reflect basic homophobia—imitating same sex eroticism, calling someone queer, or mincing about with limp wrists—are also about policing gendered identities and practices. Through making homophobic jokes, calling other boys gay and imitating effeminate men boys attempt to assure themselves and others of their masculinity. For contemporary American boys, the definition of masculinity entails displaying power, competence, a lack of emotions, heterosexuality, and dominance. Says Kevin, for instance, to be masculine is to be "tough." The ideal man is "strong" and he "can't be too emotional" adds Erik. Maleness does not confer masculinity upon a given boy. Rather masculinity is the repeated signaling to self and others that one is powerful, competent, unemotional, heterosexual and dominant.

This signaling appears in two ways, through practices of repudiation and confirmation. Repudiatory practices take the form of a "fag discourse," consisting of homophobic jokes, taunts, and imitations through which boys publicly signal their rejection of that which is considered unmasculine. Boys confirm masculine selves through public enactments of compulsive heterosexuality which include practices of "getting girls," physically confining girls under the guise of flirtation, and sex talk. For many contemporary American boys masculinity must be repeatedly proven as one's identity as masculine is never fully secured. This essay unpacks adolescent boys' public enactments of homophobia and heterosexuality, examining them as sexualized as well as gendered processes which have ramifications for all teenagers—male, female, straight and gay.

The Fag Discourse

Boys repeatedly tell me that "fag" is the ultimate insult for a boy. Darnell stated, "Since you were little boys you've been told, 'hey, don't be a little faggot.'" Jeremy emphasized that this insult literally reduced a boy to nothing, "To call someone gay or fag is like the lowest thing you can call someone. Because that's like saying that you're nothing." Indeed, much like the boys terrorized by Brian and Craig, boys often learn long before adolescence that a "fag" was the worst thing a guy could be. Thus boys' daily lives often consist of interactions in which they frantically lob these epithets at one another and try to deflect them from themselves.

Many boys explained their frequent use of insults like queer, gay and fag by asserting that, as Keith put it, "guys are just homophobic." However, analyzing boys' homophobic practices as a "fag discourse" shows that their behavior reflects not just a fear of same sex desire, but a specific fear of *men's* same sex desire. Many told me that homophobic insults applied primarily to boys, not to girls. While Jake told me that he didn't like gay people, he quickly added, "Lesbians, okay, that's good!" Now lesbians are not "good" because of some enlightened approach to sexuality, but because, as Ray, said, "To see two hot chicks banging bodies in a bed, that's like every guy's fantasy right there. It's the truth. I've heard it so many times." So their support of lesbians is more about heterosexual fantasy than about a progressive attitude (Jenefsky and Miller 1998).

Furthermore, several boys argued that fag, queer and gay had little to do with actual sexual practices or desires. Darnell told me "It doesn't have anything to do with being gay." Adding to this sentiment, J. L. said, "Fag, seriously, it has nothing to do with sexual preference at all. You could just be calling somebody an idiot, you know?" As David

explained, "Being gay is just a lifestyle. It's someone you choose to sleep with. You can still throw a football around and be gay." David's final statement clarifies the distinction between popular understandings of these insults and teens' actual use of them. That is, that they have to do with men's same sex eroticism, but at their core discipline gendered practices and identities (such as the ability, or lack thereof, to throw a football). In asserting the primacy of gender to the definition of these seemingly homophobic insults boys reflect what Riki Wilchins (2003) calls the Eminem Exception, in which Eminem explains that he doesn't call people "faggot" because of their sexual orientation, but because they are weak and unmanly. While it is not necessarily acceptable to be gay, if a man were gay *and* masculine, as in David's portrait of the football throwing gay man, he does not deserve the insult.

What renders a boy vulnerable to homophobic epithets often depends on local definitions of masculinity. Boys frequently cited exhibiting stupidity, femininity, incompetence, emotionality or same sex physicality as notoriously non-masculine practices. Chad, for instance, said that boys might be called a fag if they seemed "too happy or something" while another boy expounded on the dangers of being "too smiley." Ironically, these insults are pitched at boys who engage in seemingly heterosexual activities. Kevin, when describing his ideal girlfriend said, "I have to imagine myself singing, like serenading her. Okay, say we got in a fight and we broke up. I have to imagine myself as a make-up gift to her singing to her out of her window." Kevin laughed as he said that when he shares this scenario with his friends "the guys are like, 'dude you're gay!'"

Because so many activities could render a boy vulnerable to these insults perhaps it is little surprise that Ben asserted that one could be labeled for "anything, literally anything. Like you were trying to turn a wrench the wrong way, 'dude you're a fag.' Even if a piece of meat drops out of your sandwich, 'you fag!'" While my research shows that there are a particular set of behaviors that could get a boy called the slur, it is no wonder that Ben felt a boy could be called it for "anything." In that statement he reveals the intensity and extent of the policing boys must do of their behaviors in order to avoid the epithet.

The sort of homophobic harassment detailed above has as much to do [with] definitions of masculinity as it does with actual fear of other gay men (Corbett 2001, Kimmel 2001). Being subject to homophobic harassment has as much to do with failing at masculine tasks of competence, heterosexual prowess or in any way revealing weakness as it does with a sexual identity. Homophobic epithets such as fag have gendered meanings *and* sexual meanings. The insult is levied against boys who are not masculine, even momentarily, and boys who identify (or are identified by others) as gay. This sets up a very complicated daily ordeal in which boys continually strive to avoid being subject to the epithet, but are simultaneously constantly vulnerable to it.

This sort of homophobia appears frequently in boys' joking relationships. Sociologists have pointed out that joking is central to men's relationships in general (Kehily and Nayak 1997, Lyman 1998). Through aggressive joking boys cement friendship bonds with one another. Boys often draw laughs though imitating effeminate men or men's same sex desire. Emir frequently imitated effeminate men who presumably sexually desired other men to draw laughs from students in his introductory drama class. One day his teacher, disturbed by noise outside the classroom, turned to close the door saying, "We'll shut this unless anyone really wants to watch sweaty boys playing basketball." Emir lisped, "I wanna watch the boys play!" The rest of the class cracked up at his imitation. No one [in] the class actually though[t] Emir was gay, as he purposefully mocked both same sex sexual desire and an effeminate gender identity. This sort of ritual reminded other youth that masculine men did not desire other men, nor did they lisp or behave in other feminine manners. It also reminded them that men who behaved in these ways were worthy of laughter and derision.

These everyday joking interchanges, however, were more than "just jokes." For some boys, such as Lawrence King, the intolerance for gender differences espoused by these joking rituals have serious, if not deadly, consequences. Ray and Peter underscore this in their conversation. Ray asserted "I can't stand fags. Like I've met a couple. I don't know. The way they rub you. Gay people I don't care. They do their thing in their bedroom and that's fine. Feminine guys bother me." Peter, his friend, continued "If they try to get up on you. I'll kill you." Ray and Peter illuminated the teenage boys' different responses to gay and unmasculine men as Ray espouses tolerance for the presumably gender normative former and Peter threatens violence against [the] latter. In this sense the discourse runs a continuum from joking to quite violent harassment. While boys said that the "fag" insult was more about failing at masculinity than about actually being gay, it seemed that a gay and unmasculine boy suffered the most under this "gender regime" (Connell 1987).

As a talented dancer who frequently sported multicolored hair extensions, mascara and wore baggy pants, fitted tanktops and sometimes a skirt, Ricky violated these norms of gender *and* sexuality. He told me that harassment started early, in elementary school. "I'm talking like sixth grade, I started being called a fag. Fifth grade I was called a fag. Third grade I was called a fag." Though he moved schools every two years or so, this sort of harassment continued and intensified as he moved into high school. At his school's homecoming game (for which Ricky had choreographed the half time show) he was harassed until he left after hearing things like "there's that fucking fag" and "What the fuck is that fag doing here? That fag has no right to be here." When watching him dance with the school's all female dance team other boys reacted in revulsion. Nils said, "it's like a car wreck, you just can't look away." J. R., the captain of the football team, shook his head and muttered under his breath, "That guy dancing, it's just disgusting, Disgusting!" shaking his head and stomping off. Even though dancing is the most important thing in his life, Ricky did not attend school dances because he didn't like to "watch my back" the whole time. He had good reason for this fear. Brad said of

[the] prom, "I heard Ricky is going in a skirt, it's a hella short one." Sean responded with "I wouldn't even go if he's there." Topping Sean's response Brad claimed, "I'd probably beat him up outside."

The harassment suffered by Ricky featured none of the joking or laughter exhibited in other interchanges. Very real threats of violence under-girded boys' comments about him. Ricky told me that he walked with his eyes downcast, in order to avoid boys' eye contact fearing that they would see such eye contact as a challenge. Similarly he varied his route home from school each day and carried a rock in his hand to protect himself. For many boys, in order to maintain a sense of themselves as masculine, they felt they had to directly attack Ricky, a symbol of what they feared most.

Compulsive Heterosexuality

If daily life for many boys entails running a gauntlet of homophobic insults, how do they avoid being permanently labeled as Ricky was? Boys defend against homophobic teasing and harassment by assuring others of their heterosexuality. In the same way that boys' homophobia is not specifically about a sexual identity, compulsive heterosexuality[1] is not only about expressing love, desire and intimacy, but about showing a sexualized dominance over girls' bodies. The sort of gendered teasing in which boys engage in takes a toll on girls as well as other boys. In my research I found three components of compulsive heterosexuality: rituals of getting girls, rituals of touch, and sex talk.

Perhaps the most obvious example of "getting girls" is having a girlfriend. Having a girlfriend seems a normal teen behavior. For boys who are identified as feminine and teased for unmasculine practices, having a girlfriend functions as some sort of protection against homophobic harassment. Justin told me that some boys have girlfriends "so they look like they're not losers or they're not gay." David told me that a lot of the kids at his high school think that he is gay because of his preppy clothing choices and his lisp such that for him "it's better to have a girlfriend . . . because people think I'm gay. I get that all the time." In order to defend against

teasing and harassment boys like David need to establish a short of baseline heterosexuality by proving they can "get a girl." Because of the difficulty in avoiding all of the behaviors that might render one vulnerable to teasing, having a girlfriend helps to inure one to accusations of the "fag discourse."

Similarly, cross gender touching rituals establish a given boy's heterosexuality. These physical interchanges may first appear as harmless flirtation, but upon closer inspection actually reinforce boys' dominance over girls['] bodies. The use of touch maintains a social hierarchy (Henley 1977). Superiors touch subordinates, invade their space and interrupt them in a way [that] subordinates [do] not to do [to] superiors and these superior inferior relationships are often gendered ones. Boys and girls often touch each other as part of daily interaction, communication and flirtation. In many instances cross-sex touching was lightly flirtations and reciprocal. But these touching rituals ranged from playfully flirtations to assault-like interactions. Boys might physically constrain girls under the guise of flirtation. One time in a school hallway a boy wrapped his arms around a girl and started to "freak" her, or grind his pelvis into hers as she struggled to get away. This sort of behavior happened more often in primarily male spaces. One day for instance, in a school weight room, Monte wrapped his arms around a girl's neck as if to put her in a headlock and held her there while Reggie punched her in the stomach, albeit lightly and she squealed. A more dramatic example of this was during a passing period in which Keith rhythmically jabbed a girl in the crotch with his drumstick, while he yelled "Get raped! Get raped!" These examples show how the constraint and touch of female bodies gets translated as masculinity, embedding sexualized meanings in which heterosexual flirting is coded as female helplessness and male bodily dominance.

While people jokingly refer to boys' sex talk as "boys will be boys" or "locker room" talk, this sex talk plays a serious role in defending against acquiring an identity like Ricky's. Boys enact and naturalize their heterosexuality by asserting "guys are horndogs" or by claiming that it is "kind of impossible for a guy" to not "think of sex every two minutes" as Chad does. Thinking about boys' sexual performance in terms of compulsive heterosexuality shows that asserting that one is a horndog and cannot help but think about sex is actually a gendered performance. Boys' sex talk often takes the form of "mythic story telling" in which they tell larger than life tales about their sexual adventures, their bodies and girls' bodies that do not reflect love, desire or sensuality, but rather dominance over girls' bodies. Pedro, for instance, laughed and acted out having sex with his girlfriend by leaning back up against the wall, legs and arms spread and head turning back and forth as he continued to say proudly "I did her so hard when I was done she was bleeding. I tore her walls!" The boys surrounding him cheered and oohed and aahhed in amazement. Violence frequently frames these stories. Much like the touching rituals in which boys establish dominance over girls' bodies these stories show what boys can make girls' bodies do. Rich, after finishing lifting weights in his school's weight room, sat on [a] weight bench and five boys gathered around him as he told a story, after much urging, about sex with his now ex-girlfriend. He explained that they were having sex and "she said it started to hurt. I said we can stop and she said no. Then she said it again and she started crying. I told her to get off! Told her to get off! Finally I took her off," making a motion like he was lifting her off of him. He continued, there was "blood all over me! Blood all over her! Popped her wall! She had to have stitches." The boys started cracking up and moaning. Not to be outdone, the other boys in the circle began to chime in about their sexual exploits. Even those who didn't have stories about themselves, asserted their knowledge of sex through vicarious experiences. Troy joined the discussion with a story about his brother, a professional basketball player for a nearby city. He "brought home a 24 year old drunk chick! She *farted* the whole time they were doing it in the other room! It was *hella* gross!" All the boys cracked up again. Adam, not to be outdone, claimed "my friend had sex with a drunk chick.

He did her in the butt! She s*** all over the place!" The boys all cracked up again and yelled out things like "hella gross!" or "that's disgusting!" These graphic, quite violent stories detail what boys can make girls' bodies do—rip, bleed, fart and poop.

To understand the role of sexuality in maintaining gender inequality, it is important to look at sexuality and specifically heterosexuality, not as a set of desires, identities or dispositions, but as an institution. Adrienne Rich (1986) does this when she argues that heterosexuality is an institution that systematically disempowers women. Similarly compulsive heterosexuality is a set of practices through which boys reinforce linkages between sexuality, dominance, and violence. This heterosexuality is a defensive heterosexuality, not necessarily a reflection of an internal set of emotions.

Conclusion

Many boys' school based lives involve running a daily gauntlet of sexualized insults, as they simultaneously try to lob homophobic epithets at others and defend themselves from the said epithets. In this sense masculinity becomes the daily interactional work of repudiating the labels of fag, queer or gay. Unpacking the definition of what appears to be homophobia clarifies the gender policing at the heart of boys' harassment of one another and of girls. Homophobic epithets may or may not have explicitly sexual meanings, but they always have gendered meanings. Many boys are terrified of being permanently labeled as gay, fag or queer since to them, such a label effectively negates their humanness. As a part of boys' defensive strategies, girls' bodies become masculinity resources deployed in order to stave off these labels.

The practices of compulsive heterosexuality indicate that control over girls' bodies and their sexuality is central to definitions of adolescent masculinity. If masculinity is, as boys told me, about competence, heterosexuality, being unemotional, and dominance, then girls' bodies provide boys the opportunity to ward off the fag discourse by demonstrating mastery and control over them. Engaging in compulsive heterosexuality also allows boys to display a lack of emotions by refusing to engage the empathy that might mitigate against such a use of girls and their bodies. It is important to note that many of these boys are not unrepentant sexists or homophobes. In private and in one on one conversations many spoke of sexual equality and of tender feelings for girls. For the most part these were social behaviors that boys engaged in when around other boys, precisely because they are less reflections of internal homophobic and sexist dispositions and more about constituting a masculine identity, something that is accomplished interactionally.

This gendered homophobia as well as sexualized and gendered defenses against it comprise contemporary adolescent masculinity. Fear of any sort of same sex intimacy (platonic or not) polices boys' friendships with one another. The need to repudiate that which is not considered masculine leads to a very public renunciation of same sex desire. Heterosexual flirtation becomes intertwined with gendered dominance. What this means is that the public face of adolescent sexuality is rife with reproduction of gender inequality, through processes of the fag discourse and compulsive heterosexuality.

Note

1 This concept draws upon Adrienne Rich's (1986) influential concept of "compulsory heterosexuality" as well as Michael Kimmel's (1987) notion of "compulsive masculinity."

References

A.A.U.W. 2001. *Hostile Hallways*. Washington, D.C.: American Association of University Women.

Connell, R. W. 1987. *Gender and Power*. Stanford: Stanford University Press.

Corbett, Ken. 2001. "Faggot = Loser." *Studies in Gender and Sexuality* 2(1):3–28.

Henley, Nancy. 1977. *Body Politics: Power, Sex, and Nonverbal Communication*. Englewood Cliffs, N.J.: Prentice-Hall.

Jenefsky, Cindy and Diane H. Miller. 1998. "Phallic Intrusion: Girl–Girl Sex in Penthouse." *Women's Studies International Forum* 21(4):375–385.

Kehily, Mary J. and Anoop Nayak. 1997. "'Lads and Laughter': Humour and the Production of Heterosexual Masculinities." *Gender and Education* 9(1):69–87.

Kimmel, Michael. 1987. "The Cult of Masculinity: American Social Character and the Legacy of the Cowboy." pp. 235–249 in *Beyond Patriarchy: Essays by Men on Pleasure, Power and Change*, edited by M. Kaufman. New York: Oxford University Press.

——. 2001. "Masculinity as Homophobia: Fear, Shame, and Silence in the Construction of Gender Identity." pp. 266–287 in *The Masculinities Reader*, edited by S. Whitehead and F. Barrett. Cambridge: Polity.

Kimmel, Michael S. 2003. "Adolescent Masculinity, Homophobia, and Violence: Random School Shootings, 1982–2001." *American Behavioral Scientist* 46(10):1439–1458.

Lyman, Peter. 1998. "The Fraternal Bond as a Joking Relationship: A Case Study of the Role of Sexist Jokes in Male Group Bonding." pp. 171–193 in *Men's Lives*, 4th ed., edited by M. Kimmel and M. Messner. Boston: Allyn and Bacon.

National Mental Health Association. 2002. *What Does Gay Mean? Teen Survey Executive Summary*.

Newman, Katherine, Cybelle Fox, David J. L. Harding, Jal Mehta and Wendy Roth. 2004. *Rampage: The Social Roots of School Shootings*. New York: Basic Books.

Rich, Adrienne. 1986. "Compulsory Heterosexuality and Lesbian Existence." pp. 23–74 in *Blood, Bread and Poetry*. New York: W.W. Norton & Company.

Wilchins, Riki. 2003. "Do You Believe in Fairies?" *The Advocate*, February 4, pp. 72.

Youth Risk Behavior Survey—Washington. 1995.

Men and Work

In what ways is work tied to male identity? Do men gain a sense of fulfillment from their work, or do they view it as necessary drudgery? How might the organization of workplaces play on, reinforce, or sometimes threaten the types of masculinity that males have already learned as youngsters? How does the experience of work (or of not having work) differ for men of different social classes, ethnicities, and sexual preference groups? And how do recent structural changes in society affect the masculinity–work relationship? The articles in this part address these issues and more.

The rise of urban industrial capitalism saw the creation of separate "public" and "domestic" spheres of social life. As women were increasingly relegated to working in the home, men were increasingly absent from the home, and the male "breadwinner role" was born. The sexual division of labor, this gendered split between home and workplace, has led to a variety of problems and conflicts for women and for men. Women's continued movement into the paid labor force, higher levels of unemployment, and the rise of a more service-oriented economy have led to dramatic shifts in the quality and the quantity of men's experiences in their work.

In her article, Marianne Cooper examines the consequences of gender stereotypes on men who work in Silicon Valley as they struggle to balance work and family. Kristen Barber looks at the ways that gendered spaces of consumption work to "masculinize" men—and simultaneously "feminize" women.

Sociologists have long noted that when men work in female-dominated occupations, they often receive unearned privileges, like the "glass escalator effect" for male elementary teachers noted by sociologist Christine Williams. However, as the article by Adia Harvey Wingfield illustrates, men's gender privilege in workplaces largely evaporates when race is taken into account: there is no glass escalator for black males. Deploying yet another angle on intersectional studies of men in workplaces, Kristen Schilt shows how the experience of transgendered (female to male) people illuminates the informal workings of men's continued privilege in workplaces.

PART III DISCUSSION QUESTIONS

1. How do gender-neutral workplace policies end up producing unequal outcomes for differently raced and gendered workers? Is a gender-neutral workplace possible?
2. Marianne Cooper's article showed how "superdads" take on a second shift in much the same way that mothers in the paid economy have. What is the likelihood that these experiences for men will foster solidarity with women? What might this look like?
3. What advantages and disadvantages do men in general experience in the workplace? How do these change when intersectionality is considered?
4. What does Kristen Schilt's article tell us about the role of bodies in gender privilege and performance?
5. Considering the hair salons in Kristen Barber's article, is there an equivalent space for women where men shore up the heterosexuality of women clients? Why or why not?

Being the "Go-To Guy"

Fatherhood, Masculinity, and the Organization of Work in Silicon Valley

MARIANNE COOPER

Introduction

Driving down a busy freeway into the heart of Silicon Valley, one sees billboards everywhere heralding the arrival of the new economy. Ads for e-tailing, high-speed Internet connections, and dot. com job openings permeate the skyline. Even a sign for *Forbes* magazine announces "high octane capitalism ahead." While it is undeniable that the new economy is here, it is also undeniable that this is largely a male endeavor. A recent report by the American Association of University Women (2000) found that women make up only about 20% of information technology professionals and that they receive less than 28% of the computer science bachelor's degrees. . . .

It is within this male-dominated, turbo-capitalism environment that the fathers I interviewed negotiate their work and family lives. The intent of my study was to explore the mostly ignored experiences of working fathers. What I discovered through my examination of these men's work and family lives was the emergence of a newly constituted masculinity that coincides with the new way work is organized in the new economy. Two questions addressing both sides of the work–family equation flowed from this discovery: How does this new masculinity articulate with processes of labor control? And, how does it articulate with processes of family life, particularly fathering?

Thus, my findings are twofold. First, they show that as a gendered construct, this new masculinity functions as a key mechanism of control in high-tech workplaces that rely on identity-based forms of control. Second, they show that the successful enactment of this new masculinity shapes how these fathers both think about and manage their work and family lives.

Methods

. . . I sent out an e-mail message requesting one-hour interviews with fathers working in high-tech companies to discuss how they balance work and family life. . . . I received over thirty e-mail responses. I ruled out those who were self-employed, since I wanted to get information about workplace culture, interactions with co-workers, etc. . . .

The interviewees work in all different types and sizes of high-tech companies. While some work for large companies that make millions of dollars a year, others work for small start-ups. Thirteen interviewees are software engineers, one is a service engineer, one an engineering project manager, three are in sales/business development/management, and two are computer researchers.

My informants ranged in age from thirty to forty-four; the average age was thirty-seven. Though incomes ranged from $60,000 to $200,000, most were concentrated in the $80,000 to $150,000

Marianne Cooper, "Being the 'Go-To Guy': Fatherhood, Masculinity, and the Organization of Work in Silicon Valley," from *Qualitative Sociology,* 23(4): 379–405. Copyright 2000 by Springer Nature, reprinted by permission of the publisher.

range. Except for one informant who was Mexican-American and did not have a bachelor's degree, the rest were white and held college degrees. Three participants had Ph.D.s, two had MBAs, three had master's degrees in computer science, and one had a master's degree in math. All fathers are currently married. Seven of their spouses work full-time, four work part-time, three are students, and six are stay-at-home mothers.

A New Masculinity for the New Economy

In recent years, there has been a growing interest in the definition and practice of masculinity reflected by the emergence of the "New Men's Studies" (Carrigan et al. 1985; Brod and Kaufman 1994; Connell 1995; Mac An Ghaill 1996). Much of this scholarship draws upon R. W. Connell's theory of hegemonic masculinity. For Connell (1995), hegemonic masculinity "is the configuration of gender practices which embodies the currently accepted answer to the problem of legitimacy of patriarchy, which guarantees (or is taken to guarantee) the dominant position of men and the subordination of women" (p. 77). While there is a hegemonic form of masculinity, which in the U.S. could be seen as a rich, good-looking, popular, athletic, white, heterosexual man, masculinity is not unitary or homogeneous. Rather, there are "multiple masculinities," some subordinate and some dominant, which are created by differences in ethnicity, race, class, sexual orientation, age, and occupation (Connell 1987).[1]...

Given that the form and content of hegemonic masculinity is dependent upon the social and historical context in which it operates, it follows that the Silicon Valley context should shape the particular type of masculinity found in the high-tech world of the new economy. Indeed, scholars have already established that technical knowledge and expertise are socially defined as masculine (Cockburn 1988; Turkle 1984, 1988; Hacker 1990) and that within these male domains computing cultures possess a specific masculinity (Wright 1996; Kendall 1999, 2000). For example, ... Kendall (2000) found that the masculinity enacted by young male participants

in an on-line interactive text-based forum was constructed around a "nerd" identity. . . .

This nerd masculinity, common in the high-tech world, is glorified in depictions of Silicon Valley life. Even the success story of the founders of Silicon Valley is a phenomenon often referred to as "The Revenge of the Nerds." Men who in their youth were marginalized for being geeks and nerds came back as adults to get the last laugh. Using their intellect, they launched a technological revolution and in the process of changing the world became very rich and very powerful.

. . . In the Valley, competition isn't waged on the basketball court or by getting girls. Here men compete in cubicles to see who can work more hours, who can cut the best code, and who can be most creative and innovative. As one interviewee put it:

> Guys constantly try to out-macho each other, but in engineering it's really perverted because out-machoing someone means being more of a nerd than the other person. It's really geeky. It's really sad. It's not like being a brave firefighter and going up one more flight than your friend. There's a lot of see how many hours I can work whether or not you have a kid. That's part of the thing, how many hours you work. He's a real man, he works ninety-hour weeks; he's a slacker, he works fifty hours a week. (Scott Webster)

Moreover, high-tech companies are organized in ways that deviate from traditional masculinity. . . . Alvesson (1998) makes this point, noting that in knowledge intensive jobs,

> there may be limited space for employment of many of the traditionally used sources of male power and male identity associated with bureaucracy and rationality. New discourses advocated by management theorists as well as by corporate practitioners instead construct work and organizations in terms of creativity, intuition, flexibility, flattened hierarchy, social interaction, and team building, etc. (p. 2)

Thus, the Valley is based upon a masculinity that corresponds with what the technology industry needs to satiate and expand its markets.

Ideological reasons, and in some cases biographical ones as well, also underpin this new masculinity. All of the high-tech workers I spoke with profess an egalitarian gender ideology in regard to women in the work force. They feel it is important for more women to go into the high-tech industry, and many of the fathers I interviewed wished they worked with more women. In fact, in an effort to diversify their teams, several said that they go out of their way to recruit women, extending searches longer than necessary to try to find qualified women candidates.

To be sure, the majority of my sample perceive themselves to be qualitatively different from other men in terms of their more enlightened personal attitudes towards and relationships with women. This self-perception is evident through comparisons the interviewees make between themselves and men who they feel are sexist or stereotypically macho.

I don't drive a pick-up truck and wear tattoos. I'm very modern. I believe in sharing the household work and believe that my wife's career is important. (Rich Kavelin)

Communication is something that is important to us. So when something goes wrong, when we have a disagreement or a misunderstanding, my wife feels doubly hurt. Because she thinks, well we put such a value on trying to communicate and it failed. I think it makes it worse than if she were married to Joe Six-Pack. (Jay Masterson)

. . . Biography may also underpin this new masculinity. Though not a focal point of my study, my perception is that as nerds, approximately two-thirds of my sample were victims of traditional hegemonic masculinity in their earlier lives. Accordingly, they may also have personal as well as ideological reasons to oppose a traditionally macho masculinity.

Taken together, type of work, ideology, and, in some cases, biography, work against the form of masculinity that remains dominant in much of society. Nonetheless, there is still a hegemonic masculinity in the new economy, but one that takes on somewhat different characteristics. Though the essence of this masculinity is rooted in technical expertise, its other characteristics involve working a lot of hours and working with a small team of *great* people to get things done. James McNichol and Scott Webster, both software engineers, describe the team dynamic:

James: It's like a sports team. Not in the sense of locker room, but in the sense that there is just a natural order, and everybody gets their place and you work together. There are lots of models that boys grow up with for how that kind of team works and what you do and don't do. Like not questioning the coach and there's a lot of doing and thinking about it afterwards instead of considering the options beforehand. It's not an articulate culture.

Scott: The key element of this whole environment is the team mentality. It's an idea derived from male tradition probably. Even as a contractor you have to live with it too. You have to be part of the team, you can't fall out. If you get injured, you come back as fast as you can or you play with your injury whether it's emotional or physical.

The successful enactment of this masculinity involves displaying one's exhaustion, physically and verbally, in order to convey the depth of one's commitment, stamina, and virility.

Engineers have this idea that you are out there and you are building something and these small companies are going to do huge things and lots of people are going to get rich and it's gonna happen because we are great. Even under normal circumstances when there are no extraordinary demands you see people working thirty-six hours straight just because they are going to meet the deadline. They are going to get it done and everybody walks around proud of how exhausted they were last week and conspicuously putting in wild hours. It's a status thing to have pizza delivered to the office. So I don't know why it happens, but I really feel like it is kind of a machismo thing, I'm tough, I can do this thing. Yeah I'm tired but I'm on top of it, you guys don't worry about me, I can get my thing done . . . The people who conspicuously overwork are guys and I think it's usually for the benefit of other guys. (Kirk Sinclair)

Theoretically, the knowledge work these men do is gender-neutral. As opposed to manual work that requires physical strength, knowledge work requires only mental ability. Therefore, either men or women can perform knowledge work. Yet, as Leidner (1993) found and the above quotations illustrate, most jobs can be constructed as either masculine or feminine by emphasizing certain aspects of the job and de-emphasizing and reinterpreting other dimensions. The gendering of jobs that are potentially gender-neutral illustrates how gender is constructed through work, how gendered subjectivities are formed. In this case, masculinity is constructed by imbuing knowledge work with a masculine sensibility that isn't intrinsic to the work. . . .

> There's a certain glamour to heroic efforts. If you look at a well-managed company that delivers a reliable product on time with no fuss, there's no talk of it. But the release of an important product becomes lore when the engineering team worked for a week solid to get it done. Those kind of amazing efforts are talked about. (Kirk Sinclair)

Remarkably, poor planning is reinterpreted as a test of will, a test of manhood for a team of engineers (men). Sheer determination and strength of character achieve the task, releasing a product on time. Presented with an overwhelming challenge, it takes masculine capabilities to complete the mission, to overcome the odds. . . .

Gender and the Labor Process

Not surprisingly, the new masculinity and the workplace practices associated with the achievement of this gendered subjectivity benefit the technology industry. Technical brilliance, innovation, creativity, independent work ethics, long hours, and complete dedication to projects are the main requirements for companies trying to position themselves on the cutting edge. This link between gendered subjectivity and labor process conditions suggests that masculinity may then be a way to

control worker's participation in the labor process. Despite the likely link between gender and strategies of control, scholars have noted the absence of research about gender in organizations and about how gender works in the dynamic processes of consent and control (Kanter 1977; Acker 1990; Collinson 1992; Collinson and Hearn 1996b; Mac An Ghaill 1996; Pierce 1996; Alvesson and Billing 1997; Lee 1998).

. . . Lee (1998) addresses this lack of gender analysis and develops a feminist theory of production politics which takes account of the role gender plays in the development of control strategies. Lee's theory argues that "factory regimes are gendered institutions in which gender is a central and primary organizing principle of production politics" (p. 165).[2] Lee draws upon Acker's (1992) definition which states that a gendered institution is one in which "gender is present in the processes, practices, images and ideologies, and distributions of power in the various sectors of social life" (p. 567). . . .

With labor process scholars looking at how gender works on the shop floor (Collinson 1992; Lee 1998), it would make sense for scholars concerned with identity-based forms of control to also pay attention to gender, a key aspect of an individual's identity. Identity-based forms of control, or what Etzioni (1961) termed normative control, is control which works by laying claim to the worker's sense of self, engendering in them a deep personal commitment to the goals and values of the company. . . .Thus, this type of control is a self-surveilling one which monitors work behavior by eliciting thoughts, feelings, and emotions that correspond with the interests of the company. However, research on normative control has not looked through a gendered lens (Edwards 1979; O'Reilly and Chatman 1986; Kunda 1992). Instead, it has focused on mechanisms through which organizations attain identity-based consent, like strong workplace cultures, and on the characteristics of the organizational identity without discussing what the gender, racial, or class dimensions of this identity might be.

Kunda (1992) is particularly guilty of this omission in his ethnography of normative control in the engineering division of a high-tech company. Though Kunda convincingly illustrates how the company engineered its culture so as to create a member role that was internalized by employees, his analysis omits the way in which gender intersects with corporate culture, giving rise to a particular type of normative control operating in this firm. . . . His argument rests on the assumption that a workplace comprised mostly of men is actually gender-neutral.

. . . Mumbly (1998) provides this alternative reading, arguing that Kunda unwittingly offers an analysis of the social construction of white-collar masculinity. . . . Mumbly notes that the self-identity of these engineers is so embedded in their work that there is almost no distinction between their private and public selves. Indeed, he illustrates how the acceptance and enactment of organizational membership can lead to a devaluation of family life and can, in its extreme, cause burnout. The type of masculinity constructed among these engineers is rooted in technical expertise, mental ability, and mental, emotional, and physical endurance, not physical prowess. Ultimately, Mumbly illuminates what Kunda doesn't see—that masculine subjectivities are created and constructed through participation in the labor process itself, that normative control is gendered. . . .

Masculinity—the Invisible Control Strategy

High-tech companies rely on normative control to manage the white-collar, or knowledge, workers they employ for three reasons. First, with such a tight labor market, workers are not dependent on any one company for the reproduction of their labor power. Consequently, more coercive tactics, already thought to be incompatible with managing educated and highly skilled workers, are untenable because employees would just leave oppressive work environments. Second, normative control is seen to be well-suited to companies that want to encourage creativity and innovation, characteristics which aren't associated with coercive, technical, or bureaucratic styles of control (Kunda and Van

Maanen 1999). Third, at this point in the technological revolution, the member role and work behaviors that high-tech companies seek are so pervasive and diffuse throughout Silicon Valley itself that little articulation of these practices is needed in order to guide workers' thoughts and actions. Dylan Fitzgerald describes this collective consciousness:

> My sense is that being in Silicon Valley that [the culture] is already so much around that [description of it] isn't needed. I mean you almost just have to refer to it and everyone goes yeah. They know what you are talking about. And everyone here knew that. They knew they were signing up for a start-up company in Silicon Valley and that was part of the expectation. It was going to involve a commitment to a small group of people whom [sic] are all counting on each other to make the thing work and there was a potentially big financial pay-off if the whole thing worked out.

These workplace practices are so entrenched that interviewees often used the term Silicon Valley as shorthand for what is to them a clearly defined way of being and of doing. Companies can then rely on the internalization of these shared understandings to regulate workers. . . .

. . . A "masculine ethic" (Kanter 1977, p. 22), or the assumption that a worker doesn't have any outside obligations that conflict with their ability to put work first, makes ten-hour days the norm. Yet, this market logic is made palatable because it is cloaked in a youthful playfulness that pervades the Valley. . . . But behind the flex-time and casual dress is a culture in which the viewpoint of the shareholder reigns supreme. Beneath the playfulness a serious adult game is being played, a game in which large amounts of money can be won or lost. In order to win in this world, you have to be inventive and brilliant, you have to squash your competitors by cornering the market, and you have to do it all quickly. The pace is intense; if you stop to take a breath you might miss out.

The fast pace, frenzied lifestyle, and devotion to work are norms clearly internalized by my interviewees. This internalization process is evident when my interviewees report feeling pressure to work, but view the pressure as emanating from an internal rather than an external source. Accordingly, the interviewees more often attribute intense work ethics to individual personality traits than to management and co-worker expectations.

For example, Dylan Fitzgerald's daughter had health problems when she was born. As a principal founder of the start-up in which he currently works, he feels he was given a lot of flexibility to take care of family matters. He said that he took five months off for paternity leave and felt no pressure from his co-workers to return. Yet, as we continued the interview it became clear that he in fact had worked during this time and that he was under pressure, but in his view it was his own.

> [After my daughter was born] I didn't come back to work at all for about two months and was part-time for about six months and I was just extremely fortunate to have the flexibility. I'm sure my co-workers would rather have had me back but I didn't get any pressure.

> I tried to keep up with e-mail. I tried to keep up with what was going on. I probably came in once or twice a week for particular meetings. But it wasn't that people were pressuring me but my own sense of things that needed to happen, that I knew people were counting on getting done. So there was kind of a self-generating pressure.

> I think what really happened was that I worked a couple hours a day, maybe even half-time towards the end. But because I was not actually meeting any of the deadlines that I had planned for myself, I kept feeling like I wasn't doing what I was supposed to be doing.

In reality, Dylan did not take time off from work. Instead, he worked less than the amount he expected of himself as a member of a start-up. This pattern of actually working when an interviewee stated that he had taken time off for paternity leave occurred several times.

> When I was on paternity leave with my first child, I actually did a fair amount of work. At the time

I was writing programs that really ran on a standard PC, so while Brad was sleeping I wrote. Basically I built an entire product so I had no compunction about work because I was actually working. (Alan Payne)

The desire to work all the time is seen by James McNichol as arising out of an addiction to work as well as workplace expectations:

> So I think there are a couple things going on. First, if you are talking about software guys, most of these guys are just addicts. It's one of the most addictive professions that I know. And it attracts addicts so they are just strung out. They just can't withdraw from working. They can't withdraw from programming especially. Second, the level of management in high-tech companies is just for shit. I mean you've got these nerd addict engineers managing other nerd addict engineers. The managers are giving the engineers the message all the time that you've got to work and most of them don't know how to delegate, it's just pitiful, it's just awful. My god, I mean talk about sweatshops, I mean they are oblivious. The managers have no idea what an altered state they are in all the time while they are managing these guys. So I think engineers are getting constant messages that if they are not working all the time then they will be replaced. I mean their entire self-esteem is based on the code they are cutting, it's really sad. But give an addict any free time at all and they will work.

Interestingly, though James thinks that managers pressure people to work, he believes that he works so much because of his own individual desire to work, his own addiction.

> I work way more than anyone gives me the message to work. I give myself the message that I have to work all the time. I struggle with that all the time. I'm just as much an addict as the rest of these guys, but it's just intrinsic to personality types . . . I'm getting better though. It used to be just because I was an addict. I was just anxious as hell unless I was working. This sense of mastery that you have over this piece of computer software is just astounding, it's just unrivalable in the real world.

The real world looks like a series of terrible mishaps that you have very little control over. So you know, the lure of spending your time in front of a machine where you just have complete control over is pretty extraordinary.

I think lately I've gotten much better. I'm working a lot right now because we are very close to bringing out a new product, but I've gotten much better. Hey, when you got here I was fixing my bike, I mean I'm not working right now. It took me a long time to realize that just because I wasn't working 9 to 5 doesn't mean I have to work all the time. I just learned that I had to take time for myself, take time away from work when things weren't busy. And I think that's taken just years and twelve-step programs literally just to learn not to fall into those traps.

Despite James' belief that he works a lot because of his own individual desire to work, it is clear that internal and external pressures go hand in hand. . . . It seems that the interviewees compare themselves to some real or mythic person (male) who works when they are asleep, who cuts code that doesn't have bugs, who scores the deal that they just lost, who takes his company public while they struggle to get theirs off the ground. . . . Thus, the force causing them to work both surrounds them and is internalized by them, creating normative patterns, understandings, and definitions about work. These normative beliefs are so shared and internalized that the control strategy has no obvious or definite point of origin. . . . This is precisely the self-enforcing type of discipline characteristic of normative control. As Kunda points out, under normative control "discipline is not based on explicit supervision and reward, but rather on peer pressure and more crucially, internalized standards of performance" (p. 90).

High-tech companies rely on normative control, control that depends on the knowledge worker's identity. However, these identities, . . . are not gender-neutral. . . . The masculinity created and constructed by the labor process borrows from, but is not identical to, traditional masculinity. It does not emphasize physical strength, but mental toughness. It does not require hazing women but does require a willingness to be absorbed in one's work that, by effect if not design, excludes both women and family responsibilities. . . .

So where do these identifications with work come from? How are they created? Do organizations produce them and/or are there wider structural causes? Though my data cannot offer definitive answers since I did not study any one organization in depth, I can posit some preliminary explanations that future research should more thoroughly examine. As discussed earlier, the culture of Silicon Valley is diffuse, not organizationally bound. Consequently, organizations may not have to actively or consciously engender identities in employees by manufacturing their culture. . . . In addition, the focus on casual and flexible workplaces eliminates bureaucratic elements. Although this can't, on its own, produce identifications with work, it does get rid of the formal apparatuses, which could otherwise cause the organizational identity to appear external and therefore distinct from one's own identity. Finally, in the new economy, lifetime, even long-term, employment is a thing of the past. For most workers, and particularly for high-tech workers, short-term employment and job-hopping among firms is common practice. In this new type of career structure, one's career is one's own possession, independent of any particular firm. Thus, concern over employability may serve as a powerful tool for creating identities rooted in work.

Fatherhood in the New Economy

This new masculinity is primarily constructed in the public sphere, for it is only by living up to expectations at work that these men can become *genius warriors, tough guys* who get the job done no matter what. It is only in the public arena that they become *heroes* and *go-to guys* by delivering on the projects they *sign up for*. However, as fathers, these men have private lives and personal responsibilities which conflict with these public requirements. . . . Though most of my interviewees did less around the house and less with their children than did their wives, the majority of them expressed a sincere interest in being active fathers. . . . Thus, the new masculinity contains an internal contradiction: How can anyone simultaneously be the go-to guy at work and at home?

Superdads

Three ways of resolving this contradiction emerged among my interviewees. Seven of them attempt to meet all work and family obligations without sacrificing anything in either sphere. The result is that these Superdads sacrifice themselves. . . . These fathers tend to have a more egalitarian gender ideology . . . [and] a care orientation which engenders a strong emotional connection between them and their families.

This care orientation has two components. First, these fathers talk about being attentive to the emotional, physical, and spiritual needs of those around them. Second, this attentiveness coincides with a broader definition of care which includes emotion work and care work, as well as paid work. Superdads seem to notice when caring work like laundry or shopping needs to be done and don't appear to resent doing it. This attentiveness and broader definition of care enables them to anticipate the needs of their family and, most importantly, it enables them to empathize with their wives. Rich Kavelin, a Superdad who works in business development, illustrates this caring orientation when he describes a typical evening at home with his three-month-old son and his wife Joan, a social worker on an eight-month maternity leave:

> When I get home at 6:30 p.m. the baby is essentially my child for the rest of the evening. My wife very often goes out and just hands me the baby and says here is he, he loves you, here's your daddy. She grabs the car keys and splits because she's with the child non-stop for 10 to 12 hours during the day and she needs a little personal time. So she will go out and generally she's out for about an hour or so and I'll hang out with the baby. I'll feed him, play with him, talk to him. When she gets home, it alternates. About half the time I'll make dinner, and half the time she makes dinner. If there are

chores to be done like dishes or laundry, I'll pitch in and help with that. So I don't expect her to do everything.

Rich's acknowledgement that his wife both needs and is entitled to "personal time" reflects his ability to empathize with her and to recognize the actual work involved in taking care of a child. . . . The possession of such a care orientation is stressful and overwhelming for Superdads because, in addition to demands at work, these fathers feel responsible for demands at home as well.

Traditionals

Three[3] participants resolved the new masculinity contradiction by approaching work and family through a traditional male model. Despite these interviewees' ideological belief in egalitarianism, especially in the workplace, they didn't seem to practice what they preached at home. . . . They speak about their families in emotionally disconnected ways and talk about caring for their family in a limited fashion, placing more emphasis on work and the income it provides. . . . They either don't notice or overlook the work required for family life, leaving it instead for their wives. . . . They also appear to be less stressed than Superdads because their energy and emotions are less divided between work and home. Interestingly, Traditionals took the least amount of time off for paternity leave.

. . . Edward, an engineering project manager, is married to Jessica, a full-time homemaker who cares for their two young sons. Edward describes their domestic division of labor:

> My wife does most of the home care. Occasionally I'll do some vacuuming and I gotta make sure I pick up my own clothes and keep the closet clean or else she gets on me about that a little bit. She does the general cleaning and I do all the outside stuff, cutting the lawn, and maintenance or repairs. I do usually end up loading the dishwasher after dinner cause I normally get done first. See, my wife has it timed perfectly. I go over and I load my dishes in the dishwasher. And by that time the kids are starting to finish a little bit so she starts handing

stuff over to the counter to me. So by the time I get out of there, everybody is done and I've got all the dishes to do so that's really the only inside task that I do on a regular basis.

In contrast to Rich, who doesn't expect his wife to do everything around the house and wants to do his part, Edward not only expects his wife to do everything but feels manipulated by her when he does a single domestic task.

Fathers who relinquish their part of the caring work and expect their wives to be responsible for all domestic chores sometimes encounter resistance. In Edward's case, he and his wife have fights about who does more work for the family.

> We fight occasionally. She feels like she's doing more and I feel like I'm doing more. Like in the fall when football season starts, I'll sit down and watch two football games in a row, six hours worth. She isn't very happy about that. She's running around chasing the kids all day and feeding them and then she's like "You don't do anything around here." And I'll say, "I go to work for forty, fifty hours a week." And then she's like "Don't you think I'm working around here?" So it goes back and forth like that.

Ironically, Edward recognizes the work his wife does while he is relaxing on the couch. Yet he detaches himself from any obligation to share in this type of family work because he feels he has already done his part by working at the office.

Transitionals

Between the Superdads and the Traditionals sits the largest group, the Transitionals. Similar to the Traditionals, the Transitionals partially resolve the new masculinity contradiction by reneging on their egalitarian ideology somewhat and instead leaving a lot of the family work to their wives. Yet, like Superdads, the Transitionals want to be involved fathers and are responsible for at least some of the family work. Consequently, Transitionals have a harder time balancing work and family than the Traditionals. However, they are not as conflicted as the Superdads because they hold onto the care orientation more loosely, frequently

handing off duties, obligations, and emotion work to their wives. While some Transitionals lean towards being a Superdad, others lean towards being a Traditional.

Like Edward Vicker, Chris Baxter, a Transitional father in business development, also has clashes with his wife when he "backslides into assuming that because she's home full-time she has all this extra time to clean the bathrooms and cook dinner." Chris and his wife Emma have two children, a girl who is seven and a boy who is four. It seems that ideally Chris would like Emma to be a traditional stay-at-home mom. Yet Emma sees motherhood in more professional terms. She is at home to raise the children, not to be a homemaker or a maid. A recent clash over decorating illustrates this tension:

> I think in terms of motherhood, one of the things that I see her having a greater responsibility for than I is home decorating, and sometimes she accepts it and other times she really pushes back. A part of it is that we are both terrible at it. But I think she's better than I am so I kind of push that on her. So I'll say, "You're staying here at home and part of staying at home is making it a wonderful home, right?" And she's like, "I'll sign up for leading the brainstorming on that but I'm not signing up for doing that as well as deciding what to put here and there and finding the contractor, while you just sign up for writing the check because you are the one working." So although at times it would be nice if she did that, in the end I think it's better if we do it together because then we are both doing it.

Chris is caught between his wish for his wife to be traditional and his knowledge that a more egalitarian partnership is fairer and more rewarding in the long run. . . .

Being the Go-To Guy

Scholars have found that a father's masculinity is called into question when his family obligations encroach upon his work obligations (Pleck 1993; Hochschild 1997; Levine and Pittinsky 1997). These findings suggest that ideas, norms, and expectations about what is and is not masculine have a regulating effect on the thoughts, choices, and actions of fathers. Indeed, an examination of the work–family practices my interviewees engage in shows that the strategies they employ to manage their work and family lives reflect a desire to personify and embody the public aspects of the new masculinity. To maintain the image and the reality that they are go-to guys, these fathers rely on a combination of the following practices: self-sacrifice, silencing work–family conflict, disguising the care they do perform, and turning to women, both at work and at home, to help them mediate between their public and private responsibilities. Moreover, even the way these fathers think about and conceptualize care reflects a desire to make family fit within the demands of the high-tech world, to make family fit within the narrow boundaries of this gendered subjectivity. Thus, the internalization of the Silicon Valley member role not only impacts how these fathers work, but also spills over into how they think about and participate in family life.

Self-Sacrifice

To reconcile their desire to be involved in family life with their desire to be a serious player at work, Superdads, and some Transitionals, pay a tremendous personal cost. . . . Rich Kavelin articulates the stress this causes in his life:

> The most difficult thing about having a kid has been letting go of personal time. I don't mind the work, it doesn't bother me . . . But now and then I'd like to be able to go play golf with my friends. My wife still has some personal life because we make an extra effort. She goes to girls' night, to ladies' night, she has a mothers' group and support groups. It's actually more important to me that she has a social life because if you think about it I'm here all day. I have people that I interact with at work, adult conversation, and I'm using my mind. Whereas she's at home with somebody who is drooling and spitting up and going "ahhh" so her need for human contact is much higher and I'm okay with that. But every now and then I get a bit grumpy and think, "Why the hell can't I just go get a beer with Neil tonight, I miss my friend Neil."

Like Rich, Dylan Fitzgerald, also a Superdad, is overwhelmed with work and being there for his two-year-old daughter Anna. . . . This tension leaves him feeling as if he's underperforming in both realms.

> I'm continually feeling like I'm not quite doing what I want to be doing in either place and I'm doing absolutely nothing else that isn't one of those two things. I mean the concept of free time or hobbies, well it seems kind of laughable at this point.

Not only do the Superdads sacrifice personal time, they also survive on minimal amounts of sleep in order to meet conflicting obligations. Often they work during the day, come home to help with dinner and put the kids to bed, then work more after their kids and their spouses fall asleep. Alan Payne, a software engineer, conceptualizes his workday in two shifts.

> In engineering there just isn't a sharp divide between work and family. I've finally been able to turn that to my advantage but it has cost me a lot of sleep because what I do is I work two shifts. I work a shift in the day at the company starting at around 10 a.m. and ending at 6 p.m. Then I come home and spend time with my family. When the kids go to bed, I log on and work another shift from about 10 p.m. to 2 a.m.

By forfeiting sleep and personal time, Superdads constantly scramble to meet competing commitments, which leaves them feeling exhausted and overwhelmed. Rich Kavelin expresses this fatigue:

> I signed up for this life, right. . . and you pay a price if you have a high-paying job or a career that you are really fulfilled by. So my price is that I'm exhausted. I hardly get any sleep.

Superdads attribute their exhaustion to career demands. Yet, what really seems to be causing their fatigue is that they possess a caring orientation within a social world so dominated by the market that there is little space, time, or energy left for care. So within this context, their attentiveness to the emotional and care needs of their families makes their work load triple that of other fathers who aren't as attentive to the needs of those around them. The Superdads' unwillingness to cut back either at work or at home, and their willingness to live a completely insane lifestyle, signify how central both home and work are to their identities. . . .

Silencing Conflict and Care

A prerequisite to being a committed team player is a devotion to work that borders on addiction. . . . Addiction means you bring work home— you don't bring home to work. This devaluing of private needs and overvaluing of public needs is quite evident in the hesitancy many fathers feel about bringing up work–family conflicts at the workplace. Instead of openly discussing conflicts, most fathers I interviewed keep problems to themselves, thereby conveying the impression that work comes first.

Rich Kavelin managed a recent work–family conflict with silence. His boss wanted him to leave on a business trip the same day that he and his wife needed to meet with their priest to discuss their son's christening. . . . Here is Rich's description of the incident:

> So here I am talking to the VP on the phone and he's like "We need to do this now, we need to hook up with these guys from X, we need to set this up, here are my contacts, we are going on the 29th, and I looked at my calendar and literally I started to sweat. I'm going "Umm that day is difficult for me, is there any other day we can go?" and he's like "I don't think so Rich, my calendar is pretty full but check with my secretary tomorrow." So I called up the secretary the next day and I was sweating like a horse. I said, "Hey, you gotta get me out of this because my baby is getting christened and if I don't meet with the priest it's not going to happen and my family is going to kill me and my wife will divorce me and I won't have any kids, and life will be terrible." So she looked, and the only day I could replace that with was 4 weeks away so I said, "What is he doing in between?" She said, "He's going to Germany for a week, then Mexico, then to England, then to Boston, then California and then he can meet with you in New York." And the guy lives

in Pennsylvania and he has two kids and a wife, and I'm going he doesn't have two kids and a wife, he has people that live in his house, that's basically what he has.

Though Rich is willing to express that the day is difficult, he's not willing to explain the real reason he cannot leave, that he has a family conflict. He told me that he didn't want to tell his boss about the christening because right now he's the VP's "go-to guy." The VP depends on him, gives him interesting assignments, and is clearly impressed with Rich's work. Despite Rich's disdain for the way his boss puts work before family, he does not want to jeopardize his position by identifying himself as someone who prioritizes both work and family. It's as if any connection with the private sphere will be a mark against him. Thus, Rich consents to the logic of the market, to the requirements of the new masculinity. He does whatever it takes to convey that he does not have other needs, that he is autonomous and independent and always ready to go when the boss calls.

Like Rich, other fathers dealt with work–family conflict with silence.

> I can remember various times when I had to leave in the middle of the day to drop my son off at baseball practice. I might not have been real forthcoming about that because that may seem a little less important to somebody, particularly if they are not a parent. It would be a lot easier for them to understand if I said my son is at his school and the school is going to close in half an hour and I've got to pick him up before it closes. That's like an emergency. But when it sounds like something that is more optional, I might not be so quick to volunteer it. (Stan Espe)

The hesitancy and silence about work–family conflict maintains the idea that these fathers do not have any obligations outside of work. The above quotation also points out that the most legitimate way in which the family can come into the workplace is through an emergency: In emergency situations it is clear that family comes before work. But when things are functioning smoothly in normal, everyday life, family is less of a priority than work.

When personal things come up in people's lives, like losing a parent or something like that, there is absolutely no question that people would get time to go take care of that. Of course there is also the expectation that when just day-to-day stuff comes up, you will be willing to rearrange your family life to put in extra hours that week or spend a Saturday doing work so we get things done on time. So in real crisis situations there would be no question that family life would get taken care of but there might be week-to-week conflict that's just kind of unavoidable given the way the company has set its goals. (Dylan Fitzgerald)

. . . In addition to the silence surrounding work–family conflict, there is also silence about paternity leave. A curious discovery is that ten fathers in my sample were given paid time off, ranging from two to three weeks. This paid leave was not an explicit policy or benefit. Rather, these leaves were secretly arranged through managers who granted the leave but didn't inform the human resources department. The other ten took vacation time and unpaid leave. The desire by some managers to give their employees paternity leave could, if discussed openly, be mobilized to institutionalize men's parenting. Regrettably, however, this countervailing force remains shrouded and untouched, a sign of just how inhospitable the high-tech world is to matters of the heart. . . . Taken together, the silencing and disguising of care is a strategy that allows fathers to parent while preserving the idea that their parental duties do not come before their workplace obligations.

Turning to Women in Order to Care

Through Rich's incident with the VP about his son's christening, we can see the way in which women help men mediate between home and work without being detected. Rich feels comfortable telling the secretary the real reason he cannot leave on that date because he has no fear that she will think he is less committed to work or less of a player. . . . The secretary solves Rich's problem by finding an alternative date which enables him to keep his commitments to his job and to his family. . . . A common theme that emerged was that wives often set times at which their husbands had to be home. The wives enforce these times by telling their husbands the time they need to leave work in order to get home on schedule and by calling or paging to remind them. These reminders can also serve as "excuses" for fathers to go home, since it conveys to others that it is the wife, not the husband, who is responsible for the father leaving work. Thus, women become symbols, interpreters, and mediators of care in a world where "real" men are not allowed, or at least are not supposed, to care.

Market Language

The degree to which the new masculinity is internalized and embodied by my interviewees can be seen in the way some fathers draw upon market language and market concepts to make sense of their intimate relationships and personal lives. In describing his relationship with his wife, Chris Baxter said:

Our pediatrician tells us that we are supposed to go out on a date once a month but we get busy so we go out about once a quarter. We know mentally what we are supposed to do, but whether we execute on that, well it depends.

This statement "once a quarter" reveals a temporal order dominated by the fiscal year. It also reduces an intimate aspect of personal life to a task that if "executed" can be scratched off the "to do" list, analogous to something being moved from the in box to the out box. . . .

Several fathers portrayed their personal lives in contractual terms. In the same way they "sign up" for projects at work, they "signed up" for a particular family life too. Dylan Fitzgerald used this contractual talk:

I'm very conscious of the fact that if I had an extra two to three hours a day to do work I could be getting more done here, improving the company's odds of succeeding. I'm also very conscious that I'm not spending as much time around the house with my daughter as I committed to when we planned the whole thing out.

It appears that Dylan and his wife carefully planned out caring for their child, in the same way that projects are planned out at work. Like transactions in the market, the care for their child too is arranged on the basis of a contract, with each party agreeing to perform different parts. Now Dylan is caught in the "time bind" (Hochschild 1997), unable to "deliver" in the way he would like in either part of his life. . . .

The embodiment of the new masculinity can also be seen in the way some fathers shape and curtail their beliefs about care in order that family life does not interfere with the demands of the market. By reshaping and redefining care, family life is made compatible with the bottom line. Eric Salazar expressed this sentiment when he discussed his paternity leave. His supervisor gave him a paid two-week leave when his daughter was born:

> On the one hand I was very grateful that I was being paid for the leave and that I wasn't taking it out of vacation or sick time. But at the same time I honestly felt that it was something I deserved. So I was thankful, but I wasn't overwhelmed by the gift from my boss. I think that it's something that really should be the norm. It's never enough, but realistically I think two weeks would be capitalistically fair for the company to offer that.

Eric assesses the needs for his family within the constraints of capitalism. In doing so, we can see how the market creates the terms within which family policies are negotiated. Ultimately, what is fair for capitalism is by default both fair for the family and a suitable practice for a man who is both a father and a serious high-tech worker.

Chris Baxter also reveals the priority given to market needs, at the expense of familial needs, when he discussed which employees are entitled to flexibility in their job:

> As a manager I have a much easier time giving extra flexibility to folks I know will get the job done and come in on the weekend because Thursday afternoon they took off to go to their child's check-up or whatever. Somebody missing deadlines, who is always over their budget, they are not going to

get that flexibility. I hate to sound like a capitalist but at the end of the day, the company shareholders aren't holding shares so that we have flexible lives. They are holding the shares because they are expecting a return on them. So if you can generate some return and balance your life then it's great. But job one is the return.

For Chris, not only do market demands come before family concerns, but a worker must also earn the privilege to meet family demands by first meeting all market requirements. Interestingly, though he is obviously a free market supporter, Chris tries to distance himself from sounding like a capitalist. Sensing the coldness of his outlook he points to real world constraints, not his own belief system, to justify his opinion about flexibility. . . . By characterizing care needs in a way that is congruent and acceptable to capitalism, these fathers construct family life in a way that is compatible with the workplace expectations of the new masculinity. In this way, care never infringes on the market, but the market continually intrudes upon care. . . .

Resistance

The extent to which individual fathers will go to achieve and enact this gendered subjectivity varies. There do seem to be limits to how far some men will go for their job. Several fathers told cautionary tales about absentee fathers whom they refused to be like. Rich Kavelin will not be like his boss, the senior VP who travels all the time. He also will not be like his former boss at a start-up he used to work for:

> The CEO of this start-up company had three kids, 4, 7, 10, nice kids but he never ever ever sees them because he's at work seven days a week. He does triple sevens. He works from 7 in the morning until 7 in the evening 7 days a week. He thought he was a good father because once a year he'd go camping for a week with his kids or one day on a weekend he would take them out to ice cream for two hours and he'd say it's not the quantity of time it's the quality of time. And I'm just thinking, his kids aren't going to have any idea who he is, he

doesn't think these little moments matter but they do. I mean the guy was a real shit when it came to his kids, I'm sorry. He's forty and he's bound and determined that he's going to make his multimillions and he thinks he is doing the right thing for his kids, because he thinks he's doing all this for them since one day they will be rich. They will be rich with money but poor as people.

Rich recognizes that his former boss led an "emotionally downsized" life and refuses to buy into "a reduction of needs" ideology (Hochschild 1997). Yet, it remains unclear how Rich will maintain his line in the sand when he wouldn't even tell his current boss about his son's christening.

. . . Kirk Sinclair is a defector from the triple seven world. He works from home and is in charge of sales for a small software company, but formerly he worked as an engineer who wanted to be known in his field. After spending a year as a vice president of engineering in a struggling firm, working so much that he never saw his children, he decided to change his quality of life. Kirk has changed his priorities.

> I still want to be successful financially. I still want to be respected in my field. But I'm not out for fame and glory any longer. And I think I've got a much more reasonable balance of life.

An in-depth look at the process Kirk went through in order to change his life highlights the contours of the new masculinity and its relationship to work and family life. Kirk's reputation was made through his involvement in a start-up called Innovate that was very successful. At that point in his life he personified the Silicon Valley warrior:

> I worked hard at my start-up because I was Ali, that was my log-in name. I was famous at the company and I was infamous. Salespeople and marketing people would come and talk to me, they wanted me to meet with customers and really decisions didn't get made unless I got to play and I just liked it. I liked being in charge, I never had that in my life, and it was just a lot of fun. I got to make decisions that were worth huge amounts of money and I had never done that before.

When his second child Andi was born, he took only a couple of days off from work. This was and continues to be a "sore point" with his wife, who wanted him to take more time off. Kirk's quick return to work stemmed from his desire to get back to the office, not from management expectations.

> I had a very supportive management structure above me. The woman who I reported to was a strong family supporter. And it would have been absolutely okay for me not to be there, which is to say, clock out . . . So I can't say that I was under any pressure from the office. I was under a fair bit of pressure from myself. Then I was mostly doing engineering work. There's this kind of machismo culture among young male engineers that you just don't sleep. So Andi was born and I went back to the office and I didn't have a lot of people saying to me "Jesus, what are you doing here?" My boss was saying "Hey, what are you doing here?" but none of my colleagues were surprised that I was there.

. . . When his start-up went public, it was bought by a larger competitor. Unhappy with the management changes that resulted, Kirk left and went to work as the vice president of engineering at a small biotech start-up.

> . . . So the job sucked and the commute was driving me nuts. I would get up at 4 a.m. and be at the office by 6 so that I could beat the commute rush down. I didn't see the kids in the morning and then there would be a board meeting or something so I would stay until 9 or 10 at night, get in the car and drive home and I wouldn't see them when I got home. So really I went for a year seeing them almost not at all and it was a very, very tough year for my wife. I mean every time the phone rang it was me on my cell phone saying I wouldn't be home. She was supportive of me taking the job, it was clear she hated me having that job and I just was not having any fun. It took me a long time to give myself permission to quit that job, to admit that I had made a mistake. So I resigned in October of last year, nine months after I took the job, and was talked into a fairly extended transition that saw me there basically until the end of May. And at that point I was exhausted,

emotionally and intellectually, I didn't have anything left so I took all of the next summer off and we traveled a bunch and just hung out with the kids.

I started looking around for other jobs, there is a lot of hiring going on. I have a good track record and know a lot of people. So lots of other vice president jobs were available at companies that was [sic] venture-backed and you know it was a chance to get on the Innovate rocketship again and make a lot of money. But the problem is that with those jobs you need to be at the office early, they need you to stay late. They need the job to come first and I had spent a year letting a real crappy job come first. The family really suffered. The kids didn't see me. And frankly I didn't want to do that again.

The reason it was so difficult for Kirk to walk away from his job was because he had "signed up" to do the job and in doing so his name and his capabilities became responsible for making it work. Thus, he committed himself mentally and emotionally to getting the job done.

We all knew walking into it that this was something that needed to be turned around, it was broken. I don't know if it's machismo or not, I mean I was committed to make this thing work. And it was very, very hard to quit 'cause I had convinced myself that I would do that job and so I had to convince myself that it was okay to fail.

In order for Kirk to allow himself to quit, he had to renegotiate aspects of his identity. He had to come to terms with the fact that he was not the person (man) to accomplish "the task." . . . Poignantly, he derides himself for even thinking that he could rise to this insane challenge and feels that he set himself up for failure. It is interesting that Kirk's desire to quit is seen and experienced by him as acceptance of failure. In Kirk's mind, then, you either win or lose, you deliver or you don't. What has changed for him now is that his identity is no longer solely based on the paid work he performs, what his colleagues think of him, and whether or not he's the go-to guy.

Until not too long ago, a huge part of my identity was wrapped up in what I did for a living and was

I famous in my field. Did people call me to solicit my opinion on developments in the industry, and now I don't care about that so much, I don't need to see my name in print, I don't need to see my papers cited in other people's papers.

Now, his identity is built more around his family and less around his work.

With the job I have now, I'm working with people who I intellectually respect, the product is outstanding, it's very easy to sell. I'm getting to do some stuff that is professionally very important and I get to see my kids every morning and be here in the afternoon when they get home. I chose this job not because it's the one that is going to make us rich. It probably won't. On the other hand, it's a good living. I'm having a fun time and I get to be around the kids all the time.

In order for Kirk to resist the organization of work in the Valley he had to reconstruct his identity, particularly his gendered subjectivity. He had to let go of the desire to outperform others, win battles, and be the best. In essence, Kirk had to let go of the public requirements of the new masculinity in order to embrace its private dimensions. He had to let go of being the go-to guy at work in order to be the go-to guy at home. In reordering his life, he revalued care and recognized that he and his family had needs.

Conclusion

The examination of the work–family phenomenon requires a bridging and reworking of different domains of theorizing so that instead of sitting in either the public or the private, analysis can move back and forth between the public and the private, the market and the home. . . .

What I found is that fathers internalize the characteristics of the new masculinity, which shapes both how they work and how they parent. To achieve this gendered subjectivity, men must be technically brilliant and devoted to work. They must be tough guys who get the job done no matter what. Fathers so identify with these qualities that their desire to work all the time is experienced by them as emanating from their own personality traits rather than from co-worker or management expectations. Consequently, the type of control these fathers experience is an identity-based one. However, this identity is not gender-neutral. Rather, because workplace practices are suffused with masculine qualities, performance of them achieves a masculinized subjectivity. . . .

These findings have important implications for labor process and work–family scholars. For labor process scholars, my findings highlight the centrality of gender in the organization of work. Therefore, research about processes of control, particularly research on identity-based forms of control, must analyze the gendered dimensions of the phenomenon they describe in order to gain an accurate and complete understanding. For work–family scholars, my findings highlight the need to think about the ways in which gendered subjectivities explain work and family practices. For example, when taken into consideration, gendered subjectivities may account for the failure of people to make use of family-friendly policies even in ostensibly open organizations. In sum, my study illustrates the importance of studying work and family issues in a holistic manner that more accurately reflects the holistic nature of peoples' everyday lives.

Notes

1. Though some scholars take a more essentialized view of masculinity (and femininity), believing that certain practices indicate that a person is a man or woman (Collinson and Hearn 1994), I take a less embodied viewpoint. I agree with Alvesson and Billing (1997), who see masculinity and femininity as "traits or forms of subjectivities (orientations in thinking, feeling, and valuing) that are present in all persons, men as well as women" (p. 85).

2. Lee is working from Burawoy's (1985) theory of factory regimes which entails two components: the labor process, meaning the technical and social organization of production, and the production apparatuses, meaning the institutions that regulate and shape the workplace politics (p. 19).

3. I am invoking the typology Hochschild (1989) used as it conveys and describes the three distinct positions held by the interviewees. The terms Traditional and Transitional come directly from Hochschild (p. 16).

References

Acker, J. (1990). "Hierarchies, Jobs, Bodies: A Theory of Gendered Organizations." *Gender and Society* 4:2 139–158.

Acker, J. (1992). "Gendered Institutions: from Sex Roles to Gendered Institutions." *Contemporary Sociology* 21: 139–158.

Alvesson, M. and Billing, Y. D. (1997). *Understanding Gender and Organizations*. London: Sage Publications.

Alvesson, M. (1998). "Gender Relations and Identity at Work: a Case Study of Masculinities and Femininities in an Advertising Agency." *Human Relations* 51:8 969–1006.

American Association of University Women. (2000). "Tech-Savvy: Educating Girls in the New Computer Age." Washington, DC: American Association of University Women. Retrieved May 28, 2000 (http://www.aauw.org/2000/techsavvybd.html).

Brod, H. and Kaufman, M. (1994). *Theorizing Masculinities*. Thousand Oaks: Sage Publications.

Carrigan, T., Connell, R. W. and Lee, J. (1985). "Towards a New Sociology of Masculinity." *Theory and Society* 14: 551–604.

Cockburn, C. (1988). *Machinery of Dominance: Women, Men, and Technical Know-how*. Boston: Northeastern University Press.

Collinson, D. L. (1992). *Managing the Shopfloor*. New York: Walter de Gruyter.

Collinson, D. L. and Hearn, J. (1994). "Naming Men as Men: Implications for Work, Organization and Management." *Gender, Work and Organization* 1:1 2–22.

Collinson, D. L. and Hearn, J. (1996). "Breaking the Silence On men, masculinities and managements." In D. L. Collinson & J. Hearn (Eds.), *Men as managers, managers as men* (pp. 1–24). London: Sage Publications.

Connell, R. W. (1987). *Gender and Power*. Cambridge: Polity Press.

Connell, R.W. (1995). *Masculinities*. Berkeley: University of California Press.

Edwards, R. (1979). *Contested Terrain*. New York: Basic Books.

Hacker, S. (1990). *"Doing It the Hard Way"*: *Investigations of Gender and Technology*. Boston: Unwin Hyman.

Hochschild, A. (1989). *The Second Shift*. New York: Avon Books.

Hochschild, A. (1997). *The Time Bind*. New York: Metropolitan Books.

Kanter, R. M. (1977). *Men and Women of the Corporation*. New York: Basic Books.

Kendall, L. (2000). "'Oh no! I'm a Nerd!' Hegemonic Masculinity on an Online Forum." *Gender and Society* 14:2 256–275.

Kendall, L. (1999). "'The Nerd Within': Mass Media and the Negotiation of Identity Among Computer-Using Men." *Journal of Men's Studies* 7:3 353.

Kunda, G. (1992). *Engineering Culture*. Philadelphia: Temple University Press.

Kunda, G. and Van Maanen, J. (1999). "Changing Scripts at Work: Managers and Professionals." *Annals of the American Academy of Political and Social Science* 561: 64–80.

Lee, C. K. (1998). *Gender and the South China Miracle*. Berkeley: University of California Press.

Leidner, R. (1993). *Fast Food, Fast Talk*. Berkeley: University of California Press.

Levine, J. A. and Pittinsky, T. L. (1997). *Working Fathers*. San Diego: Harcourt Brace & Company.

Mac An Ghaill, M. E. (1996). *Understanding Masculinities*. Philadelphia: Open University Press.

Mumbly, D. K. (1998). "Organizing Men: Power, Discourse, and the Social Construction of Masculinity(s) in the Workplace." *Communication Theory* 8:2 164–179.

Pierce, J. L. (1996). "Reproducing Gender Relations in Large Law Firms: The Role of Emotional Labor in Paralegal Work." *Working in the Service Society*, edited by C. Macdonald and C. Sirianni. Philadelphia: Temple University Press.

Pleck, J. (1993). "Are 'Family-Supportive' Employer Policies Relevant to Men?" *Men, Work, and Family*, edited by J. C. Hood. Newbury Park: Sage Publications.

Turkle, S. (1984). *The Second Self: Computers and the Human Spirit*. New York: Simon and Schuster.

Turkle, S. (1988). "Computational Reticence: Why Women Fear the Intimate Machine." Pp. 41–61 in *Technology and Women's Voices: Keeping in Touch*, edited by C. Kramarae. New York: Routledge Kegan Paul.

Wright, R. (1996). "The Occupational Masculinity of Computing." Pp. 77–96 in *Masculinities in Organizations*, edited by C. Cheng. Thousand Oaks: Sage Publications.

Racializing the Glass Escalator

Reconsidering Men's Experiences with Women's Work

ADIA HARVEY WINGFIELD

Sociologists who study work have long noted that jobs are sex segregated and that this segregation creates different occupational experiences for men and women (Charles and Grusky 2004). Jobs predominantly filled by women often require "feminine" traits such as nurturing, caring, and empathy, a fact that means men confront perceptions that they are unsuited for the requirements of these jobs. Rather than having an adverse effect on their occupational experiences, however, these assumptions facilitate men's entry into better paying, higher status positions, creating what Williams (1995) labels a "glass escalator" effect.

The glass escalator model has been an influential paradigm in understanding the experiences of men who do women's work. Researchers have identified this process among men nurses, social workers, paralegals, and librarians and have cited its pervasiveness as evidence of men's consistent advantage in the workplace, such that even in jobs where men are numerical minorities they are likely to enjoy higher wages and faster promotions (Floge and Merrill 1986; Heikes 1991; Pierce 1995; Williams 1989, 1995). Most of these studies implicitly assume a racial homogenization of men workers in women's professions, but this supposition is problematic for several reasons. For one, minority men are not only present but are actually overrepresented in certain areas of reproductive work that have historically been dominated by white women (Duffy 2007). Thus, research that focuses primarily on white men in women's professions ignores a key segment of men who perform this type of labor. Second, and perhaps more important, conclusions based on the experiences of white men tend to overlook the ways that intersections of race and gender create different experiences for different men. While extensive work has documented the fact that white men in women's professions encounter a glass escalator effect that aids their occupational mobility (for an exception, see Snyder and Green 2008), few studies, if any, have considered how this effect is a function not only of gendered advantage but of racial privilege as well.

In this article, I examine the implications of race–gender intersections for minority men employed in a female-dominated, feminized occupation, specifically focusing on Black men in nursing. Their experiences doing "women's work" demonstrate that the glass escalator is a racialized as well as gendered concept.

Theoretical Framework

In her classic study *Men and Women of the Corporation*, Kanter (1977) offers a groundbreaking analysis of group interactions. Focusing on high-ranking

Adia Harvey Wingfield, "Racializing the Glass Escalator: Reconsidering Men's Experiences with Women's Work," *Gender & Society*, 23(1). Copyright 2009. Reprinted by permission of SAGE Publications, Inc.

women executives who work mostly with men, Kanter argues that those in the extreme numerical minority are tokens who are socially isolated, highly visible, and adversely stereotyped. Tokens have difficulty forming relationships with colleagues and often are excluded from social networks that provide mobility. Because of their low numbers, they are also highly visible as people who are different from the majority, even though they often feel invisible when they are ignored or overlooked in social settings. Tokens are also stereotyped by those in the majority group and frequently face pressure to behave in ways that challenge and undermine these stereotypes. Ultimately, Kanter argues that it is harder for them to blend into the organization and to work effectively and productively, and that they face serious barriers to upward mobility.

Kanter's (1977) arguments have been analyzed and retested in various settings and among many populations. Many studies, particularly of women in male-dominated corporate settings, have supported her findings. Other work has reversed these conclusions, examining the extent to which her conclusions hold when men were the tokens and women the majority group. These studies fundamentally challenged the gender neutrality of the token, finding that men in the minority fare much better than do similarly situated women. In particular, this research suggests that factors such as heightened visibility and polarization do not necessarily disadvantage men who are in the minority. While women tokens find that their visibility hinders their ability to blend in and work productively, men tokens find that their conspicuousness can lead to greater opportunities for leadership and choice assignments (Floge and Merrill 1986; Heikes 1991). Studies in this vein are important because they emphasize organizations—and occupations— as gendered institutions that subsequently create dissimilar experiences for men and women tokens (see Acker 1990).

In her groundbreaking study of men employed in various women's professions, Williams (1995) further develops this analysis of how power relationships shape the ways men tokens experience work in women's professions. Specifically, she introduces the concept of the glass escalator to explain men's experiences as tokens in these areas. Like Floge and Merrill (1986) and Heikes (1991), Williams finds that men tokens do not experience the isolation, visibility, blocked access to social networks, and stereotypes in the same ways that women tokens do. In contrast, Williams argues that even though they are in the minority, processes are in place that actually facilitate their opportunity and advancement. Even in culturally feminized occupations, then, men's advantage is built into the very structure and everyday interactions of these jobs so that men find themselves actually struggling to remain in place. For these men, "despite their intentions, they face invisible pressures to move up in their professions. Like being on a moving escalator, they have to work to stay in place" (Williams 1995, 87).

The glass escalator term thus refers to the "subtle mechanisms in place that enhance [men's] positions in [women's] professions" (Williams 1995, 108). These mechanisms include certain behaviors, attitudes, and beliefs men bring to these professions as well as the types of interactions that often occur between these men and their colleagues, supervisors, and customers. Consequently, even in occupations composed mostly of women, gendered perceptions about men's roles, abilities, and skills privilege them and facilitate their advancement. The glass escalator serves as a conduit that channels men in women's professions into the uppermost levels of the occupational hierarchy. Ultimately, the glass escalator effect suggests that men retain consistent occupational advantages over women, even when women are numerically in the majority (Budig 2002; Williams 1995).

Though this process has now been fairly well established in the literature, there are reasons to question its generalizability to all men. In an early critique of the supposed general neutrality of the token, Zimmer (1988) notes that much research on race comes to precisely the opposite of Kanter's conclusions, finding that as the numbers of minority group members increase (e.g., as they become less likely to be "tokens"), so too do tensions between the majority and minority groups. For instance, as minorities move into predominantly white neighborhoods, increasing numbers do not create the likelihood of greater acceptance and better treatment. In contrast, whites are likely to relocate when neighborhoods become "too" integrated, citing concerns about property values and racialized ideas about declining neighborhood quality (Shapiro 2004). Reinforcing, while at the same time tempering, the findings of research on men in female-dominated occupations, Zimmer (1988, 71) argues that relationships between tokens and the majority depend on understanding the underlying power relationships between these groups and "the status and power differentials between them." Hence, just as men who are tokens fare better than women, it also follows that the experiences of Blacks and whites as tokens should differ in ways that reflect their positions in hierarchies of status and power.

The concept of the glass escalator provides an important and useful framework for addressing men's experiences in women's occupations, but so far research in this vein has neglected to examine whether the glass escalator is experienced among all men in an identical manner. Are the processes that facilitate a ride on the glass escalator available to minority men? Or does race intersect with gender to affect the extent to which the glass escalator offers men opportunities in women's professions? In the next section, I examine whether and how the mechanisms that facilitate a ride on the glass escalator might be unavailable to Black men in nursing.[1]

Relationships with Colleagues and Supervisors

One key aspect of riding the glass escalator involves the warm, collegial welcome men workers often receive from their women colleagues. Often, this reaction is a response to the fact that professions dominated by women are frequently low in salary and status and that greater numbers of men help improve prestige and pay (Heikes 1991). Though some women workers resent the apparent ease with which men enter and advance in women's professions, the generally warm welcome men receive

stands in stark contrast to the cold reception, difficulties with mentorship, and blocked access to social networks that women often encounter when they do men's work (Roth 2006; Williams 1992). In addition, unlike women in men's professions, men who do women's work frequently have supervisors of the same sex. Men workers can thus enjoy a gendered bond with their supervisor in the context of a collegial work environment. These factors often converge, facilitating men's access to higher-status positions and producing the glass escalator effect.

The congenial relationship with colleagues and gendered bonds with supervisors are crucial to riding the glass escalator. Women colleagues often take a primary role in casting these men into leadership or supervisory positions. In their study of men and women tokens in a hospital setting, Floge and Merrill (1986) cite cases where women nurses promoted men colleagues to the position of charge nurse, even when the job had already been assigned to a woman. In addition to these close ties with women colleagues, men are also able to capitalize on gendered bonds with (mostly men) supervisors in ways that engender upward mobility. Many men supervisors informally socialize with men workers in women's jobs and are thus able to trade on their personal friendships for upward mobility. Williams (1995) describes a case where a nurse with mediocre performance reviews received a promotion to a more prestigious specialty area because of his friendship with the (male) doctor in charge. According to the literature, building strong relationships with colleagues and supervisors often happens relatively easily for men in women's professions and pays off in their occupational advancement.

For Black men in nursing, however, gendered racism may limit the extent to which they establish bonds with their colleagues and supervisors. The concept of gendered racism suggests that racial stereotypes, images, and beliefs are grounded in gendered ideals (Collins 1990, 2004; Espiritu 2000; Essed 1991; Harvey Wingfield 2007). Gendered racist stereotypes of Black men in particular emphasize the dangerous, threatening attributes associated with Black men and Black masculinity, framing Black men as threats to white women, prone to criminal behavior, and especially violent. Collins (2004) argues that these stereotypes serve to legitimize Black men's treatment in the criminal justice system through methods such as racial profiling and incarceration, but they may also hinder Black men's attempts to enter and advance in various occupational fields.

For Black men nurses, gendered racist images may have particular consequences for their relationships with women colleagues, who may view Black men nurses through the lens of controlling images and gendered racist stereotypes that emphasize the danger they pose to women. This may take on a heightened significance for white women nurses, given stereotypes that suggest that Black men are especially predisposed to raping white women. Rather than experiencing the congenial bonds with colleagues that white men nurses describe, Black men nurses may find themselves facing a much cooler reception from their women coworkers.

Gendered racism may also play into the encounters Black men nurses have with supervisors. In cases where supervisors are white men, Black men nurses may still find that higher-ups treat them in ways that reflect prevailing stereotypes about threatening Black masculinity. Supervisors may feel uneasy about forming close relationships with Black men or may encourage their separation from white women nurses. In addition, broader, less gender-specific racial stereotypes could also shape the experiences Black men nurses have with white men bosses. Whites often perceive Blacks, regardless of gender, as less intelligent, hardworking, ethical, and moral than other racial groups (Feagin 2006). Black men nurses may find that in addition to being influenced by gendered racist stereotypes, supervisors also view them as less capable and qualified for promotion, thus negating or minimizing the glass escalator effect.

Suitability for Nursing and Higher-Status Work

The perception that men are not really suited to do women's work also contributes to the glass escalator effect. In encounters with patients, doctors, and other staff, men nurses frequently confront others who do not expect to see them doing "a woman's job." Sometimes this perception means that patients mistake men nurses for doctors; ultimately, the sense that men do not really belong in nursing contributes to a push "*out* of the most feminine-identified areas and *up* to those regarded as more legitimate for men" (Williams 1995, 104). The sense that men are better suited for more masculine jobs means that men workers are often assumed to be more able and skilled than their women counterparts. As Williams writes (1995, 106), "Masculinity is often associated with competence and mastery," and this implicit definition stays with men even when they work in feminized fields. Thus, part of the perception that men do not belong in these jobs is rooted in the sense that, as men, they are more capable and accomplished than women and thus belong in jobs that reflect this. Consequently, men nurses are mistaken for doctors and are granted more authority and responsibility than their women counterparts, reflecting the idea that, as men, they are inherently more competent (Heikes 1991; Williams 1995).

Black men nurses, however, may not face the presumptions of expertise or the resulting assumption that they belong in higher-status jobs. Black professionals, both men and women, are often assumed to be less capable and less qualified than their white counterparts. In some cases, these negative stereotypes hold even when Black workers outperform white colleagues (Feagin and Sikes 1994). The belief that Blacks are inherently less competent than whites means that, despite advanced education, training, and skill, Black professionals often confront the lingering perception that they are better suited for lower-level service work (Feagin and Sikes 1994). Black men in fact often fare better than white women in blue-collar jobs such as policing and corrections work (Britton 1995), and this may be, in part, because they are viewed as more appropriately suited for these types of positions.

For Black men nurses, then, the issue of perception may play out in different ways than it does for white men nurses. While white men nurses enjoy the automatic assumption that they are qualified, capable, and suited for "better" work, the experiences of Black professionals suggest that Black men nurses may not encounter these reactions. They may, like their white counterparts, face the perception that they do not belong in nursing. Unlike their white counterparts, Black men nurses may be seen as inherently less capable and therefore better suited for low-wage labor than a professional, feminized occupation such as nursing. This perception of being less qualified means that they also may not be immediately assumed to be better suited for the higher-level, more masculinized jobs within the medical field.

As minority women address issues of both race and gender to negotiate a sense of belonging in masculine settings (Ong 2005), minority men may also face a comparable challenge in feminized fields. They may have to address the unspoken racialization implicit in the assumption that masculinity equals competence. Simultaneously, they may find that the racial stereotype that Blackness equals lower qualifications, standards, and competence clouds the sense that men are inherently more capable and adept in any field, including the feminized ones.

Establishing Distance from Femininity

An additional mechanism of the glass escalator involves establishing distance from women and the femininity associated with their occupations. Because men nurses are employed in a culturally feminized occupation, they develop strategies to disassociate themselves from the femininity associated with their work and retain some of the privilege associated with masculinity. Thus, when men nurses gravitate toward hospital emergency wards rather than obstetrics or pediatrics, or emphasize that they are only in nursing to get into hospital administration, they distance themselves from the femininity of their profession and thereby preserve their status as men despite the fact that they do "women's work." Perhaps more important, these strategies also place men in a prime position to experience the glass

escalator effect, as they situate themselves to move upward into higher-status areas in the field.

Creating distance from femininity also helps these men achieve aspects of hegemonic masculinity, which Connell (1989) describes as the predominant and most valued form of masculinity at a given time. Contemporary hegemonic masculine ideals emphasize toughness, strength, aggressiveness, heterosexuality, and, perhaps most important, a clear sense of femininity as different from and subordinate to masculinity (Kimmel 2001; Williams 1995). Thus, when men distance themselves from the feminized aspects of their jobs, they uphold the idea that masculinity and femininity are distinct, separate, and mutually exclusive. When these men seek masculinity by aiming for the better paying or most technological fields, they not only position themselves to move upward into the more acceptable arenas but also reinforce the greater social value placed on masculinity. Establishing distance from femininity therefore allows men to retain the privileges and status of masculinity while simultaneously enabling them to ride the glass escalator.

For Black men, the desire to reject femininity may be compounded by racial inequality. Theorists have argued that as institutional racism blocks access to traditional markers of masculinity such as occupational status and economic stability, Black men may repudiate femininity as a way of accessing the masculinity—and its attendant status—that is denied through other routes (hooks 2004; Neal 2005). Rejecting femininity is a key strategy men use to assert masculinity, and it remains available to Black men even when other means of achieving masculinity are unattainable. Black men nurses may be more likely to distance themselves from their women colleagues and to reject the femininity associated with nursing, particularly if they feel that they experience racial discrimination that renders occupational advancement inaccessible. Yet if they encounter strained relationships with women colleagues and men supervisors because of gendered racism or racialized stereotypes, the efforts to distance themselves from femininity still may not result in the glass escalator effect.

On the other hand, some theorists suggest that minority men may challenge racism by rejecting hegemonic masculine ideals. Chen (1999) argues that Chinese American men may engage in a strategy of repudiation, where they reject hegemonic masculinity because its implicit assumptions of whiteness exclude Asian American men. As these men realize that racial stereotypes and assumptions preclude them from achieving the hegemonic masculine ideal, they reject it and dispute its racialized underpinnings. Similarly, Lamont (2000, 47) notes that working-class Black men in the United States and France develop a "caring self" in which they emphasize values such as "morality, solidarity, and generosity." As a consequence of these men's ongoing experiences with racism, they develop a caring self that highlights work on behalf of others as an important tool in fighting oppression. Although caring is associated with femininity, these men cultivate a caring self because it allows them to challenge racial inequality. The results of these studies suggest that Black men nurses may embrace the femininity associated with nursing if it offers a way to combat racism. In these cases, Black men nurses may turn to pediatrics as a way of demonstrating sensitivity and therefore combating stereotypes of Black masculinity, or they may proudly identify as nurses to challenge perceptions that Black men are unsuited for professional, white-collar positions.

Taken together, all of this research suggests that Black men may not enjoy the advantages experienced by their white men colleagues, who ride a glass escalator to success. In this article, I focus on the experiences of Black men nurses to argue that the glass escalator is a racialized as well as a gendered concept that does not offer Black men the same privileges as their white men counterparts.

Data Collection and Method

I collected data through semistructured interviews with 17 men nurses who identified as Black or African American. Nurses ranged in age from 30 to 51 and lived in the southeastern United States. Six worked in suburban hospitals adjacent to major cities, six were located in major metropolitan urban care centers, and the remaining five worked in rural hospitals or clinics. All were registered nurses or licensed practical nurses. Six identified their specialty as oncology, four were bedside nurses, two were in intensive care, one managed an acute dialysis program, one was an orthopedic nurse, one was in ambulatory care, one was in emergency, and one was in surgery. The least experienced nurse had worked in the field for five years; the most experienced had been a nurse for 26 years. I initially recruited participants by soliciting attendees at the 2007 National Black Nurses Association annual meetings and then used a snowball sample to create the remainder of the data set. All names and identifying details have been changed to ensure confidentiality (see Table 12.1).

I conducted interviews during the fall of 2007. They generally took place in either my campus office or a coffee shop located near the respondent's home or workplace. The average interview lasted about an hour. Interviews were tape-recorded and transcribed. Interview questions primarily focused on how race and gender shaped the men's experiences as nurses. Questions addressed respondents' work history and current experiences in the field, how race and gender shaped their experiences as nurses, and their future career goals. The men discussed their reasons for going into nursing, the reactions from others on entering this field, and the particular challenges, difficulties, and obstacles Black men nurses faced. Respondents also described their work history in nursing, their current jobs, and their future plans. Finally, they talked about stereotypes of nurses in general and of Black men nurses in particular and their thoughts about and responses to these stereotypes. I coded the data according to key themes that emerged: relationships with white patients versus minority patients, personal bonds with colleagues versus lack of bonds, opportunities for advancement versus obstacles to advancement.

The researcher's gender and race shape interviews, and the fact that I am an African American woman undoubtedly shaped my rapport and the interactions with interview respondents. Social desirability

Table 12.1 Respondents

Name	Age	Specialization	Years of Experience	Years at Current Job
Chris	51	Oncology	26	16
Clayton	31	Emergency	6	6
Cyril	40	Dialysis	17	7
Dennis	30	Bedside	7	7 (months)
Evan	42	Surgery	25	20
Greg	39	Oncology	10	3
Kenny	47	Orthopedics	23	18 (months)
Leo	50	Bedside	20	18
Ray	36	Oncology	10	5
Ryan	37	Intensive care	17	11
Sean	46	Oncology	9	9
Simon	36	Oncology	5	5
Stuart	44	Bedside	6	4
Terrence	32	Bedside	10	6
Tim	39	Intensive care	20	15 (months)
Tobias	44	Oncology	25	7
Vern	50	Ambulatory care	7	7

bias may compel men to phrase responses that might sound harsh in ways that will not be offensive or problematic to the woman interviewer. However, one of the benefits of the interview method is that it allows respondents to clarify comments diplomatically while still giving honest answers. In this case, some respondents may have carefully framed certain comments about working mostly with women. However, the semistructured interview format nonetheless enabled them to discuss in detail their experiences in nursing and how these experiences are shaped by race and gender. Furthermore, I expect that shared racial status also facilitated a level of comfort, particularly as respondents frequently discussed issues of racial bias and mistreatment that shaped their experiences at work.

Findings

The results of this study indicate that not all men experience the glass escalator in the same ways. For Black men nurses, intersections of race and gender create a different experience with the mechanisms that facilitate white men's advancement in women's professions. Awkward or unfriendly interactions with colleagues, poor relationships with supervisors, perceptions that they are not suited for nursing, and an unwillingness to disassociate from "feminized" aspects of nursing constitute what I term *glass barriers* to riding the glass escalator.

Reception from Colleagues and Supervisors

When women welcome men into "their" professions, they often push men into leadership roles that ease their advancement into upper-level positions. Thus, a positive reaction from colleagues is critical to riding the glass escalator. Unlike white men nurses, however, Black men do not describe encountering a warm reception from women colleagues (Heikes 1991). Instead, the men I interviewed find that they often have unpleasant interactions with women coworkers who treat them rather coldly and attempt to keep them at bay. Chris is a 51-year-old oncology nurse who describes one white nurse's attempt to isolate him from other white women nurses as he attempted to get his instructions for that day's shift:

> She turned and ushered me to the door, and said for me to wait out here, a nurse will come out and give you your report. I stared at her hand on my arm, and then at her, and said, "Why? Where do you go to get your reports?" She said, "I get them in there." I said, "Right. Unhand me." I went right back in there, sat down, and started writing down my reports.

Kenny, a 47-year-old nurse with 23 years of nursing experience, describes a similarly and particularly painful experience he had in a previous job where he was the only Black person on staff:

> [The staff] had nothing to do with me, and they didn't even want me to sit at the same area where they were charting in to take a break. They wanted me to sit somewhere else . . . . They wouldn't even sit at a table with me! When I came and sat down, everybody got up and left.

These experiences with colleagues are starkly different from those described by white men in professions dominated by women (see Pierce 1995; Williams 1989). Though the men in these studies sometimes chose to segregate themselves, women never systematically excluded them. Though I have no way of knowing why the women nurses in Chris's and Kenny's workplaces physically segregated themselves, the pervasiveness of gendered racist images that emphasize white women's vulnerability to dangerous Black men may play an important role. For these nurses, their masculinity is not a guarantee that they will be welcomed, much less pushed into leadership roles. As Ryan, a 37-year-old intensive care nurse says, "[Black men] have to go further to prove ourselves. This involves proving our capabilities, *proving to colleagues that you can lead*, be on the forefront" (emphasis added). The warm welcome and subsequent opportunities for leadership cannot be taken for granted. In contrast,

these men describe great challenges in forming congenial relationships with coworkers who, they believe, do not truly want them there.

In addition, these men often describe tense, if not blatantly discriminatory, relationships with supervisors. While Williams (1995) suggests that men supervisors can be allies for men in women's professions by facilitating promotions and upward mobility, Black men nurses describe incidents of being overlooked by supervisors when it comes time for promotions. Ryan, who has worked at his current job for 11 years, believes that these barriers block upward mobility within the profession:

> The hardest part is dealing with people who don't understand minority nurses. People with their biases, who don't identify you as ripe for promotion. I know the policy and procedure, I'm familiar with past history. So you can't tell me I can't move forward if others did. [How did you deal with this?] By knowing the chain of command, who my supervisors were. Things were subtle. I just had to be better. I got this mostly from other nurses and supervisors. I was paid to deal with patients, so I could deal with [racism] from them. I'm not paid to deal with this from colleagues.

Kenny offers a similar example. Employed as an orthopedic nurse in a predominantly white environment, he describes great difficulty getting promoted, which he primarily attributes to racial biases:

> It's almost like you have to, um, take your ideas and give them to somebody else and then let them present them for you and you get no credit for it. I've applied for several promotions there and, you know, I didn't get them. . . . When you look around to the, um, the percentage of African Americans who are actually in executive leadership is almost zero percent. Because it's less than one percent of the total population of people that are in leadership, and it's almost like they'll go outside of the system just to try to find a Caucasian to fill a position. Not that I'm not qualified, because I've been master's prepared for 12 years and I'm working on my doctorate.

According to Ryan and Kenny, supervisors' racial biases mean limited opportunities for promotion and upward mobility. This interpretation is consistent with research that suggests that even with stellar performance and solid work histories, Black workers may receive mediocre evaluations from white supervisors that limit their advancement (Feagin 2006; Feagin and Sikes 1994). For Black men nurses, their race may signal to supervisors that they are unworthy of promotion and thus create a different experience with the glass escalator.

Strong relationships with colleagues and supervisors are a key mechanism of the glass escalator effect. For Black men nurses, however, these relationships are experienced differently from those described by their white men colleagues. Black men nurses do not speak of warm and congenial relationships with women nurses or see these relationships as facilitating a move into leadership roles. Nor do they suggest that they share gendered bonds with men supervisors that serve to ease their mobility into higher-status administrative jobs. In contrast, they sense that racial bias makes it difficult to develop ties with coworkers and makes superiors unwilling to promote them. Black men nurses thus experience this aspect of the glass escalator differently from their white men colleagues. They find that relationships with colleagues and supervisors stifle, rather than facilitate, their upward mobility.

Perceptions of Suitability

Like their white counterparts, Black men nurses also experience challenges from clients who are unaccustomed to seeing men in fields typically dominated by women. As with white men nurses, Black men encounter this in surprised or quizzical reactions from patients who seem to expect to be treated by white women nurses. Ray, a 36-year-old oncology nurse with 10 years of experience, states,

> Nursing, historically, has been a white female's job [so] being a Black male it's a weird position to be in. . . . I've, several times, gone into a room and a male patient, a white male patient has, you know,

they'll say, "Where's the pretty nurse? Where's the pretty nurse? Where's the blonde nurse?". . . "You don't have one. I'm the nurse."

Yet while patients rarely expect to be treated by men nurses of any race, white men encounter statements and behaviors that suggest patients expect them to be doctors, supervisors, or other higher-status, more masculine positions (Williams 1989, 1995). In part, this expectation accelerates their ride on the glass escalator, helping to push them into the positions for which they are seen as more appropriately suited.

(White) men, by virtue of their masculinity, are assumed to be more competent and capable and thus better situated in (nonfeminized) jobs that are perceived to require greater skill and proficiency. Black men, in contrast, rarely encounter patients (or colleagues and supervisors) who immediately expect that they are doctors or administrators. Instead, many respondents find that even after displaying their credentials, sharing their nursing experience, and, in one case, dispensing care, they are still mistaken for janitors or service workers. Ray's experience is typical:

> I've even given patients their medicines, explained their care to them, and then they'll say to me, "Well, can you send the nurse in?"

Chris describes a somewhat similar encounter of being misidentified by a white woman patient:

> I come [to work] in my white uniform, that's what I wear—being a Black man, I know they won't look at me the same, so I dress the part—I said good evening, my name's Chris, and I'm going to be your nurse. She says to me, "Are you from housekeeping?" . . . I've had other cases. I've walked in and had a lady look at me and ask if I'm the janitor.

Chris recognizes that this patient is evoking racial stereotypes that Blacks are there to perform menial service work. He attempts to circumvent this very perception through careful self-presentation, wearing the white uniform to indicate his position as a nurse. His efforts, however, are nonetheless met with a racial stereotype that as a Black man he should be there to clean up rather than to provide medical care.

Black men in nursing encounter challenges from customers that reinforce the idea that men are not suited for a "feminized" profession such as nursing. However, these assumptions are racialized as well as gendered. Unlike white men nurses who are assumed to be doctors (see Williams 1992), Black men in nursing are quickly taken for janitors or housekeeping staff. These men do not simply describe a gendered process where perceptions and stereotypes about men serve to aid their mobility into higher-status jobs. More specifically, they describe interactions that are simultaneously raced *and* gendered in ways that reproduce stereotypes of Black men as best suited for certain blue-collar, unskilled labor.

These negative stereotypes can affect Black men nurses' efforts to treat patients as well. The men I interviewed find that masculinity does not automatically endow them with an aura of competency. In fact, they often describe interactions with white women patients that suggest that their race minimizes whatever assumptions of capability might accompany being men. They describe several cases in which white women patients completely refused treatment. Ray says,

> With older white women, it's tricky sometimes because they will come right out and tell you they don't want you to treat them, or can they see someone else.

Ray frames this as an issue specifically with older white women, though other nurses in the sample described similar issues with white women of all ages. Cyril, a 40-year-old nurse with 17 years of nursing experience, describes a slightly different twist on this story:

> I had a white lady that I had to give a shot, and she was fine with it and I was fine with it. But her husband, when she told him, he said to me, I don't have any problem with you as a Black man, but I don't want you giving her a shot.

While white men nurses report some apprehension about treating women patients, in all likelihood this experience is compounded for Black men

(Williams 1989). Historically, interactions between Black men and white women have been fraught with complexity and tension, as Black men have been represented in the cultural imagination as potential rapists and threats to white women's security and safety—and, implicitly, as a threat to white patriarchal stability (Davis 1981; Giddings 1984). In Cyril's case, it may be particularly significant that the Black man is charged with giving a shot and therefore literally penetrating the white wife's body, a fact that may heighten the husband's desire to shield his wife from this interaction. White men nurses may describe hesitation or awkwardness that accompanies treating women patients, but their experiences are not shaped by a pervasive racial imagery that suggests that they are potential threats to their women patients' safety.

This dynamic, described primarily among white women patients and their families, presents a picture of how Black men's interactions with clients are shaped in specifically raced and gendered ways that suggest they are less rather than more capable. These interactions do not send the message that Black men, because they are men, are too competent for nursing and really belong in higher-status jobs. Instead, these men face patients who mistake them for lower-status service workers and encounter white women patients (and their husbands) who simply refuse treatment or are visibly uncomfortable with the prospect. These interactions do not situate Black men nurses in a prime position for upward mobility. Rather, they suggest that the experience of Black men nurses with this particular mechanism of the glass escalator is the manifestation of the expectation that they should be in lower-status positions more appropriate to their race and gender.

Refusal to Reject Femininity

Finally, Black men nurses have a different experience with establishing distance from women and the feminized aspects of their work. Most research shows that as men nurses employ strategies that distance them from femininity (e.g., by emphasizing nursing as a route to higher-status, more masculine jobs), they place themselves in a position for upward mobility and the glass escalator effect (Williams 1992). For Black men nurses, however, this process looks different. Instead of distancing themselves from the femininity associated with nursing, Black men actually embrace some of the more feminized attributes linked to nursing. In particular, they emphasize how much they value and enjoy the way their jobs allow them to be caring and nurturing. Rather than conceptualizing caring as anathema or feminine (and therefore undesirable), Black men nurses speak openly of caring as something positive and enjoyable.

This is consistent with the context of nursing that defines caring as integral to the profession. As nurses, Black men in this line of work experience professional socialization that emphasizes and values caring, and this is reflected in their statements about their work. Significantly, however, rather than repudiating this feminized component of their jobs, they embrace it. Tobias, a 44-year-old oncology nurse with 25 years of experience, asserts,

> The best part about nursing is helping other people, the flexibility of work hours, and the commitment to vulnerable populations, people who are ill.

Simon, a 36-year-old oncology nurse, also talks about the joy he gets from caring for others. He contrasts his experiences to those of white men nurses he knows who prefer specialties that involve less patient care:

> They were going to work with the insurance industries, they were going to work in the ER where it's a touch and go, you're a number literally. I don't get to know your name, I don't get to know that you have four grandkids, I don't get to know that you really want to get out of the hospital by next week because the following week is your birthday, your 80th birthday and it's so important for you. I don't get to know that your cat's name is Sprinkles, and you're concerned about who's feeding the cat now, and if they remembered to turn the TV on during the day so that the cat can watch *The Price is Right*. They don't get into all that kind of stuff. OK, I actually need to remember the name of your cat so

that tomorrow morning when I come, I can ask you about Sprinkles and that will make a world of difference. I'll see light coming to your eyes and the medicines will actually work because your perspective is different.

Like Tobias, Simon speaks with a marked lack of self-consciousness about the joys of adding a personal touch and connecting that personal care to a patient's improvement. For him, caring is important, necessary, and valued, even though others might consider it a feminine trait.

For many of these nurses, willingness to embrace caring is also shaped by issues of race and racism. In their position as nurses, concern for others is connected to fighting the effects of racial inequality. Specifically, caring motivates them to use their role as nurses to address racial health disparities, especially those that disproportionately affect Black men. Chris describes his efforts to minimize health issues among Black men:

> With Black male patients, I have their history, and if they're 50 or over I ask about the prostate exam and a colonoscopy. Prostate and colorectal death is so high that that's my personal crusade.

Ryan also speaks to the importance of using his position to address racial imbalances:

> I really take advantage of the opportunities to give back to communities, especially to change the disparities in the African American community. I'm more than just a nurse. As a faculty member at a major university, I have to do community hours, services. Doing health fairs, in-services on research, this makes an impact in some disparities in the African American community. [People in the community] may not have the opportunity to do this otherwise.

As Lamont (2000) indicates in her discussion of the "caring self," concern for others helps Chris and Ryan to use their knowledge and position as nurses to combat racial inequalities in health. Though caring is generally considered a "feminine" attribute, in this context it is connected to challenging racial health disparities. Unlike their white men colleagues, these nurses accept and even embrace certain aspects of femininity rather than rejecting them. They thus reveal yet another aspect of the glass escalator process that differs for Black men. As Black men nurses embrace this "feminine" trait and the avenues it provides for challenging racial inequalities, they may become more comfortable in nursing and embrace the opportunities it offers.

Conclusions

Existing research on the glass escalator cannot explain these men's experiences. As men who do women's work, they should be channeled into positions as charge nurses or nursing administrators and should find themselves virtually pushed into the upper ranks of the nursing profession. But without exception, this is not the experience these Black men nurses describe. Instead of benefiting from the basic mechanisms of the glass escalator, they face tense relationships with colleagues, supervisors' biases in achieving promotion, patient stereotypes that inhibit caregiving, and a sense of comfort with some of the feminized aspects of their jobs. These "glass barriers" suggest that the glass escalator is a racialized concept as well as a gendered one. The main contribution of this study is the finding that race and gender intersect to determine which men will ride the glass escalator. The proposition that men who do women's work encounter undue opportunities and advantages appears to be unequivocally true only if the men in question are white.

This raises interesting questions and a number of new directions for future research. Researchers might consider the extent to which the glass escalator is not only raced and gendered but sexualized as well. Williams (1995) notes that straight men are often treated better by supervisors than are gay men and that straight men frequently do masculinity by strongly asserting their heterosexuality to combat the belief that men who do women's work are gay. The men in this study (with the exception of one nurse I interviewed) rarely discussed sexuality except to say that they were straight and were not bothered by "the gay stereotype." This is consistent with Williams's findings. Gay men, however,

may also find that they do not experience a glass escalator effect that facilitates their upward mobility. Tim, the only man I interviewed who identified as gay, suggests that gender, race, and sexuality come together to shape the experiences of men in nursing. He notes,

> I've been called awful things—you faggot this, you faggot that. I tell people there are three *F*s in life, and if you're not doing one of them it doesn't matter what you think of me. They say, "Three *F*s?" and I say yes. If you aren't feeding me, financing me, or fucking me, then it's none of your business what my faggot ass is up to.

Tim's experience suggests that gay men—and specifically gay Black men—in nursing may encounter particular difficulties establishing close ties with straight men supervisors or may not automatically be viewed by their women colleagues as natural leaders. While race is, in many cases, more obviously visible than sexuality, the glass escalator effect may be a complicated amalgam of racial, gendered, and sexual expectations and stereotypes.

It is also especially interesting to consider how men describe the role of women in facilitating—or denying—access to the glass escalator. Research on white men nurses includes accounts of ways white women welcome them and facilitate their advancement by pushing them toward leadership positions (Floge and Merrill 1986; Heikes 1991; Williams 1992, 1995). In contrast, Black men nurses in this study discuss white women who do not seem eager to work with them, much less aid their upward mobility. These different responses indicate that shared racial status is important in determining who rides the glass escalator. If that is the case, then future research should consider whether Black men nurses who work in predominantly Black settings are more likely to encounter the glass escalator effect. In these settings, Black men nurses' experiences might more closely resemble those of white men nurses.

Future research should also explore other racial minority men's experiences in women's professions to determine whether and how they encounter the processes that facilitate a ride on the glass escalator. With Black men nurses, specific race or gender stereotypes impede their access to the glass escalator; however, other racial minority men are subjected to different race or gender stereotypes that could create other experiences. For instance, Asian American men may encounter racially specific gender stereotypes of themselves as computer nerds, sexless sidekicks, or model minorities and thus may encounter the processes of the glass escalator differently than do Black or white men (Espiritu 2000). More focus on the diverse experiences of racial minority men is necessary to know for certain.

Finally, it is important to consider how these men's experiences have implications for the ways the glass escalator phenomenon reproduces racial and gendered advantages. Williams (1995) argues that men's desire to differentiate themselves from women and disassociate from the femininity of their work is a key process that facilitates their ride on the glass escalator. She ultimately suggests that if men reconstruct masculinity to include traits such as caring, the distinctions between masculinity and femininity could blur and men "would not have to define masculinity as the negation of femininity" (Williams 1995, 188). This in turn could create a more equitable balance between men and women in women's professions. However, the experiences of Black men in nursing, especially their embrace of caring, suggest that accepting the feminine aspects of work is not enough to dismantle the glass escalator and produce more gender equality in women's professions. The fact that Black men nurses accept and even enjoy caring does not minimize the processes that enable *white* men to ride the glass escalator. This suggests that undoing the glass escalator requires not only blurring the lines between masculinity and femininity but also challenging the processes of racial inequality that marginalize minority men.

Author's Note

Special thanks to Kirsten Dellinger, Mindy Stombler, Ralph LaRossa, Cindy Whitney, Laura Logan, Dana Britton, and the anonymous reviewers for their insights and helpful feedback. Thanks also to Karyn Lacy, Andra Gillespie, and Isabel Wilkerson for their comments and support. Correspondence concerning this article should be addressed to Adia Harvey Wingfield, Department of Sociology, Georgia State University, P.O. Box 5020, Atlanta, GA 30302-5020; phone: 404-413-6509; e-mail: aharvey@gsu.edu.

Note

1. I could not locate any data that indicate the percentage of Black men in nursing. According to 2006 census data, African Americans compose 11 percent of nurses, and men are 8 percent of nurses (http://www.census.gov/compendia/statab/tables/08s0598.pdf). These data do not show the breakdown of nurses by race and sex.

References

Acker, Joan. 1990. Hierarchies, jobs, bodies: A theory of gendered organizations. *Gender & Society* 4:139–58.

Britton, Dana. 1995. *At work in the iron cage.* New York: New York University Press.

Budig, Michelle. 2002. Male advantage and the gender composition of jobs: Who rides the glass escalator? *Social Forces* 49(2): 258–77.

Charles, Maria, and David Grusky. 2004. *Occupational ghettos: The worldwide segregation of women and men.* Palo Alto, CA: Stanford University Press.

Chen, Anthony. 1999. Lives at the center of the periphery, lives at the periphery of the center: Chinese American masculinities and bargaining with hegemony. *Gender & Society* 13:584–607.

Collins, Patricia Hill. 1990. *Black feminist thought.* New York: Routledge.

———. 2004. *Black sexual politics.* New York: Routledge.

Connell, R. W. 1989. *Gender and power.* Sydney, Australia: Allen and Unwin.

Davis, Angela. 1981. *Women, race, and class.* New York: Vintage.

Duffy, Mignon. 2007. Doing the dirty work: Gender, race, and reproductive labor in historical perspective. *Gender & Society* 21:313–36.

Espiritu, Yen Le. 2000. *Asian American women and men: Labor, laws, and love*. Walnut Creek, CA: AltaMira.

Essed, Philomena. 1991. *Understanding everyday racism*. New York: Russell Sage.

Feagin, Joe. 2006. *Systemic racism*. New York: Routledge.

Feagin, Joe, and Melvin Sikes. 1994. *Living with racism*. Boston: Beacon Hill Press.

Floge, Liliane, and Deborah M. Merrill. 1986. Tokenism reconsidered: Male nurses and female physicians in a hospital setting. *Social Forces* 64:925–47.

Giddings, Paula. 1984. *When and where I enter: The impact of Black women on race and sex in America*. New York: HarperCollins.

Harvey Wingfield, Adia. 2007. The modern mammy and the angry Black man: African American professionals' experiences with gendered racism in the workplace. *Race, Gender, and Class* 14(2): 196–212.

Heikes, E. Joel. 1991. When men are the minority: The case of men in nursing. *Sociological Quarterly* 32:389–401.

hooks, bell. 2004. *We real cool*. New York: Routledge.

Kanter, Rosabeth Moss. 1977. *Men and women of the corporation*. New York: Basic Books.

Kimmel, Michael. 2001. Masculinity as homophobia. In *Men and masculinity*, edited by Theodore F. Cohen. Belmont, CA: Wadsworth.

Lamont, Michelle. 2000. *The dignity of working men*. New York: Russell Sage.

Neal, Mark Anthony. 2005. *New Black man*. New York: Routledge.

Ong, Maria. 2005. Body projects of young women of color in physics: Intersections of race, gender, and science. *Social Problems* 52(4): 593–617.

Pierce, Jennifer. 1995. *Gender trials: Emotional lives in contemporary law firms*. Berkeley: University of California Press.

Roth, Louise. 2006. *Selling women short: Gender and money on Wall Street*. Princeton, NJ: Princeton University Press.

Shapiro, Thomas. 2004. *Hidden costs of being African American: How wealth perpetuates inequality*. New York: Oxford University Press.

Snyder, Karrie Ann, and Adam Isaiah Green. 2008. Revisiting the glass escalator: The case of gender segregation in a female dominated occupation. *Social Problems* 55(2):271–99.

Williams, Christine. 1989. *Gender differences at work: Women and men in non-traditional occupations*. Berkeley: University of California Press.

——. 1992. The glass escalator: Hidden advantages for men in the "female" professions. *Social Problems* 39(3): 253–67.

——. 1995. *Still a man s world: Men who do women s work*. Berkeley: University of California Press.

Zimmer, Lynn. 1988. Tokenism and women in the workplace: The limits of gender neutral theory. *Social Problems* 35(1): 64–77.

Just One of the Guys?

How Transmen Make Gender Visible at Work

KRISTEN SCHILT

Theories of gendered organizations argue that cultural beliefs about gender difference embedded in workplace structures and interactions create and reproduce workplace disparities that disadvantage women and advantage men (Acker 1990; Martin 2003; Williams 1995). As Martin (2003) argues, however, the practices that reproduce gender difference and gender inequality at work are hard to observe. As these gendered practices are citations of established gender norms, men and women in the workplace repeatedly and unreflectively engage in "doing gender" and therefore "doing inequality" (Martin 2003; West and Zimmerman 1987). This repetition of well-worn gender ideologies naturalizes workplace gender inequality, making gendered disparities in achievements appear to be offshoots of "natural" differences between men and women, rather than the products of dynamic gendering and gendered practices (Martin 2003). As the active reproduction of gendered workplace disparities is rendered invisible, gender inequality at work becomes difficult to document empirically and therefore remains resistant to change (Acker 1990; Martin 2003; Williams 1995).

The workplace experiences of female-to-male transsexuals (FTMs), or transmen, offer an opportunity to examine these disparities between men and women at work from a new perspective. Many FTMs enter the workforce as women and, after transition, begin working as men.[1] As men, they have the same skills, education, and abilities they had as women; however, how this "human capital" is perceived often varies drastically once they become men at work. This shift in gender attribution gives them the potential to develop an "outsider-within" perspective (Collins 1986) on men's advantages in the workplace. FTMs can find themselves benefiting from the "patriarchal dividend" (Connell 1995, 79)—the advantages men in general gain from the subordination of women—after they transition. However, not being "born into it" gives them the potential to be cognizant of being awarded respect, authority, and prestige they did not have working as women. In addition, the experiences of transmen who fall outside of the hegemonic construction of masculinity, such as FTMs of color, short FTMs, and young FTMs, illuminate how the interplay of gender, race, age, and bodily characteristics can constrain access to gendered workplace advantages for some men (Connell 1995).

In this article, I document the workplace experiences of two groups of FTMs, those who openly transition and remain in the same jobs (open FTMs) and those who find new jobs posttransition as "just men" (stealth FTMs).[2] I argue that the positive and negative changes they experience when they become men can illuminate how gender discrimination and gender advantage are created and maintained through workplace interactions. These experiences also illustrate that masculinity is not a fixed character type that automatically commands privilege but rather that the relationships between competing hegemonic and marginalized masculinities give men differing abilities to access gendered workplace advantages (Connell 1995).

Theories of Workplace Gender Discrimination

Sociological research on the workplace reveals a complex relationship between the gender of an employee and that employee's opportunities for advancement in both authority and pay. While white-collar men and women with equal qualifications can begin their careers in similar positions in the workplace, men tend to advance faster, creating a gendered promotion gap (Padavic and Reskin 2002; Valian 1999). When women are able to advance, they often find themselves barred from attaining access to the highest echelons of the company by the invisible barrier of the "glass ceiling" (Valian 1999). Even in the so-called women's professions, such as nursing and teaching, men outpace women in advancement to positions of authority (Williams 1995). Similar patterns exist among blue-collar professions, as women often are denied sufficient training for advancement in manual trades, passed over for promotion, or subjected to extreme forms of sexual, racial, and gender harassment that result in women's attrition (Byrd 1999; Miller 1997; Yoder and Aniakudo 1997). These studies are part of the large body of scholarly research on gender and work finding that white- and blue-collar workplaces are characterized by gender segregation, with women concentrated in lower-paying jobs with little room for advancement.

Among the theories proposed to account for these workplace disparities between men and women are human capital theory and gender role socialization. Human capital theory posits that labor markets are neutral environments that reward workers for their skills, experience, and productivity. As women workers are more likely to take time off from work for child rearing and family obligations, they end up with less education and work experience than men. Following this logic, gender segregation in the workplace stems from these discrepancies in skills and experience between men and women, not from gender discrimination. However, while these differences can explain some of the disparities in salaries and rank between women and men, they fail to explain why women and men with comparable prestigious degrees and work experience still end up in different places, with women trailing behind men in advancement (Valian 1999; Williams 1995).

A second theory, gender socialization theory, looks at the process by which individuals come to learn, through the family, peers, schools, and the media, what behavior is appropriate and inappropriate for their gender. From this standpoint, women seek out jobs that reinforce "feminine" traits such as caring and nurturing. This would explain the predominance of women in helping professions such as nursing and teaching. As women are socialized to put family obligations first, women workers would also be expected to be concentrated in part-time jobs that allow more flexibility for family schedules but bring in less money. Men, on the other hand, would be expected to seek higher-paying jobs with more authority to reinforce their sense of masculinity. While gender socialization theory may explain some aspects of gender segregation at work, however, it leaves out important structural aspects of the workplace that support segregation, such as the lack of workplace child care services, as well as employers' own gendered stereotypes about which workers are best suited for which types of jobs (Padavic and Reskin 2002; Valian 1999; Williams 1995).

A third theory, gendered organization theory, argues that what is missing from both human capital theory and gender socialization theory is the way in which men's advantages in the workplace are maintained and reproduced in gender expectations that are embedded in organizations and in interactions between employers, employees, and coworkers (Acker 1990; Martin 2003; Williams 1995).

However, it is difficult to study this process of re-production empirically for several reasons. First, while men and women with similar education and workplace backgrounds can be compared to demonstrate the disparities in where they end up in their careers, it could be argued that differences in achievement between them can be attributed to personal characteristics of the workers rather than to systematic gender discrimination. Second, gendered expectations about which types of jobs women and men are suited for are strengthened by existing occupational segregation; the fact that there are more women nurses and more men doctors comes to be seen as proof that women are better suited for helping professions and men for rational professions. The normalization of these disparities as natural differences obscures the actual operation of men's advantages and therefore makes it hard to document them empirically. Finally, men's advantages in the workplace are not a function of simply one process but rather a complex interplay between many factors, such as gender differences in workplace performance evaluation, gendered beliefs about men's and women's skills and abilities, and differences between family and child care obligations of men and women workers.

The cultural reproduction of these interactional practices that create and maintain gendered workplace disparities often can be rendered more visible, and therefore more able to be challenged, when examined through the perspective of marginalized others (Collins 1986; Martin 1994, 2003; Yoder and Aniakudo 1997). As Yoder and Aniakudo note, "marginalized others offer a unique perspective on the events occurring within a setting because they perceive activities from the vantages of both nearness (being within) and detachment (being outsiders)" (1997, 325–26). This importance of drawing on the experiences of marginalized others derives from Patricia Hill Collins's theoretical development of the "outsider-within" (1986, 1990). Looking historically at the experience of Black women, Collins (1986) argues that they often have become insiders to white society by virtue of being forced, first by slavery and later by racially bounded labor

markets, into domestic work for white families. The insider status that results from being immersed in the daily lives of white families carries the ability to demystify power relations by making evident how white society relies on racism and sexism, rather than superior ability or intellect, to gain advantage; however, Black women are not able to become total insiders due to being visibly marked as different. Being a marginalized insider creates a unique perspective, what Collins calls "the outsider-within," that allows them to see "the contradictions between the dominant group's actions and ideologies" (Collins 1990, 12), thus giving a new angle on how the processes of oppression operate. Applying this perspective to the workplace, scholars have documented the production and reproduction of gendered and racialized workplace disparities through the "outsider-within" perspective of Black women police officers (Martin 1994) and Black women firefighters (Yoder and Aniakudo 1997).

In this article, I posit that FTMs' change in gender attribution, from women to men, can provide them with an outsider-within perspective on gendered workplace disparities. Unlike the Black women discussed by Collins, FTMs usually are not visibly marked by their outsider status, as continued use of testosterone typically allows for the development of a masculine social identity indistinguishable from "bio men."[3] However, while both stealth and open FTMs can become social insiders at work, their experience working as women prior to transition means they maintain an internalized sense of being outsiders to the gender schemas that advantage men. This internalized insider/outsider position allows some transmen to see clearly the advantages associated with being men at work while still maintaining a critical view to how this advantage operates and is reproduced and how it disadvantages women. I demonstrate that many of the respondents find themselves receiving more authority, respect, and reward when they gain social identities as men, even though their human capital does not change. This shift in treatment suggests that gender inequality in the workplace is not continually reproduced only because women make different education and workplace choices than men but rather because coworkers and employers often rely on gender stereotypes to evaluate men's and women's achievements and skills.

Method

I conducted in-depth interviews with 29 FTMs in the Southern California area from 2003 to 2005. My criteria for selection were that respondents were assigned female at birth and were currently living and working as men or open transmen. These selection criteria did exclude female-bodied individuals who identified as men but had not publicly come out as men at work and FTMs who had not held any jobs as men since their transition, as they would not be able to comment about changes in their social interactions that were specific to the workplace. My sample is made up of 18 open FTMs and 11 stealth FTMs.

At the onset of my research, I was unaware of how I would be received as a non-transgender person doing research on transgender workplace experiences, as well as a woman interviewing men. I went into the study being extremely open about my research agenda and my political affiliations with feminist and transgender politics. I carried my openness about my intentions into my interviews, making clear at the beginning that I was happy to answer questions about my research intentions, the ultimate goal of my research, and personal questions about myself. Through this openness, and the acknowledgment that I was there to learn rather than to be an academic "expert," I feel that I gained a rapport with my respondents that bridged the "outsider/insider" divide (Merton 1972).

Generating a random sample of FTMs is not possible as there is not an even dispersal of FTMs throughout Southern California, nor are there transgender-specific neighborhoods from which to sample. I recruited interviewees from transgender activist groups, transgender listservers, and FTM support groups. In addition, I participated for two years in Southern California transgender community events, such as conferences and support group meetings. Attending these community events gave

me an opportunity not only to demonstrate long-term political commitment to the transgender community but also to recruit respondents who might not be affiliated with FTM activist groups. All the interviews were conducted in the respondents' offices, in their homes, or at a local café or restaurant. The interviews ranged from one and a half to four hours. All interviews were audio recorded, transcribed, and coded.

Drawing on sociological research that reports long-standing gender differences between men and women in the workplace (Reskin and Hartmann 1986; Reskin and Roos 1990; Valian 1999; Williams 1995), I constructed my interview schedule to focus on possible differences between working as women and working as men. I first gathered a general employment history and then explored the decision to openly transition or to go stealth. At the end of the interviews, I posed the question, "Do you see any differences between working as a woman and working as a man?" All but a few of the respondents immediately answered yes and began to provide examples of both positive and negative differences. About half of the respondents also, at this time, introduced the idea of male privilege, addressing whether they felt they received a gender advantage from transitioning. If the concept of gender advantage was not brought up by respondents, I later introduced the concept of male privilege and then posed the question, saying, "Do you feel that you have received any male privilege at work?" The resulting answers from these two questions are the framework for this article.

In reporting the demographics of my respondents, I have opted to use pseudonyms and general categories of industry to avoid identifying my respondents. Respondents ranged in age from 20 to 48. Rather than attempting to identify when they began their gender transition, a start date often hard to pinpoint as many FTMs feel they have been personally transitioning since childhood or adolescence, I recorded how many years they had been working as men (meaning they were either hired as men or had openly transitioned from female to male and remained in the same job). The average time of working as a man was seven years. Regarding race and ethnicity, the sample was predominantly white (17), with 3 Asians, 1 African American, 3 Latinos, 3 mixed-race individuals, 1 Armenian American, and 1 Italian American. Responses about sexual identity fell into four main categories, heterosexual (9), bisexual (8), queer (6), and gay (3). The remaining 3 respondents identified their sexual identity as celibate/asexual, "dating women," and pansexual. Finally, in terms of region, the sample included a mixture of FTMs living in urban and suburban areas. (See Table 13.1 for sample characteristics.)

The experience of my respondents represents a part of the Southern California FTM community from 2003 to 2005. As Rubin (2003) has demonstrated, however, FTM communities vary greatly from city to city, meaning these findings may not be representative of the experiences of transmen in Austin, San Francisco, or Atlanta. In addition, California passed statewide gender identity protection for employees in 2003, meaning that the men in my study live in an environment in which they cannot legally be fired for being transgender (although most of my respondents said they would not wish to be a test case for this new law). This legal protection means that California transmen might have very different workplace experiences than men in states without gender identity protection. Finally, anecdotal evidence suggests that there are a large number of transgender individuals who transition and then sever all ties with the transgender community, something known as being "deep stealth." This lack of connection to the transgender community means they are excluded from research on transmen but that their experiences with the workplace may be very different than those of men who are still connected, even slightly, to the FTM community.

Transmen as Outsiders Within at Work

In undergoing a physical gender transition, transmen move from being socially gendered as women to being socially gendered as men (Dozier 2005). This shift in gender attribution gives them the potential to develop an "outsider-within" perspective (Collins 1986) on the sources of men's advantages in the workplace. In other words, while they may find themselves, as men, benefiting from the "patriarchal dividend"(Connell 1995, 79), not being "born into it" can make visible how gendered workplace disparities are created and maintained through interactions. Many of the respondents note that they can see clearly, once they become "just one of the guys," that men succeed in the workplace at higher rates than women because of gender stereotypes that privilege masculinity, not because they have greater skill or ability. For transmen who do see how these cultural beliefs about gender create gendered workplace disparities, there is an accompanying sense that these experiences are visible to them only because of the unique perspective they gain from undergoing a change in gender attribution. Exemplifying this, Preston reports about his views on gender differences at work posttransition: "I swear they let the guys get away with so much stuff! Lazy ass bastards get away with so much stuff and the women who are working hard, they just get ignored. . . . I am really aware of it. And that is one of the reasons that I feel like I have become much more of a feminist since transition. I am just so aware of the difference that my experience has shown me." Carl makes a similar point, discussing his awareness of blatant gender discrimination at a hardware/home construction store where he worked immediately after his transition: "Girls couldn't get their forklift license or it would take them forever. They wouldn't make as much money. It was so pathetic. I would have never seen it if I was a regular guy. I would have just not seen it. . . . I can see things differently because of my perspective. So in some ways I am a lot like a guy because I transitioned younger but still, you can't take away how I was raised for 18 years." These comments illustrate how the outsider-within perspective of many FTMs can translate into a critical perspective on men's advantages at work. The idea that a "regular guy," here meaning a bio man, would not be able to see how women were passed over in favor of men makes clear that for some FTMs, there is an ability to see how gender stereotypes can advantage men at work.

Table 13.1 Sample Characteristics

Pseudonym	Age	Race/Ethnicity	Sexual Identity	Approximate Number of Years Working as Male	Industry	Status at Work
Aaron	28	Black/White	Queer	5	Semi-Professional	Open
Brian	42	White	Bisexual	14	Semi-Professional	Stealth
Carl	34	White	Heterosexual	16	Higher Professional	Stealth
Christopher	25	Asian	Pansexual	3	Semi-Professional	Open
Colin	31	White	Queer	1	Lower Professional	Open
Crispin	42	White	Heterosexual	2	Blue-Collar	Stealth
David	30	White	Bisexual	2	Higher Professional	Open
Douglas	38	White	Gay	5	Semi-Professional	Open
Elliott	20	White	Bisexual	1	Retail/Customer Service	Open
Henry	32	White	Gay	5	Lower Professional	Open
Jack	30	Latino	Queer	1	Semi-Professional	Open
Jake	45	White	Queer	9	Higher Professional	Open
Jason	48	White/Italian	Celibate	20	Retail/Customer Service	Stealth
Keith	42	Black	Heterosexual	1	Blue-Collar	Open
Kelly	24	White	Bisexual	2	Semi-Professional	Open
Ken	26	Asian/White	Queer	6 months	Semi-Professional	Open
Paul	44	White	Heterosexual	2	Semi-Professional	Open
Peter	24	White/Armenian	Heterosexual	4	Lower Professional	Stealth
Preston	39	White	Bisexual	2	Blue-Collar	Open
Riley	37	White	Dates women	1	Lower Professional	Open
Robert	23	Asian	Heterosexual	2	Retail/Customer Service	Stealth
Roger	45	White	Bisexual	22	Lower Professional	Stealth
Sam	33	Latino	Heterosexual	15	Blue-Collar	Stealth
Simon	42	White	Bisexual	2	Semi-Professional	Open
Stephen	35	White	Heterosexual	1	Retail/Customer Service	Stealth
Thomas	42	Latino	Queer	13	Higher Professional	Open
Trevor	35	White	Gay/Queer	6	Semi-Professional	Open
Wayne	44	White/Latino	Bisexual	22	Higher Professional	Stealth
Winston	40	White	Heterosexual	14	Higher Professional	Stealth

However, just as being a Black woman does not guarantee the development of a Black feminist perspective (Collins 1986), having this critical perspective on gender discrimination in the workplace is not inherent to the FTM experience. Respondents who had held no jobs prior to transition, who were highly gender ambiguous prior to transition, or who worked in short-term, high-turnover retail jobs, such as food service, found it harder to identify gender differences at work. FTMs who transitioned in their late teens often felt that they did not have enough experience working as women to comment on any possible differences between men and women at work. For example, Sam and Robert felt they could not comment on gender differences in the workplace because they had begun living as men at the age of 15 and, therefore, never had been employed as women. In addition, FTMs who reported being very "in-between" in their gender appearance, such as Wayne and Peter, found it hard to comment on gender differences at work, as even when they were hired as women, they were not always sure how customers and coworkers perceived them. They felt unable to speak about the experience of working as a woman because they were perceived either as androgynous or as men.

The kinds of occupations FTMs held prior to transition also play a role in whether they develop this outsider-within perspective at work. Transmen working in blue-collar jobs—jobs that are predominantly staffed by men—felt their experiences working in these jobs as females varied greatly from their experiences working as men. This held true even for those transmen who worked as females in blue-collar jobs in their early teens, showing that age of transition does not always determine the ability to see gender discrimination at work. FTMs working in the "women's professions" also saw a great shift in their treatment once they began working as men. FTMs who transitioned in their late teens and worked in marginal "teenage" jobs, such as fast food, however, often reported little sense of change posttransition, as they felt that most employees were doing the same jobs regardless of gender. As a gendered division of labor often

does exist in fast food jobs (Leidner 1993), it may be that these respondents worked in atypical settings, or that they were assigned "men's jobs" because of their masculine appearance.

Transmen in higher professional jobs, too, reported less change in their experiences posttransition, as many of them felt that their workplaces guarded against gender-biased treatment as part of an ethic of professionalism. The experience of these professional respondents obviously runs counter to the large body of scholarly research that documents gender inequality in fields such as academia (Valian 1999), law firms (Pierce 1995), and corporations (Martin 1992). Not having an outsider-within perspective, then, may be unique to these particular transmen, not the result of working in a professional occupation.

Thus, transitioning from female to male can provide individuals with an outsider-within perspective on gender discrimination in the workplace. However, this perspective can be limited by the age of transition, appearance, and type of occupation. In addition, as I will discuss at the end of this article, even when the advantages of the patriarchal dividend are seen clearly, many transmen do not benefit from them. In the next section, I will explore in what ways FTMs who expressed having this outsider-within perspective saw their skills and abilities perceived more positively as men. Then, I will explore why not all of my respondents received a gender advantage from transitioning.

Transition and Workplace Gender Advantages[4]

A large body of evidence shows that the performance of workers is evaluated differently depending on gender. Men, particularly white men, are viewed as more competent than women workers (Olian, Schwab, and Haberfeld 1988; Valian 1999). When men succeed, their success is seen as stemming from their abilities while women's success often is attributed to luck (Valian 1999). Men are rewarded more than women for offering ideas and opinions and for taking on leadership roles in group settings (Butler and Geis 1990; Valian 1999). Based on these findings, it would be expected that stealth transmen would see a positive difference in their workplace experience once they have made the transition from female to male, as they enter new jobs as just one of the guys. Open FTMs, on the other hand, might find themselves denied access to these privileges, as they remain in the same jobs in which they were hired as women. Challenging these expectations, two-thirds of my respondents, both open and stealth, reported receiving some type of posttransition advantage at work. These advantages fell into four main categories: gaining competency and authority, gaining respect and recognition for hard work, gaining "body privilege," and gaining economic opportunities and status.

Authority and Competency

Illustrating the authority gap that exists between men and women workers (Elliott and Smith 2004; Padavic and Reskin 2002), several of my interviewees reported receiving more respect for their thoughts and opinions posttransition. For example, Henry, who is stealth in a professional workplace, says of his experiences, "I'm right a lot more now. . . . Even with folks I am out to [as a transsexual], there is a sense that I know what I am talking about." Roger, who openly transitioned in a retail environment in the 1980s, discussed customers' assumptions that as a man, he knew more than his boss, who was a woman: "People would come in and they would go straight to me. They would pass her and go straight to me because obviously, as a male, I knew [sarcasm]. And so we would play mind games with them. . . . They would come up and ask me a question, and then I would go over to her and ask her the same question, she would tell me the answer, and I would go back to the customer and tell the customer the answer." Revealing how entrenched these stereotypes about masculinity and authority are, Roger added that none of the customers ever recognized the sarcasm behind his actions. Demonstrating how white men's opinions are seen to carry more authority, Trevor discusses how, posttransition, his ideas are now taken more seriously in group situations—often to the

detriment of his women coworkers: "In a professional workshop or a conference kind of setting, a woman would make a comment or an observation and be overlooked and be dissed essentially. I would raise my hand and make the same point in a way that I am trying to reinforce her and it would be like [directed at me], 'That's an excellent point!' I saw this shit in undergrad. So it is not like this was a surprise to me. But it was disconcerting to have happen to me." These last two quotes exemplify the outsider-within experience. Both men are aware of having more authority simply because of being men, an authority that happens at the expense of women coworkers.

Looking at the issue of authority in the women's professions, Paul, who openly transitioned in the field of secondary education, reports a sense of having increased authority as one of the few men in his work environment:

> I did notice [at] some of the meetings I'm required to attend, like school district or parent involvement [meetings], you have lots of women there. And now I feel like there are [many times], mysteriously enough, when I'm picked [to speak] . . . I think, well, why me, when nobody else has to go to the microphone and talk about their stuff? That I did notice and that [had] never happened before. I mean there was this meeting . . . a little while ago about domestic violence where I appeared to be the only male person between these 30, 40 women and, of course, then everybody wants to hear from me.

Rather than being alienated by his gender tokenism, as women often are in predominantly male workplaces (Byrd 1999), he is asked to express his opinions and is valued for being the "male" voice at the meetings, a common situation for men in "women's professions" (Williams 1995). The lack of interest paid to him as a woman in the same job demonstrates how women in predominantly female workspaces can encourage their coworkers who are men to take more authority and space in these careers, a situation that can lead to the promotion of men in women's professions (Williams 1995).

Transmen also report a positive change in the evaluation of their abilities and competencies after transition. Thomas, an attorney, relates an episode in which an attorney who worked for an associated law firm commended his boss for firing Susan, here a pseudonym for his female name, because she was incompetent—adding that the "new guy" [i.e., Thomas] was "just delightful." The attorney did not realize that Susan and "the new guy" were the same person with the same abilities, education, and experience. This anecdote is a glaring example of how men are evaluated as more competent than women even when they do the same job in careers that are stereotyped requiring "masculine" skills such as rationality (Pierce 1995; Valian 1999). Stephen, who is stealth in a predominantly male customer-service job, reports, "For some reason just because [the men I work with] assume I have a dick, [they assume] I am going to get the job done right, where, you know, they have to second guess that when you're a woman. They look at [women] like well, you can't handle this because you know, you don't have the same mentality that we [men] do, so there's this sense of panic . . . and if you are a guy, it's just like, oh, you can handle it." Keith, who openly transitioned in a male-dominated blue-collar job, reports no longer having to "cuddle after sex," meaning that he has been able to drop the emotional labor of niceness women often have to employ when giving orders at work. Showing how perceptions of behavior can change with transition, Trevor reports, "I think my ideas are taken more seriously [as a man]. I had good leadership skills leaving college and um . . . I think that those work well for me now. . . . Because I'm male, they work better for me. I was 'assertive' before. Now I'm 'take charge.'" Again, while his behavior has not changed, his shift in gender attribution translates into a different kind of evaluation. As a man, being assertive is consistent with gendered expectations for men, meaning his same leadership skills have more worth in the workplace because of his transition. His experience underscores how women who take on leadership roles are evaluated negatively, particularly if their leadership style is perceived as assertive, while men are rewarded for being aggressive leaders (Butler and Geis 1990; Valian 1999).[5]

This change in authority is noticeable only because FTMs often have experienced the reverse: being thought, on the basis of gender alone, to be less competent workers who receive less authority from employers and coworkers. This sense of a shift in authority and perceived competence was particularly marked for FTMs who had worked in blue-collar occupations as women. These transmen report that the stereotype of women's incompetence often translated into difficulty in finding and maintaining employment. For example, Crispin, who had worked as a female construction worker, reports being written up by supervisors for every small infraction, a practice Yoder and Aniakudo (1997, 330) refer to as "pencil whipping." Crispin recounts, "One time I had a field supervisor confront me about simple things, like not dotting i's and using the wrong color ink. . . . Anything he could do, he was just constantly on me. . . . I ended up just leaving." Paul, who was a female truck driver, recounts, "Like they would tell [me], 'Well we never had a female driver. I don't know if this works out.' Blatantly telling you this. And then [I had] to go, 'Well let's see. Let's give it a chance, give it a try. I'll do this three days for free and you see and if it's not working out, well then that's fine and if it works out, maybe you want to reconsider [not hiring me].'" To prove her competency, she ended up working for free, hoping that she would eventually be hired.

Stephen, who was a female forklift operator, described the resistance women operators faced from men when it came to safety precautions for loading pallets:

[The men] would spot each other, which meant that they would have two guys that would close down the aisle . . . so that no one could go on that aisle while you know you were up there [with your forklift and load] . . . and they wouldn't spot you if you were a female. If you were a guy . . . they got the red vests and the safety cones out and it's like you know—the only thing they didn't have were those little flashlights for the jets. It would be like God or somebody responding. I would actually have to go around and gather all the dykes from receiving to come out and help and spot me. And I can't tell you how many times I nearly ran over a kid. It was maddening and it was always because [of] gender.

Thus, respondents described situations of being ignored, passed over, purposefully put in harm's way, and assumed to be incompetent when they were working as women. However, these same individuals, as men, find themselves with more authority and with their ideas, abilities, and attributes evaluated more positively in the workforce.

Respect and Recognition

Related to authority and competency is the issue of how much reward workers get for their workplace contributions. According to the transmen I interviewed, an increase in recognition for hard work was one of the positive changes associated with working as a man. Looking at these stories of gaining reward and respect, Preston, who transitioned openly and remained at his blue-collar job, reports that as a female crew supervisor, she was frequently short staffed and unable to access necessary resources yet expected to still carry out the job competently. However, after his transition, he suddenly found himself receiving all the support and materials he required:

I was not asked to do anything different [after transition]. But the work I did do was made easier for me. [Before transition] there [were] periods of time when I would be told, "Well, I don't have anyone to send over there with you." We were one or two people short of a crew or the trucks weren't available. Or they would send me people who weren't trained. And it got to the point where it was like, why do I have to fight about this? If you don't want your freight, you don't get your freight. And, I swear it was like from one day to the next of me transitioning [to male], I need this, this is what I want and [snaps his fingers]. I have not had to fight about anything.

He adds about his experience, "The last three [performance] reviews that I have had have been the absolute highest that I have ever had. New management team. Me not doing anything different than I ever had. I even went part-time." This comment shows that even though he openly transitioned and remained in the same job, he ultimately finds himself rewarded for doing less work and having to fight less for getting what he needs to effectively do his job. In addition, as a man, he received more positive reviews for his work, demonstrating how men and women can be evaluated differently when doing the same work.

As with authority and competence, this sense of gaining recognition for hard work was particularly noticeable for transmen who had worked as women in blue-collar occupations in which they were the gender minority. This finding is not unexpected, as women are also more likely to be judged negatively when they are in the minority in the workplace, as their statistical minority status seems to suggest that women are unsuited for the job (Valian 1999). For example, Preston, who had spent time in the ROTC as a female cadet, reported feeling that no matter how hard she worked, her achievements were passed over by her men superiors: "On everything that I did, I was the highest. I was the highest-ranking female during the time I was there. . . . I was the most decorated person in ROTC. I had more ribbons, I had more medals, in ROTC and in school. I didn't get anything for that. There was an award every year called Superior Cadet, and guys got it during the time I was there who didn't do nearly what I did. It was those kinds of things [that got to me]." She entered a blue-collar occupation after ROTC and also felt that her workplace contributions, like designing training programs for the staff, were invisible and went unrewarded.

Talking about gender discrimination he faced as a female construction worker, Crispin reports,

I worked really hard. . . . I had to find myself not sitting ever and taking breaks or lunches because I felt like I had to work more to show my worth. And though I did do that and I produced typically more than three males put together—and that is really a statistic—what it would come down to a lot of times was, "You're single. You don't have a family."

That is what they told me. "I've got guys here who have families." . . . And even though my production quality [was high], and the customer was extremely happy with my work . . . I was passed over lots of times. They said it was because I was single and I didn't have a family and they felt bad because they didn't want Joe Blow to lose his job because he had three kids at home. And because I was intelligent and my qualities were very vast, they said, "You can just go get a job anywhere." Which wasn't always the case. A lot of people were—it was still a boy's world and some people were just like, uh-uh, there aren't going to be any women on my job site. And it would be months . . . before I would find gainful employment again.

While she reports eventually winning over many men who did not want women on the worksite, being female excluded her from workplace social interactions, such as camping trips, designed to strengthen male bonding.

These quotes illustrate the hardships that women working in blue-collar jobs often face at work: being passed over for hiring and promotions in favor of less productive male coworkers, having their hard work go unrecognized, and not being completely accepted.[6] Having this experience of being women in an occupation or industry composed mostly of men can create, then, a heightened appreciation of gaining reward and recognition for job performance as men.

Another form of reward that some transmen report receiving posttransition is a type of bodily respect in the form of being freed from unwanted sexual advances or inquiries about sexuality. As Brian recounts about his experience of working as a waitress, that customer service involved "having my boobs grabbed, being called 'honey' and 'babe.'" He noted that as a man, he no longer has to worry about these types of experiences. Jason reported being constantly harassed by men bosses for sexual favors in the past. He added, "When I transitioned it was like a relief! [laughs] . . . I swear to God! I am not saying I was beautiful or sexy but I was always attracting something." He felt that becoming a man meant more personal space and less

sexual harassment. Finally, Stephen and Henry reported being "obvious dykes," here meaning visibly masculine women, and added that in blue-collar jobs, they encountered sexualized comments, as well as invasive personal questions about sexuality, from men uncomfortable with their gender presentation, experiences they no longer face posttransition. Transitioning for stealth FTMs can bring with it physical autonomy and respect, as men workers, in general, encounter less touching, groping, and sexualized comments at work than women. Open FTMs, however, are not as able to access this type of privilege, as coworkers often ask invasive questions about their genitals and sexual practices.

Economic Gains

As the last two sections have shown, FTMs can find themselves gaining in authority, respect, and reward in the workplace posttransition. Several FTMs who are stealth also reported a sense that transition had brought with it economic opportunities that would not have been available to them as women, particularly as masculine women.

Carl, who owns his own company, asserts that he could not have followed the same career trajectory if he had not transitioned:

I have this company that I built, and I have people following me; they trust me, they believe in me, they respect me. There is no way I could have done that as a woman. And I will tell you that as just a fact. That when it comes to business and work, higher levels of management, it is different being a man. I have been on both sides [as a man and a woman], younger obviously, but I will tell you, man, I could have never done what I did [as a female]. You can take the same personality and it wouldn't have happened. I would have never made it.

While he acknowledges that women can be and are business entrepreneurs, he has a sense that his business partners would not have taken his business venture idea seriously if he were a woman or that he might not have had access to the type of social networks that made his business venture possible. Henry feels that he would not have reached the same level in his professional job if he were a woman because he had a nonnormative gender appearance:

> If I was a gender normative woman, probably. But no, as an obvious dyke, I don't think so . . . which is weird to say but I think it's true. It is interesting because I am really aware of having this job that I would not have had if I hadn't transitioned. And [gender expression] was always an issue for me. I wanted to go to law school but I couldn't do it. I couldn't wear the skirts and things females have to wear to practice law. I wouldn't dress in that drag. And so it was very clear that there was a limit to where I was going to go professionally because I was not willing to dress that part. Now I can dress the part and it's not an issue. It's not putting on drag; it's not an issue. I don't love putting on a tie, but I can do it. So this world is open to me that would not have been before just because of clothes. But very little has changed in some ways. I look very different but I still have all the same skills and all the same general thought processes. That is intense for me to consider.

As this response shows, Henry is aware that as an "obvious dyke," meaning here a masculine-appearing woman, he would have the same skills and education level he currently has, but those skills would be devalued due to his nonnormative appearance. Thus, he avoided professional careers that would require a traditionally feminine appearance. As a man, however, he is able to wear clothes similar to those he wore as an "obvious dyke," but they are now considered gender appropriate. Thus, through transitioning, he gains the right to wear men's clothes, which helps him in accessing a professional job.

Wayne also recounts negative workplace experiences in the years prior to his transition due to being extremely ambiguous or "gender blending" (Devor 1987) in his appearance. Working at a restaurant in his early teens, he had the following experience:

> The woman who hired me said, "I will hire you only on the condition that you don't ever come in the front because you make the people uncomfortable." 'Cause we had to wear like these uniforms or something and when I would put the uniform on, she would say, "That makes you look like a guy." But she knew I was not a guy because of my name that she had on the application. She said, "You make the customers uncomfortable." And a couple of times it got really busy, and I would have to come in the front or whatever, and I remember one time she found out about it and she said, "I don't care how busy it gets, you don't get to come up front." She said I'd make people lose their appetite.

Once he began hormones and gained a social identity as a man, he found that his work and school experiences became much more positive. He went on to earn a doctoral degree and become a successful professional, an economic opportunity he did not think would be available had he remained highly gender ambiguous.

In my sample, the transmen who openly transitioned faced a different situation in terms of economic gains. While there is an "urban legend" that FTMs immediately are awarded some kind of "male privilege" posttransition (Dozier 2005), I did not find that in my interviews. Reflecting this common belief, however, Trevor and Jake both recount that women colleagues told them, when learning of their transition plans, that they would probably be promoted because they were becoming white men. While both men discounted these comments, both were promoted relatively soon after their transitions. Rather than seeing this as evidence of male privilege, both respondents felt that their promotions were related to their job performance, which, to make clear, is not a point I am questioning. Yet these promotions show that while these two men are not benefiting undeservedly from transition, they also are not disadvantaged.[7] Thus, among the men I interviewed, it is common for both stealth and open FTMs to find their abilities and skills more valued posttransition, showing that human capital can be valued differently depending on the gender of the employee.

Is It Privilege or Something Else?

While these reported increases in competency and authority make visible the "gender schemas" (Valian 1999) that often underlie the evaluation of workers, it is possible that the increases in authority might have a spurious connection to gender transitions. Some transmen enter a different work field after transition, so the observed change might be in the type of occupation they enter rather than a gender-based change. In addition, many transmen seek graduate or postgraduate degrees posttransition, and higher education degrees afford more authority in the workplace. As Table 13.2 shows, of the transmen I interviewed, many had higher degrees working as men than they did when they worked as women. For some, this is due to transitioning while in college and thus attaining their bachelor's degrees as men. For others, gender transitions seem to be accompanied by a desire to return to school for a higher degree, as evidenced by the increase in master's degrees in the table.

A change in educational attainment does contribute to getting better jobs with increased authority, as men benefit more from increased human capital in the form of educational attainment (Valian 1999). But again, this is an additive effect, as higher education results in greater advantages for men than for women. In addition, gender advantage alone also is apparent in these experiences of increased authority, as transmen report seeing an increase in others' perceptions of their competency outside of the workplace where their education level is unknown. For example, Henry, who found he was "right a lot more" at work, also notes that in daily, nonworkplace interactions, he is assumed, as a man, to know what he is talking about and does not have to provide evidence to support his opinions. Demonstrating a similar experience, Crispin, who had many years of experience working in construction as a woman, relates the following story:

> I used to jump into [situations as a woman]. Like at Home Depot, I would hear . . . [men] be so confused, and I would just step over there and say, "Sir, I work in construction and if you don't mind me helping you." And they would be like, "Yeah, yeah, yeah" [i.e., dismissive]. But now I go [as a man] and I've got men and women asking me things and saying, "Thank you so much," like now I have a brain in my head! And I like that a lot because it was just kind of like, "Yeah, whatever." It's really nice.

His experience at Home Depot shows that as a man, he is rewarded for displaying the same knowledge about construction—knowledge gendered as masculine—that he was sanctioned for offering when he was perceived as a woman. As a further example of this increased authority outside of the workplace, several FTMs report a difference in their treatment at the auto shop, as they are not assumed

Table 13.2 Highest Level of Education Attained

Highest Degree Level	Stealth FTMs		Open FTMs	
	As Female	As Male	As Female	As Male
High school/GED	7	2	3	2
Associate's degree	2	3	3	3
Bachelor's degree	2	4	7	4
Master's degree	0	1	2	4
Ph.D.	0	1	1	2
J.D.	0	0	1	2
Other	0	0	1	1
Total	11	11	18	18

Note: FTMs = female-to-male.

to be easy targets for unnecessary services (though this comes with an added expectation that they will know a great deal about cars). While some transmen report that their "feminine knowledge," such as how to size baby clothes in stores, is discounted when they gain social identities as men, this new recognition of "masculine knowledge" seems to command more social authority than prior feminine knowledge in many cases. These stories show that some transmen gain authority both in and out of the workplace. These findings lend credence to the argument that men can gain a gender advantage, in the form of authority, reward, and respect.

Barriers to Workplace Gender Advantages

Having examined the accounts of transmen who feel that they received increased authority, reward, and recognition from becoming men at work, I will now discuss some of the limitations to accessing workplace gender advantages. About one-third of my sample felt that they did not receive any gender advantage from transition. FTMs who had only recently begun transition or who had transitioned without using hormones ("no ho") all reported seeing little change in their workplace treatment. This group of respondents felt that they were still seen as women by most of their coworkers, evidenced by continual slippage into feminine pronouns, and thus were not treated in accordance with other men in the workplace. Other transmen in this group felt they lacked authority because they were young or looked extremely young after transition. This youthful appearance often is an effect of the beginning stages of transition. FTMs usually begin to pass as men before they start taking testosterone. Successful passing is done via appearance cues, such as hairstyles, clothes, and mannerisms. However, without facial hair or visible stubble, FTMs often are taken to be young boys, a mistake that intensifies with the onset of hormone therapy and the development of peach fuzz that marks the beginning of facial hair growth. Reflecting on how this youthful appearance, which can last several years depending on the effects of hormone therapy, affected his work

experience immediately after transition, Thomas reports, "I went from looking 30 to looking 13. People thought I was a new lawyer so I would get treated like I didn't know what was going on." Other FTMs recount being asked if they were interns, or if they were visiting a parent at their workplace, all comments that underscore a lack of authority. This lack of authority associated with looking youthful, however, is a time-bounded effect, as most FTMs on hormones eventually "age into" their male appearance, suggesting that many of these transmen may have the ability to access some gender advantages at some point in their careers.

Body structure was another characteristic some FTMs felt limited their access to increased authority and prestige at work. While testosterone creates an appearance indistinguishable from bio men for many transmen, it does not increase height. Being more than 6 feet tall is part of the cultural construction for successful, hegemonic masculinity. However, several men I interviewed were between 5′1″ and 5′5″, something they felt put them at a disadvantage in relation to other men in their workplaces. Winston, who managed a professional work staff who knew him only as a man, felt that his authority was harder to establish at work because he was short. Being smaller than all of his male employees meant that he was always being looked down on, even when giving orders. Kelly, who worked in special education, felt his height affected the jobs he was assigned: "Some of the boys, especially if they are really aggressive, they do much better with males that are bigger than they are. So I work with the little kids because I am short. I don't get as good of results if I work with [older kids]; a lot of times they are taller than I am." Being a short man, he felt it was harder to establish authority with older boys. These experiences demonstrate the importance of bringing the body back into discussions of masculinity and gender advantage, as being short can constrain men's benefits from the "patriarchal dividend" (Connell 1995).

In addition to height, race/ethnicity can negatively affect FTMs' workplace experience posttransition. My data suggest that the experiences of

FTMs of color is markedly different than that of their white counterparts, as they are becoming not just men but Black men, Latino men, or Asian men, categories that carry their own stereotypes. Christopher felt that he was denied any gender advantage at work not only because he was shorter than all of his men colleagues but also because he was viewed as passive, a stereotype of Asian men (Espiritu 1997). "To the wide world of America, I look like a passive Asian guy. That is what they think when they see me. Oh Asian? Oh passive. . . . People have this impression that Asian guys aren't macho and therefore they aren't really male. Or they are not as male as [a white guy]." Keith articulated how his social interactions changed with his change in gender attribution in this way: "I went from being an obnoxious Black woman to a scary Black man." He felt that he has to be careful expressing anger and frustration at work (and outside of work) because now that he is a Black man, his anger is viewed as more threatening by whites. Reflecting stereotypes that conflate African Americans with criminals, he also notes that in his law enforcement classes, he was continually asked to play the suspect in training exercises. Aaron, one of the only racial minorities at his workplace, also felt that looking like a Black man negatively affected his workplace interactions. He told stories about supervisors repeatedly telling him he was threatening. When he expressed frustration during a staff meeting about a new policy, he was written up for rolling his eyes in an "aggressive" manner. The choice of words such as "threatening" and "aggressive," words often used to describe Black men (Ferguson 2000), suggests that racial identity and stereotypes about Black men were playing a role in his workplace treatment. Examining how race/ethnicity and appearance intersect with gender, then, illustrates that masculinity is not a fixed construct that automatically generated privilege (Connell 1995), but that white, tall men often see greater returns from the patriarchal dividend than short men, young men, and men of color.

Conclusion

Sociological studies have documented that the workplace is not a gender-neutral site that equitably rewards workers based on their individual merits (Acker 1990; Martin 2003; Valian 1999; Williams 1995); rather "it is a central site for the creation and reproduction of gender differences and gender inequality" (Williams 1995, 15). Men receive greater workplace advantages than women because of cultural beliefs that associate masculinity with authority, prestige, and instrumentality (Martin 2003; Padavic and Reskin 2002; Rhode 1997; Williams 1995)—characteristics often used to describe ideal "leaders" and "managers" (Valian 1999). Stereotypes about femininity as expressive and emotional, on the other hand, disadvantage women, as they are assumed to be less capable and less likely to succeed than men with equal (or often lesser) qualifications (Valian 1999). These cultural beliefs about gender difference are embedded in workplace structures and interactions, as workers and employers bring gender stereotypes with them to the workplace and, in turn, use these stereotypes to make decisions about hiring, promotions, and rewards (Acker 1990; Martin 2003; Williams 1995). This cultural reproduction of gendered workplace disparities is difficult to disrupt, however, as it operates on the level of ideology and thus is rendered invisible (Martin 2003; Valian 1999; Williams 1995).

In this article, I have suggested that the "outsider-within" (Collins 1986) perspective of many FTMs can offer a more complex understanding of these invisible interactional processes that help maintain gendered workplace disparities. Transmen are in the unique position of having been socially gendered as both women and men (Dozier 2005). Their workplace experiences, then, can make the underpinnings of gender discrimination visible, as well as illuminate the sources of men's workplace advantages. When FTMs undergo a change in gender attribution, their workplace treatment often varies greatly—even when they continue to interact with coworkers who knew them previously as women. Some posttransition FTMs, both stealth and open, find that their coworkers, employers, and customers attribute more authority, respect, and prestige to them. Their experiences make glaringly visible the process through which gender inequality is actively created in informal workplace interactions. These informal workplace interactions, in turn, produce and reproduce structural disadvantages for women, such as the glass ceiling (Valian 1999), and structural advantages for men, such as the glass escalator (Williams 1995).

However, as I have suggested, not all of my respondents gain authority and prestige with transition. FTMs who are white and tall received far more benefits posttransition than short FTMs or FTMs of color. This demonstrates that while hegemonic masculinity is defined against femininity, it is also measured against subordinated forms of masculinity (Connell 1995; Messner 1997). These findings demonstrate the need for using an intersectional approach that takes into consideration the ways in which there are cross-cutting relations of power (Calasanti and Slevin 2001; Collins 1990; Crenshaw 1989), as advantage in the workplace is not equally accessible for all men. Further research on FTMs of color can help develop a clearer understanding of the role race plays in the distribution of gendered workplace rewards and advantages.[8]

The experiences of this small group of transmen offer a challenge to rationalizations of workplace inequality. The study provides counterevidence for human capital theories: FTMs who find themselves receiving the benefits associated with being men at work have the same skills and abilities they had as women workers. These skills and abilities, however, are suddenly viewed more positively due to this change in gender attribution. FTMs who may have been labeled "bossy" as women become "go-getting" men who seem more qualified for managerial positions. While FTMs may not benefit at equal levels to bio men, many of them do find themselves receiving an advantage to women in the workplace they did not have prior to transition. This study also challenges gender socialization theories that account for inequality in the workplace. Although all of my respondents were subjected to gender socialization as girls, this background did not impede their success as men. Instead, by undergoing a change in gender attribution, transmen can find that the same behavior, attitudes, or abilities they had as females bring

them more reward as men. This shift in treatment suggests that gender inequality in the workplace is not continually reproduced only because women make different education and workplace choices than men but rather because coworkers and employers often rely on gender stereotypes to evaluate men and women's achievements and skills.

It could be argued that because FTMs must overcome so many barriers and obstacles to finally gain a male social identity, they might be likely to overreport positive experiences as a way to shore up their right to be a man. However, I have reasons to doubt that my respondents exaggerated the benefits of being men. Transmen who did find themselves receiving a workplace advantage posttransition were aware that this new conceptualization of their skills and abilities was an arbitrary result of a shift in their gender attribution. This knowledge often undermined their sense of themselves as good workers, making them continually second-guess the motivations behind any rewards they receive. In addition, many transmen I interviewed expressed anger and resentment that their increases in authority, respect, and recognition came at the expense of women colleagues. It is important to keep in mind, then, that while many FTMs can identify privileges associated with being men, they often retain a critical eye to how changes in their treatment as men can disadvantage women.

This critical eye, or "outsider-within" (Collins 1986) perspective, has implications for social change in the workplace. For gender equity at work to be achieved, men must take an active role in challenging the subordination of women (Acker 1990; Martin 2003; Rhode 1997; Valian 1999; Williams 1995). However, bio men often cannot see how women are disadvantaged due to their structural privilege (Rhode 1997; Valian 1999). Even when they are aware that men as a group benefit from assumptions about masculinity, men typically still "credit their successes to their competence" (Valian 1999, 284) rather than to gender stereotypes. For many transmen, seeing how they stand to benefit at work to the detriment of women workers creates a sense of increased responsibility to challenge the gender discrimination they can see so clearly. This challenge can take many different forms. For some, it is speaking out when men make derogatory comments about women. For others, it means speaking out about gender discrimination at work or challenging supervisors to promote women who are equally qualified as men. These challenges demonstrate that some transmen are able, at times, to translate their position as social insiders into an educational role, thus working to give women more reward and recognition at these specific work sites. The success of these strategies illustrates that men have the power to challenge workplace gender discrimination and suggests that bio men can learn gender equity strategies from the outsider-within at work.

Notes

1. Throughout this article, I endeavor to use the terms "women" and "men" rather than "male" and "female" to avoid reifying biological categories. It is important to note, though, that while my respondents were all born with female bodies, many of them never identified as women but rather thought of themselves as always men, or as "not women." During their time as female workers, however, they did have social identities as women, as coworkers and employers often were unaware of their personal gender identities. It is this social identity that I am referencing when I refer to them as "working as women," as I am discussing their social interactions in the workplace. In referring to their specific work experiences, however, I use "female" to demonstrate their understanding of their work history. I also do continue to use "female to male" when describing the physical transition process, as this is the most common term employed in the transgender community.

2. I use "stealth," a transgender community term, if the respondent's previous life as female was not known at work. It is important to note that this term is not analogous with "being in the closet," because stealth female-to-male transsexuals (FTMs) do not have "secret" lives as women outside of working as men. It is used to describe two different workplace

choices, not offer a value judgment about these choices.

3. "Bio" man is a term used by my respondents to mean individuals who are biologically male and live socially as men throughout their lives. It is juxtaposed with "transman" or "FTM."

4. A note on pronoun usage: This article draws from my respondents' experiences working as both women and men. While they now live as men, I use feminine pronouns to refer to their female work histories.

5. This change in how behavior is evaluated can also be negative. Some transmen felt that assertive communication styles they actively fostered to empower themselves as lesbians and feminists had to be unlearned after transition. Because they were suddenly given more space to speak as men, they felt they had to censor themselves or they would be seen as "bossy white men" who talked over women and people of color. These findings are similar to those reported by Dozier (2005).

6. It is important to note that not all FTMs who worked blue-collar jobs as women had this type of experience. One respondent felt that he was able to fit in, as a butch, as "just one of the guys." However, he also did not feel he had an outsider-within perspective because of this experience.

7. Open transitions are not without problems, however. Crispin, a construction worker, found his contract mysteriously not renewed after his announcement. However, he acknowledged that he had many problems with his employers prior to his announcement and had also recently filed a discrimination suit. Aaron, who announced his transition at a small, medical site, left after a few months as he felt that his employer was trying to force him out. He found another job in which he was out as a transman. Crispin unsuccessfully attempted to find work in construction as an out transman. He was later hired, stealth, at a construction job.

8. Sexual identity also is an important aspect of an intersectional analysis. In my study, however, queer and gay transmen worked either in lesbian, gay, bisexual, transgender

work sites, or were not out at work. Therefore, it was not possible to examine how being gay or queer affected their workplace experiences.

References

Acker, Joan. 1990. Hierarchies, jobs, bodies: A theory of gendered organizations. *Gender & Society* 4: 139–58.

Butler, D., and F. L. Geis. 1990. Nonverbal affect responses to male and female leaders: Implications for leadership evaluation. *Journal of Personality and Social Psychology* 58: 48–59.

Byrd, Barbara. 1999. Women in carpentry apprenticeship: A case study. *Labor Studies Journal* 24 (3): 3–22.

Calasanti, Toni M., and Kathleen F. Slevin. 2001. *Gender, social inequalities, and aging*. Walnut Creek, CA: Alta Mira Press.

Collins, Patricia Hill. 1986. Learning from the outsider within: The sociological significance of Black feminist thought. *Social Problems* 33 (6): S14–S31.

———. 1990. *Black feminist thought*. New York: Routledge.

Connell, Robert. 1995. *Masculinities*. Berkeley: University of California Press.

Crenshaw, Kimberle. 1989. Demarginalizing the intersection of race and sex: A Black feminist critique of antidiscrimination doctrine, feminist theory, and antiracist politics. *University of Chicago Legal Forum* 1989: 139–67.

Devor, Holly. 1987. Gender blending females: Women and sometimes men. *American Behavioral Scientist* 31 (1): 12–40.

Dozier, Raine. 2005. Beards, breasts, and bodies: Doing sex in a gendered world. *Gender & Society* 19: 297–316.

Elliott, James R., and Ryan A. Smith. 2004. Race, gender, and workplace power. *American Sociological Review* 69: 365–86.

Espiritu, Yen. 1997. *Asian American women and men*. Thousand Oaks, CA: Sage.

Ferguson, Ann Arnett. 2000. *Bad boys: Public schools in the making of Black masculinity*. Ann Arbor: University of Michigan Press.

Leidner, Robin. 1993. *Fast food, fast talk: Service work and the routinization of everyday life*. Berkeley: University of California Press.

Martin, Patricia Yancy. 1992. Gender, interaction, and inequality in organizations. In *Gender, interaction, and inequality*, edited by Cecelia L. Ridgeway. New York: Springer-Verlag.

———. 2003 "Said and done" versus "saying and doing": Gendering practices, practicing gender at work. *Gender & Society* 17: 342–66.

Martin, Susan. 1994. "Outsiders-within" the station house: The impact of race and gender on Black women police officers. *Social Problems* 41: 383–400.

Merton, Robert. 1972. Insiders and outsiders: A chapter in the sociology of knowledge. *American Journal of Sociology* 78 (1): 9–47.

Messner, Michael. 1997. *The politics of masculinities: Men in movements*. Thousand Oaks, CA: Sage.

Miller, Laura. 1997. Not just weapons of the weak: Gender harassment as a form of protest for army men. *Social Psychology Quarterly* 60 (1): 32–51.

Olian, J. D., D. P. Schwab, and Y. Haberfeld. 1988. The impact of applicant gender compared to qualifications on hiring recommendations: A meta-analysis of experimental studies. *Organizational Behavior and Human Decision Processes* 41: 180–95.

Padavic, Irene, and Barbara Reskin. 2002. *Women and men at work*. 2nd ed. Thousand Oaks, CA: Pine Forge Press.

Pierce, Jennifer. 1995. *Gender trials: Emotional lives in contemporary law firms*. Berkeley: University of California Press.

Reskin, Barbara, and Heidi Hartmann. 1986. *Women's work, men's work: Sex segregation on the job*. Washington, DC: National Academic Press.

Reskin, Barbara, and Patricia Roos. 1990. *Job queues, gender queues*. Philadelphia: Temple University Press.

Rhode, Deborah L. 1997. *Speaking of sex: The denial of gender inequality*. Cambridge, MA: Harvard University Press.

Rubin, Henry. 2003. *Self-made men: Identity and embodiment among transsexual men*. Nashville, TN: Vanderbilt University Press.

Valian, Virginia. 1999. *Why so slow? The advancement of women*. Cambridge, MA: MIT Press.

West, Candace, and Don Zimmerman. 1987. Doing gender. *Gender & Society* 1: 13–37.

Williams, Christine. 1995. *Still a man s world: Men who do "women's" work*. Berkeley: University of California Press.

Yoder, Janice, and Patricia Aniakudo. 1997. Outsider within the firehouse: Subordination and difference in the social interactions of African American women firefighters. *Gender & Society* 11: 324–41.

"Men Wanted"

Heterosexual Aesthetic Labor in the Masculinization of the Hair Salon

KRISTEN BARBER

The emerging literature on aesthetic labor foregrounds the role retail workers' appearances play in successful corporate branding and in the sale of products and services. This is particularly true for frontline service workers who mediate the relationship between customer and product. Corporations hire workers with the "right" aesthetic qualities to support their brand images and this often translates into social inequalities, particularly in high-end retail that privileges white, middle-class, conventionally gendered workers. Retail brands also create sexualized—and often subordinating—marketing strategies that shape employment experiences (Hochschild 1983; Loe 1996; McBride 2005; Mills 1996, 2006). Sexuality, however, remains an undertheorized aspect of aesthetic labor and thus of corporate efforts to create gendered brands and consumer identities. In this article, I ask: How exactly does sexuality shape aesthetic labor?

Turning my attention to two high-service men's salons in Southern California, Adonis and The Executive, I argue that beauty workers suffer the demands of heterosexual aesthetic labor, whereby management mobilizes employees' heterosexual identities and heterogendered appearances to enhance both their corporate brands and their clients' social status.[1] By hiring for, developing, and mobilizing the sexual identities and gender habitus of heterofeminine women, Adonis and The Executive "pull against the grain of the original coding" (Craig and Liberti 2007, 678) of the hair salon to masculinize a historically feminized space and consumer practice. Aesthetic labor scholars conceptualize workers as living breathing mannequins and decorative hardware that reflects customers' identities back to them (Williams and Connell 2010; Witz, Warhurst, and Nickson 2003). This highlights the objectifying effect of aesthetic labor but also glosses over the organizational and interpersonal heterogendering of service relationships through which frontline workers become "identity resources" (Pascoe 2007) for customers' projections of social locations.

While we know how men deploy classed and raced masculinity to make sense of their beauty consumption (Barber 2008, 2015), we know less about how the organization of labor supports these consumer habits. I unpack four main themes of heterosexual aesthetic labor to better understand this link between work, consumption, and gender: (1) the corporate practice of hiring for and developing heterosexual workers, (2) the commercialization of workers' hetero-gendered habitus, (3) workers' professionalizing efforts to reroute resulting identity threats, and (4) workers' denial and gender essentialism as strategies for neutralizing interpersonal effects. I discuss how the masculinizing and high-service culture of Adonis and The Executive create identity dilemmas for women working at these salons at the same time it produces professional-class masculine beauty consumers. Moving beyond the point of recruitment, I show how heterosexual aesthetic labor affects hiring practices as well as worker–client interactions and the sociopsychological meaning-making strategies women deploy to maintain their professional identities and legitimize their work. The resistant potential of these coping strategies, however, is limited by the institutionalized link between heterosexual femininity and the salons' and employees' success. Findings reveal that the symbolic exchanges between management, workers, and customers are important analytic sites for developing theories on aesthetic labor.

Aesthetic Labor in Service Work

In her study of Delta flight attendants, Hochschild (1983) explored the way airlines require their frontline service workers to perform "emotional labor." Emotions, she found, are commercialized so that workers manage their "authentic" feelings of exhaustion, frustration, and anger in order to smile at, defer to, and ultimately to produce happy customers. Since women are supposed natural nurturers and expected to be deferential, emotional labor in service work becomes feminized and linked to the production of gender—as well as race and class—inequalities (Duffy 2007; Ehrenreich and Hochschild 2004; Kang 2003, 2010; MacDonald and Merrill 2008). Hochschild's study drew attention to service work as an important site for understanding worker exploitation in the new economy and has encouraged research on other

undertheorized aspects of service work. Building on the concept of emotional labor as an embodied process and drawing from Bourdieu's (1984) theory of habitus, aesthetic labor scholars have begun investigating corporate requirements for service workers to "look good" and "sound right" (Warhurst and Nickson 2001, 2007; Williams and Connell 2010; Witz, Warhurst, and Nickson 2003). Particular to habitus is the idea that class locations shape people's behaviors, tastes, and dispositions, which are taken for granted as second nature. Aesthetic labor ties workers' commercial value to such socially informed behaviors as bodily comportment, style, and speech and thus produces discriminatory hiring practices (Mears 2014). Williams and Connell (2010) show that high-end retailers like Banana Republic, for example, often hire white middle-class workers to sell goods to white middle-class customers. Corporations rely on a pool of ready-made workers to act as extensions of their brand images. Brands, Pettinger (2010) notes, "are presented back to the customer not merely through logos, the arrangement of the shop, and such like, but also through the bodies of employees." While aesthetic labor moves beyond the emotions of service work, it adds to rather than replaces emotional labor as a means by which customers and corporations are commercially crafted (Cohen et al. 2013). . . .

The Gender and Sexuality of Aesthetic Labor

The aesthetic labor literature focuses on how corporations use race, class, and gender in hiring workers and to sort workers into different jobs. Employees of color might find themselves working in the stockrooms of especially high-end retail outlets while white women cashiers act as the face of stores (Williams 2006). In fashion retail, corporations expect sales associates to model their clothing, therefore capitalizing on existing "cultural forms of feminization" whereby women are rewarded for maintaining normative femininity (Pettinger 2005). While this concept highlights the diversity of femininities, I argue that *gender habitus* more fully captures the socially informed, ingrained, and habitual character of thinking, speaking, and behaving in masculine and feminine ways, making hegemonically gendered workers widely available to support mainstream corporate brands. . . .

Feminist scholars contend that the study of sexuality is integral to understanding structural, organizational, and micro-level processes that support and sometimes challenge the gender order. Heterosexuality, for example, is a key component of hegemonic masculinities, whereby boys and men gain gender privilege through the projection of heterosexual prowess (Connell 1995; Kimmel 1994). And lesbians are culturally masculinized as "dykes" or failed women (Halberstam 1998) who cannot serve as resources for men's projections of hetero-desires. Yet aesthetic labor scholarship has largely overlooked the role sexuality plays in gendering both brands and worker–consumer relationships. . . . "Strategically sexualized" work should be considered in the study of aesthetic labor, since it supports brands and fattens corporate revenues at workers' expense (Warhurst and Nickson 2009, 399). . . .

Managing Sexuality in Service Work

Conceptualizing workers as models, decorative hardware, and mirrors importantly points to their objectification but also portrays workers as passive props rather than dynamic actors who manage interactions with customers, dilemmas at work, and the meaning of their labor. Women already have a more difficult time gaining professional recognition and respect than their male peers, since people are likely to see them as "gendered personas" rather than as disembodied workers (Forseth 2005, 443). Aesthetic labor threatens to compound this difficulty by emphasizing workers' bodies, and heterosexual aesthetic labor especially draws attention to women's sexual identities and appeal. Women service workers thus come up against dilemmas on the shop floor, which "represent[s] a minefield of threats to the dignity and virtue of female workers" (Otis 2008, 360). While the aesthetic labor literature leaves out workers' agency—instead focusing on how corporations shape employees' labor (Guerrier and Abid 2004)—workers

may indeed resist and rearrange social relations on the job. . . . They may use "professionalizing protocols" to distinguish themselves as legitimate workers (Otis 2008), "coyly deflect" sexual attention (Parreñas 2009), and police their clothing to avoid drawing attention to their bodies (Giuffre and Williams 2000). Slippages between feminized service work and sex/sex work motivate workers to emphasize professional identities, to cast the workplace as reputable (Gimlin 1996), and to draw intimacy boundaries between themselves and clients (Sherman 2007). Displaying professionalism therefore includes "keeping one's distance from close relationships with clients," or otherwise avoiding "excess merger" and "over rapport" (Oerton 2004, 104). Some workers are highly invested in containing the effects sexuality has on their work experiences, identities, and status, while others come to accept and enjoy some sexuality in the workplace via a "period of adjustment" (Dellinger and Williams 2002; 247). Either way, organizational cultures enable and constrain workers' abilities to resist and cope with sexuality and to forge powerful, dignified identities. . . .

In the high-service men's salons, Adonis and The Executive, employees do not look like their customers. The mainly female beauty workers do not mirror their male clients' social identities back to them. These women do, however, perform aesthetic labor that supports the organizational heterogendering of the salon brand and consumer experience. By emphasizing the women's agency and the dynamic interactions between management, workers, and clients, I consider the women's roles as *interactive* identity resources and answer the following questions: How do these organizations capitalize on heterosexual aesthetic labor to create a masculinizing and high-end consumer experience for men in a historically feminized space? How does this labor create dilemmas for the women workers? And what coping strategies do the women deploy to manage these dilemmas?

Men's Salons

The hair salon is a historically feminized space in which women gossip, build communities, and shore up their appearances. . . . Since hegemonic masculinity is produced via the repudiation of the feminine (Connell 1995; Kimmel 1994), it seems counterintuitive that men and masculinity might be reproduced in this space. However, while working-class men are unlikely to identify with or feel comfortable in a salon (see Paap 2006), class-privileged men can use salons to produce a high-end gendered aesthetic (Barber 2008, 2015). Dedicated men's salons help these men purchase aesthetic-enhancing and pampering services without fear of feminization. Southern California is replete with luxury hair and nail salons and is on the forefront of the growing men's grooming industry, with high-service salons dedicated to the primping and preening of men's bodies. While California excels in men's grooming, there is also a nationwide expansion in the production and purchase of services, spaces, and products designed for and marketed specifically to men (Euromonitor International 2010, 2015; IBISWorld 2010, 2015). . . .

Adonis and The Executive have clean lines, leather chairs, and charge upwards of $39 for a haircut. This cost allows middle- and upper-middle-class men to regularly patronize the salons while also excluding working-class men who might be unable or unwilling to pay this much for a haircut. Both salons offer manicures and pedicures, hair coloring, and straight razor shaves. Adonis provides massages and facials, is located in a hip beach community, and attracts casually dressed yet trendy clients in their 20s and 30s. . . . The Executive offers men body waxing, is situated in a sprawling suburb with big box stores and office buildings, and attracts many clients in their 50s and 60s. These men generally get a haircut during their lunch breaks or after work; they come to the salon dressed in slacks, button-up shirts, and ties. . . . The salons provide snacks, beer, wine, and "men's" magazines, including *GQ* at Adonis and *Golf* at The Executive. Clients are welcomed by the warm smile of a pretty receptionist and appear comfortable waiting for their appointments and chatting with stylists.

Methods

Data for this article come from a larger research project that explores how women beauty workers are the cornerstones of the men's grooming industry (Barber 2016). I spent nine months studying Adonis and The Executive. As luxury spaces, they are likely less racially diverse than more economical men's salons like Sports Clips. But unlike Sports Clips, they offer an array of grooming services, allowing me to study a male clientele that demonstrates an interest in and ability to afford the careful commercial fashioning of their bodies. To better understand how heterosexual aesthetic labor operates on both an organizational and interpersonal level, I draw from 34 in-depth interviews with workers who greet and groom men, and who manage the overall operations of the salons. These employees include licensed hairstylists, barbers, nail technicians, and estheticians, as well as one massage therapist, four receptionists, and Veronica, owner of The Executive. Tyler, owner of Adonis, was unwilling to be interviewed. Despite having varying technical responsibilities, all of these employees were occupationally required to talk to and care for male clients, and all but the receptionists touched men's bodies. Employees averaged 25 years old at Adonis and 34 years old at The Executive. Reflecting the predominance of women in this line of work,[2] all but three of these employees were women. Four women working at The Executive were hired before I exited the field, and their position as newcomers offered insight into the processes involved in adjusting to the salons' work cultures. . . . Interviews lasted an average of one hour and covered how employees came to work in men's grooming, what they believe the salons offer men, and their relationships with clients and management. I open-coded interview transcripts to identify themes around workers' formal and informal labor. I then analyzed these themes for gender effects while leaving room for sexuality, class, and race to emerge as mitigating structures of the gendered interactions between employees, clients, and management.

Male clients were racially diverse but largely white. While Latino and Asian men frequented both salons, I never saw a Black man purchase services or products. Demographic information I collected from 12 client interviews at The Executive (and another at Adonis) shows that men were generally upper-middle class, with an average income of $152,150, and held jobs in professional occupations such as law and civil engineering. Ten of the men identified as "heterosexual," and the others reported their sexuality as "male," "married," or "I didn't answer the sexual orientation question, but I'm married." The owner of Adonis did not permit me to interview clients (I interviewed one client I knew personally), but my recorded observations suggest they were well-to-do (signaled by their brand name clothing and ability to afford salon services) and often younger than those at The Executive. I conducted interviews with clients both in-person and over the phone to accommodate their busy schedules. Questions centered on how they became clients of Adonis or The Executive, their relationships with the staff, and why they believe men go to the salons. Interviews lasted 20 to 45 minutes and were audio-recorded and transcribed. I sorted data by how the men experienced the services, amenities, and interpersonal relationships at the salons. As men's relationships with workers rose to the forefront of emerging themes, I conceptualized their descriptions as reflections of heterogendered and classed structures, organizations, and identities.

The Organization of Heterosexual Aesthetic Labor

Four themes arose that speak to the way heterosexual aesthetic labor organizes the gender of work, consumption, and corporate branding in men's salons. The first two themes focus on how Adonis and The Executive hire straight, conventionally feminine women, develop these women's appearances, and mobilize them as gendered brand representatives. Themes three and four emphasize how the women perform emotional labor via professionalizing and gender essentialism to manage

resulting identity dilemmas at work. I unpack these themes in turn and highlight when emotional labor and aesthetic labor operate independently from each other or together. What emerges is a story about both the corporate commodification of workers' heterosexual identities and the agency these workers deploy to deflect heteromasculine performances while also supporting a masculine brand image and a heteromasculinizing consumer experience.

Hiring and Developing Straight Aesthetics

Trish, a 29-year-old massage therapist, was the only lesbian at either salon. This "outsider within" (Collins 1986) status makes her especially attuned to the way heterosexual aesthetic labor drives hiring practices at Adonis. She told me it is obvious Tyler prefers to hire pretty straight women and so she must have been hired by mistake. "Tyler picks girls that are attractive, for sure," she said.

> I don't know how I got the job. I had longer hair then, that's probably why. He didn't know I was a queer then. But he definitely wants to know if they're cute . . . . Tyler definitely hires pretty girls, for sure. And if you show up without makeup on, he'll be mad.

Long hair and makeup act as indicators of heterofeminine gender identity and influence Tyler's hiring decisions, advantaging straight women and creating employment barriers for genderqueer applicants. Depicting herself as having slipped through the cracks, Trish sported short spiky blonde hair, tattoos, and a makeup-free face at the time of my study. Although she no longer met the salon's demands for heterosexual aesthetic labor, she also did not pose a threat to Adonis's heteromasculine consumer experience because her position as massage therapist kept her largely out of sight in a back room marked "spa area."

Tyler relied on the gender habitus of straight women to help him hire the "right" kind of worker, but there were times when he also enforced heterosexual aesthetic labor by policing the women's bodies. When I asked Connie, a 24-year-old stylist, if any unwritten rules shape her work experiences, she said the women have to "look good" or else Tyler will send them home to change. He reminds the women that their appearances are just as commercially valuable as their technical skills, and he is known to say, "You look like crap, go home and change." The women understand that at Adonis "looking good" means appealing to the presumed heterosexual desires of their male clients. Mary, another 24-year-old stylist, explained:

—say they come in and there's a girl wearing just sloppy jeans with a T-shirt and tennis shoes and their hair is in a ponytail. Or you come in and the girl has her hair done, it's styled really cute, they have a lot of makeup on, they're dressed real trendy and cute, a cute little dress on or tight jeans or whatever, where would you rather go?

Women who wear little dresses, tight jeans, and obvious makeup, and who have carefully coiffed hair, support an institutionalized heteromasculine consumer experience at the salon. In a larger cultural context where hegemonic masculinity is tied to heterosexuality and straight women are readily objectified, this appears an obvious way to recode beauty so it is palatable to a straight male clientele. Overlooking the organizational production of clients' entitlement to women's bodies and sexualities, Mary suggested it makes sense men choose a salon that provides them heterosexual titillation.

Exemplifying the gendered character of heterosexual aesthetic labor, Adonis's two male stylists, Joshua and Ryan, said they do not have to adhere to any particular appearance rules at work. Joshua, a 31-year-old licensed barber, explained:

For me, I think it's different, because I was the only guy for a long time, so I just made up my own [dress code]. I felt this was nice, so I'll wear this; I think it'll work, so I'll just do that. I've never been bothered. [Tyler] always says, "Oh, you always look good!"

By virtue of being a man, Joshua does not suffer the same objectifying demands on his sexuality as the women. He instead focuses on carving out

"brotherly" relationships with clients, who he said sometimes want advice from and to confide in another man. This does not mean he completely escapes the demands of heterosexual aesthetic labor, though; rather, these demands look different for men. Joshua and Ryan, a 34-year-old stylist, still project heteromasculine identities that mitigate clients' potential homophobic fears of being touched, groomed, and cared for by another man. So, while Tyler may not police their appearances, he relies on Joshua and Ryan to possess a straight masculine habitus that helps to make Adonis a comfortable place for other straight men.

Women who worked at The Executive did not tell me stories about heterosexist hiring practices or being sent home to change into more heterosexually appealing clothing. But when I asked them why they believe men patron the salon, many of them said, "sex sells," and as evidence pointed to online reviews in which clients described them as "hot chicks." Veronica, owner of The Executive, believed hiring a mostly female staff set the stage for heterosexualized worker–client interactions and tried to stem this by enforcing a dress code. She boasted that her dress code controls shop floor interactions to create a professional organizational aesthetic. "Every salon has a dress code . . . ours is professional attire," she said:

No jeans. It's nothing low-cut, nothing too short, because it's a male environment. You've got to be familiar with what would provoke unwanted attention. So [a] dress code in the aspect of keeping it nice and professional.

Veronica understands that men's entitlement to women's bodies might impact service encounters at the salon, but the dress code supports the idea that it is women's bodies, not men's actions, that are the problem. She also overlooks how this entitlement is supported by implicit organizational demands on women's heterofeminine identities and appearances.

The institutionalization of this dress code does not mean women at The Executive escape the demands of heterosexual aesthetic labor. Rather, the salon is organized around classed expressions of heterofemininity (Trautner 2005), so that what counts as "professional" includes tight black dress slacks with fitted button-up shirts and spandex leggings with off-the-shoulder tops, and almost always a pair of heels. It is a sexualized professional aesthetic that does double-duty in a salon set up to appeal to and reinforce the distinction of straight businessmen. By mandating her stylists adhere to a professional yet heterosexual aesthetic, Veronica secures a brand image that resonates with a high-status, straight, and largely white male clientele. She said, "It is discussed in our employee handbook, absolutely. We talk about attire, how you present yourself. . . . We're a brand, and we want to support that brand in what we wear to work every day." This appearance-disciplining policy sets workers up as extensions of the brand, whereby they ease men's relationships to a historically feminized institution by appealing to both their racialized class privileges and heterosexual identities. This labor also reinforces the women's paradoxical class positions. Appearing professional, the women at The Executive project a similar class location as their clients, and they often told me that their clients see them as fellow professionals. But they are not the men's peers. They sit at men's feet to shore up their toenails and wax their unwanted nose and ear hair. And while the women are solidly middle-class, they also rely on clients for commission and tips. This mimics conventional gender relations and symbolic gender expectations whereby women are financially dependent on and subservient to men.

Commercializing Heterofeminine Habitus

Organizational demands for heterosexual aesthetic labor situate the women salon workers as ideal commodities to promote a heteromasculine consumer experience. Both Adonis and The Executive feature these conventionally feminine employees on company websites, postcards, and television commercials, and Adonis has women hit the streets to solicit new business. With the exception of The Executive's website, male employees are conspicuously absent from these marketing

strategies. When the men do appear, they look as if they are clients rather than employees. The Executive's online photo gallery included a group photo of the women gathering around two men who were seated in vintage reproduction barbershop chairs. While some women posed smiling at the camera, others appeared to be cutting the men's hair. Only regular clients might recognize one of the men as Randy, a barber at the salon, and the other as Antonio, one of the salon's two shoe shiners. By making male employees invisible, the salon invites clients to imagine a grooming experience unfettered by the homophobic discomfort of being touched by another man (see Alexander 2003 on the secret pleasures of homosocial barbershop touch), and instead gives the impression that clients will have beautiful women touching and talking to them. Such promotional efforts help to assure that men's association with hegemonic masculinity will be enhanced not despite of, but because of purchasing salon services.

Adonis more blatantly commodifies its employees to encourage men to make appointments. Slippages between sexuality and aesthetic labor in the salons set up the women as recognizable identity resources (Pascoe 2007) for clients' projections of heteromasculine desires and thus as secondary sites of consumption. One client I spoke with described the salon's online commercial as "porn." The commercial featured eight young, thin, and attractive women in miniskirts—all employees at the time—clawing at the salon's front door. They slid around on stilettos, pushing each other while trying to break into the salon to reach the tall and freshly coiffed man inside. Whitney, the 24-year-old manager and receptionist, licks the man's black dress shoe just before she pulls him toward her open mouth for a kiss. This commercial looped on a small flat screen television at the front desk, just to the left of where Whitney worked. Noah, the 34-year-old client who called it porn, said the commercial invited men to believe that having their haircut at Adonis will result in women "crawling all over each other" to date them. More specifically, the commercial allows men to imagine sexual exchanges with their hairstylists and nail technicians, or the salon's receptionist.

Trish described a marketing event during a local classic car show. Tyler required women employees to wear suggestive tank tops and hit the streets to lure men into the salon:

> [T]here was a car show on [Main] Street, classic cars all over the place. We had to stand out in the front handing out water bottles with [Adonis's] label on it, trying to advertise. . . . But [the stylists] all were wearing, and [Tyler] made me wear this, too, the tank top says "Men Wanted" on the front, and it says "follow me to [Adonis]" on the back. I had to wear that shirt! I was gonna' shoot myself. I was like, "There's no way!" And you're walking around and the guys were like, "Men *wanted*?!"

This marketing strategy played on sexual innuendo, inviting men to approach the women as if they were personally soliciting sexual attention. While Trish had to presumably downplay her sexuality (Williams, Giuffre, and Dellinger 2009) to successfully act as heterosexual bait, she was likely not the only woman to feel uncomfortable with this objectifying marketing strategy. She also did not believe that she had much of a choice in resisting participation since as a new hire she "did not want to upset" Tyler and jeopardize her employment.

The availability of women's bodies and sexualities was not lost on men who reported enjoying their interactions with the "pretty women." Dan, a 61-year-old client of The Executive, told me that a friend of his came to the salon, pointed to "a stunning blonde," and asked the receptionist, "When does *she* have an appointment?" Choosing a stylist for her heterofeminine presentation highlights the women's commercial value as gendered persons. Another client, 34-year-old Warren, told me, "There's a tremendous amount of sex appeal at [The Executive], and most guys, that's what they like. They like being waited on hand and foot by beautiful women." Heterosexual aesthetic labor reaffirms straight women's roles as servers of men and highlights the emotional labor involved in being both sexy and caring. Acting as identity resources,

these women are supposed to make clients feel catered to as straight, class-privileged men. The men often flirt with employees and make sexual remarks that take advantage of the women as obligated identity resources for men's displays of hetero-desires, and that consequently threaten the women's professional identities.

Professionalizing Rhetoric and Protocols

Professionalism in service work denotes a kind of behavior that is emotionally constrained and focused on the customer, and so at Adonis and The Executive it reflects men's high-status social locations back to them at the same time it creates subordinate women. Women at the salons repeatedly explained that the client "is number one." Professionalism is also a contextually specific and readily available rhetoric with which the women deny men's sexual behavior and reroute potential threats to their professional dignity. When I asked June, a 29-year-old stylist at The Executive, if clients flirt with her, she replied: "For the most part, they know they're in a professional business, so they are not going to cross the line." Kendra, a 35-year-old stylist, agreed: "It's not that big of a deal. We're in a professional environment, so it's not gonna get out of hand." Claiming men do not bring sexuality into the salon fails to acknowledge that sexuality is an organizing aspect of service organizations and retail brands, that men regularly objectify women in the workplace, and that displays of heterosexuality commonly associate men with privileged masculinity (Connell 1995; Kimmel 1994).

Imagining clients see them and the salons as professional allows the women to paint their work as devoid of over rapport (Oerton 2004) and casts the worker–client relationship as shaped by unspoken yet understood boundaries. However, cracks in the workers' depictions of clients as sexually constrained appeared when they admitted that they sometimes have to remind men they are professionals. Just minutes after claiming men do not "cross the line," June explained she sometimes has to tell clients she is "serious" about her work.

When men flirt with June, her status as a straight, heterosexually desirable woman becomes salient and she attempts to manage their impression of her: "I think you just have to be really up front with it." She tells men, "I take my job seriously. This is a professional place. I would appreciate if you just leave it at that." The regularity with which women working at the salons told me stories of having to deploy professionalizing rhetoric reveals that clients do not always self-regulate their heteromasculine performances. In fact, these performances are organizationally supported.

The degree to which women can contain men's heterosexual behavior is constrained by the link between heterofemininity and the salons' success. Adonis and The Executive operate under the assumption that happy clients who experience ego-inflating appointments are more likely to come back. Good service is defined by seamless interactions between customers and workers, and so while women working at Adonis and The Executive expressed to me a sense of frustration with men staring at their breasts or asking them on dates, they often coyly deflect (Parreñas 2009) unwanted attention rather than confront clients directly. Kendra, for example, teases men who flirt with her, "I'll jokingly say, . . . 'This isn't that type of place.'" Turning men's heteromasculine displays into a joke demonstrates the emotional labor women do to manage the interactional effects of heterosexual aesthetic labor. The agency women exercise to discipline clients, though, ultimately undermines their ability to be strong sexual subjects (Giuffre, Dellinger, and Williams 2008) and might appear to clients as rhetorical sexual banter.

Stylists and receptionists also manage the emotions of jealous wives and girlfriends. One day, while Brinn, a 24-year-old receptionist, was making her usual string of confirmation calls, I overheard her assuring someone that she was calling from The Executive:

> Brinn hangs up the phone and sighs, "You know what really bothers me? When I make a confirmation call and the guy's wife says, 'This is Joe's *wife.*' I'm not here to steal your man, lady!" She tells me

this happens often; wives and girlfriends do not know their husbands or boyfriends are expecting a confirmation call from the salon and wonder why a woman is calling. "Yeah; they're like, 'Who *is* this?!'"

Wives and girlfriends call into question the legitimacy of Brinn's relationships with clients. By framing women's suspicions as irrational, Brinn individualizes their reactions and makes invisible the salon's commercialization of women's hetero-feminine habitus. Isabel, a 31-year-old stylist, told me she constantly reminds clients' wives that although she is touching and talking with their husbands, she does so in a professional space. She tried to place one wife at ease: "I'm like, 'Now you know where your husband comes is a really, really respectful salon, it's really professional, it's nothing to be scared [of].'" Isabel challenges the idea that her relationships with clients are sexual and uses professionalizing rhetoric to separate The Executive from supposedly less respectful salons. The context in which she evokes a professional affiliation, however, has the unintentional effect of highlighting the slippages between sexuality and the labor of masculinizing the salon and the salon experience for men.

In addition to using professionalizing rhetoric, the women rely on two professional protocols to mitigate the interpersonal effects of heterosexual aesthetic labor (Otis 2008): (1) monitoring what they wear to work and (2) drawing social boundaries between themselves and clients. "You wouldn't want to wear anything that's too crazy, too short or whatever, be uncomfortable all day working around all men," Jesse explained. She suggests women should expect to endure flirting and ogling by clients, and that men's heterosexually aggressive behavior is normal and natural. It is up to women to control men's behavior by finding work attire that abates unwanted sexual attention while also meeting organizational demands for heterosexual aesthetic labor. Personalizing the management of clients' heterosexual performances lets men off the hook for their bad behavior and further veils the operations of heterosexual aesthetic labor. Stylists also draw social boundaries between themselves and clients to avoid overrapport. Mary, for example, sometimes socializes with clients in larger groups but will not date clients. "I try to keep it professional in certain ways...now that I'm single," she said. "...I just don't think I could date a client. So I kind of keep it on that level." All of the women share this "no dating" policy, and most of them refuse to spend any time fraternizing with clients outside of work. Bridgette, a 41-year-old nail technician, told me: "I don't really have any clients I have friendships with, no. I like to keep my work life separate from my private life." Neither salon have written rules regulating worker–client relationships, but the women take it upon themselves to draw intimacy boundaries (Sherman 2007) important for avoiding unwanted familiarity and for casting clear divisions between their personal (sexualized) selves and their more public professional identities.

Naturalizing and Neutralizing Heteromasculine Performances

The women admitted that clients often ask them on dates, make sexual remarks, and even purchase them gifts and send them flowers at work. They sometimes made these come-ons into non-issues by denying and essentializing men's sexual behaviors....Bridgette used to feel so uncomfortable with men's advances that she had considered quitting,

> A lot of my clients that were married were hitting on me, and it was kind of getting to the point where I was a bit tired of it....So as far as—it kind of crossed my mind that I wouldn't work here any more. But that was a phase for, like, six weeks, and then it stopped.

Client come-ons created a hostile work environment for Bridgette, but she felt unable to confront clients or to discuss her discomfort with Veronica. Her only option for escaping heterosexualized workplace interactions, she suggested, was to quietly leave her job. Jessie, a 28-year-old stylist at Adonis, said that while some clients flirt with her, they are mostly

"harmless." "Maybe some guys might [flirt]....But they might just be like that," she said. "I'd say 90% of the time they're probably married anyway. I don't think—they're pretty harmless,...not too many creepers....Not really anymore." Jessie paints clients as flirts instead of "creepers" and naturalizes men's behavior by claiming they "might just be like that."

I found that the more seasoned workers often denied men's sexual behaviors while the new hires had not yet moved through the necessary period of adjustment (Dellinger and Williams 2002), whereby they become accustomed to the interpersonal effects of heterosexual aesthetic labor. The four new hires at The Executive expressed surprise and frustration with management's demands on their bodies and heterosexual identities. Veronica encouraged employees to greet clients with a hug and to even kiss them on the cheek. Nell, a 26-year-old new stylist, said, "Veronica does encourage that we hug our clients. I have a big problem with that. But that's only because I feel that's outside my job duties." Male beauty workers at the salons rarely hug their clients. They instead shake clients' hands or firmly pat them on the back. Expectations that women hug clients illustrates that their jobs are about more than cutting hair and clipping cuticles. Their jobs also require mediating men's relationships with beauty by serving up a caring and physically intimate consumer experience. Ruth, a 30-year-old newcomer, explained that it is important to keep these interactions with clients from being read as sexual: "Being in this industry, you have to be comfortable with touching people. But everybody knows if it's a weird touch or not, or where it crosses the line into being unprofessional." New stylists revealed that management encourages physical intimacy to capitalize on women's heterosexual aesthetic labor and were the most in tune to tensions between this labor and a sense of professionalism.

Like Jessie, who suggested men "might just be like that," many women evoked essentializing rhetoric to neutralize the consequences of men's sexual behavior. . . . When describing her interactions with clients, for example, Emily, a 21-year-old stylist at Adonis, told me that men are "wired" to see women as sexual objects, but that she and the other stylists try not to encourage their sexual fantasies: "Obviously, a lot of guys probably come in here because there are all these—'Hot chicks gonna cut my hair, it's gonna be so cool.' Like, we don't act like, 'Oooh!' Like a Playboy Bunny . . . . So, I'm sure they have it in their heads, guys are wired like that, but we don't play into it." . . . This sort of perspective is vital to understanding the perpetuation of sexism, since the dictum that "men will be men" stems from and supports rampant victim-blaming rhetoric. This rhetoric excuses men's supposedly uncontrollable heterosexual urges that objectify, subordinate, delegitimize, and harm the dignity of women, and that often excuse rape and other forms of sexual assault. In another example, Holly, a 22-year-old stylist and nail technician at Adonis, catches men ogling her breasts while she bends over in front of them to cut their bangs. She claimed this does not bother her because men simply cannot help themselves,

> Whatever. [I] laugh it off. They're fricking guys. Like my boyfriend says, boys think with their unh-unh. They don't think with their brains most of the time. So I just try to keep that in mind, and I'm like, whatever.

Accepting this ogling as part of men's biological makeup may help to protect Holly from the sociopsychological harm of objectification, but it also allows her interactions with clients to go on uninterrupted so that she can cut hair without offending men's sense of heterosexual entitlement. Evoking what McCaughey (2007) calls the "caveman mystique," Emily and Holly uphold the myth that men are so close to their primitive roots that their sexual behavior cannot be altered; that misogyny, as it were, is written into their DNA. The question of what sort of men get away with this behavior also points to race and class privilege.

Most of the men who patronize Adonis and The Executive are white, and it is unlikely the women would be so be so quick to describe Black and Latino men as "harmless." After all, the same racist and classist stereotypes that allow the objectifying behavior of privileged white men also cast poor men of color as criminal, dangerous, and hypersexual.

Holly argued that men are inferior to women, despite their performances of heteromasculine dominance, because "they don't think with their brains." This rationalization suggests that even when women fail to directly discipline clients, they still dismiss the harmful consequences of men's behavior. The problem is that men's bad behavior goes unchallenged, reflecting a larger culture of silence around men's sense of entitlement to women's bodies. Clients are not at the salon to be lectured about their misogynistic remarks or their ogling of women, and salon employees understand this. The women learn that when they speak to clients it is only to make the men feel funny, cared for, and attractive. A sign that hangs above the shampoo bowl at Adonis reminds stylists, "This is your clients [sic] time to relax . . . do not engage in conversation." So when the women do encounter uncomfortable interactions in which men make claims to their bodies, they often remain silent. Emily tried to muffle the noises of one client who moaned while she shampooed his hair. "I have this one guy and he's like, 'unnnh, unnnh,'" she said.

> And I'm like, "Ok, I get it, you like this head massage. You don't have to make those groaning noises, please." I had [another stylist] standing there, and I was just looking at my coworker. "Stop!" [I] put a towel on his face. "Why do you have to do that?" It's so weird.

Emily expressed frustration with her moaning client and worked within the constraints of her job to control an otherwise uncomfortable interaction. In a workplace that relies on the organizational commodification and interpersonal consumption of heterosexual women—and emphasizes client privilege and worker deference—all she could do was cover his mouth with a hot towel that was already part of a free mini-facial.

Conclusion

Moving beyond the idea that aesthetic labor situates retail workers as models, decorative hardware, and mirrors, this article emphasizes the interactive aspect of aesthetic labor by exploring how service workers more generally both become identity resources for customers' projections of social identities and navigate the objectifying effects of aesthetic labor. By bringing sexuality to the same analytic level as race, class, and gender, I show how the organizational processes of hiring for, developing, and mobilizing workers' sexual identities and appearances help to create a heterogendered brand and consumer experience. Adonis and The Executive rely on heterosexual, heterofeminine women workers to organize and recode the historically feminized salon around notions of hegemonic masculinity. This creates a consumer environment in which high-status straight men are created at the point of purchase, so that men can avoid feelings of effeminacy while having their hair coiffed and nails buffed. Working for an organization capitalizing on gender hierarchies, women who labor on men's bodies become more than skilled workers, they become gender and sexual persons ripe for consumption.

At the same time the salons regulate employees' labor, workers find space to exercise agency. Worker agency is revealed when women at Adonis and The Executive discipline clients via professionalizing rhetoric and protocols, and when they engage gender essentialism to deny men's heteromasculine behavior. These reactions aid the women in managing their discomfort and maintaining legitimate workplace identities yet also maintain unequal gender and class relations. So the question remains: Why don't the women do more to manage slippages of sexuality at work? The answer is that as extensions of the brand, the women are responsible for creating seamless interactions that promote the heteromasculine and class privileges of their clients. They are commission- and tip-based employees, and so their livelihood is tied to the success of corporations engaged in the commercialization of heterofemininity. A culture of silence around men's behavior also persists at the salons, and it is difficult to reject something that seemingly does not exist. Gender and sexual hierarchies therefore end up unfairly advantaging straight female applicants at the point of hire and become the personal burden of workers who (at least early on) see heterosexual aesthetic labor as a problem in the workplace.

Theories of aesthetic labor build on Hochschild's concept of emotional labor, but at Adonis and The Executive it is clear they work together. Heterosexual aesthetic labor requires emotional labor as the women manage their clients' sexual behavior and enact silent subordination, by which Adonis in particular creates privileged salon experiences for men. Emotional deference to heterosexually performing clients reflects the gendered habitus of women as servers, and this deference helps to create successful masculinizing branding efforts. Organizational emphasis on professionalism at The Executive also calls for a constrained disposition focused on providing class-privileged customers with "good" (heteromasculine) customer service. Looking ahead to the future of service work research, I suggest scholars should consider the micro- and organizational-level heterogendering of retail workplaces and how gendered branding draws from and informs the inequalities of both labor and consumption. Focusing on the processes by which organizations become raced, classed, and gendered, we can see how sexuality differently shapes men and women's work responsibilities. This research also encourages scholars to investigate the sociopsychological meaning-making strategies of workers to better understand how aesthetic labor shapes the informal job requirements of and the identities of workers responsible for reproducing others' social privileges.

Notes

1. While the literature on service work and consumption generally refer to the "customer," employees at Adonis and The Executive use the term "client." Therefore, when specifically discussing the salons, I use "client/s" to conform to their preferred language.
2. The U.S. Bureau of Labor Statistics (2014) shows women make up 94.6 percent of 760,000 hairdressers, hairstylists, and other cosmetologists and 16.8 percent of 110,000 barbers.

Author's note: I am thankful to Dana Britton, Catherine Connell, Edward Flores, Pierrette Hondagneu-Sotelo, Lanita Jacobs, Kelsy Kretschmer, and Michael A. Messner for their helpful comments on previous drafts of this article, as well as to Joya Misra, Jo Reger, and the anonymous reviewers of *Gender & Society*. I am also indebted to the owners, staff, and clients at Adonis and The Executive for their willingness to partake in this study. Correspondence concerning this article should be addressed to Kristen Barber, Southern Illinois University, Carbondale, 3436 Faner Hall, MC 4524, Carbondale, IL 62901, USA; e-mail: barber@siu.edu.

References

Alexander, Bryant Keith. 2003. Fading, twisting, and weaving: An interpretive ethnography of the black barbershop as cultural space. *Qualitative Inquiry* 9 (1): 105–28.

Barber, Kristen. 2008. The well-coiffed man: Class, race, and heterosexual masculinity in the hair salon. *Gender & Society* 22 (24): 455–76.

Barber, Kristen. 2015. Styled masculinity: Men's consumption of salon hair care and the construction of difference. In *Exploring masculinities: Identity, inequality, continuity and change*, edited by C. J. Pascoe and Tristan Bridges. Cambridge, UK: Oxford University Press.

Barber, Kristen. 2016. *Styling masculinity: Gender, class, and inequality in the men's grooming industry*. New Brunswick, NJ: Rutgers University Press.

Bourdieu, Pierre. 1984. *Distinction: A social critique of the judgment of taste*. Cambridge, MA: Harvard University Press.

Bureau of Labor Statistics, U.S. Department of Labor. 2014. *Household data annual averages: Employed persons by detailed occupation, sex, race, and Hispanic or Latino ethnicity*. Washington, DC: Bureau of Labor Statistics.

Cohen, Rachel Lara, Kate Hardy, Teela Sanders, and Carol Wolkowitz. 2013. Introduction: The body/sex/work nexus. In *Body/sex/work: Intimate, embodied and sexualized labor*, edited by Carol Wolkowitz, Rachel Lara Cohen, Teela Sanders, and Kate Hardy. London: Palgrave Macmillan.

Collins, Patricia Hill. 1986. Learning from the outsider within: The sociological significance of Black feminist thought. *Social Problems* 33 (6): 14–32.

Connell, R. 1995. *Masculinities*. Berkeley: University of California Press.

Craig, Maxine Leeds, and Rita Liberti. 2007. "Cause that's what girls do": The making of a feminized gym. *Gender & Society* 21 (5): 676–99.

Dellinger, Kristen, and Christine L. Williams. 2002. The locker room and the dorm room: Workplace norms and the boundaries of sexual harassment in magazine editing. *Social Problems* 49 (2): 242–57.

Duffy, Mignon. 2007. Doing the dirty work: Gender, race, and reproductive labor in historical perspective. *Gender & Society* 21 (3): 313–36.

Ehrenreich, Barbara, and Arlie Russell Hochschild. 2004. *Global woman: Nannies, maids, and sex workers in the new economy*. New York: Holt Paperbacks.

Euromonitor International: Country Sector Briefing. May 2010. *Men's grooming products–U.S.*

Euromonitor International: Country Sector Briefing. May 2015. *Men's grooming products–U.S.*

Forseth, Ulla. 2005. Gender matters? Exploring how gender is negotiated in service encounters. *Gender, Work & Organization* 12 (5): 440–59.

Gimlin, Debra. 1996. Pamela's place: Power and negotiation in the hair salon. *Gender & Society* 10 (5): 505–26.

Giuffre, Patti A., and Christine L. Williams. 2000. Not just bodies: Strategies for desexualizing the physical examination of patients. *Gender & Society* 14 (3): 457–82.

Giuffre, Patti, Kirsten Dellinger, and Christine L. Williams. 2008. "No retribution for being gay?" Inequality in gay-friendly workplaces. *Sociological Spectrum* 28: 254–77.

Guerrier, Yvonne, and Amel Abid. 2004. Gendered identities in the work of overseas tour reps. *Gender, Work and Organizations* 11 (3): 334–50.

Halberstam, Judith. 1998. *Female masculinity.* Durham, NC: Duke University Press.

Hochschild, Arlie Russell. 1983. *The managed hand: Commercialization of human feeling.* Berkeley: University of California Press.

IBISWorld. 2010. Hair and nail salons in the U.S.: 81211. *IBISWorld Industry Report.*

IBISWorld. 2015. Hair and nail salons in the U.S.: 81211. *IBISWorld Industry Report.*

Kang, Miliann. 2003. The managed hand: The commercialization of bodies and emotions in Korean immigrant-owned nail salons. *Gender & Society* 17 (6): 820–39.

Kang, Miliann. 2010. *The managed hand: Race, gender, and the body in beauty service work.* Berkeley: University of California Press.

Kimmel, Michael S. 1994. Masculinity as homophobia: Fear, shame and silence in the construction of gender identity. In *Theorizing masculinities,* edited by Harry Brod and Michael Kaufman. Thousand Oaks, CA: Sage.

Loe, Meika. 1996. Working for men—At the intersection of power, gender, and sexuality. *Sociological Inquiry* 66 (4): 399–42.

MacDonald, Cameron Lynne, and David Merrill. 2008. Intersectionality in the emotional proletariat: A new lens on employment discrimination in service work. In *Service work: Critical perspectives,* edited by Cameron MacDonald and Marek Korczynski. New York: Routledge.

McBride, Dwight. 2005. *Why I hate Abercrombie & Fitch: Essays on race and sexuality.* New York: New York University Press.

McCaughey, Martha. 2007. *The caveman mystique: Pop-Darwinism and the debates over sex, violence, and science.* London: Routledge.

Mears, Ashley. 2014. Aesthetic labor for the sociologies of work, gender, and beauty. *Sociology Compass* 8 (12): 1330–43.

Mills, Albert J. 1996. Strategy, sexuality and the stratosphere: Airlines and the gendering of

organizations. In *Gender relations in public and private: New research perspectives,* edited by Lydia Morris and E. Stina Lyon. London: Palgrave Macmillan.

Mills, Albert J. 2006. *Sex, strategy, and the stratosphere: The gendering of airline culture.* London: Palgrave Macmillan.

Oerton, Sarah. 2004. Bodywork boundaries: Power, politics and professionalism in therapeutic massage. *Gender, Work and Organization* 11 (5): 544–65.

Otis, Eileen M. 2008. The dignity of working women: Service, sex, and the labor politics of localization in China's city of eternal spring. *American Behavioral Scientist* 52 (3): 356–76.

Pascoe, C. J. 2007. *Dude you're a fag: Masculinity and sexuality in high school.* Berkeley: University of California Press.

Paap, Kris. 2006. *Working construction: Why white working class men put themselves—and the labor movement—in harm's way.* Ithaca, NY: Cornell University Press.

Parreñas, Rhacel Salazar. 2009. Hostess work: Negotiating the morals of money and sex. *Economic Sociology of Work* 18: 207–32.

Pettinger, Lynne. 2005. Gendered work meets gendered goods: Selling and service in clothing retail. *Gender, Work and Organization* 12 (5): 460–78.

Pettinger, Lynne. 2010. Branded workers. *Nowaytomakealiving.net/post/844/* (accessed on April 4, 2014).

Sherman, Rachel. 2007. *Class acts: Service and inequality in luxury hotels.* Berkeley: University of California Press.

Trautner, Mary Nell. 2005. Doing gender, doing class: The performance of sexuality in exotic dance clubs. *Gender & Society* 19 (6): 771–88.

Warhurst, Chris, and Dennis Nickson. 2001. *Looking good and sounding right: Style counselling and the aesthetics of the new economy.* London: Industrial Society.

Warhurst, Chris, and Dennis Nickson. 2007. Employee experience of aesthetic labour in retail and hospitality. *Work, Employment & Society* 21 (1): 103–20.

Warhurst, Chris, and Dennis Nickson. 2009. "Who's got the look?": Emotional, aesthetic and sexualized labour in interactive services. *Gender, Work and Organization* 16 (3): 385–404.

Williams, Christine L. 2006. *Inside toyland: Working, shopping, and social inequality.* Berkeley: University of California Press.

Williams, Christine L., and Catherine Connell. 2010. "Looking good and sounding right": Aesthetic labor and social inequality in the retail industry. *Work and Occupations* 37 (2): 349–77.

Williams, Christine, Patti Giuffre, and Kirsten Dellinger. 2009. The gay-friendly closet. *Sexuality Research & Social Policy* 6 (1): 29–45.

Witz, Anne, Chris Warhurst, and Dennis Nickson. 2003. The labour of aesthetics and the aesthetics of organization. *Organization* 10 (1): 33–54.

Men and Health: Body and Mind

The gap between male and female life expectancy was 2 years in 1900. Why is it 5 years today? Why do men suffer heart attacks and ulcers at such a consistently higher rate than women do? Why are auto insurance rates so much higher for young males than for females of the same age? Are mentally and emotionally "healthy" males those who conform more closely to the dominant cultural prescriptions for masculinity, or those who resist those dominant ideals?

The articles in this part examine the "embodiment" of masculinity, the ways in which men's mental health and physical health express and reproduce the definitions of masculinity we have ingested in our society. Michael Kehler shows how this gendering of body and health starts so early among boys. Don Sabo offers a compassionate account of how men will invariably confront traditional stereotypes as they look for more nurturing roles. Sapna Cheryan and her colleagues show how men overcompensate when their masculinity is threatened. Gloria Steinem pokes holes in the traditional definitions of masculinity, especially the putative biological basis for gender expression.

PART IV DISCUSSION QUESTIONS

1. Cheryan et al. find that men distance themselves from femininity when they feel they are less masculine than average. How might men's compensations shift as hybrid masculinities continue to co-opt traits that are not traditionally hegemonic? How might compensation vary for men of different social positions?

2. How does the locker room body surveillance described by Kehler reinforce hegemonic masculinity? Where else is this kind of surveillance common? What are its effects on men's health?

3. How does Gloria Steinem challenge the binary that biological experiences are fixed and social experiences are fluid in her essay *If Men Could Menstruate*?

Wrestling with the Risks

A Guide to Men's Health Studies

DON SABO

My grandfather used to smile and say, "Find out where you're going to die and stay the hell away from there." Grandpa had never studied epidemiology (i.e., the study of variations in health and illness in society) but he understood that certain behaviors, attitudes and cultural practices can put individuals at risk for accidents, illness, or death. The evidence and insights presented in this article show how boys and men define and enact gender in ways that profoundly influences their well-being and life expectancy. For example, how come more teenage boys than girls die from suicide, car accidents, or gunshot wounds? Why do men generally die younger than women? Why are men with health problems less likely than women to see a doctor? The main argument developed here is that many aspects of traditional masculinity are dangerous to men's health. First, I identify how gender is connected with sickness and death, paying particular attention to how the risk for obtaining certain illnesses varies among men and in comparison to women. I then discuss an array of men's health issues and suggest possible preventive strategies for enhancing men's health.

Gender Differences in Health and Illness

British anthropologist Ashley Montagu was among the first to draw upon epidemiological data to show men are more vulnerable to mortality than women (Montagu, 1953). At the time, this groundbreaking claim contradicted hegemonic gender ideologies, which posited men as "naturally" stronger, smarter, and better than women. Montagu's assertion has been repeatedly observed by contemporary epidemiologists and demographers, which this section explores in greater depth.

Mortality and Life Expectancy

Today, females have greater life expectancy than males in the United States, Canada, and other post-industrial societies. This pattern begins at birth; as evidenced in Table 15.1, which illustrates the disparities between male and female infant mortality rates from 1940–2008 in the United States, males' chances of dying during the prenatal and neonatal stage are greater than females' (CDC, 1992, 2013a). Men's greater mortality rates persist through old age and, as Table 15.2 shows, men's death rates are higher than women's for the top ten causes of death in the United States (National Center for Health Statistics, 2016).

At first glance, these differences might appear to suggest an inherent female biological health advantage. A closer analysis of differences between women's and men's life expectancies, however, indicates that gendered health disparities are not static. Social and cultural factors shape and constrain individuals' expected health outcomes, and differences between men's and women's health patterns have changed over time. Women's relative

---

Don Sabo, "Wrestling with the Risks: A Guide to Men's Health Studies," original to this volume, by permission of the author.

Table 15.1 Gender and Infant Mortality Rates for the United States, 1940–2008

Year	Both Sexes	Males	Females
1940	47.0	52.5	41.3
1950	29.2	32.8	25.5
1960	26.0	29.3	22.6
1970	20.0	22.4	17.5
1980	12.6	13.9	11.2
1989	9.8	10.8	8.8
2008	6.9	7.2	6.0

Source: Adapted from Centers for Disease Control and Prevention, *Monthly Vital Statistics Report* 40 (8, Suppl.2), p. 41. The 2008 data are available at *National Vital Statistics Report*, Vol. 62, No. 8, December 18, 2013.

increased smoking among women, have narrowed the gender gap between men's and women's mortality rates. For example, women's life expectancy was 7.9 years greater than men's in 1979, 6.9 years in 1989 (National Center for Health Statistics, 1992), and 5.2 years greater in 2004 (Ibid, 2015). These differences, moreover, vary by race and ethnicity; in 2014, white male and white female life expectancy averaged 76.5 and 81.1 years-old respectively, compared to 72.0 and 78.1 among non-Hispanic blacks, and 79.2 and 84.0 among Hispanics (National Center for Health Statistics, 2016), thus demonstrating the ways in which sociocultural processes shape men's and women's mortality rates.

advantage in life expectancy was rather small at the beginning of the 20th century, but female mortality declined more rapidly during the mid-20th century, thereby increasing the gender gap in life expectancy. Women's decreasing maternal mortality rate, coupled with men's increased mortality from coronary heart disease and lung cancer that were, in turn, mainly due to higher rates of cigarette smoking among males, were key mechanisms contributing to these trends. In more recent years, however, some changes in gendered behaviors, such as

Morbidity

Despite outliving men, women experience acute illnesses—such as respiratory conditions, infective and parasitic conditions, and digestive system disorders—at higher rates than men (Cypress, 1981; Dawson & Adams, 1987). By contrast, Courtenay (2011) documents that men are more prone to develop chronic illnesses such as coronary heart disease, emphysema, and gout. Men also average higher injury rates, which is partly attributed to gender differences in socialization and lifestyle; for example, men are at a great risk of becoming

Table 15.2 Ratio of Male to Female Age-Adjusted Death Rates, for the Ten Leading Causes of Death for the Total U.S. Population in 2014

Cause of Death	Number of Total Deaths	Percentage	Male to Female Ratio	Black to White Ratio
Diseases of the heart	614,318	23.4	1.6	1.2
Malignant neoplasms	591,700	22.5	1.4	1.2
Chronic lower respiratory diseases	147,101	5.6	1.2	0.7
Accidents (unintentional injuries)	135,928	5.2	2.0	0.8
Cerebrovascular diseases	133,163	5.1	1.0	1.4
Alzheimer's disease	95,541	3.6	0.7	0.8
Diabetes	74,488	2.9	1.5	1.9
Influenza and pneumonia	55,227	2.1	1.3	1.1
Nephritis, nephritic syndrome, nephrosis	48,146	1.8	1.5	2.0
Intentional harm (suicide)	42,826	1.6	3.6	0.4

injured while engaging in reckless behavior, participating in contact sports, or working in risky blue-collar occupations. By contrast, women are generally more likely to experience chronic conditions such as anemia, chronic enteritis and colitis, migraine headaches, arthritis, and thyroid disease (Ibid). These differences are partially due to pharmaceutical advertising campaigns, which often aim to convince people that they are sick and need to see a doctor when, in fact, they are not clinically ill (Brownlee, 2007). Much of this type of "direct to consumer" advertising has been geared to women, but efforts aimed at men are on the rise, suggesting we may see a hike in men's rate of "morbidity" in the near future.

Biology + Society + Culture = Complexity

In addition to gender, a highly complex set of global, social, cultural, psychological, racial, and ethnic factors influence variations in men's and women's health (Broom & Tovey, 2009; W. Courtenay, 2011; Payne, 2006). Understanding the disparate mortality and morbidity rates between men and women is further complicated by the study of epidemiology itself (Sabo, 2005). The emphasis on *differences* can sometimes hide *similarities* between women's and men's health outcomes. Questioning the conventional wisdom that women in industrialized countries get sick more often than men, MacIntyre, Hunt, and Sweeting (1996) studied health data sets from both Scotland and the United Kingdom. They found that after controlling for age, statistically significant differences between many of men's and women's self-reported psychological and physical symptoms disappear. Such results suggest that both differences *and* similarities in men's and women's health exist and that changes in gender relations during recent decades "may produce changes in men's and women's experiences of health and illness" (p. 623).

To summarize, although some gender differences in mortality and morbidity are associated with biological or genetic processes, or with reproductive biology (e.g., testicular or prostate cancer), the largest variations in men's and women's health are related to social, economic, and cultural factors (W. Courtenay, 2011; W. H. Courtenay, McCreary, & Merighi, 2002). For this reason, it remains important to be critical of dominant men's health discourses. In addition to equating "men's health" to the delivery of biomedical services or the selling of private sector marketing services or products, these discourses often lump all men into the same category (Schofield, Connell, Walker, Wood, & Butland, 2000), thus obscuring important intra-gender variation among men and inter-gender variation between men and women.

Masculinities and Men's Health

There is no such thing as masculinity, there are only masculini*ties* (Connell & Messerschmidt, 2005; Sabo & Gordon, 1995). The fact is, not all men are alike, nor do all men share the same stakes in the gender order. At any given historical moment, there are competing masculinities—some dominant, some marginalized, and some stigmatized—each with their respective structural, psychosocial, and cultural moorings. This results in substantial differences in men's health outcomes. As Keeling (2000) wrote, "So it is that there is no single, unitary men's health—instead, sexual orientation, race, socioeconomic status, and culture all intervene to affect the overall health status of each man and or men of various classes or groups" (p. 101). Next, this chapter takes an intersectional approach to men's health and explores how age, race and ethnicity, sexuality, incarceration, extracurricular participation, and fatherhood differently shape men's health outcomes.

Adolescent Males

Pleck, Sonenstein, and Ku (1994) were among the first to apply critical feminist perspectives to their research on adolescent boys' health outcomes. By interviewing a national sample of adolescent boys aged 15–19, they examined whether and how identifying as traditionally masculine increased boys' risk for engaging in an array of behaviors that are associated with adverse health outcomes. Their findings revealed that boys who expressed higher levels of traditionally masculine attitudes were more likely to be suspended from school, drink and use drugs, come into contact with law enforcement, be sexually active, have more heterosexual partners in the last year, and commit sexual assault. These kinds of behavior elevate boys' risk for contracting sexually transmitted diseases and place boys at an elevated risk of early death by accident or homicide (Courtenay, 2011). Furthermore, these same behaviors can also encourage victimization of women through men's violence, sexual assault, unwanted teenage pregnancy, and sexually transmitted diseases.

Today, it may be the case that boys and young men are less likely to buy into traditional "macho" identities (Sobralske, 2006), but gender relations that encourage adolescent boys to engage in risky behaviors continue to be embedded within institutions such as the media, schools, locker rooms, peer cultures, the military, and sports. The link between masculinities and risky behaviors likely helps explain the health outcomes of 15–24 year-old males in the United States, for whom the three main causes of death are unintentional injury, suicide, and homicide (National Center for Health Statistics, 2017).

Finally, adolescence is a phase of accelerated physiological development and more boys than girls are classified as "obese." Among 13–19 year-olds, 19.8% of boys and 18.3% of girls were obese in 2012 (Carroll, Navaneelan, Bryan, & Ogden, 2015; Ogden, Carroll, Kit, & Flegal, 2012). Obesity among both boys and girls in the United States has increased since the 1970s, and adolescents from racial/ethnic minorities are especially likely to be overweight. Obese adolescents often become obese adults, thus elevating boys' and men's long-term risk for illness and diseases, including coronary heart disease, diabetes, mellitus, joint disease, and certain cancers.

Men of Color

The historical and social context of racial and economic inequality helps explains patterns of health and illness among men of color. African Americans, Hispanics, and Native Americans are disproportionately poor and are more likely to work in low-paying and dangerous occupations, live in polluted areas, be exposed to toxic substances, and experience the threat and reality of crime. People who are systematically disadvantaged by systems of inequality are also less likely to have access to high-quality health care, a trend that is particularly pronounced for African Americans (Courtenay, 2011). Although African American men have higher rates of alcoholism, infectious diseases, and drug-related conditions, for example, they are less apt to receive health care and, when they do, their care is often inferior.

Compared to whites, African Americans experience twice as much infant mortality, are twice as likely to die from diabetes-related complications, have 80% more strokes, have 20–40% higher rates of cancer, and live 5–7 fewer years on average (Burrus, Liburd, & Burroughs, 1998; Chin, Zhang, & Merrell, 1998; Straub, 1994; Wingo et al., 1996). The age-adjusted death rate is greater for men of color relative to white men: 1.7 times greater for African Americans, 1.8 times greater for Asians, and 1.5 times greater for Latinos/Hispanics (Collins, Hall, & Neuhaus, 1999; W. H. Courtenay et al., 2002). African American and American Native/Alaskan Native men are also overrepresented among those who incur non-fatal work-related injuries and illnesses, lack health insurance coverage, engage in illicit drug use, have HIV, are obese, come into contact with environmental hazards, and lack access to healthy foods (CDC, 2013b). With regards to HIV/AIDS, heart disease, prostate cancer, colon cancer, and lung cancer, African American males also have higher death rates than all other men (Artiga, Foutz, Cornachione, & Garfield, 2007). Hispanic men also show more signs of ill health than their white counterparts. One explanation is that the growing numbers of both documented and undocumented Hispanic males in the U.S. workforce in recent decades, particularly in blue-collar jobs (e.g., construction, agriculture, warehousing), contributes to high rates of work-related injuries and deaths (CDC, 2008). Those who care about men's health, therefore, need to be attuned to the interplay among gender, race/ethnicity, cultural differences, and economic conditions when working with diverse populations.

Gay and Bisexual Men

Gay and bisexual men comprise anywhere between 5 to 10 percent of U.S. men. In the past, gay men have been viewed as evil, sinful, sick, emotionally immature, and socially undesirable. Homophobic and heteronormative attitudes and practices are often embedded within the healthcare system and the public sphere more broadly, which can impact gay and bisexual men's health. Stigmatization and marginalization, for example, may lead to emotional confusion and suicide among gay youth. Although many gay men are open about their sexual and gender identities (Anderson, Magrath, & Bullingham, 2016), anxiety and stress can tax the emotional and physical health of "closeted" gay and bisexual men. Furthermore, when seeking medical services, some gay and bisexual men also deal with the homophobia of health care workers.

In the United States and Canada, men who have sex with men (MSM) often engage in sexual acts, such as unprotected anal and oral sex, that place them at risk of sexually transmitted diseases such as HIV transmission. For gay and bisexual men who are infected by the HIV virus, the personal burden of living with an AIDS diagnosis may be made heavier by homophobia. The cultural meanings associated with AIDS can also filter into gender and sexual identities. Tewksbury's (1995) interviews with 45 HIV+ gay men showed how masculinity, sexuality, stigmatization, and interpersonal commitments shape the decisions men make about engaging in risky sexual behavior. Most of the men practiced celibacy or safer sex to prevent others from contracting the disease, but several continued to have unprotected sex.

Prison Inmates

The United States has the highest incarceration rate of any nation in the world, with about 2.2 million inmates in prison or jail. Men, especially men of color, are over-represented among those behind bars. African Americans are more likely than white

Americans to be arrested, and once arrested, they are more likely to be convicted. Once convicted, they often face longer sentences. The lifetime likelihood of imprisonment rates among U.S. residents born in 2001 are 1 in 9 for all men, 1 in 17 for white men, 1 in 3 for black men, and 1 in 6 for Latino men.

The prison system acts as a pocket of health risks for incarcerated men, and is part of an institutional chain that facilitates transmission of HIV and other infections to certain North American populations, particularly those who are poor, racial and ethnic minorities, and who live in urban areas of the U.S. For example, the HIV infection rate is five times greater among state and federal inmates than in the general U.S. population (CDC, 2016). Most inmates contract HIV/AIDS *outside* state and federal prisons (Bureau of Justice Statistics, 2007), but prison conditions exacerbate incarcerated men's likelihood of contracting HIV or other infections such as tuberculosis, STDs, or hepatitis (Polych & Sabo, 2001). Inside prisons, the HIV virus is primarily transmitted through unprotected penetrative sex, which occurs primarily through consensual unions and secondarily through sexual assault and rape (Sabo, Kupers, & London, 2001). Although the amount of IV drug use behind prison walls is unknown, the scarcity of needles often leads to needle and sharps sharing, which also exacerbates HIV transmission among prisoners.

In addition to being at an elevated risk of contracting HIV and other STDs, prisoners are also burdened by high rates of mental health issues and substance abuse use that jeopardize their health. Long prison sentences, the threat and reality of violence, loneliness, separation from family, invasive noise, and solitary confinement erode prisoners' psychological health. These conditions often lead prisoners to shut down emotionally or attempt suicide (Kupers, 2017). Furthermore, because many states have lengthened prison sentences in recent decades, more prisoners are now over the age of 50. Chronic diseases like heart disease, cancer, and liver diseases top the list of ailments for the aging prison population (Bureau of Justice Statistics, 2007). Older men also comprise a significant portion of the more than half of U.S. prison and jail prisoners who are dealing with a mental illness (James & Glaze, 2006).

Despite these health risks, efforts to educate and improve the health conditions of prisoners are limited. In particular, the "graying" of the prison population highlights the importance of attending to both the physical and mental health needs of men behind bars (Aday, 2003). When left unaddressed, the health risks of prison not only jeopardize male prisoners' health, but they also put the broader public at risk as well. Prisons are not hermetically sealed enclaves; hundreds of thousands of prisoners are released each year, while hundreds of thousands return to the prison system (Eberstadt, 2016). The current system is failing many former prisoners, who return home upon release and likely find that factors such as addiction, mental illness, and STDs act as barriers when seeking jobs, rebuilding relationships with family members, and securing successful re-entry to society (Dill et al., 2016).

Male Athletes

Injury is everywhere in sport. It is evident in the lives and bodies of athletes, who regularly experience bruises, torn ligaments, broken bones, aches, lacerations, muscle tears, and concussions. Although injuries are often unavoidable in sports, participating in traditional men's sports places men at a higher risk for injury. During the 2005–06 school year, for example, there were an estimated 1,442,533 injuries to U.S. high school athletes in nine popular sports (CDC, 2006a), with football players and wrestlers averaging the highest injury rates.

Within sports such as football and hockey, where athletes regularly inflict injury on others, men often glorify pain, injury and sacrificing one's body to "win at all costs." The "no pain, no gain" philosophy, which is rooted in traditional cultural equations between masculinity and sports, also jeopardizes the health of athletes who subscribe to its ethos (Sabo, 2004, 2009). For example, Tiger Woods won the 2008 U.S. Open only weeks after a knee surgery, and he admitted that doctors had

cautioned against playing. When asked why he played despite the pain and re-injury risks, he explained, "You just keep playing. Like one of my buddies, we always used to joke 'How many reps you got?' And we used to say 'Four? No, it's forever.'" Although it paid off for Woods, this same mind-over-matter and macho-over-medicine mindset often leads to permanent damage and a sad end to many athletes' dreams.

The connections between sport, masculinity, and health risks are also evident in Klein's (1993) study of bodybuilders. Klein spent years as an ethnographic researcher in the muscled world of the bodybuilding subculture, where masculinity is equated to maximum muscularity and striving for bigness and physical strength. Although bodybuilding allows men to mask emotional insecurities and low self-esteem, doing so often requires men to engage in risky practices such as anabolic steroid use, overtraining, and extreme dieting. Klein thus lays bare a tragic irony in American culture; the powerful male athlete—a symbol of strength and health—has often sacrificed his health in pursuit of this ideal (Messner & Sabo, 1994).

Although athletes who participate in contact sports pay a high physical price for their participation, pundits and academics often give insufficient attention to the health risks associated with sport. Decades ago, George D. Lundberg (1994), a former editor of the *Journal of American Medical Association*, was among the first to draw attention to the deleterious effects of contact sports when he called for a ban on boxing in the Olympics and United States military. Despite systematically drawing upon clinical evidence laying bare the neurological harm of boxing, his editorial entreaty was largely ignored. Today, the amount of scholarly attention given to athletic injuries remains uneven. Despite the extensive participation in sport by millions of youth and young adults, for example, the Centers for Disease Control does not systematically monitor youth sports injuries and fatalities. The pervasive cultural denial surrounding sports injury is also evident in the way some researchers report sporting deaths. The following academic article on deaths among high school and college football players clearly illuminates how academic language can mystify the dangers of playing contact sports (Kucera et al., 2017):

> A high school player aged 16 years was injured at the end of the second quarter of the game while blocking on a kickoff return. The athlete lowered his helmet into the chest of an opponent and appeared unconscious when he hit the ground. He was immediately attended to by emergency medical services and transported by ambulance to a hospital. Surgery was performed to relieve pressure on the brain, but the player never recovered consciousness. He died one week following the injury. Cause of death was a traumatic brain injury.

In this article, the authors place the cause of death squarely on the individual athlete himself, who "lowered his helmet into the chest of an opponent." Outside of the clinical perspective of a journal article, this phrasing sounds preposterous. Think about it: if your friend's chest and skull were crushed during an auto accident, would you say his death happened because he lowered his upper body into the steering wheel or because he was in a car accident? Analogously, this author would label *football* as the "cause of death" for the 16-year-old high school player discussed above.

The cloak of denial is especially prevalent around the topic of traumatic brain injuries (TBIs) in youth sport. Each year more than half a million U.S. youth aged 15 or younger require some type of general hospital care, and boys—especially those who play sport—remain at a heightened risk of suffering TBIs. One study found that 16.2% of boys reported a TBI "sometime in their lifetime" compared to 12.8% of girls (Faul, Xu, Wald, & Coronado, 2010). When researchers looked at the TBI rates among Canadian youth, male athletes accounted for 63% of male TBI cases, whereas female athletes comprised 47% of female TBI cases (Ilie, Boak, Adlaf, Asbridge, & Cusimano, 2013). Regretfully, many head injuries do not fall into the "injury happens, gets treated, and disappears" category. Many of the neurological and behavioral effects of TBIs are long-term, and thus negatively impact boys' and men's cognitive capabilities, personalities, and behaviors across the life course.

Athleticism also places boys and men at an increased likelihood of using performance enhancing drugs. An early nationwide survey of American male high school seniors found that 6.6% were currently using or had previously used anabolic steroids. Athletes comprised about two-thirds of the steroid users (Buckley et al., 1988). Since then, extensive use of anabolic steroids has been uncovered in an array of sporting contexts, ranging from elite sport (professional baseball and football, Olympic weight lifting, international cycling) to youth and recreational sport (Bahrke, Yesalis, Kopstein, & Stephens, 2000). Anabolic steroid use has been linked to physical health risk such as liver disease, kidney problems, atrophy of the testicles, elevated risk for injury, and premature skeletal maturation. Furthermore, using anabolic steroids places young males at an increased risk of engaging in other health risk behaviors such as fighting, driving without a seatbelt, using drugs and alcohol, and committing suicide (Melnick, Miller, Sabo, Barnes, & Farrell, 2010; Miller, Barnes, Sabo, Melnick, & Farrell, 2002).

Although boys average higher rates of drug and alcohol use during adolescence when compared to girls (Veliz, Boyd, & McCabe, 2015), high school athletic participation appears to play a key role in moderating this relationship. Some studies have found that male high school athletes are less likely to smoke cigarettes (Melnick, Miller, Sabo, Farrell, & Barnes, 2001) and use drugs such as marijuana or cocaine (Miller, Sabo, Melnick, Farrell, & Barnes, 2001). However, other research finds that illicit substance use varies by the *type* of sport. Among 8th through 12th graders, for example, boys playing high contact sports (i.e., football, wrestling, hockey, lacrosse) reported higher rates of illicit substance use during the past 30 days when compared to boys playing semi-contact sports (i.e., baseball, basketball, field hockey, and soccer), non-contact sports (i.e., cross country, swimming and diving, tennis, track, and volleyball), and boys who were not athletes (Veliz et al., 2015). A key public health lesson here for young people and parents is that more research is needed, to fully understand the range of health outcomes associated with boys' and men's sporting participation.

Dads and Health Promotion

Understanding how men's physical and mental health unfolds inside marriage and family is an emerging concern among men's health advocates. Family life today is more diverse than ever, and many families no longer fit the "traditional" two-parent nuclear family comprised of a breadwinner dad and a stay-at-home mom. Gay marriage is now legal within the U.S., divorce is more common than it used to be, and Americans now marry at older ages. There is more diversity in the ways men parent; e.g., many single parents are men, LGBT men are raising a child under age 18 (Goldberg, Gartrell, & Gates, 2014).

One result of changing family forms is that more dads play a central role in shaping their kids' health behaviors and attitudes (Marsiglio, 2016), including providing a model for healthy or risky behaviors. For example, Canadian researchers found that preschool-aged boys with parents who encouraged and enjoyed physical activity were more physically active than boys with inactive and unsupportive parents (Zecevic, Tremblay, Lovsin, & Michel, 2010). Men also play an important role in shaping their partners' physical and emotional health. Men's choices and behaviors inside marriage and family can foster their spouses' and kids' health and physical activity levels (Bonhomme, 2007), but income and education often exert greater influence on the health-smart behaviors of adults and children than gender or race (Brown et al., 2015).

Men's Health Issues

U.S. men die for different reasons, but one leading cause of death is cancer. The three most common cancers among males are prostate (102/100,000), lung (70/100,000), and colorectal (94/100,000), but race and ethnicity shape men's odds of dying from cancer (United States Cancer Statistics, 2016). For men of all races, the leading causes of cancer death is lung cancer (54/100,000). Rates of prostate and colorectal cancer—which are 19/100,000 and 17/100,000, respectively—are the second and third most prevalent types of cancer for white, black and Hispanic men, whereas colorectal cancer is second among Asian/Pacific Islander men. Advocates for men's health struggle to understand these issues, and some are discussed below.

Testicular Cancer

Though relatively rare in the general population (1% of all cancers in men), testicular cancer is commonly identified among men aged 21–34 years old (American Cancer Society, 2005). If detected early, the cure rate is high, while delayed diagnosis can be life-threatening. Regular testicular self-examination (TSE), therefore, can be an effective preventive means for insuring early detection and successful treatment. Regretfully, however, most physicians do not teach TSE techniques, and most men are not aware of testicular cancer. Other men are reluctant to examine their testicles as a preventive measure, and even men who are taught TSE practice self-examinations less frequently over time. Men's resistance to TSE has been linked to awkwardness about touching themselves, associating the touching of their genitals with homosexuality or masturbation, or the idea that TSE is not a manly behavior. In an effort to encourage men to educate themselves and take steps to monitor and assess their overall health, Courtenay (2011) developed a "Six-Point HEALTH Plan," which encourages men to deconstruct cultural stereotypes of men as strong, invulnerable, and resistant to disease and injury. After dropping the expectation that men should be macho, men can better recognize the consequences associated with not using a seat belt, drinking and driving, engaging in unsafe sex acts, popping pills, fighting, and ignoring the possibility of testicular cancer. Integral to this plan is the practice of regular testicular self-exams, which remains a key form of preventative self-care.

Further complicating matters, however, is the fact that men sometimes postpone seeking treatment when testicular symptoms are recognized.

Men's individual reluctance to discuss testicular cancer partly derives from the widespread cultural silences that envelopes it. The penis is a cultural symbol of male power, authority, and sexual domination. Its symbolic efficacy in traditional, male-dominated gender relations, therefore, risks being eroded by the realities of testicular cancer, thus highlighting the ways in which subscribing to aspects of hegemonic masculinity places men at an increased risk of engaging in behaviors that are detrimental to their overall health.

Prostate Disease

The older men get, the more likely it is that they will develop medical problems with their prostate glands. Some men may experience benign prostatic hyperplasia, an enlargement of the prostate gland that is associated with symptoms such as dribbling after urination, frequent urination, or incontinence. Others may develop infections (prostatitis) or malignant prostatic hyperplasia (prostate cancer). Prostate cancer is diagnosed more frequently in Canada and the United States than any other cancer (McDavid, Lee, Fulton, Tonita, & Thompson, 2004). One in six men develop this cancer during their lifetime, with African American males showing higher prevalence rates than white men (American Cancer Society, 2017). Although prostate cancer rates have increased in recent decades, earlier diagnosis and treatment have reduced mortality.

Treatments for prostate problems depend on the specific diagnosis, but range from medication to radiation to surgery. As is the case with testicular cancer, survival from prostate cancer is enhanced by early detection. Raising men's awareness about the health risks associated with the prostate gland, therefore, may prevent unnecessary morbidity and mortality. Furthermore, more invasive surgical treatments for prostate cancer can produce incontinence and impotence, speaking to the importance of early detection.

Alcohol Use

When compared to women, men comprise a greater percentage of alcohol users who develop social and medical problems from alcohol abuse, a trend that occurs in part due to the connection between traditional masculinity and alcohol consumption. The media often sensationalizes links between booze and male bravado. For decades, male stereotypes have been used in beer commercials to promote beer drinking as a reward for a job well done, as a form of male bonding, or to glorify romantic success with women (Postman, Nystrom, Strate, & Weingartner, 1987). The combination of beer and liquor ads with sports imagery is a common advertising ploy to entice men to consume alcohol (Messner & Montez De Oca, 2005).

Alcohol use is now highly prevalent among U.S. teenagers. Eighteen percent of eighth graders and 55% of twelfth graders have gotten drunk "at least once" in their lives (Johnston, O'Malley, Bachman, & Schulenberg, 2008). In many high schools and colleges, girls have caught up with boys' rate of binge drinking, which is defined as drinking five drinks in rapid succession for males and four drinks for females (Wecshler, 2005). Males who were frequent binge drinkers were more likely than non-binge-drinking males to report driving after drinking, missing class, engaging in unplanned sexual behavior, falling behind in school work, being hurt or injured and having trouble with campus police. For both sexes, binge drinking is associated with other health risks such as STDs, unintended pregnancy, and sexual assault (CDC, 2012).

Although heart disease is the leading health risk for U.S. men across all age groups, unintentional injuries pose the greatest threat to men's life from childhood through age 44 (Mayo Clinic, 2008). Alcohol abuse likely helps explain this statistic. More men than women die from alcohol-induced causes (Kung, Hoyert, Xu, & Murphy, 2008). Alcohol use is frequently involved with the four leading causes of death among youth and young adults—motor vehicle accidents, unintentional injuries, homicide, and suicide (Eaton et al., 2006), and alcohol-related automobile accidents are the top cause of death among 16- to 24-year-old men. The number of automobile fatalities among male adolescents that result from a mixture of alcohol abuse and macho daring is unknown.

Men and HIV/AIDS

During the 1980s, human immunodeficiency virus (HIV) infection became a major cause of death for U.S. men. By 1990, for example, HIV infection was the second leading cause of death among men aged 25–44, versus the sixth leading cause of death among same-age women (CDC, 2006c). Today, African Americans and Hispanics/Latinos remain disproportionately overrepresented among those affected by HIV, especially among males. At the same time, however, new HIV diagnoses have decreased by 35% among all heterosexuals, 40% among all women, 42% among African American women, and 63% among those who inject drugs (CDC, 2016). The sexual behaviors among 13- to 24-year-olds accounted for 22% of new HIV/AIDS diagnoses in the US in 2015, with gay and bisexual males contributing to 81% of the total (CDC, 2017).

The sexual behaviors of young people help explain why youth and young adults continue to comprise a large percentage of U.S. individuals diagnosed with HIV. Among high school students surveyed during 2015, for example, 41% reported having sexual intercourse at least once, and 30% did so during the previous 3 months. For those surveyed, 43% did not use a condom, and 21% used drugs or alcohol before sex (CDC, 2017).

Men who are disadvantaged by race or socioeconomic inequality also remain more likely to come into contact with HIV/AIDS. CDC data show, for example, that African Americans, who are about 14% of the total U.S. population, comprised 49% of both new HIV cases and new AIDS diagnoses in 2006 (Noble, 2008). African Americans (not Hispanic) were 38.2% of all the estimated adult and adolescent males living with AIDS between 1981 and 2006 (CDC, 2006b). Courtenay (2011) reports that one in four males who die from HIV infection is African American, and among college-age African American men, the HIV infection rate is three times greater than it is for white men. The high rate of AIDS among racial and ethnic minorities can kindle racial prejudices in some minds, and AIDS is sometimes seen as a "minority disease." HIV infection is also linked to economic problems, including community disintegration, unemployment, homelessness, eroding urban tax bases, mental illness, substance use, and criminalization (Wallace, 1991). For example, males comprise the majority of homeless persons and runaway children. Poverty and adult homelessness and running away from home among children overlap with drug addiction and sexual victimization which, in turn, are linked to HIV infection. While African American men, Hispanic men, and men living in poverty may be at greater risk of contracting HIV/AIDS, it is not their race or class position that confers risk, but rather the social circumstances and inequalities shaping their lives.

Suicide

During 2013, there were 41,149 suicides in the U.S., or about one every 13 minutes (CDC, 2013b). Suicide ranks third as a cause of death among persons aged 10–14, second among 15- to 34-year-olds, and fourth among 35- to 44-year-olds. Males comprised 77.9% of all suicides, and compared to females, males typically deploy more violent means of attempting suicide and are more likely to complete the act—a preference that is consistent with traditional masculine behavior. For example, men often use firearms to kill themselves (56.9%), whereas women are more apt to use poison (38%).

The fact that men are more likely to die from suicide than women is puzzling, as suicide data consistently show that men attempt suicide less frequently. Canetto's (Canetto, 1995) pioneering interviews with male suicide survivors, however, provide lasting insights into these trends. While she recognized that men's psychosocial reactions and adjustments to nonfatal suicide vary by race/ethnicity, socioeconomic status, and age, masculinity remains an important factor shaping men's experiences. Failure is often seen as being unmanly, suggesting that developing solutions to undermine aspects of traditional masculinity might result in declines in men's suicide rates.

Erectile Dysfunction

Men often joke about their penises or tease one another about penis size and erectile potency (i.e., not being able to "get it up"). In contrast, they rarely discuss concerns about erectile dysfunction (ED) in a serious way. Men's silences about ED are regrettable in that many men, both young and old, experience recurrent or periodic difficulties getting or maintaining an erection. ED, which is defined as having a partial or complete inability to get and maintain an erection, usually has physical causes, happens mostly to older men, and is frequently treatable. Estimates of the number of American men with erectile disorders range from 10 million to 30 million (Minnesota Men's Health Center, 2008). Some main risk factors for ED are diabetes, smoking, and aging.

During the 1960s and 1970s, erectile disorders were largely thought to stem from psychological problems such as depression, financial worries, or work-related stress. Masculine stereotypes about male sexual prowess, phallic power, or being in charge of lovemaking were also identified as potentially placing too much pressure on some males to perform. Today, however, health experts increasingly emphasize *physiological* explanations of ED and medical interventions as treatment. Many men with erectile disorders are relieved to learn that the dysfunction is not "in their heads" but is something that is often medically addressed.

The marketing and availability of drugs like Viagra have inadvertently spawned a wave of recreational drug use (Brownlee, 2007). Young men may mix Viagra with other club drugs at parties or for all-night sex. Some evidence shows that Viagra use is greater among men who have sex with men and heterosexuals who use other kinds of drugs during sex which, in turn, can lead to other forms of sexual risk taking (Fisher et al., 2006).

Men's Violence

Men's violence is a major public health problem. The traditional masculine ideal calls on males to be aggressive and tough. Anger is a by-product of this aggression and toughness, a vehicle used by some men to separate themselves from women and gain status from other men. Men's anger and violence derive, in part, from gender inequality.

Women are especially victimized by men's anger and violence in the form of rape, date rape, battery, assault, sexual harassment on the job, and verbal harassment (Katz, 2006). Men use the real or perceived threat of violence to maintain their political and economic advantage over women and lesser-status men, thus reinforcing larger patterns of domination.

U.S. homicide rates have declined in recent decades (Bureau of Justice Statistics, 2011), but one pattern has remained constant—men are the most likely to commit and be victims of homicide. During the 2000s, for example, the homicide rate was highest among U.S. 15- to 19-year-old males (13/100,000 standard population) followed by 25- to 34-year-olds (11/100,000) (Kung et al., 2008). In 2005 males were almost four times more likely than females to die from homicide (9.8/100,000 and 2.5%/100,000, respectively). The convergence of race, ethnicity, and economic inequalities also shapes risk for death from homicide (Edwards, 2014).

War, a form of institutionalized violence, has always been a gendered and predominantly male activity that exacted high rates of morbidity and mortality among its participants (Malszecki & Cavar, 2001; Sjoberg, 2013). An estimated 108 million people died in wars during the 20th century, and between 150 million and 1 billion were killed in wars throughout patriarchal history (Hedges, 2003). Soldiers are taught to conform to a type of traditional masculinity that embodies violence-proneness, toughness, and obedience to male authority. The negative health consequences of war for both sexes are painfully evident. Many boys and men are killed, whereas others return from war physically and psychologically maimed. Men's violence on the patriarchal battlefields also often spills over into civilian populations where women and children are victimized (Brownmiller, 1975; Chang, 1997). As Sen (1997) observed, "Historically, wars between nations, classes, castes, races, have been fought on the battlefield on the bodies of men, and off the battlefield on the bodies of women" (p. 12). Today, expressions of the militarization of men's violence, partly inspired and fueled by traditional masculinities, are found in the Taliban of Afghanistan, the Darfur region of Sudan, terrorist movements, the warring factions in Syria or Iraq, or the bluff and bravado of male political leaders like Kim Jong Lee, Vladimir Putin, or Donald Trump.

Male Victims of Sexual Assault

Researchers and public health advocates began to recognize the sexual victimization of women in Western countries during the late 1960s. By the late 1990s, the sexual abuse of males began to receive increased attention within the media and public discourses. In Canada, for example, media coverage of the sexual abuse of youth hockey players by their coaches spurred recognition of the issue (Robinson, 1998). Reformers also decried man-on-man rape in North American prisons (Kupers, 2017). The alleged cover-ups by Catholic bishops in the United States, in relation to some priests' pedophilic exploitation of boys, and the activism and litigation of victims have expanded public awareness as well.

Despite growing public recognition, research in this area is rare. Little is known about the prevalence of sexual abuse of boys and its psychosocial effects. Campus rape is now rightfully recognized as a key social concern among women, but male students are also victimized in appreciable numbers. In a survey of nine U.S. universities during the 2014–2015 academic year 0.8% of male students reported being raped, 3.1% were sexually assaulted, and 7.0% were assaulted since entering any college; the respective percentages for women were 4.1%, 10.3% and 34.4% (Krebs, Lindquist, Berzofsky, Shook-Sa, & Peterson, 2016). Males who suffer sexual victimization as children experience lasting self-blame, feelings of powerlessness and stigmatization, suspicion of others, and confusion about sexual identity, and some eventually repeat the cycle by victimizing others as adolescents and adults (Messerschmidt, 2000; O'Leary, 2001). In summary, in our patriarchal society sexual violence against girls and women is far more pervasive than it is against boys and men

(DeKeseredy, 2011), but both are legitimate legal and public health concerns.

Summary

Images of muscled, invulnerable, daring, unemotional, and risk-taking masculinity remain prevalent within U.S. culture. Each summer, Hollywood rolls out adventure films about superheroes like The Hulk, Iron Man, Spiderman, X-Men, and the Fantastic Four. It is ironic, however, that two of the best known actors portraying Superman suffered from real-life disasters. George Reeves, who starred in the original black-and-white television show, committed suicide, and Christopher Reeves, who portrayed the "man of steel" in technicolor, was paralyzed during a high-risk equestrian event. One lesson is that behind the cultural façade of mythic masculinity, men are vulnerable. Indeed, as we have seen in this article, the cultural messages sewn into the fabric of masculinity put men at risk for illness and early death. A sensible preventive health strategy for men today is to challenge the negative aspects of traditional masculinity that endanger their health, while encouraging men to embody the positive aspects of men's lifestyles that heighten their physical vitality. To put it simply: enjoy the movies, play with the myths, but don't buy into messages about masculinity that put your well-being at risk!

Sabo and Gordon (1995) created the term "men's health studies" to describe theory and research that used gender theory and feminist vision to critically evaluate unhealthy facets of masculine identity and men's lives. The understanding and promotion of men's health requires a sharper recognition that the sources of men's risks for many diseases do not strictly reside in men's psyches, gender identities, or the activities that they enact in daily life. Men's activities, routines, and relations with others are fixed in the historical and structural relations that constitute the larger gender order. As we have seen, not all men or male groups share the same access to social resources, educational attainment, and opportunity that, in turn, can influence their health options. Yes, men need to pursue personal change in order to enhance their health, but without changing the political, economic, and ideological structures of the gender order, men's individual-level health gains can easily erode. If men are going to pursue self-healing, therefore, they need to create an overall preventive strategy that at once seeks to change potentially harmful aspects of traditional masculinity that negatively impact the health of boys and men from all walks of life.

References

Aday, R. H. (2003). *Aging prisoners: Crisis in American corrections*. New York: Praeger.

American Cancer Society. (2017). *Cancer Facts & Figures 2017*. Atlanta: American Cancer Society, 2017.

Anderson, E., Magrath, R., & Bullingham, R. (2016). *Out in Sport: The Experiences of Openly Gay and Lesbian Athletes in Competitive Sport*. New York: Routledge.

Artiga, S., Foutz, J., Cornachione, E., & Garfield, R. (2007). *Key Facts: Race, Ethnicity & Medical Care*. Henry J. Kaiser Family Foundation.

Bahrke, M. S., Yesalis, C. E., Kopstein, A. N., & Stephens, J. A. (2000). Risk Factors Associated With Anabolic–Androgenic Steroid Use Among Adolescents. *Sports Medicine, 29*(6), 397–405.

Bonhomme, J. J. (2007). Men's health: impact on women, children and society. *The Journal of Men's Health & Gender, 4*(2), 124–130.

Broom, A., & Tovey, P. (2009). *Men's health: Body, identity and social context*. West Sussex: John Wiley & Sons. Retrieved from https://books.google.nl/books?hl=en&lr=&id=9hexN6JAVrYC&oi=fnd&pg=PR8&dq=).++Men%E2%80%99s+Health:+Body,+Identity+and+Social+Context&ots=PzZ9l7h9bT&sig=wWzsqjPxzXIoRe85arJLg3HrDAg

Brown, N. A., Smith, K. C., Thornton, R. L., Bowie, J. V., Surkan, P. J., Thompson, D. A., & Levine, D. M. (2015). Gathering perspectives on extended family influence on African American children's physical activity. *Journal of Health Disparities Research and Practice, 8*(1), 10.

Brownlee, S. (2007). *Overtreated: Why too much medicine is making us sicker and poorer*. New York: Bloomsbury Publishing USA.

Brownmiller, S. (1975). *Against our will: Men, women and rape*. New York: Open Road Media.

Buckley, W. E., Yesalis, C. E., Friedl, K. E., Anderson, W. A., Streit, A. L., & Wright, J. E. (1988). Estimated prevalence of anabolic steroid use among male high school seniors. *Journal of American Medical Association, 260*(23), 3441–3445.

Bureau of Justice Statistics. (2007). *Medical Causes of Death in State Prisons, 2001–2004*. Washington, DC: U.S. Department of Justice. Retrieved from https://www.ncjrs.gov/App/AbstractDB/AbstractDBDetails.aspx?id=237953

Bureau of Justice Statistics. (2011, November 18). New Report: U.S. Homicide Rate Falls to Lowest Rate in Four Decades. Retrieved from https://www.justice.gov/archives/opa/blog/new-report-us-homicide-rate-falls-lowest-rate-fourdecades

Burrus, B. B., Liburd, L. C., & Burroughs, A. (1998). Maximizing participation by black Americans in population-based diabetes research: the Project DIRECT pilot experience. *Journal of Community Health, 23*(1), 15–28.

Canetto, S. S. (1995). Men who survive a suicidal act: Successful coping or failed masculinity. In D. Sabo & D. F. Gordin (Eds.), *Men's health and illness: Gender, power, and the body* (pp. 292–304). Newbury Park, CA: Sage.

Carroll, M. D., Navaneelan, T., Bryan, S., & Ogden, C. L. (2015). *Prevalence of Obesity among Children and Adolescents in the United States and Canada* (NCHS Data Brief No. 211). Atlanta, GA: Centers for Disease Control and Prevention. Retrieved from http://eric.ed.gov/?id=ED563900

CDC. (1992). *Advance report of final mortality statistics, 1989* (Monthly Vital Statistics Report No. 40(8), Supplement 2). Atlanta, GA: Centers for Disease Control and Prevention. Retrieved from https://www.cdc.gov/nchs/data/mvsr/supp/mv40_08s2.pdf

CDC. (2006a). *Sports-related injuries among high school athletes—United States, 2005-06 school year* (No. 55(38)). Atlanta, GA: Centers for Disease Control and Prevention.

CDC. (2006b). *Twenty-five years of HIV/AIDS—United States, 1981–2006* (No. 55(21)). Atlanta, GA: Centers for Disease Control and Prevention.

CDC. (2006c). *Update: Mortality attributable to HIV infections/AIDS among persons aged 25–55 years—United States, 1990–91* (No. 42(25)) (pp. 481–6). Atlanta, GA: Centers for Disease Control and Prevention.

CDC. (2008). *Work-related injury deaths among Hispanics—United States, 1992–2006* (No. 57(22)) (pp. 597–600). Atlanta, GA: Centers for Disease Control and Prevention.

CDC. (2012). *Fact Sheets—Binge Drinking*. Atlanta, GA: Centers for Disease Control and Prevention. Retrieved from https://www.cdc.gov/alcohol/fact-sheets/binge-drinking.htm

CDC. (2013a). *CDC Health Disparities and Inequalities Report—United States, 2013* (62(3), Supplement 3). Atlanta, GA: Centers for Disease Control and Prevention. Retrieved from https://www.cdc.gov/mmwr/pdf/other/su6203.pdf

CDC. (2013b). *WISQARS (Web-based Injury Statistics Query and Reporting System)—Injury Center*. Atlanta, GA: Centers for Disease Control and Prevention. Retrieved from https://www.cdc.gov/injury/wisqars/index.html

CDC. (2016). *HIV in the United States*. Atlanta, GA: Centers for Disease Control and Prevention. Retrieved from https://www.cdc.gov/hiv/statistics/overview/ataglance.html

CDC. (2017). *Health Services for Teens*. Atlanta, GA: Centers for Disease Control and Prevention. Retrieved from https://www.cdc.gov/healthyyouth/healthservices/index.htm

Chang, I. (1997). *The rape of Nanking: The forgotten holocaust of World War II*. New York: Penguin Books.

Chin, M. H., Zhang, J. X., & Merrell, K. (1998). Diabetes in the African American Medicare population: morbidity, quality of care, and resource utilization. *Diabetes Care, 21*(7), 1090–1095.

Collins, K. S., Hall, A., & Neuhaus, C. (1999). *U.S. minority health: A chartbook, 1999*. New York: The Commonwealth Fund.

Connell, R., & Messerschmidt, J. W. (2005). Hegemonic masculinity rethinking the concept. *Gender & Society, 19*(6), 829–859.

Courtenay, W. (2011). *Dying to be men: Psychosocial, environmental, and biobehavioral directions in promoting the health of men and boys*. New York: Routledge.

Courtenay, W. H., McCreary, D. R., & Merighi, J. R. (2002). Gender and ethnic differences in health beliefs and behaviors. *Journal of Health Psychology, 7*(3), 219–231.

Cypress, B. K. (1981). Patients' reasons for visiting physicians: National Ambulatory Medical Care Survey. United States, 1977–78. *Vital and Health Statistics. Series 13, Data from the National Health Survey, 13*(56), 1–128.

Dawson, D. A., & Adams, P. F. (1987). *Current estimates from the National Health Interview Survey*. (Vital Health Statistics Series, Series 10, No. 164 No. 87–1592) (p. 1). Washington, DC: U.S. Department of Public Health Service.

DeKeseredy, W. S. (2011). *Violence against women: Myths, facts, controversies*. Toronto, Ontario: University of Toronto Press. Retrieved from https://books.google.nl/books?hl=en&lr=&id=L7-iG-kwlw0C&oi=fnd&pg=PR9&dq=Violence+against+Women:+Myths,+Facts,+Controversies&ots=1HBSr-8E3u&sig=vAQRr5-7oR9UxGskKMMTwpHZi1M

Dill, L. J., Mahaffey, C., Mosley, T., Treadwell, H., Barkwell, F., & Barnhill, S. (2016). "I Want a Second Chance": Experiences of African American Fathers in Reentry. *American Journal of Men's Health, 10*(6), 459–465. https://doi.org/10.1177/1557988315569593

Eaton, D. K., Kann, L., Kinchen, S., Ross, J., Hawkins, J., Harris, W. A., . . . Wechsler, H. (2006). Youth risk behavior surveillance—United States, 2005. *Journal of School Health, 76*(7), 353–372.

Eberstadt, N. (2016). *Men Without Work: America's Invisible Crisis*. West Conshohocken, PA: Templeton Foundation Press.

Edwards, H. (2014). *The Dr. Harry Edwards Lecture in Sport and American Culture*. Presented at The Texas Program in Sports and Media, Austin, Texas.

Faul, M., Xu, L., Wald, M. M., & Coronado, V. G. (2010). *Traumatic brain injury in the United States: emergency department visits, hospitalizations, and deaths. Atlanta: Centers for Disease Control and Prevention*. Centers for Disease Control and Prevention, National Center for Injury Prevention and Control.

Fisher, D. G., Malow, R., Rosenberg, R., Reynolds, G. L., Farrell, N., & Jaffe, A. (2006). Recreational Viagra use and sexual risk among drug abusing men. *American Journal of Infectious Diseases, 2*(2), 107.

Goldberg, A. E., Gartrell, N. K., & Gates, G. (2014). *Research report on LGB-parent families*. Los Angeles: The Williams Institute, UCLA School of Law. Retrieved from http://williamsinstitute.law.ucla.edu/wp-content/uploads/lgb-parent-families-july-2014.pdf

Hedges, C. (2003, July 6). What Every Person Should Know About War. *The New York Times*.

Retrieved from http://www.nytimes.com/2003/07/06/books/chapters/what-every-person-should-know-aboutwar.html

Ilie, G., Boak, A., Adlaf, E. M., Asbridge, M., & Cusimano, M. D. (2013). Prevalence and correlates of traumatic brain injuries among adolescents. *JAMA*, *309*(24), 2550–2552.

James, D. J., & Glaze, L. E. (2006). *Mental health problems of prison and jail inmates* (Bureau of Justice Statistics Special Report No. NCJ 213600). Washington, DC: U.S. Department of Justice.

Johnston, L. D., O'Malley, P. M., Bachman, J. G., & Schulenberg, J. E. (2008). *Monitoring the Future: National Results on Adolescent Drug Use. Overview of Key Findings, 2008.* (NIH Publication No. 09–7401) (pp. 2550–2552). Bethesda, MD: National Institute on Drug Abuse. Retrieved from http://eric.ed.gov/?id=ED508287

Katz, J. (2006). *Macho Paradox: Why Some Men Hurt Women and How All Men Can Help.* Naperville, IL: Sourcebooks, Inc.

Keeling, R. P. (2000). College health: Biomedical and beyond. *Journal of American College Health*, *49*(3), 101–104.

Klein, A. M. (1993). *Little big men: Bodybuilding subculture and gender construction.* Albany, NY: State University of New York Press.

Krebs, C., Lindquist, C., Berzofsky, M., Shook-Sa, B., & Peterson, K. (2016). *Campus Climate Survey Validation Study Final Technical Report* (Bureau of Justice Statistics Research and Development Series). Washington, DC: Bureau of Justice Statistics, U.S. Department of Justice.

Kucera, K. L., Yau, R., Register-Mihalik, J., Marshall, S. W., Thomas, L. C., Wolf, S., . . . Guskiewicz, K. M. (2017). Traumatic Brain and Spinal Cord Fatalities Among High School and College Football Players—United States, 2005–2014. *Morbidity and Mortality Weekly Report*, *65*(52), 1465–9.

Kung, H.-C., Hoyert, D. L., Xu, J., & Murphy, S. L. (2008). *Deaths: Final data for 2005* (National Vital Statistics Report, Volume 56, Number 10). Atlanta, GA: Centers for Disease Control and Prevention, National Center for Injury Prevention and Control.

Kupers, T. A. (2017). *Solitary: The Inside Story of Supermax Isolation and How We Can Abolish It.* Oakland, CA: University of California Press.

Lundberg, G. D. (1994). Let's stop boxing in the Olympics and the United States Military. *Journal of American Medical Association*, *271*(22), 1790–1790.

Macintyre, S., Hunt, K., & Sweeting, H. (1996). Gender differences in health: are things really as simple as they seem? *Social Science & Medicine*, *42*(4), 617–624.

Malszecki, G., & Cavar, T. (2001). Men, masculinities, war, and sport. In N. Mandell (Ed.), *Feminist issues: Race, class, and sexuality* (pp. 166–192). Toronto, Ontario: Pearson Education Canada.

Marsiglio, W. (2016). *Dads, Kids, and Fitness: A Father's Guide to Family Health.* Rutgers, NJ: Rutgers University Press.

Mayo Clinic. (2008). Men's top 10 health threats: Mostly preventable. Retrieved June 1, 2017, from http://www.mayo-clinic.com/health/mens-health/MC00013

McDavid, K., Lee, J., Fulton, J. P., Tonita, J., & Thompson, T. D. (2004). *Prostate cancer incidence and mortality rates and trends in the United States and Canada.* (Public Health Reports, Volume 119 No. PMC1497609) (pp. 174–186). Atlanta, GA: Division of Cancer Prevention and Control, National Center for Chronic Disease Prevention and Health Promotion, Centers for Disease Control and Prevention. Retrieved from https://www.ncbi.nlm.nih.gov/pmc/articles/PMC1497609/pdf/15192905.pdf

Melnick, M. J., Miller, K. E., Sabo, D. F., Barnes, G. M., & Farrell, M. P. (2010). Athletic participation and seatbelt omission among US high school students. *Health Education & Behavior*, *37*(1), 23–36.

Melnick, M. J., Miller, K. E., Sabo, D. F., Farrell, M. P., & Barnes, G. M. (2001). Tobacco use among high school athletes and nonathletes: Results of the 1997 Youth Risk Behavior Survey. *Adolescence*, *36*(144), 727.

Messerschmidt, J. W. (2000). *Nine lives: Adolescent masculinities, the body, and violence.* Boulder, CO: Westview.

Messner, M. A., & Montez De Oca, J. (2005). The male consumer as loser: Beer and liquor ads in mega sports media events. *Signs*, *30*(3), 1879–1909.

Messner, M. A., & Sabo, D. F. (1994). *Sex, Violence & Power in Sports: Rethinking Masculinity.* Freedom, CA: Crossing Press.

Miller, K. E., Barnes, G. M., Sabo, D. F., Melnick, M. J., & Farrell, M. P. (2002). Anabolic–androgenic steroid use and other adolescent problem behaviors:

Rethinking the male athlete assumption. *Sociological Perspectives*, *45*(4), 467–489.

Miller, K. E., Sabo, D. F., Melnick, M. J., Farrell, M. P., & Barnes, G. M. (2001). *The Women's Sports Foundation Report: Health risks and the teen athlete*. East Meadow, NY: Women's Sport Foundation.

Minnesota Men's Health Center. (2008). Facts about Erectile Dysfunction. Retrieved from http://www.mmhc-online.com/articles/impotency.html

Montagu, A. (1953). *The natural superiority of women*. New York: MacMillan.

National Center for Health Statistics. (1992). *Advance report on final mortality statistics* (40(8) supplement 2 No. 92–1120). Hyattsville, MD: Centers for Disease Control and Prevention, National Center for Injury Prevention and Control.

National Center for Health Statistics. (2016). *Health, United States, 2015: With Special Feature on Racial and Ethnic Health Disparities* (No. 2016–1232). Hyattsville, MD: Centers for Disease Control and Prevention, National Center for Injury Prevention and Control.

National Center for Health Statistics. (2017, May 17). Mortality Data. Retrieved from https://www.cdc.gov/nchs/nvss/deaths.htm

Noble, R. (2008). United States Statistics Summary. Retrieved from http//www.avert.org/statsum.htm

Ogden, C. L., Carroll, M. D., Kit, B. K., & Flegal, K. M. (2012). Prevalence of obesity and trends in body mass index among US children and adolescents, 1999-2010. *Journal of American Medical Association*, *307*(5), 483–490.

O'Leary, P. (2001). Working with males who have experienced childhood sexual abuse. In B. Pease & P. Camilleri (Eds.), *Working with men in the human services*. Crows Nest, Australia: Allen & Unwin.

Payne, S. (2006). *The Health of Men and Women*. Malden, MA: Polity.

Pleck, J. H., Sonenstein, F. L., & Ku, L. C. (1994). Problem Behaviors and Masculinity Ideology in Adolescent Males. In R. D. Ketterlinus & M. E. Lamb (Eds.), *Adolescent Problem Behaviors: Issues and Research*. New York: Routledge. Retrieved from https://www.routledge.com/Adolescent-Problem-Behaviors-Issues-and-Research/Ketterlinus-Lamb/p/book/9780805811575

Polych, C., & Sabo, D. (2001). Sentence—Death by lethal infection: IV-drug use and infectious disease transmission in North American prisons. In D. Sabo, T. A. Kupers, & W. London (Eds.), *Prison masculinities* (pp. 173–83). Philadelphia: Temple University Press.

Postman, N., Nystrom, C., Strate, L., & Weingartner, C. (1987). *Myths, Men, & Beer: An Analysis of Beer Commercials on Broadcast Television, 1987*. Falls Church, VA: AAA Foundation for Traffic Safety.

Robinson, L. (1998). *Crossing the line: Violence and sexual assault in Canada's national sport*. Toronto: McClelland & Stewart Limited.

Sabo, D. (2004). The politics of sports injury: Hierarchy, power, and the pain principle. In K. Young (Ed.), *Sporting bodies, damaged selves: Sociological studies of sports-related injury* (pp. 59–79). Boston: Elsevier.

Sabo, D. (2005). The study of masculinities and men's health: An overview. In M. S. Kimmel, J. Hearn, & R. Connell (Eds.), *Handbook of studies on men and masculinities* (pp. 326–52). Thousand Oaks, CA: Sage.

Sabo, D. (2009). Sports Injury, the Pain Principle, and the Promise of Reform. *Journal of Intercollegiate Sport*, *2*(1), 145–152.

Sabo, D., & Gordon, D. F. (Eds.). (1995). *Men's health and illness: Gender, power, and the body*. Thousand Oaks, CA: Sage Publications.

Sabo, D., Kupers, T. A., & London, W. (Eds.). (2001). *Prison Masculinities*. Philadelphia: Temple University Press.

Schofield, T., Connell, R. W., Walker, L., Wood, J. F., & Butland, D. L. (2000). Understanding men's health and illness: a gender-relations approach to policy, research, and practice. *Journal of American College Health*, *48*(6), 247–256.

Sen, G. (1997, June). *Globalization in the 21st century: challenges for civil society*. Presented at The UNVA Development Lecture, University of Amsterdam.

Sjoberg, L. (2013). *Gendering Global Conflict: Toward a Feminist Theory of War*. New York: Columbia University Press.

Sobralske, M. (2006). Machismo sustains health and illness beliefs of Mexican American men. *Journal of the American Association of Nurse Practitioners*, *18*(8), 348–350.

Straub, N. R. (1994). African Americans: Their health and the health care system. *The Pharos*, 18–20.

Tewksbury, R. (1995). *Sexual adaptation among gay men with HIV* (D. Sabo & D. F. Gordon, Eds.). Thousand Oaks, CA: Sage Publications.

United States Cancer Statistics. (2016). *1999–2013 Cancer Incidence and Mortality Data*. Atlanta, GA: U.S. Department of Health and Human Services, Centers for Disease Control and Prevention and National Cancer Institute. Retrieved from https://nccd.cdc.gov/uscs/

Veliz, P. T., Boyd, C. J., & McCabe, S. E. (2015). Competitive sport involvement and substance use among adolescents: a nationwide study. *Substance Use & Misuse, 50*(2), 156–165.

Wallace, R. (1991). Traveling waves of HIV infection on a low dimensional "socio-geographic" network. *Social Science & Medicine, 32*(7), 847–852.

Wecshler, H. (2005). *Harvard School of Public Health, College Alcohol Study, 1999* (Computer File No. ICPSR03818-v2). Ann Arbor, MI: Inter-university Consortium for Political and Social Research [distributor], 2005-11-22. Retrieved from https://doi.org/10.3886/ICPSR03818.v2

Wingo, P. A., Bolden, S., Tong, T., Parker, S. L., Martin, L. M., & Heath, C. W. (1996). Cancer statistics for African Americans, 1996. *CA: A Cancer Journal for Clinicians, 46*(2), 113–125.

Zecevic, C. A., Tremblay, L., Lovsin, T., & Michel, L. (2010). Parental influence on young children's physical activity. *International Journal of Pediatrics, 2010*.

Manning Up

Threatened Men Compensate by Disavowing Feminine Preferences and Embracing Masculine Attributes

SAPNA CHERYAN, JESSICA SCHWARTZ CAMERON, ZACH KATAGIRI, AND BENOÎT MONIN

"It seems I had to fight my whole life through. Some gal would giggle and I'd get red And some guy'd laugh and I'd bust his head, I tell ya, life ain't easy for a boy named 'Sue'."

—Johnny Cash, "A Boy Named Sue" (1969)

How do people react when one of their important social identities is threatened? In the song "A Boy Named Sue," Johnny Cash tells the story of a boy with an emasculating name. Faced with this ever-present threat to his masculinity, Sue overcompensates by becoming "quick and mean" and fighting his "whole life through." The lyrics attest to the pressure that is placed on males to be masculine and the psychological discomfort felt when masculinity is questioned (e.g., Massad, 1981). The song also suggests that rather than simply living with the threat, men actively respond to recover their masculinity. We tested two basic strategies that men might use to compensate for masculinity threats: (i) exaggerating their masculinity and (ii) avoiding stereotypically feminine preferences. We further examined whether some strategies of reestablishing a threatened identity were favored over others, and if so, why.

Gender is one of the foremost social categories (Fiske, Haslam, & Fiske, 1991; Stangor, Lynch, Duan, & Glas, 1992; van Knippenberg, van Twuyver, & Pepels, 1994), and norms mandating gender-appropriate behaviors are instilled in the US from an early age (Cahill & Adams, 1997; Fagot, 1977; Sandnabba & Ahlberg, 1999). Men feel pressure to conform to gender-stereotypic attributes, such as being tall and athletic (Cejka & Eagly, 1999; McCreary, Saucier, & Courtenay, 2005), having an active sexual life (Gross & Blundo, 2005; Jewkes, 2005), being agentic and assertive (Eagly, 1987; Schmitt & Branscombe, 2001), and achieving status (Eagly & Steffen, 1988; Mirowsky, 1987; Moss-Racusin, Phelan, & Rudman, 2010)....

Men and women who violate gendered expectations encounter backlash in the form of social and economic penalties (Moss-Racusin et al., 2010; Rudman, 1998; Rudman, Moss-Racusin, Glick, & Phelan, 2012).... Although both men and women may change their behaviors when faced with backlash, men are a particularly appropriate population in which to investigate different identity recovery strategies because masculinity is more easily threatened than femininity (Vandello & Bosson, 2013;

Vandello, Bosson, Cohen, Burnaford, & Weaver, 2008; Winegard, Winegard, & Geary, 2014).

Responding to Masculinity Threats

Men who have less masculine facial features (e.g., "babyfaces") are more likely to win military awards (Collins & Zebrowitz, 1995), have assertive and hostile personalities (Zebrowitz, Collins, & Dutta, 1998), and to commit crimes (Zebrowitz, Andreoletti, Collins, Lee, & Blumenthal, 1998) than men whose faces appear more masculine. Similarly, men who receive feedback that they scored low on a measure of masculinity or who participated in a feminine activity were more likely to display aggressiveness (Bosson, Vandello, Burnaford, Weaver, & Wasti, 2009; Vandello et al., 2008; Willer, Rogalin, Conlon, & Wojnowicz, 2013), harass female interaction partners (Maass, Cadinu, Guarnieri, & Grasselli, 2003), and derogate other non-masculine men (Glick, Gangl, Gibb, Klumpner, & Weinberg, 2007; Schmitt & Branscombe, 2001). These findings suggest that men compensate for a masculinity threat by presenting themselves as more stereotypically masculine, in particular by displaying physical evidence of masculinity (e.g., aggressiveness; Winegard et al., 2014).

In the current paper, we examine a potential second strategy available to men in response to a masculinity threat: avoiding stereotypic femininity. Because masculinity and femininity are distinct concepts (Bern, 1974), it is important to understand whether masculinity threat causes men to distance from the outgroup, embrace the ingroup, or do both at the same time. . . . In our studies, we threaten men's masculinity and investigate whether those men are more likely to distance from feminine preferences than men who are not threatened.

Identity Signaling Strategies

The second contribution of this work is to examine whether some strategies are seen as more effective at signaling an identity than others, and are therefore more likely to be used in response to an identity threat. . . . We hypothesize that when embracing an ingroup, threatened individuals may put forth group-relevant *attributes* to establish their credentials as bona fide members of the group, but may not increase their ingroup-aligned *preferences*—perhaps because attributes, especially physical ones (Winegard et al., 2014), are more effective signals of identity than preferences. In other words, threatened men might be more likely to embrace masculine attributes than to embrace masculine preferences because knowing that someone *likes* something may be less informative than knowing that someone *is* something. . . .

We also hypothesize that in the domain of preferences, avoiding stereotypically feminine preferences will be a more commonly employed strategy than embracing stereotypically masculine preferences. For males, masculine preferences (e.g., liking football) are more common and more normative than feminine preferences (e.g., liking figure skating). Outgroup preferences, because they are not normative, serve a diagnostic function, whereas ingroup preferences are seen as normative for the group and therefore less diagnostic (Berger & Heath, 2007; Jones & Davis, 1965; Kelley, 1973; Ybarra, 2002). . . . Preferences for products—from clothing to electronics—may be particularly well suited to capturing how men respond to a threat to their masculinity because the possession of these products can signal to others the kind of person you are (Berger & Heath, 2007; Cheryan, Plaut, Davies, & Steele, 2009; Gosling, Ko, Mannarelli, & Morris, 2002). . . .

In two experiments, we examine three strategies that men might use to respond to a threat to their masculinity: avoiding feminine preferences, embracing masculine preferences, and claiming masculine attributes.[1] Pretests to Study 1 first examine the perceived effectiveness of these strategies in signaling a masculine identity. In Study 1, we give men false feedback that they failed at a test of masculinity and investigate whether they are more likely to distance themselves from feminine products than to embrace masculine ones. Then in Study 2, we employ another technique to threaten masculinity by telling men that they are physically weaker than their male peers and examine which strategies they use to reinstate their masculinity. Across both studies, we hypothesize that strategies that are seen as the most useful indicators of a masculine identity (i.e., distancing from feminine preferences and embracing masculine attributes) will be favored by men to reestablish their masculinity over strategies that are less useful indicators (i.e., embracing masculine preferences).

Study 1

The first study tested two recovery strategies that men could use to respond to a threat to their masculinity: embracing masculine preferences and distancing from feminine preferences. Two pretests were conducted. The first pretest assessed perceptions of how effectively feminine and masculine product preferences signal identity. The second pretest compared the identity signaling properties of product preferences and attributes.

. . . Our hypothesis was that distancing from feminine preferences would be a stronger signal of masculinity than embracing masculine ones, and as a result, men under threat would react by distancing from feminine products compared to non-threatened men but be less likely to embrace masculine products.

Method

Participants

Males (*N* = 36; 13 Whites, 11 Asian Americans, 4 African Americans, 4 Latinos, 3 multiracial, 1 Other) were recruited in an undergraduate dormitory and participated in exchange for a $3 gift card. One participant expressed suspicion in the open-ended data that his feedback was false, but removing his data does not change results. Two male experimenters administered the study.

Pretesting Products

In order to establish a set of products as masculine or feminine, 26 male students as part of a larger study were given a list of 15 activities (e.g., "Shopping at Home Depot"; see Appendix for full list of activities). These activities were chosen to be familiar and relevant to the student population and

range in masculinity and femininity. Participants were instructed to rate on two separate scales the masculinity and femininity of male individuals who engaged in these activities. Ratings were made on two 9-point scales (1 = *not at all masculine/feminine*, 9 = *very masculine/feminine*).

Masculine and feminine activities with confidence intervals that did not include the midpoint were selected for inclusion in this study (five masculine activities, α = .73; three feminine activities, α = .67). Correlations between masculine and feminine ratings ranged from −.75 (Armani) to .31 (Lively Arts). Each activity was converted into a product (e.g., "a $25 gift certificate to Home Depot") for the second pretest. The remaining seven neutral activities were used in Study 2 as controls.

Pretesting Preferences versus Attributes

The objective of the second pretest was to establish how effective each strategy is at signaling an identity. We asked specifically how useful the items or attributes would be in providing information about a male whom participants did not know.

A second sample of 25 students (20 women, 5 men; the majority of the sample was drawn from the female-dominated introductory psychology pool) rated the eight masculine and feminine products from the first pretest as well as an additional five masculine attributes on how useful they would be in signaling a male's identity. Attributes were established as masculine by previous literature and included height, athleticism, aggressiveness, handiness with tools, and past relationship experience (Cejka & Eagly, 1999; Gross & Blundo, 2005; Schmitt & Branscombe, 2001). Participants indicated the extent to which possession of the attribute (e.g., "his height") or interest in the receiving the product (e.g., "his interest in receiving a gift certificate to Home Depot") would "provide useful information"; see Berger and Heath (2007) for a similar measure of identity signaling. Because we were interested in the masculine identity in particular, we asked participants to indicate how useful the item would be in describing "a male student whom you do not know." Ratings were made on a scale from 1 (= *would not be useful in describing him*) to 9 (= *would be very useful in describing him*).

A repeated-measures one-way analysis of variance (ANOVA) revealed that feminine product preferences, masculine product preferences, and masculine attributes differed significantly on how much they signaled a male's identity, $F(2, 48) = 21.73$, $p < .001$. Pairwise comparisons showed that preferences for feminine products were seen as providing significantly more useful information about a male ($M = 5.24$, $SD = 1.54$) than preferences for masculine products ($M = 3.80$, $SD = 1.50$), $F(1, 24) = 20.68$, $p < .001$, $d = .91$. Thus, for men, interest in products that are masculine does not provide as much useful information about that male as interest in feminine products. In addition, the possession of masculine attributes was seen as providing significantly more useful information about a male ($M = 6.10$, $SD = 0.80$) than preferences for masculine products ($M = 3.80$, $SD = 1.50$), $F(1, 24) = 39.85$, $p < .001$, $d = 1.30$ (see Figure 16.1).

Materials and Procedure

Participants completed a computer-based masculinity test with the stated purpose "to measure the level of [their] masculinity compared to those of

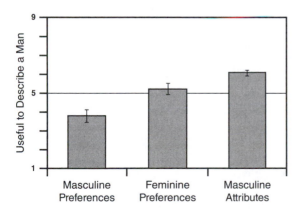

Figure 16.1 Study 1 pretest study ratings of how useful our masculine preferences, feminine preferences, and masculine attributes would be in describing a man. Error bars represent standard error.

other men" (see Rudman and Fairchild, 2004 for a similar procedure). The 17 multiple-choice questions included questions that were related to consumer preferences (e.g., "What kind of car would you prefer to drive?" Options: "Honda Civic," "Ford Taurus," "Toyota Camry," "Volvo C70") or self-related attributes (e.g., "Which of the following characteristics best describes you?" Options: "Logical," "Practical," "Intellectual," "Rational") and were designed so that no answer was obviously masculine. After taking the test, participants were told that the median score was 72 out of 100, with 100 being "completely masculine." Participants then received feedback about their performance via the computer; the experimenter was therefore blind to condition. Participants were randomly assigned to receive either a score of 26 (*threat condition*) or 73 (*non-threat condition*).

Following a reaction time task on the computer,[2] participants were asked to provide feedback about how much they "would like to receive . . . as compensation" the three most masculine and three most feminine products from the pretest (interspersed) on a scale from 1 (= *not at all*) to 7 (= *very much*). A manipulation check item asked participants how their score on the masculinity test compared to other students at their university, on a scale from 1 (= *much less masculine*) to 7 (= *much more masculine*). An open-ended question then asked how they felt about that feedback. Demographics were asked at the end.

Results and Discussion

The manipulation check revealed that threatened participants, as expected, remembered receiving a relatively lower masculinity score ($M = 1.87$, $SD = 0.99$) than non-threatened participants ($M = 4.43$, $SD = .68$), $t(34) = 9.24$, $p < .001$, $d = 3.01$.

A 2 condition (threatened, non-threatened; between) × 2 products (masculine, feminine; within) ANOVA on preference for gendered products (averaged over the three products for each gender) revealed no main effects, both $Fs < 2.0$, $ps > .17$. However, as predicted, there was a significant interaction of condition and products, $F(1, 34) = 5.81$, $p = .02$. Men under threat claimed less interest in receiving feminine products ($M = 2.91$, $SD = 1.37$) than masculine products ($M = 3.78$, $SD = 1.54$), $F(1, 34) = 4.35$, $p = .045$, $d = .66$, but non-threatened men were similarly interested in receiving the masculine ($M = 3.71$, $SD = 1.54$) and feminine products ($M = 4.16$, $SD = 1.52$), $F(1, 34) = 1.60$, $p = .21$ (see Figure 16.2). Seen another way, whereas the groups differed in how much they repudiated feminine products, $F(1, 34) = 6.37$, $p = .02$, $d = .86$, they did not differ in their interest in masculine products, $F(1, 34) = .02$, $p = .90$.

Next we disaggregated the products to establish whether one or a subset of them drove effects. While threatened men distanced at least marginally from all of the feminine products, all $ps < .10$, they did not move on any of the masculine products, all $ps > .46$. Embracing these masculine products seems to provide a less useful signal of masculinity, especially in the context of also being able to distance from feminine products. Taken together with the results of the pretest, these results suggest that threatened males assert their masculinity by

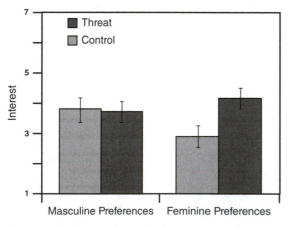

Figure 16.2 Men in Study 1 who were told that they were significantly below the median on a multiple-choice test of masculinity expressed lower preference for feminine products than men who were told that their masculinity score was close to the median for their gender. The two groups did not differ in their preferences for masculine products. Error bars represent standard error.

focusing on the most effective strategy available to them, which in this case was distancing from feminine product preferences. One limitation of this study was the relatively small sample size ($N = 36$ for two cells). We increased the sample size in Study 2 and reassessed effects on the same dependent measures.

Study 2

The results of the previous study suggested that men under masculinity threat distance from stereotypically feminine preferences but do not embrace stereotypically masculine preferences more than non-threatened men. In Study 2, we employed a different threat to masculinity: that of being physically weaker than other males. Whereas previous work on masculinity threat and Study 1 threatened masculinity in a global way (e.g., scoring low on a masculinity test), Study 2 examined whether threatening one specific aspect of masculinity causes men to embrace another aspect to compensate. . . . In this study, we gave men false feedback regarding their handgrip strength and examined whether they boosted their masculinity on a masculine domain unrelated to the one that was threatened. . . .

We predicted that men who were threatened by being told that their handgrip strength was low (despite their actual score) would report less interest in feminine products compared to non-threatened men; however, threat would be less likely to change men's interest in masculine products. In line with the identity signaling properties of masculine attributes found in the pretest data in Study 1, we anticipated that threatened men would report more masculine attributes than those who were not threatened.

Method

Participants

Undergraduate males ($N = 50$) participated in exchange for psychology participant pool credit or snacks. Information about participant race was not collected. No participants expressed suspicion during the study or during debriefing that the feedback or cover story was false. A male experimenter administered this study.

Materials and Procedure

Participants were instructed that they would be participating in a study on "effects of exertion on decision-making." Participants took part in a test of handgrip strength, using the Jamar Grip Test device, a handheld instrument that measures, in kg, the maximum pressure that participants are able to generate by squeezing. After a practice attempt, participants were told to squeeze the device with their dominant hand as hard as they could, after which the experimenter took the device from them, read their score out loud, and recorded it on the questionnaire they were to complete. False feedback on their grip strength was presented on two hand-drawn feedback sheets (dominant hand, nondominant hand) that contained the plotted distribution of scores for alleged previous male and female participants. Male and female plots made two rough, overlapping bell curves (the distribution overlap was roughly 30% for both hands). The sheets were drawn such that, at a glance, it was easy to tell that the female average was lower than the male average. The axes of the graphs were not labeled, to enable the experimenter to mark participants at a particular point in the distribution regardless of their actual performance. The experimenter made a mark on the feedback sheet in the middle of either the female distribution (*threat condition*) or the male distribution (*non-threat condition*) and wrote the score near the mark. The experimenter explained the distributions to the participants and pointed out where their scores fell on the distribution (see Maass et al., 2003 for a similar instantiation of prototypicality threat).

Participants were then given a questionnaire asking about masculine and feminine attributes including: height (*masculine*) (Cejka & Eagly, 1999), number of previous relationships (*masculine*) (Gross & Blundo, 2005), handiness with tools (*masculine*), and personality traits (*masculine and feminine*), as measured by the original Bem Sex-Role Inventory (BSRI; masculine traits α = .87 feminine traits α = .74) (Bem, 1974). . . . Embedded among the questions of interest were distracter questions (e.g., weight and major) to make the questionnaire seem like a general background instrument and minimize suspicion.

Participants repeated the grip test with their nondominant hand and were again reinforced with false feedback that corresponded to their condition. They then rated, on scales from 1 (= *not at all*) to 9 (= *very*), their interest in receiving the five masculine, three feminine, and seven neutral products from the Study 1 pretest (interspersed) as compensation for participating in the study. Participants were asked their opinions of the test (how enjoyable, easy, masculine, feminine, and related to ability; how much effort they put in; how much they cared about doing well). All ratings were made on scales from 1 (= *not at all*) to 9 (= *very*). Finally, the experimenter measured participants' actual heights.

Results

Grip Test Ratings

Participants did not differ by condition on their ratings of the grip test, including how enjoyable (M = 5.24, SD = 1.92) or easy (M = 5.58, SD = 1.89) they found the test, or how much it was a measure of ability (M = 4.84, SD = 2.49), all ts < 1.4, ps > .17. Both groups cared equally about doing well on the test (M = 6.24, SD = 1.98) and reported putting in equal effort (M = 7.18, SD = 1.26), both ts < 1, ps > .57. A 2 (grip test rating [how masculine, how feminine; within]) × 2 (condition [threatened, non-threatened; between]) ANOVA revealed no main effect of condition, $F(1, 48)$ = .00, p = 1.0, nor an interaction on how gendered they rated the grip test, $F(1, 48)$ = .02, p = .89. However, as expected, participants found the test to be more of a test of masculinity (M = 6.02, SD = 1.60) than femininity (M = 3.62, SD = 1.28), $F(1, 48)$ = 75.99, p < .001, d = 1.25. These results suggest that both groups believed the grip test was equally masculine and equally indicative of their ability after receiving the feedback.

Distancing from Feminine Products

To examine whether men reported liking feminine products less when under threat, we ran a 2 condition (threatened, non-threatened; between) × 2 products (masculine, feminine; within) ANOVA and examined preferences for the gendered products, averaged by gender. This analysis revealed no main effect of condition, $F(1, 48) = 1.36$, $p = .25$, but a main effect of products; men were less interested in feminine products than in masculine ones, $F(1, 48) = 5.75$, $p = .02$, $d = .33$. As predicted, this main effect was qualified by a significant interaction, $F(1, 48) = 4.36$, $p = .04$. Threatened men expressed less interest in feminine products than masculine products, $F(1, 48) = 10.07$, $p = .003$, $d = .68$ (see Table 16.1 for means), whereas the non-threatened group did not differ in their interest in feminine and masculine products, $F(1, 48) = .05$, $p = .83$. Seen the other way, the groups differed in interest in feminine products, $F(1, 48) = 4.88$, $p = .03$, $d = .62$, but they did not differ in their interest in masculine products, $F(1, 48) = .12$, $p = .74$. As expected, there were no differences between the groups in interest for the neutral products, $t(48) = .73$, $p = .47$.

Asserting Masculine Attributes

We computed an exaggeration score by taking the difference between their reported height and their actual height. (As would be expected with random assignment, actual height did not differ between the groups, $t(48) < 1.0$, $p = .92$.) Threatened participants exaggerated their height by over three-quarters of an inch; $t(24) = 8.51$, $p < .001$, $d = 1.70$ (one-sample t-test vs. 0), while those in the non-threatened group did not show such a difference between their reported and actual heights, $t(24) = 1.36$, $p = .19$, yielding a significant difference between the groups, $t(48) = 4.15$, $p < .001$, $d = 1.17$. Threatened participants also reported having had more relationships, $t(48) = 3.45$, $p = .001$, $d = .98$, and being marginally more handy with tools, $t(48) = 1.85$, $p = .07$, $d = .52$.

BSRI traits similarly revealed differences between the threatened and non-threatened groups. Thirty of the forty traits were in the predicted

Table 16.1 Men in Study 2 Were Given False Feedback That Their Grip Was Weak (Threatened Group) or Average (Non-Threatened Group) for a Man and Then Asked to Indicate Their Preference for Consumer Products and to Indicate Attributes about Themselves. Preferences for Products, Handiness, and BSRI (Trait) Items Were Asked on Scales from 1 (= *not at all*) to 9 (= *very*)

Strategy	Variable	Threatened		Non-threatened		Test of Difference
		M	(SD)	M	(SD)	p
Repudiating feminine preferences						
	Interest in feminine products	3.45	(1.56)	4.48	(1.72)	*
	Interest in masculine products	4.73	(1.60)	4.57	(1.73)	ns
Asserting masculine attributes						
	Height exaggeration (inches)	0.78	(0.46)	0.16	(0.59)	***
	Reported number of relationships	3.12	(1.59)	1.76	(1.17)	**
	Rating of handiness	6.80	(1.63)	5.84	(2.01)	†
	Masculine slant in BSRI (masculine traits – feminine traits)	0.82	(0.63)	0.37	(0.99)	†
	Rating of own aggressiveness (from BSRI)	4.32	(1.03)	3.40	(1.12)	**
	Rating of own athleticism (from BSRI)	5.36	(1.35)	4.44	(1.76)	*

Note: The groups differ at *$p < .05$, **$p < .01$, ***$p < .001$, †$p < .10$.

direction (binomial p = .002), with threatened participants reporting higher masculine traits and lower feminine traits than controls. A 2 (condition: threatened, non-threatened; between) × 2 BSRI subscale (masculine, feminine; within) ANOVA on the BSRI revealed no main effect of condition, $F(1, 48)$ = .31, p = .58, but a main effect of subscale, $F(1, 48)$ = 25.85, p < .001, d = .70, such that men claimed to have more masculine than feminine traits. These effects were qualified by a marginally significant interaction, $F(1, 48)$ = 3.65, p = .06. The difference between masculine and feminine traits was greater for threatened men, $F(1, 48)$ = 24.47, p < .001, d = 1.31, than for men in the non-threatened condition, $F(1, 48)$ = 5.04, p = .03, d = .37. Group differences were significant for self-ratings of aggressiveness, $t(48)$ = 3.03, p = .004, d = .86, and athleticism, $t(48)$ = 2.08, p = .04, d = .59, two traits on the BSRI related to strength and considered highly stereotypically masculine (Cejka & Eagly, 1999) (see Table 16.1 for means).

Discussion

Men who had their masculinity threatened by ostensibly doing poorly on a test of handgrip strength exaggerated their height, demonstrating that even an objective measure can be falsified when it serves an identity-enhancing function. . . . Threatened men also reported a greater number of past relationship partners and higher levels of aggressiveness and athleticism than did men who were given feedback that they were of average strength for their gender. Challenging one indicator of masculinity led men to attempt to reassert their masculinity on some of the very dimensions with which handgrip strength has been shown to be associated, such as aggressiveness and sexual experience (Gallup et al., 2007).

When not under threat, men did not differ in their preferences for feminine and masculine products. This suggests that the feminine products were no more stigmatized or less attractive for men than the masculine products when men were not under threat. However, when faced with masculine identity threat, threatened men showed less interest in feminine products than in masculine products. . . . Thus, when males in this study were made to feel that one of their masculine traits (i.e., strength) was not measuring up to what is deemed typical for their group, they made up for it indirectly by boosting otherwise unrelated aspects of themselves (e.g., number of past relationships) and distancing from feminine preferences. However, they did not assert normative masculine preferences, suggesting that they were taking into account the effectiveness of different strategies in signaling an identity.

General Discussion

Men who encountered a threat to their masculinity engaged in specific and predictable identity strategies in an attempt to reestablish that masculinity. First, threatened men expressed lower preferences for products that were rated as feminine, such as clothing and beauty products. Second, men attempted to restore their masculinity by altering seemingly indisputable facts from their lives—such as overstating their height, claiming to have had more relationship experiences, and embracing more masculine personality traits—in order to make their individual attributes seem more prototypical of their gender. Men therefore reacted to allegations that they did not live up to the prototypical image of their group by creatively using both distancing and assertion strategies to reestablish their position within that group.

The specific strategies that men used to reinstate their masculinity, however, varied in line with the extent to which they were seen as useful signals of identity. Distancing from feminine products and embracing masculine attributes were seen as more indicative of male identity than embracing masculine products. As a result, men who attempted to reassert their masculinity changed their preferences for feminine products and presented evidence about their masculine attributes, but they did not increase their preferences for masculine products.

These results may be broadly applicable to others who are undergoing a threat to their group memberships. Threatening an important identity could cause group members to distance from outgroup preferences or assert their ingroup status using evidence about themselves rather than claim ingroup preferences.

There are two reasons that men might not both distance from feminine products and embrace masculine ones. First, interest in masculine products was seen as providing less useful information about men than interest in feminine products, suggesting that this domain would be less relevant to their efforts to assert a masculine identity. Second, giving men the opportunity to distance from feminine preferences may have been sufficient to protect their masculine identity in the face of threat (Bosson et al., 2005; Monin & Miller, 2001). Future research could investigate whether embracing masculine preferences might be deployed in situations where distancing from feminine preferences is not an available option (Willer et al., 2013).

From a practical perspective, if we know which strategies are most likely to be deployed, we can focus on preventing the negative consequences that they might engender. Disavowing feminine preferences when under threat could help explain, for example, why men who earn less money than their wives—and are thus not fulfilling a traditional masculine role—are less likely to share housework duties than men who are primary breadwinners (Bittman, England, Sayer, Folbre, & Matheson, 2003). Embracing masculine attributes (i.e., aggressiveness) in response to threats could also be one potential explanation for why men who are unemployed instigate more violence against women than those who are employed (Kyriacou et al., 1999). Considering ways to validate men's masculinity or otherwise remove the threat of not being masculine, perhaps by drawing attention to more inclusive norms of masculinity (Hugenberg & Bodenhausen, 2010), may be helpful in enabling men to embrace more stereotypically feminine and egalitarian pursuits.

Limitations and Future Directions

This paper provides insight into the strategies that men use, and the ways that men use them, when confronted with a threat to their masculinity. One important limitation of this work is that we did not examine how feminine attributes are affected when men are under masculinity threat. Feminine attributes, such as being modest and caring about one's appearance, are perceived as signaling a lack of masculinity in men (e.g., Moss-Racusin et al., 2010). As a result, when men encounter a threat to their masculinity, they may distance from feminine attributes as a way to reassert their masculinity. Future research could include feminine and masculine attributes to examine whether men may be more likely to use one (or both) in response to masculinity threats.

A second limitation of this work is that we used a subset of product preferences in the two studies (e.g., five masculine products, three feminine products, and seven neutral products) and are thus unable to conclude whether results generalize to all masculine and feminine preferences. Indeed, there are likely important features that make some ingroup and outgroup preferences better suited than others to signal masculinity. For example, preferences that overshoot masculine norms and are less common among the ingroup (e.g., liking dog fighting) may say more about men than those that are more normative of men. Future work could examine a range of preferences (and attributes) to examine whether some are more susceptible to being used by men in the face of masculinity threat. . . .

Conclusion

Men whose masculine identity was threatened attempted to restore it by renouncing stereotypically feminine preferences and exaggerating other aspects of their masculinity (such as height, past relationship experience, and self-reported aggressiveness). Notably, the masculinity offered up by these participants took the form of facts from their lives, such as physical height and past relationship history, suggesting that offering seemingly indisputable evidence about one's group membership, as opposed to claiming normative preferences, is a favored strategy of those asserting an identity. The present research adds to the growing body of research evidencing that individuals are not passive recipients of identity threats but, rather, are active participants who engage in creative strategies to preserve and restore their questioned identities.

Notes

1. We did not investigate feminine attributes in this paper. As a result, we do not know whether men may disavow feminine attributes when faced with a threat to their masculinity. See the Limitations and Future Directions section in the General Discussion for more on the exclusion of feminine attributes.
2. We administered a masculine–feminine self-concept implicit association test (Greenwald & Farnham, 2000) but did not find effects of condition on men's implicit self-concept, suggesting that these identity strategies may operate on the explicit rather than implicit level.

References

Bem, S. L. (1974). The measurement of psychological androgyny. *Journal of Consulting and Clinical Psychology, 42,* 155–162.

Berger, J., & Heath, C. (2007). Where consumers diverge from others: Identity-signaling and product domains. *Journal of Consumer Research, 34,* 121–134.

Bittman, M., England, P., Sayer, L., Folbre, N., & Matheson, G. (2003). When does gender trump money? Bargaining and time in household work. *American Journal of Sociology, 109,* 186–214.

Bosson, J. K., Prewitt-Freilino, J. L., & Taylor, J. N. (2005). Role rigidity: A problem of identity misclassification? *Journal of Personality and Social Psychology, 89,* 552–565.

Bosson, J. K., Vandello, J. A., Burnaford, R. M., Weaver, J. R., & Wasti, S. A. (2009). Precarious manhood and displays of physical aggression. *Personality and Social Psychology Bulletin, 35,* 623–634.

Cahill, B., & Adams, E. (1997). An exploratory study of early childhood teachers' attitudes toward gender roles. *Sex Roles, 36,* 517–529.

Cejka, M. A., & Eagly, A. H. (1999). Gender-stereotypic images of occupations correspond to the sex segregation of employment. *Personality and Social Psychology Bulletin, 25,* 413–423.

Cheryan, S., Plaut, V. C., Davies, P. G., & Steele, C. M. (2009). Ambient belonging: How stereotypical cues impact gender participation in computer science. *Journal of Personality and Social Psychology, 97,* 1045–1060.

Collins, M. A., & Zebrowitz, L. A. (1995). The contributions of appearance to occupational outcomes in civilian and military settings. *Journal of Applied Social Psychology, 25,* 129–163.

Eagly, A. H. (1987). *Sex differences in social behavior: A social-role interpretation.* Hillsdale, NJ: Erlbaum.

Eagly, A. H., & Steffen, V. J. (1988). A note on assessing stereotypes. *Personality and Social Psychology Bulletin, 14,* 676–680.

Fagot, B. J. (1977). Consequences of cross-gender behavior in preschool children. *Child Development, 48,* 902–907.

Fiske, A. P., Haslam, N., & Fiske, S. T. (1991). Confusing one person with another: What errors reveal about the elementary forms of social relations. *Journal of Personality and Social Psychology, 60,* 656–674.

Glick, P., Gangl, C., Gibb, S., Klumpner, S., & Weinberg, E. (2007). Defensive reactions to masculinity threat: More negative affect toward effeminate (but not masculine) gay men. *Sex Roles, 57,* 55–59.

Gosling, S. D., Ko, S. J., Mannarelli, T., & Morris, M. E. (2002). A room with a cue: Personality judgments based on offices and bedrooms. *Journal of Personality and Social Psychology, 82,* 379–398.

Greenwald, A. G., & Farnham, S. D. (2000). Using the Implicit Association Test to measure self-esteem and self-concept. *Journal of Personality and Social Psychology, 79,* 1022–1038.

Gross, G., & Blundo, R. (2005). Viagra: Medical technology constructing aging masculinity. *Journal of Sociology & Social Welfare, 32,* 85–97.

Hugenberg, K., & Bodenhausen, G. V. (2010). *Effects of reference group norms and distinctiveness motives on attitudinal judgments: The case of gender deviance.* Unpublished manuscript.

Jewkes, Y. (2005). Men behind bars: "Doing" masculinity as an adaptation to imprisonment. *Men and Masculinities, 8,* 44–63.

Jones, E. E., & Davis, K. E. (1965). A theory of correspondent inferences: From acts to dispositions. *Advances in Experimental Social Psychology, 2*, 219–266.

Kelley, H. H. (1973). The processes of causal attribution. *American Psychologist, 28*, 107–128.

Kyriacou, D. N., Anglin, D., Taliaferro, E., Stone, S., Tubb, T., Linden, J. A., . . . Kraus, J. F. (1999). Risk factors for injury to women from domestic violence against women. *New England Journal of Medicine, 341*, 1892–1898.

Maass, A., Cadinu, M., Guarnieri, G., & Grasselli, A. (2003). Sexual harassment under social identity threat: The computer harassment paradigm. *Journal of Personality and Social Psychology, 85*, 853–870.

McCreary, D. R., Saucier, D. M., & Courtenay, W. H. (2005). The drive for muscularity and masculinity: Testing the associations among gender-role traits, behaviors, attitudes, and conflict. *Psychology of Men and Masculinity, 6*, 83–94.

Mirowsky, J. (1987). The psycho-economics of feeling underpaid: Distributive justice and the earnings of husbands and wives. *American Journal of Sociology, 92*, 1404–1434.

Monin, B., & Miller, D. T. (2001). Moral credentials and the expression of prejudice. *Journal of Personality and Social Psychology, 81*, 33–43.

Moss-Racusin, C. A., Phelan, J. E., & Rudman, L. A. (2010). When men break the gender rules: Status incongruity and backlash against modest men. *Psychology of Men and Masculinity, 11*, 140–151.

Rudman, L. A. (1998). Self-promotion as a risk factor for women: The costs and benefits of counterstereotypical impression management. *Journal of Personality and Social Psychology, 74*, 629–645.

Rudman, L. A., & Fairchild, K. (2004). Reactions to counter stereotypic behavior: The role of backlash in cultural stereotype maintenance. *Journal of Personality and Social Psychology, 87*, 157–176.

Rudman, L. A., Moss-Racusin, C. A., Glick, P., & Phelan, J. E. (2012). Reactions to vanguards: Advances in backlash theory. In P. G. Devine & E. A. Plant (Eds.), *Advances in Experimental Social Psychology* (vol. 45, pp. 167–228). San Diego, CA: Elsevier.

Sandnabba, N. K., & Ahlberg, C. (1999). Parents' attitudes and expectations about children's cross-gender behavior. *Sex Roles, 40*, 249–263.

Schmitt, M. T., & Branscombe, N. R. (2001). The good, the bad, and the manly: Threats to one's prototypicality and evaluations of fellow in-group members. *Journal of Experimental Social Psychology, 37*, 510–517.

Stangor, C., Lynch, L., Duan, C., & Glas, B. (1992). Categorization of individuals on the basis of multiple social features. *Journal of Personality and Social Psychology, 62*, 207–218.

van Knippenberg, A., van Twuyver, M., & Pepels, J. (1994). Factors affecting social categorization processes in memory. *British Journal of Social Psychology, 33*, 419–431.

Vandello, J. A., & Bosson, J. K. (2013). Hard won and easily lost: A review and synthesis of theory and research on precarious manhood. *Psychology of Men & Masculinity, 14*, 101.

Vandello, J. A., Bosson, J. K., Cohen, D., Burnaford, R. M., & Weaver, J. R. (2008). Precarious manhood. *Journal of Personality and Social Psychology, 95*, 1325.

Willer, R., Rogalin, C. L., Conlon, B., & Wojnowicz, M. T. (2013). Overdoing gender: A test of the masculine overcompensation thesis. *American Journal of Sociology, 118*, 980–1022.

Winegard, B., Winegard, B., & Geary, D. C. (2014). Eastwood's brawn and Einstein's brain: An evolutionary account of dominance, prestige, and precarious manhood. *Review of General Psychology, 18*, 34–48.

Ybarra, O. (2002). Naive causal understanding of valenced behaviors and its implications for social information processing. *Psychological Bulletin, 128*, 421–441.

Zebrowitz, L. A., Andreoletti, C., Collins, M. A., Lee, S. Y., & Blumenthal, J. (1998). Bright, bad, baby-faced boys: Appearance stereotypes do not always yield self-fulfilling prophecy effects. *Journal of Personality and Social Psychology, 75*, 1300–1320.

Zebrowitz, L. A., Collins, M. A., & Dutta, R. (1998). The relationship between appearance and personality across the life span. *Personality and Social Psychology Bulletin, 24*, 736.

Appendix

List of Activities and Products Used in Studies 1 and 2

Activities (pretest)	Products (Studies 1 and 2)
Masculine	
Attending a Cardinal basketball game	Two tickets to a Cardinal basketball game
Attending Big Game	Two tickets to the Big Game
Shopping at Home Depot	A $25 gift certificate to Home Depot
Watching a movie at a movie theater, a drink and popcorn	Two movie passes with free drinks and with popcorn
Buying an unassembled desk from Ikea	A free desk from Ikea unassembled
Feminine	
Going to Health and Body Day Spa	A free trial day at Health and Body Day
Spa shopping at Banana Republic	A $25 gift certificate to Banana Republic
Attending a Lively Arts performance	Two tickets to a Lively Arts performance
Neutral	
Wearing a Stanford sweatshirt from the bookstore	A free Stanford University sweatshirt from the bookstore
Eating at Bucca di Beppo	A free dinner at Bucca di Beppo
Shopping at the Stanford bookstore	A $25 gift certificate for the Stanford bookstore
Buying a preassembled desk from Ikea	A free desk from Ikea preassembled
Shopping at Armani Exchange	A $25 gift certificate to Armani Exchange
Getting a haircut at Supercuts	A free haircut at Supercuts
Participating in a session with a personal trainer at 24 Hr Fitness	A free trial day 24 Hr Fitness with a personal trainer

If Men Could Menstruate

GLORIA STEINEM

A white minority of the world has spent centuries conning us into thinking that a white skin makes people superior—even though the only thing it really does is make them more subject to ultraviolet rays and to wrinkles. Male human beings have built whole cultures around the idea that penis-envy is "natural" to women—though having such an unprotected organ might be said to make men vulnerable, and the power to give birth makes womb-envy at least as logical.

In short, the characteristics of the powerful, whatever they may be, are thought to be better than the characteristics of the powerless—and logic has nothing to do with it.

What would happen, for instance, if suddenly, magically, men could menstruate and women could not?

The answer is clear—menstruation would become an enviable, boastworthy, masculine event:

Men would brag about how long and how much.

Boys would mark the onset of menses, that longed-for proof of manhood, with religious rituals and stag parties.

Congress would fund a National Institute of Dysmenorrhea to help stamp out monthly discomforts.

Sanitary supplies would be federally funded and free. (Of course, some men would still pay for the prestige of commercial brands such as John Wayne Tampons, Muhammad Ali's Rope-a-dope Pads, Joe Namath Jock Shields—"For Those Light Bachelor Days," and Robert "Baretta" Blake Maxi-Pads.)

Military men, right-wing politicians, and religious fundamentalists would cite menstruation ("*men*-struation") as proof that only men could serve in the Army ("you have to give blood to take blood"), occupy political office ("can women be aggressive without that steadfast cycle governed by the planet Mars?"), be priests and ministers ("how could a woman give her blood for our sins?"), or rabbis ("without the monthly loss of impurities, women remain unclean").

Male radicals, left-wing politicians, and mystics, however, would insist that women are equal, just different; and that any woman could enter their ranks if only she were willing to self-inflict a major wound every month ("you *must* give blood for the revolution"), recognize the preeminence of menstrual issues, or subordinate her selfness to all men in their Cycle of Enlightenment.

Street guys would brag ("I'm a three-pad man") or answer praise from a buddy ("Man, you lookin' *good*!") by giving fives and saying, "Yeah, man, I'm on the rag!"

TV shows would treat the subject at length. ("Happy Days": Richie and Potsie try to convince Fonzie that he is still "The Fonz," though he has missed two periods in a row.) So would newspapers.

(SHARK SCARE THREATENS MENSTRUATING MEN. JUDGE CITES MONTHLY STRESS IN PARDONING RAPIST.) And movies. (Newman and Redford in "Blood Brothers"!)

Men would convince women that intercourse was *more* pleasurable at "that time of the month." Lesbians would be said to fear blood and therefore life itself—though probably only because they needed a good menstruating man.

Of course, male intellectuals would offer the most moral and logical arguments. How could a woman master any discipline that demanded a sense of time, space, mathematics, or measurement, for instance, without that in-built gift for measuring the cycles of the moon and planets—and thus for measuring anything at all? In the rarefied fields of philosophy and religion, could women compensate for missing the rhythm of the universe? Or for their lack of symbolic death-and-resurrection every month?

Liberal males in every field would try to be kind: the fact that "these people" have no gift for measuring life or connecting to the universe, the liberals would explain, should be punishment enough.

And how would women be trained to react? One can imagine traditional women agreeing to all these arguments with a staunch and smiling masochism ("The ERA would force housewives to wound themselves every month": Phyllis Schlafly. "Your husband's blood is as sacred as that of Jesus—and so sexy, too!": Marabel Morgan.) Reformers and Queen Bees would try to imitate men, and *pretend* to have a monthly cycle. All feminists would explain endlessly that men, too, needed to be liberated from the false idea of Martian aggressiveness, just as women needed to escape the bonds of menses-envy. Radical feminists would add that the oppression of the nonmenstrual was the pattern for all other oppressions. ("Vampires were our first freedom fighters!") Cultural feminists would develop a bloodless imagery in art and literature. Socialist feminists would insist that only under capitalism would men be able to monopolize menstrual blood. . . .

In fact, if men could menstruate, the power justifications could probably go on forever.

If we let them.

Examining Boys, Bodies, and PE Locker Room Spaces

"I Don't Ever Set Foot in That Locker Room"

MICHAEL KEHLER

For many boys, time spent in high school gym, or what is formally known as "physical education" (PE), is a fond and distant memory. The fondness does not, however, imply it was enjoyable for all. Rather, it conveys happiness that PE is over and done with, a memory that some would rather forget. Secondary school PE in particular is often characterized by a competitive model that promotes and encourages one-upmanship among boys. Striving to out run, pump more iron, or do more push-ups than your classmate, while not always intended, is nonetheless part of the culture in many boys' PE classes. Proving to your peers that you are stronger, faster, and more able-bodied is often accepted and encouraged in PE classes. Boys need to be tough; competition in sport is what makes them men! Reaffirming to some, this masculine culture oppresses and silences other boys. However, it is prevalent in many schools and regularly considered normal, "boys being boys." Sports, masculinity, and schooling have long been associated with a problematic culture that has been more about "measuring up" and performing or expressing a hypermasculinity and less about promoting healthy life practices. There is an accepted and unquestioned practice in PE that *all* boys adhere to a shared set of normative practices that make them boys (Paechter 2003).

Today there is a noticeable reconfiguration of the visual landscape of billboard and magazine advertising. Once dominated by women, it is now increasingly shared with scantily clad muscled bodies of men. . . . The impact of this shift on how boys define themselves through the body is significant and at the heart of this chapter. For some adolescent boys, high school PE is a time characterized by fear, anxieties, and outward alienation. The constant bodily surveillance and harassment some boys experience leave many feeling anxious and ashamed of their bodies and, moreover, less likely to continue in PE (Atkinson and Kehler 2012). . . .

In this chapter I examine the conceptual and practical challenges adolescent boys face as they manage both their bodily practices in school PE classes and the broader ideological accounts of masculinity that inform these everyday practices. I argue that with the expansion of a visual landscape that has increasingly commodified male bodies, adolescent boys are under increased public as well as private scrutiny in what Liz Frost (2003, 54) describes as an "intensified engagement with the visual self-production" of youth. In other words, I draw a connection between the growing awareness boys have of their physical bodies and the possibilities to speak to and from their bodies in relation to prevailing masculine ideologies. I extend understandings of youth identities, and more specifically adolescent masculinities, that are routinely negotiated among and between boys in high school locker rooms. . . . Observing these youth interactions helps us to better understand the ways boys come to name themselves through the body. Moreover, I argue throughout this chapter that there is a growing need in education to broaden our repertoire of ways for identifying and acknowledging adolescent masculinities through bodily practices and the performative subjectivities that emerge in the interactions among boys in an unsupervised space such as secondary school PE locker rooms.

Navigating the Bodily Practices of Boys

At a time when we are increasingly told to look, feel, and be certain ways, it is particularly salient to consider how youth make sense of these messages, especially in light of a dominant discourse intersecting health, body image, and masculinities. Youth and a growing number of adolescent boys in particular are confronted with a barrage of images depicting buff boys with ripped abs (Gill, Henwood, and McLean 2005; Krayer, Ingledew, and Iphofen 2008; Shilling 2010). They are told directly that tight bodies and well-defined muscles make a man. And if muscles alone don't make them a man, boys are led to believe that muscles do allow them to show others who is the man. . . . Adolescent boys' relationship to sport is often traced to the sex-segregated experiences they have in school PE. It is during this significant and formative time in early adolescence that young men are increasingly engaged in the competing and sometimes conflicting ways of being boys among boys, particularly in masculinized spaces such as school locker rooms and PE sex-segregated classes where participation and attendance are compulsory.

This study builds on previous theorizing and research that locate the bodily practices of youth as a significant means through which to better understand, name, and know how boys interpret masculinities through gender performativity. Raewyn Connell (1995, 45) argues that "true masculinity is almost always thought to proceed from men's bodies—to be inherent in a male body or to express something about a male body." She argues that our

bodies are more than the physical; they are the emblematic representation of specific versions of masculinity. The masculine body is imbued with all that it means to be a man. Strength, dominance, and aggression contrast with the more vulnerable, weaker, and less able-bodied boys we often recount from childhood days. The outward expression of bodily practices that capture and affirm narrow, heteronormative masculinities while excluding, marginalizing, and oppressing others emerges as significant and troubling findings in the study that follows. . . .

The performativity of gendered identities, particularly in sex-segregated situations such as high school locker rooms, allows young men to reproduce hegemonic masculinities and reaffirm heteronormative masculinity among their peers. Sex-segregated contexts provide a domain within which expectations and terms of engagement, such as gender-normative behaviors, attitudes, and expressions, are routinely operationalized and moreover manifest themselves without interrogation or critical scrutiny. These spaces within schools allow stereotypical attitudes and behaviors to go unchecked and in some cases actually promote and encourage sexism, misogyny, and heterosexism to be legitimated and valorized. As Chris Shilling (2004, 482) argues, "dominant conceptions of masculinity encourage boys to participate in body-building activities that increase their strength, self-confidence, and capacity to occupy space." In his research, Moss Norman (2011, 441, 442) explains that even when there are "multiple and contradictory performances of masculinity, there were nonetheless contextually regulated limits to this multiplicity where gendered subjectivities were policed through discourses of gender and heterosexuality." His research illustrates how boys "deploy dominant discourses of masculinity that position the feminine as appearance-oriented and masculinity as performance-oriented, thereby laying out, reproducing, and naturalizing the 'proper' way for young men to relate to their gendered bodies." Locker rooms and change areas are perhaps one of the most troubling sex-segregated school spaces where the conduct, behaviors, and attitudes of youth remain out of the purview of adults and thus are problematic because they are not well monitored for inappropriate, threatening, and aggressive conduct among students.

Whose Body Is It Anyway? When the Body Is Named

I begin this section by raising a series of questions that guide this section and invite the reader to consider when and how the male body is named. It is worth asking for example: Under what conditions do boys and men have license to see or look upon other males' bodies? How in/visible is the male body? To what extent has the hypervisibility of the masculine body contributed to the naming and defining of male bodies? How does the increased visibility contribute to men's/boy's bodies as textual representations of raced, classed, and sexualized masculinities? To what extent has the growing consumption and availability of masculine bodies in the public mainstream allowed for or inhibited reconfigurations of masculine identities through the body? . . . The implications of this study and others that aim at opening up conversations of bodily practices and sex-segregated spaces such as locker rooms and PE classes are significant for school policies, curriculum development, and promoting healthier, safer school climates (Martin and Govender 2011; O'Donovan and Kirk 2007).

Contextually located and bounded by the practices promoted and supported in PE, the adolescent male body is emerging as a wider representational tool of masculinities in both the public consumer culture as well as the private spaces of school locker rooms/changing rooms. . . . The body is increasingly monitored, surveyed, and accounted for in schools, especially within the current climate of "panic," mobilizing an obesity discourse that, according to Emma Rich (2010, 806), has led to a damaging set of conditions and predispositions imbedded in policies and practices aimed at "children as subjects particularly in terms of a developing sense of embodiment."

Drawing on Judith Butler's (2004) theory of gender performativity, I argue that boys routinely navigate gender spaces in very regulated and normatively sanctioned ways. . . . Gender and the expression of masculinities is an outward display and expression of valued and often valorized forms of masculinities intentionally produced and reproduced to ensure membership and acceptance within and across peers (Smolak 2004). "Students' gendered bodies and behaviors are both scrutinized and disciplined by their peer group, with public and negative labeling for those unwilling or unable to conform to group norms" (Paechter 2003, 49). In other words, with regard to changing gender relations and power dynamics among boys, the climate in schools in particular has witnessed a shift to not only an acknowledgment of the body as present but moreover an acknowledgment of the body as imminent, dominant, active, and visually ever present in the constant surveillance of schooled bodies (Frost 2003; Paechter 2011; Rich 2010).

. . . We must examine further how the rise in the commodification of male body images in the media has allowed for or tailored the ways in which boys understand their bodies. Bodies of other boys are powerful reference points. Schools are ubiquitous sites in which competing discourses of masculinity, particularly within PE, invoke skills-based, strength-based, and performance-based models that promote boys "doing" bodies in particularly narrow and restrictive ways. And while admittedly the physicality, muscularity, and general awareness of the masculine body are not new, what is increasingly under investigation of importance in schools is how and when adolescent men engage in body projects and what conditions allow men to operate within and beyond such boundaries imposed by, for example, a health, obesity, or fat phobia discourse (see, for example, Evans, Davies, and Rich 2008; Norman 2011; Sykes and McPhail 2008) that operates in tandem with various discourses of masculinity. . . .

PE and PE locker rooms are unsettling places because of the ways in which they promote and even perpetuate bodily practices that revolve around a culture of privilege, power, and popularity among boys. Many adolescent bodies, I argue, have remained a relative source of power, dominance, and oppression, while others have not. Our understandings of the strains and tensions that inhere in processes of embodiment among adolescent males have been limited, curtailed, and silenced, as I argue elsewhere (Kehler and Atkinson, forthcoming), because of the gatekeeping that occurs in schools to prevent the body from being seen and heard (see also Paechter 2011; Shilling 2010). My research makes visible these processes of embodiment.

The Study

Conducted over a three-year period (2008–2011), this qualitative study examined the reasons some adolescent boys are reluctant to participate in required secondary school PE classes in three major cities across Canada. Funded by the Social Science and Humanities Research Council of Canada, this collaborative project was conducted with two other researchers who shared in data collection and analysis. The goal was to more closely examine the issues adolescent boys identified as factors negatively influencing their experience of health education in ninth grade PE, the introductory secondary level class. . . . Ethics approval was received at the University of Western Ontario, and the project was later granted ethics approval from three different school boards. The data presented in this chapter are a partial representation but reflect a consistent and recurring set of themes and analysis that emerged across the larger study. Our aim was not to make generalizations beyond this study but rather to look across different geographical contexts in similar school spaces, namely high school locker rooms. . . .

Data were collected using participant observation and semistructured interviews. Our team recruited seventy-seven boys, between the ages of fourteen and fifteen, using a variety of techniques. . . . Semistructured interviews lasting between forty-five minutes and one and a half hours were conducted at times and places chosen by the participants, including guidance counselor offices, empty classrooms, coffee shops, restaurants, and libraries. In line with a more collaborative research approach and to promote a participatory and respectful dialogue with the participants, boys chose their own pseudonyms, thus allowing the young men more control over how they are named in this study. Interviews were audio-taped and transcribed. Interview data were shared across researchers, and emerging themes were identified through consistent and recurrent patterns. Participant observations during structured PE class time were conducted as a way to contrast students' narratives with their daily experiences in PE. Students were observed during class time over a period of two to three days depending on schedules, teacher permissions, and interruptions at individual schools.

Locker Rooms and the Private Spaces That Hide Us

Boys actively make sense of their bodies in relation to the self-identities they negotiate in high school locker rooms, and these male self-identities are often calibrated against the sorts of masculinities that are routinely constructed within specific sporting contexts (Pringle and Hickey 2010). Drawing on the school context, I identify two relatively distinct spaces within locker rooms in which boys are regularly positioned among other boys. I refer to these spaces as identifiably separate on the basis of the amount or level of privacy and protection they allow boys within locker rooms. Either normative or nonnormative, these spaces allow for boys to adhere to or transgress bodily practices dictated and predicated upon heteronormative codes of masculinity. I draw attention to these spaces as powerful and troubling contexts within which adolescent boys routinely become hyperconscious of the meanings of their own and other boys' bodies. The bodily practices of boys in PE locker rooms have a significant bearing on the long-term healthy life practices among adolescent boys.

Protected Spaces and Avoidance Strategies

For some boys, going to the locker room was anxiety-inducing, and they dreaded PE because of the interactions they had with their peers in the space. As a result, many of the boys expounded strategies they used to avoid locker rooms. I argue that there remains a private discomfort and set of anxieties in which adolescent young men are very body conscious and fearful and (a)shamed in many cases by how their body is viewed. . . . What I describe as *nonnormative spaces* are areas of the locker room that are not easily viewed by others outside of those boys who already have membership in this confined space. Nonnormative spaces also allow boys a different level of personal security and safety not found in normative spaces. Membership in this case is based on a common or shared access—namely, these boys were ninth grade PE students. Other students were not allowed in the locker room at this time, so access was restricted to this population of students. These spaces are distinct because they do not require normative conduct, behavior, or attitudes to be openly expressed while using them. These are relatively private spaces and include stalls, or areas of the locker room that are sheltered or shielded, including corners. . . . Boys purposefully use these spaces in locker rooms because of the level of protection and safety they provide.

The privacy and the ability to skirt or avoid peer surveillance were important in locker room maneuvers among the young men in this study. In a conversation, Connor made a distinction identifying specific safe spaces, including the washroom stall, where some boys change "so that other people don't watch them." During our research, the boys consistently referred to zones or spaces in school locker rooms that had an impact on how they managed and conducted themselves. Different groups of boys regularly took up space and used separate parts of the locker room. Just as classrooms often have seating plans, the locker room too was organized by different groups of boys in different areas.

Many of the boys identified groups within PE class based on "athleticity" and level of caring or investing in the class. Chewi describes one group of boys by saying, "They really just don't do anything because they don't try and they don't care and

maybe some of the people in the low athletic group might eventually switch over there because they don't like being made fun of and they'll just stop trying." According to many of the boys the "jocks" and the "popular" boys were regularly found in the center of the locker rooms. The less athletic boys often changed at lockers or in spaces just beyond the central area. . . . I refer to the washroom within locker rooms as *a nonnormative space*. As such boys are more easily able to escape the surveillance of their peers and avoid harassment and belittling comments made by the "popular boys" who control the central change area or what I refer to as the *normative space*. The *normative spaces* are more public and open to peer scrutiny, verbal harassment, and physical banter among boys. The boys purposefully use washrooms and changing room stalls to remove themselves from the larger population of their classmates. They avoid changing with their peers, conversing, and participating as regular class members. In the following conversation James explains he does not go into the locker room, but he nonetheless has a strong opinion and developed a strategy to avoid using the locker room. John similarly had managed to avoid changing in the locker room. He had been shamed and ridiculed in the past and had since developed a routine for avoiding this harassment. Such a strategy reflects significantly on the anxieties the boys have about using or entering the locker room:

See these clothes I'm wearing? These are my gym clothes. I wear these clothes to school. I wear gym shoes to school. I don't ever set foot in that locker room just because I don't want to be in there and I don't want to be half naked in there. (James)

Okay, therein lies where it's really gone wrong for me because I have not brought my gym uniform, my gym clothes to school on so many occasions that if I don't pass the exam I'm not going to get the credit for gym and that was a conscious choice on my part because I did not want to participate because I brought it [my gym uniform] a few times but I would wear it underneath my other clothes and I would just take those off in the change room and have my gym uniform on because I was uncomfortable with my body and I was afraid of what other kids would say to me because in grade eight I know in the change room I got made fun of a lot. When I would take my shirt off to change into my other shirt other people would scream and look away and stuff just to make fun of me. So I had enough of that and I decided that I was either not going to bring my uniform or just not participate at all. (John)

John continues to explain his discomfort with other people seeing him and a history of weight-based teasing in school locker rooms. "When I was in the change room and I'd forgotten to wear my gym clothes underneath my other clothes and so I would actually take my shirt off just by the sleeves and then I put my other shirt on and then I would kind of pull my other shirt off at the same time. So I'm not comfortable with people seeing me because I'm not comfortable with myself and that's because I have been made fun of before." James made a clear and firm decision to never "set foot in that locker room," just as John decided he had "had enough of that" and would either "bring my uniform or just not participate at all." The culture of the changing room, including its characteristics, rules, and features, both physically and socially impacts the ways students engage or disengage from PE class. . . . Both James and John developed ways to respond to a threatening and unwelcoming climate. Each strategy was intentional and purposeful to protect themselves from teasing and peer scrutiny of their bodies. John's eighth grade experience in changing rooms was damaging and unchecked by teachers. As none of the boys in our study referred to any adult supervision in the changing rooms, they were left alone to change and prepare themselves for class.

The *normative spaces* in school locker rooms are delineated and maintained through routine and frequent social coercion and verbal taunts. Largely open spaces, these areas are purposefully and aggressively maintained on the basis of rules and codes of normative masculinity. The boys themselves carefully monitor outward physical and

verbal exchanges or interactions among boys in these spaces. Anything that appears less than masculine or contravenes acceptably masculine conduct becomes easy fodder for public humiliation. Conversations in these areas typically focus on sport performance or athletic prowess. Chewi, for example, describes that after class "it would just be like walking into the change room and then they all start saying, 'oh you just fell' and 'that was terrible' kind of stuff and that always happens after gym." Similarly Joey commented that in class "I usually drop balls if they're thrown to me and that kind of gets people mad that are on my team. They always tell me when we're changing." The more popular boys, often those with considerable physical prowess, regularly exchanged barbs with the less athletic students. Both skill-based and appearance-based teasing among boys was similarly found by Linda Smolak (2004).

Relative comparisons are made among boys as a means to maintain a hierarchical structure. Athletic ability and physical attributes are often cited as points of comparison and contribute to growing body dissatisfaction among more adolescent boys than previously thought (Krayer, Ingledew, and Iphofen 2008). In the following excerpt Dave describes the intimidation some boys experience in the locker room: "I know in some schools, some of the skinny, small guys . . . all the big guys kind of pick on them for not being as good and they don't like going in the locker room because they might get bullied or stuffed in a locker." This accepted culture of locker rooms is often dismissed as "normal" boy culture. Stereotypes of boys jockeying for position, flexing muscles, and demonstrating prowess at the expense of other, often weaker boys has been a regular part of the boys' characterizations of their locker room and class experiences across the schools in our study. . . . In the next instance, Chewi describes his strategy for getting to the changing room ahead of his classmates to avoid the awkwardness of changing with his peers: "I was always on time and I always got changed and in the gym by the time they all already came in but still, it was awkward, yeah." This strategic and careful planning to avoid being with his peers while changing reveals unexplained anxieties some boys have in these masculinized spaces. This awkwardness was also evident with regard to showering after PE class. Chewi remarks, "I actually never ever once stepped in there, never showered once in the change room. Thankfully I had last period gym so I'd just come home after." And while Chewi was able to avoid using the showers, this was nonetheless an issue the PE teacher directly addressed with the students: "Like our teacher even said, you can use the showers if you want. If you feel uncomfortable, bring a swimsuit, but no one still did. No one used the showers and I don't know why. I guess just the whole security thing. . . . Like the way they're feeling, their security." . . .

The level of anxiety and uncertainty about nudity as well as personal safety is striking. In fact, Jarred Martin and Kaymarlin Govender (2011, 235–236) found that the intersections between concerns for perceived body ideals, muscularity, and traditional masculine beliefs "are constricting and damaging as they enforce and perpetuate a culture of secrecy and silence over talking about one's vulnerabilities and anxieties as a male." In Chewi's case the teacher was aware of the discomfort among his students and offered a coping strategy but failed to actually address the insecurities. There is a deeply held belief that boys can navigate, participate, and enter highly masculinized places such as boys' and men's locker rooms because of an assumed acceptance of and comfort with normative masculine ideology.

In an interview Bob similarly expresses a discomfort in boy's locker rooms: "Maybe the guys like seeing each other but I don't think so. I don't know why they have open showers for guys but you get used to it and actually I don't [shower] anymore." Bob explains that while he eventually accepted the lack of privacy he opts not to shower and thus avoids his peers' surveillance. Interestingly, Bob also comments on the possible pleasure in seeing each other in the showers, but quickly dismisses it. His discomfort is related to "open showers for guys." He does not make any explicit comparison to

the showers provided for girls, which at that school were closed and separated by curtains. . . . In the following conversation, Rod describes the showers as a space where "you're kind of away from the teacher" and where boys are able to do "things to harass you." "I don't shower anymore. I just shower when I get home and again, the guy who bugged me, he's like, 'Why don't you take a shower.' So I said, 'Because I don't feel like it.' . . . It's like when you're kind of away from the teacher, they want to pick on you more like in the showers or the stalls, they would pick on you more and you would feel uncomfortable just being in there with a group of naked boys just playing around, doing things to harass you." But as Andrew explains, although the "big kids" avoid the locker room so as not to be seen changing, the privileged-bodied boys understand and notice the strategy:

> He won't go in the change room. He will change in the bathroom upstairs. He'll come down and he will smell because he doesn't . . . they don't shower after gym. They don't put on deodorant. They'll just go in the change room but wear their gym clothes under their normal clothes and they'll just take them off. So they don't have to go in and take off their shirt or they don't have to take off their pants and put on their shorts. They'll do it in the bathroom. They'll go into a stall or stuff like that so they don't have to be seen without their shirt. They shouldn't have to do that because he will . . . and everyone notices, like what's the point of doing that when everyone knows that you're doing it because of that. Like everyone will be like, "Oh where is he?" Like they'll notice that he's not there. "Where's the big kid?" Oh he must . . . you wonder where he is and then he just pops out and he's all changed. So they realize that the overweight kids, they don't go in the change room.

The exchange Bob had with his peer reflects one example of surveillance in segregated locker room spaces. Rod describes a sense of bodily discomfort "just being in there with a group of naked boys" but also a sense of fear of the harassment that occurs "away from the teacher." Across the boys in this study, many like Chewi, Bob, and Rod developed strategies of avoidance and withdrawal. The discomfort, anxieties, and concerns these young men expressed about their bodies and the locker room harassment in particular are troubling. Harrison Pope, Katharine Phillips, and Roberto Olivardia (2000, 60) explain, "Because men aren't supposed to worry or complain about their looks, few would ever admit that they'd secretly like to have a steroid-sized body or that they fret about their inadequacies when examining their bodies in the mirror. Fewer still would acknowledge that their obsessions about body appearance have anything to do with threatened masculinity." If left unaltered, unsupervised spaces like school locker rooms will continue to foster and perpetuate normative codes of masculinity that threaten to alienate and marginalize boys, particularly those who do not agree with the rules and codes of behavior generally accepted in these spaces. . . .

In the following conversation James demonstrates a keen awareness of the kind of cultural capital masculine athletic and able bodies were granted in this PE culture. James describes a community of adolescent bodies where he is located and subjugated. "I guess other people are like, 'Hey, look at me flex.' You know, like Harley: 'Why don't you flex? . . . Look at that. That's epic. I have an entire straight line.' I guess that's how I became aware that I was weak but again I don't care. I guess I became aware I was weak when I couldn't run for more than a bit without getting out of breath. I couldn't throw the ball when everyone else could. Seeing their abilities compared to mine made me realize that I'm not very good at gym and then I realized I don't really want to be." The ripped body of Harley with "an entire straight line" extending down his abdomen was an invitation for James to gaze upon his body and moreover to critically assess his own body and abilities in sport. Harley's invitation suggests that adolescent boys are increasingly defining themselves through their bodies. Being big, strong, and ripped and being able to show it to classmates matter. Boys are "subject to a set of evaluative standards relating to their physicality, about which they frequently have little control and may, even with hours in the gym or training for sports, be able to do little about" (Frost 2003, 67).

Teasing in the Boy's Room

Teasing, especially weight-based teasing, is a powerful and damaging form of peer control exerted among adolescent boys in locker rooms. Appearance-related teasing, weight-related comments, and degrading other boys for having what are referred to as "man boobs" occur regularly as a form of social control within boy peer groups (see Krayer, Ingledew, and Iphofen 2008; Smolak 2004; Taylor 2011). In her study of gender- and weight-based teasing in secondary schools, Nicole Taylor (2011, 191) describes teasing's enduring damage that not only is common but has become part of "the verbally and physically abusive culture of the boys' locker room." There is growing evidence that boys regularly deploy both verbal and physical intimidation in school locker rooms and succumb to various forms of hazing, which tends to be underreported (Taylor 2011). During our interview, Spikeshade describes the kind of teasing he experienced while contrasting it between elementary school and secondary school: "One of the reasons for my poor self-image would probably be people making fun of me in elementary school and even a little bit here too. I had some kids. . . . I'm not going to name any names but some kids in my gym class would make fun of me for my weight." He continues, "It was more accepting [in elementary school] like in gym class they wouldn't make fun of you because you couldn't run or anything like that but here [in secondary school] I would get made fun of for my weight or when I run because you know, I'm overweight and people. . . . I've received a lot of comments that I care not to repeat really but they've basically been about my weight and how when I run it's just like, my fat bounces. So it's just . . . I didn't get that so much in elementary school really because people were just there to have fun and we were kids."

Spikeshade further explains the impact appearance-based teasing has on him in PE class: "I know that the experiences that stand out for me are probably when somebody would make a rude comment to me about my weight and I just wouldn't retaliate because there's just no point. I'm not sinking to their level. They can say whatever they want. It doesn't really affect me but well, evidently it does because years of it has led to my poor body image but at the moment it doesn't affect me and there have been a few times where I'm just going to come right out and say this, where I've been like people have smacked my fat and laughed at it because it jiggled and I've been smacked right across, well, my man boobs." Spikeshade contrasts this weight-based teasing to the privilege associated with being thin: "Well, they're thin, that's the thing. They're not necessarily buff or really muscular but they're all thinner than I am, most of them, like 99 percent of them and so they really have no problems with it. I mean I'm pretty sure in the summer if they got hot and sweaty, they'd just take their shirt off and walk around shirtless. . . . Usually me and the other big guys are usually the ones that would get made fun of and not the thin guys." Spikeshade is clear about the ridicule and teasing directed at him, that being thin is more desirable and less likely to be a source of teasing. He also demonstrates the gradual shift in locker room climate between the elementary and secondary levels. At elementary PE Spikeshade and classmates "were kids and just there to have fun"; in secondary school he endures the teasing but reluctantly acknowledges the long-term impact: "They can say whatever they want. It doesn't really affect me but well, evidently it does because years of it has led to my poor body image but at the moment it doesn't affect me."

Like many of the boys subject to weight-based teasing, Spikeshade developed strategies that denied the impact the ridicule had and justified the others' behavior. During our interview he explained the behavior of the "jocks" this way: "It could be that they were just brought up differently and not, now I don't want to call parenting into question but not properly disciplined and it could also be the fact that they get with their friends and they actually think that this is acceptable because their friends are

doing it." Spikeshade justifies the bullying and harassment he experiences from the "jocks" because of parenting, being raised differently, and peer pressure. The locker room teasing has made Spikeshade, like many other boys, self-conscious, aware of his body and of thinness and the privilege extended to thin boys. He does not outwardly respond to the teasing because he refuses to "sink to their level." And while Spikeshade suggests he is not affected by the teasing, the opposite is evident. His bodily fears are best captured as he explains, "I'm afraid of what I look like and how other people perceive me and I know . . . it's kind of a gray area because I'm not sure what a healthy body weight for my height would be yet. I don't want to get too thin either from exercises. So what I'm really trying to do is lose the fat and build muscle. So I may weigh the same. I may end up weighing more but weight isn't really as important to me as physique." Spikeshade is concerned about his appearance and how others perceive him. He also understands that some bodies are privileged while others remain a pubic source for ridicule. . . .

. . . In the following interview excerpt Mythic further illustrates how changing room conversation influences his impression of his own abilities. The impact of social comparison among boys further reveals the kind of climate they endure coming and going to PE class. Mythic states, "Probably the most nerve-wracking thing would have to be is just people comparing me to themselves, maybe like 'God dude, you suck and gym is really bad for you' and you know they say that I'm not a team person and they say I'm not physical. They say I'm un-athletic sometimes, like it's a bad thing." Mythic illustrates the divisive manner in which boys compare one another based on athletic prowess. The changing room allows for uncensored conversation in which boys succumb to the verbal abuse of others who have become respected, regarded, and feared because of their athletic cachet both with peers and importantly oftentimes with teachers as well. The conversation, impressions, and experiences these boys have in school changing rooms contribute to how they define themselves, their bodies, and their relationship to physical activity in particular. The location provides a secluded, private, and unsupervised space in which masculinities and physical activity are seamlessly bound to youth identities. Unless this culture and the climate that prevails are more closely scrutinized, boys will continue to withdraw and decide that they "don't really want to be" good at gym.

Conclusion

In this chapter I have described how adolescent boys name and understand the relationship between adolescent bodies and masculinities in a PE context and offered a way of looking inward toward and outward from high school locker rooms, spaces that heretofore have been largely closed, private, or taboo within both research and school communities. The process of negotiating adolescent male bodies is not well understood, but is routinely accepted and interpreted within and among boys, viewed as simply "boys will be boys." People believe that the locker room towel whipping, ball tossing, wrestling, and banter are simply what happens when boys congregate. But research is starting to illuminate the costs of such "normal," taken-for-granted masculine culture.

. . . As Mona-Iren Hauge and Hanne Haavind (2011) have argued, and as this study further illustrates, boys produce and reproduce various masculinities through their bodies. They impose their bodies through physical means on other boys and occupy physical space in ways that marginalize and oppress weaker bodies. Locker rooms and PE classes form a private space in which bodily practices among boys reveal a troubling geography of masculinities regularly enacted away from the supervision of adults. More vulnerable boys hide their bodies to protect themselves and secure their bodies from stronger, dominant, and aggressive others. Ordered by codes of masculinity and unspoken rules for maneuvering masculinities in school, locker rooms remain a forbidden and threatening space for some boys.

Messner and Musto (2014, 107) have argued the significance of studying "kids not simply as future adults, but as active subjects who create their own social worlds." . . . As I have shown in this chapter,

adolescent boys are both concerned about their bodies and willing to talk about them. Our participants were incredibly attuned to the meanings associated with masculine bodies among men and the implications in the social context of their everyday relations. Until researchers engage with youth, sports, and particularly the cultures and changing rooms that are oftentimes restricted to understand youth identities and sport, these spaces will remain much the same, simply boys *doing* boy.

References

Atkinson, Michael, and Michael Kehler. 2012. "Boys, Bullying, and Biopedagogies in Physical Education." *Thymos: Journal of Boyhood Studies* 6.1–2: 166–185.

Butler, Judith. 2004. *Undoing Gender*. New York: Routledge.

Connell, Raewyn. 1995. *Masculinities*. Berkeley: University of California Press.

Evans, John, Brian Davies, and Emma Rich. 2008. "The Class and Cultural Functions of Obesity Discourse: Our Later Day Child Saving the Moment." *International Studies in Sociology of Education* 18.2: 117–132.

Frost, Liz. 2003. "Doing Bodies Differently? Gender, Youth, Appearance, and Damage." *Journal of Youth Studies* 6.1: 53–70.

Gill, Rosalind, Karen Henwood, and Carl McLean. 2005. "Body Projects and the Regulation of Normative Masculinity." *Body and Society* 11.1: 37–62.

Hauge, Mona-Iren, and Hanne Haavind. 2011. "Boys' Bodies and the Constitution of Adolescent Masculinities." *Sport, Education, and Society* 16.1: 1–16.

Kehler, Michael, and Michael Atkinson. Forthcoming. "The Space Between: Boys, Bodies, and Negotiating Research Subjectivities in Physical Education." *International Journal of Men's Health*.

Krayer, Anne, David K. Ingledew, and Ron Iphofen. 2008. "Social Comparison and Body Image in Adolescence: A Grounded Theory Approach." *Journal of Health Education Research* 23.5: 892–903.

Martin, Jarred, and Kaymarlin Govender. 2011. "'Making Muscle Junkies': Investigating Traditional Masculine Ideology, Body Image Discrepancy, and the Pursuit of Muscularity in Adolescent Males." *Men's Health* 10.3:220–239.

Messner, Michael, and Michela Musto. 2014. "Where Are the Kids?" *Sociology of Sport Journal* 31.1: 102–122.

Norman, Moss. 2011. "Embodying the Double-Bind of Masculinity: Young Men and Discourses of Normalcy, Health, Heterosexuality, and Individualism." *Men and Masculinities* 14.4: 430–449.

O'Donovan, Toni M., and David Kirk. 2007. "Managing Classroom Entry: An Ecological Analysis of Ritual Interaction and Negotiation in the Changing Room." *Sport, Education, and Society* 12.4: 399–413.

Paechter, Carrie. 2003. "Power, Bodies and Identity: How Different Forms of Physical Education Construct Varying Masculinities and Femininities in Secondary Schools." *Sex Education* 3.1: 47–59.

———. 2011. "Gender, Visible Bodies, and Schooling: Cultural Pathologies of Childhood." *Sport, Education, and Society* 16.3: 309–322.

Pope, Harrison G., Katharine A. Phillips, and Roberto Olivardia. 2000. *The Adonis Complex: The Secret Crisis of Male Body Obsession.* New York: Free Press.

Pringle, Richard G., and Christopher Hickey. 2010. "Negotiating Masculinities via the Moral Problematization of Sport." *Sociology of Sport Journal* 27: 115–138.

Rich, Emma. 2010. "Obesity Assemblages and Surveillance in Schools." *International Journal of Qualitative Studies in Education* 23.7: 803–821.

Shilling, Chris. 2004. "Physical Capital and Situated Action: A New Direction for Corporeal Sociology." *British Journal of Sociology of Education* 25.4: 473–487.

———. 2010. "Exploring the Society–Body–School Nexus: Theoretical and Methodology Issues in the Study of Body Pedagogics." *Sport, Education, and Society* 15.2: 151–167.

Smolak, Linda. 2004. "Body Image in Children and Adolescents: Where Do We Go from Here?" *Body Image* 1:15–28.

Sykes, Heather, and Deborah McPhail. 2008. "Unbearable Lessons: Contesting Fat Phobia in Physical Education." *Sociology of Sport Journal* 5.1: 66–96.

Taylor, Nicole L. 2011. "'Guys, She's Humongous!' Gender and Weight-Based Teasing in Adolescence." *Journal of Adolescence Research* 26.2: 178–199.

Men, Sex, and Relationships

Why do many men have problems establishing and maintaining intimate relationships with women? What different forms do male–female relational problems take within different socioeconomic groups? How do men's problems with intimacy and emotional expressivity relate to power inequities between the sexes? Are rape and domestic violence best conceptualized as isolated deviant acts by "sick" individuals, or are they the illogical consequences of male socialization? This complex web of male–female relationships, intimacy, and power is the topic of this part.

And what is the nature of men's relationships with other men? Do men have close friendships with men, or do they simply "bond" around shared activities and interests? How do competition, homophobia, and violence enter into men's relationships with each other? For example, a student recently commented that when he goes to movies with another male friends, they always leave a seat between them, where they put their coats, because they don't want anyone to think they are there "together."

But what are the costs of this emotional and physical distance? And what are the costs of maintaining emotionally impoverished relationships with other men? How is this emotional distance connected to men's intimate relationships with women? Is it related to Billy Crystal's line in *When Harry Met Sally* that women and men can never be friends because "the sex thing always gets in the way"?

Do young guys together constantly brag about heterosexual conquests, real or imagined? Neill Korobov's analysis of young men's conversations with their friends suggests a different sort of gamesmanship and bonding is going on among some male friends: Men become "lovable losers" by telling sexual stories about embarrassing romantic and sexual mishaps and gaffes. Stefan Robinson and his colleagues focus on the changing nature of men's friendships: Does the "bromance" indicate a breaking down of homophobia and the emergence of a new era of male–male intimacy? Not so fast, say Tristan Bridges and Chong-Suk Han. Bridges observes how homophobia still structures men's relationships with each other, while Han shows how racial and ethnic stereotypes continue to organize gay men's relationships as well.

PART V DISCUSSION QUESTIONS

1. The concept of hybrid masculinities is a concept with significant explanatory power. What new insights does it introduce? What might be overlooked by applying this approach to masculinities?
2. What does Neill Korobov mean when he writes, "the *spectacle* of emasculation . . . is a useful rhetorical ploy for simultaneously embracing and disavowing the role of victim. What remains is a quiet reassertion of traditional masculinity" (page 228)? How is this emasculation used by men when their masculinity is threatened?
3. Does the increasing acceptance of homosexuality and homosociality (the "bromance") between men challenge patriarchal power? Why or why not?
4. It's often considered that racism, sexism, and classism are interlocking systems of oppression. How are changes to masculinity limited by these systems? How do they challenge them? What is the role of sexuality in this oppression?

A Very "Gay" Straight?

Hybrid Masculinities, Sexual Aesthetics, and the Changing Relationship between Masculinity and Homophobia

TRISTAN BRIDGES

There has been little attention paid to the queer practices of people who identify as heterosexual, and further research in this area is needed (Schippers 2000, 760).

This article explores the gender and sexual dynamics of three groups of men—with varying commitments to feminist ideals (from anti- to pro-) and levels of interest in gender and sexual inequality (from highly concerned to apathetic)—to investigate heterosexual men's relationships with gender, sexuality, and inequality, and the potential for change embedded within a peculiar practice. Heterosexual men in each group defined aspects of themselves as "gay." But they did so in a way that allowed them to retain a "masculine" distance from homosexuality. The practice initially appears to be the mirror image of Connell's (1992) research on gay men classifying themselves as "a very straight gay." Rather than gay men co-opting elements of "straight" culture and style, I discuss straight men borrowing elements of "gay" culture and discursively framing themselves as "gay." Compared with Connell's (1992) "straight gay" men, however, the men in this study engage in this practice for different reasons and with distinct consequences. They rely on "gay aesthetics" to construct *hybrid masculinities* (Demetriou 2001; Messner 1993) that work to distance them

in subtly different ways from stigmatizing stereotypes of masculinity.

While scholarship discusses homophobia as a fundamental element of contemporary masculine identities (Connell 1992; Herek 1986; Kimmel 1994; Lehne 1976; Pascoe 2007), the practices of the men I studied—straight men who identify with some "gay" cultural styles—appear to challenge this relationship. I theorize "sexual aesthetics" to make sense of this apparent contradiction. "Sexual aesthetics" refer to cultural and stylistic distinctions used to delineate boundaries between gay and straight cultures and individuals. The ways in which heterosexual men in each group deploy gay aesthetics reveal group-specific meanings and consequences. Broadly speaking, straight men's reliance on aspects of gay culture illustrates some of the ways that sexual prejudice, inequality, and the relationship between masculinity and homophobia are better understood as transforming than disappearing. Similar to other analyses of contemporary hybrid masculine practices, these men's behavior conceals privileges associated with white, heterosexual masculinity.

This article addresses three issues: (1) the hybridization of straight men's identities through the use of gay aesthetics; (2) the social construction of sexual aesthetics; and (3) the motivations for and consequences of this practice.

Hybrid Masculinities

Hybrid masculinities refer to gender projects that incorporate "bits and pieces" (Demetriou 2001) of marginalized and subordinated masculinities and, at times, femininities. "Hybrid" is used in the social sciences and humanities to address processes and practices of cultural integration or mixing (Burke 2009). . . .

A central issue in research on hybrid masculinities is whether they challenge and/or perpetuate systems of inequality. There are three streams of research that address this question: One questions the extent of hybridization (e.g., Connell and Messerschmidt 2005); a second considers hybridization as pervasive and as illustrating a unilateral move toward greater gender and sexual equality (e.g., Anderson 2009; McCormack 2012); and a third—agreeing that hybridization is significant—argues that it perpetuates inequalities in new and "softer" ways (e.g., Demetriou 2001; Messner 1993).

Connell and Messerschmidt, briefly addressing hybrid masculinities, acknowledge that "specific masculine practices may be appropriated into other masculinities" (Connell and Messerschmidt 2005, 845). Yet, they are not convinced that hybrid masculine forms represent anything beyond local subcultural variation. Others have been less dismissive. For example, Anderson's (2009) theory of "inclusive masculinity" argues that contemporary transformations in men's behaviors and beliefs are pervasive and undermine gender and sexual hierarchies and inequality. While many stress an intimate connection between masculinity and homophobia (Kimmel 1994; Pascoe 2007), Anderson proposes that this connection exists only in social contexts with high levels of "homohysteria,"[1] a condition that, he argues, does not characterize contemporary Western societies (see also McCormack 2012). Anderson frames contemporary masculinities as characterized by increasing levels of "inclusivity" and equality.

. . . As Messner argues, hybrid masculinities

represent highly significant (but exaggerated) shifts in the cultural and personal styles . . . but these changes do not necessarily contribute to the undermining of conventional structures of men's power. Although "softer" and more "sensitive" styles of masculinity are developing among some privileged groups of men, this does not necessarily contribute to the emancipation of women; in fact, quite the contrary may be true. (Messner 1993, 725)

More recently, Messner (2007) theorized a culturally ascendant hybrid masculinity combining "toughness" with "tenderness" in ways that work to obscure power and inequality. Similarly, Demetriou (2001) addresses the appropriation of elements of subordinated and marginalized "Others" by white heterosexual men that ultimately work to recuperate white, heterosexual, masculine privilege. Focusing on the incorporation of gay male culture, Demetriou illustrates how hybrid masculinities can be understood as contemporary expressions of existing forms of inequality. "New, hybrid configurations of gender practice . . . enable [heterosexual men] to reproduce their dominance . . . in historically novel ways" (Demetriou 2001, 351). . . . That these changes have primarily emerged among groups of young, heterosexual, white men speaks to the flexibility of identity afforded privileged groups.

Sexual Aesthetics

The literature on hybrid masculinities focuses on the assimilation of aspects of cultures and performances associated with various marginalized and subordinated "Others." A significant strand in this research deals with the incorporation of "gay" cultural styles to enact masculine gender identities (e.g., Anderson 2009; Bridges 2010; Demetriou 2001; McCormack 2012; Pascoe 2007; Wilkins 2009). Theorizing the "aesthetic" elements of sexualities enables a more thorough analysis of the consequences of their incorporation into hybrid masculine identities and practices.

Scholars understand gender and sexuality as co-constructed (e.g., Pascoe 2007; Schippers 2000; Seidman 1996; Stein and Plummer 1994; Ward 2008) and unstable (Butler 1990; Seidman 1996), prompting research into the cultural work that maintains identity categories. Connell's (1992) work on gay men who identify as "a very straight gay" is a useful illustration. Connell found that gay men's use of "straight" had less to do with cultural subversion and more to do with safety and gender identification. Gay men who incorporate elements of "straight" masculinity are a powerful illustration of the co-construction of gender and sexuality (e.g., Hennen 2005; Ocampo 2012; Ward 2008). . . .

Sexualities are communicated and adopted to define one's self and others based on a wide array of sexual aesthetics. Sexual aesthetics refer to cultural and stylistic distinctions utilized to delineate symbolic boundaries between gay and straight cultures and individuals. . . .

A variety of things can "count" as sexual aesthetics: interests, material objects, styles of bodily comportment, language, opinions, clothing, and behaviors. Theorizing sexual aesthetics enables an analysis of sexuality as both a *sexual* and *cultural* category (e.g., Halperin 2012; Ward 2008). Connell's (1992) and Ward's (2008) research considers why men engaging in same-sex behavior might rely on what I am calling straight aesthetics, but— as Schippers (2000) notes—less research considers straight-identified men who rely on gay aesthetics.

Like hybrid masculinities, there is a dual potential embedded within sexual aesthetics to challenge and/or reproduce inequality. Whether this potential is realized is an empirical question. While capable of being used to subvert gender and sexual boundaries and inequality, this shift can also work to obscure inequality in new ways by relying on an aesthetic discourse that (implicitly) disregards its existence.

Data and Methods

I selected groups of men for this study based on two axes of variation: their gender-political affiliations and the level of reflexivity with which they consider gender-political concerns. The three groups vary on both axes[2]: fathers' rights activists, pro-feminist men, and a group without formal gender-political affiliation—bar regulars. The majority of the men

in my sample are white (56 of 63) and all but two identify as heterosexual (61 of 63). Thus, my sample is consistent with other research that discusses the flexibility afforded contemporary straight, white masculinities (e.g., Anderson 2009; Messner 1993; Pascoe 2007; Ward 2008; Wilkins 2009).

The behavioral pattern I discuss—heterosexual men's reliance upon gay aesthetics—was not present among every member of every group. Seventeen out of the 63 men in the study explicitly engaged in this practice. The practice did, however, appear among all three groups. It is not my intention to claim that my findings are statistically representative. Rather, this article is concerned with theorizing a term that helps examine the motivations behind and consequences of an interesting pattern of behavior (Small 2009). . . .

. . . Following is a brief overview of each group.

Men Can Parent Too is a fathers' rights activist organization attempting to raise awareness about and protest what they perceive as gender inequality in divorce and custody proceedings. Ask any member if gender inequality exists and he will give you an answer similar to Dave, a 35-year-old lawyer who volunteers his time providing information and support to divorcing fathers: "Men and women are not equal. It's really as simple as that. Women get more than men. They get more from men in their marriages just like they get more when those marriages break up. Inequality exists. Men are getting screwed."

Guys for Gender Justice is a pro-feminist group of men who meet regularly to discuss gender and sexual inequality, raise money for non-profit organizations dealing with violence against women, and volunteer for feminist organizations and causes. Ask a member about the existence of gender inequality, and he will likely tell you something akin to Dan, a 25-year-old graphic designer: "Women have been getting the shaft for millennia. . . . Men don't get how they are actually a part of it. Women and men are unequal and we all have a part to play to fix it."

The Border Boys are a group of bar regulars at a small, privately owned restaurant and bar. Their weekly meetings are less structured than the other two groups, though no less frequent. They are also less reflexive about gender and inequality, but gender, sexuality, and inequality are popular topics of conversation. Ask one of The Border Boys whether gender inequality exists and he might give you an answer like Jeffrey's, a 29-year-old restaurant employee still uncertain of his life ambitions: "I don't know. . . . Actually, let me qualify that: I don't care. If men and women are unequal, they are, and if not, they're not. Everybody has to deal with the shit they are dealt."

Each of the groups kept regular meeting times. I observed participants both in and out of their meeting settings. I informally interviewed men throughout the study, but formal, in-depth, semi-structured interviews were conducted at the conclusion of my study as well. Interviews ranged from 45 to 90 minutes. As a young, white man, my own identity was consistent with most of the men I studied. These factors certainly played a role in the data I was able to collect and the interactions I observed. It may, for instance, have contributed to me being less noticed than I might have been otherwise. It might have also produced a level of comfort due to potentially assumed similarities in our values and beliefs. Conversely, respondents may not have explained some things to me out of a belief that I "must know." So, I could have also missed out on aspects of their lives because both they and I neglected them as significant. Interview questions dealt with friendships, romantic relationships, work lives, family, and beliefs about more abstract issues like power and inequality, and whether and how they saw these issues at work in their own lives.

Field notes and interviews were transcribed and coded according to a grounded theoretical method, allowing findings to emerge from the data (Strauss and Corbin 1998). Open coding revealed the framing of behavior, opinions, speech, dress, and tastes as "gay" among all three groups. I initially relied on gay aesthetics as a sensitizing concept (Blumer 1954), providing a framework to consider the practice.

A Very "Gay" Straight?

Dan is a member of Guys for Gender Justice, a group he says meets for two purposes:

> We . . . talk about how guys are a part of inequality and how we can change that. . . . We try to, like, volunteer our time and stuff to other groups . . . you know, that are for gender equality. . . . So, basically, we say we're feminist in two ways: how we think and how we act.

I asked whether the majority of the members of his organization identified as heterosexual. "They're straight . . . they're all straight," Dan told me. Jokingly, he continued, "And it's funny, 'cause we're all involved in this totally *gay* thing, but we're all straight . . . you know?" When I asked whether Dan also identified as straight, his response was interesting: "Yeah, I'm straight. I've always been straight. . . . But actually, I'm also pretty gay in *how* I'm straight." While only a minority of the men in my study relied on gay aesthetics in this way, heterosexual men in all three groups defined aspects of themselves as "gay" in similar ways.

Identifying Gay Aesthetics

Sexual aesthetics are best identified by how they are used rather than from what they are composed. Thus, gay aesthetics do *not* refer to the universal components of gay identity and culture. Rather, they are used in ways that suggest universal elements of sexual identities and cultures. So, when Matt, one of The Border Boys, stated, "I can tell a dude's gay by the way he walks," he implies universal standards. As I define sexual aesthetics, it is less important that Matt's belief is accurate; what matters is that he believes it is. Many men in this study felt they could easily "spot" gay men.

When I began my study of Men Can Parent Too, Dave—the group organizer—and I talked in his office at a small law firm about the group and my research. I told him I was interested in studying men who were attempting to figure out "how to be a man." Dave immediately responded that I'd "want to meet" Luke. Luke was getting a divorce because he had recently come out as gay. He came to the first two meetings only, but remained a part of the study.[3] He came to the group after recently separating from his wife and concerned that he would lose access to his children.

When Luke first talked with me about deciding to come out, he discussed the realization of how it might affect his relationship with his children (because of both his wife's feelings about homosexuality and Luke's struggle to obtain steady employment). He had some difficult, but interesting, things to say. I asked whether he always knew he was gay: "Well, I *was* always gay, but also not . . . I mean, I was gay even when I was straight . . . I always had, you know, certain things about me that made me realize . . . you know, little things, but important still." When asked about the "little things," Luke illustrates his understanding of the nuances of gay aesthetics:

I mean, I didn't play with dolls or anything . . . though I might have if my mother let me [laughs] . . . I mean, I like fish more than steak, you know? I don't like cars or driving. I actually prefer to bike or walk. Just little things like that. I prefer to go to museums over action movies. I'd rather watch the Food Network than something like "The Man Show." I'm just gay!

Here, Luke relies on gay aesthetics to identify the seeds of belonging to gay culture long before adopting a gay identity. Specific features of life narratives are an important piece of gay identities; having the "right" sexual aesthetics is often part of framing oneself as *authentically* gay. Interestingly, the gay aesthetics Luke discusses are also markers of class status (e.g., Halperin 2012; Valocchi 1999). Straight participants in this study also framed middle- and upper-class tastes as "gay."

. . . Despite variation in what qualified as gay aesthetics, however, all of my participants discussed them as universal features of gay culture. For example, at Guys for Gender Justice meetings, men often discussed having been mistaken for gay. Shane shared one experience:

People sometimes think I'm gay. . . . They just think I, like, might be or something. . . . I take it

as an opportunity to help gay people. . . . I'll usually say something like, "Because I'm stylish? Or because I'm nice to people? . . . What? Because I'm healthy and care about my clothes and the way I look?" You know? Like, "Oh, because I have good taste in music?"

Shane's point here illustrates one way he resists heterosexism: by strategically reframing the implications of being called "gay." Rather than as an insult, Shane reinterprets the "insult" as a compliment by guessing at why he might be taken for gay and claiming those traits as his own. While attempting to neutralize differences, however, Shane's comments simultaneously reinforce symbolic boundaries separating gay from straight by (re)classifying those tastes and behaviors as gay.

A separate way that gay aesthetics were identified was through the use of "gaydar"—a portmanteau combining "gay" and "radar." "Gaydar" was discussed by men in all three groups to suggest that an individual was particularly well attuned to gay aesthetics, or to more forcefully argue that gay men are easily identified. Henry, one of The Border Boys, illustrates one use:

I just have good gaydar. . . . I'm not gay, but I know the signs. . . . I have gay friends. . . . Actually, some gay guys I know think I have better gaydar than them. . . . I'm in the know, that's all I'm saying.

Henry's use here was similar to the ways that "gaydar" was employed by men in Guys for Gender Justice as well. "Gaydar" was used most frequently by the pro-feminist men. Andrew, a young economics professor at a community college, said:

My gaydar is pretty sensitive. . . . It's not that I'm, like, always on the lookout or whatever, but my gaydar picks it up [cups his hand above his head, imitating a satellite dish]. I think when you're involved in a group like [Guys for Gender Justice], you're just thinking about more than your average man on the street. Gaydar's part of that.

While Henry's and Andrew's uses of gaydar are fairly innocent, both participate in the reification of sexual differences. Beyond that, they demonstrate some of the ways these men framed themselves as *different from* and often *better than* "most men" by claiming a better cultural (and sometimes political) "fit" (Ward 2008) with gay culture, illustrated by their knowledge of and comfort with gay aesthetics.

Regardless of whether or not they called it "gaydar," men in this study felt confident they "could tell" whether or not someone was gay. For instance, in a separate conversation with Dave (Men Can Parent Too), he brought up Luke again:

> I knew he was gay. . . . Okay, so, when he came into my office . . . he sat down like this [gingerly sits down, slightly pursing his lips]. He shook my hand like this [softly]. He's a nice guy . . . don't get me wrong . . . but, you know . . . I knew it. The handshake took me off guard, but with the whole sitting thing . . . I can typically call that kind of thing.

. . . Sexual aesthetics are often understood as a proxy for other dimensions of sexuality and used to promote understandings of sexuality wherein "gay" and "straight" are constructed as unavoidably different. The ability to identify gay aesthetics and a belief in their meaning and importance relies on an understanding of essential differences. And while straight men's use of gay aesthetics might belie an essentialist understanding of sexuality, these data support a different conclusion. Though gay aesthetics play a critical role in defining group boundaries for claims to rights and recognition, they take on distinct consequences, which I discuss further, when wielded by straight men.

On the Elements of Gay Aesthetics

In an interview with Richard (The Border Boys), he told me: "I'm emotional, man. I cry at movies. I cry when my friends hurt my feelings. . . . That's what you need to know. I'm not your average man . . . all masculine and all that. . . . And if that makes me gay, then fuck it, I'm gay . . . but, of course, I'm not *gaaaay*." When pressed to explain, Richard delineated some of the elements that make up gay aesthetics:

> Well, of course, it's gay if you go like this [cocks his wrists] and if you're all pansy or whatever. It's gay

to talk like this [affects his voice]. But, it's also gay if you're, like, into how you look too much. . . . It's gay if you're all emotional . . . like if you cry or . . . or even if you care too much about your friends. That's gay! It's gay to read, or . . . like, if you like novels rather than books. That's fucking gay. It's also gay to be into gay rights . . . or even women's rights. That's totally gay! Basically, being kinda gay could be a lot of things. . . . For me . . . I'm gay in like how I'm not all into bein' manly.

As Richard explains, gay aesthetics are composed of diverse elements. For the purposes of this article, I discuss three: (1) Sexual aesthetics can be *tastes*, as Richard characterizes concern with appearance or interest in certain kinds of literature as gay; (2) sexual aesthetics can be *behavioral*, such as Richard's mention of bodily comportment and speech patterns; (3) sexual aesthetics can be *ideological*, as Richard identifies support for certain issues as gay. Though Richard identifies three elements, he and the Border Boys relied on only two when identifying aspects of themselves as gay. Each group relied on different elements (see Table 19.1), and tastes were by far the most common.

Tastes

Similar to Luke's analysis of his preferences for museums, seafood, and certain kinds of television programs, straight men in each group identified some of their own tastes as gay. Ralph, a member of Men Can Parent Too, made similar comments:

> RALPH: The guys I work with are just not the same kinda guy as me. . . . All of 'em . . . want action. . . . I'm just trying to be a dad and make a paycheck. . . . I actually am not all

Table 19.1 Group Use of Elements of Gay Aesthetics

	Tastes	Behaviors	Ideologies
Men Can Parent Too	✓		
The Border Boys	✓	✓	
Guys for Gender Justice	✓	✓	✓

into this action . . . you know . . . like, a action kinda mindset . . . I don't drink beer. . . . I really don't like it. I mainly drink wine. But, I'm gay like that and it doesn't bug me.

INTERVIEWER: What do you mean?

RALPH: Oh, no . . . no, no, no. I'm not a fag or something like that. I just mean I'm into kinda gay stuff like that, you know? I mean, you've been over to my house. I'm a neat freak. It's just how I am.

Only men in The Border Boys and Men Can Parent Too used the word "fag." Ralph's use strategically distances himself from homosexuality, illustrating how men can utilize gay aesthetics while simultaneously promoting gender and sexual inequality. Thus, Ralph's reliance on gay aesthetics to discursively distance himself from a stereotype of masculinity is not necessarily indicative of a weakening relationship between masculinity and homophobia or sexual prejudice (e.g., Anderson 2009). Rather, it illustrates the ways that hybrid masculine practices can perpetuate inequality in new ways (Demetriou 2001; Messner 1993).

All three groups talked about various tastes as gay as a way of creating some symbolic distance between themselves and "other men." Only men in Guys for Gender Justice, however, also attempted to garner status as politically progressive by employing gay aesthetics. Many members of Guys for Gender Justice excitedly shared experiences of being "confused for gay." Indeed, at several group meetings, this kind of storytelling often turned into a contest. The youngest member of the group, Peter, explained:

People always think I'm gay . . . always! . . . People meet me and they just don't know what to do with me. They see what I wear and . . . and they see how I talk. . . . Maybe I'm just too nice. Maybe that's the problem. I always tell people that I constantly have to come out. . . . I come out as straight every time I meet someone new . . . I mean, I was in the closet and I didn't even know it. That's me, though . . . [pursing his lips] I like to sprinkle some gay on my straight.

Peter's comments frame his appearance and demeanor as gay. Like Ralph, Peter uses gay aesthetics to discursively situate himself as a hybrid masculinity. The practice allows both men to distance themselves from stereotypes of masculinity. But, unlike Ralph, Peter also attempts to frame himself as politically progressive. Peter proudly flaunts being "mistaken for gay," and later matter-of-factly stated, "It's basically impossible to be homophobic if people think you're gay." In the process, however, Peter implicitly neutralizes power relations that make "the closet" a meaningful metaphor. The closet is born from social oppression, requiring individuals to conceal their identities (Seidman 2002). Peter's use casually disguises heterosexual privilege and implicitly deflates claims to sexual inequality made by truly gay individuals. While much less overt than Ralph's use of the word "fag," Peter's discursive performance more indirectly constructs his own straight identity through a disavowal of gay identity.

Similarly, and somewhat ironically, Travis, a member of The Border Boys, identified himself as gay because of his interest in women:

I'm into hanging out with women. . . . I'm not a man's man or whatever. I'm more of a woman's man. I like art, jazz, and . . . I hate to say it this way, but I just actually think I'm a lot better than [The Border Boys]. . . . Sure, some of that is gay . . . but I mean . . . sometimes I feel like I really get along with gay men. . . . We just have a lot of things in common, with one *really* big difference.

Travis defines himself as distinct from The Border Boys. This was a common practice among all of The Border Boys, though not all of them sought to illustrate the ways they perceived themselves to be different with gay aesthetics. It is also significant that while Travis never said "fag" (as Ralph did), he is similarly careful to disavow gay identity by explaining the "*really* big difference" between *having* gay tastes and *being* gay.

These men are all participating in an essentialist discourse that reestablishes boundaries between gay and straight individuals and cultures. While all of the men are interested in framing themselves as different from "most men," some of them (particularly those in Guys for Gender Justice) also use gay aesthetics to frame themselves as politically tolerant. Thus, as Gary (Guys for Gender Justice) said, "If people thinking you're gay doesn't bug you, it's a good sign that you're on the right side." Yet, as Peter illustrates, men in Guys for Gender Justice also "outed" themselves as straight in various ways.

Despite these differences, the men in this study seemed to understand the relationship between gay aesthetics and gender and sexual inequality as relatively autonomous. Conversely, Connell's (1992) "straight gay" participants understood systems of aesthetic evaluation as producing the very hierarchies from which they are said to emerge. Connell (1992) argued that the "straight gay" men in her study relied upon what I call "straight aesthetics" for safety and gender identification. They were cognizant of the relationship between their performances of gender and sexuality and violence and inequality. This illustrates something important about the straight men's use of gay aesthetics in this study—the practice was not associated with an understanding of sexual aesthetics as part of systems of power and inequality.

Behaviors

A second dimension of gay aesthetics is behavioral—inscribing sexual meaning to individuals' actions. For instance, Doug, a therapist and member of Guys for Gender Justice, explained to the group, "You can't hide your sexuality . . . You can try, but it comes out. Gay guys are more flamboyant and they can't hold it in. . . . It's science." Doug's comment illustrates how beliefs about gay aesthetics come to be more than just beliefs. . . . The behavioral dimensions of gay aesthetics are typically signifiers of gender as well, illustrating the co-construction of gender and sexuality (Pascoe 2007; Schippers 2000; Ward 2008). Gender transgressive behavior was understood as a gay aesthetic among all three groups, though only members of Guys for Gender Justice and The Border Boys discussed some of their own behaviors as gay.

Henry (The Border Boys) claimed the behavioral dimension of gay aesthetics: "That's just me. I'm not gay . . . but I've got flair, dude." Affecting his voice, he continued, "I've got tons of flair and I don't care." Laughing, Jeffrey rejoined, "This is my fucking voice, man. It's the way I talk." Jeffrey has a higher-pitched voice and enunciates. . . . They participate in promoting stereotypes of effeminacy as a natural part of being a gay man by identifying with aspects of these qualities.

Behavioral gay aesthetics were much more common among members of Guys for Gender Justice. A conversation between these two illustrates this dynamic:

PETER: I mean . . . I don't know. I walk, sit, and talk funny. I just do. Actually, I get a lot of shit for it. I'm just more . . . you know. I'm ladylike . . . but it's like, get over yourself.

GARY: I actually get that at school. I had a group of students ask me if I was gay. I asked, "And why would you think that?" They said that it was because . . . how I speak or wave my hands around . . . I was like, "What?" I teach English, you know? I'm being emphatic!

PETER: Exactly . . . but who cares? I like the attention. . . .

GARY: I don't mind either. If the way I speak makes you think I'm gay, think away. . . . Some of the greatest writers of all times were gay. . . .

. . . Peter's self-reference as "ladylike" also illustrates how gay aesthetics are gendered by conflating gender and sexual transgressions. Thus, the hybrid masculinities these men perform co-opt elements of gender culturally coded as "feminine," which are simultaneously sexualized when adopted by men. Messerschmidt writes:

Hegemony may be accomplished . . . by the incorporation of certain aspects of [marginalized and subordinated masculinities or femininity] into a functioning gender order rather than by active oppression. . . . In practice, of course, incorporation and oppression can occur together. (Messerschmidt 2010, 39)

Consistent with Demetriou's (2001) analysis, these hybrid masculine forms are not subverting systems of inequality. Rather, they illustrate the transformative potential of inequality. To understand this, we must consider power and inequality as flexible. Similar to their use of tastes, from the way these men identified their participation in behavior culturally coded as gay, they conceal the ways this practice helps reproduce existing systems of power and inequality.

Ideologies

A third dimension of gay aesthetics is ideological. Ideological stances taken by individuals can be marked with sexual meaning. Feminism was the most frequently discussed ideology with sexual connotations. Situating masculinity and feminism as opposed causes men's engagements with feminism to be understood as emasculating (Bridges 2010). The men in this study were acutely aware of this fact. For instance, when Dan (Guys for Gender Justice) says, "They're straight . . . they're all straight. And it's funny, 'cause we're all involved in this totally gay thing," he is referring to feminism. Similarly, and noted above, Richard (*The Border Boys*) states, "It's . . . gay to be into gay rights . . . or even women's rights. That's totally gay!"

Of all the groups, only Guys for Gender Justice utilized ideological positions to identify aspects of themselves as gay. This highlights an important distinction between the groups. All three relied on gay aesthetics to distance themselves from what they understood as stigmatizing stereotypes of masculinity. But only the pro-feminist men also relied on gay aesthetics to situate themselves as *authentically* politically progressive. Indeed, they seemed to be attempting to discursively "queer" themselves to demonstrate their feminist convictions.

Saul (Guys for Gender Justice) epitomizes this position. When we met, he was wearing a T-shirt with "Feminist chicks dig me!" on the front and an AIDS awareness ribbon on his bag.

> I initially got involved with a sexual violence resource center as a volunteer. . . . All the ladies I worked with there . . . they all totally thought I was gay. . . . It's funny how people think you're gay if you, like, are for gay marriage. . . . Apparently even being against sexual violence is gay. . . . It's like clothes. . . . I don't wear straight guy clothes and I don't have straight guy politics . . . and to be perfectly honest, that's one of a few reasons I'm different from most guys. I'm better.

On Motivations and Consequences

In this section, I explore the incentives men found in relying on gay aesthetics. All three groups used gay aesthetics to distance themselves from various groups of men. Men in Men Can Parent Too seem to be seeking distance from toxic heterosexual masculinities, allowing them to frame themselves as "good guys" by more explicitly labeling the "bad." Similarly, The Border Boys' use of gay aesthetics was often aimed at illustrating their moral worth. Guys for Gender Justice, however, traded on gay aesthetics as feminist political currency. Motivated to prove themselves "on the right side," they actively "queered" their straight identities. In spite of these differences in motivations, however, there are common consequences that worked to reproduce systems of inequality in new ways.

Thomas, a member of The Border Boys, is openly gay, Black, and though he was present fewer nights a week than the others, he was central to the group when he joined them at the bar. He spoke directly about straight men's interest in an affiliation with gay men and how he believes this has changed:

> When I was in college, having a friend who was gay, even if people just thought he was gay, meant you were gay . . . like, having a gay friend [now] is totally in. . . . If you've got a gay friend . . . you aren't a piece of shit. People think gay people are really discriminating too, I think . . . If you hang out with a gay person, you must be really "down" or whatever.

Thomas's assertion seems to have been correct, but much more so for men in The Border Boys and Guys for Gender Justice than those in Men Can Parent Too.

Many members of Guys for Gender Justice felt that heterosexuality was somewhat dull and meaningless, and voiced a desire to distance themselves from stereotypes of masculinity. This seemed to be a primary motivation for relying on gay aesthetics. Jacob (Guys for Gender Justice) put it this way:

> Being straight is lame. There's just nothing exciting about saying, "Mom, Dad . . . I turned out just like you expected." . . . There was a time when I actually really wanted to be gay . . . not to, like, get with guys or whatever . . . but just 'cause . . . gay people are just more fun. Straight men are probably the most boring, cardboard people ever. So, I certainly do stuff that makes people question if I'm gay or not, 'cause I might not be gay, but I'm not going to be a robot.

Jacob explains some of the reasons that he "queers" his performance of masculinity. It's a contradictory practice, and all of the men in this study either smiled or laughed when I asked them to talk more about calling aspects of themselves gay. They did so in ways that implied the answer was self-evident, at least to them.

Similarly, Doug (Guys for Gender Justice) said, "Guys . . . hold that . . . straight guys are pretty boring for the most part. That's part of the reason I joined this group. . . . They might be straight, but they fooled me when I first met 'em." Doug and Jacob not only distance themselves from "most men," but also use gay aesthetics to forge hybrid masculinities that are experienced as more exciting than the options they perceive themselves as having access to as young, straight, white men.

Like Jacob and Doug, almost all of the men presented themselves as unique from other men, as Bob's (Men Can Parent Too) comments illustrate as we talked in the office of a restaurant he manages:

> Being a regular guy is, like, being a regular dad . . . it's not good enough. . . . If you want to go through your whole life playing by all the rules, you're gonna be a kinda "Who cares?" kinda guy.

Most guys just wanna prove they're, like, tough guys or something. I'm not like that . . . I mean, in some ways I think my marriage ended 'cause I'm just not an average guy.

Men in each group echoed Bob's expressing an urge to distance himself from "regular guys." Yet, what qualified as a "regular guy" was subtly different among the three groups. For instance, Bob relied on gay aesthetics as a mechanism symbolically creating some discursive space between himself and "tough guys." Bob later said,

> It's gay that I'm all into my family. I get teased [by some of my employees] for havin' pictures of my kids all up in my office. They say, "That's gay!" and all that. And I'm like, "Okay, I'm gay, then." You know? If yer not a dickwad, you get called gay. . . . I'll just be like, "I'd rather be gay than a dick."

Bob is not attempting to distance himself from *all* heterosexual men here—just *those* heterosexual men (the "dickwads"). It's a discursive strategy allowing him to create some rhetorical space in which he frames his own masculinity as not the "real problem."

The men in Men Can Parent Too use gay aesthetics in ways that simultaneously disavow homosexuality, consistent with practices of "othering." Yet, the men in Guys for Gender Justice (and, to a lesser extent, The Border Boys) are doing something more complicated. They attempt to "queer" their straight masculine identities with gay aesthetics to prove their moral worth, or with the understanding that gay aesthetics serve as evidence of "authentic" feminist politics. . . .

The men in this study utilized gay aesthetics to fill the perceived emptiness of straight masculinities—but they maintained a heterosexual identity and thus continued to benefit from the privileges associated with heterosexuality. This finding corroborates Seidman's claim that gender and sexual inequality are alive and well, but something significant has changed: "the formation of a self-conscious, deliberate public culture of heterosexuality" (Seidman 2002, 115). Thus, while perhaps insensitive, Peter's comment "I come out as straight every time I meet someone new" is indicative of this transformation. This change, however, does not necessarily indicate that inequality no longer exists or that masculinity's relationship with homophobia is disappearing. Rather, it is part of a hybridization of masculinity that works in ways that obscure contemporary inequality (e.g., Demetriou 2001; Messner 1993; Messerschmidt 2010).

Bertrand Russell argued that oppression assumes diverse forms. One form that Russell found particularly curious was a strategy whereby oppressed groups were constructed as "virtuous":

> It begins only when the oppressors come to have a bad conscience, and this only happens when their power is no longer secure. The idealizing of the victim is useful for a time: if virtue is the greatest of goods, and if subjection makes people virtuous, it is kind to refuse them power, since it would destroy their virtue. (Russell 1937, 731)

Russell argues that the "superior virtue of the oppressed" is a discourse enabling inequality to go unquestioned, providing new ideological supports for continued oppression when others begin to crumble.

Straight men's use of gay aesthetics may illustrate that stereotypes of homosexuality are not viewed negatively by all straight men. Yet, this simple change is not sufficient evidence of a unilateral move toward greater gender and sexual equality (e.g., Anderson 2009; McCormack 2012). Rather, these findings corroborate other research on contemporary hybrid masculine forms (Demetriou 2001; Messerschmidt 2010; Messner 1993, 2007), suggesting that they are pervasive and work to obscure (rather than weaken) existing systems of power and inequality. Thus, as Demetriou writes, "Hybridization in the realm of representation and in concrete, everyday practices make [new iterations of inequality] appear less oppressive and more egalitarian" (Demetriou 2001, 355).

For instance, Seidman's claim that Americans are becoming both more attentive to homosexuality and "skilled at reading signs of sexual identity" (Seidman 2002, 56) is a significant part of this cultural process. There is, however, no intrinsic relationship between this ability and sexual equality. Thus, while it may be tempting to label some of the men in this study as participating in "undoing gender" (Deutsch 2007) and perhaps sexuality as well by illustrating that straight men can "look" and "act" gay too, this is an inaccurate reading of what is being accomplished. There are at least three distinct consequences.

First, the belief in the pre-social nature of gay aesthetics is part of an essentialist discourse that identifies and fortifies symbolic sexual boundaries between gay and straight aesthetics, and solidifies social boundaries between gay and straight individuals. These men's identity work could contribute to disrupting gendered sexual boundaries by illustrating our collective capacity to "play" with gender and sexual aesthetics. Yet, in practice, these men's behaviors are best understood as reinvigorating symbolic sexual boundaries and recuperating gender and sexual privilege in historically novel ways.

Second, these men—seemingly unintentionally—capitalize on symbolic sexual boundaries to distance themselves from specific configurations of hegemonic masculinity, but not necessarily the associated privileges. The effect is to disguise gender and sexual privilege by crafting hybrid masculinities with gay aesthetics. By framing themselves as gay, they obscure the ways they benefit from being young, mostly white, heterosexual men.

Third, straight men's reliance on gay aesthetics to enrich their heterosexual gender identities implicitly softens more authentic claims to sexual inequality. As Doug put it, "Face it, gay guys are just more colorful.... They're just more fun." The men in Guys for Gender Justice were motivated to engage in this practice out of more than a desire to distance themselves from stigmatized masculinities (i.e., to prove feminist authenticity). But, comments like Doug's were common among this group and illustrate that the practice is also a hybrid masculine strategy associated with cultural miscegenation and its associated problems and critiques.

In a similar way, bell hooks argues that whites desire "a bit of the Other" to help fill the emptiness of white identity (hooks 1992). Hughey's (2012) analysis comparing a nationalist and antiracist organization fits within this framework as well. Men in both groups framed whiteness as "cultureless," seeking to associate with nonwhite culture to alleviate these feelings. Though both groups participated in this practice for different reasons, Hughey (2012) illustrates how this cultural appropriation works to further entrench and disguise systems of power and inequality. Indeed, Wilkins (2004) identified a similar process at work among white youth performing and identifying with aspects of Puerto Rican culture and identity.

For the men in this study, heterosexuality lacked the luster of an identity forged in a struggle for equal rights and recognition. However, while they symbolically invert the sexual hierarchy for aesthetics (i.e., gay is more desirable that straight), they simultaneously maintain heteronormative hierarchies for sexual acts, desires, and orientations. By casually framing being gay only as fun and exciting, this practice allows these men to ignore the persistence of extreme sexual inequality and the hardships that actual gay men face every day.

Conclusion

. . . Hybrid masculinities illustrate the flexibility of contemporary masculinities (perhaps particularly young, white, straight masculinities), and straight men's reliance on gay aesthetics is one kind of hybridization. These "gay straight" men might appear to blur the boundaries between gay and straight through assimilating a variety of gay aesthetics. Yet, this move toward "inclusivity" (Anderson 2009) can be interpreted in more than one way and does not necessarily indicate declining levels of gender and sexual inequality.

Research and theory suggest a more nuanced interpretation of the motivations behind and consequences of these kinds of practices. Straight men who identify aspects of themselves as gay in this study draw on varied resources to simultaneously assert heterosexual masculine identities, to distance themselves from stigmatizing stereotypes of masculinity, and—for some—to communicate authentic allegiance with groups to which they claim no formal membership.

Future research is necessary to examine how prevalent these practices are, and the diverse ways in which gay aesthetics are understood and utilized by straight men. It will also be important to continue to address the ways in which the aesthetic elements of identity categories operate throughout social life in ways that both empower and oppress.

Drawing connections to a large body of research on contemporary transformations in masculinity, this article suggests that hybrid masculinities are a significant social phenomenon. Consistent with other research implying that hybridization may be a social practice more available to socially privileged groups of men (e.g., young, straight, and white), this research also implies that the existence of hybrid masculinities does not inherently imply that social inequalities are diminishing. Rather, as Messner (1993, 2007), Demetriou (2001), and Messerschmidt (2010) all argue, this research supports the notion that hybrid masculinities are perpetuating inequality in new (and less easily identifiable) ways. Using Messner's (1993) language, these practices are illustrative of a transformation in the "style but not substance" of contemporary gender and sexual inequality.

While the gay men in Connell's (1992) research rely on straight aesthetics for gender *identification*, the straight men in this study are doing something else. Their use of gay aesthetics is better understood as gender *dis-identification*. These men's reliance upon gay aesthetics expands "acceptable" performances of straight masculinity, but does so without challenging the systems of inequality from which they emerge.

Notes

1. "Homohysteria" is a measure of popular awareness of gay identity, disapproval of homosexuality, and the extent to which homophobia is fundamental to masculine identification.
2. Messner (1997) situates fathers' rights groups and pro-feminist groups of men at the poles of men's gender-political activism in the United States.
3. Luke is not an example of a straight-identified man using "gay aesthetics." I bring him up here because he is helpful in defining what sexual aesthetics are and why they matter.

Author's note

Thanks to Tara Tober and CJ Pascoe for critical feedback and ongoing support, and Rae Blumberg, Michael Kimmel, Greta Snyder, Elizabeth Gorman, Rachel Rinaldo, Jane Ward, Dana Britton, Neal King, Jennifer Silva, Lawrie Balfour, Benjamin Snyder, Matthew Morrison, Matthew Hughey, Portia Levasseur, and John Bridges. Thanks also to Joya Misra and Mary Bernstein for editorial guidance, and anonymous reviewers at *Gender & Society*. Correspondence concerning this article should be addressed to Tristan Bridges, The College at Brockport, SUNY, 350 New Campus Drive, Brockport, NY 14420, USA; e-mail: TBridges@Brockport.edu.

References

Anderson, Eric. 2009. *Inclusive masculinity*. New York: Routledge.

Blumer, Herbert. 1954. What is wrong with social theory? *American Sociological Review* 19:3–10.

Bridges, Tristan. 2010. Men just weren't made to do this: Performances of drag at "Walk a Mile in Her Shoes" marches. *Gender & Society* 24:5–30.

Burke, Peter. 2009. *Cultural hybridity*. Malden, MA: Polity Press.

Butler, Judith. 1990. *Gender trouble*. New York: Routledge.

Connell, Raewyn W. 1992. A very straight gay. *American Sociological Review* 57:735–51.

Connell, Raewyn W., and James Messerschmidt. 2005. Hegemonic masculinity: Rethinking the concept. *Gender & Society* 19:829–59.

Demetriou, Demetrakis. 2001. Connell's concept of hegemonic masculinity: A critique. *Theory and Society* 30:337–61.

Deutsch, Francine. 2007. Undoing gender. *Gender & Society* 21:106–27.

Halperin, David. 2012. *How to be gay*. Cambridge, MA: Harvard University Press.

Hennen, Peter. 2005. Bear bodies, bear masculinity. *Gender & Society* 19:25–43.

Herek, Gregory. 1986. On heterosexual masculinity. *American Behavioral Scientist* 29:563–77.

hooks, bell. 1992. Eating the other. In *Black looks: Race and representation*. Boston: South End Press.

Hughey, Matthew. 2012. *White bound*. Stanford, CA: Stanford University Press.

Kimmel, Michael. 1994. Masculinity as homophobia. In *Theorizing masculinities,* edited by Harry Brod and Michael Kaufman. Thousand Oaks, CA: Sage.

Lehne, Gregory. 1976. Homophobia among Men. In *The forty-nine percent majority,* edited by Deborah David and Robert Brannon. Reading, MA: Addison-Wesley.

McCormack, Mark. 2012. *The declining significance of homophobia*. New York: Oxford University Press.

Messerschmidt, James. 2010. *Hegemonic masculinities and camouflaged politics*. Boulder, CO: Paradigm.

Messner, Michael. 1993. "Changing men" and feminist politics in the United States. *Theory and Society* 22:723–37.

Messner, Michael. 1997. Politics of masculinities. New York: Alta Mira.

Messner, Michael. 2007. The masculinity of the Governator. *Gender & Society* 21: 461–80.

Ocampo, Anthony. 2012. Making masculinity: Negotiations of gender presentation among Latino gay men. *Latino Studies* 10:448–72.

Pascoe, CJ. 2007. *Dude, you're a fag*. Berkeley: University of California Press.

Pfeil, Fred. 1995. *White guys*. New York: Verso Books.

Russell, Bertrand. 1937. The superior virtue of the oppressed. *The Nation* 26: 731–32.

Savran, David. 1998. *Taking it like a man*. Princeton, NJ: Princeton University Press.

Schippers, Mimi. 2000. The social organization of sexuality and gender in alternative hard rock. *Gender & Society* 14:747–64.

Seidman, Steven. 1996. Introduction. In *Queer theory/ sociology,* edited by Steven Seidman. Oxford, UK: Blackwell.

Seidman, Steven. 2002. *Beyond the closet.* New York: Routledge.

Small, Mario Luis. 2009. How many cases do I need? *Ethnography* 10:5–38.

Stein, Arlene, and Ken Plummer. 1994. "I can't even think straight": "Queer' theory and the missing sexual revolution in sociology. *Sociological Theory* 12:178–87.

Strauss, Anselm, and Juliet Corbin. 1998. *The basics of qualitative research.* New York: Routledge.

Valocchi, Steve. 1999. The class-inflected nature of gay identity. *Social Problems* 46:207–24.

Ward, Jane. 2008. Dude-sex: White masculinities and "authentic" heterosexuality among dudes who have sex with dudes. *Sexualities* 11:414–34.

Wilkins, Amy. 2004. Puerto Rican Wannabes. *Gender & Society* 18:103–21.

Wilkins, Amy. 2009. Masculinity dilemmas. *Signs* 34:343–68.

"He's Got No Game"

Young Men's Stories about Failed Romantic and Sexual Experiences

NEILL KOROBOV

Introduction

During the last decade, there has been an increasing amount of theoretical and analytic attention to masculinity from a discursive orientation (Wetherell and Edley 1999, Gough 2001, Riley 2003, Korobov 2004, 2005, 2006, Korobov and Bamberg 2004). In seizing on rigorous analytic procedures for the close study of talk, discursive work has been instrumental in revealing how oppressive forms of masculinity are not only discursively produced and reproduced, but also how they are routinely denied, inoculated from challenge, and mitigated through irony, humor and parody. It has been in this second vein of analysis, in exposing the plausibly deniable features of masculinity, that discursive work has uniquely illuminated Connell's (1995) argument concerning the flexible, formidably resourceful, and inscrutable composition of what is hegemonic about masculinity. Whereas traditional psychological work often conflates "hegemonic masculinity" with "heroic masculinity" (bread-winner, heterosexual, tough, virile), discursive work has revealed that what is sometimes most hegemonic are masculine positions that are knowingly non-heroic or ordinary, i.e., the self-reflexive varieties that casually and playfully parody traditional male stereotypes.

Nowhere is this more obvious than in the textual and visual construction of masculinities in popular culture magazines, television and films. For instance, consider the interminable barrage of men's lifestyle magazines (*Maxim, Details, FHM, Stuff, Loaded*, etc.) that proffer, in tongue-in-cheek ways, a kind of "new laddism"—an educated, middle-class, and witty version of masculinity that eschews the wimpishness of the sensitive "new man" while seeking to re-claim the conservative ethos of beer, women and sport (Benwell 2002). Or consider the television sitcom trend of presenting men as anti-heroes—as hapless, yet affably befuddled and domesticated, who nevertheless remain eminently likable and successful. There are also series such as MTV's *Jackass*, where a group of unassuming white working-class guys turn failure and bodily injury into a "carnivalesque sadomasochism" that relentlessly mocks heroic masculinity (Brayton 2007). Also popular is the "white-guy-as-loser" trope that is ubiquitous in beer commercials (Messner and Montez de Oca 2005). This "lovable loser" finds himself routinely humiliated, usually as a result of pursuing unattainably beautiful women. Yet, he is blissfully self-mocking and ironic about his loser-status, for he is a loser only in contrast to the outdated macho versions of masculinity typical of beer ads in the past. In whatever form, these various media gambits have been successful in serving up an average and ordinary "everyman"—a youthful

Neill Korobov, "He's Got No Game: Young Men's Stories about Failed Romantic and Sexual Experiences," *Journal of Gender Studies,* 18(2):99–114. Copyright 2009, reprinted by permission of Taylor & Francis.

and predominately white version of masculinity that is playfully ironic and self-mocking.

When interpreted in the wake of significant post–civil rights advances by women, sexual minorities and ethnic minorities, these new masculine tropes appear as a form of anxious "white male backlash" (Savran 1996, Robinson 2000), albeit an intentionally mitigated backlash. Commercial forces have commodified these anxious and self-deprecating tendencies, creating a simulacrum of marginalized and victimized masculine positionalities and disseminating them throughout culture (see Benwell 2002, Brayton 2007). Unfortunately, there is a paucity of micro-level research detailing how ordinary young men occasion such positions within mundane social contexts. As these visual and textual depictions of failed masculinity become increasingly woven into the fabric of everyday culture, we are left to wonder if and how young men are adopting them as part of the project of doing homosociality and, if so, how the face of hegemonic masculinity may be slowly changing as a result.

The present study thus takes a keen interest in how young men occasion a variety of self-deprecating masculine tropes in their stories about romantic mishaps and gaffes, often resulting in rejection and embarrassment. These types of stories are the focus of the present study. The aim in studying self-deprecation in the context of romantic experiences is not to voyeuristically indulge in young men's immature behavior; rather, the aim is to use a critical-discursive perspective to examine how young men formulate stories that, at least on the surface, seem contrary to traditional masculine norms, and to finally suggest how a new variety of male homosociality and hegemonic masculinity is emerging as a result.

The "Ordinariness" of Hegemonic Masculinity

Insight into this new variety of hegemony is not without precedent. In one of the more widely cited discursive studies on masculinity, Wetherell and Edley (1999) found that the most common form of self-positioning with young men did not involve "heroism" or "rebelliousness," but rather "ordinariness." Most men resisted the macho and "bad-boy" masculine ideals in favor of positioning themselves as normal and conventional guys. Wetherell and Edley (1999) noticed, however, that their "ordinariness" was actually a gender-oppressive method of self-presentation. They argue that sometimes one of the most effective ways of endorsing hegemonic masculinity is to demonstrate one's distance from it—that is, to show, with all the weapons of rhetoric, that one has the courage and confidence, as an "ordinary" man, to resist (and even mock) heroic and macho forms of masculinity.

This lampooning of heroic and macho masculinity and embracing of the "everyman" is a type of masculine subjectivity slowly being illuminated in a range of subsequent studies (see Gough 2001, Korobov 2005, 2006, Korobov and Thorne 2006, Brayton 2007, Gilmartin 2007). In remarking on the "generous nonchalance" in heterosexual college-aged men's stories about romantic breakups, Gilmartin (2007) noticed that young men put a considerable amount of effort into making romance a casual, easily-jettisoned topic. In two similar studies, Korobov and Thorne (2006, 2007) found that young men often playfully mitigated the seriousness of their romantic problems so as to appear nonchalant, un-invested, and at times mildly amused by their own and each other's romantic troubles. Gough (2001) found that young men often discursively suppressed their thoughts in particular contexts in order to manage potentially sexist sentiments. The common thread in these studies is not that young men are, as men, simply "ordinary" sorts of people. Rather, it is that young men are, occupationally speaking, increasingly finding themselves in a culture that mandates the social business of what Harvey Sacks (1984) calls "doing being."

For Sacks (1984), "ordinariness" is not an aspect of one's personality, but rather is a concerted interactive accomplishment. Sacks (1984, p. 414) notes that "it is not that somebody *is* ordinary; it is perhaps that that is what one's business is, and it takes work, as any other business does." As social business, doing being ordinary becomes an attributional issue with deviance and normalcy at stake. It is a way of being "reciprocally witnessable" or intelligible to members of a social group (Sacks 1984). As a member of a social group, one must not only monitor one's experiences for features that are story-worthy, but one must also take care to assure that what gets storied are those experiences that one is, as an ordinary member, entitled to have. As a way of creating sociality, group members are thus obliged to bind up their experiences by borrowing from the group's common stock of knowledge. The work of being ordinary thus becomes crucially important for telling stories that break with convention, such as romantic/sexual failures.

The central premise of this study is that formulations of ordinariness are likely to be features in young men's stories about romantic and/or sexual mishaps. At stake for these young men is not ordinariness in the sense of their heterosexual *orientation* or their heterosexual *desire*. Those canonical or "ordinary" heterosexual and masculine elements are secured by virtue of the fact that the young men's stories are clearly about pursuits, albeit unsuccessful pursuits, of romantic and sexual experiences with women. At stake are other aspects of ordinary masculinity, such as skillful and successful seduction, prowess, glibness, bravura, or what is sometimes euphemistically referred to as "game," as in the sports metaphor of "he's got game" (Brooks 1997, Levant 1997).

Being normatively masculine is thus only partially about displaying heterosexual orientation or heterosexual desire; it is also about having "game," which is to say, being able to display a set of well-honed romantic skills. Because these young men's stories celebrate gaffes leading to embarrassment and sometimes rejection, they break with the canonical masculine norms of cool seduction or gamesmanship. A new form of homosociality is thus being created here, where stories of romantic failure function as a strategy for coping with the shifting meaning of "successful" masculinity. The focus of this study is to understand how positions of failed gamesmanship function in the accomplishment of these young men's masculine subjectivities, how a sense of conventionality or ordinariness is reclaimed, and what these processes reveal about the shifting nature of hegemonic masculinity in contemporary culture.

Background to the Study

Twelve group discussions were conducted with three young-adult male friends per group, plus an adult-male moderator. Each of the 36 participants was between the ages of 18 and 23 ($M = 19.8$ years, $SD = 0.8$ years), and was living away from home while enrolled in a public university in Northern California. Small and casual group discussions were chosen, as opposed to one-on-one interviews, so as to create a fluid, symmetrical and collaborative context in which to share stories about potentially delicate topics. Each triad was required to have known each other for at least six months and to have been "good friends" at the time of the group discussion. The large majority (89%) of the sample self-identified as either "Caucasian" or "white"; the remainder declined to state ethnicity, or indicated either "Asian" or "Latino" descent. The entire sample self-identified as "heterosexual."

Participants were enlisted informally through general requests for volunteers in both upper and lower-level social science university courses. The study was described as a research project looking at how young adult same-sex friends talk about their romantic experiences. Each conversation was audio recorded with permission and fully transcribed (see Appendix 20.1 for transcription conventions). Each group discussion lasted approximately 1.5h and generated a total of approximately 980 pages of transcribed dialogue.

The group conversations were relatively unstructured. The moderator casually asked for small stories about everyday events (see Ochs and Capps 2001, Bamberg 2004). The discussions were littered with colorfully co-constructed small stories. It is quite possible that, as a male moderator in his mid-thirties of a similar ethnicity and class as the majority of the participants, the young men felt less inhibited with me than they would with a female or older male researcher. My aim, therefore, was to create a space where the participants felt free to engage in the kinds of conversations that occurred naturally in their everyday contexts. With that in mind, I did not simply remain on the periphery back-channeling the young men with "mmhs" and "yeahs," but rather cautiously engaged them, challenged them, and cajoled them when appropriate.

Analysis

The analytic focus is a critical discursive analysis of "small stories," aligned closely with programs of discursive research that have detailed the subtle and often indirect ways that young men transact compliance and resistance to normative masculinity in everyday conversations (Wetherell and Edley 1999, Gough 2001, Korobov 2004, 2006). The central focus in this form of analysis is how young men indirectly align themselves with the stereotypical aspects of normative masculinity while *at the same time* engaging in talk that is meant to sound sensitive, self-deprecating or vulnerable. This requires an examination of how self-deprecation and self-derogation is *rhetorically* built to simultaneously accommodate and resist an array of social expectations, potential interlocutor challenges and cultural assumptions. It is in this vein that the analyses extend into a discussion of the ideological and gender-political nature of how formulations of self-deprecation and "failure" become strategically useful for the overall survivability and adaptability of hegemonic masculinity.

Analyses proceeded by first identifying any story that involved talk about romantic or sexual experiences which failed or were embarrassing in some way, i.e., stories about romantic mishaps, gaffes and bad decisions that resulted in embarrassment, anxiety or rejection. Inductive analyses revealed that these kinds of stories generally touched on one of three general themes. First, many of the failed romantic stories seemed to involve experiences with what some of the participants called "*crazy bitches*." From what could be gleaned from the conversations, "crazy bitch" is a colloquially popular, misogynistic phrase used to describe women

who are erratic, overly jealous, insecure, vengeful, and sometimes violent. A second common theme was failure in the context of attempted "*hook-ups*." "Hook-ups" referred to some form of casual, no-strings-attached sexual experience. And finally, many of the young men told stories of times they made fools out of themselves while being inebriated. The subjects talked about alcohol as providing a kind of "*liquid courage*" that often backfired on them. The analyses that follow examine, in a broad and critical-discursive way, paradigmatic stories for each of the three themes.

Theme 1: "*Crazy Bitches*"

In this first story, Hal recounts a relatively recent dating experience in which his girlfriend reveals that she might have contracted herpes from another man and that she has continued to have sex with her ex-boyfriend while dating Hal. Rather than disparage this, Hal creates an ironic and bemused incongruity between his ex-girlfriend's outlandish actions/statements and his nonchalant reactions, thus creating a palpable tension the young men find funny.

Story 1

Participants: Hal (H), Gary (G), and Cory (C), Moderator (M)

1. H: maybe a week yeah I'd say about a week
2.   into the school year I got a phone call
3.   from her and she said "um I'm sorry but
4.   I may have herpes" ((laughter, 2.0))
5. H: yeahha ((laughing)) whic(hah) was a fun
6.   phone call to get and then so she told me
7.   and what was funny was that on the first
8.   date uh one of the things she told me was
9.   like uhh "<u>hey</u> I just got tested and I'm clean
10.   so you don't have to worry" and I said
11.   "<that's gre::at> that's wonderful" umm::
12.   and so> but every time we had sex I used
13.   a condom <and so but she called me and
14.   she's like yeah uh about a week before she
15.   met me she said she was at this party and
16.   she ended up getting drunk and her (.)

17. this is an exact quote "<ended up having
18. sex with some Asian dude in the back of
19. his van>"[. . .] and so I said "<okay::: um
20. let me call you back in like a day or two
21. once I think about some things>"[. . .]
22. G: and then two weeks later he gets a text
23. message and he looks at it and he just
24. starts (.) I guess he just started laughing
25. or something I don't really remember but
26. it said something along the lines of "hey
27. what up I'm uh oh what was it I'm back=
28. H: =I'm back with Bruce again"(.) yeah with
29. Bruce [. . .] she's crazy she been dating this
30. guy for about two years and like recently
31. broke up with him but <did:::n't tell him>
32. or something cause like when I talked to
33. her she said "yeah me and my boyfriend
34. broke up" and then later that day her boy-
35. friend called her ex-boyfriend called her
36. and she picked up n' was like "oh hey honey
37. what's up?" and I'm like uh::: so does he
38. know that he's been broken up with an' I'm
39. like well:: I think he knows and so <I don't
40. think she ever actually stopped having sex
41. with him> while we were dating

Although Hal notes that he had sex with this woman, he deviates from the heroic masculine script by positioning himself not as hero but as a victim. He positions her as having a questionable sexual past that put his health in jeopardy; she also cheats on him with her ex-boyfriend. Nevertheless, Hal exploits the self-deprecating aspect of his victim status to both entertain his male friends and, by extension, to position himself as confidently detached and even slightly amused by the "crazy" behavior of this woman. Hal's casual position of ordinariness is principally brought off through a series of carefully crafted juxtapositions between his girlfriend's reported speech and his own sarcastic or deadpan reactions to it. For instance, in response to her admission that she is disease-free, Hal slows his speech in an audibly long and drawn-out sarcastic way as he says "<that's gre::at> that's wonderful." His slow and deliberate staging of this evaluation, common in sarcastic rejoinders, instructs the

others to hear her admission as odd and to see him as nonchalant about it. Later, after she casually calls him up to alert him about her sexual encounter with "some Asian dude in the back of his van" and of the chance they both might now have herpes, he is again affectedly nonchalant as he replies "<okay::: um let me call you back in like a day or two once I think about some things>." Coupled with Hal's instructive laughter, there are other instances (lines 5, 36–39) where Hal reports his own speech in an exaggerated, slow and sarcastic way so as to forward a surprised but cool and ordinary reaction to "crazy" admissions from his girlfriend. This ironic tension works to procure laughter, as it illuminates the extraordinariness of his girlfriend's non-normative actions in contrast to his own subdued and ordinary reactions.

As seen in the first story, a defensively built form of misogyny often lurks in stories about failed romantic experiences that involve "crazy" women. This next story is no exception. In it, Gus weaves a very colorful account about a recent run-in with his angry ex-girlfriend, Noel. Prior to this story we learn that Gus recently broke up with Noel, immediately following their first sexual encounter.

Story 2

Participants: Noah (N), Gus (G), Chris (C), Moderator (M)

1. G: so I see Noel at a party last week and um
2. she's like "hey Gus" an I was like "hey"
3. and she's like "HEY I got something to tell
4. you" and I was like "oh shit" so like she
5. like walks over to me pretty upset look-
6. ing and she's like um just went off (.) she's
7. like "YOU THINK YOU CAN HAVE SEX
8. WITH ME AND JUST NEVER DEAL
9. WITH IT AGAIN" an blah blah an' she's
10. like <"I outta make you feel the pain you
11. made me feel"> ((laughter, 1.0))
12. G: and so she went like this ((makes clenched
13. fist)) and she grabbed my balls and was
14. like <"I hope you're feeling the same pain
15. I was"> an I was like "AGGHH SHOOT"
16. an I didn't know what to do

17. N: ((smile voice)) and how long was she
18.   grabbin em?
19. G: for a good while like=
20. M: =and you just stood there?
21. G: well I put my hand over my balls and then
22.   she like she's like "it's a good thing you cup-
23.   ping em cause I'm squeezing really hard
24.   right now" an I'm like "ALL:::RIGHT"[. . .]
25. N: ((laughing)) it was AWESOME
26. G: she was freakin out she grabbed my
27.   balls and then like for a good like thirty
28.   seconds she was like ((inhales loudly))
29.   and like staring in my eyes [. . .] I didn't
30.   know what to say like I was trying to say
31.   ((in falsetto)) "I'm sorry" an trying to
32.   like explain myself but at the same time
33.   my balls=
34. M: = you're talking in falsetto
35. G: there was no point in like trying to explain
36.   anything.

Although Gus had sex with Noel, the story is not about bragging about that, but instead is a colorful and self-deprecating admission of how Noel enacted a publicly and personally humiliating form of revenge. Why, we might wonder, would Gus spend an entire story ratcheting up the details of this embarrassing incident? Before focusing on the details of the story, imagine that instead of getting angry, Noel approached Gus with a controlled anger or sadness at having been rejected after having sex with him for the first time. Had that happened, it is unlikely that Gus's story would have worked. In other words, Gus's self-deprecating story, and the victim status that ensues, only works if he can construe her vis-à-vis the irrational "crazy bitch" trope (see Gilmartin 2007). Moreover, her craziness needs to be illustrated in a remarkably weighty and colorful way so that it serves as a clear foil to his relatively calm response. As Gilmartin (2007) observed in her study of college-aged men's experiences of romance, guys expected to end relationships and break hearts, and expected women to get really angry with them. Unlike sadness, anger enables

a traditionally masculine response (remain stoic, take it, say nothing). Noel's anger confirms Gus's standing in the gender order. Had she not cared, Gus might be less certain of where he stood as a man. And the crazier she seems, the more difficult it becomes to empathize with her pain. By extension, it becomes more difficult to condemn Gus for sexually exploiting her.

The "crazy bitch" trope is but one essential ingredient in this story. The other essential ingredient, the one that drives the self-deprecation, centers on the spectacle of having one's testicles squeezed by an angry woman in a public setting. Of the image of Gus standing there cupping his testicles in pain, Noah laughingly remarks, "it was AWESOME" (line 25). It is "awesome" for these guys both for its physical comedy and for what it represents at a gender-political level. The punishment of the white male body is yet another prop in the project of creating a white-male backlash rhetoric (Savran 1996). The effect is (yet again) a victimized male identity, or more accurately, the simulacrum of a fractured abject hero (see Brayton 2007). Whereas emasculation in-and-of-itself is not "awesome," the *spectacle* of emasculation, particularly when cloaked in irony, is a useful rhetorical ploy for simultaneously embracing and disavowing the role of victim. What remains is a quiet reassertion of traditional masculinity. In effect, the misogynistic message is: "these women are crazy, but we can take it and we can laugh about it."

Theme 2: "Hook-ups"

This simulacrum of victimization can appear in a variety of forms. Aside from being scared by venereal diseases or accosted, many of the young men in this study told stories highlighting their floundering oafishness in sexual "hook-ups" with women. In the following story, Terry talks about his recent attempt to "make out" with a young woman. Kyle and Cal have heard the story before, and prompt him (beginning in line 4) to focus on an awkward expression that he apparently used the first time he told them the story.

Story 3

*Participants: Kyle (K), Terry (T), Cal (C),
Moderator (M)*

1. T: we're just getting kind of flirty and I try
2. making out with her and she totally just
3. like blocks me n' stuff
4. K: but later you were like outside sitting on
5. this thing and she was sitting on your lap
6. and you started to:::?
7. T: ((in deadpan)) playing the vagina ((laugh-
8. ter, 2.0))
9. M: ((laughing)) wait(hah) <u>playing</u> the
10. vagina>?
11. K: they weren't even making out he was just
12. <<u>playing</u> the vagina>
13. T: ((laughing)) I dunno what(hah) I'm doing
14. down there
15. M: ((laughing)) you can't say "playing the
16. vagina" what's that? but no wait ((dead-
17. pan)) no seriously keep saying it it's cool
18. T: so um we go back in her house and I hop
19. in her bed an' she's like "oh no you gotta
20. go" and I'm just like "<u>what</u>?" I was like
21. "what the fuck" like "why are you telling
22. me to leave like after all this?"
23. C: right (.) you've already touched her vagina
24. K: YEAH
25. T: YEAH
26. C: no <u>played</u> the vagina
27. T: ((laughing)) ex(h)actly
28. K: you played the vagina
29. C: ((deadpan)) what sport did you play with
30. her vagina?
31. T: pretty much things just didn't happen
32. C: no duh

Kyle's interrupted narration in lines 4–6 and the dangling "and you started to:::" works as a prompt in the first part in a kind of adjacency pair, which Terry completes with staged deadpan in line 7 when he says "playing the vagina." Terry apparently used the expression in an earlier telling of this story where Kyle was present (instead of using more common terms, like "touching" or "fingering," or

even the expression "playing *with her* vagina"). "Playing the vagina" is a verbal gaffe that his friends find entertaining. Terry's deadpan in line 7 reveals his willingness to be complicit with the joke so as to produce the expected group laughter (lines 7 and 8). What makes the gaffe additionally funny is that they were not, according to Kyle, even "making out" (line 11) when Terry attempted to touch her vagina. He was only "trying" to "make out," as Terry himself attests (lines 1 and 2). In accounting for this, Terry displays ignorance and laughs as he says "I dunno what I'm doing down there" (lines 13 and 14), a concession that admits to a general clumsiness in sexual situations. His laughter, though, mitigates the seriousness of the self-criticism, lacing it with a kind of knowing or hipster irony. In other words, because he knows he's not cool with the ladies, he is in a way, cool. His friend's laughter is also ambiguous. Are they laughing at the courage or the stupidity required to attempt to touch a woman like that while not even really "making out" to begin with?

When Terry tries to get the story back on track (line 18), thus displaying more of the details of his rejection and of how he feels he was sexually led on by this woman, his friends initially agree (lines 23–25), thereby securing for him a victim status; yet, they quickly derail him yet again and return to enjoying Terry's humorous malapropism. This derailing is a form of displacement (see Edwards 2005), which involves the use of displaced buffer topics, particularly in cases where complaints or troubles are being articulated, that are biased towards a nonserious treatment. It is particularly useful for taking the sting out of sensitive topics, like sexual failure. In lines 1–2 and 18–22, Terry attempts to launch his rejection story, only to have it displaced each time. His friends are arguably helping him out, in a way, to mitigate his romantic failure. Terry displays complicity in both instances (lines 7 and 27), thereby colluding in the fun of laughing at his gaffe. In this particular example, Terry is positioned not simply as a victim of his own fumbling hands, but also of the young woman's (alleged) capriciousness when it comes to sending sexual signals and setting clear boundaries.

In this next story, Kyle talks about a recent attempt to ask a young woman over to his house for a "hook-up." What makes the story tellable is not that Kyle was rejected *per se*, which seemed inevitable, but is the way he went about trying to persuade her to come back to his house and his nonchalant reaction to her rejection.

Story 4

Participants: Kyle (K), Terry (T), Cal (C), Moderator (M)

1. K: like two weeks ago I went over to Ali's
2.   house and there was this girl Jaime that
3.   I'd hooked up with in the past a few times
4.   an I was trying to get her to go back to
5.   my place but she wasn't really having it
6.   ((laughter, 1.0))
7. M: what were you saying to try to get her to
8.   come back?
9. K: tha:::t's the thing uhmm(hahuh) ((laughs))
10. T: I was there I can vouch [it was like]
11. K: [yea what] I say?
12. T: pretty much that=
13. K: =just "<u>hey</u> let's go back to my place"
14.   ((laughter, 2.0))
15. T: it's "are you coming home with me" n'she's
16.   like "nope I'm going to sleep"[. . .]
17. M: I think you got dissed ((all laugh, 1.0)) is
18.   that what you think?
19. T: I thought it was pretty funny when we
20.   were going home and he calls her again on
21.   the phone n'he's like "so are you coming
22.   over soon?" ((laughter, 2.0))
23. K: an she did [°not°
24. T: [not ((laughing)) you tried
25. K: I tried (.) that's all that counts

At stake in this story are Kyle's seduction skills, which Kyle formulates in a *knowingly* glib and unadorned way. Kyle assumes the position of the "underachieving pick-up artist" who admittedly dispenses with curt pick-up lines ("hey let's go back to my place"; "are you coming home with me?"; "so are you coming over soon?") so lacking in creativity or romance that they clearly violate the masculine dictum to display "game." What function, we might ask, does his self-deprecating story of failed seduction achieve, other than a laugh or the opportunity to display nonchalance? At the end, Terry and Kyle note that it is the "trying" that counts. Is this a kind of valorization of a blue-collar work ethic when it comes to romantic seduction? Or is this irony yet again? After all, Kyle's seduction repertoire is blissfully lazy. His gamesmanship is entirely lacking. He is not *really* trying, though, which seems to be exactly the point. His laziness, and the subsequent rejection that predictably follows, is the formula that makes the story funny to his friends and therefore tellable in the first place.

One way to understand the logic of such failed masculine positions is to interpret them on a broader gender-political level. They reflect what Messner and Montez de Oca (2005) argue is men's increasingly unstable status in contemporary culture when it comes to understanding how to initiate romantic endeavors. Being ironic or self-mocking about such complexities is one way of coping with this tension, or more broadly, with the erosion of the masculine norm to have seduction skills. Kyle's lazy seduction (i.e., "are you coming home with me?") can thus be viewed as a misogynistic, albeit tongue-in-cheek, backlash against women's increasing autonomy and social power. Rather than risk being genuinely humiliated, either via rejection for actually trying or by appearing genuinely (not playfully) ignorant about the evolving rules of gender relations, men might opt for a kind of "boys-will-be-boys" defensive ironic posture. The obvious playfulness and staged certitude of quips like "hey let's go back to my place" inoculates it from charges of blatant sexism. When seen in this light, the "trying is all that counts" adage is not an endorsement for an actual roll-your-sleeves-up approach to figuring out how to appropriately talk to women, but is a way of rationalizing failure. "Trying" is futile, in other words, so one might as well have a laugh. It allows men to indirectly define themselves as victims, as the purveyors of a now endangered form of suave masculinity.

Theme 3: *"Liquid Courage"*

Being drunk was another common resource in these young men's self-deprecating stories. There were generally two types of stories involving alcohol and romantic embarrassment. The first type, as illustrated in the next story, usually involved getting drunk and making daring, but foolish, attempts to flirt with attractive women. The second type, as illustrated in Story 6, often involved getting drunk with a woman (usually at a party) and then having something embarrassing happen. In this first story, Ron and Seth co-narrate a recent incident where Ron "got sloshed," took his pants off, and approached a very attractive and sober female friend and asked her for a date.

Story 5

Participants: Ron (R), Zach (Z), Seth (S), Moderator (M)

1. R: apparently I don't remember this but I lost
2. my pants somehow ((laughter, 2.0)) [. . .]
3. R: and pounded on one of my housemate's
4. doors and said like "we should go on a date"
5. and then "let's set a date" an'she's like =
6. S: = oh that was so funny
7. R: she's "you won't remember Ron you're
8. sloshed"
9. M: and she's like "uh:: you're in your under-
10. wear Ron"
11. S: this is our other female housemate from
12. this year Ashley
13. Z: she's pretty hot
14. R: yea she's very hot [. . .] so yea apparently
15. I guess someone had or I guess I had started
16. going to bed and then I went outside and
17. I knocked on Ashley or I <u>pounded</u> I don't
18. know on Ashley's door (.) she was kind of
19. asleep being it four in the morning and uh
20. I just said ((in drunk voice)) "we should go
21. on a date" you know an it wasn't knowing me
22. it wasn't very sexual at all (.) it was more like
23. cause she's into a lot of guy things she's into
24. Family Guy she's into video games you know
25. so she's pretty cool I have a good time around

26. her you know (.) I can joke around like a guy
27. I don't have to kind of censor myself cause
28. it's a girl and yea so (.) and I just said "you
29. know what we should go out sometime I
30. like you you're cool you're fun to be around"
31. and <yeah::::> she says <"Ron you're drunk
32. and you won't remember this"> and um of
33. course I didn't the next morning and I get
34. up and Seth's like "guess what you did last
35. night" and I'm like "oh god"
36. S: he just wanted me to shut up (.) he just
37. wanted some orange juice and like I just
38. started just started harassing him and
39. asking him if he remembered ANY of the
40. night before and does he remember talk-
41. ing to Ashley and he says "NO NO NO
42. WAY I didn't do that" ((laughing)) and
43. he(huh) goes "really I did that?" and he's
44. like "fu:::ck"

At least three discursive elements intersect to make this kind of story work. First, inebriation stories allow for hazy recollections, where the narrator is able to play "mind" against "world" (Edwards 1997). Phrases like "apparently," "I don't remember," "somehow," "that's a little fuzzy," "I hear different stories," and "I guess" are littered throughout Ron's narrative. These rhetorical constructions of ignorance (see Potter 1996, Edwards 1997) make the veracity of the events being narrated a function of the "world out there," of what his friends have told him, rather than being a product of Ron's actual memory, which is liable to be biased by his own interests. It is, however, counterintuitive it may seem, absolutely crucial that Ron *not* remember. Not remembering insulates Ron from the counter that he was intentionally trying to be cool or courageous, which works against the masculine dictum to be effortless and nonchalant. Not remembering also allows his friends (see Seth's contributions) to own the story, in a way, since they get to remember it, interpret it as cool or funny, pass it along, and most importantly, hold the one who experienced it accountable in terms of masculine norms. In this way, self-deprecating stories are essential for promoting homosociality.

A second way that Ron manages this kind of story is by scripting his actions according to a pervasive and stable dispositional tendency (Edwards 1995). From lines 23–26, Ron suggests that given what is "known" about him and Ashley, i.e., that they joke around a lot and that she is cool and into guy things, it is likely that his flirtation was meant playfully and not sexually. Where there is a predictable way of acting, then whatever happens (here, Ron taking his pants off and asking Ashley on a date) can be attributed to a kind of scripted repartee between the participants. The effect is that it situates Ron's actions within a pre-established frame of playfulness, thus mitigating the potential for his actions to appear perverse, harassing or desperate. The self-deprecation reveals that he can be himself around her, that he can be playful and boyish, or as he puts it (line 27), "I don't have to censor myself." His self-deprecation is thus proof of their chemistry.

Finally, from a gender-political perspective, the entire story treats failure as patriarchal male privilege, and a supposedly endearing one at that, thus reincarnating the "loser motif" and "everyman" trope (see Messner and Montez de Oca 1995). It involves male "buddies" drinking beer together at a house party, a woman who is constructed as a fantasy object or "hottie," and precarious attempts by one or more "buddies" to risk humiliation by attempting to broach the space of the "hottie." While this happens, the other "buddies" gleefully enjoy their beer and the voyeurism of watching their friend make his moves (Seth listened through the door, line 19). The attempt at the "hottie" inevitably fails, and is followed by the kind of rejection that occasions high-fives from the other "buddies." They are thus outed as "losers" but do not seem to care because they have each other, their beer, and now a good story to tell (see Messner and Montez de Oca 1995). When seen this way, stories of failed seduction, though deceptively playful in their telling, cater exclusively to men's insecurities about their unstable status within the contemporary gender order. They invite men to not only take refuge in the victim identity occasioned by this loser status, but to exploit it through irony, and to finally recognize that while "hotties" may be unavailable, the one thing that men can count on is their shared fraternal bond.

In this second type of inebriation story, Shawn relates a time when he and his girlfriend, Kaly, got drunk at a big fraternity party and went to an upstairs room to have sex.

Story 6

Participants: Shawn (S), Mod (M)

1. S: I brought Kaly with me and uh it was a
2.   big party and we were both fairly inebri-
3.   ated and I uh took her by the hand and
4.   lead her into my buddy's room [. . .] and
5.   all my other friends are very aware of it
6.   and we're takin off each other's clothes and
7.   then there's this like pounding on the door
8.   "SHAWN" ((laughing)) hahan' I say "GO
9.   AWAY" and they say "NO:: what are you
10.   doing come out here" (.) and I guess one of
11.   my other drunk buddy's was getting a lap
12.   dance like outside in the main room (.) so
13.   they're like banging down the door and at
14.   one point they were really like harassing us
15.   like I guess like the door had a crappy lock
16.   and there was a way to exploit it um and
17.   so they were coming in the room as I was
18.   getting a blow job ((laughing)) hahhuh
19.   yeah so like Kaly was awesome she like
20.   leans against the door to block em so I
21.   thought that was pretty cool (.) so we're in
22.   this bedroom and we had just finished and
23.   we're lying there on the bed and my buddy
24.   Paul stumbles in and uh I say "Paul what
25.   are you doing get out of here now" and he
26.   just kind of like looks at me with this you
27.   know this goofy expression and he kind of
28.   like starts stumbling over towards the bed
29.   and I say "Paul what are you doing LEAVE
30.   RIGHT NOW" and I'm like yelling at him
31.   an uh he goes <"nah::: man it's cool">
32.   ((laughing)) and(ha) so he(huh) sits he
33.   like sits down like Indian style just like

34.   plops down at the corner of the bed and he
35.   goes <"I'm just getting my gum"> and like
36.   ((laughing)) and he pulls out this pack of
37.   like I dunno Orbitz or something ((laugh-
38.   ing)) and I'm(ha) like I'm like <u>screaming</u> at
39.   him and he uh he says "Kaly do you want
40.   some gum?" and she says "NO" and she
41.   slaps his hand awayn' I said "Paul get out
42.   of here" so I jump off the bed like totally
43.   naked I'm like grabbing and I lift him up
44.   and I say "get out" and I throw him out the
45.   door and like slammed it shut
46. M: holy crap
47. S: and as I throw Paul out and slam the door
48.   I hear my friend Judy scream ((in a high
49.   pitched voice)) "I saw Sean's lil' penis!"
50.   hahhe an (ha)so now all my friends=
51. M: = you're like legend there now

This story oscillates between being a traditionally heroic masculine story and an anti-heroic and somewhat humiliating one. With regard to the former, Shawn is having spontaneous sex with his drunk girlfriend at a fraternity party while his buddies are in the other room getting lap dances. Yet, when one looks at how Shawn positions his own character in the telling of the story, his character appears anxious, frustrated and embarrassed. His narration involves people trying to barge in on them and how Paul's nonchalance exposes his own frustration. And finally, Judy sees his penis and yells out to everyone that it was small. There is very little that is cool or suave about the way his character is presented in this narration of sexual activity. It is only in the re-retelling, with the embedded laughter at certain points and with evaluative tags like "it was awesome" or "it was funny" that we see he has a different, more nonchalant perspective now.

Like the last story, the self-deprecating aspects of his narrated character allow for "mind" (i.e., Shawn's intentions and expectations concerning the events at the party) and "world" (i.e., the actual events at the party) to be played against one another for rhetorical purposes. In allowing his character to appear anxious and embarrassed by the fracas,

Shawn-the-narrator is doing interactive work. He is guarding against the view that he intentionally orchestrated the types of events that occur at these parties. As Coates (2003) has shown, although men enjoy telling wild stories, it is a violation of the "ordinariness" norm to appear to have a hand in making wild things happen for the purpose of having a good story (Sacks 1984). The party needs to have a life of its own. Allowing oneself to appear accidentally, or even reluctantly, embarrassed in the melee of a wild party, is part of the rhetorical project of accounting for potentially anti-normative events. While Shawn can certainly laugh at the events now, as narrator, he must present his character in the story differently. As is true for the other stories analyzed, Shawn's self-deprecation is at the service of creating a discursive identity that is marginalized and victimized by events "out there."

Conclusion

The analysis of young men's stories about romantic experiences found that, contrary to the expectation that male friends will boast about their romantic endeavors, young men are apt to display self-deprecating positions about romantic and sexual mistakes and gaffes. However, like the "lovable loser" laddishness that parades itself in the media, these forays into non-heroic masculinity are not straightforward. They are cloaked in a self-reflexivity that makes it difficult to determine whether the young men are complying with or resisting normative masculinity. The analyses lend empirically-grounded weight to discussions about the use of play and irony in masculine gender construction, discussions that, to date, have largely been confined to more macro-level cultural analyses. The micro-level analysis of young men's small stories reveal how formulations of self-deprecation occasion a victim identity that effaced the young men's agency.

If scored on a psychological inventory or scale measuring adherence to traditional masculinity, these young men's stories would not represent paradigmatic complicity; but when analyzed within the sequential arrangement of turns, where double-voicing, irony and innuendo are played up, displays of self-deprecation buy back complicity with traditional masculine norms. While the young men resist looking straightforwardly or obviously macho, they also work to safeguard the traditional masculine values of appearing confident, secure and knowing about what is at stake in displaying their views. As Wetherell and Edley (1999) argue, one of the more subtle ways for young men to reclaim the control associated with hegemonic masculinity is to appear ordinary, flouting the social expectation that their romantic and sexual agenda is simply about mastering seduction and gamesmanship.

This study found that managing ordinariness through candor meant negotiating an ideological dilemma (Billig *et al.* 1988)—the tension between acquiescing to a transparent conformity to stereotypical masculine norms, and working to avoid the perception that one's resistance somehow portrays one as romantically challenged. Displays of failure allowed these young men to deflate the bravado of heroic masculinity while not appearing to be genuine losers. In other words, they seemed discursively skilled at coming off non-seriously, not because success in romantic relationships is unimportant, but as a strategy for coping with the ambiguities of contemporary gender relations. The types of subjectivities evinced in these stories aptly reflect a crisis in masculinity that encourages men to be independent, confident and secure in their masculinity, while simultaneously not taking themselves too seriously, and also being advised to reform or abandon their oppressive habits, to be more open and tolerant, and to practice sensitivity and compassion.

While this may or may not be a tall order, the young men in this study were skilled at indirectly seizing on it in working up the sheen of victimization. While they certainly implicate themselves in the failures narrated, they also work to position women as irrational, capricious or hostile. For instance, the "crazy bitch" trope is useful for mitigating sexual exploitation. By presenting Noel as crazy, and himself as being able to take it (as well as being entertained by it), Gus works to turn the tables. He tells a humorous story that circumvents the cause of Noel's anger, namely that he used her for sex.

While he does nothing to suggest that Noel did not have the right to be angry, his narration construes her as *excessively* angry, thus mitigating his culpability. It is in this vein that I have argued that self-deprecation is often camouflage for sexism.

This has direct repercussions for research concerning the relationship between "new prejudice" and hegemonic masculinity. "New prejudice" refers to forms of prejudice that are accomplished in subtle and intricate ways—often, paradoxically, by the speaker espousing egalitarian or liberal values (see Billig *et al.* 1988, Wetherell and Potter 1992). The paradox is that as young men become more socialized to resist "old fashioned" forms of sexism, while attempting to accommodate women's increased power in heterosexual relationships, the better they may become at normalizing the new sexism found in contemporary, media-driven forms of "lad-masculinity." Strategic displays of self-deprecation are one example of a burgeoning discursive practice for trying out "new" forms of staged sexism. To date, very few discursive researchers (and even fewer psychologists) have examined how these practices are worked-up and managed, or how they become psychologically relevant in the formation of young men's masculinities.

Given the limited sample size and its demographic homogeneity—largely white, heterosexual college-age students—there are limitations regarding the generalizability of this study's findings. Messner and Montez de Oca (2005) have argued that the "lovable loser" trope popularized in the media caters almost exclusively to young *white* men, rather than men of color. Ethnic minorities may not as easily identify with the playfulness of self-deprecation or the irony of the loser-motif and, as such, may resist them. This remains an open research question, as are questions pertaining to impact of socio-economic status, sexual orientation and age. It is also important to consider whether the context of the adult-moderated group discussions pressed for self-deprecating stories about romantic mishaps. This setting may have been an optimal climate for telling embarrassing romantic stories. Since most of the stories had already been told in previous settings, the threat of teasing, ridicule or rejection is lessened. Future research will have to be more innovative in capturing a variety of conversations in a variety of settings.

To conclude, I return to an issue raised at the beginning: how are we to think about what is currently "hegemonic" about masculinity? This study has shown that for young heterosexual white males, heroic masculinity may be increasingly supplanted with an "everyman" form of masculinity that achieves hegemony through knowing self-deprecation, ordinariness and nonchalance. This supplanting is not simply a media phenomenon, but is alive in the quotidian details of men's discursive practices. Being hegemonic in a constantly changing landscape of gender relations means learning to manage a variety of social and cultural expectations within specific contexts while neither over- or under-indulging in traditional masculine norms. By examining these projects in detail, we can productively begin to identify hegemonic practices as the gradual fine-tuning of a range of discursive techniques that allow men to maintain *multiple* ideological positions within a variety of situations. To do so in ways that become routinely normalized is to effectively and unfortunately guarantee, as Connell (1995) argues, an iterative process of dominance for men. Preventing this kind of iterative recuperation of hegemony will thus require equally creative interventions that alter the discursive resources of men in ways that promote counter-sexist social practices.

References

Bamberg, M., 2004. I know it may sound mean to say this, but we couldn't really care less about her anyway. Form and functions of "slut-bashing" in male identity constructions in 15-year-olds. *Human development*, 47, 331–353.

Benwell, B., 2002. Is there anything "new" about these lads? The textual and visual construction of masculinity in men's magazines. *In*: L. Litosseliti and J. Sunderland, eds. *Gender identity and discourse analysis*. Amsterdam/Philadelphia: John Benjamins Publishing.

Billig, M., *et al.*, 1988. *Ideological dilemmas: a social psychology of everyday thinking*. London: Sage.

Brayton, S., 2007. MTV's *Jackass*: transgression, abjection, and the economy of white masculinity. *Journal of gender studies*, 16 (1), 57–72.

Brooks, G. R., 1997. The centerfold syndrome. *In*: R. F. Levant and G. R. Brooks, eds. *Men and sex. New psychological perspectives*. New York: John Wiley & Sons.

Coates, J., 2003. *Men talk: stories in the making of masculinities*. Malden, MA: Blackwell Publishers.

Connell, R. W., 1995. *Masculinities*. Berkeley, CA: University of California Press.

Edwards, D., 1995. Two to tango: script formulations, dispositions, and rhetorical symmetry in relationship troubles talk. *Research on language and social interaction*, 28 (4), 319–350.

Edwards, D., 1997. *Discourse and cognition*. London: Sage.

Edwards, D., 2005. Moaning, whining and laughing: The subjective side of complaints. *Discourse studies*, 7, 5–29.

Gilmartin, S., 2007. Crafting heterosexual masculine identities on campus. *Men and masculinities*, 9, 530–539.

Gough, B., 2001. "Biting your tongue": negotiating masculinities in contemporary Britain. *Journal of gender studies*, 10(2), 169–185.

Korobov, N., 2004. Inoculating against prejudice: a discursive approach to homophobia and sexism in adolescent male talk. *Psychology of men and masculinity*, 5, 178–189.

Korobov, N., 2005. Ironizing masculinity: how adolescent boys negotiate hetero-normative dilemmas in conversational interaction. *The journal of men's studies*, 13, 225–246.

Korobov, N., 2006. The management of "nonrelational sexuality": positioning strategies in adolescent male talk about (hetero)sexual attraction. *Men and masculinities*, 8, 493–517.

Korobov, N. and Bamberg, M., 2004. Positioning a "mature" self in interactive practices: how adolescent males negotiate "physical attraction" in group talk. *British journal of developmental psychology*, 22, 471–492.

Korobov, N. and Thorne, A., 2006. Intimacy and distancing: young men's conversations about romantic relationships. *Journal of adolescent research*, 21, 27–55.

Korobov, N. and Thome, A., 2007. How late adolescent friends share stories about relationships: the importance of mitigating the seriousness of romantic problems. *Journal of social and personal relationships*, 24 (6), 971–992.

Levant, R. F., 1997. Nonrelational sexuality in men. *In*: R. F. Levant and G. R. Brooks, eds. *Men and sex. New psychological perspectives*. New York: John Wiley & Sons.

Messner, M. and Montez de Oca, J., 2005. The male consumer as loser: beer and liquor ads in mega sports media events. *Signs: journal of women in culture and society*, 30, 1870–1909.

Ochs, E. and Capps, L., 2001. *Living narrative: creating lives in everyday storytelling*. Cambridge, MA: Harvard University Press.

Potter, J., 1996. *Representing reality: discourse, rhetoric, and social construction*. London: Sage.

Riley, S. C. E., 2003. The management of the traditional male role: a discourse analysis of the constructions and functions of provision. *Journal of gender studies*, 12 (2), 99–113.

Robinson, S., 2000. *Marked men: white masculinity in crisis*. New York: Columbia University Press.

Sacks, H., 1984. On doing "being ordinary." *In*: J. M. Atkinson and J. Heritage, eds. *Structures of social action. Studies in conversational analysis*. Cambridge: Cambridge University Press.

Savran, D., 1996. The sadomasochist in the closet: white masculinity and the culture of victimization. *Journal of feminist cultural studies*, 8, 127–152.

Wetherell, M. and Edley, N., 1999. Negotiating hegemonic masculinity: imaginary positions and pscyho-discursive practices. *Feminism and psychology*, 9 (3), 335–356.

Wetherell, M. and Potter, J., 1992. *Mapping the language of racism: discourse and the legitimation of exploitation*. Hemel Hempstead: Harvester Wheatsheaf.

Appendix 20.1

Transcription Conventions

(.)	Short pause of less than 1 second
(1.5)	Timed pause in seconds
[overlap	Overlapping speech
?	Rising intonation/question
°quieter°	Encloses talk that is quieter than the surrounding talk
LOUD	Talk that is louder than the surrounding talk
Underlined	Emphasis
>faster<	Encloses talk that is faster than the surrounding talk
<slower>	Encloses talk that is slower than the surrounding talk
((comments))	Encloses comments from the transcriber
Rea:::ly	Elongation of the prior sound
=	Immediate latching of successive talk
[…]	Where material from the tape has been omitted for reasons of brevity.

They Don't Want to Cruise Your Type
Gay Men of Color and the Racial Politics of Exclusion

CHONG-SUK HAN

Introduction

Thirty minutes after the posted starting time, men, and a handful of women, continue to wander into the second floor auditorium of a long neglected performance hall in the center of the city's gayborhood. Like many things gay, the scheduled forum on race, sponsored by one of the largest gay-identified organization in the city, begins on gay time. As the audible levels of conversations begin to wane, organizers urge the audience of some 200 men, and a handful of women, to take their seats so we can all begin. Within minutes, a representative of the host agency lays out the ground rules of discussion—most noticeably that we will not, given the limited time, try to define racism while quickly offering that, "everyone is capable of racism," a definition that many men of color in the audience would, if given the chance, vehemently dispute. Perhaps it wouldn't have been such an issue if members of the community who were invited to help plan the forum hadn't spent weeks arguing for the need to discuss racism in the gay community, rather than focus solely on race. Or perhaps it wouldn't have been such a slight if they were asked to provide an alternative definition of racism, particularly who is able, within the larger social structure, to practise it rather than being left with only one definition of it.

In fact, the title "Race Forum" was specifically chosen, against the suggestions offered by members of the community, so that the focus could be on "race" rather than the trickier topic of "racism."

"It's like they didn't hear a thing," a member of the "community" told me immediately after the announcement. "Why did we go to the meetings? It's like we weren't even there. We might as well be invisible." Though flabbergasted, he also told me that, "It's no surprise." It seems that for this member of the community, speaking up and being ignored has come to be a common occurrence. After all, being a gay man of color is to experience the unnerving feeling of being invited to a potluck while being told not to bring anything since nobody would be interested in what you bring, and then not being offered any food since you didn't bring anything anyway.

Looking around the audience, two things become immediately clear. First, the auditorium is noticeably empty given the tendency of other forums hosted by this agency to fill to capacity and then some. More importantly, the faces are overwhelmingly darker than those at other forums sponsored by this organization. One could conclude, if one were so inclined, that this forum on race was not as popular with many of the gay men who normally attend while bringing out other men who wouldn't normally attend events that would have a broader gay appeal. However, the composition of the audience reflects a larger picture of the broader gay community where issues of race and racism are often ignored.

Looking around any gayborhood, something becomes blatantly clear. Within the queer spaces that have sprung up in once neglected and forgotten neighborhoods, inside the slick new storefronts and trendy restaurants, and on magazine covers—as well as between the covers for that matter—that are no longer covered in plain brown paper and kept behind the counter, gay America has given a whole new meaning to the term "whitewash."

We, as a collective, have rehabilitated homes in neglected neighborhoods. We've planted flowers, we've painted the walls, fixed old roofs, and generally have increased the "value" of areas that were once in urban decline. Whitewash.

We've revived old storefronts, bringing a multitude of retail shops (and the accompanying tax base) to streets once reserved for activities outside the law—not that everything we do within our own houses, or behind the storefronts for that matter, are well within the comfortable boundaries of a legally sanctioned activity. Whitewash.

We've fought hard to counter the stereotypes so famous in mainstream culture of the nellie queens or the lecherous sex stalker and replace them with images that reflect the "true" gay experience. Rather than accept the images thrown upon us by the mainstream press, we've given gay American a face we can all be proud of. Whitewash.

Whiteness in the gay community is everywhere, from what we see, what we experience, and more importantly, what we desire. The power of whiteness, of course, derives from appearing to be nothing in particular (Lipsitz, 1998). That is, whiteness is powerful precisely because it is everywhere but nowhere in particular. When we see whiteness, we process it as if it doesn't exist or that its existence is simply natural. We don't see it precisely because we see it constantly. It blends into the background and then becomes erased from scrutiny. And this whiteness is imposed from both outside and inside of the gay community. According to Allan Bérubé, the gay community is overwhelmingly portrayed in the heterosexual mind as being "white and well-to-do" (2001, p. 234). Media images now popular in television and film such as *Will and Grace, My Best Friend's Wedding, In and Out, Queer as Folks, Queer Eye for the Straight Guy*, etc. promote a monolithic image of the gay community as being overwhelmingly upper-middle class—if not simply rich—and white. For example, in the movie, *Boat Trip*, about the comic misadventures of two straight men booked on a gay cruise by a gay travel agent hellbent on preserving the honor of his lover, all the gay men, with one exception, are white. The juxtaposition of Cuba Gooding Jr. as the protagonist who stumbles his way through a boat filled with hundreds of gay men, also works to mark racial boundaries. Gay men are white and the straight man is not. Clearly, in this movie, "men of color" and "gay" are mutually exclusive categories. While mass media will often use stereotypes to sell minority characters to majority audiences, the gay media are no less to blame for the promotion of the "gay equals white" misconception. Even the most perfunctory glance through gay publications exposes the paucity of non-white gay images. It's almost as if no gay men of color exist outside of fantasy cruises to Jamaica, Puerto Rico, or the "Orient." And even then, they exist only to fulfill the sexual fantasies of gay white men. "Exotic" vacations to far away places are marketed to rich white men and poor colored bodies are only another consumable product easily purchased with western dollars. As such, gay men of color, whether found within western borders or conveniently waiting for white arrival in the far off corners of the globe, are nothing more than commodities for consumption.

It's not just the media, both straight and gay, that robs gay men of color of equal representation, the gay "community" is no less to blame. Gay organizations themselves promote and reinforce the whiteness of gay life. The gay movement that once embodied the ideals of liberation, freedom, and social justice quickly turned to the causes of

promoting gay pride through visibility and lob-
bying efforts that forced established institutions—
particularly media institutions—to re-examine
mainstream heterosexist bias against gay men and
women. Doing so, however, led to the unfortunate
consequence of ignoring non-gay issues such as
"homelessness, unemployment, welfare, universal
health care, union organizing, affirmative action,
and abortion rights" (Bérubé, 2001, p. 235). Promoting gay issues meant promoting acceptance rather
than liberation. To do so, gay activists adapted various whitening practices to sell gay America to the
heartland of America by:

> *mirroring* the whiteness of men who run power-
> ful institutions as a strategy for winning credibil-
> ity, acceptance, and integration; *excluding* people
> of color from gay institutions; *selling* gay as white
> to raise money, make a profit, and gain economic
> power; and daily wearing the *pale protective color-
> ing* that camouflages the unquestioned assump-
> tions and unearned privileges of gay whiteness.
> (Bérubé, 2001, p. 246)

Unfortunately, this mirroring of the mainstream
community to promote gay causes has meant ignoring the "non-gay issues" that impact the lives
of gay men and women of color as members of
racial minority groups such as affirmative action,
unemployment, educational access, etc. It has even
ignored immigration debates, as is evident in a
recent Advocate.com editorial which suggested
that focusing on immigrant rights would take away
from gay rights. What such arguments ignore is
that many in the gay community are members of
immigrant groups. As such, to be gay in America
today is to be white. More specifically, it means
to be white and well-to-do. This is obvious in the
ways that gay organizations and businesses mark
and market themselves to the larger community, both gay and straight. Gay publications tout
the affluence of the gay community when fighting for advertising dollars. Non-profit organizations (NPO) and gay-identified businesses that
serve a multi-racial clientele are marked as being
raced and, in turn, mark themselves as such. For

example, organizations such as Brother to Brother,
Gay Asian Pacific Support Network, Hombres Latinos, etc. mark the racial borders of patronage. Gay
businesses, too, mark these borders. Bars populated
by non-white clients exist merely to support white
male fantasies about gay men of color are marked
with appropriately fetishized names such as the
Voodoo Lounge in Seattle, Papicock in New York,
and Red Dragon in Los Angeles. The Blatino Bronx
Factory not only marks the club as raced but also
quite blatantly specifies which races they are marking. Yet gay-identified organizations with mostly,
and sometimes exclusively, white clientele—both
businesses and NPOs—are never marked in this
way. In fact, they vehemently oppose such characterizations, arguing instead that they serve all gay
people. It is never the "Gay White Support/Social
Organization," but rather, "Gay Support/Social Organization." In doing so, the implication is that they
speak for all gay people, a claim they make while
ignoring certain voices. Their concerns, those of
largely gay white men, become the *de facto* concerns for gay men of color. As such, whiteness takes
center stage and it becomes synonymous with gay
where gay comes to mean white and white comes
to mean gay.

Despite all of this, it would be a mistake to
assume that whiteness is not actively maintained.
Rather, the illusion of normalcy requires active
maintenance of racial borders. "White" doesn't
become normal because it is so, it becomes normal
because we make it so. More often than not, whiteness is maintained through active exclusion of
those who are non-white. In this paper, I examine
the forms of racism that are found in gay communities and show how race is implicated in the
construction of gay identities. Particularly, I focus
on subtle forms and blatant forms of racism that
negate the existence of gay men of color and how
racism affects the way we see gay men. In this way,
I hope to add another dimension to Bérubé's theory
about how "gay" remains white. In addition, I examine the homophobia found in racial and ethnic
communities to examine the further marginalization of gay men of color.

Of course, in discussing gay men of color, it is important to point out that this group includes people with vastly different backgrounds along every imaginable social delineation. Care should be taken when referencing the experiences of this group. At the same time, this essay is not about gay men of color as it is about racism in the larger gay community, as well as homophobia found elsewhere, and how that racism and homophobia, both subtle and overt, manifests itself. I'm not so much interested here in the values, beliefs, and cultures of gay men of color as I am with the discriminatory practices of gay white men and the institutions that they control. I'm certain that the racist discourse that justifies such behavior is uniquely modified to fit different racial/ethnic groups that are targeted. My interest is to point out that despite different constructions of race and ethnicity, the end results of exclusion and objectification are similar for racialized groups. As such, this paper should not be read as an exploration into the lives of gay men of color but to the practices of gay white men that work to marginalize the previous group.

Invisible . . . You Make Me Feel Invisible: Subtle Forms of Racism

Not surprisingly, allusions to invisibility are common in the writings and media productions created by gay men of color. For example, in *Tongues untied*, black film maker Marlon Riggs had this to say about San Francisco:

> I pretended not to notice the absence of black images in this new gay life, in bookstores, poster shops, film festivals, even my own fantasies. Something in Oz was amiss, but I tried not to notice. I was intent on my search for my reflection, love, affirmation, in eyes of blue, gray, green. Searching, I discovered something I didn't expect, something decades of determined assimilation cannot blind me to. In this great, gay Mecca, I was an invisible man. I had no shadow, no substance, no place, no history, no reflection. (Riggs, 1989)

Likewise, Joseph Beam (1986) in his work, *In the Life* wrote:

> Visibility is survival . . . It is possible to read thoroughly two or three consecutive issues of the *Advocate*, the national biweekly gay news-magazine, and never encounter, in the words or images, Black gay men . . . We ain't family. Very clearly, gay male means: White, middle-class, youthful, nautilized, and probably butch, there is no room for Black gay men within the confines of this gay pentagon. (quoted in Manalansan, 1996, p. 402)

Standing at the door of various gay bars, I've been asked, on several occasions, by doormen if I was aware that it was a gay bar. In one particular instance, one doorman added after I answered in the affirmative, "You must really want a drink." In these instances, unlike other instances of blatant racism that I discuss below, it just didn't occur to the doormen that being gay *and* Asian was within the realm of the possible. Following their logic, if gay men are white, non-white men must not be gay. As such, the non-white man entering this "gay" establishment must obviously be in great need of libation rather than sexual encounter. In addition to lived experiences, this sense of invisibility is found in writings by gay Asian men as well. Song Cho writes:

> The pain of being a gay Asian, however, is not just the pain of direct discrimination but the pain of being negated again and again by a culture that doesn't acknowledge my presence . . . Not only did I have to deal with the question of sexual invisibility as a gay man, there was also the issue of racial invisibility. (Cho, 1998, p. 2)

Another writer describes his experiences at gay bathhouses in this way:

> When I go to the baths, I usually go home empty handed without even one guy having hit or making a pass at me. . . . When I first started going to the baths, I could not understand why no one was interested in me. I would hang out for hours and hours and no one would give me a second look. What was more disheartening was the fact that I saw some weird combinations at the baths.

Drop dead gorgeous white men would not even give me a second look, yet be with someone who (in my mind) was below average in the looks department... When I came out, it never occurred to me that I would become invisible and undesirable and truly worthless in the eyes of so many gay men... Gay Asians are invisible to the gay white community. (Anonymous, n.d.)

At the same time that they are invisible, gay Asian men are also seen as being exotic, submissive fantasies for white men. However, being seen as exotic and submissive is yet another form of subtle racism where gay Asian men are not seen as individuals but as a consumable product for white male fantasy (Ayres, 1999).

Gay Native American men also felt this "disconnection" from the gay community, even when they are active in gay politics. Jaline Quinto quotes one gay Native American activist as stating:

I was doing a lot of things in the community, but feeling still that disconnection from the larger mainstream gay community because I was Native... There was this ideal of what constituted beauty, part of it had to do with if you don't have blonde hair and blue eyes, you don't meet the standard. (Quinto, 2003, p. 14)

Gay Latino men don't fare much better in the larger gay community. As Munoz (1999) points out, the mainstream gay community either ignores or exoticizes Latino bodies. That is to say, Latino men, like other men of color, also fall into two categories within the gay community. Either they are invisible or exist only as props for white male consumption. Miguel Flores is quoted by Joel P. Engardio as stating:

I hate being a fetish. They don't see you as a person. Just an object, Latin meat... When I found out about this city, it seemed like a dream. But when I got here [San Francisco], I realized even in the gay capital of the U.S., I'm still Mexican... I didn't come all this way to go through the same shit. (Engardio, 1999, p. 7)

Perhaps no example of racial fetishization of gay men of color is more blatant than the use of the "Indian" character in the 1970s disco group, Village People. Singing songs embedded with gay metaphors, the Village People rose to cult status among both gay and straight listeners and were, perhaps, the most popular music group during the gay-active 1970s. A brain child of music producer, Jacques Morali, each "character" in the band represented a gay fetish. While the "Indian" was a character unto his own, representing the idea that a man of color can be a fetish just by being a man of color, the other characters were given an occupational or behavioral role often fetishized within the gay community such as cowboy, biker, construction worker, soldier, and cop. The implication, of course, is that while men of color are fetishized for what they are, white men are fetishized for what they do. Thus, white men can choose when they want to be objectified, but men are color are simply objects.

As discussed above, existing only as props for white male consumption represents another subtle form of racism. As Tony Ayres notes:

First, there is overt belligerence: the drunk queens who shout in my face, "Go back to your own country"; the tag line at the end of gay personal classifieds—"No Fats, Femmes, or Asians"; the guys who hissed at me in the back room, "I'm not into Asians." Still, these incidents are rare and easily dealt with. The second response is the exact opposite of this racist antagonism. It is an attraction to me because of my Asianness, my otherness... This has nothing to do with my individual qualities as a person. It is the fact that I conveniently fit into someone else's fantasy. They expect me to be so flattered by the attention of a white man that I will automatically bend over and grab my ankles. (1999, p. 89)

Whereas Asian men become the object of white male fantasy due to their perceived feminine qualities, Black men suffer the opposite stereotype. Rather than subservient geishas who will submissively tend to all of the white male fantasies of domination, black men are the overly sexual predators racially capable of fulfilling white male sexual lust. If Asian men are the vassals for white men's domination fantasies, black men are the tools required for white male submissive fantasies. As Frantz Fanon explains, the black "man" no longer exists in the white sexual imagination. Instead, "one is no longer aware of the negro, but only of a penis. The Negro is eclipsed. He is turned into a penis. He is a penis" (1970, p. 120). Rather than existing as individuals, black men exist as sexual tools, ready to fulfill, or violate, white male sexual fetishes. This fetishization of the black man's penis is perhaps most evident in nude photographs of black men, taken by white men, and meant for white (straight, gay, male and female) consumption. Perhaps nowhere is this more evident than in the photography of Robert Mapplethorpe, particularly the collection of photographs published in *Black Book*. As Mercer (1991) points out, images, such as those presented by Mapplethorpe, help to objectify and fetishize black men as being nothing more than giant penises. Ironically, whereas the objectification of Asian men is largely based on the desire to dominate, the objectification of black men is based on the fear of domination (Fung, 1991; Marriott, 2000).

They Don't Want to Cruise Your Type: Blatant Forms of Racism

Sometimes racism in the gay community takes on more explicit forms. Like racism everywhere, these forms tend to operate with the goal of excluding, in this case, men of color from gay institutions. Perhaps the most notorious has been the events surrounding Badlands, a popular bar in the Castro district in San Francisco. In the summer of 2004, Badlands became the site of weekly picketing after a group of racially diverse Bay Area residents filed a complaint with the San Francisco Human Rights Commission, the San Francisco Entertainment Commission, the California Department of Fair Employment and Housing, and the state Alcoholic Beverage Control Department claming racial discrimination at the bar. Among the complaints were that not only was the owner practising job discrimination at the bar but also that non-white customers were being either turned away at the door or were being expunged from the bar. According to complainants, people of color were routinely denied employment and promotional opportunities and entrance into the establishment. Most obvious incidents were the fact that black men were required to provide two forms of I.D. at the door while white men were required to only show one. Michael Kinsley, a former bouncer at the club, stated:

> One of my tasks while working at the Badlands was to stand guard and judge whether or not to allow entrance into the bar. Introductory bouncer etiquette, courtesy of Les (the owner), was a short course in discriminating between "Badlands" and "non-Badlands" customers. During this introduction there were continual references to the characteristics of the undesirable customers—if they looked like "street people" or if they were not "dressed" like "Badlands customers." As a new initiate into the field of adult door monitor there were, in the first few weeks, instances where Les would politely walk a person to the door and escort them from the premises. These instances were all accompanied by an admonishing, "This person was not a Badlands customer," or "He had a backpack. We don't let in people with backpacks. They are often street people or have no money." All of these individuals had one common feature and it was painfully obvious to me—everyone escorted out was black. (And Castro for All, 2004)

Max Killen, another former Badlands doorman, was also quoted as stating:

> He (Les Natali, the owner) sat me down and he told me, "There are certain types of people that we don't want in here. And those people can go across the street." He didn't say the Pendulum (another Castro street bar with a large black clientele), but . . . it was really obvious that he was talking about the bar. He wasn't talking about hanging out in the parking lot or at the other places there. It was the Pendulum. (And Castro for All, 2004)

It is interesting to note that the racist policies are cloaked in discourses of class. By doing so, it allows gay businesses to escape the stigma of racism while ultimately maintaining racial borders. Ironically, the mirroring of the gay community with the white mainstream, as discussed earlier, contributes to such actions. Such mirroring actions allow gay business owners to mask issues of race and class under the justification of running a "successful" business.

An isolated incident might have been easily forgotten, but the events at Badlands struck a cord with the city's non-white gay and lesbian residents. For them, it was just another incident in a long history of racial discrimination in the city's gayborhood. As Don Romesburg (2004) notes,

> The most recent troubles surrounding the Badlands [were] just the latest incarnation of a longstanding struggle in the Castro's LGBT community regarding racial discrimination and exclusion.

In fact, the policy of requiring multiple forms of I.D. from non-white patrons had a long history in the Castro, starting with the Mine Shaft, a Castro bar that required three forms of I.D. for men of color during the mid-1970s. Rodrigo Reyes, in an interview with Richard Marquez in 1991, recalls this about the early 1980s:

> There were also some racist discriminatory practices on the part of the bars in that sometimes they would ask for an inordinate amount of IDs from people of color ... They would ask for two, three picture IDs. So it wasn't a very happy time for Latino gays ... We were still a marginal group. The dominant group was still white gay men. (quoted in Ramirez, 2003, p. 232)

Also during the early 1980s, an informal study conducted by the Association of Lesbian and Gay Asians (ALGA) found that multiple carding was a fairly widespread practice among gay bars throughout San Francisco, not just in the Castro district. Recalling the ensuing boycott following the release of the study, Dinoa Duazo notes:

> The most insidious aspect of the whole situation was how proprietors felt completely justified to practice such casual discrimination. Unfortunately, just because a community has faced oppression, there's no guarantee that its members won't practice it themselves. (1999, p. 5)

In fact, during an on-air debate on KPFA, a local radio station, one bar owner told Randy Kikukawa, one of the organizers of the boycott, that "Your people don't drink. We have to make money," and "It's a cruise bar, we would lose money because they don't want to cruise your type" (Duazo, 1999, p. 5). Also, the practice of multiple carding was not unique to San Francisco. In Washington, DC, two bars, Lost & Found and Grand Central, were targeted by community activists for blatantly requiring two forms of I.D. from non-white patrons while allowing white patrons easy access. In 1984, the "Boston Bar Study" conducted by Men of All Colors Together Boston (MACTB) cited numerous examples of widespread discrimination at gay bars in Boston against black men. Similar types of discrimination have also been cited in Los Angeles and New York (Wat, 2002). Even more troubling is that this type of behavior seems to be international as well—anywhere that gay white men come into contact with gay men of color (Ridge, Hee & Minichiello, 1999). One can only imagine how many others never make it into the new stories. Rather than isolated events attributable to racist owners of single bars, the attempt to patrol the borders of whiteness in gay-owned business establishments seems to be a systematic practice to ensure only certain types of people are allowed into "gay" bars.

I Just Want an "All American" Boy

The primacy of white images in the gay community often leads to detrimental results for gay men of color, particularly manifested as internalized racism. In "No blacks allowed," Keith Boykin argues that "in a culture that devalues black males and elevates white males," black men deal with issues of self-hatred that white men do not. "After all," he notes, "white men have no reason to hate themselves in a society that reinforces their privilege." Boykin argues that this racial self-hatred makes gay black men see other gay black men as unsuitable sexual partners. Obviously, such racial self-hatred rarely manifests itself as such. Instead, gay black men who don't want to date other black men simply rely on stereotypes to justify their behavior rather than confront their own self-hatred. For example, Boykin notes that most of these men justify excluding other black men as potential partners by relying on old stereotypes of the uneducated, less intelligent black male. Ironically, the same black men who rely on these stereotypes to exclude members of their own race rarely enforce them on gay white men, as evidenced by Boykin's example of the gay black man who has no problem with dating blue-collar white men but excludes black men on the assumption that they are, "uneducated and less successful than he is." What's worse is that not only do gay black men fail to see each other as sexual partners, white men also ignore them. In such an environment, black men compete with each other for the allusive white male partner (Boykin, 2002, p. 1).

This desire for white male companionship is not limited just to black men, and neither is racial self-hatred. Rather, it seems to be pandemic among many gay men of color. For example, Tony Ayres explains that:

> The sexually marginalized Asian man who has grown up in the West or is western in his thinking is often invisible in his own fantasies. [Their] sexual daydreams are populated by handsome Caucasian men with lean, hard Caucasian bodies. (1999, p. 91)

Likewise, Kent Chuang writes about how he tried desperately to avoid anything related to his Chinese heritage and his attempts to transform his "shamefully slim Oriental frame . . . into a more desirable western body" (1999, p. 33). Asian men, too, rely on stereotypes to justify their exclusive attraction to white men. For example, a gay Asian man is cited as stating:

> For me, I prefer dating white men because I want something different from myself. I think that dating another Asian would be like dating my sister. I mean, we would have so much in common, what would there be for us to learn about? Where would the excitement come from? (Han, 2005)

Here, gay Asian men rely on the old stereotype of an "Asian mass" to justify their own prejudices towards other Asian men. All Asians are presented as homogenous masses with each person being interchangeable with another. Ironically, white men who exclusively date white men rarely rely on such tactics. There is no need to argue, from a white male position, that dating other white men would be like "dating their brothers." Also, the man's characterization of other Asian men as "sister" also points to the stereotypical ways that Asian men are seen in the larger gay community. Stereotyped as overly feminine, gay Asian men become unappealing to gay men who desire men who are masculine or "straight acting."

Partner preference among Latino men also seems to follow the hierarchy of the "white is best" mentality. Ramirez notes that the competition for a white "trophy" boyfriend among gay Latino men has often hindered community formation. Rather than seeing each other as allies, gay Latino men may see each other as competitors for the attention of the few white men who prefer Latino men to other white men. For example, one Latino man was quoted as saying:

> One of the things that I saw that really bothered me and I told them, I said, "What the problem here is everybody is after the white trophy. That's the problem here. And unless two people are comadres [godmothers], you don't want to have nothing to do with each other. But that's the problem. After the white trophy, nobody has time. And it's like, you tear each other down . . . viciousness, because you're after the white trophy. And to have a white lover is ooohhh! Don't you see?" (Ramirez, 2003, p. 229)

After complaining to other Latino men about the pedestalization of white men among gay Latino men, this particular gay Latino man was labeled a "radical lesbian." The implication here is that any Latino man who chooses to be with another Latino man, rather than a white man that has come to dominate gay male sexual fantasies, must be a "lesbian," a woman who prefers other women. The limited definition of desirable masculinity within the gay community leads to white males as being "men" while men of color are placed lower on the hierarchy much in the same way that the mainstream creates a hierarchy of men and women. As such, men of color are seen lower on the gendered hierarchy within the gay community where white masculinity is valued over all other forms of masculinity. Should they prefer other men of color, they are easily conflated with "lesbians," two people lower on the gender hierarchy who prefer the sexual companionship of each other over that of the gender dominant group.

While information about racial preference for Native American men is scarce, Brown (1997) reported that only one of their five gay Native American male informants reported ever having a sexual relationship with another Native American male.

Rather than less, race seems to matter more to gay men than to straight men when it comes to mate selection. Examining personal ads, Phua and Kaufman (2003) found that gay men were significantly more likely to prefer one race and suggest that they may be more likely to exclude certain races as well. According to their data, gay men of color were much more likely to explicitly exclude members of their own race and much more likely to request another race (overwhelmingly white) than even gay white men.

There's No Name for This

It would be too easy to throw racism at the doorstep of gay white men and blame them for all of the problems encountered by gay men of color. But racial and ethnic communities must also take some of the blame for whatever psychological assaults gay men of color have endured. If we are invisible in the dominant gay community, perhaps we are doubly so in our racial/ethnic communities.

In the film, *There is no name for this*, produced by Ming-Yuen S. Ma and Cianna Pamintuan Stewart, Chwee Lye Chng, a gay Asian man explains:

There are words in Malay, in Chinese, or what have you that describes, you know, that is used in the culture. But it's more akin to the word, a transvestite. We just don't know, there is no vocabulary for that and I think that's why it was so difficult

to, to perhaps, come out because if I thought I'm gay, I almost have to accept the very distorted definition in the culture of, I'm going to be a cross dresser, I'm going to stand in the street corner and service me. (Ma & Stewart, 1997)

As can be noted from the above quote, the prominence of negative gay stereotypes in Asian cultures makes it difficult for them to discuss their sexual orientation with their families. In addition, the absence of vocabulary also makes it difficult to discuss sexual matters. Anna Jiang in describing the difficulty of discussing her sister's sexuality with her parents stated:

I have some relatives who only speak Chinese. When I tried to explain Cecilia's character to them, I don't know how to do it. I don't know how to explain the term "gay" and "lesbian" to them. (Ma & Stewart, 1997)

Likewise, Doug Au explained:

It's not just coming out, it's not just saying that I'm queer or that I'm gay but really being able to sit down with someone and explain to them in a way they could understand. (Ma & Stewart, 1997)

Gay and lesbian Asians are not alone in feeling invisible within their ethnic communities. One gay Latino man was quoted by Edgar Colon as stating:

My family acts as if my sexual orientation does not exist. Moreover, I have no ongoing contact with my family. In this way, we can make sure that I remain invisible. (2001, p. 86)

In Latino cultures, much as in some Asian cultures, "there is no positive or self-validating word for one who identifies himself as homosexual" (Manalansan, 1996, p. 399). Rather, to self-identify as "gay" means taking on the maligned and feminine label of *maricon*, implying that one takes the passive role in sexual intercourse. Embedded within the *machisimo* framework of Latin male sexuality, the passive partner during gay intercourse is doubly stigmatized as not only being one who engages in sexual acts with other men but also as taking the feminine, passive role during execution.

Likewise, many Native American gay men have also been forced to leave reservations and families after disclosing that they are gay. As Karina Walters notes:

> In some cases, [first nations gay, lesbian, bisexual, transgendered, two-spirits] leave reservations at very young ages and with little education, eventually trading sex to survive in cities. Prejudice in [first nations] communities manifests itself in the denial of the existence of [first nations gay, lesbian, bisexual, transgendered, two-spirits], avoidance in discussing the subject, and cultural beliefs that nonhetero-sexual behavior is sinful, immoral, and against traditions. (Walters *et al.*, 2002, p. 317)

In black communities, much has been debated recently regarding the "down low" phenomenon when men, who may be either bisexual or closeted homosexuals, have openly heterosexual lives but engage in covert sexual acts with other men (King, 2004). While it should be noted that black men are not the only men to engage in homosexual activity while leading heterosexual lives, the common belief is that they are more likely than white men to engage in such behavior. True, there are ample examples of homophobia in the black community. At the same time, there is evidence to indicate that it is a mistake to attribute homophobia as simply a black phenomenon, or a phenomenon specific to any racial/ethnic community. Rather, as Manalansan (1996) explains, homophobia in the black community may have much to do with class, self-identification of gay men and women, and other situational factors associated with being a minority group in a racialized society than with blacks being inherently more homophobic than whites.

Borrow the Words but Ignore the Meaning

The irony, of course, is that even as the "gay" community uses the language of the civil rights movement to further the cause of equality for gays and lesbians, many within the community continue to ignore the lessons that should be apparent within the language that they have adopted. For example,

the National Gay and Lesbian Task Force describes itself in this way:

> Founded in 1973, the National Gay and Lesbian Task Force Foundation (the Task Force) was the first national lesbian, gay, bisexual and transgender (LGBT) civil rights and advocacy organization and remains the movement's leading voice for freedom, justice and equality. We work to build the grassroots political strength of our community by training state and local activists and leaders, working to strengthen the infrastructure of state and local allies, and organizing broad-based campaigns to build public support for complete equality for LGBT people.

The use of the terms civil rights, movement, justice, equality, grassroots, activist, etc., clearly harkens back to the language of the civil rights movement. The language of the civil rights movement has resonated with numerous "gay" organizations and as such, they have presented the movement as being one of equality and justice rather than sexual preference. While the Task Force has done an admirable job in promoting issues of race within the gay community, and several men and women of color hold leadership positions on their board of directors, the majority of other gay organizations have not followed suit, particularly at the local level.

Predictably, the use of civil rights language has been met with contesting viewpoints about its validity when applied to gay rights. On the one hand, it has been met positively with Julian Bond, board chairman of the NAACP stating:

> Are gay rights civil rights? Of course they are. "Civil rights" are positive legal prerogatives—the right to equal treatment before the law. These are rights shared by all—there is no one in the United States who does not—or should not—share in these rights . . . We ought to be flattered that our movement has provided so much inspiration for others, that it has been so widely imitated, and that our tactics, methods, heroines and heroes, even our songs, have been appropriated by or served as models for others . . . Many gays and lesbians worked side by side with me in the '60s Civil Rights

Movement. Am I to tell them "thanks" for risking life and limb helping me win my rights—but they are excluded because of a condition of their birth? They cannot share now in the victories they helped to win? (Bond, 2004, p. 142)

Others have been less generous with their support, such as the Reverend Fred L. Shuttlesworth, the interim president of the Southern Christian Leadership Conference:

I was among the original five who started the Southern Christian Leadership Conference (SCLC), and our primary focus back then was to put an end to racial segregation under the Jim Crow system. As SCLC's first secretary, I never took down anything in our minutes that addressed the issue of gay rights. The issue of gay rights was not our focus, and should not be confused with the Civil Rights Movement. (Shuttlesworth, 2004, p. 142)

The problem here is that whether one supports the analogy with the civil rights movement or not, both perspectives seem to negate the possibility that people can be both gay and a racial minority, a point made clear by Mary F. Morten, the former liaison to the gay community under Chicago mayor Richard Daley, when she states:

A major problem is that gay and lesbian life is associated with privilege because it is depicted far too often from a white perspective. We have few positive images of African American gays and lesbians, and we rarely see African American gays and lesbians on TV. So for many people being gay is associated with being white ... We have always had visibly gay and lesbian folks in our community, whether we talked about it or not ... We need to be much more open about the reality that you live next door to some gays and lesbians, that we're in your family, that we're literally everywhere in our community. (Morten, 2004, p. 144)

Clearly, for Morten, acknowledging that racial communities include gay members and, by extension, acknowledging that gay communities include members of racial minority groups, is a top priority.

Discussion

Given the prevalence of negative racial attitudes in the larger gay community and the homophobia in racial communities, gay men of color have had to build identities along the margins of both race and sexuality. More often than not, this has been a difficult road. Looking for a space to call his own, Eric Reyes asks, while referring to Michiyo Cornell's early writing that America is a "great lie":

I ask which America should I call a lie. Is it the Eurocentric and heterosexual male-dominated America, the white gay male-centered Queer America, the marginalized People of Color (POC) America, or our often-romanticized Asian America? As a Queer API, I ask where is this truth situated that betrays our belief that we have a space here in this place called America? Locating this space from which we draw our strength and our meaning is the part of coming out that never ends. (Reyes, 1996, p. 85)

The difficulty for gay men of color in coming out as gay has to do with both the homophobia found in racial communities and the racism found in gay communities. True, men of color are dependent on ethnic communities. Michiyo Cornell explains, "because of Asian American dependence on our families and Asian American communities for support, it is very difficult for us to be out of the closet" (1996, p. 83). At the same time, this "dependence" may have more to do with lacking alternatives rather than self-inflicted internal homophobia. As Richard Fung points out:

As is the case for many other people of color and especially immigrants, our families and our ethnic communities are a rare source of affirmation in a racist society. In coming out, we risk (or feel that we risk) losing this support. (Fung, 1991, p. 149)

Other gay men of color have also pointed out the need to maintain ties to their racial and ethnic communities in order to maintain a sense of self-esteem. In fact, the two-spirit movement among gay Native Americans has played a powerful part in bolstering self-esteem among gay Native

American men and women. Rather than attempting to "fit" into white definitions of "gay" or "lesbians," Native Americans have reclaimed a long cultural practice of valuing a third gender that is not rigidly linked to the European definitions of "man" and "woman" (Brown, 1997; Quinto, 2003; Walters, 1999). In fact, Walters demonstrates that enculturation into Native communities is critical for mental health among gay Native Americans (Walters, 1999).

In this paper, I examined both the racism found in the gay community and the homophobia found in racial and ethnic communities and argue that both racism and homophobia affect men of color negatively in ways that may be multiplicative rather than additive. That is, gay men of color don't simply experience racism because they are racial minorities and homophobia because they are sexual minorities. Instead, they experience a unique type of racism and homophobia because they are gay and of color. Certainly, gay Asian men experience these forces differently from gay black men. In addition, the mirroring of the mainstream by the gay community can also be seen to occur in communities of color, where they favor heterosexuality above homosexuality in an attempt to mirror the dominant society. Within this framework, gay men and women of color are relegated to the bottom of the hierarchy in both communities. While I have limited my discussion to gay men, it is likely that examining the lives of bisexual men of color, bisexual women of color, and lesbian women of color, would lead to a fuller understanding of multiple sites of oppression. Future research and theoretical work will need to tease out the specific experiences of multiply marginalized groups in order to truly understand how race, sexuality, class, etc. may be intersected in the lives of subaltern groups rather than focus on single categories of oppression and expect these to be additive rather than multiplicative. Only then can we truly understand the methods of domination and oppression that mark groups and the implications that such categorization may have.

References

And Castro for All. (2004). Is badlands bad? Retrieved 10 August 2005 from www.isbadlandsbad.com

Anonymous. (n.d.). *Racism or preference (at the baths?).* Retrieved 10 February 2005 from *Bathhouse Diaries*, www.bathhouseblues.com/racism.html

Ayres, T. (1999). China doll: The experience of being a gay Chinese Australian. In P. A. Jackson & G. Sullivan (Eds.), *Multicultural queer: Australian narratives.* New York: The Haworth Press.

Beam, J. (1986). Introduction. In J. Beam (Ed.), *In the life: A Black gay anthology.* Boston: Alyson.

Bérubé, A. (2001). How gay stays white and what kind of white it stays. In B. Brander Rasmussen, E. Klinenberg, I. J. Nexica & M. Wray (Eds.), *The making and unmaking of whiteness.* Durham, NC: Duke University Press.

Bond, J. (2004). Is gay rights a civil rights issue? Yes. *Ebony, 59*(9), 142–46.

Boykin, K. (2002). No blacks allowed. Retrieved 25 September 2005 from *Temenos*, www.temenos.net/articles/12-23-04.shtml

Brown, L. (1997). Women and men, not-men and not-women, lesbians and gays: American Indian gender style alternatives. *Journal of Gay and Lesbian Social Services, 6*(2), 5–20.

Cho, S. (1998). *Rice: Explorations into gay Asian culture and politics.* Toronto: Queer Press.

Chuang, K. (1999). Using chopsticks to eat steak. *Journal of Homosexuality, 36*(3/4), 29–41.

Colon, E. (2001). An ethnographic study of six Latino gay and bisexual men. *Journal of Gay and Lesbian Social Services, 12*(3/4), 77–92.

Cornell, M. (1996). Living in Asian America: An Asian American lesbian's address before the Washington Monument (1979). In R. Leong (Ed.), *Asian American sexualities: Dimensions of the gay and lesbian experience.* New York: Routledge.

Duazo, D. (1999). Looking back in homage. *Lavender Godzilla*, April, 1–5.

Engardio, J. P. (1999). You can't be gay, you're Latino: A gay Latino identity struggles to emerge, somewhere between the macho Mission and Caucasian Castro. *SF Weekly*, 7.

Fanon, F. (1970). *Black skin, white masks.* London: Paladin.

Fung, R. (1991). Looking for my penis: The eroticized Asian in gay video porn. In Bad Object-Choice (Ed.),

How do I look: Queer film and video. Seattle: Bay Books.

Han, C.-S. (2005). Gay Asian men and negotiating race and sexual behavior. Unpublished manuscript.

King, J. L. (2004). *On the down low: A journey into the lives of "straight" black men who sleep with men.* New York: Broadway Books.

Lipsitz, G. (1998). *Possessive investment in whiteness.* Philadelphia: Temple University Press.

Ma, M.-Y. S., & Stewart, C. P. (1997). *There is no name for this.* API Wellness Center.

Manalansan, M. R. (1996). Double minorities: Latino, black and Asian men who have sex with men. In R. Savin Williams & K. Cohen (Eds.), *The lives of lesbians, gays, and bisexuals: Developmental, clinical and cultural issues.* Fort Worth, TX: Harcourt, Brace and Co.

Marriott, D. (2000). *On black men.* New York: Columbia University Press.

Mercer, K. (1991). Skinhead sex thing: Racial difference and the homoerotic imaginary. In Bad Object-Choice (Ed.), *How do I look: Queer film and video.* Seattle: Bay Books.

Morten, M. (2004). Is gay rights a civil rights issue? Maybe. *Ebony, 59*(9), 142–46.

Munoz, J. E. (1999). *Disidentifications: Queers of color and the performance of politics.* Minneapolis: University of Minnesota Press.

National Gay and Lesbian Task Force Foundation. (1973). Retrieved from www.thetaskforce.org/aboutus/whatwedo.cfm

Phua, V., & Kaufman, G. (2003). The crossroads of race and sexuality: Date selection among men in internet "personal" ads. *Journal of Family Issues, 24*(8), 981–94.

Quinto, J. (2003). Northwest two-spirit society. *Colors Northwest, 3*(3), 12–15.

Ramirez, H. N. R. (2003). "That's my place!": Negotiating racial, sexual, and gender politics in San Francisco's Gay Latino Alliance, 1975–1983. *Journal of the History of Sexuality, 12*(2), 224–58.

Reyes, E. (1996). Strategies for queer Asian and Pacific Islander spaces. In R Leong (Ed.), *Asian American sexualities: Dimensions of the gay and lesbian experience.* New York: Routledge.

Ridge, D., Hee, A., & Minichiello, V. (1999). "Asian" men on the scene: Challenges to "gay communities." *Journal of Homosexuality, 36*(3/4), 43–68.

Riggs, M. (1989). *Tongues untied.* MTR Production.

Romesburg, D. (2004). Racism and reaction in the Castro: A brief, incomplete history. Retrieved 20 October 2005 from www.isbadlandsbad.com/archives/000039.html

Shuttlesworth, F. (2004). Is gay rights a civil rights issue? No. *Ebony, 59*(9), 142–46.

Walters, K. (1999). Negotiating conflicts in allegiances among lesbians and gays of color: Reconciling divided selves and communities. In G. P. Mallon (Ed.), *Foundations of social work practice.* New York: Harrington Park Press.

Walters, K., Longress, J., Han, C.-S., & Icard, L. (2002). Cultural competence with gay and lesbian persons of color. In D. Lum (Ed.), *Culturally competent practice: A framework for understanding diverse groups and justice issues.* Pacific Grove, CA: Thomson Brooks/Cole.

Wat, E. C. (2002). *The making of a gay Asian community: An oral history of pre-AIDS Los Angeles.* Lanham, MD: Rowman & Littlefield.

The Bromance

Undergraduate Male Friendships and the Expansion of Contemporary Homosocial Boundaries

STEFAN ROBINSON, ERIC ANDERSON, AND ADAM WHITE

Whereas most of the twentieth century investigations of male friendship explicitly focused on missing emotional and physical intimacy, compared to what exists in women's friendships (Lewis 1978), the concept of the bromance has been recently used to describe a new form of friendship between men: one based in intimacy. The term has been used, variably, by scholars (DeAngelis 2014; Thompson 2015), normally as a cultural discourse on friendship. DeAngelis (2014, p. 1) describes a *bromance* as "a term denoting an emotionally intense bond between straight men," and Davies (2014) goes as far to say that a bromance often surpasses the romantic closeness that men share with their wives and girlfriends.

Although recent research has discussed the emergence of bromances and how they connect to homosociality (Anderson 2014; Chen 2011; Hammarén and Johansson 2014), there are no known systematic examinations of its conceptualization, behavioral requisites, or limitations. . . .

. . . In order to address: (a) the lack of definitional literature on bromances and (b) the implications of having such relationships, we carried out in-depth interviews with 30 male university students in the United Kingdom who identified as heterosexual or mostly heterosexual.

Male Friendship: Non-Intimate Connections

The level of physical and emotional intimacy expressed between men in a given context is highly contingent on their awareness and inclusion or rejection of homosexuality. When examining heterosexual men's preference for same-sex socializing and friendship—known as *homosociality*—in the past 50 years, significant regulation of masculinity related to men's socially perceived sexuality is evident (Lipman-Blumen 1976; Sedgwick 1985). This is despite men's same-sex friendships being described as highly intimate (Deitcher 2001), even romantic (Rotundo 1989), before the modern era. . . .

At the turn of the twentieth century, the western population's awareness of homosexuality grew (Miller 1995). At the same time, Sigmund Freud published three influential essays on the *Theory of Sexuality* (1905). His works proposed that young men were being converted to homosexuality as a consequence of a feminine upbringing and socialization process. He further suggested that absent fathers, as well as a lack of male role models, contributed to the homosexualization of children. Cancian (1986) explains that these concerns were propagated by certain social, economic, and

Stefan Robinson, Eric Anderson, and Adam White, "The Bromance: Undergraduate Male Friendships and the Expansion of Contemporary Homosocial Boundaries," *Sex Roles,* January 1975, Springer Science and Business Media, reprinted by permission of the publisher.

geographic shifts that occurred during the second industrial revolution. The mass migration of workers from the agrarian to industrial lifestyle destined men to work extended shifts away from home, contributing to the demise of rural and family life.

At this time, the general public broadly believed that sexuality was socially constructed as part of a child's upbringing and was widely understood to be a permanent, "other" sexuality (Foucault 1984). Simply, Anglo-American societies believed that the embodiment of femininity caused homosexuality (Weeks et al. 2003). Although not intending to stigmatize homosexuality, Freud inadvertently promoted the structure of the nuclear family, something for which homosexuality was a direct threat (Anderson 2009).

Consequently, the late Victorian era is described as a homophobic one (Kimmel 1994). The same-sex intimacy that Tripp (2005) describes began to be socially policed as awareness of homosexuality grew in the twentieth century. By the 1980s, the romantic friendships that Rotundo (1989) highlighted became entirely limited to gay men and lesbians (Diamond et al. 1999). In other words, straight men feared being socially perceived as gay for displaying physical or emotional intimacy with other men. This constriction had significant implications for the development of close friendships between men (Morin and Garfinkle 1978; Komarovsky 1974). . . .

Anderson's (2009) concept of homohysteria explains the shift in the physical and emotional dispositions of men before the first half of the twentieth century and the decades of the latter half. McCormack and Anderson (2014) define *homohysteria* as the fear of being socially perceived as gay— something made possible because heterosexuality cannot be definitively proven among straight men in a culture that is both aware and fearful of homosexuality. Subsequently, men were culturally compelled both to perform certain overtly heterosexual behaviors and to avoid engaging in those that would feminize them.

It is important to understand that this cultural landscape has left a generation of heterosexual men with a life of non-intimate connections, as well as with friendships that may never achieve the level of intimacy to which they should have been entitled (Collins and Sroufe 1999; Connolly et al. 2000). We cannot say for certain that men are inherently predisposed to be less emotive and expressive than women, but scholars would argue that twentieth century culture has certainly predisposed men's emotional boundaries to be more rigid and distant (Anderson 2014; Connell 1995; Hruschka 2010; McCormack 2012). As Fehr (1996) explains, men have traditionally chosen to align with orthodox masculine archetypes, even when they may internally desire open, emotional, and tactile contact with other men. Importantly for our study, cultural restrictions on male emotionality have drastically affected men's ability to emote and confide (Bowman 2008), significantly reducing their coping strategies to deal with internal conflicts such as depression, anxiety, and suicidal thoughts (Cleary 2012; Scourfield 2005). . . .

Inclusive Masculinity Theory

In recent years, scholars have noted a rapid decline in the prevalence of cultural homophobia (Anderson 2014; McCormack 2012; Savin-Williams 2005) and a consequent expansion of social landscapes for not only gay men, but also young men altogether, esteeming more inclusive and emotive masculine identities than previously observed (Anderson 2005; McCormack 2012; Murray and White 2015; Murray et al. 2016; Weeks 2007; White and Hobson 2015; White and Robinson 2016). . . .

Inclusive masculinity is based on the social inclusion of those traditionally marginalized by hegemonic masculinity. Inclusive masculinity can now be observed with prominence in major social institutions including education (McCormack 2011), sport (Adams 2011; Magrath et al. 2015) and social media (Morris and Anderson 2015). Young men in these forums have progressively aligned themselves away from orthodox tropes of masculinity and are less concerned about whether others perceive them to be gay or straight, masculine or feminine (Anderson 2014; Savin-Williams 2005). Because of the campaigning of oppressed gay men and lesbians, among others, a dramatic shift in attitudes was stimulated in the late twentieth century and early twenty-first century that recognized and accepted homosexuality as a legitimate orientation. Anderson (2009) argues that this has permitted young men to embrace feminine, inclusive, and intimate behaviors because they have far less fear of being labelled as gay. . . .

. . . The decline of cultural homophobia has relinquished men's burden to police their gendered behaviors. Like men of the 1980s, they still make friends through sports, drinking, and exercising, but they can now also bond over shopping or dining together. Unlike men of the 1980s, they form deep emotional relationships, based on emotional disclosure with one another. Thus, whereas Bank and Hansford (2000) previously found that male friendships struggle due to emotional restraint, masculine hierarchies and homophobia, many scholars now suggest that the millennial generation espouses a culture that is much more inclusive and cohesive (Adams 2011; McCormack 2012; Thurnell-Read 2012). With the present research, we build on this body of evidence and explore homosociality in the form of a bromance. We seek to know how men conceptualize a bromance, how a bromance differs from a friendship, and the roles that physical and emotional intimacy play in these classifications.

Method

Participants

Over a 3-month period, between August 2014 and November 2014, we conducted semi-structured interviews into the friendship experiences of 30 undergraduate men who identified as heterosexual or mostly heterosexual and who were enrolled in one of four undergraduate sport-degree programs at one university in the United Kingdom. . . . The sample comprised men aged 18–22 years (18 years, $n = 1$; 19 years, $n = 15$; 20 years, $n = 9$; 21 years, $n = 4$; 22 years, $n = 1$), and although not selected for race, the near-exclusively White student body of this British university limited our analysis to that of

only White men. Our sample was also populated by participants from self-identified, middle-class backgrounds. Thus our findings are limited to a somewhat homogeneous sample of young, largely White, heterosexual men. . . .

Procedures

We used a guided interview that aimed to determine the characteristics of this sample's bromance relationships. The interviewer was selected because he already had a good rapport with the collective student body surveyed on homophobia 18 months earlier. This is evidenced by outstanding, anonymous, teacher evaluations performed on this 46-year-old White, gay man at the end of the class he taught in the first semester (which all student were compelled to take). The benefit of this method was that students had already developed a level of rapport with the interviewer, allowing sensitive topics to be more easily discussed (Hutchinson et al. 2002).

The one-on-one interviews began by verbally briefing participants about the nature of the study and then furnishing them with a participant information sheet and copy of ethics approval. Participants were then required to sign a consent form, and simultaneously verbally reminded of their rights to withdraw from the study, to refuse to answer questions, and to review transcripts from the interview. All ethical procedures of the British Sociological Association have been followed. Participants were provided with an information sheet with the investigators' contact information, aims of the study, consent forms, and indication that there was no penalty for not participating.

Through a variety of questions (available as an on-line supplement), participants were then asked to discuss their understandings and experiences of bromances and the homosocial aspects of their same-sex friendships. For the purposes of our research, questions concerned real experiences and not hypothetical situations. The line of questioning broadly intended to tease out what the men understood bromances to be, whether they existed in their lives, and how they were enacted. . . .

Analytic Methods

Given that our aim was to understand the operational definition of what a bromance is, and how they are embodied within the participants' lives, we used an inductive approach concerned with extracting thematic categories based on consistent, repetitive, and recurring experiences of related data (Braun and Clarke 2006). We intended to draw out the key patterns in data that express a level of consensus and unanimity in the views expressed (Joffe 2012). This approach was also valued for its theoretical flexibility and roundedness in data (Braun and Clarke 2006).

After transcribing the digitally recorded interviews, data analysis occurred in a three-step processes. First, participants' narratives were coded by the first and third authors for themes relating to their views about bromances and same-sex friendships, as well as their perception of the boundaries of such friendships. This step utilized broad codes of "emotional disclosure," "body comfort," and "similarities." The second round of coding added more detail, producing more complex codes, including: "Expressions of Physical Tactility," "Love," and "Emotional Vulnerability." At this point, the codes identified were collated in order to develop the themes that emerge in the data presented here: (a) bromantic intimacy as unique compared to friendships and romances, (b) the embodiment of a bromance (coded into three sections on kissing, cuddling, and nudity), and (c) the bromance as being inclusive of poly-amorous (albeit nonsexual) affection. An external academic was independently consulted because of his expertise in the area. Codes were discussed between these two authors until interpretations were agreed (Goetz and LeCompte 1984). For that reason, the process permitted a level of mutual consistency, principally generating more valid data (Denscombe 2002).

As is consistent with the intentional design of our study, we prompted for and selected accounts of the personal over the general. In cases where participants provided both an example of how others do, view, or enact a bromance, as well as how they themselves do, view and enact a bromance, we always took the personal account (Kerrick and Henry 2017). We should acknowledged that participants deployed the bromance term in a grammatically unconventional way. Participants variably used the word "bromance(s)" as both a way of identifying their close friend(s) and their relationship with that person, invoking the word awkwardly at times as a pronoun. The authors have left these inconsistencies as stated by the participants so as not to skew the accuracy of the data. For clarity, the authors invoke the term "bromance" to describe a relationship type and "bromantic friend" to describe the people in those relationships.

Results

During interviews, it was revealed that each of the 30 men had at least one bromantic friend, either in the past or at the present time. This was true regardless of whether one defined as exclusively or mostly heterosexual (see Table 22.1 for information about individual men, listed by assigned pseudonym, who are quoted here). There was [a] high level of consistency and confirmation between the men on what bromances were and how they impacted on their lives. The principal characteristics of a bromance concerned having shared interests as well as maintaining emotional and physical intimacy.

Defining the Bromance

Before trying to unpack the bromance for its detailed constituent parts and characteristics, and with respect to the fluid and holistic nature of relationships, it is worthwhile briefly setting out the overarching insights that the men had in defining the bromance. In presenting his definition of a bromance, Patrick, for example, said:

> A bromances is someone who is literally there for you all the time. Someone you can relate to on an emotional level. Someone you can share secrets and pain with, and love, but there is no sort of sexual attraction. It can be intimate though. (Patrick)

Similarly, Mark said:

> I've got really good friends that are guys and we call it a bromance. You can fully discuss your fears and

Table 22.1 Participants' Characteristics

Pseudonym	Age	Sexual Orientation	Ethnicity
Aaron	19	Heterosexual	White
Alan	21	Mostly heterosexual	White
Beck	20	Heterosexual	White
Ben	20	Heterosexual	White
Bruce	20	Heterosexual	White
Chris	19	Heterosexual	White
Dan	21	Mostly heterosexual	White
Derek	19	Heterosexual	White
Gavin	19	Mostly heterosexual	White
George	19	Heterosexual	White
Hamish	19	Mostly heterosexual	White
Harvey	20	Heterosexual	White
Henry	19	Heterosexual	White
Ivan	20	Heterosexual	Eastern European
Jay	22	Heterosexual	White
Jack	19	Mostly heterosexual	White
Jason	20	Mostly heterosexual	White
Jim	19	Heterosexual	White
Liam	20	Heterosexual	White
Luke	19	Mostly heterosexual	White
Mark	21	Heterosexual	White
Martin	19	Heterosexual	White
Max	19	Mostly heterosexual	White
Patrick	19	Heterosexual	White
Reese	21	Heterosexual	White
Regi	19	Mostly heterosexual	White
Robbie	20	Heterosexual	White
Samuel	20	Mostly heterosexual	White
Theo	18	Heterosexual	White
Tony	19	Heterosexual	White

problems with them, all of that. We are completely comfortable with each other and kiss and hug every now and then. You know they will always be there to back you up if you need it. (Mark)

And Henry said:

I have one [bromance] with my best friend. Like, he will do something for me and I'll feel really sentimental, like you really shouldn't have done that, but you did. He does more for me than a normal friend would. It creates a love feeling for me, not sexual though. (Henry)

These extracts provide rich examples of how our participants experience and define their bromances. When asked about the difference between a friendship and a bromance, participants were clear to differentiate between the two, arguing that bromances were more important. Luke said: "You have people that you are really close to, and get on with really well, but a bromance is closer." He added: "With a bromance you can talk about anything, with friends you can't." Aaron said: "They are a lot more than just a mate." Bruce compared his experience of a bromance to a romance: "We are basically like a couple . . . we get called like husband and wife all the time." Martin agreed: "It's like having a girlfriend, but then not a girlfriend."

Just as a bromance was compared by some to having a romantic relationship with a girlfriend, many said it was like having a brother. Mark said: "You always hear guys say they are brothers-from-another-mother. It shows that they are close, like family." Many of the other participants were familiar with this term. Chris added: "You look out for each other, like brothers." This comparison to family members and romances conveys the profound connection that is definitional to bromances. Illustrating this connectedness, Robbie said: "We pretty much know each other's minds inside-out." Jason added: "With the guy it's like you can relate straight to each other, and know what each other is thinking. You are always on the same wavelength." Thus, we highlight that the participants situate bromances somewhere within the dimensions of romance, friendship, and family relationships.

Unlike a heterosexual romance, a bromance need not be predicated in monogamy. Participants unanimously suggested that men are permitted to have more than one bromance. Some of our participants have several. Ivan said: "It's so easy to have bromances." Dan said: "I'm in probably seven or eight bromances which I will cuddle with."

George said: "I have about four," and Chris said: "I've got lots." These men show us not only that they are permitted to have multiple bromantic friendships, but that there is acceptance among peers for whom having another bromance is not a betrayal to other bromantic relationships.

Characteristics of a Bromance

Shared Interests

All participants believed that having shared interests is a necessary requisite for having a bromance. Sharing the same context of being students involved in sport was not itself enough to develop a bromance. Regi explained: "A bromance works best when those involved share similar interests and personalities." Samuel agreed: "For me, you have to have extremely similar interest and it has to build from that." Harvey said a bromance is formed "when two boys meet and they get on well and have similar interests. They bounce off one another . . . they will be similar in personality." Hamish said: "We share interests and like the same things."

Team sports served as one space where males could meet to develop emotional bonds (Anderson et al. 2012a; Baker and Hotek 2011). Martin, for example, was a member of the university rugby team, and he suggested that most of his relationships with teammates are also bromances: "I have lots of bromances . . . I've never seen more penises and bollocks in one space, it's very much more open." Gavin also thought rugby was a catalyst for bonding: "I went from a school where touching guys was stigmatized, to men's rugby where they are all in the showers intentionally dropping soap. I think the stigma is changing with youth." Jay agreed: "I think the fact that I play rugby encourages it . . . they [bromances] are a lot more common among rugby players." Jack has a bromance with his housemates who all share an interest in rugby:

> Sometimes, like three of us will have a lecture that finishes at 6 pm on a Monday, and the fourth lad will have dinner ready for us: it's cute, it's thoughtful . . . when I finish [lectures] before them, and we go clubbing, I have pizzas ready for them. It benefits all of us. (Jack)

Although there is a clear recognition that sport provides men with a social space for accelerated social bonding, as well as homosocial and bromantic development (see also Adams 2011; Anderson and McCormack 2015), it is having shared interests that normally leads to the friendship creation (Parks and Floyd 1996; Seiden and Bart 1975) that then advances into a bromance. This was an absolute requisite for the development of a bromance. Samuel said: "Quite honestly, it can only work with someone who shares the exact same interests on the exact same level: whether you're into sport, films, studying the same stuff, or whatever." This emphasis on interests and shared experiences was articulated by participants as being pivotal to the start of a bromance and, as Ben said, "Before you know it, you are doing everything together." Through sharing interests and social spaces, these men were able to cultivate close and intimate friendships with their analogous peers.

Emotional Intimacy

All participants suggested that bromances differ from friendships through the level of emotional disclosure that is permissible to one another. This included sharing secrets and confiding exclusively with their bromantic friend(s). They were clear that a bromance offers a deep sense of unburdened disclosure and emotionality based on trust and love. Hence, these undergraduate men inform us that they desire to develop relationships with other men premised on companionship and intimacy where complete emotional disclosure is possible.

The vulnerability and connection expressed by these men toward their bromantic friends was so profound that many spoke of their love for one another in endearing terms. Jack said: "I love him to bits, he's my man crush," and Theo said: "I can happily say, 'oh I love him.'" This declaration of love contravenes the heterosexual vocabulary of previous decades when men even avoided using the word "like" because it was perceived as being too affectionate (Lewis 1978). Conversely, men in our sample expressed a much more affectionate sentiment. Max, for example, said: "I feel free to tell him I love him, because I do. There is no attraction, but also no embarrassment."

Although he does not use the word homosocial, Jason made clear that there is a difference between homosocial attraction and homosexual desire. He argued that "There is no sort of sexual attraction in this love." This is the feeling expressed by all the men we interviewed, whereby they separate emotional desire from physical desire. The absence of sexual attraction distinguishes these men as heterosexual to both themselves and others. More importantly, these men share a progressive understanding that love can exist between two people without the need or requirement for sex with each other. Harvey said: "The only difference [between a romance and bromance] is the sexual desire." Sam said: "Everything is close in a bromance, just not the sexual stuff." Aaron said: "When you have a bromance with a friend, it's motivated by your interest in that person, love and friendship, and not because you want sex [unlike with a woman]."

It is not just the ability to express love in a bromance that is valued, but also the reaction that one is likely to receive from that disclosure. . . . "You can say stuff to him without offending him," Harvey said, ". . . and it feels like there are no boundaries between us and what we can say." Jay said: "I trust him with a lot more than I trust a normal friend. We tell each other everything." Joe had the same experience, saying ". . . you just click. You tell them stuff you don't tell other people. Everything is generally closer." George explained: "It's that guy or two that you need, who is always there for you. You can talk to him about anything. It doesn't matter what you tell him, he is always there to listen." . . . George even gave an example where he spoke of his desire for his girlfriend to finger him—an increasingly common phenomenon among this cohort of men (Branfman et al. 2017). However, knowing his girlfriend had hinted at being opposed to this activity, he had only told his bromantic friend and not his girlfriend about his sexual desires. Gavin similarly

reserved the disclosure of certain intimacies to his bromantic friend, modifying the number of sexual conquests he had depending on the person to whom he was speaking. "My bro is the only person that knows the exact amount," Gavin said.

Many others identified sexual desires and health issues as subjects that could only be fully discussed with their bromantic friends. When asked how one defines the difference between a friend and a bromantic friend, Regi summarized: "It's in the ability to completely confide." Beck believed that this heightened capacity for disclosure was because "A bromance will never judge you . . . you're just so relaxed around each other." Jay felt more free to act, suggesting that he does not need to "keep up a figure of masculinity; a bromance isn't going to care." Dan said: "I hold nothing back in my bromance." Finally, speaking about emotionality and what emotions were not permissible to share, Regi said: "In my bromance nothing is off limits."

The emotional intimacy expressed by these young men represents a core foundation of what it means to have a bromance. When these men feel so relaxed with each other and free to divulge all, they are invoking a profound trust and dependence in their bromantic relationships. Whereas this openness emanated as the primary underpinning characteristic of a bromance, there were other, more physical behaviors that were typical too.

Physical Intimacy

While being emotionally intimate, these men also valued physical intimacy as an integral benefit of having a bromance. Although this was viewed as nonessential to the creation or maintenance of a bromance, physical intimacy was routine and enjoyed by these men. They spoke about their desire to cuddle and hug with their bromantic friends. Some agreed that this was the case when asked, whereas others offered it unsolicited as part of their definition of a bromance. For example, Robbie said: "You can lie in bed with your bromance, have a cuddle and just talk." Patrick said: "Part of my understanding of it [a bromance] is having a cuddle buddy." Martin also thought physical embracement was a core part of a bromantic friendship. "It's cuddling, hugging, sex jokes . . . you have the emotions, feelings and the hugging [again]." This research, therefore, confirms Anderson and McCormack's (2015) earlier findings of men (at a different British university) where they found 37 of 40 undergraduate heterosexual male sportsmen had cuddled in bed with their male friends. In the present research, cuddling occurred with 29 of the 30 men. For Lee, who had not cuddled with his bromantic friend, he said: "It's not that I wouldn't; I just don't feel the need to."

Also consistent with other research on British undergraduate men at other universities, where 89% of 145 undergraduate heterosexual men had kissed on the lips (Anderson et al. 2012), men in our study readily talked about kissing their bromantic friends. Tony said: "I kiss him all the time." Derek said: "You see guys kissing and cuddling loads. It's never an issue to anyone." Beck agreed: "Guys nowadays, in my generation, there is so much kissing between guys because it's showing affection." Max said that with his bromantic friend, "I hug him and kiss him and tell him I love him."

Participants also discussed being comfortable when they are physically naked around their bromantic friends. They indicated that it is not common to appear nude in front of other men, that they do not regularly shower in the presence of other men, and that nudity is generally considered a private issue. However, men in bromances appear naked more easily around one another. Jack said:

> I live in a house with three other guys, and there are massive bromances going on between us. We walk around naked. I got no problems standing naked in a room with my housemates. We feel comfortable being naked around each other. (Jack)

Liam, who has bromantic friendships with several of his housemates, said: "I can come out of the shower naked and nobody bats an eyelash." These men did not describe casual nudity among peers as a finite requirement for having a successful bromance, but they did identify it as a useful bonding mechanism. However, there did seem to be an implication that nudity around each other was a step, and perhaps served as a form of symbolic proof, of heterosexuality, social comfort, and bromantic interest.

Explicating this finding, George suggested that casual nudity in bromantic friendships also ". . . frees up the opportunity for shared sexual experiences." When talking about his experience of a male–male–female threesome, he said: "We're best mates, so we've seen each other naked before, so that wasn't much of a bother. You're both not shy about it at all, and it's a good way to bond with him in that sort of way." For Jack, this occurred in reverse; he had a foursome with another male and two women (Scoats et al. 2017). "We weren't good friends, but now [after the foursome], we are good friends and play for the same football team. I guess he is a bromance to me." This is again resonant of the requisite for shared interests and experiences in a bromance—whether it is liking the same football team or sharing sexual partners. This is consistent with research on male–male–female sexual threesomes which finds that heterosexual men are more likely to engage in such with a bromantic friend (Scoats et al. 2017). Like others who had a threesome with their bromantic friend, or say that if the opportunity arose they would, Jim explained how it can occur without it homosexualizing its participants:

> A bro is someone that you genuinely don't have any boundaries with. So when you are having a threesome with your bro and a girl, it's something that you high five each other about, and not something that you'd feel awkward about, even if one of you did come out as gay, it's no different. (Jim)

The participants made clear that the affection they feel for one another was not restricted to the private realm. When discussing whether a bromance is something that is broadcast to others, all participants agreed that a bromance did not need to be silenced. On the contrary, the men we interviewed suggested that there is *no* desire to shield their bromantic love or how they feel for each other. The physically intimate activities in which they engage were socially permissible in the public realm. Evidencing this, Alan said: "There's a great photo of me and [bro] on Facebook cuddling," and Reese said: "We hug when we meet, and we sleep in the same bed when we have sleepovers. Everyone knows it, and nobody is bothered by it because they do it as well."

Gavin spoke about public displays of affection between bromantic friends as a source of publicly declaring one's homosociality: "If you need a hug he will be there for you. It doesn't matter if it's in public 'cause no one will judge, it just shows you care." Chris, like many heterosexual men in other studies (Anderson 2014; Morris and Anderson 2015), also expressed his love for his bromantic friend through multiple modalities, including Facebook and other forms of social media. Ben spoke about when he goes clubbing with his friends, he, even if inadvertently, makes his bromance publicly visible: "We will drink quite a bit and sometimes kiss when we're out; no one thinks much of it." Like Ben, many of the men in our study engaged in public kissing behaviors and were unmindful of what others thought, largely because they say others do not judge it. In other research, Peterson and Anderson (2012) highlight that the university dancefloor has become a popular space for homosocial touch and kissing, and Scoats (2015) shows that pictures of such intimate acts are generously available on students' Facebook accounts, without shame or regulation.

Discussion

With the present research, we addressed the lack of definitional literature on bromances and the implications of having such relationships. There is little research that explores the bromance's conceptual underpinnings and its position is a legitimate relationship within the literature (Thompson 2015). Our results show that bromances have achieved a deep resonance in UK university culture and that men interpret these relationships as real and important, and not as a fantasy or as comedic like depicted in popular television programs and films (Boyle and Berridge 2012). We found no variance in

how they defined or experienced a bromance based upon their self-definition as either exclusively heterosexual or mostly heterosexual.

The most salient feature these 30 men described about a bromance—even if overly idealized—was that they were free of judgment, which permits them to push the cultural margins of traditional masculinity toward more intimate and expressive behaviors than previously occurred between male friends (Lewis 1978; Williams 1985). In fact, it was the degree of emotional disclosure that differentiates a friendship from a bromance. Emotional intimacy was articulated to be of great importance in bromances, and the unburdened disclosure possible in these relationships enabled men to profess love for one another.

This intimacy was not limited to the emotional realm, however. The use of cuddling was recognized by many to be a benefit of having a bromance, and it was a physically demonstrative way of showing affection for each other. This was supplemented by other experiences of kissing, casual nudity, and shared sexual encounters, such as threesomes, which have been suggested elsewhere to improve bonding in male–male friendships (Flood 2008; Scoats et al. 2017). Same-sex sexuality outside the presence of women, however, does not seem to be a normal component of the bromance. These men have thus enjoyed homosocial physical affection, disassociating the intimacies of same-sex touch from homosexuality. We found that this distinction had freed up the opportunity for both emotional and physical intimacies to be shown in public spaces between bromantic friends, and this freedom highlights the significant value that these relationships hold in their social world.

The lack of physical and emotional boundaries in these friendships represents a significant sequential shift in permissible masculine identity. Ward (2015) draws upon Anderson's body of research (cf. Anderson 2014) to suggest that straight, White men are even able to have sex with one another without jeopardising their heterosexual identity. This is not to say that men no longer police their gendered behaviors, but rather that they are permitted more flexibility to socialize and relate in a way that would have been formerly branded as feminine, and as gay, in the late twentieth century.

Limitations

As part of the coding process, it became clear that the participants in our study were not asked to what degree their bromantic relationships were formally constituted or simply assumed. When we consider the way in which romantic relationships are constituted, there is usually an explicit commitment and labelling of being in a formal relationship. We recognize that our presentation structure lends itself to suggest that the bromance is a developmental process, but in this instance, more qualitative work would be welcomed around the establishment of bromances, in terms of their official or assumed constitution.

Our conclusions concerning the definition and significance of the bromance are limited to our sample; we do not claim that our results are generalizable to those who are not of our participants' age, race, and social class. However, the dialogue and narrative of the young men's accounts of same-sex relations are broadly consistent with other research on heterosexual, university-aged British men (aged 18–22 years-old).

We consider the breadth and depth of bromances to be just as complex and vast as romantic relationships. To this end, we were compelled to be very selective and discerning in the themes that are featured in the present paper. Indeed, although there was a wealth of data brought forward here, we felt it necessary to unpack the foundational elements of the relationship rather than complicate and confuse the research with multiple avenues of sub-interests. Accordingly, we consider our study to be a high-level investigation into these young men's definitions and experiences of the bromance, not a systematic account of all elements of the relationship.

Future Research Directions

Many of our participants had multiple bromances, bringing with it questions around the number of bromances one is permitted to have and expected to be able to maintain. Indeed, research in this area would benefit from considering the poly-amorous nature of bromances, their alignment and cohesion with romances, and issues of jealousy and emotional monogamy. Although these bromances permit more inclusive, liberal, and tactile behaviors between men, as well as represent improved liberality in contemporary masculinity, they may not altogether benefit cross-sex relations.

Also, throughout our results, there was no indication that these men's increased appreciation for femininity and expressiveness strengthened their relationships with women. On the contrary, the ability to emote, confide and cuddle with male friends may in fact reduce men's appetite for interaction with women and intensify the exclusivity of male friendships. More research into how bromances affect heterosexual men's understandings of and views of women, as well as their romantic relationships, is needed. Although the men in our study made some interesting suggestions about how bromance and romances conflict, reflect, and impact one another, this area was not fully addressed in our paper. For example, given that the young men in our study can have heterosexual sex and emotional support without romantic commitment (Anderson 2014; Bogle 2008), further research is required to assess whether this has reduced their desire to find early romantic attachment.

This point raises further implications around the potential for men to privilege their same-sex friendships over their cross-sex friendships and romances. Mehta and Strough (2009) suggest that the reinforcement and strengthening of homosocial bonds may contribute to the devaluing and discouraging of cross-sex socialization, although, this is not necessarily a problem given the importance of same-sex friendships for socio-emotional development. However, because data increasingly show a delayed onset into family life for Anglo-American men (Arnett 2004), it is worthwhile considering that bromantic co-habitations may already be happening in larger numbers than expected, although more research is needed.

Practice Implications

The overarching implication of our research, beyond defining and situating the bromance in the context of contemporary masculinity, hinges on the impact that these bromances may be having on men's emotional well-being. We are encouraged to see that these men are engaging on a deep emotional level with their bromances to better theirs, and their significant others', emotional well-being. We recognize that sharing emotional and physical closeness with others serves an important purpose in maintaining one's mental well-being (Hruschka 2010; Scourfield 2005). Mental health practitioners should recognize bromances as legitimate influential relationships in the everyday lives of young men. For instance, these men often suggested that they could only fully discuss concerns over their health and sexual lives with their bromances, not with their families or romantic partners. Practitioners should recognize the implicit benefit of these relationships, having almost unbound limits in what can be disclosed. For those who are dealing with depressive symptoms or social anxieties, bromances may offer a way forward and a coping strategy.

Cultural Implications

The present research shows that these heterosexual undergraduate men, enrolled in one of four undergraduate sport-degree programs at one university in the United Kingdom, developed attachment bonds premised on self-disclosure and intimacy with other men. This likely occurs for two reasons. First, intimate bonding helps men achieve independence from their parents because they may receive advice and companionship elsewhere (Collins and Repinski 1994; Collins and Sroufe 1999). Second, adolescent masculinity has undergone substantial change in relation to multiple social structures (Kozloski 2010; Luttrell 2012; McCormack 2012) as the decline of homohysteria has eroded some traditional conceptions of orthodox masculinity. This shift has created a space in which young men have re-evaluated and reinvented masculinity and friendships to be more emotionally and physically

intimate. Zorn and Gregory (2005, p. 211) conclude that men now swiftly develop close friendships at university, offering them "valuable, tangible and socioemotional support." . . .

We argue that the decrease in cultural homohysteria recently documented in studies of males aged 16–24 years-old (Channon and Matthews 2015; McCormack 2012) has enabled our participants to both emotionally disclose their fears and anxieties, as well as be physically intimate with other men. Moreover, they do so without fear of social judgment or peer-ridicule. The bromance has been deeply situated within homosociality with an emphasis on trust, longevity and mutual love. They are not one-off temporal experiences; rather, they are relationships that are dependent on both men being entirely open and supportive of one another. These relationships embody the kind of emotional support and intimacy that young men need as part of healthy development (Courtenay 2000; Floyd et al. 2005; Way 2011, 2013).

Given the socio-economic differences between the present generation and the last, particularly concerning significantly delayed entry into professional occupations, higher education, fatherhood, and marriage (Arnett 2004; Dermott 2008; Hagestad and Call 2007; Office for National Statistics 2012), the idea that these college men might maintain their bromantic relationships in their current manner well beyond their university years is tenable. However, as a *New York Times* article which recently featured American men doing (Howard 2012), our participants might carry on privileging bromances long into their adult lives.

This could be possible for several reasons. Young men in the United Kingdom today are not afforded the same economic solidarity that their fathers were granted. For example, they are experiencing a housing affordability crisis, whereby the equity of co-habitation with friends has become more appealing (Hilber and Vermeulen 2016). Indeed, the recent passing of same-sex marriage legislation in the United Kingdom would suggest that improved social attitudes exist toward same-sex co-habitation, making the reality of living with friends altogether more normative. Moreover, because young men in the twenty-first century, unlike in previous generations, can have unsanctioned heterosexual sex without romantic commitment (Bogle 2008), as well as emotional disclosure with male friends (McCormack 2012), they are less pressed to find early attachment with romantic partners. Certainly, because data consistently show a delayed onset into family life for Anglo-American men (Arnett 2004), it is worthwhile considering that these bromantic co-habitations may already be happening in larger numbers than expected, although more research is needed.

Conclusion

Our study set out to respond to a deficit in the research literature around the prospect of Hollywood-depicted bromances occurring in everyday life (Thompson 2015). . . . In exploring how these relationships are constituted, we found that bromances were likely to develop in an environment where interests could be shared, where emotional intimacy flourished, and physical intimacy could be enjoyed. The men we interviewed show consistency in attitudes with other research on young men in esteeming more emotionally charged and physically tactile same-sex friendships compared to recent decades (Magrath et al. 2015; McCormack 2012). Crucially, we recognize a great willingness among these heterosexual-identified men to disassociate with previous modes of masculinity that would have sanctioned such interactions.

The social freedoms the bromance permits are undoubtedly productive towards fostering a more emotive and expressive masculine culture that is more in line with women's modes of interaction. Results support the view that declining homophobia and its internalization has had significant positive implications for men's expressiveness and intimacy. . . . In our study, . . . men were emoting widely and with great trust in their bromances. Therefore, we conclude firstly that the bromance term has been widely invoked within the university community to characterize the new deeply intimate, emotive, and trusting nature of close male

friendships in the twenty-first century. Secondly, we find that bromances are offering a legitimate and important space for college men to broaden their emotional coping strategies and manage their personal lives.

Compliance with Ethical Standards

Conflicts of Interest

There are no conflicts of interest to report.

Research Involving Human Subjects

This research included qualitative interviews with human subjects. As highlighted in the article, "The ethical procedures of the British Sociological Association have been followed. This includes participants' right to view transcripts, the right to withdraw from the study, making anonymous the participants' names and the name of their university. Participants were provided with an information sheet with the investigators' contact information, aims of the study, consent forms and indication that there was no penalty for not participating."

Ethical Approval

Ethical approval was obtained from the University of Winchester, Research Ethics Committee.

References

Adams, A. (2011). Josh wears pink cleats: Inclusive masculinity on the soccer field. *Journal of Homosexuality, 58*(5), 579–596. doi:10.1080/00918369.2011.563654.

Anderson, E. (2005). *In the game: Gay athletes and the cult of masculinity*. New York: University of New York Press.

Anderson, E. (2009). *Inclusive masculinity: The changing nature of masculinities*. New York: Routledge.

Anderson, E. (2014). *21st century jocks: Sporting men and contemporary heterosexuality*. New York: Macmillan.

Anderson, E., Adams, A., & Rivers, I. (2012). I kiss them because I love them: The emergence of heterosexual men kissing in British institutes of education. *Archives of Sexual Behaviour, 41*(2), 421–430. doi:10.1007/s10508-010-9678-0.

Anderson, E., & McCormack, M. (2015). Cuddling and spooning heteromasculinity and homosocial tactility among student-athletes. *Men and Masculinities, 18*(2), 214–230. doi:10.1177/1097184X14523433.

Arnett, J. (2004). *A longer road to adulthood.* New York: Oxford University Press.

Baker, P., & Hotek, D. (2011). Grappling with gender: Exploring masculinity and gender in the bodies, performances, and emotions of scholastic wrestlers. *Journal of Feminist Scholarship, 1*, 1–15. Retrieved from http://www.jfsonline.org/issue1/pdfs/jfs_issueFINAL.pdf#page=53.

Bank, B, & Hansford, S. (2000). Gender and friendship: Why are men's best same-sex friendships less intimate and supportive? *Personal Relationships, 7*(1), 63–78. doi:10.1111/j.1475-6811.2000.tb00004.x.

Bogle, K. (2008). *Hooking up: Sex, dating, and relationships on campus.* New York: New York University Press.

Bowman, J. (2008). Gender role orientation and relational closeness: Self-disclosive behavior in same-sex male friendships. *The Journal of Men's Studies, 16*, 316–330. doi:10.3149/jms.1603.316.

Boyle, K., & Berridge, S. (2012). I love you, man: Gendered narratives of friendship in contemporary Hollywood comedies. *Feminist Media Studies, 14*(3), 353–368. doi:10.1080/14680777.2012.740494.

Branfman, J., Stiritz, S., and Anderson, E. (2017). Relaxing the straight-male anus: Decreasing homohysteria around anal eroticism. *Sexualities.* Advance online publication. doi:10.1177/1363460716678560.

Braun, V., & Clarke, V. (2006). Using thematic analysis in psychology. *Qualitative Research in Psychology, 3*(2), 77–101. doi:10.1191/1478088706qp063oa.

Cancian, F. (1986). The feminization of love. *Signs, 11*(4), 692–709. doi:10.1086/494272.

Channon, A., & Matthews, C. (2015). It is what it is: Masculinity, homosexuality, and inclusive discourse in mixed martial arts. *Journal of Homosexuality, 62*(7), 936–956. doi:10.1080/00918369.2015.1008280.

Chen, E. J. (2011). Caught in a bad bromance. *Texas Journal of Women and Law, 21*(2), 241–267. Retrieved from http://heinonline.org/HOL/Page?handle=hein.journals/tjw121anddiv=12andg_sent=1and collection=journals.

Cleary, A. (2012). Suicidal action, emotional expression, and the performance of masculinities. *Social Science and Medicine, 74*(4), 498–505. doi:10.1016/j.socscimed.2011.08.002.

Collins, W., & Repinski, D. (1994). Relationships during adolescence: Continuity and change in interpersonal perspective. In R. Montemayor, G. Adams, & T. Gullotta (Eds.), *Personal relationships during adolescence* (pp. 7–36). Thousand Oaks: Sage.

Collins, W., & Sroufe, L. (1999). Capacity for intimate relationships. In W. Furman, B. Brown, & C. Feiring (Eds.), *The development of romantic relationships in adolescence* (pp. 125–147). Cambridge: Cambridge University Press.

Connell, R. (1995). *Masculinities.* Berkeley: University of California Press.

Courtenay, W. H. (2000). Constructions of masculinity and their influence on men's well-being: A theory of gender and health. *Social Science and Medicine, 50*(10), 1385–1401. doi:10.1016/S02779536(99)00390-1.

Davies, N. (2014). I love you hombre. In M. DeAngelis (Ed.), *Reading the bromance: Homosocial relationships in film and television* (pp. 109–138). Detroit: Wayne State University Press.

DeAngelis, M. (2014). *Reading the bromance: Homosocial relationships in film and television.* Detroit: Wayne State University Press.

Deitcher, D. (2001). *Dear friends: American photographs of men together, 1840–1918.* New York: Harry N. Abrams Inc..

Denscombe, M. (2002). *Ground rules for good research.* Leicester: Open University Press.

Dermott, E. (2008). *Intimate fatherhood: A sociological analysis.* New York: Routledge.

Diamond, L., Savin-Williams, R., & Dube, E. (1999). Intimate peer relations among lesbian, gay and bisexual adolescence. In W. Furman, B. Brown, & C. Feiring (Eds.), *The development of romantic relationships in adolescence* (pp. 175–210). Cambridge: Cambridge University Press.

Fehr, B. (1996). *Friendship processes.* Thousand Oaks: Sage.

Flood, M. (2008). Men, sex, and homosociality: How bonds between men shape their sexual relations with women. *Men and Masculinities, 10*(3), 339–359. doi:10.1177/1097184X06287761.

Floyd, K., Hess, J. A., Miczo, L. A., Halone, K. K., Mikkelson, A. C., & Tusing, K. J. (2005). Human affection exchange: VIII. Further evidence of the benefits of expressed affection. *Communication Quarterly, 53*(3), 285–303. doi:10.1080/01463370500101071.

Foucault, M. (1984). *The Foucault reader*. New York: Pantheon Books.

Freud, S. (1905). *Three essays on the theory of sexuality*. London: Hogarth Press.

Goetz, J., & LeCompte, M. (1984). *Ethnography and qualitative design in educational research*. Orlando: Academic Press.

Hagestad, G., & Call, V. (2007). Pathways to childlessness a life course perspective. *Journal of Family Issues, 28*(10), 1338–1361. doi:10.1177/0192513X07303836.

Hammarén, N., & Johansson, T. (2014). Homosociality in between power and intimacy. *SAGE Open, 4*(1), 1–11. doi:10.1177/2158244013518057.

Hilber, C., & Vermeulen, W. (2016). The impact of supply constraints on house prices in England. *The Economic Journal, 126*(591), 358–405. doi:10.1111/ecoj.12213.

Howard, H. (2012). A confederacy of bachelors. *New York Times*. Retrieved from https://mobile.nytimes.com/2012/08/05/nyregion/four-men-sharing-rent-and-friendship-for-18-years.html.

Hruschka, D. (2010). *Friendship: Development, ecology, and evolution of a relationship* (Vol. 5). Berkeley: University of California Press.

Hutchinson, S., Marsiglio, W., & Cohan, M. (2002). Interviewing young men about sex and procreation: Methodological issues. *Qualitative Health Research, 12*, 42–60. doi:10.1177/1049732302012001004.

Joffe, H. (2012). Thematic analysis. In D. Harper & A. Thompson (Eds.), *Qualitative research methods in mental health and psychotherapy: An introduction for students and practitioners* (pp. 209–224). Chichester: Wiley.

Kerrick, M. R., & Henry, R. L. (2017). "Totally in love": Evidence of a master narrative for how new mothers should feel about their babies. *Sex Roles, 76*(1–2), 1–16. doi:10.1007/s11199-016-0666-2.

Kimmel, M. (1994). *Manhood in America*. New York: Free Press.

Komarovsky, M. (1974). Patterns of self-disclosure of male undergraduates. *Journal of Marriage and the Family, 36*(4), 677–686. doi:10.2307/350349.

Kozloski, M. (2010). Homosexual moral acceptance and social tolerance: Are the effects of education changing? *Journal of Homosexuality, 57*(10), 1370–1383. doi:10.1080/00918369.2010.517083.

Lewis, R. (1978). Emotional intimacy among men. *Journal of Social Research, 34*(1), 108–121. doi:10.1111/j.1540-4560.1978.tb02543.x.

Lipman-Blumen, J. (1976). Toward a homosocial theory of sex roles: An explanation of the sex segregation of social institutions. *Signs, 1*(3), 15–31.

Luttrell, W. (2012). Making boys' careworlds visible. *Thymos: Journal of Boyhood Studies, 6*(2), 186–202. doi:10.3149/thy.0601.186.

Magrath, R., Anderson, E., & Roberts, S. (2015). On the door-step of equality: Attitudes toward gay athletes among academy-level footballers. *International Review for the Sociology of Sport, 50*(7), 804–821. doi:10.1177/1012690213495747.

McCormack, M. (2011). Hierarchy without hegemony: Locating boys in an inclusive school setting. *Sociological Perspectives, 54*(1), 83–101. doi:10.1525/sop.2011.54.1.83.

McCormack, M. (2012). *The declining significance of homophobia: How teenage boys are redefining masculinity and heterosexuality*. New York: Oxford University Press.

McCormack, M., & Anderson, E. (2014). The influence of declining homophobia on men's gender in the United States: An argument for the study of homohysteria. *Sex Roles, 71*(3–4), 109–120. doi:10.1007/s11199-014-0358-8.

Mehta, C., & Strough, J. (2009). Sex segregation in friendships and normative contexts across the life span. *Developmental Review, 29*(3), 201–220. doi:10.1016/j.dr.2009.06.001.

Miller, N. (1995). *Out of the past: Gay and lesbian history from 1869 to the present*. London: Vintage.

Morin, S., & Garfinkle, E. (1978). Male homophobia. *Journal of Social Issues, 34*(1), 29–47. doi:10.1111/j.1540-4560.1978.tb02539.x.

Morman, M. T., & Floyd, K. (2006). Good fathering: Father and son perceptions of what it means to be a good father. *Fathering, 4*(2), 113–136.

Morris, M., & Anderson, E. (2015). Charlie is so cool like: Authenticity, popularity and inclusive masculinity on YouTube. *Sociology, 49*(6), 1200–1217. doi:10.1177/0038038514562852.

Murray, A., & White, A. (2015). Twelve not so angry men: Inclusive masculinities in Australian contact sports. *International Review for the Sociology of Sport*. Advance online publication. doi:10.1177/1012690215609786.

Murray, A., White, A., Scoats, R., & Anderson, E. (2016). Constructing masculinities in the National Rugby League's footy show. *Sociological Research Online, 21*(3), 11. doi:10.5153/sro.4044.

Office for National Statistics. (2012). *Marriages in England and Wales, provisional 2012*. Retrieved from http://www.ons.gov.uk/ons/dcp171778_366530.pdf.

Parks, M., & Floyd, K. (1996). Meanings for closeness and intimacy in friendship. *Journal of Social and Personal Relationships, 13*(1), 85–107. doi:10.1177/0265407596131005.

Peterson, G., & Anderson, E. (2012). The performance of softer masculinities on the university dance floor. *The Journal of Men's Studies, 20*(1), 3–15. doi:10.3149/jms.2001.3.

Rotundo, A. (1989). Romantic friendship: Male intimacy and middle-class youth in the northern United States, 1800–1900. *Journal of Social History, 23*(1), 1–25.

Savin-Williams, R. (2005). *The new gay teenager*. Cambridge: Harvard University Press.

Scoats, R. (2015). Inclusive masculinity and Facebook photographs among early emerging adults at a British university. *Journal of Adolescent Research*, 1–23. doi:10.1177/0743558415607059.

Scoats, R., Joseph, L., & Anderson, E. (2017). "I don't mind watching him cum": Heterosexual men, male–male–female threesomes, and the erosion of the one-time rule of homosexuality. *Sexualities. Advance online publication*. doi:10.1177/1363460716678562.

Scourfield, J. (2005). Suicidal masculinities. *Sociological Research Online, 10*(2). Retrieved from http://www.socresonline.org.uk/10/2/scourfield.html.

Sedgwick, E. K. (1985). *Between men: English literature and male homosocial desire*. New York: Columbia University Press.

Seiden, A., & Bart, P. (1975). Woman to woman: Is sisterhood powerful? In N. Glazer-Malbin (Ed.), *Old family/new family* (pp. 189–228). New York: Van Nostrand.

Thompson, L. (2015). Reading the bromance: Homosocial relationships in film and television. *Journal of Gender Studies, 24*(3), 368–370. doi:10.1080/09589236.2015.1005976.

Thurnell-Read, T. (2012). What happens on tour: The premarital stag tour, homosocial bonding, and male friendship. *Men and Masculinities, 15*(3), 249–270. doi:10.1177/1097184X12448465.

Tripp, C. (2005). *The intimate world of Abraham Lincoln*. New York: Free Press.

Ward, J. (2015). *Not gay: Sex between straight White men*. New York: New York University Press.

Way, N. (2011). *Deep secrets: Boys' friendships and the crisis of connection*. Cambridge: Harvard University Press.

Way, N. (2013). Boys' friendships during adolescence: Intimacy, desire, and loss. *Journal of Research on Adolescence, 23*(2), 201–213. doi:10.1111/jora.12047.

Weeks, J. (2007). *The world we have won: The remaking of erotic and intimate life*. New York: Routledge.

Weeks, J., Holland, J., & Waites, M. (2003). *Sexualities and society: A reader*. Oxford: Polity Press.

White, A., & Hobson, M. (2015). Teachers' stories: Physical education teachers' constructions and experiences of masculinity within secondary school physical education. *Sport, Education and Society*. Advance online publication. doi:10.1080/13573322.2015.1112779.

White, A., & Robinson, S. (2016). Boys, inclusive masculinities and injury: Some research perspectives. *Boyhood Studies, 9*(2), 73–91. doi:10.3167/bhs.2016.09206.

Williams, D. G. (1985). Gender, masculinity–femininity, and emotional intimacy in same-sex friendship. *Sex Roles, 12*(5–6), 587–600. doi:10.1007/BF00288179.

Zorn, T., & Gregory, K. (2005). Learning the ropes together: Assimilation and friendship development among first-year male medical students. *Health Communication, 17*(3), 211–231. doi:10.1207/s15327027hc1703.

Men in Families

Are men still taking seriously their responsibilities as family breadwinners? Are today's men sharing more of the family housework and child care than those in previous generations? The answers to these questions are complex, and often depend on which men we are talking about and what we mean when we say "family."

Many male workers long ago won a "family wage" and, with it, made an unwritten pact to share that wage with a wife and children. But today, as Barbara Ehrenreich argues in her influential book *The Hearts of Men*, increasing numbers of men are revolting against this traditional responsibility to share their wages, thus contributing to the rapidly growing impoverishment of women and children. Ehrenreich may be correct, at least with respect to the specific category of men who were labeled "yuppies" in the 1980s. But if we are looking at the growing impoverishment of women and children among poor, working-class, and minority families, the causes have more to do with dramatic shifts in the structure of the economy—including skyrocketing unemployment among young black males—than they do with male irresponsibility. Increasing numbers of men have no wage to share with a family.

But how about the new dual-career family? Is this a model of egalitarianism, or do women still do what sociologist Arlie Hochschild called "the second shift"—the housework and child care obligations that come after their workplace shift is done? In this section, Sarah Thébaud and David Pedulla, and Daniel Carlson and his colleagues examine the contemporary division of labor in families. Carlson finds that more egalitarian division of labor results in a better sex life—for both women and men. Dana Berkowitz examines how gay men negotiate housework and masculinity, while Allen Kim and Karen Pyke provide an intersectional analysis of ethnicity and gender in the context of the family.

PART VI DISCUSSION QUESTIONS

1. With reference to the Berkowitz piece, why would gay men encourage norms of hegemonic masculinity in their sons?
2. South Korea's Father Schools mobilize a static, white, idealized form of American fatherhood to discipline and shame Korean men into more affectionate familial relationships. How might such an approach work in the United States?
3. Why do you think the gendered division of domestic labor (housework) is so resistant to change?
4. Thébaud and Pedulla illustrate the power of perceived norms in shaping men's work/family preferences. How might gender equality activists make use of their findings?

Can a Gay Man Be a Housewife?

Gay Fathers Doing Gender, Family, and Parenting

DANA BERKOWITZ

Heteronormative assumptions about appropriate parents, gender norms, and child socialization continue to underpin the hegemonic view of family. Lesbian and gay families challenge these gender and heteronormative assumptions and expose the widening gap between the complex reality of contemporary families and the simplistic ideology that pervades modern family thought, scholarship, rhetoric, and policies. This paper advances theoretical understanding on how gay men discursively construct their procreative consciousness and fathering experiences. I maintain that attention to such discourse opens doors to new understandings of how societal surveillance fueled by heterosexism, homophobia, and constricting gender norms shapes gay men's fathering thoughts and experiences.

I draw upon my current research that explores the narratives of 22 gay fathers and 19 childless gay men. I detail how many of the men I spoke with relied upon dominant narratives of gender, kinship, biogenetics, and responsibility in the context of the interview setting. Participants described how they negotiate gender, sexuality, and real or imagined families within explicit gendered and heterosexist social boundaries; ultimately reifying certain discourses that I expected them to subvert or at least transgress. I argue that because these men and their families are under extreme surveillance and public scrutiny,

they are forced to draw upon the very discourses that many family scholars expect them to reject.

Background

I expand upon the procreative identity framework—a conceptual lens that was initially developed to explain how heterosexual men experience the procreative arena (Marsiglio & Hutchinson, 2002). The procreative identity framework is a useful conceptual lens to explore gay men's experiences in the reproductive realm because procreative consciousness is viewed as the cognitive and emotional awareness and expression of self as a person capable of creating and caring for life. Moreover, the framework treats this self-expression as a process-oriented phenomenon tied to situational contingencies, global sentiments, and romantic relationships. Although gay men's experiences are distinct in some ways, the basic conceptual lens is relevant to gay men because it accentuates how men's procreative consciousness is activated and evolves. Furthermore, the model's emphasis on both individual-based and relationship-based modes for expressing procreative consciousness draws attention to how gay men, on their own and in conjunction with partners, learn to frame their view about becoming fathers.

While it is sensible to extend the procreative identity framework to the experiences of gay men,

Dana Berkowitz, "Can a Gay Man Be a Housewife? Gay Fathers Doing Gender, Family and Parenting," edited from a version first presented at the American Sociological Association Annual Meeting, August 2007. Reprinted by permission of the author.

extending a model originally conceptualized for heterosexual men is complicated. I hesitate to take knowledge developed by and for heterosexual men and risk incorrectly extending this knowledge to the experience of gay men. Although gay men's desire for parenthood may be similar in some situations to heterosexuals' feelings, gay men's access to fatherhood and fathering experiences are constructed within a heterosexually defined realm embedded with ideological proscriptions. To address this consideration, I draw upon the theoretical contributions of feminist sociologist Dorothy Smith. Smith maintains that women's consciousness has been created by men occupying positions of power (1987, 1990). I borrow from and expand on this framework positing that gay men's procreative consciousness has been constructed within a world that has traditionally assumed heterosexuality and continues to privilege heterosexual parenting. Smith maintains that consciousness is not merely something going on in people's heads, rather it is produced by people and it is a social product (Smith, 1990). Thus, in order to more completely understand gay men's procreative consciousness and their possible fantasies of fathering, there is a necessity to link this consciousness with the institutions that create, maintain, challenge, and eventually change how gay men have historically imagined fatherhood and families. Smith's framework helps to anchor gay men's personal thoughts and experiences about fatherhood within the political, historical, economic, and social process that shapes them. Smith's theoretical paradigm highlights how certain institutions and ruling relations, such as adoption and fertility agencies, and the institutionalization of both fatherhood and the gay subculture shape the processes by which gay men contemplate and experience fatherhood. For example, even though gay men's desire for parenthood and experiences of fathering may be similar in some situations to heterosexuals' feelings, gay men's access to adoption and assisted reproductive technologies is mediated by a bureaucratic apparatus that affects the conditions under which they can father (Lewin, 2006). This is especially important for this study because

the majority of data were collected in Florida and New York. The former is currently one of the only states with explicit statutes prohibiting adoption by gay men and lesbians and in the latter state all use of surrogate mothers is illegal (Horowitz & Maruyama, 1995; Mallon, 2004; Weltman, 2005).

I also draw upon the concept of doing fathering to show how men engage in fathering actions, behaviors, and processes. This concept emerges from West and Zimmerman's construct of doing gender (1987). The metaphor of doing gender was one of the first to reconceptualize gender as not so much a set of traits residing with individuals, but as something people do in their social interactions. "A person's gender is not simply an aspect of what one is, but more fundamentally, it is something that one does, recurrently, in interaction with others" (West and Zimmerman, 1987: 126). By using this conceptual lens to frame my analysis, fathering and more broadly family are viewed as situated accomplishments of my participants, and when fathering and family are viewed as such, the focus of analysis moves from matters internal to the individual to interactional and eventually institutional arenas. Thus, one is not only a father but one does fathering, just as one does gender. The concept of accountability is of primary significance here because given that much of society still defines family as a heterosexual two-parent nuclear structure, the families in my study came to be held accountable for every action each member performed. Accountability is relevant to both those actions that conform and deviate from prevailing normative conceptions about family. I stress that while individuals are the ones who do fathering and family, the process of rendering something accountable is both interactional and institutional.

The concept of accountability becomes critical as I move into a theoretical discussion of how heterosexual domination influences how gay men discursively do fathering and family. Accountability is of primary importance in the specific context of gay and lesbian headed families. Gay fathers are consistently viewed with suspicion because of myths surrounding issues of pedophilia, a desire to "replicate their lifestyle" and a perceived lack of ability to properly socialize children and inscribe them with stereotypical gendered norms.

Gay men's thoughts about fatherhood and fathering experiences are complex and dynamic. Thus, each of these theoretical lenses is necessary to expand the procreative identity framework and disentangle the convoluted web of gay men's fathering talk.

Method

As a qualitative method, in-depth interviewing accentuates the subjective quality of different life experiences, the contextual nature of knowledge, the production of social meanings, and the interactive character of human action. I use this interviewing technique to study the process by which gay men express their procreative consciousness, father identities, and fathering experiences.

Recruitment

Analysis draws on audiotaped, in-depth interviews conducted with a sample of 19 childless gay men and 22 gay fathers who have created families through nonheterosexual means. The participants were recruited through a variety of methods in diverse locales from 2004–2006. In South and North Central Florida, I used both snowball sampling and posted fliers in areas frequented by members of the gay community such as gay community centers, shopping malls, eating and drinking establishments, hair salons, and gay activist organizations. The fliers for the recruitment of childless gay men were a broad call for participants who might be interested in discussing their thoughts about fatherhood, without screening them for whether they intended to have children. The fliers for gay fathers specified that we were searching for men who had become fathers through any means other than heterosexual intercourse.

Participants

The group of childless gay men differed substantially from those who chose to become fathers through nonheterosexual means. These differences

should not be regarded as a substantive finding of my research, but an artifact of my recruitment strategies. The childless gay participants were more racially, ethnically, and economically diverse than the fathers. Three of the childless men were African American, 1 was Chinese-American, 2 were Latino, and 13 were White. Three participants had not completed college, 5 were enrolled in college with the intentions of graduating, 7 had graduated from a four-year university, and 4 had an advanced graduate degree. Two participants were Jewish, 1 was Presbyterian, 3 were Christian, 4 were Catholic, 1 was Buddhist and Catholic and 8 reported to have no religious affiliation. Six participants were students and the remaining participants were employed in either the service sector or the professional sector. Annual income for these men ranged from under $15,000 to over $75,000 annually. Ages of the childless men ranged from 19–53 and the mean age was 31.

Consistent with other research on gay fathers (Johnson & Connor, 2002; Mallon, 2004), the gay fathers participating in this research were White and predominantly upper middle class. All but 2 of these men earned over $75,000 annually, the remaining 2 earned between $30,000–$60,000, and the majority of participants were employed in the professional sector. Similarly, all participants except 2 had completed college and 8 had an advanced graduate degree. Fathers' ages ranged from 33–55 with a mean age of 43.5. Nine participants were Jewish, 5 were Catholic, 4 were Christian, 2 were Unitarian, and 3 claimed to have no religious affiliation. Participants created their families in diverse ways, including various forms of adoption, traditional and gestational surrogacy arrangements, and co-parenting with a lesbian woman or women.

Interviews

Semi-structured interviews were conducted that lasted from 45–120 minutes. They took place in a variety of settings (e.g., participants' households or work offices, coffee shops, eating and drinking establishments, the researcher's office, and over the telephone). Although it was my intention to conduct all interviews individually, 6 men who were coupled and had young children opted to be interviewed together. The qualitative interviews were preceded by a brief sociodemographic background survey. Interviews were open-ended and designed to generate rich, detailed information. Participants were encouraged to discuss their thoughts, feelings, experiences, and personal narratives regarding their images and decisions about fatherhood. Interviews were designed to explore the men's emerging identity as a prospective or real father, including how their father identity emerged out of interactions with other children, friends, family members, birth mothers, agency coordinators, and romantic partners.

Analysis

The initial textual material was analyzed with grounded theory methodology for qualitative data analysis (Glaser & Strauss, 1967; Strauss & Corbin, 1998). As ideas, terms, moods, and so on surfaced in multiple interviews, they were coded and given tentative labels during the open phase of coding. Open coding is a process of comparing concepts found in the text for classification as examples of some phenomenon. As similarities in experience, patterns, and emergent themes appeared, categories of phenomena were labeled and entered into a code list. This process of open coding enabled me to create an analytic process for identifying key categories and their properties (Strauss & Corbin, 1998).

My final stage of selective coding allowed me to compare themes identified in this study to existing literature exploring fathering talk among both gay and heterosexual men. The themes derived from this work unveil the dynamic and complex process of how gay men discursively construct their procreative and father identities in a socially constructed world that privileges heterosexuality.

Findings

The remainder of this paper addresses how the men I spoke with drew upon dominant gender and familial discourses. First, I explore how men's descriptions of their procreative consciousness was framed within an essentialized context. Next, I move to a discussion of how men described their ideal fathering experiences and detail aspects related to the privileging of biological ties and the dominant two-parent nuclear family. Finally, I examine how participants narrated their thoughts about engendering their children and their experiences of gender accountability. In each and every phase of procreative and fathering talk, men drew upon a discourse associated with the hegemonic family and/or normative gender stereotypes.

An Essentialized Procreative Consciousness

Regardless of one's sexuality, parenthood has become a reflective process in contemporary Western society. "Paths to parenthood no longer appear natural, obligatory, or uniform, but are necessarily reflexive, uncertain, self-fashioning, plural, and politically embattled" (Stacey, 2006, p. 28). Children have moved from an economic asset to an economic responsibility and even a liability. Thus, "an emotional rather than economic calculus governs the pursuit of parenthood" (Stacey, 2006, p. 28). Openly identified gay men who seek fatherhood face these dimensions of postmodern parenting in an exaggerated way. Furthermore, it has been documented that the thought processes that gay men undergo to become fathers are quite different from those experienced by their heterosexual counterparts (Barret & Robinson, 2000; Bigner & Jacobsen, 1989; Mallon, 2004). Many of the men I spoke with were well aware of emerging legal and reproductive opportunities that made their once outlandish daydreams of becoming a father now a viable reality. Yet, they also were well aware of how structural and institutional constraints shaped their experiences in the procreative realm.

More interestingly however was how some men explained their fathering desires within the constraints of dominant gender discourse. Nick, a soft-spoken 26-year-old who moved from the Midwest to Miami Beach a year earlier eloquently discussed his burning desire to father as equivalent to a woman's natural drive to mother:

> Because I was always gay and I did have some maternal instinct. Maybe at the time that women first, whenever, somewhere in adolescence, was when I

first started thinking I want to have a child . . . the older I got the more I considered it the same way as finding Mr. Right . . . this very important thing that would complete me. The only thing that could [complete me].

Nick cited identifying as gay as being tantamount to having a maternal urge. Further, he recognized that as a human being, the only thing that would fully complete him was creating a family of his own. Ross, a childless single man, echoed Nick's sentiments regarding a desire to father. He asserted that fatherhood is "the greatest thing that somebody can do. I think it enriches your life . . . you can give back to someone your good experiences, so they can become a good person."

That men discussed their procreative fantasies in terms of having a "maternal instinct," "the greatest thing that somebody can do" and "needing something to complete me" clearly speaks to our contemporary pronatalist milieu. It also touches on the notion of generativity, or the nurturing quality in individuals whereby they seek to "create and guide younger generations" (Marsiglio, 1995, p. 84). While some refer to gay men choosing fatherhood as postmodern pioneers (Stacey, 2006), the yearning to procreate, father, nurture, and have someone depend on you is a particularly modern characteristic. What is unique about this desire is only that it is being articulated by gay men, a population who because of gender and heterosexist norms are not expected to have these yearnings. Clearly, because gay men are raised within a socially constructed society that stresses pronatalism and generativity, their procreative desires and discourses are not so different from their heterosexual counterparts.

However, when we listen to how gay men negotiate these modern desires for fatherhood with their gay identity, essential ideologies associated with gender and sexuality surface. For example, while Luke wanted children in his future, he maintained that:

Gay men were not meant to be that way, if it was meant to be that way then two people would have stood beside each other and had a baby. Obviously there is a reason that our bodies are built to procreate and for a woman to go through that process.

Luke described his procreative urges within the constraints of a heteronormative discourse. If we take Luke's statement and juxtapose it against those of Nick and Ross, it illuminates how gay men's reliance on dominant familial, heterosexual, and gender discourse underscores the need for a more inclusive way of talking about parenting. Furthermore, because we live in a society that conflates and confuses gender and sexuality, gay men's procreative fantasies are narrated within the constraining framework of Western conceptions of gender and sexuality. Yet while many of the men describe their procreative desires within a gendered and heteronormative context, there were a few exceptions. Not surprisingly, one of these exceptions surfaced in my conversation with Segal, a fellow sociologist who is a leading scholar on gender and sexuality. He mentioned that my study should critically examine how heterosexism "hinders and hurts gay men." This reliance upon dominant gender and familial discourse is a theme that surfaced more than I would have ever imagined and confirms Segal's statement of how heterosexism constrains gay men's narrative abilities.

Essentializing Biology

The formation of a father identity for some of the men is mediated by the anticipated or actual presence of biological ties. Childless participants diverged in whether they desired a child who was biologically related to them. Some men explained that they preferred a child who would have blood ties to them, whereas others talked about wanting to adopt their future child. Zach, a childless 33-year-old Chinese-American restaurant manager, confessed that the only way he would have a child was if that child was biologically related to him. He elaborated:

I would love more than anything to have a child. My own as well. . . . If I am going to have a child, I want it to be a part of me . . . I want it to have some of my characteristics . . . I want to have a little piece of me . . . I think that if anything, that is really what drives all of it. I do want to have someone, a little piece of me out there doing a little something to contribute to the world.

Zach was one of the few childless men who was so explicit in his desire for a biological child. A handful of other childless men claimed that although a biological tie was preferred, adoption would be a second option. Taylor, also childless, explained, "adoption would just be the second option, like a fall back . . . I'd rather conceive a child with someone I know and trust . . . I guess I would rather have my own . . . but if that's not an option, adoption wouldn't change anything." Although Taylor and a few other men ideally preferred a biological relation between themselves and their child, as gay men and as prospective fathers, they realized their options were quite limited. Many other men, both childless and fathers, questioned their ability to feel the same level of affection for a child not biologically related to them as compared to a genetically related child. These statements illuminate how the men I spoke with still greatly valued biogenetic ties. Although I found a great deal of creative negotiation within these families, it is significant to recognize that such negotiations were regulated with the conventional privileging of biological relatedness at the forefront of these men's consciousness.

The Essential Family

The majority of childless men I spoke with perceived their futures as residing in an intimate partnership raising children. Noah articulated that, "I know that that's going to be the only way for me to have a kid, but I would like to, I would like to provide that child with more of a structured family than just a single parent." Walter echoed Noah's sentiments when he explained, "I'm not religious, but I think God made it so that two people have to create a child because it usually takes two people to parent a child." In an ideal family, most of these men saw themselves raising children in a (post)modern nuclear family: two men, two children, a pet, a suburban style house and a white picket fence. While gay men are marginalized from traditional family

arrangements, my participants' narratives underscore that their ideal visions of family and fatherhood are forged within a dominant understanding of normative images of family. Moreover, men's visions of an ideal family were fashioned with the dominant mother as nurturer, father as provider familial ideology.

Noah fantasized his ideal parenting experience:

I definitely see myself being like the quintessential little housewife, if a gay man can be a housewife. Like, I very much and like take on the maternal role in the family, and in a relationship, I'm very much like the little wife. And I'm always cooking and cleaning for them, and like taking care of them, and so I think it's, when I think of myself having kids, I very much think of myself being like the soccer mom . . . I think about . . . where we would live and our family and I'd have my Volvo Sedan, my Sedan, my Volvo SUV with my SLK hardtop convertible, for when I want to have like mommy time, and be the soccer mom.

Noah's ideal fathering—or rather, mothering—visions take place within a 1950s glorified and somewhat postmodern conception of a Leave It to Beaver–esque family. The reliance by so many men on a dominant gender and family discourse points to a very uninclusive way of speaking about family. That Noah envisioned his parenting roles as a caretaker and nurturer and automatically equates these roles with taking on the role of a soccer mom speaks to the insidiousness of socially constructed gender norms within the family.

Gender Essentialism

A final theme that surfaced was how men spoke about negotiating the real or imagined gender of children. Many of the gay men's narratives underscored uncertainty with regards to how they envisioned coping with public bathroom issues, menstruation, bra-shopping, and the first dates of their future or present daughters. A vast majority of gay fathers painted a mental picture of a menstruating, bra-shopping, sexually active teenager and I heard constant concern from these men wondering if two dads could adequately deal with the "harsh" realities of a thirteen-year-old girl's pubescent phase. Rick and Art, fathers of a three-year-old boy spoke about how they fantasized about the challenges of having a little girl because, "We knew boy issues; we knew what to expect . . . we also thought girls were more difficult in terms of later on, with puberty and all that." Both Rick and Art questioned if two dads could adequately deal with the realities of a 13-year-old girl's pubescent phase.

When envisioning raising a girl child, many men discussed the importance of securing a suitable role model for her, particularly during her pubescent phase. Noah explained:

> I like to think that like my mother or my partner's mother or my female friends would be there and that they would . . . like help her out and like if she's having like maybe, if I had a daughter and she's 12 years old, and she's got her period, and like I'd like to have help with that, but I understand where she would feel uncomfortable coming to me, so, I see that you know the presence of like other women or a mother or someone who'd be involved is beneficial.

When men envisioned taking up the tasks of raising a girl, preparation and planning become critical. Such planning always includes guaranteeing a suitable role model for their girl children to assist with milestones like menstruation.

If I were to follow a folk logic, it makes sense that two men would have anxiety about raising a girl child because in their minds, their own experiences would not easily parallel hers. However, some participants wondered how their gender and sexuality would interact to negatively affect their boy children's future socialization. Marc, the proud single father of a four-year-old girl explained, "If I have a boy, will I be as good as a role model? You know, dads take their sons to ball games and things like that, which I am just not into . . . if I had a boy, it might be somewhat difficult to do that 'macho' role model." Because Marc was never the stereotypical masculine athlete, he questioned whether he could participate with his imagined son in

"normal" male-bonding activities. In most cases, it is taken for granted that someone can appropriately raise a child of the same gender, but in some cases, like Marc's own, gender atypical behavior is cited as a reason for not being a suitable role model for children of the same gender. Hence, the men's perceptions of their future children's gender socialization helped forge the men's child and fathering visions as well as their procreative and father identities. However, such considerations were clearly framed within rigid gender stereotypes.

Sanctions against gay men for doing gender incorrectly are rampant in heterosexist U.S. society. These sanctions are exacerbated in the case of gay parents, in that they have a unique type of surveillance surrounding both their own normative gendered behavior as well as their children's gendered actions and attitudes. Because the heterosexual nuclear family has become institutionalized as an "ideological code" (Smith, 1990), gay fathers are held accountable for the gendered outcomes of their children. Thus, the panoptic gaze of the heterosexual eye serves as a surveillance mechanism that commands these fathers to engage in self-monitoring their children's gendered actions, to become per Foucault (1977) "docile bodies" inscribed with normative gender standards.

This becomes more lucid when we explore how men spoke about how they actually did fathering. Lawrence is a gay father with two teenage sons who never doubted his own ability to instill his teenage boys with "proper" masculine ideals. Nevertheless, he recalled a scenario when an outsider who happened to be in close proximity to him and his son scrutinized his fathering skills:

> I remember once Issac [older son] was crying, he was like 3-years-old, and he hurt himself and he was crying, and there was this painter in the house, and the painter kept saying, "be a man, be a man." And my instinct is to hug him and wait until he stopped crying, and let him sit there and calm down, you know. But this man's thing was "be a man" which is I think what many people would say. . . . So, I just took him away, and I didn't say any more.

Gender scholars have argued that normative definitions such as No Sissy Stuff, The Big Wheel, The Sturdy Oak, and Give 'em Hell give men a blueprint for how to live their lives (Brannon, as cited in Connell, 1995 and Kimmel, 1994). As an adult gay man reared with these gendered blueprints, Lawrence was acutely aware of the rigid definitions of masculinity in contemporary society. As such, he was keenly attentive to the pressures of raising a man in a socially constructed world that defines masculinity in such strict terms. In contemporary society, raising a boy to be a "proper" and "suitable" man is simultaneous with preparing him to fit into the historically and socially constructed version of hegemonic masculinity that is culturally dominant (Connell, 1995).

Lawrence also elaborated on another time when an outsider commented on his son's masculine development. Many years prior to the interview, Lawrence was with his two young sons at a local playground. He clearly remembered another father approaching his younger son, who had recently been wounded and was wailing at the pain. The man exclaimed, "Oh stop crying, you're acting like a girl" to the young boy. Although Lawrence was tempted to retort "What is wrong with being a girl?" he quickly stopped himself from succumbing to his immediate response and simply picked up his boy and walked away. Lawrence explained that he was uncomfortable with having another adult man fill his son's head with stereotypical masculine ideals. At the same time, Lawrence clearly did not want to get in a verbal argument in a public playground about the unfairness of the expectation that boys should not display emotion. Furthermore, Lawrence was in a paradoxical dilemma: he should not want his son to have to act in accordance with hegemonic ideals of masculinity, yet he understood that in order to survive as a man in contemporary society, one needs to adapt to certain normative gender standards.

Discussion

This paper details how gay men discursively construct their procreative and father identities within the constrictions of a gendered and heteronormative discourse. My analysis underscores the needs to move beyond the social and structural constraints in attaining fatherhood to distinguish what type of father identities and families are produced in these distinct settings. Expanding the pro-creative identity framework developed for heterosexual men with Smith's feminist sociology, West and Zimmerman's (1987) concept of accountability and a Foucaultian power/knowledge (1977) framework brings us closer to grasping the insidious effects of heterosexual surveillance on gay and lesbian parents.

Whereas the closet as a strategy of accommodating to heterosexual domination is becoming less salient, this does not necessarily denote that heterosexual domination is a remnant of the past. The discourses of my participants demonstrate that whether it is the 1970s, 80s, 90s or today, gay men are still growing up in a world organized by heterosexuality. Although many individuals today can choose to live beyond the closet, they must still reside in a world where most institutions maintain heterosexual domination. My conversations with these men show how heterosexual dominance is deeply rooted in the institutions and culture of American society and must be understood as not simply a product of laws or individual prejudice, but institutionalized pervasive dominance (Seidman, 2004).

The insights I generate about gay men and their fathering talk should be viewed in context and their limitations noted. Meanwhile, because the process of becoming a gay father through nonheterosexual means is often financially costly, and because of my recruitment strategies, the fathers who participated in my study were primarily white and in the professional class. Regrettably, I am unable to speak to how minority men and gay men of more limited financial means discursively construct their procreative and father identities. That is an area for further research.

Literature Cited

Barret, R. L., & Robinson, B. E. (2000). *Gay Fathers*. San Francisco: Jossey-Bass.

Bigner, J. J., & Jacobsen, R. B. (1989). The value of children to gay and heterosexual fathers. *Journal of Homosexuality*, 18:12, 163–172.

Connell, R. W. (1995). *Masculinities*. Berkeley: University of California Press.

Foucault, M. (1977). *Power/Knowledge: Selected interviews and other writings, 1972–1977*. New York: Pantheon.

Glaser, B. G., & Strauss, A. L. (1967). *The discovery of grounded theory: Strategies for qualitative research*. Hawthorne, NY: Aldine de Gruyter.

Horowitz, R. M., & Maruyama, H. (1995). *Legal issues in gay and lesbian adoption: Proceedings from the Fourth Annual Pierce-Warwick Adoption Symposium*. Washington, DC: Child Welfare League of America.

Johnson, S. M., & Connor, E. M. (2002). *The gay baby boom: The psychology of gay parenthood*. New York: New York University Press.

Kimmel, M. (1994). Masculinity as homophobia: Fear, shame, and silence in the construction of gender identity. In Harry Brod and Michael Kaufman (Eds.), *Theorizing masculinities* (pp. 119–141). Thousand Oaks, CA: Sage.

Lewin, E. (2006). Family values: Gay men and adoption in America. In K. Wegar (Ed.) *Adoptive families in a diverse society* (pp. 129–145). New Brunswick, NJ: Rutgers University Press.

Mallon, G. P. (2004). *Gay men choosing parenthood*. New York: Columbia University Press.

Marsiglio, W. (1995). *Procreative man*. New York: New York University Press.

Marsiglio, W., & Hutchinson, S. (2002). *Sex, men, and babies: Stories of awareness and responsibility*. New York: New York University Press.

Seidman, S. (2004). *Beyond the closet: The transformation of gay and lesbian life*. New York: Routledge.

Smith, D. (1987). *The everyday world as problematic: A feminist sociology*. Toronto: University of Toronto Press.

Smith, D. (1990). *Conceptual practices of power: Toward a feminist sociology of knowledge*. Boston: Northeastern University Press.

Stacey, J. (2006). Gay parenthood and the decline of paternity as we knew it. *Sexualities, 9*, 27–55.

Strauss, A., & Corbin, J. (1998). *Basics of qualitative research: Techniques and procedures for developing grounded theory* (2nd ed.). Newbury Park, CA: Sage.

Weltman, J. J. (2004, August 26). Surrogacy in New York. *Resolve of New York*. Retrieved September 1, 2005, from http://www.surrogacy.com/Articles/news_view.asp?ID=128.

West, C., and Zimmerman, D. (1987). Doing gender. *Gender & Society*, 1, 2: 125–151.

Taming Tiger Dads

Hegemonic American Masculinity and South Korea's Father School

ALLEN KIM AND KAREN PYKE

When globalization, Western neo-colonialism, economic crises, and modernity destabilize gender arrangements in non-Western regions, men face masculinity crises that necessitate the reconstitution of their masculinity practices and identities (Kimmel 2003). Examining how men in such situations engage with and understand white Western masculinity and the extent to which they internalize or resist Western hegemonic gender logics—or what they interpret as such—can reveal the power of Western hegemonic masculinity in an emerging global society. These concerns inform our study of how notions of white Western manhood inform the teachings of the South Korean Father School movement, which trains men to adopt an emotionally involved, gender progressive family role. The concept of Western hegemonic masculinity orients our analysis of the movement's discourse.

Hegemonic masculinity is a configuration of masculinity practices associated with the major forms of social power. A by-product of domination, it is defined in relation to subordinates, including the masculinities identified with "other" nonwhite, lower-class, and/or non-Western men, and the femininity associated with women (Connell 1995; Heath 2003; Pyke 1996). For example, as an ideal type, hegemonic masculinity in the United States is associated with a white class-privileged professionally successful man who is highly involved with

his family, nurturing, and emotionally expressive. This is often called the "New Man" masculinity or "New Fatherhood" (Adams and Coltrane 2008; Hondagneu-Sotelo and Messner 1994).... Hegemonic masculinity is adaptable; it is an ideal type associated with the most elite positions of power and presented as the form to which all men should aspire, but to which many are excluded (e.g., men who are nonwhite, gay, or lower income; Chen 1999; Connell 1995; Pyke 1996). For the hegemonic masculinity of North America, Europe, and Australia to acquire global hegemony, its coercive effects must be evident among non-Western and nonwhite men.... How do non-Western men in such situations engage with and understand Western hegemonic masculinity as they reconstitute their masculinity? This question orients our study of the (re)construction of masculinity among leaders and participants of the South Korean Father School movement. The Father School movement, which grew during the 1997 Asian economic crisis when middle-class "salarymen" faced joblessness, attempts to remedy what movement leaders describe as a crisis in Korean masculinity. Because Father School uses images of hegemonic white American masculinity to train Korean men to be involved, loving family men, it is a particularly fitting site to explore the global domination of Western masculinity.

A Globally Hegemonic Masculinity

The masculinity practices of elite men in North America, Europe, and Australia radiate internationally through Western-dominated multinational corporations, mass media, education, government, and the Christian church. Some suggest Western hegemonic masculinity is acquiring prominence in an emerging world culture. "By virtue of the cultural, political, and economic dominance of the institutions of multinational business, the masculinity formed in their matrix is in a strong position to claim hegemony in the gender order of the societies they dominate" (Connell and Wood 2005, 362). . . . Western hegemonic masculinity is cast as the most developmentally advanced form, superior to all others (Kimmel 2003).

Scholars have examined masculinity among non-Western men in the context of migration and transnational families (Dreby 2006; Hondagneu-Sotelo and Messner 1994; Mirandé, Pitones, and Díaz 2011; Montes 2013; Thai 2008) and among nonwhite and lower-class men in Western societies (Chen 1999; Connell 1995; Pyke 1996). We know less, however, about how a wide-reaching hegemonic masculinity rooted in Western domination impinges on masculinities in non-Western regions, threatening them with actual or symbolic subordination (Connell and Messerschmidt 2005). Non-Western men confronting a "masculinity crisis" in the context of Western dominance can resist and maintain ascendancy through coordinated "compensatory manhood acts" or "protest masculinities" forged around racial/ethnic, national, class, political, or religious identities and institutions (Kimmel 2003; Pyke 1996; Shrock and Schwalbe 2009). In turn, the West constructs these oppositional masculinities as backward, inferior, and threatening, thereby justifying Western containment, monitoring, and control of the bearers of such masculinities. . . . Consider, for example, current East–West tensions pivoting around the gender order and the definition of masculinity. The Islamic fundamentalist masculinity of the Taliban and al Qaida is a protest masculinity marked by violence, extreme subordination of women, and denigration of Western masculinity practices as the behavior of enemy infidels (Kimmel 2003). Meanwhile, the West deploys "Orientalist" imagery of Islamic "terrorist" masculinity as fanatical, misogynistic, illogical, and backward in projecting Western masculinity as gender progressive, rational, modern, and developmentally superior (Said 1978).

Hegemony occurs when the oppressed accepts the worldview of the oppressor, including the form of masculinity associated with the oppressor (Chen 1999; Pyke 1996). . . . This is more likely when there is broad recognition among non-Western men that the masculinity they are "doing" is failing in the context of a changing local or global gender order. Such conditions can ignite new masculinity practices that hold the promise of human progress and ascendancy in a changing world, and thus a turn toward that form of masculinity acquiring global ascendancy, raising the following questions: Do we find evidence in non-Western regions of the hegemony of Western masculinity? And, specifically, do non-Western men internalize Western hegemonic masculinity as a standard for rejecting and denigrating their own previously ascendant local masculinity? Our analysis considers these questions.

The Destabilization of South Korean Masculinity

The locally hegemonic masculinity in urban South Korea has been that of the white-collared "salaryman" who works long days after which he joins colleagues at business meetings in hostess bars, drinking well into the night. The work-obsessed salaryman can go days without seeing his family, contributing to "fatherless households" (Taga 2005, 132–33). . . . Traditional Korean family customs stress strong parental control, emotional restraint, a rigid gender order, strong role prescriptions, family obligation, self-sacrifice for the good of the family, and instrumental care and support of children until marriage. Under Confucianism, children, even as adults, are expected to show deference and respect toward parents (Kim 2008). This ethos contrasts with an American individualist emphasis on independence, self-reliance, and a definition of love that values intimacy, emotional expressiveness, and close talk (Cancian 1987); and self-development, individual happiness even at the expense of family ties, and egalitarianism across gender and generational status (Bellah et al. 1985). . . .

Prior to the 1990s, the vast majority of married Korean women focused on domesticity but entered the labor force in greater numbers after the 1997 Asian economic crisis when men lost jobs and earnings, and bankruptcies, divorce, and domestic violence increased (Kwon et al. 2003; Oh 2009; Sung 1998). Men's inability to fulfill the breadwinning role led to a masculinity crisis (Kwon and Roy 2007, 288), marked by increased rates of depression, alcoholism, and suicide among men (Khang et al. 2005; Yoon 2010). The government launched suicide prevention campaigns emphasizing men's emotional well-being and family connection. These therapeutic themes are also salient in the Father School movement and indicate a society-wide attempt to shift Korean masculinity away from an emphasis on emotional endurance and stoicism.

The decline of the "good provider" role occurred over several decades in the United States. In its stead emerged the "New Man" who shares breadwinning and child care roles with his wife, though this is an ideal type to which some men aspire but few actually attain (Adams and Coltrane 2008; Bernard 1981). By contrast, the Asian crisis prompted swift and dramatic changes in Korean gender arrangements, including men's job and earnings instability and women's entry into the paid labor force (Choi and Chang 2012; Kim et al. 2009).

Alongside demographic changes in family life was a shift in Korean media imagery of fathers. Involved fathering became the topic of several reality television shows, including *The Return of Super Man*, about four celebrity fathers who care for their children two days a week without their wives' assistance (Sung 2014). Similarly, the portrait of Korean family men in television ads shifted from the absent "salaryman" patriarch to the kind, emotionally present family man. The new family man media imagery mirrored new expectations occurring throughout Korea (Kwon and Roy 2007; Son 2013). . . .

Korean Father School Movement's "Gender Boot Camp"

At Father School, I learned that the most important thing about caring for your family as a father is communication and expressing your feelings.

(56-year-old father)

The Father School movement, which began in Seoul in 1995 at Duranno Bible College and spread to 53 countries, attempts to help men become healthier fathers and husbands by aligning their masculine identity and practices with "contemporary" gender norms and general Christian values, in contradistinction to the "misguided" practices of earlier generations of Korean fathers who stressed authoritarianism and family hierarchy (Father School USA brochure 2012). Given the focus and intensity of Father School training, it has been likened to a 12-step program by the *New York Times* (Laporte 2011) and a "gender boot camp" (Kim 2014). . . . According to Father School, men's reasons for participation include (1) pressure from family, friends, and Father School volunteers; (2) a desire to improve family communication and emotional connection; and (3) wanting to learn about men's positive role in the family. By 2013, there were 175,000 graduates of Father School in South Korea. . . . [O]ur analysis centers on the gender component of Father School teachings in the field, not on its religious roots (Heath 2003).

Father School conferences of 30 to 150 participants meet for five consecutive Saturdays and include presentations and small accountability discussion groups with trained facilitators. Presenters include professors, government officials, entertainers, athletes, clergy, and former Father School graduates. Workshops involve hugging rituals and the writing of "confessional" letters to family members in which men share both good and painful memories, regrets, and love for family members. The writing and public reading of men's handwritten missives function as the core of Father School activities. Additionally, between meetings, men have homework assignments designed to improve family relations, such as expressing verbal and physical affection, helping with domestic tasks, and dating family members.

Father School draws extensively on the once popular U.S. evangelical Promise Keeper men's movement. Like Promise Keepers, Father School emerged around concern for a growing epidemic of "abusive, ineffective and absentee fathers . . ." with the goal of strengthening men's community roles through "healthy communication" and greater family engagement (Father School brochure 2010a). . . . Father School participants commonly weep when sharing regrets or describing their own fathers' harsh and distant parenting. . . .

There are also some important distinctions. While Promise Keepers leaders had financial and political ties to the anti-feminist fundamentalist right, Father School has no links to conservative gender movements. Some who study Promise Keepers rhetoric note that while it engaged some progressive gender language regarding husbands and wives as partners, it . . . blamed the feminization of men for the decline of family life and aimed to revitalize men's authority (Bartkowski 2004; Heath 2003). Although Father School also promotes greater gender equality alongside men's "benevolent" headship of the family, the "take charge" rhetoric of Promise Keepers is antithetical to the Father School goal of softening intense patriarchal masculinity. . . . While Promise Keepers was criticized for excluding women at their events, Father School regards wives (and children) as integral to men's masculine reconstitution, and asks the women to read letters they have written to their husbands at the final Father School meeting. . . .

. . .While Father School draws on images of Euro-American men, thus suggesting a distinctly American form of hegemonic masculinity, this form of masculinity is not so distinct from the hegemonic masculinity scholars find in all Anglophone societies (Connell 2005). So while we refer to American hegemonic masculinity in our analysis, we join other scholars and our respondents in regarding this reference to be largely synonymous with Western hegemonic masculinity, especially in terms of the dynamics by which Western masculinity is acquiring global ascendancy.

Methods

Much research on U.S. men's movements analyzes only the leadership and literature (Brickner 1999; Donovan 1998). Yet the reconstitution of men's gender identities in terms of the movement's discourse unfolds among participants, typically in the context of small groups (Heath 2003). . . . Hence we consider the goals of Father School as defined by its leaders and literature—a "top down" organizational view—as well as the experiences of participants at the "bottom" of the organization.

Our Korean data are from the first author's larger project on Father School in Seoul and the United States. Korean Father School leaders gave the first author, who previously graduated from the Father School program in Los Angeles, permission to collect data as an observer. He had access to preconference prep meetings, debriefing sessions with volunteers, and Father School conferences, where he rotated among small groups during which participants shared personal experiences. Because of his previous knowledge of Father School, fluency in Korean, and donning of the Father School uniform, he blended in easily.

The first author observed 25 Father School meetings in and around Seoul from July 2010 to April 2012, which included 15 guest speakers, 15 videos, 35 small group discussions, and more than 100 public readings of letters (approximately 90 by men to their family members, 22 by wives to their husbands, and 8 by children to their fathers). In addition to field notes and Father School documents, data for this study include 145 handwritten letters from men participants: 50 letters to their fathers and 25 to their wives; 35 "confessional" letters; and 20 letters by participants' wives and 15 by their children.

We analyzed the data related to the "top" and "bottom" of the organization separately so as to compare the construction of masculinity at these different sites. We draw on constructivist grounded theory (Charmaz 2000) in analyzing the meanings

Father School leaders and participants bring to the project of reconstituting masculinity. The first author open coded memos from field observations. Using a constant comparative method, he reread coded data to refine coding categories and capture emergent themes (Strauss and Corbin 1998). He sorted images of Korean and American men in Father School videos and lecture slides as negative, positive, or neutral. Negative images are those Father School used as examples of the "problem," such as an angry, screaming father. Positive images are those used to illustrate the solution or a model to emulate, such as a man hugging his son. He coded as neutral those images containing no strongly marked positive or negative behaviors and that Father School presented as neither problematic nor a model to emulate, such as men at work or riding a subway train. In analyzing Father School lecture content, the first author coded depictions of Korean men's "failures" as negative assessments and examples of remedial behaviors and attitudes as positive assessments. He similarly coded the references to Korean and American masculinity in participant letters.

Through the Western Looking Glass

Father School leaders critically scrutinize the ideals and practices of what they construct as a distinctly Korean masculinity. Using references to Euro-American men, leaders prescribe the masculinity of the "New Man"—an involved, loving family man (Adams and Coltrane 2008; Hondoneu-Sotelo and Messner 1994). Father School presents this form of hegemonic masculinity, which has been much discussed in all Anglophone countries (Connell 2005), as the modern, "healthy" antidote to a problematic Korean masculinity. Our analysis of the rhetoric of Father School leaders and documents indicates the reproduction of "Orientalist" views promulgated in the United States. . . . Father School glorifies Euro-American masculinity as a superior example to emulate. . . .

Our analysis of the participants' letters and small group discussions also finds that most embrace the rhetoric of Father School leaders by contrasting a glorified Euro-American "New Man" ideal with a denigrated Korean masculinity. . . . In the sections below, we present an analysis of the discourse of a problematic Korean masculinity in Father School, and follow with evidence of the Father School endorsement of the white "New Man" masculinity, which Father School presents as the hegemonic form of American masculinity. We then present our analysis of Father School participant data.

Denigrating Korean Masculinity

Father School presenters describe Korean men as distant, uncommunicative, and abusive. They blame, in part, Confucianist traditions that emphasize men's superiority and "unhealthy forms of patriarchal authority . . . passed down generation to generation" (Father School 2010b). One speaker explains, "Our fathers were harsh, and expressing emotions was a sign of weakness. Korean fathers have inherited this legacy and therefore we are unable to . . . share kind and loving words." Father School describes men's family ties and communication as "broken." One presenter cites a study that finds only "five percent of [Korean] teenagers share their problems with their dad." Another refers to the traditional Korean expression, "Men are heaven; women are earth," as "backwards," "mistaken," and insulting to "modern Korean women," including "men's daughters." Their solution is a "modern" family that is less gender polarized, more emotionally expressive, and "stronger and more united." . . .

Father School repeatedly problematizes the "salaryman" culture in various training formats. For example, guest speakers reiterate the advice manual and describe Korean men as "victims" of a "shallow culture" that values "pride, military toughness, golfing skills, drinking, sexual virulence, and economic status markers" (Father School 2010b, 14) more than family. The Father School manual also blames family problems on men's workaholism, alcoholism, late-night meetings with coworkers, extramarital sexual liaisons, a selfish "recreational appetite," domestic abuse, and emotional and physical absence. The Korean man, according to the manual, "believes that making money is sufficient for his role in the family," has "difficulty control-ling his temper," and feels entitled to leisure away from his family (Father School 2010b, 6). Further, the manual charges, the Korean father "does not know how to affirm and encourage his wife and children," causing "broken communication," deep emotional wounds, and alienation. As a remedy, the manual (2010, 23) advises men to end all "sharp, loud words" and violence toward family members because the "hand of the father should be a hand of blessing and not of violence." Korean men are nega-tively depicted in ten of 23 images in Father School video and slide presentations. There are eight neu-tral images. The five positive images of Korean men are of prominent entertainers and Father School graduates who share their personal testimonies of transformation from distant fathers to emotionally expressive, family-focused men.

In pushing men to adopt "contemporary" family arrangements, Father School casts middle-class families in urban Seoul as old-fashioned and back-ward, characteristics taken directly from the West-ern "Orientalist" construction of Asian cultures (Pyke 2010). In blaming a distinctly Korean form of masculinity, Father School ignores the structural forces of late capitalism and corporate institutional practices not limited to Korean society that require men's long workdays. Father School does not ad-vocate change in Korea's relation to capitalism or in the gendered structure of the workplace. Nor does Father School suggest that women share the breadwinning role to ease their husband's burden. The Father School remedy is not one of structural change but of personal transformation through the assimilation of a masculinity deemed superior to that of traditional Korean culture.

Glorifying White Masculinity

. . . Father School refers to white American family men as embodiments of the ideal. The Father School manual describes a good father and husband as one who spends time with his family, is emotion-ally expressive and affectionate, and empowers his children to learn to be independent . . . [em-phasizing] Western values that differ from Korean principles of instrumental love and the interdepen-dence of family members from birth until death. Father School incorporates images of white men from Promise Keepers materials, popular Ameri-can Christian publications, and U.S. cinema into video and slide presentations. While Father School presents Korean men as examples of a problematic masculinity, there is not one negative image of a white man in their materials. . . .

Father School leaders rely on the Promise Keep-ers movement as a vehicle for glorifying white mas-culinity, including the use of scenes from a Promise Keepers video with (mostly) white American men at a large Promise Keepers stadium rally. The video shows men hugging, crying, holding hands in prayer, confessing regrets, and pledging to become better family men. After the video, a Father School leader praises the Promise Keepers men's display of family commitment and instructs attendees to em-ulate the emotional vulnerability and self-reflection of these "American" men. . . . In a seminar on "Fa-thers' Influence," a Father School speaker shows a slide of Rick, a white American father, pushing his wheelchair-bound son, Dick, in a marathon. In an-other slide, the father and son are embracing and crying at the finish line. Korean subtitles describe the pair as "inseparable" for "Dick is the heart and Rick is the body." Explaining they trekked 3,770 miles across America, the Father School presenter describes Rick as "an amazing" exemplar of a fa-ther's love and dedication. A recording of Ameri-can pop singer Josh Groban's song "You Raise Me Up" ends the presentation.

Father School presentations rely heavily on scenes of Euro-American men in happy family situations: a man walking hand-in-hand with his wife, son, and daughter and a man throwing a base-ball with his son—an archetypical symbol of father/ son bonding in U.S. culture. Father School deploys white American iconography not only as a posi-tive model but also in the relational construction of Korean fathers as severely deficient.

In addition, some Father School speakers refer to their experiences in the U.S. and the "good" American fathers they met, juxtaposing these accounts with criticism of Korean fathers. For example, one guest speaker shared this observation with conference members:

> When I worked in the United States, I would overhear American fathers planning their weekends with family members and they always say, "I love you." They always seemed to look forward to spending time with their family after work. Most Korean dads have work or leisure activities with friends or coworkers as their focus—not the family.

...While criticizing Korean men for being unloving, Father School does not acknowledge how providing financial support is an instrumental show of love and commitment. Through this interpretive lens that glorifies American manhood and celebrates the American family ideal, racial/ethnic and non-Western family forms and practices are denigrated as deficient, abnormal, and unhealthy—and in need of Western liberation (see Pyke 2000, 2010).

White Masculinity to the Rescue

... Father School gives assignments to participants steeped in the images and therapeutic ethic of U.S. culture.... Specifically, participants are told to hug family members, say "I love you," change from authoritarian to expressive and supportive forms of communication, plan outings with family members, and write confessional letters about their regrets and hopes for the future (Kim 2013). Citing the popular American self-help book, *The Five Languages of Love* (Chapman 1995), the Father School manual instructs participants to set up a romantic date with their wife and ask what he can do to make her feel more loved, respected, understood, and secure.

While Father School does not specifically advocate gender equality, ... Father School leaders nonetheless instruct men to help wives with domestic tasks, ... [telling] participants not to address their wives using the common terms *gyp-saram* [housewoman] and *an-saram* [inside women], and use instead *anea*, meaning beloved spouse. Similarly, Father School advocates the flattening of vertical family structures that include children's

quiet deference marked by emotional restraint and the avoidance of eye contact. The manual tells men to "be eager to listen and understand ... and meet your children at the heart and eye level." ... In emulating the softer, more emotionally expressive "New Man" and rejecting what it constructs as a distinctive Korean masculinity, Family School guides men in the assimilation of a new, superior culture and the rejection of "erroneous" and "unhealthy" indigenous ways.

Participant Accounts

Denigrating Korean Patriarchy and Benchmarking Western Fathers

... Many men, and in some cases their family members, [seized] on the language of the "New Father" ideal, including the glorification of white American masculinity. However, some participants resist the glorification of white American men.... In this section, we present our analysis of men's letters as they pertain to the masculinity teachings of Father School.

In 79 of the 110 participant letters to family members, participants reiterated the Father School monolithic construction of Korean men as dictatorial, emotionally distant, and overly focused on work.... [S]ome participants might go along with the program without really believing its teachings. However, the depth of emotion and details that many men provide in their letters suggests a more than superficial engagement with the Father School discourse.

... [A]nalysis of 145 letters by participants and family members finds 26 authors who refer explicitly to a uniquely Korean masculinity to which they uniformly attribute negative traits. In letters to their fathers, two participants write (emphasis added):

> You were a *typical Korean father* and I barely have any memory of you because you were so busy. You were strict and hot-tempered, and I did not feel love from you growing up.... I was always in fear of you.

> Father, I did not like your *traditional Korean parenting style* growing up. You were harsh and would freely hit your children and forced your opinion

on all the family members. I promised not to copy your parenting style, however since growing up under *Korean ways*, it is hard to change my ways to my own family.

Another man blames "Korean Confucianism" for his family problems:

I was practically forced to admit that my own selfishness, combined with *Korean Confucianism*, was the reason why I was not able to get to know my own children through conversation. I think if I communicated more with my children I would not have so much conflict.

In letters to children, men commonly express regret for their emotional absence and abusive authoritarian parenting style, often referring to a "typical" Korean parenting style. One father writes, "For a time, dad couldn't suppress his impulsive feelings and would scold, hit, or talk down to you even for the smallest mistakes. . . . I see that everything was my fault and due to my *stubborn Korean ways*."

Fathers apologize to daughters as well as sons for curtailing their freedoms. One father writes to his daughter:

I'm sorry for hurting you in the past when I refused to accept your boyfriend. I regret raising my voice and shouting my disapproval. . . . I know I hurt you deeply through my anger and refusing to hear your feelings. It was my mistake to create such a wall between you and me after that.

Some participants refer to an image of the American father as a contrast to their poor parenting or as a goal to which they aspire. One man writes:

I am the example of a father who would buy things for my children instead of giving them my time and energy. *Like the American father playing catch with his son*, I want to strengthen bonds with my children by playing and sharing through action and dialogue.

Another participant shares his plans to adopt American practices of democratic communication:

When I did business with Americans, they speak and communicate a lot! They like talking a lot while eating with their family. These are the popular images I have of Western families too. I think it can be beneficial to increase conversation, apart from nagging as I did before, and see the children at the same heart and eye level.

A few participants say they want to adopt Western values of independence, personal freedom, and self-development. One participant shares with his small group members:

I don't want my children to have the burden to take care of me until old age. Children should live their own separate lives and have the choice to pursue their dreams. I think children need to be independent, similar to how Western fathers and mothers raise their children.

Many family members also glorify the dominant American form of masculinity. In a group discussion, one participant's wife says:

My husband is so busy and tired . . . and when he comes home he is always on the computer. *I wish he would focus more on the family and be more helpful around the home as is typical in American family life.*

On the final day of the conference, the facilitator asks family members to share how Father School is changing their husbands and fathers. One daughter benchmarks Euro-American men in her response:

Our father was not very involved in family life before, but over the last five weeks, he tries to have more conversation with us, hugging us and accepting the opinions of others more. . . . *Although it is not the same as* baeg-in abeoji *[white father] who is a close friend*, he tries to improve relationship with us more than before.

A participant's son speaks next, also using Western masculinity as a measuring stick:

At home, instead of watching TV in the living room, he helps mom with cleaning and doing kitchen chores. I think he became less stubborn and kinder to the family. Although not 100 percent, *he is trying to be more open minded, like Western style fathers.*

These examples highlight how many Father School participants internalize and reiterate widely circulating images of the "New Man" masculinity as represented by white Western family man. While this was a dominant pattern in our data, not all were as quick to blame Korean men or buy into the narrow construct of Western white masculinity.

Resistance to the Superiority of White American Masculinity

Some participants resist the glorification of Euro-American fathers either by defending Korean fatherhood or identifying weaker aspects of the "New Man" masculinity. A few participants describe Euro-American fathers as having less demanding work schedules than Korean men, being overly indulgent with their children, or having too little family authority—that is, as being too feminized. One participant states:

> Korean fathers work the most in the world according to the BBC news. Korean fathers must work to death so we don't lose our job and lose face in front of our families. I think I would be a great father if I could finish early every day like Americans and plan weekend activities with my family.... They are very fortunate and lucky.

Some participants' wives also suggest American men have it easier than Korean men. A wife shares, "I wish fathers in Korea could have more time to spend with their children like the U.S.... My husband has so little time with our children that I want them to at least have a positive image of him."

While Father School advises men to accord their children greater independence, and some participants . . . regard the . . . practice as . . . uncaring. . . . One man praises Korean fathers' breadwinning as an instrumental form of love:

> The Korean father cares just as much, if not more, than Western men. They just feel that buying and providing is their symbol of love to children. This is because Korea was once a poor country and life was very difficult. Korean men have no choice but to be loyal to their work for the sake of the nation.

Maybe Korean fathers care so much about their children's academic or job outcomes because of the difficulty of Korea's economic past and the difficulty finding a job today. This is not wrong.

An older participant whose son and grandchildren live in the U.S. praises Korean fathers' instrumental care for their children:

> In the case of American fathers, after their children grow older they want them to live separate lives. They want to be finished with parenting. Korean fathers will sacrifice eating food so their children can eat and live well, or sacrifice their retirement to put their children through school, or for them to have a wedding.

The strongest critique of white American masculinity is from a participant who has lived in the United States. He tells his group that American fathers are "not strict" with their children, have less authority in their families, and are "too accepting" of their children's bad behavior and selfishness. While he feels that Korean fathers are "too stubborn," Western fathers err on the side of "avoiding" confrontation, adding that "they prefer to be accepted so do not strongly voice their beliefs."

Despite these criticisms, . . . not a single letter or small group conversation veers from the Father School goal of emulating the emotionally expressive and involved father. . . . Participants regard these particular traits associated with Euro-American hegemonic masculinity as desirable, and draw on that ideology in denigrating Korean masculinity for failing to share them.

Even though wives engage positive images of white American masculinity as gender egalitarian and family-oriented, they were more likely than their husbands to acknowledge the challenging socioeconomic context shaping their husbands' daily lives. In 14 of 20 letters by wives, and in 15 of their 22 public confessionals, they express empathy for their husband's difficulty in balancing intensive work demands with family life. One wife writes to her husband, "I know that you faced additional burdens trying to support our family and your father who was undergoing cancer—all while you were also trying to gain a promotion." Similarly, another woman's letter reads:

> Remember that time when you were trying hard to finish your project for several months? Even now, I remember the shock and disappointment on your face when you saw a picture your son drew of our home and family and you were missing in the picture. You didn't sleep or eat well for a several days after. . . . I will do a better job to remind them that they have an honorable and hardworking father that loves them.

Father School engages a Western-oriented therapeutic ethic that emphasizes psychological transformation through collective self-help methods and feminized definitions of love that predominate in the ethos of American individualism (Cancian 1987). . . . By blaming salarymen for their long workdays, Father School fails to problematize corporate arrangements or mobilize around the need to change broader structural conditions through which local masculinities are constituted. Hence Father School leadership creates a double bind that some Father School participants and their wives acknowledge in sympathetic accounts of the difficulties salarymen face in enacting the "New Man" ideal. . . . Despite some resistance to the Father School framing of the problem, participants readily accept the Father School prescription of a softer masculinity and a shift from rigid gender and intergenerational hierarchies. Yet here again Father School does not advocate for broader social changes to enable shared breadwinning and domestic responsibilities. There are thus profound contradictions in Father School rhetoric emphasizing the personal responsibility of men to change without consideration of the larger political and institutional structures that constrain men's masculinity practices. Indeed, these same factors limit the capacity of Western men to fully engage the "New Man" ideal that Father School associates with them. It is thus likely that participants who internalize the expectation of a "New Man" masculinity might experience frustration and stress similar to what Lu and Wong (2013) found among Chinese American men living in the shadow of white American hegemonic masculinity.

Conclusion

Our analysis focuses only on the Korean Father School movement and should not be used to suggest the processes of Father School engagement with American hegemonic masculinity are shared in other sites in Korea, let alone other non-Western regions. On the other hand, our observation of the relational construction of a denigrated masculinity and a glorified Euro-American hegemonic masculinity among members of a subordinated group is not unique; other research finds similar dynamics within Western society (e.g., Chen 1999; Pyke 2010; Pyke and Johnson 2003). Our study contributes empirical evidence that these dynamics are not limited to Western societies.

. . . As the masculinity patterns and ideals associated with elite white men in Western societies gain global traction, so, too, do the controlling images and practices that denigrate and subordinate nonwhite and non-Western masculinities. Our study . . . suggests the internalization of a subordinated status in the context of a hegemonic masculinity rooted in Western society. . . . Father School situates Korean masculinity in relation to the "New Man" ideal of a nurturing, emotionally expressive family man whom it associates with American hegemonic masculinity. It does not matter that most American men do not actually achieve this hegemonic expression of masculinity; hegemonic masculinity is not "real." What matters is that this is the masculinity that Father School asserts is "real" among American men and that the movement glorifies as the modern remedy to the mistaken and outmoded Korean masculinity of the "distant patriarch." The Father School rhetoric thus reproduces for local consumption the gendered racism of Orientalism that constructs Asians as being in need of Western liberation from an antiquated gender order and authoritarian "Tiger" dads (Mohanty 1986; Pyke 2010).

Our study does not examine the extent to which individual participants actually alter their behavior in line with Father School teachings. . . . However, the voluntary nature of participants' involvement in Father School and their emotionally charged writings and personal confessions, as well as testimonials from some family members, suggest something more profound than a superficial reiteration of an imposed discourse. This begs the question: What do Father School participants have to gain in altering their familial role and ceding power in familial interactions? We provide some thoughts.

The theoretical literature on hegemonic masculinity defines it as involving both men's dominance over women and over other men . . . (Chen 1999; Connell 1995; Pyke 1996). However, . . . Father School does not encourage men to reemphasize their authority and power over women in their families but, rather, to soften "Korean patriarchy" by being more understanding and less dictatorial, less emotionally and physically distant, and more willing to help with domestic tasks and concede to the emotional needs of wives and children—that is, to give up power. . . . To understand why Father School participants might be enticed to cede such power, we draw on Chen's (1999) study of the gender strategies Chinese American men engage in "striking a bargain with hegemony" so as to elevate the status of their masculinity. Chen finds that one such strategy is the sharing of child care and housework so as to distance oneself from the stereotypical Chinese man. We speculate that something similar is occurring with the Father School movement. Specifically, Father School men might willingly trade some gender privilege, symbolically or literally, to distance themselves from notions of an archaic, patriarchal Korean masculinity as a strategy to increase the power of their masculinity by resituating it in conformity with an emerging global hegemonic masculinity.

This raises the following question: Will such bargaining with hegemony alter the subordinated status of non-Western men vis-á-vis Western hegemonic masculinity? We offer two theoretical possibilities. On the one hand, it is worth remembering that hegemonic masculinity is constructed in relation to subordinated masculinities and is dynamic and adaptable. Thus, as subordinated men attempt to bargain or comply with hegemonic masculinity, they do not cease to be subordinated by it. . . . Thus, Orientalist stereotypes that denigrate Korean masculinity might change as the gender order changes, but the underlying power processes that constitute hegemonic and subordinated masculinities very well may not.

On the other hand, it is possible that the dispersion of Western hegemonic masculinity through power relations of global capitalism and imperialism might dissipate its limited association with the geographic West. As elite men in non-Western regions join a global elite, we might see the rise of a transnational hegemonic masculinity that has its structural and cultural origins in Western hegemonic masculinity but that is no longer exclusively associated with Western elite men per se. These are questions for future research on the global implications of Western hegemonic masculinity.

Authors' Note

This research was supported by grants from the National Science Foundation (1015701) and the Korea Foundation (2012) awarded to the first author. The authors thank Joya Misra and Maxine Craig as well as the anonymous reviewers for their helpful comments. Correspondence concerning this article should be addressed to Allen J. Kim; e-mail: oneallenkim@gmail.com.

References

Adams, Michele, and Scott Coltrane. 2008. *Gender and families*, 2nd edition. Gender Lens Series. New York: Rowman & Littlefield.

Bartkowski, John. 2004. *The Promise Keepers: Servants, soldiers, and godly men*. New Brunswick, NJ: Rutgers University Press.

Bernard, Jessie. 1981. The good-provider role: Its rise and fall. *American Psychologist* 36:1–12.

Brickner, Bryan. 1999. *The Promise Keepers: Politics and promises*. Lanham, MD: Lexington Books.

Cancian, Francesca. 1987. *Love in America: Individualism and self-development*. Cambridge: Cambridge University Press.

Chapman, Gary. 1995. *The five languages of love.* Chicago: Northfield.

Charmaz, Kathy. 2000. Grounded theory: Objectivist and constructivist methods. In *Handbook of qualitative research*, 2nd edition, edited by Norman K. Denzin and Yvonna S. Lincoln, 509–35. Thousand Oaks, CA: Sage.

Chen, Anthony. 1999. Lives at the center of the periphery, lives at the periphery of the center: Chinese American masculinities and bargaining with hegemony. *Gender & Society* 13:584–607.

Choi, Sun Young, and Kyung-Sup Chang. 2012. The material contradictions of proletarian patriarchy under condensed capitalist industrialization: The instability in the working life courses of "male breadwinners" and its familial ramifications. *Korea Journal of Sociology* 46 (2): 203–30.

Connell, R. W. 1995. *Masculinities.* Cambridge, UK: Polity Press.

Connell, R. W. 2005. Change among the gatekeepers: Men, masculinities, and gender equality in the global arena. *Signs* 30:1801–25.

Connell, R. W., and James W. Messerschmidt. 2005. Hegemonic masculinity: Rethinking the concept. *Gender & Society* 19:829–59.

Connell, R. W., and Julian Wood. 2005. Globalization and business masculinities. *Men and Masculinities* 7 (4): 347–64.

Donovan, Brian. 1998. Political consequences of private authority: Promise Keepers and the transformation of hegemonic masculinity. *Theory and Society* 27:817–43.

Dreby, Joanna. 2006. Honor and virtue Mexican parenting in the transnational context. *Gender & Society* 20 (1): 32–59.

Father School. 2010a. *Duranno Father School marketing brochure.* Seoul: DFS Headquarter Office.

Father School. 2010b. *Father School advice manual.* Seoul: DFS Headquarter Office.

Father School. 2012. *Duranno Father School Marketing Brochure.* Seoul: DFS Headquarter Office.

Heath, Melanie. 2003. Soft-boiled masculinity: Renegotiating gender and racial ideologies in the Promise Keepers movement. *Gender & Society* 17 (3): 423–44.

Hondagneu-Sotelo Pierrette, and Michael A. Messner. 1994. Gender displays and men's power: The "new man" and the Mexican immigrant man. In *Theorizing Masculinities*, edited by Harry Brod and Michael Kaufman. Thousand Oaks, CA: Sage.

Y. H. Khang, J. W. Lynch, and G. A. Kaplan. 2005. Impact of economic crisis on cause-specific mortality in South Korea. *International Journal of Epidemiology* 34:1291–301.

Kim, Allen J. 2013. The changing nature of Korean American fatherhood. In *Koreans in America: History, Culture and Identity*, edited by Grace J. Yoo, 173–86. San Diego: Cognella Academic.

Kim, Allen J. 2014. Gender boot camp for Korean immigrant patriarchs: Father School and the new father conversion process. *Sociological Perspectives* 57 (3): 321–42.

Kim, Eunjung. 2008. Korean immigrant fathering: Dealing with two cultures. In *On new shores: Understanding immigrant fathers in North America*, edited by Susan S. Chuang and Robert P. Moreno, 175–96. Lanham, MD: Lexington Books.

Kim, Yu Gyung, Yang Hee Kim, and Sung Eun Lim. 2009. A study on changes of family crisis and social welfare policies in Korea with a focus on the family life cycle perspective after economic crisis. Research paper. Korea Institute for Health and Social Affairs. https://www.kihasa.re.kr/html/jsp/english/public/view.jsp?bid=30&ano=363.

Kimmel, Michael. 2003. Globalization and its mal(e) contents: The gendered moral and political economy of terrorism. *International Sociology* 18 (3): 603–20.

Kwon, Young In, and Kevin M. Roy. 2007. Changing social expectations for work and family involvement among Korean fathers. *Journal of Comparative Family Studies* 2:285–305.

Laporte, Nicole. 2011. The Korean dads' 12-step program. *New York Times Magazine*, May 6, p. MM22. http://www.nytimes.com/2011/05/08/magazine/mag-08Here-t.html?_r=0

Lu, A., and Y. J. Wong. 2013. Stressful experiences of masculinity among US-born and immigrant Asian American men. *Gender & Society* 27 (3): 345–71.

Mirandé, Alfredo, Juan M. Pitones, and Jesse Díaz. 2011. Quien Es El Mas Macho? A comparison of day laborers and Chicano men. *Men and Masculinities* 14 (3): 309–34.

Mohanty, Chandra Talpade. 1986. Under Western eyes: Feminist scholarship and colonial discourses. *Boundary* 2 12 (3): 333–58.

Montes, Veronica. 2013. The role of emotions in the construction of masculinity: Guatemala migrant men, transnational migration, and family relations. *Gender & Society* 27:469–90.

Oh, Dallan. 2009. 16% of Korean families geographically separated because of work and children's school locations. May 15, http://www.seoul.co.kr/news/newsView.php?id=20090515003007.

Pyke, Karen. 1996. Class-based masculinities: The interdependence of gender, class, and interpersonal power. *Gender & Society* 10:527–49.

Pyke, Karen. 2000. The normal American family as an interpretive structure of family life among grown children of Korean and Vietnamese immigrants. *Journal of Marriage and the Family* 62 (1): 240–55.

Pyke, Karen. 2010. An intersectional approach to resistance and complicity: The case of racialised desire among Asian American women. *Journal of Intercultural Studies* 31(1), 81–94.

Pyke, Karen, and Denise Johnson. 2003. Asian American women and racialized femininities: "Doing" gender across cultural worlds. *Gender & Society* 17:33–53.

Said, E. 1978. *Orientalism*. New York: Pantheon.

Schrock, Douglas, and Michael Schwalbe. 2009. Men, masculinity, and manhood acts. *Annual Review of Sociology* 35:277–95.

Son, So Young. 2013. A study of TV advertisements on the father role. *Korean Society of Basic Design & Art* 14 (3): 219–27.

Strauss, A., and J. Corbin. 1988. *Basics of qualitative research. Techniques and procedures for developing grounded theory*, 2nd edition. Thousand Oaks, CA: Sage.

Sung, J. (2014, March 30). Re: Look, ideal fatherhood in South Korea is in here: Korea reality show "The Return of Superman" [Web log]. http://tvcriticism2014.blogspot.kr/2014/03/look-ideal-fatherhood-in-south-korea-is.html.

Sung, S. 1998. Familism in the IMF period and gender identity crisis. *Journal of Korean Feminism* 18:75–91.

Yoon, L. 2010. South Korea's suicide problem. *Wall Street Journal*, July 21. http://online.wsj.com/article/SB1000142405274870468460457538221375237923 0.html.

Taga, Futoshi. 2005. East Asian masculinities. *Handbook of studies on men and masculinities*.

Thai, Hung Cam. 2008. *For better or for worse: Vietnamese international marriages in the new global economy*. New Brunswick, NJ: Rutgers University Press.

The Division of Child Care, Sexual Intimacy, and Relationship Quality in Couples

DANIEL L. CARLSON, SARAH HANSON, AND ANDREA FITZROY

Despite the fact that couples increasingly embrace egalitarian ideals for the division of labor (Cotter, Hermsen, and Vanneman 2014), achieving such arrangements remains difficult given persistent cultural conventions for separate gender spheres and inadequate family–workplace policies (Yavorsky, Kamp Dush, and Schoppe-Sullivan 2015). This has led many scholars to conclude that the revolution in gender equality has stalled (England 2010; Hochschild 1989). Indeed, despite steady increases in egalitarian attitudes over time in the United States, women's labor force participation rates, shares of household earnings, and shares of housework have changed little since the early 1990s (Bianchi et al. 2012).

Constructing equal partnerships can be challenging given the dearth of role models as well as numerous structural and cultural barriers to equality (Pedulla and Thébaud 2015). Research shows that sharing domestic labor and breadwinning responsibilities can be problematic for couples' happiness, stability, and sexual intimacy (Frisco and Williams 2003; Kornrich, Brines, and Leupp 2013; Rogers 2004; P. Schwartz 1995). Many of these findings, nonetheless, are based on data that are decades old. Moreover, research regarding the association between egalitarianism and couples' relationship quality has generally ignored the division of child care. Yet significant cultural and behavioral changes in parenting attitudes and practices (Bianchi et al. 2012; Dermott 2008; Hays 1999), and the centrality of the division of child care to gender inequality in the public and private spheres (Budig and England 2001; Hill 2005; Usdansky and Parker 2011), make examining the consequences of the division of child care in couples of paramount importance.

In this study, we use data from the 2006 Marital and Relationship Survey to examine how the division of child care responsibilities and decision making are associated with the quality of U.S. heterosexual couples' relationships, including their sexual frequency and the quality of their sex lives. Additionally, we examine the possible pathways through which the division of child care may affect couples' sexual intimacy, and ultimately their overall relationship quality.

The Stalled Revolution

From the 1960s to the 1990s, labor force participation among women, especially mothers with children, grew substantially in the United States. The percentage of working mothers of children under age 18 rose from approximately 28 to 68 percent (Cohany and Sok 2007). Concomitant with increases in paid labor, the percentage of married mothers who made more than their husbands increased from 3 to 17 percent (Wang, Parker, and Taylor 2013). As the division of paid labor shifted, the division of unpaid labor in the home shifted as well. Women's housework hours, on average, decreased from 30 per week in 1965 to 17.5 in 1995, while men's grew from five to 10 hours (Bianchi et al. 2012). Finally, in conjunction with these changes in behaviors, men's and women's valuation of gender equality grew over time. In 1977, 31 percent of male and 37 percent of female respondents to the General Social Survey disagreed with the statement that it is better for the man to work and the woman to tend to the home. By 1990, 57 percent of men and 60 percent of women disagreed.

Although attitudes have continued to liberalize since 1990—by 2012, the percentage disagreeing with the idea of separate spheres had increased further to 65 for men and 73 for women (Cotter, Hermsen, and Vanneman 2014)—the gendered division of labor has changed little. As of 2010, the percentage of mothers in the paid labor force had increased just 3 percent (U.S. Bureau of Labor Statistics 2014) and the percentage earning more than their husbands had grown by only 5 percent (Wang, Parker, and Taylor 2013). Moreover, men did the same amount of housework in 2010—10 hours per week—as in 1995 (Bianchi et al. 2012).

There are several forces responsible for this "stalled revolution" in gender equality (Hochschild 1989). First, couples continue to find themselves fighting against a pervasive culture of male privilege and essential gender differences in abilities and proclivities that push women away from paid work and men away from housework and caregiving (Komter 1989; Miller and Carlson 2015; Williams 2010). This cultural environment not only places women in the impossible position of being devalued for their femininity and demeaned for ignoring their role of homemaker and mother when employed (Hays 1999), but it also places pressure on men to keep their breadwinning responsibilities and eschew traditional feminine tasks in order to maintain their masculinity and avoid the perception of weakness (Williams 2010).

These cultural forces shape, and are shaped by, family and workplace policies that assume male breadwinning and female homemaking. Indeed, the absence or presence of supportive work–family policies shapes individual preferences for egalitarian arrangements (Pedulla and Thébaud 2015). Even if couples embrace egalitarian ideals and resist cultural pressures to embrace gendered roles at home, they often face institutional barriers to sharing (e.g., job inflexibility, no paid family leave, discrimination) (Capizzano, Adams, and Sonenstein 2000; Gault et al. 2014), which encourage women to leave the paid labor force and limits men's abilities to engage at home.

Perhaps no factor pushes couples toward a gendered labor arrangement like parenthood (Yavorsky, Kamp Dush, and Schoppe-Sullivan 2015). Unlike fathers, the time mothers spend with children is thought to be essential to their proper development (Hays 1999). Moreover, cultural shifts toward an ethos of intensive mothering have meant that women devote even more time to their children today than ever before (Bianchi et al. 2012). Cultural conceptions of fatherhood have also shifted, but as Dermott (2008) notes, this has not necessarily meant that mothering and fathering have become synonymous and interchangeable. Indeed, despite increases in fathers' time with children, men continue to rate mothering as more important to children than fathering.

Their actual or assumed responsibility for children means mothers face greater family–work conflict compared to fathers (Hill 2005; Usdansky and Parker 2011). With little structural support to manage competing demands, mothers, on average, decrease their time in paid work and increase their time in housework upon entering parenthood, while fathers, especially those who are unmarried, increase their time in paid work (Astone et al. 2010; Stone 2007). This has consequences, both in the short and long term, for mother's careers, not to mention gender inequality in intimate relationships (Budig and England 2001; Cha 2013). . . .

The Strains of Egalitarianism? Relationship Stability and Sexual Intimacy

Numerous studies using data from the 1980s and 1990s have intimated that egalitarianism has negative consequences for relationship quality and partners' well-being. Equal shares of paid labor and breadwinning responsibilities have been demonstrated to lower relationship quality, increase the probability of divorce, and undermine mental health, primarily through feelings of inequity or dissatisfaction regarding the division of labor (Frisco and Williams 2003; Rogers 2004; Stevens, Kiger, and Riley 2001). Such feelings of inequity and dissatisfaction are especially likely among working wives who retain responsibility for housework (Frisco and Williams 2003; Stevens, Kiger, and Riley 2001). . . . Although equal shares of housework have been found to increase feelings of fairness and relationship quality among couples (Frisco and Williams 2003; Lavee and Katz 2002; Stevens, Kiger, and Riley 2001), it has been found to undermine couples' sexual intimacy (Kornrich, Brines, and Leupp 2013; P. Schwartz 1995). . . .

The Division of Child Care and Couples' Relationship Quality

Although progress toward gender equality has stalled in many areas, one area where significant progress has been made is child care (Bianchi et al. 2012). In 1965, women spent 10.5 hours in child care per week, on average, compared to 2.6 for men. By 1995 women were performing 11.2 hours of child care per week and men 4.5 hours, and by 2010 women were doing 13.7 hours while men had further increased their contribution to 7.2 hours. Therefore, unlike other aspects of the division of labor, the gender gap in child care has continued to narrow. Whereas women used to do four times as much child care as men, today they do less than twice as much. Moreover, today couples do nearly twice as much child care as they did 50 years ago. The increase for women, however, has occurred most especially in developmental tasks (i.e., reading, playing games), while men do more of both developmental and instrumental tasks (i.e., feeding, bathing, etc.) (Sayer, forthcoming).

Of course, instrumental and developmental tasks are just two dimensions of child care. According to Craig (2006), child care, much like housework, can be divided into various kinds of tasks. Instrumental physical tasks fall into a dimension Craig labels *physical/emotional care*, which is face-to-face daily care such as feeding, bathing, dressing, putting children to sleep, carrying, holding, cuddling, hugging, and soothing. Craig titles developmental tasks *interactive child care*—those face-to-face activities such as helping children with homework, reading with them, and playing games. *Travel and communication* involves transporting children to school and lessons and discussing the child with others. Finally, *passive child care* involves supervising and monitoring children, maintaining a safe environment, and being there for the child to turn to. Like the various dimensions of housework, these activities are gendered. Mothers participate in all, spending the most time in physical/emotional care, while fathers spend their time equally in interactive and physical/emotional care. Because physical/emotional care is more routine, parenting is more intensive for mothers, while for fathers it is a shared, recreational experience (Craig and Mullan 2011). . . .

These arrangements, while good for children, may have costs for couples. Rotating shifts and working non-day shifts (i.e., second or third shift) are associated with higher levels of couple conflict, psychological distress, and less time together (Perry-Jenkins et al. 2007; Wight, Raley, and Bianchi 2008). Losing time with each other may be especially consequential to couples' relationships as time together is a primary predictor of sexual intimacy (Gager and Yabiku 2010; Kornrich, Brines, and Leupp 2013). And, subsequently, it also may affect overall relationship happiness and satisfaction, as sexually content spouses have happier and more stable relationships than those who are dissatisfied (for review, see Sprecher and Cate 2004). Despite reductions in time together, preliminary

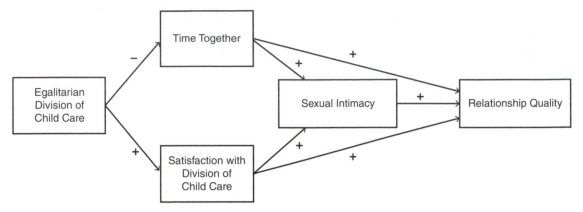

Figure 25.1 Conceptual path model of egalitarian division of child care, sexual intimacy, and relationship quality.

evidence suggests that equally sharing child care is a net positive for couples. British couples report higher levels of relationship quality when fathers are more involved in child care (Schober 2012), and father involvement in child care in nonmarried cohabiting U.S. couples lowers the likelihood of separation (McClain 2011). . . .

Figure 25.1 displays our conceptual model. As shown, we expect the division of child care to have competing consequences for couples' sexual intimacy and relationship quality. On one hand, we expect sharing child care to be associated with less time together and thus less sexual intimacy and lower relationship quality compared to having mothers retain child care responsibilities. On the other hand, we expect sharing child care to be more satisfying than having mothers do the majority of it, and thus have positive effects on sexual intimacy and relationship quality.

Fathers' participation in child care increases relationship quality, but perhaps only to a certain point. In couples where mothers work and the father cares solely for children, relationship quality has been found to decrease (Feldman 2000). This is consistent with Carlson et al. (2014), who found that couples with male homemakers are least satisfied with their division of labor, and have the least frequent and satisfying sex lives of couples. Although such arrangements are rare, the findings are consistent with a gender deviance perspective that

non-normative gender divisions of labor threaten men's masculinity and pose problems for intimate relationships (Tichenor 2005). . . . Examining whether such a pattern exists is important given increases in stay-at-home fathers in recent decades (Kramer, Kelly, and McCulloch 2013).

Method

For this study, we utilize data from the Marital and Relationship Survey, an Internet-based, nationally representative survey of U.S. adults conducted in 2006 by *Knowledge Networks* using probability sampling with random digit dialing (data is available upon request). *Knowledge Networks* provided household panelists with an Internet appliance, Internet access, Web TV, and a cash payment for completing surveys. Panelists then received unique log-in information for accessing surveys online and to ensure confidentiality. Respondents were sent emails three to four times a month inviting them to participate in research; they also were rotated in and out of the survey to ensure up-to-date nationally representative samples. In this way, the survey did not exclude members of disadvantaged backgrounds, who are the least likely to have access to the Internet (Fairlie 2004).

The Marital and Relationship Survey sample is an oversample of low to moderate income couples (income less than $50,000) and was restricted to couples with co-resident minor children and female partners under age 45. The survey was conducted in March and April of 2006. Both married and cohabiting respondents were sampled and information was collected independently from both partners. . . . Because we are interested in controlling for several couple-level variables, we limited our sample to those 487 couples where both partners completed the survey.

The primary outcomes considered in this study are couples' relationship quality and sexual intimacy. Details on variable measurement can be found in the Appendix. Two measures assess relationship quality: *relationship satisfaction*—a single-item measure ranging from 0 to 10; and *relationship conflict*—a three-item scale. Sexual intimacy is assessed with three measures of both the quantity and quality of couples' sex lives: *sexual frequency per month; satisfaction with sexual frequency*—an ordinal measure; and *quality of sexual relationship*—a four-item scale.

Analyses of sexual frequency are conducted using negative binomial regression, given the positively skewed distribution of the count of sexual encounters per month and the overdispersion of the distribution (i.e., variance is much greater than mean). Analyses of satisfaction with sexual frequency were conducted using ordered logistic regression, while analyses of relationship satisfaction, relationship conflict, and quality of sexual relationship were conducted using ordinary least squares (OLS) regression. All analyses used clustered standard errors to account for nonindependence of reports, since respondents are nested within couples.

Our primary independent variable is the division of child care. This measure taps three of the four dimensions of child care noted by Craig (2006)—passive child care (rule making), physical/ emotional child care (praising child), and interactive child care (playing with child, rule enforcement). Although we acknowledge that these items are not an exhaustive list of child care tasks, they were the only ones available. Each item indicated who was responsible for the task on a 5-point scale from 0 (female partner only) to 2 (shared equally) to 4 (male partner only). We summed these five items and averaged the total to create a summary measure, indicating the *Male partners' share of*

child care. To assess possible nonlinearity in the association of the division of child care with sexual intimacy and relationship quality, we created three dummy variables: *female partner does majority of child care* (male partner does approximately <40% and the score on his share of child care was less than 1.6); *child care shared equally* (male partner does approximately 40%–60% and the score for his share of child care was between 1.6 and 2.4); and *male partner does majority of child care* (male partner does approximately >60%, and his share of child care was equal to or greater than 2.4). Alternative specifications of the division of child care (e.g., 35/65 splits) produced identical results. Two variables are assessed as mediators—satisfaction with child care arrangement and couples' time alone together. *Satisfaction with child care* is a five-item summed scale, while *time spent alone together* is a Likert-type item ranging from 1 = never to 5 = almost every day.

A number of variables were employed as controls. These include dummy variables for respondents' *gender, race/ethnicity, union status, division of routine housework*, respondents' *education, child with disability in home*, and *religious affiliation*, as well as continuous measures for *his* and *her hours of housework per weekday*, respondent's *age, his* and *her hours spent in paid labor, number of children less than age 2 in household, number of children ages 2 to 5 in household, number of children ages 6 to 12 in household, age of youngest child in household, couples' total income*, and *female partner's share of couple's income*. Finally, we include ordinal measures for *self-rated health* (0 = poor health to 4 = excellent) and *religious attendance* (0 = never to 5 = more than once a week). We found missing values on more than 5% of cases for sexual frequency, male partners' share of child care, satisfaction with division of child care, age of youngest child, and couples' total income. We adjusted by imputing missing values for all variables using the "mi impute" procedure in Stata 12. In total, data were imputed 10 times.

Descriptive Statistics

Descriptive statistics for our sample are presented in Table 25.1. On average, both male and female partners were very satisfied in their relationships and reported little conflict. Men reported having sex on average 7.054 times a month and female partners reported 6.911 times a month. Both partners reported being satisfied with their sexual frequency. Men, however, were slightly less often satisfied with the amount of sex they were having than women. The mean for the quality of sexual relationship scale was 7.660 out of 12 for men and 7.658 out of 12 for women.

We found that the vast majority of couples shared child care tasks. Nonetheless, there were discrepancies in respondents' reports. Overall, women reported sharing the child care with their partner 73.4% of the time compared to 80.0% for men. Women reported that they did most of the child care 24.0% of time. Men reported that their female partners did the majority of child care 7.2%

of the time. Men reported they did the majority of child care 10% of the time compared to 13.3% for their female partners. We ran supplemental analyses and found no evidence that discrepancies in partners' reports were related to relationship quality, satisfaction with child care arrangements, and sexual intimacy. This gap in reports in the division of domestic labor is consistent with past findings (e.g., Lee and Waite 2005; Parker and Wang 2013). These discrepancies are attributable, in part, to the higher likelihood of women to report time spent on secondary activities than men. Moreover, while both men and women tend to inflate time spent in domestic activities, women are more likely to inflate their own time but not their male partners', while men inflate equally for both themselves and their partners (Lee and Waite 2005).

Table 25.1 Descriptive Statistics

	Men (n = 487)		Women (n = 487)	
	Mean/Proportion	**Standard Deviation**	**Mean/Proportion**	**Standard Deviation**
Individual measures				
Relationship quality measures				
Relationship satisfaction	8.435	1.707	8.194	1.952
Relationship conflict	1.700	0.737	1.709	0.774
Sexual intimacy measures				
Sexual frequency per month	7.054		6.911	7.071
Proportion satisfied with sexual frequency	0.619		0.671	
Quality of sexual relationship	7.660	2.777	7.658	2.921
Child care measures				
Male partner does majority of the child care	0.128		0.026	
Female partner does majority of the child care	0.072		0.240	
Child care shared equally	0.800		0.734	
Individual-level mediators				
Satisfaction with division of child care	3.392	0.449	3.221	0.613
How often spend time together alone	2.981	1.752	2.916	1.775
Individual-level controls				
Hours spent in paid labor per week	36.926	21.229	15.308	18.500

Protestant	0.370		0.395	
Catholic	0.183		0.205	
Other religion	0.217		0.236	
No religion	0.231		0.164	
Religious attendance[a]	4.089	1.900	3.809	1.970
Age	37.880	7.884	34.602	6.191
Self-reported health[b]	2.517	0.985	2.462	0.963
Number of children less than age 2 in household	0.107	0.316	0.107	0.316
Number of children age 2 to 5 in household	0.572	0.729	0.569	0.728
Number of children age 6 to 12 in household	0.860	0.946	0.860	0.946
Less than high school	0.096		0.092	
High school	0.349		0.324	
Some college	0.370		0.400	
Bachelor's degree or more	0.185		0.183	
He does most of the routine housework	0.063		0.045	
She does most of the routine housework	0.560	0.692		
Routine housework shared equally	0.377	0.263		
Hours of housework per weekday	2.206	3.171	3.818	3.386
Black	0.057		0.037	
Hispanic	0.080		0.074	
Other race/ethnicity	0.039		0.041	

Couple-level controls	Mean	Standard deviation
Currently cohabiting	0.108	
Cohabited prior to marriage	0.488	
Married directly	0.403	
Couples' total income	40,937.46	20,997.82
Her share of income	0.290	0.285
Age of youngest child	5.958	4.786

[a]Ranges from (0) never to (5) more than once a week.
[b]Ranges from (0) poor to (4) excellent.

The Association of the Division of Child Care with Sexual Intimacy and Relationship Quality

Table 25.2 shows results of analyses examining the association of the division of child care with couples' sexual intimacy and relationship quality. Panel 1 of Table 25.2 shows results from analysis of our summary measure of the male partner's share of child care. The male partner's share of child care is positively associated with relationship satisfaction (b = 0.624, p < .001), satisfaction with sexual frequency (b = 0.294, p < .10), and sexual relationship

Table 25.2 Negative Binomial, Ordered Logistic, and OLS Regression of Division of Child Care on Relationship Quality and Sexual Intimacy (N = 974)

	Relationship Satisfaction	Relationship Conflict	Sexual Frequency Per Month	Satisfaction with Sexual Frequency	Quality of Sexual Relationship	Satisfaction with Division of Child Care	Time Spent Alone Together
	b (SE)	b (SE)	b (SE)	b (SE)	b (SE)	b (SE)	b (SE)
Panel 1: Ordinal measure of child care							
Male partners' share of child care	0.621*** (0.157)	−0.291*** (0.064)	0.003 (0.076)	0.296† (0.168)	0.602** (0.186)	0.320*** (0.046)	0.086 (.118)
Intercept[a]	7.709*** (0.915)	2.755*** (0.490)	2.678** (0.932)	−0.989 (1.092)	6.569*** (1.502)	2.843*** (0.334)	3.854** (1.273)
Panel 2: Dummy variables for division of child care							
Division of child care (ref = shared equally)							
Female partner does majority of child care	−1.055*** (0.190)	0.460*** (0.083)	−0.128 (0.096)	−0.501** (0.194)	−1.088*** (0.271)	−0.419*** (0.061)	−0.178 (0.171)
Male partner does majority of child care	−0.225 (0.220)	0.034 (0.086)	−0.246† (0.133)	−0.215 (0.264)	−0.459 (0.367)	−0.028 (0.059)	0.014 (0.228)
Intercept[a]	9.133*** (0.812)	2.098*** (0.463)	2.749** (0.899)	−1.687† (1.019)	7.534*** (1.397)	3.565*** (0.326)	4.033*** (1.193)

[a]Intercept for satisfaction with sexual frequency is first cut point for ordered logistic regression (OLS).

***$p < .001$; **$p < .01$; *$p < .05$; †$p < .10$; all models include controls.

quality (b = 0.595, p < .001), while it is negatively associated with relationship conflict (b = −0.291; p < .001). We find no evidence using this measure of the division of child care that the male partner's share of child care is associated with reports of sexual frequency.

We hypothesized that linear measures of the division of child care may ignore important differences across child care arrangements. Therefore, we separate the division of child care into three categories in panel 2 of Table 25.2 and examine their association with couples' sexual intimacy and relationship quality. Results indicate significant differences, and in some cases the absence of difference, that are not apparent when a linear measure of the division of child care is used. As expected, results indicate that couples where the female partner is primarily responsible for child care have lower relationship quality, more couple conflict, less satisfaction with how often they have sex, and lower quality sexual relationships compared to couples who share child care equally. We find only one difference between egalitarian couples and couples where the male partner is largely responsible for child care. Couples with father-centered child care have sex marginally less often than egalitarian couples, though the difference is substantively small and amounts to only one-quarter of a sexual encounter per month between the two groups.

Mediators: Time Together and Satisfaction with Child Care Arrangement

. . . Results from Table 25.2 show that men's shares of child care are positively associated with satisfaction with the division of child care (b = 0.321, p < .001). However, in panel 2 we see that although couples where the female partner is largely responsible for housework are significantly less satisfied with the division of child care compared to those who share it equally (b = −0.421, p < .000), there is no difference between egalitarian couples and those where the male partner is largely

responsible for child care. We find no evidence that the division of child care is associated with couples' time together.

Table 25.3 shows results from analyses of satisfaction with the division of child care as a mediator of the association between couples' child care arrangements, sexual intimacy, and relationship quality. Results of formal Sobel–Goodman tests of mediation are also presented. We find that satisfaction with the division of child care mediates the effect of division of child care on satisfaction with sexual frequency and sexual relationship quality. Satisfaction with the division of child care is not associated with sexual frequency, and therefore does little to account for differences across child care arrangements in sexual frequency. When satisfaction with the division of child care is accounted for, the difference between female-centered arrangements and egalitarian arrangements in satisfaction with sexual frequency decreases 63.3% from −0.501 to −0.184 and to nonsignificance. The largest change across models is found in sexual relationship quality. When satisfaction with division of child care is accounted for, the difference between female-centered and egalitarian child care arrangements is reduced by 86.2% from −1.088 to −0.150 and to nonsignificance.

Results indicate that satisfaction with the division of child care is also a mediator of the association between the division of child care and couples' relationship quality. Accounting for satisfaction with the division of child care reduces differences in relationship satisfaction between egalitarian couples and couples where the female partner is responsible for child care by 70.1% and to marginal significance. Satisfaction with the division of child care is also an important mediator for relationship conflict. When included in the model, it accounts for more than half of the effect of the division of child care on relationship conflict. Our conceptual model indicated that sexual intimacy is likely an important factor linking satisfaction with child care to relationship quality. When measures of sexual intimacy are included

Table 25.3 Mediating Effect of Satisfaction with the Division of Child Care for Association of Division of Child Care with Sexual Intimacy and Relationship Quality

	Sexual Frequency Per Month		Satisfaction with Sexual Frequency		Quality of Sexual Relationship		Relationship Satisfaction			Relationship Conflict		
	Model 1	Model 2	Model 3	Model 4	Model 5	Model 6	Model 7	Model 8	Model 9	Model 10	Model 11	Model 12
	b (SE)	b (SE)	b (SE)	b (SE)	b (SE)	b (SE)	b (SE)	b (SE)	b (SE)	b (SE)	b (SE)	b (SE)
Division of child care (ref = shared equally)												
Female partner does majority of child care	-0.128 (0.076)	0.076 (0.095)	-0.501** (0.194)	-0.184 (0.198)	-1.088*** (0.271)	-0.150 (0.244)	-1.055*** (0.190)	-0.351† (0.181)	-0.313† (0.169)	0.460*** (0.083)	0.198** (0.072)	0.191** (0.072)
Male partner does majority of child care	-0.246† (0.133)	-0.231† (0.132)	-0.215 (0.264)	-0.181 (0.262)	-0.459 (0.367)	-0.364 (0.357)	-0.225 (0.220)	-0.177 (0.203)	-0.089 (0.188)	0.034 (0.086)	0.016 (0.079)	0.002 (0.076)
Satisfaction with division of child care		0.115 (0.102)		0.830*** (0.146)		2.227*** (0.180)		1.679*** (0.136)	1.152*** (0.133)		-0.625*** (0.054)	-0.471*** (0.058)
Sexual frequency									-0.002 (0.008)			0.011** (0.003)
Satisfaction with sexual frequency									0.020 (0.044)			-0.024 (0.021)
Quality of sexual relationship									0.233*** (0.026)			-0.067*** (0.012)
Intercept[a]	2.749** (0.889)	2.338 (0.980)	-1.687 (1.019)	1.192 (1.209)	7.534*** (1.397)	0.039 (1.525)	9.133*** (0.812)	3.145** (1.057)	3.143** (1.047)	2.098*** (0.463)	4.325*** (0.474)	4.202*** (0.442)
Sobel–Goodman test of mediation		-0.089 (0.091)		-0.348*** (0.059)		-1.330*** (0.153)		-1.003*** (0.105)	0.594*** (0.058)		0.376*** (0.042)	-0.163*** (0.023)

[a]Intercept for satisfaction with sexual frequency is first cut point for ordered logistic regression.

***p < .001; **p < .01; *p < .05; †p < .10; all models include controls.

in Table 25.3, we see that they in fact account for a fair proportion of the effect of child care satisfaction on relationship quality. These measures explain nearly one-third of the association of child care satisfaction with relationship satisfaction and one-quarter of its association with relationship conflict.

Since research has found gender differences in the consequences of the gendered division of labor for couples (e.g., Kornrich, Brines, and Leupp 2013), we conducted analyses of possible gender interactions (results not shown; available upon request). . . . Only one significant difference emerged. For men, being responsible for child care results in significantly lower reports of sexual relationship quality (b = −0.762, p < .05) compared to sharing it with their partners. For women, having a male partner who is largely responsible for child care results in reports of significantly higher sexual relationship quality compared to egalitarian arrangements (b = 2.117, p < .01). For women, the effect of the division of child care appears linear, with increases in men's share of child care resulting in an increasingly higher quality sex life. For men, sexual relationship quality appears lowest when they are primarily responsible for the children, and is highest when the responsibility is shared equally.

Conclusions

. . . We found that heterosexual couples are generally the worst off when female partners are primarily responsible for child care. Individuals who noted that the female partner does the majority of child care were least satisfied with their child care arrangement, the least satisfied with their sexual relationships, and subsequently had the lowest levels of relationship satisfaction and highest levels of relationship conflict. Although we expected that the division of child care may lower relationship quality and sexual intimacy by negatively affecting couples' time together, we found no evidence of this. Indeed, the amount of time couples spent together was unrelated to their division of child

care. Nonetheless, we did find strong support for our hypothesis that the effect of child care arrangements on sexual intimacy and relationship quality would be mediated by satisfaction with the division of child care. Satisfaction with one's child care arrangement accounted for more than 50% and as much as 86% of the variation in these relationships. This finding highlights the role of sentiment override in couples' relationships (Baxter and Western 1998) by indicating that subjective assessments of one's relationship are just as important as actual arrangements and behaviors to overall relationship quality. This of course should not mask the fact that satisfaction in all domains, on average, was most strongly related to egalitarian arrangements. . . .

Male-centered care arrangements resulted in the lowest sexual relationship quality for men, but the highest quality sex for women. This singular gender difference aside, the benefits of egalitarianism for relationship quality and sexual intimacy were similar for both men and women. This is a major finding that we think speaks to the state of hegemonic masculinity and the patriarchal dividend in the United States (Connell 1998). Because a patriarchal gender structure—which includes female responsibility for unpaid labor at home—benefits men, one might expect men with a vested interest in maintaining their privilege to be most satisfied with their arrangements and relationships when their female partners are responsible for unpaid care work. Yet, this is not the case. Rather, egalitarian arrangements are most common (at least along the child care dimensions we examined), and both men and women benefit maximally from an egalitarian division of child care. This pattern departs from past findings showing that egalitarianism posed problems for couples' relationships. Whether this apparent shift stems from increases in the costs of patriarchy or from the benefits of egalitarianism is unclear, although both may be at play. Nevertheless, sharing certain aspects of child care appears now to be acceptably masculine. As Connell (2014) notes, one of the costs of patriarchy is men's loss of time and intimacy with children, which men greatly value as central to fatherhood (Dermott 2008). Although intimacy with children is not necessary for, nor does it entail, an equal sharing of child care, sharing child care means closer relationships with one's children and also with one's partner. The interpersonal benefits of egalitarianism appear to outweigh any patriarchal privilege lost by sharing child care.

While these results suggest a gender shift, they do not indicate a complete transformation. First, although this study speaks to the consequences of sharing child care, it cannot speak to couples' abilities to achieve equality.... Indeed, parenthood itself pushes couples into conventional family roles (Yavorsky, Kamp Dush, and Schoppe-Sullivan 2015) due to unresponsive workplaces and other patriarchal practices. Second, while the benefits of men's child care performance increase arithmetically for women, full responsibility for child care has at least some negative consequences for men's sexual satisfaction. This is consistent with a gender deviance perspective, although, generally, egalitarian and male-centered child care produce similar outcomes. Nonetheless, this suggests that although men and women now embrace egalitarianism, men are not entirely comfortable reversing roles....

Although this study demonstrates that the majority of couples in the Marital and Relationship Survey share child care responsibilities with beneficial results, our measure of child care is not an exhaustive assessment of child care activities. Indeed, our measure accounts for only three dimensions of child care—physical/emotional, interactive, and passive—and does not account for travel and communication tasks or include numerous kinds of tasks within each dimension. Of significant importance are the nonexistent instrumental tasks in the Marital and Relationship Survey data. It is therefore unclear how the

inclusion of other dimensions and tasks may affect our findings. Indeed, our inability to assess physical care may explain why so many of the couples report sharing child care equally. Moreover, instrumental tasks are those most traditionally feminine. As such, performing these tasks may be more emasculating to men, and thus egalitarian arrangements of instrumental care may be less satisfying and more conflictual than sharing in other domains. Future work should include these missing dimensions and tasks if possible.

An additional limitation is that the Marital and Relationship Survey is a sample of straight, lower middle-class, mostly white American couples. A more diverse sample that more closely represents couples with children would help us understand the nuances of how the division of child care affects couples' relationships and sexual intimacy. Attention to possible differences across race, sexual orientation, and social class is recommended. We conducted supplemental interaction tests on potential differences by race and education but found no evidence that the effect of the division of child care varied along these lines. Nonetheless, sample limitations may affect these results.

Its limitations aside, this study is one of the first to consider how the division of child care in couples affects relationship quality and sexual intimacy. It adds to a growing body of research that challenges the costs of egalitarianism. Unlike the past, egalitarianism today is associated with better, more intimate relationships than gender traditional arrangements. Importantly, this aligns with the desires of the majority of Americans who strive for equality within their partnerships. Although couples still face unresponsive workplaces and unwilling political structures that have stalled the gender revolution, these results suggest that the promise of the revolution may be reignited in the twenty-first century.

Appendix

Variable	Question(s)	Measurement	Reliability; Range
Relationship satisfaction		Continuous	0–10
Relationship conflict	In the past year, how often has your partner: (a) yelled or screamed at you, (b) treated you like an inferior, and (c) blamed you for his/her problems?	(0) never–(3) a few times a week or more Mean Scale	Alpha = .83; 0–3
Sexual frequency per month		Continuous	0–124
Satisfaction with sexual frequency		(0) very dissatisfied–(4) very satisfied	0–4
Quality of sexual relationship	For each of the following statements, please tell us how much you agree or disagree: (a) I feel our sex life really adds a lot to our relationship; (b) We have problems in our relationship because one of us has become less interested in sex; and (c) I am satisfied with our sexual relationship	(0) strongly disagree, (1) disagree, (2) agree, and (3) strongly agree	Alpha = .78; 0–12
	(d) How often do you and your partner have arguments about sex?	(0) never–(3) a few times a week or more. Summed Scale	
Male partners' share of child care	Each parent may have different responsibilities for each child in the household. How do you and your [spouse/partner] divide up the child care and parenting responsibilities for this child? (a) Who is responsible for making rules for the child? (b) Who enforces the rules for this child or punishes child when rules are broken? (c) Who praises child for his/her accomplishments? (d) Who plays with the child, including sports and games?	(0) female partner only, (1) mostly female partner, (2) both equally, (3) mostly male partner, (4) male partner only Mean Scale	Alpha = .72; 0–4
Female partner does majority of child care		Male partners' share of child care <1.6 (approximately <40%) (0) no; (1) yes	
Child care shared equally		Male partners' share of child care ≥1.6 and ≤2.4 (approximately 40%–60%) (0) no; (1) yes	
Male partner does majority of child care		Male partners' share of child care >2.4 (approximately >60%) (0) no; (1) yes	
Satisfaction with child care	For each of the following statements, please tell us how much you agree or disagree: (a) My spouse/partner is the type of parent I want for my child(ren); (b) Having child(ren) has brought us closer together; (c) My spouse/partner is completely committed to being there for the child(ren); (d) The importance my spouse/partner places on the children bothers me (reverse coded). (e) How often do you and your partner have arguments about raising the children?	(0) strongly disagree–(3) strongly agree (0) never–(3) a few times a week or more.	Alpha =.74; 0–15
Time spent alone together		Summed Scale (1) almost never–(5) almost every day	1–5

Author's Note

The authors would like to thank Sharon Sassler for her helpful comments on early drafts of this manuscript. The Marital and Relationship Survey (MARS) was supported by the Initiative in Population Research at The Ohio State University (Daniel T. Lichter, PI). Correspondence concerning this article should be addressed to Daniel L. Carlson, Georgia State University, Atlanta, GA, USA; e-mail: dcarlson@gsu.edu.

References

Astone, Nan Marie, Jacinda K. Dariotis, Freya L. Sonenstein, Joseph H. Pleck, and Kathryn Hynes. 2010. Men's work efforts and the transition to fatherhood. *Journal of Family and Economic Issues* 31: 3–13.

Baxter, Janeen, and Mark Western. 1998. Satisfaction with housework: Examining the paradox. *Sociology* 32 (1): 101–20.

Bianchi, Suzanne M., Liana C. Sayer, Melissa A. Milkie, and John P. Robinson. 2012. Housework: Who did, does or will do it, and how much does it matter? *Social Forces* 91 (1): 55–63.

Budig, Michelle J., and Paula England. 2001. The wage penalty for motherhood. *American Sociological Review* 66 (2): 204–25.

Capizzano, Jeffrey, Gina Adams, and Freya Sonenstein. 2000. Child care arrangements for children under five: Variation across states. The Urban Institute Series B, no. B-7. http://www.urban.org/publications/309438.html (accessed March 15, 2000).

Carlson, Daniel L., Amanda J. Miller, Sharon Sassler, and Sarah Hanson. 2014. The gendered division of housework and couples' sexual relationships: A reexamination. Presented at the Annual Meeting of the American Sociological Association, San Francisco, CA.

Cha, YoungJoo. 2013. Overwork and the persistence of gender segregation in occupations. *Gender & Society* 27 (2): 158–84.

Cohany, Sharon R., and Emy Sok. 2007. Trends in labor force participation of married mothers of infants. *Monthly Labor Review* 130: 9–16.

Connell, R. W. 1998. Masculinities and globalization. *Men and Masculinities* 1 (1): 3–23.

Connell, R. W. 2014. Change among the gatekeepers: Men, masculinities, and gender equality in the global arena. *Signs* 40 (1): 1801–25.

Cotter, David, Joan M. Hermsen, and Reeve Vanneman. 2014. *Back on track? The stall and rebound in support for women's new roles in work and politics, 1977–2012.* Council on Contemporary Families Gender Rebound Symposium. https://contemporaryfamilies.org/category/publications/brief-reports/.

Craig, Lyn. 2006. Does father care mean fathers share? A comparison of how mothers and fathers in intact families spend time with children. *Gender & Society* 20 (2): 259–81.

Craig, Lyn, and Killian Mullan. 2011. How mothers and fathers share childcare: A cross-national time-use comparison. *American Sociological Review* 76 (6): 834–61.

Dermott, Esther. 2008. *Intimate fatherhood: A sociological analysis.* New York: Routledge.

England, Paula. 2010. The gender revolution: Uneven and stalled. *Gender & Society* 24 (2): 149–66.

Fairlie, Robert W. 2004. Race and the digital divide. *Contributions in Economic Analysis & Policy* 3 (1): 1–40.

Feldman, Ruth. 2000. Parents' convergence on sharing and marital satisfaction, father involvement, and parent–child relationship at the transition to parenthood. *Infant Mental Health Journal* 21 (3): 176–91.

Frisco, Michelle L., and Kristi Williams. 2003. Perceived housework equity, marital happiness, and divorce in dual-earner households. *Journal of Family Issues* 24 (1):51–73.

Gager, Constance T., and Scott T. Yabiku. 2010. Who has the time? The relationship between household labor time and sexual frequency. *Journal of Family Issues* 31 (2): 135–63.

Gault, Barbara, Heidi Hartmann, Ariane Hegewisch, Jessica Milli, and Lindsey Reichlin. 2014. *Paid parental leave in the United States: What the data tell us about access, usage, and economic health benefits.* Institute for Women's Policy Research, Washington, DC. http://www.iwpr.org/publications/pubs/paid-parental-leave-in-the-united-states-what-the-data-tell-us-about-access-usage-and-economic-and-health-benefits (accessed October 14, 2014).

Hays, Sharon. 1999. *The cultural contradictions of motherhood.* New Haven: Yale University Press.

Hill, E. Jeffrey. 2005. Work–family facilitation and conflict, working fathers and mothers, work–family stressors and support. *Journal of Family Issues* 26: 793–819.

Hochschild, Arlie, with Anne Machung. 1989. *The second shift: Working families and the revolution at home.* London: Penguin.

Komter, Aafke. 1989. Hidden power in marriage. *Gender & Society* 3(2): 187–216.

Kornrich, Sabino, Julie Brines, and Katrina Leupp. 2013. Egalitarianism, housework, and sexual frequency in marriage. *American Sociological Review* 78 (1): 26–50.

Kramer, Karen Z., Erin L. Kelly, and Jan B. McCulloch. 2013. Stay-at-home father's definition and characteristics based on 34 years of CPS data. *Journal of Family Issues.* doi:10.1177/0192513X13502479.

Lavee, Yoav, and Ruth Katz. 2002. Division of labor, perceived fairness, and marital quality: The effect of gender ideology. *Journal of Marriage and Family* 64: 27–39.

Lee, Yun-Suk, and Linda J. Waite. 2005. Husbands' and wives' time spent on housework: A comparison of measures. *Journal of Marriage and Family* 67: 328–336.

McClain, Lauren Rinelli. 2011. Better parents, more stable partners: Union transitions among cohabiting parents. *Journal of Marriage and Family* 73 (5): 889–901.

Miller, Amanda J., and Daniel L. Carlson. 2015. Great expectations? Working- and middle-class cohabitors' expected and actual divisions of housework. *Journal of Marriage and Family.* doi:10.1111/jomf.12276.

Parker, Kim, and Wendy Wang. 2013. *Modern parenthood: Roles of moms and dads converge as they balance work and family.* Washington, DC: Pew Research Center.

Pedulla, David S., and Sarah Thébaud. 2015. Can we finish the revolution? Gender, work–family ideals, and institutional constraint. *American Sociological Review* 80 (1): 116–39.

Perry-Jenkins, Maureen, Abbie E. Goldberg, Courtney P. Pierce, and Aline G. Sayer. 2007. Shift work, role overload, and the transition to parenthood. *Journal of Marriage and Family* 69: 123–38.

Rogers, Stacy J. 2004. Dollars, dependency, and divorce: Four perspectives on the role of wives' income. *Journal of Marriage and Family* 66 (1): 59–74.

Sayer, Liana C. Forthcoming. Trends in women's and men's time use, 1965–2012: Back to the future? In *Gender and couple relationships*, edited by Susan M. McHale, Valerie King, Jennifer Van Hook, and Alan Booth. Pennsylvania State University National Symposium on Family Issues (NSFI) book series. New York: Springer.

Schober, Pia S. 2012. Paternal child care and relationship quality: A longitudinal analysis of reciprocal associations. *Journal of Marriage and Family* 74 (2): 281–96.

Schwartz, Pepper. 1995. *Love between equals: How peer marriage really works.* New York: Simon & Schuster.

Sprecher, Susan, and Rodney M. Cate. 2004. Sexual satisfaction and sexual expression as predictors of relationship satisfaction and stability. In *The handbook of sexuality in close relationships*, edited by John H. Harvey, Amy Wenzel, and Susan Sprecher. Mahwah, NJ: Lawrence Erlbaum.

Stevens, Daphne, Gary Kiger, and Pamela J. Riley. 2001. Working hard and hardly working: Domestic labor and marital satisfaction among dual-earner couples. *Journal of Marriage and Family* 63 (2): 514–26.

Stone, Pamela. 2007. *Opting out? Why women really quit careers and head home.* Berkeley: University of California Press.

Tichenor, Veronica. 2005. Maintaining men's dominance: Negotiating identity and power when she earns more. *Sex Roles* 53: 191–205.

U.S. Bureau of Labor Statistics. 2014. Women in the labor force: A databook. *BLS Reports* (May 2014) Rep. No. 1049. Washington, DC.

Usdansky, Margaret L., and Wendy M. Parker. 2011. How money matters: College, motherhood, earnings, and wives' housework. *Journal of Family Issues* 32(11): 1449–73.

Wang, Wendy, Kim Parker, and Paul Taylor. 2013. *Breadwinner moms.* Pew Social & Demographic Trends. Washington, DC: Pew Research Center.

Wight, Vanessa R., Sara B. Raley, and Suzanne M. Bianchi. 2008. Time for children, one's spouse and oneself among parents who work nonstandard hours. *Social Forces* 87: 243–71.

Williams, Joan. 2010. *Reshaping the work–family debate: Why men and class matter.* Cambridge, MA: Harvard University Press.

Yavorsky, Jill E., Claire M. Kamp Dush, and Sarah J. Schoppe-Sullivan. 2015. The production of inequality: The gender division of labor across the transition to parenthood. *Journal of Marriage and Family* 77: 662–79.

Masculinity and the Stalled Revolution

How Gender Ideologies and Norms Shape Young Men's Responses to Work–Family Policies

SARAH THÉBAUD AND DAVID S. PEDULLA

In recent years, scholars have repeatedly documented that progress toward gender equality has stalled in both the workplace and the home. Women's labor force participation has leveled off (Bureau of Labor Statistics 2012), occupational integration has slowed (England 2010), the gender gap in wages has stagnated (Cha and Weeden 2014), and women still do the lion's share of housework and caregiving (Bianchi 2011). At the same time, men's pace of change has been sluggish. Men have demonstrated relatively low rates of entry into traditionally female-dominated occupations, modest increases in household work and child care, and more limited propensities to endorse progressive gender ideologies than their female counterparts (Bianchi 2011; Cotter, Hermsen, and Vanneman 2011; England 2010). One leading explanation for these trends is that work and family institutions remain based on outdated notions of workers and families, which impose constraints on an individual's ability to equally share earning and caregiving with a spouse or partner (Cha 2010; Gerson 2010; Stone 2007). For instance, in recent decades, employers have increasingly demanded longer and/or more unpredictable hours, an arrangement premised on an "ideal worker" who has few responsibilities outside of the workplace (Acker 1990; Williams 2001). At the same time, there has been an increasing cultural trend toward time-intensive parenting practices (Blair-Loy 2003; Hays 1998; Milkie et al. 2010), which limits one's ability to put in long hours at work or to be constantly available to an employer.

In light of these conflicting pressures, young American men and women often doubt that it will be feasible to share work and caregiving responsibilities equally with their future spouse, despite the fact that this egalitarian arrangement is what the majority of them now say they would ideally prefer (Gerson 2010; Pedulla and Thébaud 2015). For instance, in in-depth interviews, Gerson (2010) found that young, unmarried men cited the intense social and economic demands of workplaces for their time and energy as a reason for such doubts. Believing that an egalitarian relationship was out of reach, these young men gravitated toward a fallback plan that was neotraditional in nature—an arrangement where they would be the primary breadwinner and their spouse would be primarily (though not solely) responsible for housework and caregiving. . . .

However, several studies show that men's lack of responsiveness to supportive work–family policies is not simply rooted in material considerations, but also in the potential threat of these interventions to their personal beliefs, masculinity, and/or

Sarah Thébaud and David S. Pedulla, "Masculinity and the Stalled Revolution: How Gender Ideologies and Norms Shape Young Men's Responses to Work–Family Policies," *Gender & Society*, 30(4), August 2016, 590–617. Copyright 2016 by the authors, reprinted by permission of SAGE Publications.

social status. For instance, more men than women still endorse the prescriptive belief that women *ought* to be primarily responsible for caregiving (Cotter, Hermsen, and Vanneman 2011); thus, even when policies are in place that otherwise mitigate financial risks, men may be unlikely to change their behavior on ideological grounds and/or to view such policies as solving "women's problem" of balancing work and care (Duvander 2014; Padavic, Ely, and Reid 2013). Additionally, even if a man does not personally endorse a traditional gender ideology, he may still hold the descriptive belief that most other people, especially *other men*, prefer a more gender-traditional relationship and, by implication, would hold him accountable to that model. . . . Accordingly, studies find that men often face negative social stigma when they take advantage of leave policies or flexible work arrangements, and that such stigma is rooted in their violation of this normative vision of masculinity (Berdahl and Moon 2013; Rudman and Mescher 2013; Vandello et al. 2013). Thus, men's nominal response to work–family policies can be understood as a form of "doing gender" (West and Zimmerman 1987) that is geared toward maintaining an appropriately masculine social identity and status via the approval of other men (Kimmel 2008; Pascoe 2007). Taken together, the null effect of supportive work–family policy interventions on young men's relationship preferences is likely rooted not only in their relatively advantaged structural position in the workplace and in families but also in gender ideologies and norms. . . .

The goal of this study is to disentangle these processes in the U.S. context by employing a novel survey-experimental design. Specifically, we investigate the extent to which the causal effect of supportive work–family policies on young, unmarried men's preferred work–family arrangement is conditioned by their ideological and normative beliefs about gender. In particular, we focus on (1) men's personal endorsement of a gender-egalitarian ideology (i.e., their *prescriptive* beliefs about how most men and women *should* organize work and family responsibilities) and (2) men's perceptions of

normative masculinity as it pertains to work and family life (i.e., their *descriptive* beliefs about how most of their male peers *actually* prefer to organize their future work and family responsibilities). Our findings demonstrate that beliefs about what other men *actually* want, not beliefs about what they *should* want, shape men's responses to supportive work–family policies. Specifically, when supportive work–family policies are thought to be in place, men who believe that the majority of their male peers want gender-progressive relationships are significantly more likely to prefer a progressive relationship.

Work–Family Policies, Men's Behavior, and Men's Ideals

Scholars have long argued that work–family policies, when designed effectively, can help ameliorate the gendered structural constraints that characterize workplaces and families. By providing workers with the time and resources needed to simultaneously manage employment and caregiving responsibilities, policy interventions can make it more feasible for partners to pursue an egalitarian, "dual-earner, dual-caregiver" arrangement if that is what they prefer (Gornick and Meyers 2009). . . .

Notwithstanding these positive consequences of supportive policies, scholars note that the size of such effects is often modest, and the gender division of labor in countries even with the most progressive policies remains far from equal (Kotsadam and Finseraas 2011). One recent study also suggests that despite their increased propensity to take leave after the introduction of the "use it or lose it daddy month," Swedish men's propensity to use sick leave to care for children later on was unaffected by the introduction of the policy (Ekberg, Eriksson, and Friebel 2013). Thus, it is possible that progressive paternity leave policies mitigate men's fears of a career penalty in the short term, without fundamentally undermining the "ideal worker" norm that makes the adoption of a flexible work routine risky over the longer term. Furthermore, critics of supportive work–family policies have argued that they could unintentionally promote a traditional division of labor, given that women disproportionately take advantage of them (Bergmann 2009). . . .

One limitation of this literature, however, is that most studies have been based on a relatively small number of cases (e.g., comparing a few countries) with key variables measured at one point in time. In addition, they are often fraught with selection processes that prevent them from establishing causal effects. For instance, although men's takeup of parental leave is higher in countries like Sweden with policies aimed at alleviating material constraints on men, the men in these contexts are also more likely to express gender-progressive ideologies in the first place (Sjöberg 2004). . . . Therefore, the extent to which men's responses to supportive work–family policies are directly contingent upon key *cultural* forces, such as an individual's gender ideology or the masculinity norms to which he feels he is held accountable, remains an open question.

The Role of Men's Gender Ideologies and Masculinity Norms

Although men are, on average, less likely to endorse egalitarian gender ideologies than their female counterparts, when they do, they are more likely to take an active role in housework (Grunow and Baur 2014; Kroska 2004) and child care (Evertsson 2014). That is, men who hold the prescriptive belief that men *ought to* be primarily breadwinners and women *ought to* be primarily homemakers are, not surprisingly, less likely to share household and family responsibilities with their spouse. There is also evidence from Sweden that men who hold a progressive gender ideology are more likely to take advantage of parental leave than their more traditional counterparts (Duvander 2014). Thus, men's relatively modest responses to supportive work–family policies may be rooted in their tendency to be less likely to subscribe to an egalitarian gender ideology.

However, masculinity scholars have also demonstrated that regardless of their personal ideological beliefs about gender, men's preferences and behaviors (especially those of *young* men) can be best understood by their sense of social expectations and approval from other *men* (Connell 1995; Kimmel 2008; Pascoe 2007). . . . This is not surprising given that a strong commitment to work is a core dimension of masculine identity for both professional and nonprofessional men (Connell 1995; Cooper 2000; Williams 2010).

The expectations to which men may feel they are held accountable, as well as the culturally "masculine" aspects of identity and practice that they adopt, are also known to vary widely between social groups (e.g., class, race, sexual orientation), over time, and across cultural and institutional settings (Connell 1995; Kimmel 1996; Bridges and Pascoe 2014). Thus, the extent to which men believe that they will be stigmatized by other men for taking on substantial responsibility for housework and caregiving likely varies substantially across individuals. Yet, regardless of its social or demographic determinants, simply believing that such stigma exists has been shown to be powerful enough to prevent men from taking or wanting to take advantage of supportive policies, even when they report being just as dissatisfied with long and inflexible work hours as their female counterparts (Kelly et al. 2010; Munsch, Ridgeway, and Williams 2014). It is possible, however, that the relevance of such norms wanes as more and more men take leave. For instance, a recent study suggests that men in Norway are much more likely to take advantage of paternity leave if their male coworkers or brothers have taken it (Dahl, Løken, and Mogstad 2014). . . .

Empirical Predictions

Building on the aforementioned theoretical insights, we develop empirical predictions about how the relationship structure preferences of young, unmarried men without children will be affected by the presence of supportive work–family policies. We evaluate whether the effect of supportive work–family policies on young men's preferences for organizing their future work and family life are dependent upon (1) their gender ideology and (2) their perception of masculinity norms regarding work and family life. Gender ideology captures men's *prescriptive* beliefs about which division of labor is most appropriate or acceptable. In contrast, perceptions of masculinity norms capture men's *descriptive* beliefs about which division of labor other young men *actually* prefer. Specifically, this construct measures whether a man believes that the majority of his male peers ideally want to have progressive, dual-earner, dual-caregiver relationships, or whether they would prefer to structure their work and family life with a more traditional gender boundary between earning and housework and/or caregiving. Importantly, these two types of beliefs are analytically distinct, given that beliefs about what others want may not necessarily align with beliefs about what others *should* want.

Extant theory suggests that both men's gender ideologies and their perceptions of masculinity norms could play an important role in moderating the effect of supportive work–family policies on men's work–family preferences. . . . Therefore, we posit:

> *Hypothesis 1:* Supportive work–family policies will have a stronger and more positive effect on the odds of preferring an egalitarian or counternormative work–family arrangement among men who endorse progressive gender ideologies than among those who do not.

> . . .

> *Hypothesis 2:* Supportive work–family policies will have a stronger and more positive effect on the odds of preferring an egalitarian or counternormative work–family arrangement among men who believe that the majority of their male peers prefer progressive relationship structures than among those who do not.

Examining this set of issues with empirical data is challenging. First, it requires measuring men's preferences about how they would ideally like to structure their future work–family relationships while systematically exposing some, but not others, to supportive work–family policy conditions. Second, it requires measuring men's gender ideologies as well as men's perceptions of other men's relationship structure preferences. Whereas the second task can be easily executed with standard survey research methods, the first requires exogenous variation in exposure to work–family policies. Given that the selection into environments with supportive work–family policies is likely correlated with a set of other sociodemographic and attitudinal dispositions—including the type of relationship structure that an individual desires—we use a survey-experimental research design.

Methods

Our empirical analysis draws on novel survey-experimental data. The data collection process was conducted by a survey research company, Gfk (formerly "Knowledge Networks"), that maintains a national probability-based online panel of respondents that is representative of the U.S. population. The panel was built using random-digit dialing and address-based sampling methods. Households selected for the panel who need computers or access to the Internet are provided with those resources. Thus, the sample was *not* limited to computer and Internet users. Additionally, the Gfk panel is *not* an opt-in panel and, thus, does not suffer from the same concerns as opt-in panels about respondents being a highly selected group of individuals. Given that our hypotheses center on the future relationship structure preferences of young men, our analytic sample is limited to respondents between 18 and 32 years old. We also only included unmarried men without any children.[1] . . . This sample closely parallels the demographics of the individuals that Gerson (2010) interviewed in her study of young people's work–family ideals. Although our sample includes respondents of all sexual orientations, we do not have information about whether our respondents identify as gay, bisexual, or transgender (GBT). Importantly, though, the random assignment of respondents across experimental conditions prevents any systematic differences between GBT and non-GBT individuals from biasing our findings. . . .

The survey was fielded between August 3, 2012, and August 9, 2012.[2] The completion rate was 44.6 percent, which is generally consistent with Gfk surveys and significantly higher than nonprobability, opt-in, web-based panels (Knowledge Networks 2012). . . .

Experimental Design

Respondents were randomly assigned to one of two experimental conditions, summarized in Figure 26.1.[3] In the first condition (Condition 1: No Supportive Work–Family Policies), respondents were asked to report their relationship structure preference (i.e., how they would like to share work and household responsibilities with their future spouse or partner) and were provided with four options. The response options closely parallel the types of relationships that Gerson (2010) uncovered. The first option reflects a "self-reliant" preference.[4] Specifically, respondents indicate that they would prefer to maintain personal independence

and focus on a career, even if that would mean forgoing marriage or a lifelong partner. As Gerson (2010) notes, for men, maintaining self-reliance means absolving oneself from the responsibility of caring and/or providing for a family. The second and third options reflect neotraditional and counternormative arrangements by asking whether one would prefer to be *primarily* responsible for either (a) bread-winning or (b) managing the household (which may include housework and/or caregiving). In the "primary breadwinner" option (which would be considered a neotraditional arrangement for men), the respondent would be primarily responsible for financially supporting the family, whereas his spouse would be primarily responsible for managing the household. In the "primary homemaker/caregiver" option (which would be considered a counternormative arrangement), the respondent would be primarily responsible for managing the household, whereas his spouse would be primarily responsible for financially supporting the family. Importantly, these options do not preclude dual-earner arrangements. For instance, the "primary breadwinner" category

Condition #1:
No Supportive Work–Family Policies

We are interested in learning about the ways that people hope to structure their future work and family lives.

Which of the following options best describes how you would ideally structure your future work and family life?

1) Self-reliant
2) Primary breadwinner
3) Primary homemaker
4) Egalitarian

Condition #2:
Supportive Work–Family Policies

We are interested in learning about the ways that people hope to structure their future work and family lives.

Raising children, caring for ill family members, and/or taking care of household responsibilities involves a considerable amount of time and energy. In the United States, the cost of paying others to help with these responsibilities (such as child care) is also high. However, if policies were in place that guaranteed all employees access to subsidized child care, paid parental and family medical leave, and flexible scheduling (such as the ability to work from home one day per week), which of the following options best describes how you would ideally structure your future work and family life?

1) Self-reliant
2) Primary breadwinner
3) Primary homemaker
4) Egalitarian

Figure 26.1 Experimental design.

reflects a respondent's preferred level of responsibility for earning *relative* to his spouse. Thus, a respondent who selects the primary homemaker/caregiver option could also plan to work outside the home. The final response option was an egalitarian relationship structure in which paid employment, housework, and child care would be shared equally by both partners.

In the second experimental condition (Condition 2: Supportive Work–Family Policies), respondents were presented with the same question and response options as Condition 1 but also received information about supportive work–family policies in the framing of the question. Specifically, they were told to imagine that there were supportive policies in place that ease the challenges associated with work–family balance. Following Gornick and Meyers' (2009) earner-carer policy model, they were told to imagine that all workers had access to paid family leave, subsidized child care, and flexible work options (such as the opportunity to work from home one day per week). To ensure that our results are not confounded by the possible influence of attitudes toward government spending, or by heterogeneous prior or current exposure to employer-based policies, the prompt does not specify whether these policies are made available by governments or employers. Rather, the goal of Condition 2 is to provide a context in which respondents state what their future relationship preferences would be under conditions where they would have access to supportive work–family policies. . . .

Key Variables

The primary dependent variable in our analysis is built from the relationship structure preference selected by respondents (i.e., egalitarian, self-reliant, primary breadwinner, or primary homemaker). We are particularly interested in men's odds of preferring gender-progressive relationship structures. Thus, we code a respondent's relationship structure preference as progressive (equal to "1") if he selects the "egalitarian" or "primary homemaker" option and nonprogressive (equal to "0") if he selects the

"self-reliant" or "primary breadwinner" option, given that both of these arrangements allow a man to maintain a central focus on paid work while absolving him from substantially engaging in household work or caregiving.[5] The primary independent variable for our analysis is whether or not the respondent was randomly assigned to the "Supportive Work–Family Policies" condition.

Theoretically, we are interested in understanding how men's gender ideologies and their perceptions of masculinity norms moderate the effects of supportive work–family policies. To measure respondents' gender ideologies, we generated a scale from five standard survey items. On a five-point scale ranging from "strongly agree" to "strongly disagree," respondents were asked to respond to the following statements: (1) A man's job is to earn the money; a woman's job is to look after the home and family. (2) A job is alright, but what most women want is a home and children. (3) All in all, family life suffers when the wife has a full-time job. (4) A preschool child is likely to suffer if his or her mother works. (5) Being a housewife is just as fulfilling as working for pay ($\alpha = .81$). We then calculated respondents' mean value across the five items to generate a continuous gender ideology measure. Next, we dichotomized this measure, coding individuals above the mean as 1 and below the mean as 0. While our results are substantively very similar when utilizing the original gender ideology scale measure, the binary measure of gender ideology enables us to present a more straightforward comparison with our other moderating variable of interest—masculinity norms—and eases the presentation of results.

To measure perceptions of masculinity norms regarding relationship structures, we asked respondents: "In your opinion, which of the following options best describes the way that most men your age would ideally like to structure their future work and family life?" They could then select one of the four response choices that were available in the main experimental item: self-reliant, primary homemaker, primary breadwinner, or egalitarian. We generated a variable equal to 1 if the respondent indicated that he thought other men would want to have an egalitarian relationship or that other men would want to be primarily homemakers, and equal to 0 if the respondent indicated that he thought other men would want to be self-reliant or primary breadwinners. Thus, this variable is equal to 1 if the respondent believes that most other men actually want progressive rather than nonprogressive relationship structures.[6]

To ensure that our measures of gender ideology and perceived masculinity norms were empirically distinct, we examined the proportion of respondents with progressive gender ideologies in the two masculinity norms categories. The weighted proportions are nearly identical: 45.1 percent in the nonprogressive norms category and 45.3 percent in the progressive norms category.[7] Additionally, a chi-square test indicates that there is no evidence of an association between these two variables (p = 0.99).[8]

Control Variables

Since respondents are randomly assigned to one of the two experimental conditions, our research design enables us to estimate the direct effect of the "supportive policies" treatment without including control variables in our statistical models. However, men's gender ideologies and their perceptions of masculinity norms are not randomly assigned to respondents. Therefore, in our regression analyses, we adjust for a set of key covariates that might be both correlated with these moderating variables as well as respondents' relationship structure preferences. Specifically, we control for respondents' education level (at least some college or not), household income (logged), age (in years), political ideology (a seven-point scale), race/ethnicity, region (lives in the south or not), and employment status (working or not).

Manipulation Check

At the end of the survey, respondents were asked to recall whether or not they were told anything about supportive work–family policies.[9] While the majority of respondents accurately answered

the manipulation check, there were some respondents in each condition who did not. It is unclear how to interpret the findings for these respondents because if they did not notice the "supportive policies" prime, it could not have meaningfully affected their responses. Therefore, we follow the common practice among experimentalists of limiting our analysis to respondents who accurately recalled the manipulation. We discuss the robustness of the results to this analytic decision below. Our final analytic sample includes 104 respondents (47 respondents were in the "Supportive Policies" condition and 57 respondents were in the "No Supportive Policies" condition). Table 26.1 shows weighted descriptive statistics for the key characteristics of our sample.

Supportive Policies and Men's Relationship Ideals

We begin by presenting the proportion of respondents that selected a progressive relationship structure, broken down by experimental condition (i.e., no supportive workplace policies vs. supportive workplace policies), gender ideology, and perceptions of masculinity norms. Notably, the majority of respondents in each group express a preference for a progressive (egalitarian or primary homemaker) relationship structure. The top row in Table 26.2, for example, presents the proportion of men selecting a progressive relationship structure for the whole sample, by experimental condition. While the vast majority of respondents (more than 70 percent) chose a progressive relationship, on average men's relationship structure preferences do not appear to substantially differ depending on whether or not they are exposed to the supportive policy prime.

In the next two rows of Table 26.2, we separately examine the consequences of supportive policies among men with conservative and progressive gender ideologies. Not surprisingly, men with progressive gender ideologies appear to be more likely, on average, to select a progressive relationship structure than men with conservative gender ideologies. Although a slightly larger percentage

Table 26.1 Weighted Descriptive Statistics of Respondent Characteristics

	Mean/Proportion	Minimum	Maximum
Supportive work–family policies condition	0.40	0	1
Progressive gender ideology	0.42	0	1
Progressive masculinity norms	0.51	0	1
Proportion with some college	0.65	0	1
Household income (median)	$55,000	$2,500	$175,000
Proportion currently working	0.53	0	1
Age (years)	23.19	18	32
Race/ethnicity			
Proportion white, non-Hispanic	0.62	0	1
Proportion black, non-Hispanic	0.10	0	1
Proportion other, non-Hispanic	0.05	0	1
Proportion Hispanic	0.20	0	1
Proportion two or more races	0.03	0	1
Proportion southern resident	0.31	0	1
Political ideology (7 = extremely conservative)	3.65	1	7
Sample size		104	

Note: Weights used to produce descriptive statistics. Listwise deletion used to deal with missing data.

Table 26.2 Proportion of Respondents Selecting a Progressive Relationship Structure, by Supportive Policy Prime, Gender Ideology, and Masculinity Norms

	No Supportive Workplace Policies	Supportive Workplace Policies
Average effect of supportive policy prime	70.8%	73.6%
Gender ideology		
Conservative gender ideology	57.0%	67.8%
Progressive gender ideology	87.1%	84.3%
Masculinity norms		
Nonprogressive masculinity norms	78.6%	54.5%
Progressive masculinity norms	61.3%	87.1%

Note: Weights used to produce proportions.

of conservative men (67.8 percent) opt for a progressive relationship when they are exposed to the supportive policy prime compared to when they are not (57.0 percent), it does not appear as if the presence of supportive work–family policies has a systematically larger or smaller effect for men who endorse progressive versus conservative gender ideologies. In other words, men's gender ideologies

do not appear to influence their degree of receptivity to supportive work–family policies.

The bottom two rows of Table 26.2 present the relationship structure preferences for men with different perceptions of masculinity norms. Here, important differences emerge. Among male respondents who do *not* think that other men want gender-progressive relationships (e.g., those who perceive a more restrictive set of masculinity norms), supportive work–family policies seem to lower the chances of selecting a progressive relationship structure (78.6 percent vs. 54.5 percent). However, men who perceive that most other young men want progressive relationships respond quite differently to supportive policies. Among this subgroup, supportive work–family policies appear to increase the chances of selecting a progressive relationship structure (61.3 percent vs. 87.1 percent).[10]

Although the descriptive evidence in Table 26.2 provides some initial insights into the heterogeneity of men's responses to supportive work–family policies, it does not test for the statistical significance of the differences between these groups. In Table 26.3, we use logistic regression models to test for the statistical relationships of interest, controlling for race, age, education, income (logged), political views, region, and employment status. Model 1 examines the direct effect of supportive policies on men's progressive relationship structure preferences. Confirming the descriptive evidence from Table 26.2, there is no statistically significant average effect of supportive policies on men's relationship structure preferences. In Model 2, we test hypothesis 1 by including an interaction

between receiving the supportive work–family policies prime and having a progressive gender ideology. As expected, the "progressive gender ideology" coefficient is positive and marginally significant ($p < .10$), indicating that, among men who did not receive the supportive policy prime, men with progressive gender ideologies are somewhat more likely to select a progressive relationship structure. However, the interaction term between supportive policies and progressive ideology is *not* statistically significant. This finding indicates that the consequences of supportive work–family policies for men's relationship preferences do not vary systematically with men's gender ideologies. Thus, our data do not provide support for hypothesis 1. Next, in order to test hypothesis 2, model 3 includes an interaction between men's perceptions of masculinity norms and supportive work–family policies. The interaction term is positive and statistically significant, providing evidence that perceptions of masculinity norms moderate men's responses to supportive work–family policies. Hypothesis 2 is therefore supported by our data. Finally, in Model 4, we include both interaction terms and the aforementioned result holds: progressive masculinity norms, but not progressive gender

Table 26.3 Logistic Regression Models of the Effect of Supportive Work–Family Policies on Men's Preferences for a Progressive Relationship Structure

	No Interactions (1)	Gender Ideology Interaction (2)	Masculinity Norms Interaction (3)	Both Interactions (4)
Supportive work–family policies	0.103 (0.584)	0.620 (0.734)	−1.725 (1.103)	−1.082 (1.227)
Progressive gender ideology	–	1.522[†] (0.850)	–	1.446 (0.924)
Progressive masculinity norms	–	–	−0.956 (0.802)	−0.747 (0.859)
Supportive policies × progressive ideology	–	−1.243 (1.362)	–	−1.305 (1.511)
Supportive policies × progressive norms	–	–	3.480[*] (1.336)	3.281[*] (1.353)
n	104	104	104	104

Note: Log-odds presented. Standard errors in parentheses. All models control for respondent race, age, education, income (logged), political views, region, and employment status. Statistical significance (two-tailed tests): [†]$p < .10$; [*]$p < .05$.

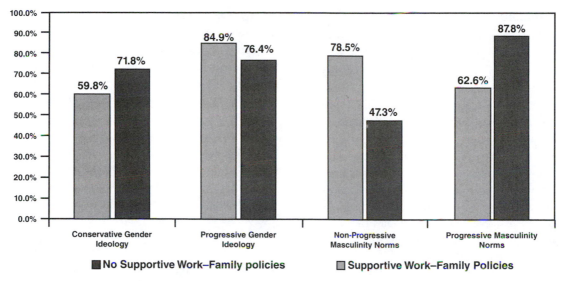

Figure 26.2 Predicted probabilities of men selecting a progressive relationship structure, by gender ideology, masculinity norms, and supportive policy prime.

Note: Predicted probabilities generated from Model 2 and Model 3 in Table 26.3. All covariates are held at their means.

ideologies, moderate the consequences of supportive work–family policies among men.

To ease interpretation of these results, Figure 26.2 presents predicted probabilities of selecting a progressive relationship structure, broken down by whether the respondent received the supportive work–family policy prime, the gender ideology of the respondent, and the respondent's perceptions of masculinity norms. The first four bars suggest that the gender ideology (conservative vs. progressive) of the respondent does not substantially influence the probability that a respondent will select a progressive relationship. In contrast, the four bars on the right side of the figure indicate that the effect of the supportive policy prime differs substantially depending on a young man's perceptions of masculinity norms. Whereas the presence of the policy prime decreases the probability of selecting a progressive relationship among men who perceive nonprogressive masculinity norms (78.5 percent vs. 47.3 percent), it increases the probability of doing so among men who perceive progressive masculinity norms (62.6 percent vs. 87.8 percent).[11]

In sum, our findings show that, on average, supportive work–family policies do not significantly affect men's work–family ideals. Additionally, while there is a generally positive association between holding a progressive gender ideology and a preference for progressive relationships (among those in the "no supportive policies" condition), having a progressive gender ideology does not make men any more or less likely to alter their ideal relationship preferences in response to work–family policy interventions. However, perceptions of normative masculinity do appear to condition men's responses to work–family policies: supportive policies have a strong, positive effect on men's propensity to prefer progressive relationships, but only if they believe that the majority of their male peers also prefer progressive relationships. Thus, our analysis points to norms of masculinity, and specifically, individual men's perceptions of those norms, as a key source of heterogeneity in men's responses to work–family policy interventions.

• • •

Conclusion

Among the many reasons that the movement toward gender equality has stalled in recent years is the resistance of men's attitudes and behaviors to interventions aimed at supporting dual-earning, dual-caregiving couples. While multiple factors likely undergird men's resistance in these areas, in this article we examine the role of ideological and normative forces in shaping how young men respond to supportive work–family policies. Specifically, we investigate whether men with progressive gender ideologies respond differently than men with conservative gender ideologies to supportive work–family policy interventions. Additionally, we examine whether differences in men's perceptions of masculinity norms as they pertain to work and family life interact with supportive work–family policies to determine their own ideal relationship structure. Consistent with previous research, we find that the majority of young men express a preference for gender-progressive relationship structures, but that, on average, there is no direct effect of supportive policies on these preferences. Additionally, there is no empirical evidence that the effect of supportive work–family policies on men's preferences is contingent on their gender ideology (hypothesis 1). However, in support of hypothesis 2, we find compelling evidence that men's perceptions of masculinity norms play an important role in shaping how they respond to work–family policies. Specifically, the supportive work–family policy prime significantly increases the likelihood of men stating a preference for a progressive relationship structure among those men who believe that the majority of their male peers prefer gender-progressive arrangements. This finding is consistent with previous work indicating that social stigma pertaining to normative masculinity plays a role in men's responses to policy interventions (e.g., Vandello et al. 2013). When men hold the descriptive belief that gender-egalitarian relationships are consonant with masculinity norms, they are more likely to recognize supportive policies as a mechanism that better enables them to contribute at home.

However, we also find that the policy prime moderately *decreases* the likelihood of preferring a progressive relationship among men who believe their male peers prefer less progressive relationship arrangements. This finding suggests that, for men in social circles that are focused on men's traditional role as workers and providers, supportive policies may have unintended consequences. For instance, it is possible that when men perceive gender-egalitarian relationships to be inconsistent with masculinity norms, they may not only fear social stigma for making significant contributions at home, but they actually may interpret work–family policies as mechanisms that better enable them to live up to neotraditional norms. These men may interpret such policies as reducing the need for them to contribute at home, given that supportive policies better enable women to be employed while also being primarily responsible for the housework and child care. We encourage future research to investigate this possibility.

Overall, our findings offer powerful evidence that masculinity norms play a role in shaping men's responsiveness to interventions aimed at gender equality. These results have important implications for gender scholarship as well as for policy interventions aimed at promoting gender equality. To begin, men's resistance, on average, to changing institutions and policies masks important heterogeneity among men. Men's responses to supportive work–family policies depend largely on their perceptions of what they believe their male peers want, and by extension, what kind of behavior they would hold them accountable to. This finding underscores the fundamentally relational, contextual, and multidimensional nature of masculinity and its role in determining men's preferences and behaviors. Our findings also point to the importance of perceptions of normative masculinity in shaping individuals' responses to work–family policies. First, policies that have the power to change norms are likely to have deeper, more fundamental consequences for gender equality than those that leave norms unchanged. This insight should encourage workplace organizations, states, and other social, political, and religious communities to consider their existing norms about gender as they design and implement various types of policies. It also resonates with evidence that "use it or lose it," and universal work–family policy interventions tend to be most effective in promoting men's takeup. Second, our findings provide evidence that ideological changes—such as changes in men's fundamental beliefs about how men and women *ought* to behave—may not be sufficient to increase men's receptivity to particular work–family policy interventions. Our data suggest that progressive gender ideologies are positively associated with desiring progressive relationships, but that they do not shift men's responses to work–family policy interventions. Rather, what appears necessary to increase the impact of supportive policies on men's work–family preferences is a change in what they believe most other men want—and by implication, a change in the gendered expectations to which they believe others will hold them accountable.

While providing important insights about masculinity, work, and family life, this study is not without limitations. Although the survey-experimental design enables us to exogenously manipulate respondents' exposure to different policy interventions, that exposure is hypothetical. The men in our sample do not actually live in two different policy regimes. Additionally, our study measures preferences, not behaviors. While useful in understanding how young men think about structuring their future work and family lives, we do not have evidence about whether preferences will affect behavior. Furthermore, it is likely that older men, as well as young married men and fathers, may express different types of ideal relationship structures, and as such, their ideals may be differentially affected by the presence of a supportive policy prime. Studying these different populations is therefore an important task for future research.

Notwithstanding these limitations, . . . our study identifies one key mechanism that currently contributes to persistent patterns of inequality in the workplace at home, but if leveraged strategically by policy makers, our identification of this mechanism could also help dismantle these patterns. Our findings also suggest that, if gender-egalitarian relationships continue to become a more normative ideal among men in the future—a distinct possibility given that young men today espouse more gender-egalitarian ideals than previous generations—supportive work–family policy interventions *do* hold promise for changing men's preferences and behaviors. . . .

Notes

1. Our survey was only administered to individuals who were "never married" or "living with a partner."
2. Data are publically available at www.tessexperiments.org and were collected as part of a larger survey experiment that included both men and women. Median completion time was three minutes.
3. Pilot testing on Amazon.com's Mechanical Turk indicated that respondents were able to understand and respond to the items in the survey experiment.
4. We did not use analytic terms—such as "self-reliant"—in the experimental prompt. . . .
5. Findings are consistent if the primary dependent variable is coded 1 only for respondents who selected an egalitarian relationship. We also estimated multinomial logistic regressions, which separate the relationship structure variable into three categories (combining egalitarian and primary homemaker). These models produce similar results. . . .
6. In the survey, respondents first provided their own relationship structure preference, then indicated what types of relationships they believe other men ideally want. The gender ideology items and manipulation check came at the end of the survey. It is possible that stating a personal preference first may shape responses to subsequent questions. Unfortunately, we are unable to empirically examine that issue with these data.

7. Unweighted proportions are 49.0 percent in the nonprogressive norms category and 51.0 percent in the progressive norms category.

8. There also is no relationship between masculinity norms and gender ideology when the full gender ideology scale is examined.

9. Respondents were unable to go back and change their answers in the survey, removing concerns that respondents may have altered the relationship structure preferences after being presented with the manipulation check.

10. Interestingly, when no supportive policies are primed, a smaller fraction of men who perceive progressive masculinity norms select a progressive relationship structure than men who perceive nonprogressive masculinity norms. However, subsequent analyses show that this difference is not statistically significant, and it therefore should not be interpreted as indicating meaningful variation in men's relationship structure preferences.

11. Supplementary analyses indicate that the supportive work–family policy prime has a positive and statistically significant effect on the odds of selecting a gender-progressive relationship structure among the subset men who perceive progressive masculinity norms ($p < .05$) and a negative and marginally significant effect on the odds of selecting a gender-progressive relationship structure among the subset of men who do not perceive progressive masculinity norms ($p = .06$).

Authors' Note

Both authors contributed equally to this article. We thank Joya Misra, Jo Reger, and four anonymous *Gender & Society* reviewers for helpful comments and suggestions. Support for this project was provided by Time-sharing Experiments for the Social Sciences, the Center for the Study of Social Organization at Princeton University, and NICHD. Correspondence concerning this article should be addressed to: Sarah Thébaud, Department of Sociology, University of California, Santa Barbara, CA 93106, USA; e-mail: sthebaud@soc.ucsb.edu and David S. Pedulla, Department of Sociology, University of Texas at Austin, 305 E. 23rd Street, A1700; Austin, TX 78712, USA; e-mail: dpedulla@utexas.edu.

References

Acker, Joan. 1990. Hierarchies, jobs and bodies: A theory of gendered organizations. *Gender & Society* 4 (2): 139–58.

Berdahl, Jennifer L., and Sue H. Moon. 2013. Workplace mistreatment of middle class workers based on sex, parenthood, and caregiving. *Journal of Social Issues* 69 (2): 341–66.

Bergmann, Barbara R. 2009. Long leaves, child wellbeing, and gender equality. In *Gender equality: Transforming family divisions of labor*, edited by Janet C. Gornick and Marcia Meyers. London: Verso.

Blair-Loy, Mary. 2003. *Competing devotions: Career and family among women executives*. Cambridge, MA: Harvard University Press.

Bianchi, Susan M. 2011. Family change and time allocation in American families. *Annals of the American Academy of Political and Social Science* 638 (1): 21–44.

Bridges, Tristan, and Cheri J. Pascoe. 2014. Hybrid masculinities: New directions in the sociology of men and masculinities. *Sociology Compass* 8 (3): 246–58.

Bureau of Labor Statistics. 2012. Labor force projections to 2020: A more slowly growing workforce. *Monthly Labor Review* 135:43–65.

Cha, Youngjoo. 2010. Reinforcing separate spheres: The effect of spousal overwork on the employment of men and women in dual-earner households. *American Sociological Review* 75 (2): 303–29.

Cha, Youngjoo, and Kim A. Weeden. 2014. Overwork and the slow convergence in the gender gap in wages. *American Sociological Review* 79 (3): 457–84.

Connell, R. 1995. *Masculinities*. Los Angeles: University of California Press.

Cooper, Marianne. 2000. Being the "go-to guy": Fatherhood, masculinity, and the organization of work in Silicon Valley. *Qualitative Sociology* 23 (4): 379–405.

Cotter, David A., Joan M. Hermsen, and Reeve Vanneman. 2011. The end of the gender revolution? Gender role attitudes from 1977 to 2008. *American Journal of Sociology* 117:259–89.

Dahl, Gordon B., Katrine V. Løken, and Magne Mogstad. 2014. Peer effects in program participation. *American Economic Review* 104 (7): 2049–74.

Duvander, Anne-Zofie. 2014. How long should parental leave be? Attitudes to gender equality, family, and work as determinants of women's and men's parental leave in Sweden. *Journal of Family Issues* 35 (7): 909–26.

Ekberg, John, Rickard Eriksson, and Guido Friebel. 2013. Parental leave—A policy evaluation of the Swedish "daddy month" reform. *Journal of Public Economics* 97:131–43.

England, Paula. 2010. The gender revolution: Uneven and stalled. *Gender & Society* 24 (2): 149–66.

Evertsson, Marie. 2014. Gender ideology and the sharing of housework and childcare in Sweden. *Journal of Family Issues* 35 (7): 927–49.

Gerson, Kathleen. 2010. *The unfinished revolution: How a new generation is reshaping family, work, and gender in America*. Oxford, UK: Oxford University Press.

Gornick, Janet C., and Marcia Meyers. 2009. Institutions that support gender equality in parenthood and employment. In *Gender equality: Transforming family divisions of labor*, edited by Janet C. Gornick and Marcia Meyers. London: Verso.

Grunow, Daniela, and Nina Baur. 2014. The association between norms and actions: The case of men's participation in housework. *Comparative Population Studies* 39 (3): 521–58.

Hays, Sharon. 1998. *The cultural contradictions of motherhood*. New Haven, CT: Yale University Press.

Kelly, Erin L., Samantha Ammons, Kelly Chermack, and Phyllis Moen. 2010. Gendered challenge, gendered response: Confronting the ideal worker norm within a white-collar organization. *Gender & Society* 24:281–303.

Kimmel, Michael. 1996. *Manhood in America: A cultural history*. New York: Free Press.

Kimmel, Michael. 2008. *Guyland: The perilous world where boys become men*. New York: HarperCollins.

Knowledge Networks. 2012. Knowledge panel design summary. http://www.knowledgenetworks.com/knpanel/docs/knowledgePanel(R)-design-summary-description.pdf (accessed March 29, 2013).

Kotsadam, Andreas, and Henning Finseraas. 2011. The state intervenes in the battle of the sexes: Causal effects of paternity leave. *Social Science Research* 40 (6): 1611–22.

Kroska, Amy. 2004. Divisions of domestic work: Revising and expanding the theoretical explanations. *Journal of Family Issues* 25 (7): 890–922.

Milkie, Melissa A., Sarah M. Kendig, Kei M. Nomaguchi, and Kathleen E. Denny. 2010. Time with children, children's well-being, and work–family balance among employed parents. *Journal of Marriage and Family* 72 (5): 1329–43.

Munsch, Christin, Cecilia Ridgeway, and Joan Williams. 2014. Pluralistic ignorance and the flexibility bias: Understanding and mitigating flextime and flex-place bias at work. *Work and Occupations* 41 (1): 40–62.

Padavic, Irene, Robin Ely, and Erin Reid. 2013. The work–family narrative as a social defense. In *Gender & work: Challenging conventional wisdom*. Research Symposium Proceedings. Boston, MA: Harvard Business School.

Pascoe, Cheri J. 2007. *Dude, you're a fag: Masculinity and sexuality in high school*. Berkeley: University of California Press.

Pedulla, David S., and Sarah Thébaud. 2015. Can we finish the revolution? Gender, work–family ideals, and institutional constraint. *American Sociological Review* 80 (1): 116–39.

Rudman, Laurie A., and Kris Mescher. 2013. Penalizing men who request a family leave: Is flexibility stigma a femininity stigma? *Journal of Social Issues* 69 (2): 322–40.

Sjöberg, Ola. 2004. The role of family policy institutions in explaining gender-role attitudes: A comparative multilevel analysis of thirteen industrialized countries. *Journal of European Social Policy* 14 (2): 107–23.

Stone, Pamela. 2007. *Opting out? Why women really quit careers and head home*. Berkeley: University of California Press.

Vandello, Joseph A., Vanessa E. Hettinger, Jennifer K. Bosson, and Jasmine Siddiqi. 2013. When equal isn't really equal: The masculine dilemma of seeking work flexibility. *Journal of Social Issues* 69 (2): 303–21.

West, Candace, and Don Zimmerman. 1987. Doing gender. *Gender & Society* 1:125–51.

Williams, Joan. 2001. *Unbending gender: Why family and work conflict and what to do about it*. Oxford, UK: Oxford University Press.

Williams, Joan. 2010. *Reshaping the work–family debate: Why men and class matter*. Cambridge, MA: Harvard University Press.

Masculinities in Religion

GOD IS A MAN! was the full-page headline of the *New York Post*, a local tabloid newspaper, on June 17, 1991. Apparently, during a Father's Day sermon, John Cardinal O'Connor, then the Archbishop of New York City, had excoriated radical feminists who had suggested the possibility of a more androgynous, all-embracing deity.

Well, is he—or she? All the monotheistic religions tend to think so: in Islam, Christianity, and Judaism, God is always depicted and understood as masculine (not necessarily so in other religious traditions).

And what does it mean? All over the globe, the twin trends are dramatic secularization—as scientific criteria dominate more and more of our understanding of life itself—and dramatic religious resurgence (except in Europe), as people return to the faiths of their forbears to explain the most basic questions of existence.

More than just the gender of God, masculinity is deeply implicated in all aspects of religion—from the gender of canonical texts to the gender of the people who are authorized to speak.

In this part, we present several different approaches to thinking about the relationship between masculinity and religion. Michael Kimmel uses his own experiences to explore the associations between Judaism, masculinity, and feminism. Zhera F. Kabasakal Arat and Abdullah Hasan look at the textual meanings of masculinities in the Qur'an, and Sarah Diefendorf reveals what male abstinence pledgers experience about the sexuality after they are married. Finally, Amy D. McDowell looks at the ways in which religion and masculinity intersect in the music scene, especially in Christian punk.

PART VII DISCUSSION QUESTIONS

1. In Diefendorf's article, Christian men lose their social support system of fellow men after marriage, coming to blame themselves or their wives for subsequent struggles with their sexuality. How does masculinity as an institution benefit from this shift?

2. How does McDowell's discussion of "aggressive and loving men" demonstrate the tension between structure and agency for Christian rockers who negotiate with competing concepts of manhood?

3. In Michael Kimmel's essay, how does the intersection of his gender and his religion explain his deep political motivation? What other cases of simultaneous advantage and disadvantage might have similar outcomes?

4. Typically, when we think of the effects of media and culture on men's lives, we think of modern sources like advertising and social media. How does Arat and Hasan's article complicate this approach? What are the intersections of religion, texts, and culture in Arat and Hasan's piece? How do they affect men's lives?

After the Wedding Night

Sexual Abstinence and Masculinities over the Life Course

SARAH DIEFENDORF

About three years ago I was 20 and she was 17. And she was convinced she was gonna get me in bed. But I told her—I was very blunt and I was a little angry too—I said I'm going to be very clear: I may be a lot of things, and I may be incredibly imperfect, but my virginity is very sacred and I will not get rid of it until I get married. . . . She didn't get that. Maybe because, you know, maybe she was sexually active at an early age, maybe that's what she thought love was.

Jason, 23

Jason has pledged sexual abstinence until marriage. Jason believes that sex is a gift from God, and, in line with the larger evangelical Christian culture of which he is a part, believes that such a gift is meant exclusively for the marriage bed. As a 23-year-old bachelor, however, Jason is transgressing normative understandings of gender that equate performances of masculinity with sexual activity. This study seeks to answer the following questions: Do young men who pledge sexual abstinence until marriage challenge normative definitions of masculinity in the United States? Second, once these men become sexually active, do their performances of masculinity change?

This article examines how young evangelical men like Jason understand and enact masculinity while maintaining strong commitments to sexual abstinence until marriage. Through interviews with men before and after marriage, the findings complicate relationships between masculinities and sexual purity by highlighting the ways that social structures and interactions shape individuals' understandings of sexuality and gender. Findings indicate that these men make sense of sex and sexuality through a shifting balance of both sacred and beastly discourses, calling into question static understandings of gender as an identity uninformed by age, relationship status, or life stage. I argue that we should account for life course transitions in our theories of masculinities (Carpenter and DeLamater 2012). Using a framework of hybrid masculinities (Bridges and Pascoe 2014), this longitudinal qualitative approach allows us to better understand both how and why seemingly transgressive, or varied, gendered practices do not always result in decreased inequalities.

Hybrid Masculinities and Heterosexuality

Masculinity is not composed of one set of behaviors, characteristics, or enactments, but rather a multitude of hierarchically organized gender projects (Connell 1987). Hegemonic masculinity rests at the top of this gender hierarchy and is best understood as the currently accepted strategy, or

Sarah Diefendorf, "After the Wedding Night: Sexual Abstinence and Masculinities over the Life Course," *Gender & Society*, 29(5) 647–669. Copyright 2015 by the authors, reprinted by permission of SAGE Publications.

conglomeration of practices, that works to both legitimate patriarchy and ensure hierarchies between men and women and among men (Messerschmidt 2012). Hegemonic masculinity is temporally specific, relational, and unattainable; it is a form of masculinity that no individual is able to fully embody (Connell 1990). Wilkins argues that this elusive component of hegemonic masculinity creates "gender dilemmas" for those who are working to create strategies and practices that both reinforce these hierarchies and are socially recognizable (Wilkins 2009).

A key feature of contemporary hegemonic masculinity is its heterosexuality (Connell 1987, 1992; Wilkins 2009). Heterosexuality is understood through a gendered language of desires and drives that are often "uncontrollable" and "relentless" among young men (Wilkins 2009). . . . Pascoe's ethnographic study of masculinity and sexuality in high school highlights the abundance of sexualized discourse present in interactions between young men, or what Pascoe (2007) calls "compulsive heterosexuality." Such innuendo and bravado are not indicative of sexual desire, nor just a way to be "one of the guys" (2007, 86). Rather, these interactions serve as a way in which young men symbolically display their power over women in an effort to reinforce their masculinity (Fine et al. 1997; Pascoe 2007; Renold 2007; Rich 1980; Thorne 1993). Not surprisingly, then, those who pledge sexual abstinence until marriage are more likely to be girls and young women (Bersamin et al. 2004). Sexual purity is congruent with cultural understandings of femininity in the United States, but is incongruent with culturally normative understandings and enactments of hegemonic masculinity.

More recent articulations of hegemonic masculinity (e.g., Connell 2005; Connell and Messerschmidt 2005; Messerschmidt 2012) conceptualize masculinities as influencing each other through micro-level processes, thus incorporating a variety of practices to create the most appropriate strategies for the reproduction of patriarchy (see also Demetriou 2001). As such, ideals of sexual abstinence and hegemonic masculinity need not be thought of as mutually exclusive. Rather, by acknowledging the agency of nonhegemonic masculinities in both their contributions to and contestations of hegemonic masculinity, we might ask how a pledge of sexual abstinence is just one of many strategies used to reinforce and benefit from hegemonic masculinity.

Hybrid masculinity is a theoretical extension of these recent articulations of hegemonic masculinity, focusing on the ways that (mostly) straight, young, white men selectively incorporate performances of masculinity that are historically, structurally, and culturally associated with nonhegemonic masculinities (Bridges 2014; Bridges and Pascoe 2014, 250). . . . Through methods of "strategic borrowing" and "discursive distancing," men create symbolic distance between themselves and hegemonic masculinity while simultaneously aligning themselves with it via more subtle means (Bridges 2014; Bridges and Pascoe 2014). Wilkins' interviews with men who have pledged abstinence until marriage serve as an example of this concept. Wilkins (2008) finds that in emphasizing that abstinence is a *choice*, men are able to maintain their authority and credibility as hegemonically masculine. In place of sexual activity, these men enact "collective processes of temptation," strategically emphasizing the difficulty in abstaining from sexual activity and thus reasserting themselves as highly sexual men. . . .

Evangelical Men

Work on evangelical men corroborates Wilkins's more general finding that transgressive practices do little to challenge boundaries and hierarchies. Evangelical men who engage in erotic cross-dressing and "pegging"[1] practices construct an understanding of gender that Burke (2014) calls *gender omniscience*, whereby men are able to justify nonnormative sexual practices through a discourse that places emphasis on God's all-knowing certainty in their heterosexuality and masculinity. In ex-gay therapies, the "healing" of homosexual men is done through a "doing" of hegemonically masculine behaviors and interactions (Robinson and Spivey 2007). Evangelical ex-gay ministries employ "queerish" strategies that ground gender essentialism in creation, and thus highlight the ability of gender to change, while also maintaining a commitment to heterosexual normativity through these strategies (Gerber 2008). . . .

Donovan argues that the Promise Keepers movement[2] might best illustrate what Schwalbe (1996) terms "loose essentialism," the idea that men can change through redefining feminine traits as masculine. Bridges and Pascoe (2014) posit that evangelical Christian men may be the "quintessential example" of this concept of "loose essentialism." Additionally, if we consider nonhegemonic traits along with those coded as "feminine"—in line with the framing of hybrid masculinity—we see how the practices of evangelical men occur in ways that often conceal gendered systems of power and inequality.

Sexuality and Masculinities over the Life Course

In framing masculinities as temporal, influential, and agentic, and as a result of myriad and changing practices and strategies in an effort to maintain legitimacy and power, we open the analytic possibility of looking at transformations in gendered identities over time. . . . Through interviews conducted both before and after marriage, my study seeks to analyze enactments of masculinity around the turning point of marriage. My analyses of the data captured lend insight to the ways in which the hybrid masculinity these young men employ shifts over life course transitions through varying processes of strategic borrowing and discursive distancing (Bridges and Pascoe 2014). . . .

Methods

The data from this study come from participant observation, focus groups, and individual semistructured, in-depth interviews with young men who attended The Message of Truth,[3] a nondenominational megachurch in the Southwest. The Message of Truth cycles about 14,000 individuals through its church doors for Sunday services, and 2,000

individuals every Friday night at The Gathering. The Gathering is a service directed toward "college students and twenty-somethings," and includes an hour of live music before a sermon on topics ranging from the meanings of Lent to the meanings of lust.

Because of the large constituency of The Message of Truth, special needs of the parish are met in small groups (Erzen 2006). These special interest groups focus on a variety of topics, from "Adult Worship Dance" to "Police Officer Law Enforcement Fellowship" to "The River"—a small group of men supporting each other in their decisions to remain abstinent until marriage. The River is dedicated to "applying biblical principles of love and respect into every portion of our lives as men of God."[4] The group meets once a week for pizza and conversation about "difficult and hard-hitting topics." . . .

In 2008, I conducted three focus groups with the men of The River, interviewed all fifteen members individually, and conducted participant observation at The Gathering services and the Sunday Worship services at The Message of Truth. Between 2008 and 2011, all but one of the members of The River got married. I conducted one focus group and follow-up interviews with all members of The River in 2011. The unit of analysis for this work is the individual men, although the shifting group dynamic of The River provides insight into the situational components of construction of gendered identities. I focus on interactions from the focus group in 2011 in the data on married life to highlight this shifting group dynamic. Internal Review Board (IRB) for human subjects approval was obtained in both 2008 and 2011, and in 2011 IRB approval included the potential to interview the wives of the 2008 respondents. The research presented here focuses on these 40 interviews and four focus groups.

Data were coded initially for general themes, which were then used to develop analytic categories that were used to recode the data, with a focus on sacred and beastly discourses (Glaser and Strauss 1967). Sacred discourses are defined as the understanding of sex and sexual practices as the gifts from God meant for the marriage bed; beastly discourses are defined as the understanding of sex and sexual practices that detract from the sacred, such as masturbation, lust, pornography, and extramarital affairs.... I use the term *discourse* in line with Farvid and Braun, who state, "Discourses about sex are the means by which people come to understand sexuality and to produce/experience their sexual behavior" (2006, 297).

I began each focus group with a question. During the first focus group, I asked the men present to describe when and how they took a pledge of sexual abstinence. Individuals took turns responding to my question in detail before delving into a larger group conversation. The men of The River would often engage in both debates and supportive dialogue in my presence about their views and understandings of sex and sexuality as sacred and beastly. My emerging analysis of the sacred and beastly discourses these men employed informed the questions I used at the beginning of each subsequent focus group, as I would often follow up on themes and questions from previous focus groups (Charmaz 2001). While I often asked questions of clarification during these conversations, the group was so used to these weekly debates that they would quickly engage in them after I asked initial questions. However, when I would ask clarifying questions, the men of The River were explaining their answers to me as a secular woman, which clearly differentiated the focus groups from their usual weekly meetings, and contributed to their length. Each focus group lasted between two and four hours....

Premarried Life: Controlling A Dangerous Sexuality

The young men of The River understand sex as both sacred and beastly. While sex *within* marriage is "sacred," sex *before* marriage is a "beast" that must be controlled. To control sex and sexuality, the men of The River rely on both small groups and "accountability partners" to maintain their pledges of abstinence. This bifurcated understanding of sex and sexuality dictates these men's understandings and enactments of their masculine selves both before and after marriage.

In individual interviews, both Derek and Jason stated that sex is a "beautiful gift." Kevin referred to sex as a "precious gift," and during our first focus group Derek added that such a gift is "meant for the marriage bed." To keep it there, sex is also something that requires boundaries. These same men who celebrate sex also acknowledge its darker sides. For Jason, sex is something that can cause "hurt, torments, guilt, and pain." During our first focus group, Aidan referred to sex as a "beast"—a temptation that can cause issues with salvation and morality if it is not controlled. Further, premarital sex is understood in gendered and biological terms. Derek stated, "Girls are responsible and courteous as far as what goes on with their bodies.... For guys it can be hard because of hormone levels."

These men lament the church dictate that sex is bad without telling them *why*. The River is a space in which participants can talk through and better understand these "beastly" threats to their pledges of abstinence. The importance of this small group echoes Donovan's (1998) work on the Promise Keepers movement, where the necessity of confessing sexual sins to fellow members is heavily stressed. Specifically, topics relating to pornography, masturbation, and lust were recurring themes in our conversations, and central to the ways in which these men understand their pledges of abstinence, sexuality, and gender.

Pornography, Masturbation, and Lust: Small Group Discussions

The members of The River believe that the use of pornography is prevalent within the Christian community. While these men attest that the problem is not growing as quickly within the church as in "secular society," many of them admit to struggles with pornography use. In the first focus group, respondents describe pornography as something "destructive" and "bad for individual or mutual use." Anything from "two clicks away" on a computer to a "JCPenney's catalog," pornography fits a wide-ranging definition and is thus a constant threat....

The men of The River understand masturbation and pornography to be heavily related. Pornography helps men, who Aidan calls "visual animals," with masturbation. For Aidan, masturbation before marriage is fine, with certain boundaries in place: "Simply pleasuring yourself without porn is fine, as long as you're not always relying on it or scheduling time around it." In our second focus group, the following interaction occurred:

CHASE: I personally disagree. . . .
AIDAN: Like I said, there are pastors who agree with me and pastors who disagree with me.
CHASE: See, that's the thing, even about stuff you disagree, you still have to talk about it.
AIDAN: I've gotten into almost full-blown shouting matches with people over it, and, you know, I don't think it's a salvation issue by any means, but it is a hot topic issue, and I think that is really why Christianity in general has avoided the topic, because there is no solid answer.

During individual interviews, Levi stated his belief that any form of masturbation before marriage is bad, and Chase discussed his worries that masturbation could substitute for sex with his (future and imagined) wife. As both marriage and the act of sex within marriage are sacred, anything that could hinder that act remains a sin that must be controlled.

For Jason, masturbation is heavily related to lust, a feeling these young men consider very dangerous. . . . Jason, however, believes that one can "masturbate not just because of lust—you can do it to deal with stress, to help you fall asleep—to give you that high just before you go to bed." Disputes play a central role in the small group. In discussing masturbation, lust, and pornography, sexually abstinent men work with others to define appropriate boundaries between the sacred and beastly to maintain their pledges. . . . Men of The River appear to challenge dominant understandings of masculinity and its relationship to sexuality by indicating that sex is something that requires premarital abstinence, constant negotiation, and control.

While these young men are not actively exploring sexual behaviors or interests, they are able to refrain in a way that does not disrupt their power over women. Tolman (2005) builds on Fine's (1988) conceptualization of "the missing discourse of desire" among teenage girls and argues that young women experience "dilemmas of desire." While the men of The River have their own dilemmas of desire, such dilemmas do not eliminate desire; rather, as beneficiaries of compulsive heterosexuality (Pascoe 2007), these men are able to tackle desire head on, and do so in ways that leave them in control of their future sexual desire. The discourse of sexual behavior and lust as a "beast" can be understood as a "discursive distancing" (Bridges and Pascoe 2014) that works to draw symbolic boundaries between these men and elements of hegemonic masculinity from which they seek distance. Simultaneously, the "sacred" discourse resituates them as beneficiaries of their future sexual lives. This hybrid masculine strategy engages with a "loose essentialism" (Schwalbe 1996) that does little to challenge long-term gendered power relations.

"Accountability Partners"

While the men of The River take part in nonnormative conversations about sexual activity, the ways in which these men control and monitor theirs and others' behaviors hint at much more "socially acceptable" masculinity practices. The River, as both a small group and a mechanism for maintaining control, sets the scene for the formation of an intricate network of "accountability partners." The second focus group collectively described accountability partners as close friends that "you can be completely honest with." Accountability partners hold an individual to his promise of abstinence until marriage. The members of The River have accountability partners for pornography, masturbation, and sexual activity with girlfriends or fiancées, and they were a common topic in focus groups and individual interviews.

Derek has one accountability partner for pornography use, and is also the accountability partner for another individual for excessive masturbation.

Eric has one accountability partner for masturbation, and serves as an accountability partner for a few men he has known since high school. Levi does not currently have an accountability partner, but relies on the small group for support. Aidan has two different accountability partners. One receives a report from Aidan's laptop every week with a list of every website Aidan has visited. If Aidan visits a pornographic website, his accountability partner will call him and talk through ways in which Aidan can avoid viewing pornography the following week. Aidan's girlfriend also receives a copy of the weekly report, but they are directly archived in her e-mail account, and Aidan believes that she does not look at the weekly reports. While this is described by Aidan as a symbolic act of trust, and understood by the second focus group in this way, this may also further indicate the views these young men hold toward women as less sexual beings. Aidan presumes his girlfriend would not have the desire to look as such reports, nor be tempted by their content. Aidan receives a text message every night at 9:00 from a second accountability partner with the simple question: "Are you behaving?" This text holds Aidan accountable for issues relating to masturbation and sexual activity with his girlfriend.

Accountability partners are not randomly chosen. Chase, a soft-spoken, determined 23-year-old, emphasizes that

> it's not the same as just confessing to your friends. One of the big things . . . is that when you confess, you should know who you confess to, because it has to be someone that you can trust, and two, they have to be spiritually stable and also because you can't just pick a random Joe and reveal to them, or your group of friends.

. . . During our third focus group Chase adds to the explanation of accountability partners: "One of the mistakes I made is I thought, well, I'll be accountable to my girlfriend. I'll tell her the things that I've done in the past, and that doesn't help. It needs to be someone you know and trust in the

same sex." Aidan interjects: "Yeah, it's a very dangerous thing, especially for couples who are dating or engaged, I would not ever ask my fiancée to be my sole accountability partner. It *has* to be somebody of the same sex as you are."

Accountability partners are a strategy through which these men can display and reinforce temptation. By insisting that accountability partners must be of the same sex, men hint at the possibility of "slipping" if they are talking openly about issues of sex and sexuality with their girlfriends/fiancées. In this sense, we can think of accountability partners and small group interactions as both the mechanisms for collective processes of temptation (Wilkins 2008) and the mechanisms through which these collective processes of temptation are encouraged and even heightened. Donovan argues that the act of confessing sexual temptation and sin produces possibilities for "new forms of heterosexuality" (1998, 832), and Kimmel's interviews with age-20-something men in *Guyland* leads him to suggest that "the actual experience of sex pales in comparison to the experience of talking about sex" (2008, 206). . . . In talking about sex as something that needs to be controlled, the men of The River discursively distance themselves from their less exalted and "secular" hegemonically masculine peers through a hybrid masculinity. These confessions, however, also enable these men to demonstrate a connection with hegemonic masculinity through claims of desire for future heterosexual practices.

While the maintenance of networks of accountability are time consuming and require commitment, Derek stated at the end of our individual interview, "It will all be worth it in the end." Through accountability partners and small group conversations about the beastly, these young men provide an example of masculinity best understood through the framework of hybrid masculinities. Before marriage, their understandings of masculinity are tied to somewhat "unmasculine" understandings of sex as something that needs to be controlled, while the mechanisms for enforcing control work to reinforce gendered hierarchies. Interviews after the "turning point" of marriage (Carpenter and DeLamater 2012) highlight why these amalgamations of practices do little to challenge existing inequalities associated with gender and sexuality when the tension between sacred and beastly discourses shifts.

Married Life: Embracing a Sacred Sexuality

In the late summer of 2011, I reconnected with the members of The River. We agreed to meet at Aidan's home. Just a few minutes into the fourth focus group, it was clear these men no longer communicated about issues related to sex and sexuality. After I asked them about The River, the following interaction occurred:

> PETER: I have no desire to ask my guy friends, "How's your sex life?" I just have no desire to ask that. And I feel like I would be . . . [pause] . . . overstepping my bounds if I did.
> AIDAN [snaps back]: Well, you would be.
> PETER: Because I want to respect their wives too, right?
> AIDAN: Yeah.

These men, who, four years prior, engaged in an open discourse about sex and sexuality, now find discussing it both inappropriate and awkward. There is a new, gendered component to these conversations, as men are now talking about themselves *and* their wives when discussing sex.

The Beastly Remains, Support Disappears

While sex postmarriage is presumed sacred, "wonderful," and a "gift from God," these married men still think of sex in beastly terms. In focusing solely on the goal of abstinence until marriage, conversations concerning healthy sexuality *within* marriage were never part of the discussion for these young men. Seth states,

> Before you get married, the biggest thing you struggle with, usually, is premarital sex, but once you are married, you can't be tempted by that anymore, so you get attacked by completely different things . . . like pornography or having sex outside

of marriage. And that was kind of striking to me. . . . Essentially, Satan has to find a new angle to attack on, and I was like, oh, hadn't really thought about that.

Like Seth, Chase admitted during an individual interview to worrying about the temptation to cheat on his wife. Aidan adds,

> It's a myth that I think is kind of perpetuated by the lack of communication, is that once you get married, suddenly all those desires are fulfilled in your spouse. It's not true. Guys are so visually driven. The desire for porn, especially if you struggled with that in the past, is still there. It doesn't go away once the ring slips on!

The beastly elements surrounding sex do not disappear with the transition to married life. Rather, they still exist, and still tempt, but these men no longer have support in the form of small groups or accountability partners to navigate these issues.

The church teaches men to keep struggles of sex and sexuality "in the light" of premarriage. Through membership in The River and the support of accountability partners, these men create space in which they can be open about their struggles. Peter reiterates, however, that the church teaches "once you are married, everything should be kept behind closed doors." Upon transition to marriage, it is assumed that couples become each other's support regardless of the issue at hand. The church's expectation that spouses should talk to each other instead of their community about issues of sexuality is not unusual. These men also face structural barriers to communication; because of a married man's presumed role as provider, small groups for married men (although not related to sexual issues) are scheduled as early as 5:00 A.M. to allow time for small group meetings, worship, and breakfast before the workday. Further, given that marriage is framed in such a sacred and positive light (see Luker 2006), married men are presumed to not need support groups to deal with issues of sexuality. This is, rather, the reward for which they have all been waiting.

A Gendered, "Sacred" Sexuality

When I first asked respondents if they were discussing their sex lives postmarriage, the following exchange occurred:

AIDAN: I guess, you know, you hear locker room talk, not that I find myself in many locker rooms, but I can't think of really any opportunity that I would have with my quote–unquote guy friends, to have those conversations, and frankly, it is none of their business, and I don't want to know about theirs either. And most of the friends that we run with are other couples, so unless all of us are sitting around sipping coffee, talking about sex—

SETH: That would be *so* awkward!

AIDAN: I don't think it would happen, maybe only in a situation like this [referring to the interview].

PETER: It's definitely not a social lubricator.

AIDAN: No, no, it's not something you just casually talk about.

SETH: At least in our circles.

AIDAN: Maybe a swinger circle! [Everyone laughs.]

Because these men understand sex to be a gift for the marriage bed, it is unthinkable to discuss sexual activity anywhere outside of their married relationships. Positive conversations around sex do not occur, and these men assume that conversations regarding sexual practices would occur only in what they think of as promiscuous, risqué, secular scenarios (such as a swinger party). A joking reference to a swinger party also allows these men to discursively distance themselves from what is assumed to be a salacious form of sexuality that does not align with the sacred aspects of sexuality they are now supposed to enjoy.

Both the awkwardness and inappropriate nature of these potential conversations is framed in relation to their wives. Their collective performances of temptation (Wilkins 2008) have changed to individual proclamations of protection for their wives. For example, when talking, very vaguely, in the fourth focus group about their current struggles

with sex, Peter says, with a sigh, "Certainly there wouldn't be any groups where couples sit down and talk about it."

SETH: Never, ever.

PETER: Because if you're struggling with something you wouldn't even tell your spouse.

AIDAN: Yeah, it's a gender thing for one, but you know, it's not only a gender thing, but now you're . . . it's hard enough to open up in front of the guys, "I'm struggling with porn," but now you've got their spouses' judging eyes staring back at you and you can hear their thoughts, it's like they're screaming, "You dirty creep!"

SARAH: But the guys wouldn't scream that—it is just women?

AIDAN: Yeah, at least from men's perspective, that is what I would be most fearful of, if I sat down in a mixed group, and had to admit to something like that, I would fear judgment from the women more than I would fear judgment from the men.

SARAH: Why's that?

AIDAN [pause]: I think in the Christian world . . . from the men's perspective, the women are so *vehemently* anti-pornography, um, that you know, instantly, this judgment would be cast against you, so I think it would be the fear of judgment in a group setting more than anything else. And, you know, the social embarrassment too, because now you've opened up to both people.

SETH: Absolutely. And I mean anything you admit to, you are saying, "My wife isn't enough to entertain me visually or sexually."

AIDAN: So you are actually admitting to several failings.

These discussions are no longer appropriate because of the ways these married men assert their masculinity. . . . If these men are not satisfied with their sexual lives, as evident through a continued tension between the sacred and beastly, these men are admitting not only to sexual transgressions, but to failures in their goals as hegemonically masculine, Christian men.

Control of Sexuality: Wives as Accountability Partners, and Practices That Endure

The men of The River frequently referred to their wives as their new accountability partners. However, these men espouse a very different definition of accountability partners postmarriage, as they are no longer an outlet for confession and discussion to mitigate tension between sacred and beastly discourses of sexuality. Instead, postmarriage, accountability partners provide a threatening reminder of understandings of proper forms of masculinity and femininity.

For example, Seth says,

> I never want to have to tell Angela something. So it's like, okay, I should not be doing this, and if I'm in a situation where it's like, okay, I need to walk away from this. There is a part of me that's like, I *want* to do this, because I am selfish, but it's like, no, it's not worth having her cry and ask me why.

Peter told me,

> Fortunately, I think having a wife acts as its own accountability. Not . . . because you're going to openly talk about the things you struggle with—hypothetically, if I look at porn and then tell my wife, she would be *devastated*. I mean, that would *wreck* her. I mean completely. She would feel so much abandonment, and she would feel so empty inside, and I don't think . . . I mean, it's one thing to sin against God, but to sin against someone you love so much, and to see the consequences in such a tangible way, I think that would drive her to depression, you know.

If these men are not able to uphold their duties as righteous men, why should their wives, who are presumed to abhor any and all sexual transgressions, turn to them as their leader? This is what Jackson meant when he described the importance, as a new husband, of his "masculine, God-fearing attitude" at the conclusion of his interview.

I had only one interaction with Aidan's wife, Rebecca, during my multiple trips to their home. She had agreed to a couple's interview. When I arrived,

Rebecca was in the kitchen, the first time she had come downstairs during my visits. While I was hopeful that her physical presence meant a chance to talk, during the two-hour discussion she sat next to us with earphones on, typing on her laptop. Although I tried to bring her into the conversation, she refused to talk, and I didn't push it. When I asked Aidan if he thought his wife, and women in the church, spoke of issues of sex and sexuality, he responded,

> I would be kind of shocked if they were. Um, I think that it stems from the culture that the church has created. Even amongst themselves—and I could be wrong, I could be totally blown away by this—but I think the answer is no, they don't. Unless there is a *huge* problem, and then I think there is a conversation that happens.

Jason provides a similar summary when asked if he thinks his wife discusses sex and sexuality with her friends: "Our sex life is off-limits and she knows this."

Later that evening, I received an email message from Aidan:

> My wife wants me to correct something I said. She said that women, both secular and Christian, discuss sex "all the time . . . in fact its [sic] something that is discussed more than any other topic." I stand corrected. She also noted that Christian women tend to discuss only with their trusted peers or leaders, never in mixed company.

Aidan's words reflect a particular understanding of women's sexuality that complements respondents' overall understandings of men's sexuality. If Aidan thinks of Christian women as "prudish" (as he described in an individual interview), he assumes they are not talking about sex. During our interview, Rebecca sat next to him while he spoke at length about the reasons Christian women do not talk about sex, and did not correct him once. Rather, she "kept it in the dark," upholding the rules of a married couple within the church, and waited until I left to correct him. Rebecca's actions are compliant and accommodating to the transition her husband has made. She is enacting what Connell refers to as "emphasized femininity" (Connell 1987). Rebecca's actions legitimate Aidan's hegemonically masculine identity postmarriage through a ritual demonstration of her own subordinate position. Although the gendered views of sexuality held by the men of The River transform accountability partners postmarriage, it appears that their wives may also play an active role in dissuading beastly discourses in married life.

When I asked participants about conversations of sexuality, it was assumed that I was talking about the beastly elements of sexuality. While the church promises sex as a wonderful gift within the marriage bed, there is little indication as to what this "wonderful gift" is supposed to entail. In an individual interview, Seth stated,

> There is no example being set once you're married. ... You have to figure it out yourself and there is no example to look at and say ... here is how to do it that way, to go in and talk to your wife about something that we do hold in such high regard, and value that aspect of a marriage. Because I've honestly never heard anybody talk about it like that. It's like, how do you talk about it like that when nobody has set that example?

These men are left alone to navigate sexuality in married life. Instead of engaging in conversations with their partners or perusing self-help literature,[5] they fall back on the model they know: temptation and accountability. However, there are no longer outlets in place for this temptation. During individual interviews, Michael states,

> I certainly haven't sat down with her after premarital counseling, after the first few months, to say hey, and ask all the questions from pre-marital counseling: "Hey, are we having enough sex? Do you like the sex we have?," etc., etc. I mean, I would just think, yeah, it's fine.

Aidan stated that if he and his wife were going to talk about sex, it would be a very serious conversation: "It's not like I can casually come home and say, 'Hey, I just thought about this today.'" Peter adds,

"You have to be really intentional about it [conversations about sex] because conversations don't just occur about sex. ... For me to come home from work and say, 'Hey, did you like it last time?' I mean, that would be ... that would be such a weird question for me to ask."

When sex is understood as sacred, it is difficult to approach it casually. This is not due to a lack of desire for more casual conversations about sex. Many of the men called for church leadership to begin conversations about sexuality in marriage. Six of the former members of The River reported that they had checked out small groups at another local evangelical church in search of support groups for married men. Yet, these same men also said that when it comes down to it, one should not need to talk about sex with one's wife "as a strong man," because, as Peter says, "It is a confidence issue. I like to believe things are going great ... no news is good news." As a member of the IT workforce, Aidan uses a computer analogy to demonstrate this same idea: "I've never heard, 'Hey, my computer is working today!' If I heard that I might die."

Through interviews with men before and after marriage, we see that such situational constructions and understandings of gender identity shift, while aspects of collective processes of temptation (Wilkins 2008) seem to endure. These men, in heterosexual, married, sexually active relationships, attempt to focus on a sacred discourse of sexuality in married life. However, the ways in which their masculine identities were negotiated before marriage appear to linger in ways that may be destabilizing. As Aidan laments, the beastly does not disappear "once the ring slips on"; issues of sex and sexuality are constantly negotiated, albeit now with less room and little support. The River, as a support group, was not narrowly about abstinence, but rather a place where men developed a way of orienting to sex that complicated desire on a variety of fronts that included pornography, masturbation, and lust. These conversations suggest an evangelical system of orienting one's body, desires, and family through a cultivated sense of managed, unmanaged, and gendered temptations that have theoretical implications for our understandings of masculinities.

Conclusion

The Message of Truth, as a religious institution, and academics who study the abstinence movement, have paid little attention to the many conversations that surround a pledge of sexual abstinence, perhaps because such facets of an abstinence pledge, such as the management of temptations of pornography, masturbation, and lust, do not threaten to undermine men's claims to hegemonic masculinity. Yet, these facets of evangelical sexuality and the ways in which those who pledge abstinence until marriage transition to married life have implications. When the church sanctions pre- and postmarriage interactions, and removes support for small groups like The River, men struggle in isolation with how to best manage their desires. Men are encouraged to have space to talk about sex and sexuality premarriage, but these conversations (and the religious institution in which they are generated) leave them with an understanding of sex as an urge that needs to be controlled, and masculinity as being dependent on their wives as simultaneously protected, nonsexual beings *and* their sexual partners. These wives have a fairly impossible and contradictory role, with seemingly few resources to navigate such responsibilities. This highly gendered, highly contextualized understanding of sexuality as beastly, wonderful, promised, and unfulfilled requires years of premarriage conversation, and although not offered, seems to require the same after marriage. While the tensions between both sacred and beastly discourses require a constant and open dialogue about sex before marriage, the inability to balance the tension between these discourses in married life leave these men unprepared for the sexual lives for which they have spent so much time preparing. . . .

Second, these findings suggest that existing models that imply a relatively static or episodic model of gender identity are lacking. Before marriage, respondents articulate and understand their masculine identities through sacred and beastly discourses of temptation, showing the potential for both transgression and reinforcement of hegemonic understandings of masculinity. After marriage, respondents understand and assert their masculine identities in relation to their wives in ways that indicate less discursive distancing from hegemonic masculinity. This longitudinal study allows us to see that, while behaviors and decisions, such as a pledge of sexual abstinence, may indicate a departure from hegemonic performances of masculinity, what appear to be transgressive practices do not always endure, nor do they result in challenges to inequalities based on gender (Bridges and Pascoe 2014). These data lend support to Bridges and Pascoe's argument that such hybrid masculinities "fortify existing social and symbolic boundaries" (2014, 246). While these findings indicate that such a shift is not clear-cut, the *shift itself* has further implications for theories of masculinities. For instance, while Demetriou (2001) argues that masculinities change, expand, and adapt to historical junctures, this work indicates that gender practices shift during an individual's life course as well.

Third, the data indicate that a close coupling with religious institutions complicates life course transitions and the ways in which masculinities are organized around these transitions. . . . While it may not be a lack of experience that produces difficulties for these men in married life, but rather a tension between the dueling discourses around sexuality available to them, we do see that the shifts in these discourses alter men's conversations about sexuality that inform their gender identities. When we study the construction of masculinities, we should account for the ways in which a variety of processes at life course transitions work together to create, re-create, and change the ways in which masculinities are understood, produced, and transformed.

Notes

1. Pegging is a sexual act in which a woman anally penetrates a man with a strap-on dildo.
2. This is the largest evangelical men's organization, with the political goal of redefining

masculinity by "altering the way men relate to their wives, children, and other men" (Donovan 1998, 819).

3. All names have been changed to protect the confidentiality of participants.

4. Language in this section is taken from The River's Facebook page.

5. There was one exception: A few of the men recalled reading *Sheet Music: Uncovering the Secrets of Sexual Intimacy in Marriage* by Dr. Kevin Leman (2003). Peter advises, "Under no circumstances read it together before you get married, because it definitely encourages behavior." Layers of control exist within available literature for these men premarriage, and the conversations encouraged by the literature seem to "drop off" postmarriage, mirroring the structure of their small group.

Author's Note

The author wishes to thank CJ Pascoe, Tristan Bridges, Sarah Quinn, Julie Brines, Becky Pettit, Pepper Schwartz, Gail Murphy-Geiss, and the editors and anonymous reviewers at *Gender & Society* for comments on earlier drafts of this work. Correspondence concerning this article should be addressed to Sarah Diefendorf, Department of Sociology, University of Washington, 211 Savery Hall Box 353340, Seattle, WA 98195-3340; email: sdief@uw.edu. This research received no specific grant from any funding agency in the public, commercial, or not-for-profit sectors.

References

Bersamin, Melina M., Samantha Walker, Elizabeth D. Waiters, Deborah A. Fisher, and Joel W. Grube. 2004. Promising to wait: Virginity pledges and adolescent sexual behavior. *Journal of Adolescent Health* 36:428–36.

Bridges, Tristan. 2014. A very "gay" straight? Hybrid masculinities, sexual aesthetics, and the changing relationship between masculinity and homophobia. *Gender & Society* 28:58–82.

Bridges, Tristan, and C. J. Pascoe. 2014. Hybrid masculinities: New directions in the sociology of men and masculinities. *Sociology Compass* 8:246–58.

Burke, Kelsey. 2014. What makes a man: Gender and sexual boundaries on evangelical Christian sexuality websites. *Sexualities* 17:3–22.

Carpenter, Laura, and John DeLamater, eds. 2012. *Sex for life: From virginity to Viagra, how sexuality changes throughout our lives.* New York: New York University Press.

Charmaz, Kathy. 2001. Grounded theory: The logic of grounded theory. In *Contemporary field research*, edited by Robert Emerson. Long Grove, IL: Waveland Press.

Connell, Raewyn. 1987. *Gender and power: Society, the person, and sexual politics.* Stanford, CA: Stanford University Press.

Connell, Raewyn. 1990. Iron man. In *Sport, men and the gender order: Critical feminist perspectives*, edited by Michael Messner and Donald Sabo. Champaign, IL: Human Kinetics.

Connell, Raewyn. 1992. A very straight gay. *American Sociological Review* 57:735–51.

Connell, Raewyn. 2005. *Masculinities.* Berkeley: University of California Press.

Connell, Raewyn, and James Messerschmidt. 2005. Hegemonic masculinity: Rethinking the concept. *Gender & Society* 19:829–59.

Demetriou, Demetrakis. 2001. Connell's concept of hegemonic masculinity: A critique. *Theory and Society* 30:337–61.

Donovan, Peter. 1998. Political consequences of private authority: Promise Keepers and the transformation of hegemonic masculinity. *Theory and Society* 27:817–43.

Erzen, Tanya. 2006. *Straight to Jesus: Sexual and Christian conversions in the ex-gay movement.* Berkeley: University of California Press.

Farvid, Panteá, and Virginia Braun. 2006. Most of us guys are raring to go anytime, anyplace, anywhere: Male and female sexuality in *Cleo* and *Cosmo*. *Sex Roles* 55:295–310.

Fine, Michelle. 1988. Sexuality, schooling, and adolescent females: The missing discourse of desire. *Harvard Educational Review* Spring:29–54.

Fine, Michelle, Lois Weiss, Judi Addelstone, and Julia Marusza. 1997. (In)secure times: Constructing white working-class masculinities in the late 20th century. *Gender & Society* 11:52–68.

Gerber, Lynne. 2008. The opposite of gay: Nature, creation, and queerish ex-gay experiments. *Nova Religio* 11:8–30.

Glaser, Barney, and Anselm Strauss. 1967. *The discovery of grounded theory: Strategies for qualitative research*. Chicago: Aldine.

Kimmel, Michael. 2008. *Guyland: The perilous world where boys become men*. New York: HarperCollins.

Leman, Kevin. 2003. *Sheet music: Uncovering the secrets of sexual intimacy in marriage*. Carol Stream, IL: Tyndale House.

Luker, Kristin. 2006. *When sex goes to school*. New York: Norton.

Messerschmidt, James. 2012. Engendering gendered knowledge: Assessing the academic appropriation of hegemonic masculinity. *Men and Masculinities* 15:1–21.

Pascoe, C. J. 2007. *Dude, you're a fag: Masculinity and sexuality in high school*. Berkeley: University of California Press.

Renold, Emma. 2007. Primary school "studs": (De)constructing young boys' heterosexual masculinities. *Men and Masculinities* 9:275–97.

Rich, Adrienne. 1980. Compulsory heterosexuality and lesbian existence. *Signs* 5:631–60.

Robinson, Christine, and Sue Spivey. 2007. The politics of masculinity and the ex-gay movement. *Gender & Society* 21:650–75.

Schwalbe, Michael. 1996. *Unlocking the iron cage*. New York: Oxford University Press.

Thorne, Barrie. 1993. *Gender play: Girls and boys in school*. New Brunswick, NJ: Rutgers University Press.

Tolman, Deborah. 2005. *Dilemmas of desire: Teenage girls talk about sexuality*. Cambridge, MA: Harvard University Press.

Wilkins, Amy. 2008. *Wannabes, goths, and Christians: The boundaries of sex, style, and status*. Chicago: University of Chicago Press.

Wilkins, Amy. 2009. Masculinity dilemmas: Sexuality and intimacy talk among Christians and goths. *Signs* 34:343–68.

Aggressive and Loving Men
Gender Hegemony in Christian Hardcore Punk

AMY D. MCDOWELL

Scholars complicate the idea that religious conservatives behave in ways that legitimate the hegemonic authority of men. Indeed, this scholarship, typically focused on Protestant evangelical Christians, shows that "godly" men express a "soft" or more feminine side of manhood that is compassionate, emotive, and faithful (Bartkowski 2004; Brenneman 2011; Gallagher and Wood 2005; Gerber 2014; Wolkomir 2001). This softer side of manhood deviates from hegemonic masculinity, which Connell (2005) defines as a context-specific strategy and a practice of masculinity that normalizes and legitimates the subordinate position of women in society. In this scholarship, hegemonic masculinity is much "harder" than religious masculinity; it is presented as tough, violent, emotionally distant, and fixated on heterosexual conquest (Bird 1996; Grazian 2007; Kimmel 2008; Stroud 2012). But this analytic dichotomy between religious (i.e., soft) and secular (i.e., hegemonic) masculinity is problematic for two reasons. First, it downplays how soft—or in this case devotional—forms of masculinity can be a component of hegemonic masculinity (Bridges and Pascoe 2014; Diefendorf 2015; Heath 2003; Wilkins 2009) and assumes that Christian men do not combine aspects of religious and secular performances of identity to promote gender hegemony. Second, it suggests that godly masculinity is confined to religious institutions or practices and has no bearing on gender hegemony in the wider culture. But what if we examine Christian men in secular spaces?

This research uses Christian Hardcore punk music to examine how young white evangelical Christian men reinforce their hegemony in secular spaces through a hybrid performance of masculinity. Christian Hardcore is part of a larger, long-standing Protestant evangelical belief that Christians should use rock and roll music for religious ends (Howard and Streck 1999; Luhr 2009; Stowe 2011). But unlike mainstream Christian rock, which is mainly restricted to Christian radio stations and youth groups, Christian Hardcore bands tour with secular groups and headline secular show bills, allowing for contact with secular men who are fans. This secular hardcore setting illustrates how religious men draw from dominant cultural scripts to facilitate gender hegemony in secular spaces at the same time that they violate aspects of hegemonic masculinity.

Christian Hardcore punks seek to masculinize Christianity by reaching out to men in a music subculture that is already dominated by white men (Duncombe and Tremblay 2011; Haenfler 2006; Khan-Harris 2007; Mullaney 2007). A *Theology21* blog titled "Screaming Praise: The Passionate Heart of Christian Hardcore" makes this mission clear:

> In a nation where the men seem to be slipping away from the Church, and the church too often seems to be emasculating those who remain, this is the kind of movement that we need. We need strong men of God to carry Church into the next generation. (McClellan 2011)

Hardcore Christians "carry Church into the next generation" as they create a common space where Christian men can come together as men and come in contact with secular men. To build this space, hardcore Christian men present themselves as both aggressive and loving. Their aggressive style of masculinity resembles the "muscled" Christianity that other sociologists and historians have studied (Borer and Schafer 2011; Greve 2014; Kimmel 2012; Putney 2001). This involves physical violence in the mosh pit and warrior imagery in the music (McDowell 2014). On the other hand, these men vocalize their love for other hardcore men, both religious and secular. This tender side fits a sensitive evangelical ethos that encourages its men to care for other men in heartfelt ways (Gerber 2014; Heath 2003; Wolkomir 2001).

Centered on a doctrine of masculine God imagery, conservative religions present the social and spiritual authority of men over women as natural, normal, and inescapable (Pevey, Williams, and Ellison 1996; Rao 2015; Sumerau 2012). But the patriarchal gender relations that conservative religions advance are not stable and are prone "towards crisis" (Connell 2005, 84), meaning that religious institutions must continuously promote and justify the political, economic, and spiritually dominant position of men in society. One way white evangelical Christians manage "crisis tendencies" in gender relations is by seeking to recruit more white men into the Christian fold (Bederman 1989; Heath 2003; Kimmel 2008; Putney 2001). . . .

Contemporary white evangelicals also fear that U.S. society is moving away from a godly ordained gender order (Greve 2014). They cite and exaggerate recent studies that show that people are growing disenchanted with organized religion and that young white men are the most disillusioned (Chaves 2011; Pew Research Center 2012; Putnam and Cambell 2010). For evangelicals, the absence of men at church is not merely a matter of statistics: some "feel that the gender distribution in their congregations is indicative of the feminization of their religion and a broader feminization of culture" (Greve 2014, 155).

Concerned that the gender order is under attack, evangelicals are hard pressed to find new ways to reach men. The Promise Keepers is one of the most visible efforts to make Christian patriarchs out of men. In its massive campaign for a godly manhood characterized by racial reconciliation, family headship and service, the Promise Keepers organization preaches that men have a moral obligation to lead their wives spiritually, socially, and politically (Bartkowski 2004; Heath 2003). They call these family men "tender warriors"—men who balance strength with compassion, and care with determination (Bartkowski 2004). Other, younger evangelical men are not so tender. Deploying an explicitly muscled approach to Christianity (Kimmel 2012), these men lift weights for Christ and compete in Mixed Martial Arts (MMA), a violent form of fighting that links the power of God to bodily strength and stamina (Borer and Schafer 2011; Greve 2014). In contrast to the notion that Jesus was a peacekeeping pacifist, Christian MMA fighters argue that violent matches are a religious activity because these "help them spread their faith" to men in a secular world (Borer and Schafer 2011, 177). Whether practitioners of "tender" or "muscled" evangelical manhood, Christian men are coming up with new ways to maintain a patriarchal gender order.

Hybrid Masculinities

. . . Rather than stress a "tender" *or* "muscled" approach to manhood, hardcore Christians express a hybrid construction of manhood that is both aggressive and loving. Exhibited by white heterosexual men in periods of crisis, hybrid masculinities incorporate "elements of identity typically associated with various marginalized and subordinated masculinities and—at times—femininities" into masculine identities (Bridges and Pascoe 2014, 246). These elastic (Bridges and Pascoe, forthcoming) masculinities find expression through emotive sharing at college bars (Arxer 2011, 404), self-identifying with gay aesthetics (Bridges 2014, 65), openly expressing affection for other men on stag tours (Thurnell-Read 2012), or pledging sexual abstinence in Christian organizations (Diefendorf

2015; Wilkins 2009). Some scholars argue that hybrid constructions of manhood threaten the existing gender order (Anderson 2009; McCormack 2012). But as Bridges and Pascoe (forthcoming) point out, hybridity does not equate to gender equality: hybrid masculinities reinforce gender hegemony by obscuring how privileged men strengthen gender binaries that are oppressive to women and subordinate masculinities (Bridges and Pascoe 2014; Messerschmidt 2010; Messner 1993, 2007). . . .

Methods

I primarily use participant observation and semi-structured interview data, but I also reference online sources about the bands I observed during field research. Participant observation data of 285 hours comes from 10 live music shows (from 2009 to 2012), two multi-day annual Cornerstone Christian rock festivals in Bushnell, Illinois (2008 and 2010), and two weekend-long Unified Underground (UU) subcultural ministry conferences in Annapolis, Maryland (2008 and 2010). The hardcore music shows I attended took place in secular bars within a 50-mile radius of Pittsburgh, Pennsylvania, and consisted of nationally known touring acts. The bands I selected to observe at secular venues also played the UU conference and/or Cornerstone festival. I selected live music shows in this way because I wanted to see how performers who participate in Cornerstone, a legendary alternative Christian rock festival (Beaujon 2006), and UU, a subcultural ministries network, convey Christianity in secular settings.

I conducted 23 intensive one-on-one interviews and five group interviews of two to six people. Interviewees included Christian and secular hardcore band members, subcultural ministers (Christian youth who organize music shows and/or Bible studies in their hometowns), and preachers and youth pastors of nondenominational and Baptist churches that support this music ideologically and/ or materially. The total number of interviewees was 40. A handful of my interviewees self-identified as straight edge, which signified their allegiance to a hardcore music scene that emphasizes the politics

of self-control by vowing to never use drugs or alcohol and avoiding sex outside of long-term relationships (Haenfler 2006; Lahicky 1997). . . .

In a project that was designed to explore how Christian youth express religion in secular music, issues regarding gender and masculinity emerged without any specific prompting on how Christian Hardcore men think of themselves as men. I asked interviewees to describe the obstacles they face in this music, who shows up to their shows, and what they think about the involvement of women. Christian and secular hardcore interviewees were also asked how they perceive the growth of Christianity in this music. The interviews were active (Holstein and Gubrium 1995), meaning that I gave respondents room to bring up issues on their own terms. Interviewees raised the notion of a "loving" ministry without my prompting. When this was mentioned, I followed the methodological advice of Crang and Cook (2007) and asked respondents to provide examples of this love and how they practice it. . . .

Public reviews of music shows (n = 23) were another source of data. These data were analyzed in light of the codes created from participant observation and interview data. Field notes and interviews were transcribed and coded according to a grounded theoretical method, allowing patterns and themes to emerge from the data (Glaser and Strauss 1999). To create open codes, I read participant observation notes and interview transcripts line-by-line (Emerson, Fretz, and Shaw 1995) and wrote analytic memos about the themes that emerged from this careful reading. Through this method I created the codes "masculinity," "ministry," "aggression," and "love." To investigate the relationship between these codes, I developed "masculine evangelicalism" as a sensitizing concept. This sensitizing concept laid the foundation for the analysis of inductive codes (Blumer 1954; Bowen 2006) and helped me organize these data on the practice of Christian Hardcore ministry. . . .

Christianity in Hardcore Punk

The fusion of Christianity and hardcore punk music is extraordinary. U.S. hardcore punk got its start in the wake of the Reagan era, when social conservatives were championing limited government, accelerating national defense, and promoting traditional family values (Blush 2010; Rettman 2014). Outraged by this political shift to the Right, hardcore punks created a music culture that "normal people" would find offensive (Rachman 2006). Fast, furious, and loud, this music was hypercritical of conservative Christianity and the neoliberal policies that defined the 1980s. Since then, the hardcore scene has undergone several sonic, symbolic, and political changes (Blush 2010; Duncombe and Tremblay 2011; Haenfler 2006; Rettman 2014). One of the most recent changes is the growing presence of Christian bands that are unapologetic about their faith in a music culture that has a reputation for loathing social conservatism. . . .

Christian Hardcore punks critique institutional religion like their secular counterparts, yet diverge from the broader punk movement in their evangelist mission to make America a Christian nation. They reason that God calls them to be punk, as one Christian Hardcore interviewee put it, because "He" wants them "to save the nation from the underground up." In the underground, Christian Hardcore men try to "reach the rejected," who they talk about in subcultural rather than socio-economic terms. From their point of view, the rejected are young white men who feel excluded by the church and/or society at large for being social misfits in some subcultural form or fashion (McDowell 2014). This notion of the rejected is regularly expressed at the UU conference, a subcultural ministry branch of Youth for Christ that hardcore Christians launched in their effort to unite the Christian subcultures in ministry. They often describe their mission as an urgent response to the fact that the mainstream church (i.e., conventional Christian denominations) is losing members and that most dropouts are young men (Chaves 2011; Pew Research Center 2012, 2015; Putnam and Campbell 2010). From their perspective, the mainstream church is to blame for this loss because it judges and mistreats people who do not fit the mold of a stereotypical Sunday Christian.

Christian Hardcore Ministry

Christian Hardcore men mix anger and love to carry out their evangelist mission in underground *music scenes*, which sociologists define as dynamic social settings of collective meaning-making focused around music and live music shows (Bennett 2004; Futrell, Simi, and Gottschalk 2006). My participant observations confirmed this. At a Christian subcultural ministries conference, around 100 people gathered in a dimly lit room for the band *Sleeping Giant*. To get ready, a crowd of young white men and a handful of women wearing a mix of flannels, dark T-shirts, and tight jeans, formed a semi-circle in the middle of the floor, up front near the stage. The rest of the audience gathered at the back of the room, where chairs had been moved. When *Sleeping Giant* took the stage, the lyrics to "Sons of Thunder" were projected on a large screen at the front of the room, a gesture that invited everyone to sing aloud. As the crowd sang the chorus— "Overcome this world with love! Overcome my heart with love!"—the lead singer swayed side-to-side and lifted his hands in praise. Following his direction, several audience members raised their hands and mouthed prayers—movements that made this performance look more like a Sunday morning worship service than a hardcore show. Then suddenly the beat shifted from a soft melody about love to a loud thunderous growl of electric guitar riffs, deep bass, and roars. In sync with this change, several young men turned praising hands into balled fists and slung their limbs around viciously. These movements shaped a mosh pit, and, as the men moved more aggressively, the pit stretched wider. Before long, a group of about 15 men were the only ones left thrashing their bodies around in the center of the room; everyone else stood at the edges of the circle or moved to the back. Later that night, a Christian band member wept on stage as he testified about a time he had premarital sex with a woman before giving his heart to Christ. As he spoke, the men who had moshed all night paused in silence to hear his emotional testimony.

This *Sleeping Giant* show illustrates how Christian Hardcore men uphold hegemonic gender relations in hardcore music as they perform a two-sided masculinity that is both physically aggressive and emotionally loving. By participating in mosh pits, Christian Hardcore youth construct male controlled spaces for the physical expression of masculinity; and by collectively singing that they will "overcome this world with love," they make emotional commitments to the Christian men in these spaces and to the secular men that they hope to reach. I find Christian Hardcore men bond with other hardcore men through an aggressive performance of masculinity that excludes women, but, at the same time, they do a loving performance of masculinity that explicitly focuses on secular men and implicitly devalues women.

Aggressive Men

The *Sleeping Giant* concert illustrates how Christian Hardcore youth carry out subcultural ministries by linking their faith in God to the antagonistic attitudes that characterize hardcore. Like the other underground Christian music scenes (Moberg 2015; Rademacher 2015), Christian Hardcore youth use warrior imagery in their albums and stage performances to present Christianity as a fearless, macho faith (McDowell 2014). But warrior imagery is not enough to establish membership in hardcore. Hardcore Christians must also earn the respect of nonbelievers at live music shows, spaces where hardcore youth, secular and religious, come together. Affectionately termed a "brotherhood," hardcore music holds homosocial unity in high esteem and normalizes the idea that men need to express solidarity with other men. The pit is a "tough place to be" (Khan-Harris 2007, 44), but it is also a place where men express unity. In the pit, men dance violently, push and knock each other around, and help up those who have fallen down (Haenfler 2006; Khan-Harris 2007; Leblanc 1999; Mullaney 2007; Tsitsos

1999). For Christian Hardcore men then, moshing is not merely a destructive release; moshing helps them achieve membership in the hardcore brotherhood. This explains why Christian Hardcore bands use "breakdowns" to, as a few put it, "get the pit going." Breakdowns are the sonic climax of hardcore songs. Composed of a few single chords chugged slowly and rhythmically in a monotonous fashion, breakdowns are central to live hardcore shows because these inspire physical thrashing and moshing in the pit (Haenfler 2006). Christian Hardcore bands also shout their most ominous messages during breakdowns. The song "Immanuel (The Reedemer)" by the billboard-topping Christian Hardcore band *For Today* is a case in point. About midway through the track, the music drops to a deep rhythmic choppy bass just as the singer roars: "Repent or Perish!"

In hardcore, good music is brutal. This is why active pits can be used to measure a band's credibility; if the pit is "going," a band is making a good impression. Samuel, the lead singer of a longstanding Christian band, measures the success of his music by how rowdy the pit gets:

> I love it when they just go nuts! I like dancers doing their dancing thing! I like push-moshers doing their push-moshing thing! I like circle pits! I like it all! I like to see kids having fun!

. . . Secular hardcore youth also use the events of the pit to affirm the quality of Christian Hardcore music. Seth, a columnist for a newspaper in Spokane, Washington, describes the pit at *The Chariot* shows as energetic and dangerous. After describing the injury he suffered from the pit at one of these shows, Seth asserts, "The pain and the doctor's bill was worth it." Seth encourages other hardcore kids to look past the religion of *The Chariot* and join their mosh pit. He claims,

> The Chariot has always been forthcoming about the band members' Christian faith, and they have addressed it lyrically. At his core Scogin [the lead singer] is a nice, affable Southern Christian boy who just happens to make killer music to slam to.

But a lack of belief in a higher calling shouldn't dissuade listeners—Scogin welcomes everyone.

Seth's appreciation for violent mosh pits at *The Chariot* show resonates with what Sam, a hardcore blogger for the *Pittsburgh Music Report*, wrote about the rush he experienced at their show in Pittsburgh:

> It was the kind of show where you just let everything go, you hit whoever you need to, you scream at the top of your lungs, you dance like it's your last day. . . . I was in the middle of a crowd of people, being thrown around and throwing people around. (Ritzer 2010)

Sam does not talk about Christianity in his review of *The Chariot* show, nor does he make a statement about his own religious identity. Instead, he focuses on how the pit made him feel free to dance violently, a primary mechanism of hardcore solidarity and largely exclusive to men. Sam continued,

> Typing with a broken left thumb is not an easy task, especially when you could have a potential concussion, judging from the size of the bruise and lump on your forehead. (The dry blood under your nose may be a clue as well.) I am not really able to tell you exactly when any of these injuries occurred to my body, besides a general blanket statement that any hardcore music fan would understand, "I saw the Chariot last night."

Sam typifies how young men use their wounds from the pit to gain credibility in this brotherhood. His broken thumb, potential concussion, bruises, and lumps establish that he is brave enough to join a notoriously daring mosh pit. Also, his wounds from other hardcore kids communicate his commitment to the scene that *The Chariot* helped create.

Given the violent measures young Christian men take to be hardcore, it is no surprise that women get pushed to the margins of this music. The gender imbalance at Christian Hardcore shows is striking, so much so that one secular musician remarked, "If you [a woman] go to a show like that you have to feel awkward because there are so many guys there."

Joseph, the pastor of a nondenominational church, claims that hardcore is dominated by young men because of the "whole energy level." "Hardcore is supposed to be angry and violent on some level," he says, "I guess that's why they call it hardcore." Pastor Joseph is not alone in his gendered assessment of hardcore anger. Greg, who plays guitar for a Christian Hardcore group, believes women do not show up for hardcore shows because they are "passive" and not as angry as men.

Women do go to hardcore shows, but they are seldom respected in the pit (Leblanc 1999; Mullaney 2007). This was made apparent at a Christian Hardcore show in Pittsburgh. Before starting the set, the band announced that the singer had an emergency and could not be there for the show. Without pause the band opened with a fast, thunderous roar. The bass player then leaped down from the stage and started slinging his guitar around his body. But rather than move away from the bassist, the audience moved towards him to form a semi-circle around him. By the end of the first song, the rest of the band relocated to the floor in the middle of a furious mosh pit. During the set, seven different young men passed the microphone to take turns screaming the lyrics to the songs. There were a few women in the pit, moshing alongside the men. One young woman jumped up and down as she screamed the lyrics (without the microphone) and another women climbed on stage and slammed to the music. But these women were never passed the microphone or given the opportunity to scream into it, even as they struggled to reach for it. They were physically excluded from the center of the scene. I next examine how, in addition to marginalizing women in these physical ways, Christian Hardcore men focus on loving men, not women, in this scene.

Loving Men

Christian Hardcore men are vocal about their godly love for other men in hardcore music. It is not unusual to see hand-drawn "Free Hugs" cardboard signs at the merchandise tables of bands or hear Christian men use the phrase "love on" from stage either as part of a prayer, a song, or a brief sermon. In the Christian Hardcore lexicon, "love on" refers to the idea that Christian ministry is a process of homosocial bonding in a music subculture that stereotypically abhors Christianity. As these youth see it, a loving ministry does not necessarily involve talk about Jesus or salvation. Loving someone is "being there" on stage, at the T-shirt booth, or after the show. As several interviewees put it, "being there plants the seed" for a Christian foundation in the hardcore brotherhood.

Christian Hardcore men open up space for men to love on one another as they sexualize and banish women from the scene. Paul, a straight edge Christian musician, believes that women get in the way of his ministry because women represent sex. Like other straight edgers, he frowns upon casual sex (Haenfler 2006) and implies that his ministry is best when women are not around. With only men present he "avoids certain temptations like, umm . . . girls trying to 'get with' the guys in our band." Straight edge Christians are not the only ones who see women as sexual objects who get in the way of their ministries. Brad, a Christian Hardcore musician who is not straight edge, feels the music he plays is a good form of ministry because women do not show up for "darker, grungier" bands and the "chicks that dig it are not our type anyway." Brad later clarifies that the kind of "chicks" who "dig" his music are unattractive because they will "get with anybody." Brad's sexual degradation of hardcore women resonates with Pastor Frisk's statements to Christian men at the UU conference. During his spiritual speaker session, Frisk cautioned attendees against womanizing and whore mongering at live music shows. Through his discourse about men lusting after women, Frisk emphasized "compulsive heterosexuality" (Pascoe 2007) when he suggested that men have a natural urge to want women all the time. This comment not only objectified and marginalized women in the scene, but also it created a safe space where Christian men could vocalize their love for one another without losing their status as heterosexuals.

One of the primary ways that Christian Hardcore men say they "love on" nonbelieving men is by befriending them at live music shows. Samuel, the lead singer of a Christian band, claims hardcore music is "overrun by kids who are screwing up and trying to find themselves" and thinks "many of them are depressed but do not know it yet." Accordingly, he believes in counseling non-Christians by letting them know that they are broken and deserve love. To make a personal connection with someone, Samuel asks questions like: "What are you doing? Where are you going to school?" He continues, "We become friends and then you can tell me about your home life . . . and then I'll tell you a little about my home life." Samuel claims it is easier for him to love on other men than it is for secular men. This is because fans and audience members generally know which groups are Christian and have come to expect that Christians feel dialogue between men is an evangelical practice, not an expression of sexual interest.

Christian Hardcore men have reason to believe that their love for other men is working. Both Christian and secular interviewees argue that Christian Hardcore bands are accepted more now in hardcore music than ever before. Some even claim that Christian bands are the leaders, not the followers, of contemporary hardcore music. Sean, who identifies as agnostic and straight edge, admires the Christian Hardcore bands that "stand up for what they believe" but do not "shove religion down your throat." After this remark, Sean lists hardcore Christians that are nice guys—the ones who take time to get to know their audience members after a show. Other secular interviewees express a similar affinity for Christian bands. Liam, the lead singer of a secular hardcore band, respects and appreciates the Christian Hardcore musicians he meets on tour. He said he thinks Christian Hardcore has "gotten so big" because "it's just so honest." For him this means that Christian bands are brave enough to profess their faith in secular spheres but they "don't go around telling you that you're a bad person if you don't believe in Jesus." Instead, they get to know you; as several people put it, "they practice what they preach." Some secular men even suggest that Christian Hardcore music helps them stay out of trouble. During talk about the growth of Christianity in this music, the bouncer of an all-ages music venue in Nashville, Tennessee, claimed that hardcore shows saved him from "being one of those stereotypical kids who has nothing to do and is cooking meth or whatever." Greg, whom I met at a subcultural ministries conference, shared a similar story about how hardcore saved him from self-destruction. He spent his early 20s drunk. When he found hardcore music, that changed. Instead of spending his time at bars, he began going to live shows. Through the hardcore scene, Greg discovered Christian Hardcore. He says the people he met through this music rekindled his lost faith in Christ, inspiring him to "dedicate [his] life to God and hardcore music." Now Greg uses his music to love on other rejected men who he believes are looking for a change.

Christian Hardcore men insist that they are accepted in hardcore music because they put their differences aside and look out for hardcore men. Paul, a straight edge Christian Hardcore musician, has faced backlash over the years: audience members have thrown beer bottles at him and told him to "Go drown in Holy Water!" Despite these attacks, Paul insists that most non-believers respect him because he is genuine about love:

> Some of our best friends in the hardcore scene are completely opposite of what we believe. But we *loved on* them the way that Christ would *love on* them and we built a friendship. To this day they might not believe what we believe but we still love them like Christ. We're still close friends with them. We'll still talk with them on the regular and they respect where we stand. They saw that we lived out what we meant. You know, what we said we believed on stage, we practiced off stage.

When Paul shares that his secular hardcore friends "saw that we lived out what we meant," he implies that he proved to other hardcore men that he cares about them, even if they do not share his faith in Christ. Likewise Jacob insists that his Christian Hardcore band has received national acclaim

because of the rapport he and his band mates build on the road with other hardcore musicians. He says the tours give him a unique "opportunity to *love on* people, to serve them, to share Christ with them through actions."

Of course not all secular hardcore youth welcome Christians with open arms. Some told me that they were "sick and tired" of all the preaching bands. This explains why Hardcore Christians often talk about loving nonbelievers as grueling work. The song "Sons of Thunder" by *Sleeping Giant* illustrates how Christians see their ministry in this music. At first the song mirrors a typical evangelical sermon about Christian grace and forgiveness. It tells listeners to "love your enemies and pray for those who persecute you." As the song develops, it is made clear that the enemies who persecute Christians are the secular youth who *Sleeping Giant* hope to befriend at their shows. The song continues: "The stinging words of the crowd; they speak of me like I've lost my mind; like I'm some kind of joke," and these "sickening" voices, the song warns, are of the devil. For the next stanza, the singer proclaims that he is "no longer afraid" because this fight is for the souls of nonbelievers and the only way to win this fight is to "overcome this world with love!"

Overall, these findings show that Christian Hardcore men marginalize women through a hybrid mix of aggressive and loving masculinity. Their violent mosh pits at live shows physically push women to the edges of the scene; their explicit focus on loving and befriending men implicitly devalues women and, in some instances, explicitly reduces women to sexual objects.

Conclusion

Christian Hardcore men promote hegemonic gender relations as they seek to make contact with and minister to secular men in hardcore music. Their practice of ministry involves a hybrid masculinity that emphasizes aggression while at the same time embraces love as a strategy to connect to secular men. Through this two-sided expression of manhood, hardcore Christian men uphold the idea that men and women "are bearers of polarized character types" (Connell 2005, 68; Sumerau, Cragun, and Mathers 2015; West and Zimmerman 1987), even as they express qualities typically associated with femininity (being loving) alongside more conventional expressions of masculinity (being aggressive) (Bridges and Pascoe 2014). . . . In hardcore music, Christian men can compensate (Schrock and Schwalbe 2009) for a loving facade that departs from hegemonic masculinity when they mosh madly to hardcore music or talk about women in sexualized terms. These actions push women to the peripheries of this music scene and nurture the idea that women do not belong in hardcore because women come between them and other men, as well as between them and God.

This study also shows that hardcore Christians combine "soft" or religious performances of masculinity with aggressive expressions of masculinity to manage gender crises *outside of religious institutions*. These findings underscore that Christianity is a powerful institution and identity, and scholars need to pay closer attention to how men use it to legitimate and reinforce the social domination of men in secular contexts. Studies that focus on how Christian men live and embody religion outside of religious institutions will be able to see how "doing gender" and "doing religion" are co-constitutive (Avishai 2008; Rao 2015), and to what extent gendered practices of religion reinforce, subvert, or strengthen gender binaries that are oppressive to women (Diefendorf 2015; Heath 2003; Messner 1993; Wilkins 2009) beyond the confines of religious congregations and organizations. . . .

Author's Note

I thank the editor, Jo Reger, as well as the anonymous reviewers for their instructive feedback on this article. I also thank Kirsten Dellinger, Kathleen Blee, and Kelsy Burke for their support and suggestions on various stages of this project. Correspondence concerning this article should be addressed to Amy McDowell, Department of Sociology and Anthropology, University of Mississippi, University, MS 38677, USA; email: mcdowell@olemiss.edu.

Refer ences

Anderson, Eric. 2009. *Inclusive masculinity: The changing nature of masculinities.* New York: Routledge.

Arxer, Steven. 2011. Hybrid masculine power: Reconceptualizing the relationship between homosociality and hegemonic masculinity. *Humanity & Society* 35:390–422.

Avishai, Orit. 2008. "Doing religion" in a secular world: Women in conservative religions and the question of agency. *Gender & Society* 22 (4): 409–33.

Bartkowski, John. 2004. *The Promise Keepers: Servants, soldiers, and godly men.* New Brunswick, NJ: Rutgers University Press.

Bederman, Gail. 1989. "The women have had charge of the church work long enough": Men and the religion forward movement of 1911–1912 and the masculinization of middle-class Protestantism. *American Quarterly* 41 (3): 432–65.

Bennett, Andy. 2004. Consolidating the music scenes perspective. *Poetics* 32:223–34.

Beaujon, Andrew. 2006. *Body piercing saved my life: Inside the phenomenon of Christian rock.* Cambridge, MA: Da Capo Press.

Bird, Shannon. 1996. Welcome to the men's club: Homosociality and the maintenance of hegemonic masculinity. *Gender & Society* 10 (2): 120–32.

Blumer, Herbert. 1954. What is wrong with social theory? *American Sociological Review* 19 (1): 3–10.

Blush, Steven. 2010. *American hardcore: A tribal history*, 2nd ed. Port Townsend, WA: Feral House.

Borer, Michael Ian, and Tyler Schafer. 2011. Culture war confessionals: Conflicting accounts of Christianity, violence, and mixed martial arts. *Journal of Media and Religion* 10:165–84.

Bowen, Glenn. 2006. Grounded theory and sensitizing concepts. *International Journal of Qualitative Methods* 5 (3): 1–9.

Brenneman, Robert. 2011. *Homies and hermanos: Gods and gangs in Central America.* New York: Oxford University Press.

Bridges, Tristan. 2014. A very "gay" straight?: Hybrid masculinities, sexual aesthetics, and the changing relationship between masculinity and homophobia. *Gender & Society* 28 (1): 58–82.

Bridges, Tristan, and C. J. Pascoe. 2014. Hybrid masculinities: New directions in the sociology of men and masculinities. *Sociology Compass* 8 (3): 246–58.

Bridges, Tristan, and C. J. Pascoe. Forthcoming. On the elasticity of gender hegemony: Why hybrid masculinities fail to undermine gender and sexual inequality. In *Sociology and gender theory*, edited by Raewyn Connell, Patricia Yancey Martin, James Messerschmidt, and Michael Messner. New York: New York University Press.

Chaves, Mark. 2011. *American religion: Contemporary trends*. Princeton, NJ: Princeton University Press.

Connell, R. W. 2005. *Masculinities*. Berkeley: University of California Press.

Crang, Mike, and Ian Cook. 2007. *Doing ethnographies*. Thousand Oaks, CA: Sage.

Diefendorf, Sarah. 2015. After the wedding night: Sexual abstinence and masculinities over the life course. *Gender & Society* 29 (5): 647–69.

Duncombe, Stephen, and Maxwell Tremblay, eds. 2011. *White riot: Punk rock and the politics of race*. London: Verso.

Emerson, Robert, Rachel Fretz, and Linda Shaw. 1995. *Writing ethnographic fieldnotes*. Chicago: University of Chicago Press.

Futrell, Robert, Pete Simi, and Simon Gottschalk. 2006. Understanding music in movements: The white power music scene. *Sociological Quarterly* 47 (2): 275–304.

Gallagher, Sally, and Sabrina Wood. 2005. Godly manhood going wild?: Transformations in conservative protestant masculinity. *Sociology of Religion* 66 (2): 135–59.

Gerber, Lynne. 2014. Grits, guts, and vanilla beans: Godly masculinity in the exgay movement. *Gender & Society* 29 (1): 26–50.

Glaser, Barney, and Anselm Strauss. 1999. *The discovery of grounded theory: Strategies for qualitative research*. New Brunswick, NJ: Aldine Transaction.

Grazian, David. 2007. The girl hunt: Urban nightlife and the performance of masculinity as collective activity. *Symbolic Interaction* 30 (2): 221–43.

Greve, Justine. 2014. Jesus didn't tap: Masculinity, theology, and ideology in Christian Mixed Martial Arts. *Religion and American Culture: A Journal of Intepretation* 24:141–85.

Haenfler, Ross. 2006. *Straight edge: Hardcore punk, clean-living youth, and social change*. New Brunswick, NJ: Rutgers University Press.

Heath, Melanie. 2003. Soft-boiled masculinity: Renegotiating gender and racial ideologies in the Promise Keepers movement. *Gender & Society* 17 (3): 423–44.

Holstein, James, and Jaber Gubrium. 1995. The Active Interview. In *Qualitative Research Methods Vol. 37*, edited by Susan McElroy. Thousand Oaks, CA: Sage.

Howard, Jay, and John Streck. 1999. *Apostles of rock: The splintered world of contemporary Christian music*. Lexington: The University Press of Kentucky.

Khan-Harris, Keith. 2007. *Extreme metal: Music culture on the edge*. New York: Berg.

Kimmel, Michael. 2008. *Guyland: The perilous world where boys become men*. New York: HarperCollins.

Kimmel, Michael. 2012. *Manhood in America: A cultural history*, 3rd ed. New York: Oxford University Press.

Lahicky, Beth. 1997. *All ages: Reflections on straight edge*. Huntington Beach, CA: Revelation.

Leblanc, Lauraine. 1999. *Pretty in punk: Girls' gender resistance in a boys' subculture*. New Brunswick, NJ: Rutgers University Press.

Luhr, Eileen. 2009. *Witnessing suburbia: Conservatives and Christian youth culture*. Berkeley: University of California Press.

McClellan, Eric. 2011. Screaming praise: The passionate heart of Christian hardcore. *Theology 21: Renovating theology for a new generation*. http://www.theology21.com/2011/07/05/screaming-praise-the-passionate-heart-of-christian-hardcore/.

McCormack, Mark. 2012. *The declining significance of homophobia: How teenage boys are redefining masculinity and heterosexuality*. New York: Oxford University Press.

McDowell, Amy. 2014. Warriors and terrorists: Antagonism as strategy in Christian hardcore and Muslim "Taqwacore" punk rock. *Qualitative Sociology* 37 (3): 255–76.

Messerschmidt, James. 2010. *Hegemonic masculinities and camouflaged politics*. Boulder, CO: Paradigm.

Messner, Michael. 1993. "Changing men" and feminist politics in the United States. *Theory and Society* 22 (5): 723–37.

Messner, Michael. 2007. The masculinity of the governator. *Gender & Society* 21 (4): 461–80.

Moberg, Marcus. 2015. *Christian metal: History, ideology, scene*. New York: Bloomsbury.

Mullaney, Jamie L. 2007. "Unity admirable but not necessarily heeded": Going rates and gender boundaries in the straight edge hardcore music scene. *Gender & Society* 21 (3): 384–408.

Pascoe, C. J. 2007. *Dude, you're a fag: Masculinity and sexuality in high school.* Berkeley: University of California Press.

Pevey, Carolyn, Christine Williams, and Christopher Ellison. 1996. Male God imagery and female submission: Lessons from a southern Baptist ladies' Bible class. *Qualitative Sociology* 19 (2): 173–93.

Pew Research Center. 2012. "Nones" on the rise: One-in-five adults have no religious affiliation. The Pew Forum on Religion & Public Life. http://www.pewforum.org/files/2012/10/NonesOnThe Rise-full.pdf.

Pew Research Center. 2015. Changing U.S. religious landscape. The Pew Forum on Religion & Public Life. http://www.pewforum.org/2015/05/12/americas-changing-religious-landscape/pf_15–05–05_rls2_1_310px/.

Putnam, Robert, and David Campbell. 2010. *American grace: How religion divides and unites us.* New York: Simon & Schuster.

Putney, Clifford. 2001. *Muscular Christianity: Manhood and sports in Protestant America, 1880–1920.* Cambridge, MA: Harvard University Press.

Rachman, Paul. 2006. *American hardcore: The history of American punk rock 1980–1986.* Culver City, CA: Sony Pictures Home Entertainment.

Rademacher, Heidi. 2015. "Men of iron will": Idealized gender in Christian heavy metal. *Social Compass* 62 (4): 632–48.

Rao, Alya Hamid. 2015. Gender and cultivating the moral self in Islam: Muslim converts in an American mosque. *Sociology of Religion* 76 (4): 413–35.

Rettman, Tony. 2014. *NYCH: New York City hardcore 1980–1990.* Brooklyn, NY: Bazillion Points.

Ritzer, Sam. 2010. Show review—The Chariot—Altar bar. Pittsburgh music report. http://www.pittsburghmusicreport.com/2010/12/show-review-chariot-altar-bar-12110.html.

Schrock, Douglas, and Michael Schwalbe. 2009. Men, masculinity, and manhood acts. *Annual Review of Sociology* 35:277–95.

Stowe, David. 2011. *No sympathy for the devil: Christian pop music and the transformation of American evangelicalism.* Chapel Hill: University of North Carolina Press.

Stroud, Angela. 2012. Good guys with guns: Hegemonic masculinity and concealed handguns. *Gender & Society* 26 (2): 216–38.

Sumerau, J. Edward. 2012. "That's what a man is supposed to do": Compensatory manhood acts in an LGBT Christian church. *Gender & Society* 26 (3): 461–87.

Sumerau, J. Edward, Ryan T. Cragun, and Lain A. B. Mathers. 2015. Contemporary religion and the cisgendering of reality. *Social Currents* 3 (3): 293–311.

Thurnell-Read, Thomas. 2012. What happens on tour: The premarital stag tour, homosocial bonding, and male friendships. *Men and Masculinities* 15 (3): 249–70.

Tsitsos, William. 1999. Rules of rebellion: Slamdancing, moshing, and the American alternative scene. *Popular Music* 18 (3): 397–414.

West, Candace, and Don Zimmerman. 1987. Doing gender. *Gender & Society* 1 (2): 125–51.

Wilkins, Amy. 2009. Masculinity dilemmas: Sexuality and intimacy talk among Christians and goths. *Signs: Journal of Women in Culture and Society* 34 (2): 343–68.

Wolkomir, Michelle. 2001. Emotion work, commitment, and the authentication of the self: The case of gay and ex-gay Christian men. *Journal of Contemporary Ethnography* 30 (3): 305–34.

Muslim Masculinities

What Is the Prescription of the Qur'an?

ZEHRA F. KABASAKAL ARAT AND ABDULLAH HASAN

Introduction

Violence has been an important concern of gender studies. While studies that focus on women's lives and status highlight the violence against women by men as an expression of power, both stemming from the privileged position of men and being used to maintain the asymmetrical power relations, masculinity studies see violence as a significant component of masculinity. Citing rape statistics, mass shooting incidents and crime rates in the United States, Jackson Katz draws attention to the gendered character of these crimes (Katz, 2003). Michael Kimmel points to violence among males and claims that "violence is often the single most evident marker of manhood" (Kimmel, 1994, p. 132).

Violence becomes more pronounced when the subject is "Muslim masculinities." Orientalism, even when it attempted to feminize Muslim men as a part of the colonial project and define them as *the Other* of the West (Said, 1978; Schick, 1999), also tended to associate Islam with violence. Since the 1990s, this association gathered greater depth. Muslim men started to be stereotyped as terrorists, and various armed Muslim groups further cemented this stereotype. Although committing violence in the name of religion, or for other causes, is not limited to Muslim men, many ask if Islam embodies certain characteristics that encourage male violence.

Followed by over 1.5 billion people around the world, Islam is not a unified or monolithic religion.

Although there have been some common rites, rituals, values and beliefs followed by many Muslims, living in different socio-economic conditions, subject to different types of political rule, and interacting with various non-Muslim communities in varying degrees, cultures created and experienced by Muslims have varied both spatially and temporally.

This article examines the message conveyed in the Qur'an—recognized by all Muslims as the word of God and the primary, most authoritative source of Islam—to identify the masculinities prescribed, if any. A comprehensive source, the Qur'an also provides moral, spiritual and social guidelines for the believer.

Our latent content analysis of the text shows that the Qur'an promotes multiple masculinities and none can be labelled as hegemonic.[1] It reveals at least five salient character traits that may be taken as prescriptions for the believing men. These traits, which we classify as submissiveness, altruism, righteousness, steadfastness and combativeness, show a complex relationship. They are not only interrelated and overlapping but may also appear contradictory, depending on the individual's religious status, institutional context, and the overall emphasis placed on moderation and restraint. Thus, we contend that while the *holistic* application of the message of the Qur'an would yield male attitudes and behaviours much different than those attributed to the stereotypical Muslim man, a *partial* reading of the Qur'an and *selective* application of its provisions can be used (and are used) to support competing masculinities, including violent ones.

The paper is organized into four sections. After a brief review of the key issues in masculinity studies and debates on Muslim masculinities, we turn to the analysis of the Qur'an. First, we discuss gender in the Qur'an to highlight some gendered notions and roles. Then, we present our methodology and findings on Muslim masculinities in the Qur'an. We conclude with an assessment of the implications of our findings.

From "Violence and Masculinity" to Multiple Masculinities

Aggressive and violent behaviour is typically associated with manhood and treated as a male trait both in popular cultures and gender studies. . . .

However, masculinity scholars tend to reject the notion that boys and men are biologically inclined to violence and aggression; they stress that masculinities are multiple, socially constructed and sustained through a complex system of symbols, identities and forces. They shift the attention from biology to social structures and discourses that guide boys to become men by acquiring certain traits and to prove their manhood by displaying these traits that set and sustain power relations (Braudy, 2003; Butler, 1990; Connell, 2005). In this paradigm, masculinity is defined as entrenched in an institutionalized power structure and a social phenomenon that is experienced in different ways by different people at different times. A range of institutions and actors, such as family, religion, media, government, law, work and peers, influence the formation of different masculinities. Connell contends that masculinities should be understood as a "feature of world society and for thinking about men's gender practices in terms global structures" and calls attention to the impact of globalization, imperialism and global gender order on masculinities within local and transnational frameworks (2005, p. 72). What is stressed here is that there are always multiple masculinities, which are not stagnant but change through

time and space, and that men are socialized or conditioned into acquiring different masculinities, including violent and aggressive ones, by varying social conditions. . . .

As gender is defined as a "performance" (Butler, 1990) and masculinity as a "homosocial" experience (Kimmel, 2008, p. 49), masculinity is increasingly seen as a front that is put on for men by men, is judged by men, and forces conformity among men (Connell, 2005; Kimmel, 2008). However, men live in diverse and hierarchal social structures. Thus, Connell points out the multiplicity of masculinity and identifies its four overarching categories: hegemonic, complicit, marginalized and subordinated (2005). Those who exhibit hegemonic masculinity often occupy the leading position in a given pattern of gender relations. According to Connell, in contemporary Western societies, "it is the successful claim to authority," more than direct violence, that is the "mark of hegemony" (Connell, 2005, p. 77).

Masculinity as a homosocial experience has been explored also for Muslim communities. Informed by Connell's arguments on multiple masculinities and Butler's notion of gender performativity, Maleeha Aslam differentiates between "Islamic masculinities" and "Muslim masculinities" and argues that "Muslim men participate in militant-jihadist Islamism and terrorism as an act of gender performativity" (Aslam, 2012, p. 2). While Islamic masculinities illuminate the "exemplary" masculinities found in sacred texts and narratives, Muslim masculinities "locate Muslim men within their current socio-economic and political contexts" (2012, p. 5). Thus, Islamic masculinities serve as alternatives to the "dominant/hegemonic 'aggressive' Muslim masculinity" (2012, p. 91).

Amanullah De Sondy similarly argues that Muslim notions of masculinity are rooted not only in Qur'anic prescriptions of masculinity but are also informed by other expressions fostered in different local and cultural contexts (such as defence of honour and valuing of virility). He discusses various case studies (e.g., lives of Muslim men and women in contemporary Pakistan and India, stories of the various Qur'anic prophets) to illustrate that "lived gendered experiences are manifold" (DeSondy, 2013, p. 5) and contends that "a mono-lithic understanding of Islamic masculinity is often imbued in politics" (p. 183). Referring to four par-ticular stories of Abrahamic prophets recounted in the Qur'an, De Sondy concludes that while the prophets' lives "tell us much about ethics and mo-rality," they tell "little about a uniform Islamic mas-culinity" (p. 120). . . .

Scholars aptly draw attention to the diversity of Muslim communities, experiences and sources employed in the construction of masculinities, and they all recognize the Qur'an as *one* informing source. The characteristics of Muslim masculinities constructed in the Qur'an, however, remain elu-sive and call for a close reading and comprehensive analysis of the text.

Gender in the Qur'an

The Qur'an was delivered to Prophet Mohammed, from 610 until his death in 632, and ordered him to spread monotheism. Introduced to a male-dominated, polytheistic and patriarchal society that worshiped both female and male deities, the Qur'an's gendered message was delivered to men as the main audience. . . .

Many Muslim analysts claim the message of the Qur'an as an essentially egalitarian one. Focusing on the literal meaning of patriarchy as "father rule," Barlas (2002) stresses that there is no glorification or justification of father's authority in the Qur'an and the Qur'an promotes gender equality. She con-tends that the Qur'an does not define men and women in terms of binary oppositions nor does it associate sex with gender, a specific division of labour, or with masculine–feminine attributes as most essentialists do. Arguing that several of God's attributes mentioned in the Qur'an are traditionally feminine traits (e.g. loving, creating, nourishing, compassionate and patient), she makes the case that the Qur'an does not consider the feminine as inferior or subordinate.[2] She attributes gender in-equalities in past and present Muslim communi-ties to the deliberately wrong interpretation of the Qur'an. Similarly, Mahmoud Mohamed Taha refers

to some inequalities between men and women, po-lygamy, veiling (*al-hijab*), segregation of men and women, and slavery as "not an original precept in Islam" (Taha, 1987, pp. 137–145).

On the other hand, Mernissi (1991)—while agreeing that the original intent of the divine message related by Prophet Mohammed was egalitarian—claims that public resistance forced some compromises. Stressing that the Prophet's pri-mary goal was reinforcing a monotheistic faith and spreading Islam, she contends that the male elite was accommodated by more agreeable verses. She also argues that misogynist notions about women's inferiority and subordination started to appear after the Prophet's death with the proliferation of the *ahadith*, sayings of the prophet that were often falsely attributed to him to advance different politi-cal agendas. Ahmed (1992) agrees that the direction of change in the course of history has been towards reinforcing inequalities, as Islam spread and inter-acted with other patriarchal cultures.[3] However, she also recognizes patriarchal norms in early Islam and notes their similarities to the norms prevailing in the surrounding communities at the time.

It is hard to dismiss numerous verses in the Qur'an that establish different opportunities and rights for men and women. Inheritance rights, bridal wealth (*mahr*), permission for polygyny, and conditions for divorce and remarriage mark dif-ferences. There is a significant division of labour, as men are assigned the role of provider (65:6–7)—although women are not barred from earn-ing income, acquiring and inheriting property, or maintaining it in their own name even after mar-riage (Arat, 2000). Warfare is not entirely a male effort, but combat appears to be a male responsibil-ity.[4] And a controversial verse opens the door for subordination of and violence against women, at least in its common interpretations:

Men are in charge of women by [right of] what Allah has given one over the other and what they spend [for maintenance] from their wealth. So righteous women are devoutly obedient, guarding in [the husband's] absence what Allah would have them guard. But those [wives] from whom you fear arrogance—[first] advise them; [then if they persist], forsake them in bed; and [finally], strike them. But if they obey you [once more], seek no means against them. Indeed, Allah is ever Exalted and Grand. (4:34)[5]

On the other hand, there is equality in creation, as both sexes were created simultaneously (4:1; 39:6; 3:195). Men and women have the same responsibilities in fulfilling their obligations towards God (4:1; 39:6; 3:195).[6] Having the same obligations, however, may not amount to having the same level of authority. Although the Qur'an has no direct reference to gender differences in this respect, it is important to note the faith's grounding in Abrahamic tradition. The Qur'an praises Abraham as the first *hanif* (monotheist) and recognizes his lineage of prophesy in its entirety. [The s]ignificant point here is the reservation of prophethood to men only.

Sexuality is accepted as a natural part of human life and not only for procreation, but it is condoned within a heterosexual union.[7] Men and women in marriage are described as [the] garment (cover/protector) of each other (2:187) and as partners with "affection and mercy" placed between them by God (30:21). Both are also expected to be chaste, avoid temptation, conceal their private parts and "cast down their eyes" (24:30). Women are advised to cover their chest and conceal their adornments from certain kin and other people (24:31).

No further division of labour in maintaining the household (beyond designating men as providers) is prescribed in the Qur'an. Parenting and parent–child relationships are mentioned but without gendering. Contrary to common claims, there is no particular elevation of motherhood, or fatherhood. Children should respect their parents, and parents should care for their children with patience, as they are included among the trials of God (64:15).

If there are differences between men and women and some gender division of labour, then what constitutes a "proper" man or woman? Most important, what are the qualities sought in a "Muslim man" that Muslim boys should aspire to acquire and Muslim men should try to perform?

Masculinities in the Qur'an

Adopting Connell's definition of masculinity, as summarized by Schippers as "a social position, a set of practices, and the effects the collective embodiment of those practices on individuals, relationships, institutional structures, and global relations of domination" (Schippers, 2007, pp. 86–87), we examine the Qur'an to identify the venerated attitudes and behaviours prescribed to men.

Methodology

Searching for Muslim masculinities in a text, our study combines elements of exploratory, descriptive and interpretive research. It involves three successive tasks: (1) reading the Qur'an to explore and identify attributes and behaviours that are judged; (2) collapsing these characteristics into broader descriptive categories as "desirable" and "undesirable"; and (3) sorting these categories as hegemonic, subordinate, etc. masculinities.

The methodology employed is latent content analysis. However, working without pre-defined masculinity characteristics, we employed "inductive category development" method, as opposed to "deductive category application" (Mayring, 2000). Thus, we read the Qur'an with attention to what *men* are ordered or recommended to do, in order to detect praiseworthy qualities and conducts, as well as what they should avoid to do (e.g.what is discouraged or condemned).[8]

The goal was to identify a set of characteristics that we could label most "desirable" and perhaps "hegemonic" masculinities. The praised characteristics, however, turn out to be not always attributed to Muslims, and they are not always treated as "desirable" traits. Thus, as is often the case in inductive method, we had to retune our exploratory research.

Thus, the analysis included two stages. The first stage involved reading of the text to identify the attitudes and behaviours that are praised and prescribed (or conversely, criticized and forbidden) and to distinguish the *salient* ones. Once the salient characteristics were established and categorized, the text was reviewed with attention to the gender and faith of the person referred (if any) in relation to the praised/disparaged characteristics, as well as the social and institutional context in which the behaviour is (expected to be) displayed.

An English translation of the Qur'an, Sahih International, was used for analysis. Although we consulted other English translations for some verses—to verify and ensure the accurate assessment of the sentiment expressed—we employed Sahih International for all quotations from the Qur'an, unless noted otherwise.[9]

Findings

Our analysis of the Qur'an reveals at least five salient character traits that are elevated: (1) submissiveness, (2) altruism, (3) righteousness, (4) steadfastness and (5) combativeness. These traits can be embodied and displayed by any person.

We identify at least seven categories of people whose conduct are evaluated or guided in the Qur'an: the Abrahamic prophets, including Prophet Mohammed; wives, parents and other kin of prophets; devout Muslim men; devout Muslim women; people of the Book (Jews and Christians who follow the Abrahamic tradition); hypocrites (those who claim to be Muslim/monotheist but think/act in defiance); and pagans (usually used to refer to the Meccans who rejected Allah's message and persecuted Prophet Mohammad and other believers). Slaves and children are also mentioned but, perhaps due to their *dependence* on free adults, the Qur'an elaborates not on their conduct but on the believers' conduct towards them. Although not categorically (as we elaborate in the subsequent pages), Abrahamic prophets tend to illustrate good behaviour that should be emulated by the believers, and pagans represent what should be avoided.[10]

The five salient character traits tend to overlap. For example, submission to God is also a righteous act. Moreover, it demands the devotion of one's wealth to help others (altruism), the sacrifice of one's life to protect the faith (combativeness), and continuous loyalty (steadfastness). However, these traits also vary in value and at times appear contradictory, depending on the institutional context in which the person is operating, as well as his status regarding the faith. In other words, similar to modern-day masculinities, the Qur'anic ones, too, are not only multiple and constructed but are also relational and institutional. . . .

The individual categories largely correspond to one's status in Islam or relation to monotheism and vary by degree, with prophets and devout Muslims at one end of the spectrum and pagans at the other. Table 29.1 presents the traits, as well as the categories at the macro (institutional) and micro (individual) levels of construction.

At the macro level, the institutional contexts that are significant for our analysis include religion, family, the Muslim community (*umma*), other communities, and property. *Religion* is the spiritual domain that involves the relationship between God and the believer. *Family* involves the relationship between husband and wife, parents and children and other kin. The *community* of believers (*umma*) involves the arrangement and regulation of civil affairs. Other *communities* could include the human or global community where inter-community relations take place, such as inter-faith relations in the Qur'an or international and transnational relations today. War and peace are initiated and regulated in this domain. *Property* involves ownership rights and responsibilities, trade, business contracts and relations, and land use.[11]

. . . In the following pages, we describe the salient characteristics and show the meanings they

Table 29.1 Salient Character Traits and Levels of Construction

Salient Character Traits	Levels of Construction	
	Institutional Level	Individual Level
Submissiveness	Religion	Prophets
Altruism	Family	Kin of prophets
Righteousness	*Umma*	Devout Muslim men & women
Steadfastness	Other communities	Hypocrites
Combativeness	Property	Pagans

take on when subjected to particular institutional systems and individual status.

Submissiveness

Submissiveness, taken as the opposite of domination and defiance, is the primary and most exalted trait of the believer, man or woman, in the institutional context of religion. This is because Islam means surrender or submission to God. The majority of the verses in the Qur'an are about submission to God, and many others dealing with other issues tend to be concluded with a reminder of God's power and a call for submission. . . .

In marriage, the relationship between husband and wife is of mutual subservience and commitment and consensual, as illustrated by a verse on breastfeeding infants:

> . . . No person is charged with more than his capacity. No mother should be harmed through her child, and no father through his child. And upon the [father's] heir is [a duty] like that [of the father]. And if they both desire weaning through mutual consent from both of them and consultation, there is no blame upon either of them. And if you wish to have your children nursed by a substitute, there is no blame upon you as long as you give payment according to what is acceptable. . . . (2:233)

In war, however, submissiveness is portrayed as a negative trait for devout Muslims. Warriors are told not to "weaken" while "superior" (47:35). On the other hand, non-Muslims who do "not desist" are chastised (96:15). Within the *umma*, Muslims are encouraged to strike a balance between their self-interest and submitting to the needs of the community. They are directed to put their own personal goals "which dominate [them]" aside and work with "one another in good works" and strengthen the community (2:148). Thus, submissiveness, as a masculine trait, can serve as the ideal trait in one situation but as a negative or subordinated trait in another.

Altruism

We use the term altruism in reference to care and concern for others, compassion, generosity, as well as selfless acts and sacrifices. The most frequent

expression of altruism in the Qur'an is the charitable act as a duty or a way of pleasing and remembering God. One of the five pillars of Islam, *zakat*, which is sometimes referred to as a "purification tax" rather than a charity (Qutb/Kotb, 1949/1970; Ramadan, 2001, p. 139; Zaman, 1996), requires all adult Muslims to give about 2.5% of their wealth annually to the needy. Several verses remind this obligation to the believer, and one even designates categories of *zakat* recipients (9:60). While *zakat* is mandatory almsgiving, there is practically no limit to voluntary contributions, as a verse addressing the Prophet states: "And they ask you what they should spend. Say, 'The excess [beyond needs]'" (2:219). Those who are generous with their wealth and give *zakat* are included among the righteous (9:75; 57:18; 63:10).

Charity is, of course, closely tied to wealth and property. While private property ownership and inheritance rights are recognized, the Qur'an asserts that the real owner of everything on earth and beyond is God and human beings are designated as the trustees (*khalifa*). God distributes wealth unevenly (4:32), but the blessed ones are expected to use their property wisely and to benefit family, community members and others.[12] . . .

Altruism goes beyond material care and also involves compassion. In addition to the poor and destitute, orphans and slaves are frequently referred to as people who are vulnerable, deserving of kindness and protection.

The Qur'an mentions war only as a fight against the non-believers who are hostile to the believers. It is treated as a collective effort of the Muslim community, and all "those who believe in Allah and the Last Day" (with no distinction to sex or other qualities) are called upon to support the cause (9:44). Anyone who gives shelter and aid is considered an ally of the believers (8:72–74). Believers are expected to spend all they have for the cause of God:

> Not equal are those believers remaining [at home]—other than the disabled—and the mujahideen, [who strive and fight] in the cause of Allah with their wealth and their lives. Allah has preferred the mujahideen through their wealth and their lives over those who remain [behind], by degrees.

And to both Allah has promised the best [reward]. But Allah has preferred the mujahideen over those who remain [behind] with a great reward. (4:95)

Yet, participation in warfare cannot be considered fully altruistic, since fighters are also promised rewards in heaven and war "booty" on earth (48:18–20). By the same token, however, generous charitable acts are also promised to multiply wealth and yield other rewards (2:276, 28:54; 30:39).

Righteousness

Defined as morally correct behaviour and thinking, righteousness is a broad concept that cuts through all other desirable character traits. Sometimes mentioning it directly, the Qur'an also offers definitions of the concept and what constitutes righteousness:

Righteousness is not that you turn your faces toward the east or the west,[13] but [true] righteousness is [in] one who believes in Allah, the Last Day, the angels, the Book, and the prophets and gives wealth, in spite of love for it, to relatives, orphans, the needy, the traveler, those who ask [for help], and for freeing slaves; [and who] establishes prayer and gives zakah; [those who] fulfill their promise when they promise; and [those who] are patient in poverty and hardship and during battle. Those are the ones who have been true, and it is those who are the righteous. (2:177)

Honesty, justice and fairness are praised in various other verses, and arrogance and corruption are referred to as the opposite of righteousness (28:77–83). Never depicted negatively, righteousness is praised in all institutional contexts and in all people, believer or not. The verse 49:13 refers to the broad applicability of righteousness:

O mankind, indeed We have created you from male and female and made you peoples and tribes that you may know one another. Indeed, the most noble of you in the sight of Allah is the most righteous of you. Indeed, Allah is Knowing and Acquainted.

. . . The emphasis on righteousness as the fabric of cooperation extends into community and inter-community affairs as well. Men and women, as well as peoples and tribes, are created as "allies of one another to enjoin what is wrong and establish prayer and give zakah and obey Allah and His Messenger" (9:71; 49:13). Muslims are required to "establish weight in justice and . . . not make deficient the balance" (55:9) while always remembering that God is the ultimate judge (88:21–26). Directives such as "give full measure when you measure," "weight in justice" or "weight with an even balance" are given frequently and used both literally and metaphorically (7:85; 11:84–85; 17:35; 26:181–182; 55:9). In matters of property and wealth, the righteous "uses his wealth to purify himself" through almsgiving (92:18) and engages in business transactions with the utmost honesty, fairness and trust (2:279; 83:1–4). Believers are also explicitly warned against corruption (7:85; 11:84; 26:183).

Unkind behaviour is equated with injustice. Surah 107, with the word "kindness" (al-Ma'un) in the title, issues warnings against being indifferent to the plight of orphans and the poor or refraining from helping the needy.

Righteousness in war is not about being strong or using force effectively but seeking just and fair dealings. Believers are instructed to investigate before engaging in a fight and not to seek warfare with peaceful non-believers to acquire wealth—with a reminder that they, too, were once non-believers (4:94). Self-restraint is also a frequent advice: "And do not let the hatred of a people for having obstructed you from al-Masjid al-Haram lead you to transgress. And cooperate in righteousness and piety, but do not cooperate in sin and aggression" (5:2).

In sum, righteousness offers the most uniform and precise characterization of ideal masculine traits, regardless of the institutional context or individual identity. The overarching message in all of the contexts is to maintain just, honest, and fair relations, whether it is with one's wife, child, slave, business partner, customer, enemy, neighbour, or criminal.

Steadfastness

Steadfastness, which can be defined as loyalty, faithfulness, determination and patience, is another frequently mentioned trait in the Qur'an. The commitment to the faith, that is the oneness of God and Mohammed's prophesy, is the principle expression of steadfastness. Muslims should be unconditionally loyal to God and avoid the "whisperings of the sneaking whisperer," be it jinn or people (114:5). But, steadfastness is sought also in times of war, in handling property, family relations, and community affairs. . . .

In marriage, steadfastness is positive and prescribed as a man's devotion to his wife; he should refrain from adulterous relationships and avoid sinful desires (4:23–24; 5:5).[14] Divorce is not desirable and cannot be sought in haste or in a state of anger. A man must take many steps in order to lawfully divorce his wife. He must wait for a prescribed time, cannot leave home, or force his wife to leave home (65:1). He should also continue providing for the estranged wife throughout the pregnancy and nursing periods (65:6).

The commitment to family, however, becomes a negative trait if one begins to neglect his religion or responsibility to protect the faith against assailants. Family and wealth should not become a distraction from the "remembrance of Allah" (63:9), and men are reminded that "[children and wealth] are but a trial" that they must overcome (8:28; 64:15). In fact, if a Muslim man chooses his family over his religion, he is considered "defiantly disobedient" (9:24) and a hypocrite.

This extends to the battlefield, as well. The Qur'an calls upon devout Muslims to remain steadfast in battle, to join it with eagerness, zeal and courage, and to overcome any distractions, such as property and family (4:74; 10:88; 47:36; 100:1–8). As with war, men should also be steadfast in maintaining peace. They are encouraged to be patient for their Lord (74:7) and "be patient over what [non-Muslims] say and avoid them with gracious avoidance" (73:10). . . .

Combativeness

We employ the term combativeness in reference to aggression and tendency to use force to settle conflicts, assert domination and employ violence. The Qur'an treats warfare as only occurring between Muslims and non-Muslims. Conflicts among believers are expected to be resolved without allowing them to escalate to the level of warfare.

Our discussion of other traits has already shown that some verses encourage believers to fight or support the fighters through other means. This is particularly evident in numerous references to martyrdom. God calls all believers to "fight in the cause of Allah" (4:74) and glorifies those who die defending the faith (3:143, 3:157, 3:169–170, 4:69, 4:74, 4:84, 4:95). But, the fight has to be for a good cause and a just one. In other words, combat is legitimate only to defend the faith against those "who disbelieve in the signs of Allah," and it has to be carried out with restraint. . . .

The Qur'an allows retaliation in kind as a way of restoring justice. The believer is told "whoever has assaulted you, then assault him in the same way that he has assaulted you" (2:194), "if you punish, . . . punish with an equivalent of that with which you were harmed" (16:126), and "Allah will surely aid" the person who "responds [to injustice] with the equivalent of that with which he was harmed and then is tyrannized" (22:60). Yet, the believer is also advised against hasty decisions of retaliation and invited to be patient: "But if you are patient—it is better for those who are patient" (16:126).

Retaliation in kind allows for both physical and capital punishment. For the transgressor, the Qur'an states: "We ordained for them therein a life for a life, an eye for an eye, a nose for a nose, an ear for an ear, a tooth for a tooth, and for wounds is legal retribution" (5:45). . . . But these verses are concluded with lines that speak to the merits of seeking settlements without resorting to violence. . . .

Mercy and forgiveness, as opposed to the use of force and retribution, is prescribed most strongly for the Prophets, and particularly for Prophet Muhammad (7:199, 21:107–112). Ordinary Muslims, too, must be just, fair and merciful to invite more people to follow the words of God and the message of his Prophet (60:8; 8:38–40). Since "There shall be no compulsion in [acceptance of] the religion" (2:256), the spread of Islam is to take place peacefully; fighting should be in defence of Islam, not to impose it.

Among violent acts, killing is considered to be the most abhorrent. Intentional killing is permitted only against those who assault the faith and Muslims, as clearly stated in the following two verses[15]:

> You will find others who wish to obtain security from you and [to] obtain security from their people. Every time they are returned to [the influence of] disbelief, they fall back into it. So if they do not withdraw from you or offer you peace or restrain their hands, then seize them and kill them wherever you overtake them. And those—We have made for you against them a clear authorization. (4:91)

> Indeed, the penalty for those who wage war against Allah and His Messenger and strive upon earth [to cause] corruption is none but that they be killed or crucified or that their hands and feet be cut off from opposite sides or that they be exiled from the land. That is for them a disgrace in this world; and for them in the Hereafter is a great punishment. (5:33)

. . . The gravity of killing is stated powerfully in verse 5:32, which states that whoever kills an individual without a due cause, "it is as if he had slain mankind entirely. And whoever saves one—it is as if he had saved mankind entirely" (5:32). The Qur'an also speaks against infanticide, practiced because the newborn is a girl (81:8) or due to poverty, and refers to their killing as "ever a great sin" (17:31).

The verse that is often interpreted as allowing men to beat their disobedient wives (4:34) can be also taken as endorsement of combativeness in the institution of family. But as indicated in previous pages, this verse is highly controversial and attributed alternative meanings. Even in the literary interpretation of the verse, beating is the last resort and no punishment should be sought if the guilty party changes the course of action. It is important to note that there are no other verses that refer to use of force and violence, as a positive or negative trait, in connection to family. The main advice regarding familial relations appears to be showing care and kindness.

Conclusion

In analyzing the Qur'an, we should first remember that it was revealed with the ultimate aim of establishing and spreading monotheism. All of its provisions dealing with economic, social or gender issues were secondary (Mernissi, 1991). Thus, there is only one clear and noncontroversial message in the Qur'an: "There is no God but Allah, and Muhammad is Allah's messenger." Beyond the call for a monotheistic faith, the message of the Qur'an becomes conditional and very complex. Its prescriptions are not always based on the believer's gender, and they vary depending on institutional contexts. "Masculinity" in the Qur'an, therefore, is embedded within and constructed in relation to a series of institutions, resulting in fluid and multidimensional masculinities.

Invoking some verses, one can claim that the use of force and violence is prescribed, if not promoted, for the believing men. Yet, men should also be peaceful and compassionate. They should provide for their family and care for the members of the community, but they should also be willing to sacrifice their life for God and punish those who stand in their way of submitting to God. Men are given power in one instance and then stripped of it in another. These diverse and contradictory prescriptions, however, converge in a resounding message: men should use their judgement and act according to the situation. Each situation merits a unique combination of masculine ideals. These ideals do not establish hierarchal masculinities with one serving as the hegemonic one. The Qur'an points to preferable options but never makes the decision. The result is not a formula but a complex message that the Muslim man has to configure for his given situation using the wisdom also granted by God.

The application of the message faces two difficulties. First, the diversity permits selectivity, which is often applied with a desire to simplify the complex and conditional message, due to ignorance, or as a result of purposeful distortion to achieve other goals. Second, the Qur'an is not the only source that guides Muslim boys and men, as well as women who raise and support them. Alternative discourses, material conditions and structural factors are often more powerful and override the Qur'an, even if it is consulted. . . .

Thus, was our entire project a futile exercise? We think not. We believe more studies like ours are needed to challenge certain myths produced and reproduced in two domains. Our first audience is Muslim communities, especially boys and young men, who hear the justification of repressive and aggressive behaviour by invoking Islam. Second one is non-Muslims who are ready to essentialize Islam, pigeon hole Muslims, and accept individual or collective acts of violence by some Muslim men as an innate feature of Islam and "Muslim masculinity." Thus, rather than declaring what Islamic masculinities are, this study intends to open the door for discussion. Without critical examination of sources and debate of different interpretations and findings, myths would continue to circulate and be taken as "the truth."

Notes

1. On "hegemonic masculinity," see Connell and Messerschmidt (2005).
2. Although she argues against essentialism, Barlas essentializes certain traits as feminine.
3. Sufi Islam, with its emphasis on love of God and spiritual aspect of the religion rather than institutional practices, is often seen as less gendered, if not the feminine side of Islam (Aslam, 2012, pp. 91–95; Samuel, 2011, pp. 317–319). However, the practice in specific orders, as well as the writings of some prominent Sufi scholars, shows that Sufism, too, has been highly gendered. Most Sufi orders not only maintained male leadership (*Murshid*) but also assigned a lower value to women even as disciples (*Murid*). See DeSondy (2013).
4. A main challenge of interpretation is about the issues that are not directly addressed in the Qur'an. If there are no specific criticisms of the prevailing practices or prescriptions to manage things differently, can we assume the Qur'an supports the established pre-Islamic practice? Those who take *sunna* (tradition) as guidance tends to maintain this position.

5. For a discussion of different interpretations of this verse and the alternative meanings of the terms commonly translated as having authority/being in charge (*qawwam*) and stike/beat (*idrib* or *daraba*), see Wadud (1999); Stowasser (1998, 1994); Barazangi (1997); Engineer (1992).
6. See especially 33:34–35 and Arat (2000) for a more detailed analysis of equalities and inequalities in the Qur'an.
7. For an alternative reading that claims the Qur'an is open to same-sex marriage, see Kugle, 2010.
8. We deliberately avoid addressing femininities and comparing them to masculinities for multiple reasons. First, while some prescriptions directly address the believing men, many apply to all believers regardless of their gender. Second, our definition of masculinity as "a social position" and acceptance of its fluidity challenge the approaches that consider masculinity as rooted in the two-sex gender binary. Finally, numerous studies over the past decades have focused on the Qur'an's teachings on the role of women and femininity (e.g., Arat, 2000).
9. See http://quran.com/1.
10. However, the Qur'an also includes praises for some individuals who were not monotheist, such as the wife of Pharaoh who saved and raised Moses and the Queen of Sheba, for their wisdom, kind behaviour, or commitment to justice.
11. Slaves, as a category of people, illustrate the complexity of the character traits that should be adopted by the owners, because they cut through the institutional contexts. During the time of revelations, they were non-Muslims captured in war (prisoners of war), owned by their masters who could sell them as property, typically paid for their services as labourers, and considered to be members of the household/family.
12. Note that travellers are often mentioned among *zakat* recipients and those who should be cared for.
13. This is a reference to daily prayers.

14. They should avoid having sexual desires to-wards their mother, daughters, sisters, aunts, nieces, foster mothers and sisters, stepdaughters, grandmothers, and other women who are already married (4:23–24).

15. See also the pre-Islamic reference: "We decreed upon the Children of Israel that whoever kills a soul unless for a soul or for corruption [done] in the land—it is as if he had slain mankind entirely. And whoever saves one—it is as if he had saved mankind entirely . . ." (5:32).

Acknowledgements

We are grateful to our designated discussant at the 2016 ISA conference, Henri Myrttinen, and colleagues in the audience for offering insightful questions and comments. We also appreciate the constructive criticisms offered by the anonymous reviewers chosen by the journal editors, which were instrumental in improving the work. All remaining problems are, of course, our responsibility.

Disclaimer

The views and interpretation reflected in this document are those of the authors and do not reflect an expression of opinion on the part of their past or present employment or other institutional affiliations.

References

Ahmed, L. (1992). *Women and gender in Islam: Historical roots of a modern debate*. New Haven, CT: Yale University Press.

Arat, Z. F. K. (2000). Women's rights in Islam: Revisiting Qur'anic rights. In P. Schwab & A. Pollis (Eds.), *Human rights: New perspectives, new realities* (pp. 69–93). Boulder, CO: Lynne Rienner.

Aslam, M. (2012). *Gender-based explosions: The Nexus between Muslim masculinities, jihadist Islamism and terrorism*. New York, NY: UNU Press.

Barazangi, N. H. (1997). Muslim women's Islamic higher learning as a human right: The action plan. In M. Afkhami & E. Friedl (Eds.), *Muslim women and the politics of participation: Beijing platform* (pp. 43–57). New York, NY: Syracuse University Press.

Barlas, A. (2002). *Believing women in Islam: Unreading patriarchal interpretations of the Qur'an*. Austin: University of Texas Press.

Braudy, L. (2003). *From chivalry to terrorism: War and the changing nature of masculinity*. New York, NY: Vintage Books.

Butler, J. (1990). *Gender trouble: Feminism and the subversion of identity*. New York, NY: Routledge.

Connell, R. W. (2005). Globalization, imperialism, and masculinities. In M. S. Kimmel, J. Hearn, & R. W. Connell (Eds.), *Handbook of studies on men and masculinities* (pp. 71–89). Thousand Oaks, CA: Sage.

Connell, R. W., & Messerschmidt, J. W. (2005). Hegemonic masculinity: Rethinking the concept. *Gender and Society, 19*, 829–859.

DeSondy, A. (2013). *The crisis of Islamic masculinities*. New York, NY: Bloomsbury Academic.

Engineer, A. (1992). *The rights of women in Islam*. New Delhi: Sterling.

Katz, J. (2003). Advertising and the construction of violent white masculinity. In G. Dines & J. M. Humez (Eds.), *Gender, race, and class in media* (pp. 261–269). Thousand Oaks, CA: Sage.

Kimmel, M. (1994). Masculinity and homophobia: Fear, shame, and silence in the construction of gender identity. In H. Brod & M. Kuafman (Eds.), *Theorizing masculinities* (pp. 119–141). Thousand Oaks, CA: Sage.

Kimmel, M. (2008). *Guyland: The Perilous World Where Boys Become Men*. New York, NY: HarperCollins.

Kugle, S. S. (2010). *Homosexuality in Islam: Critical reflection on gay, lesbian, and transgender Muslims*. Oxford: Oneworld Publications.

Mayring, P. (2000). Qualitative content analysis. *Forum Qualitative Sozialforschung/Forum: Qualitative Social Research, 1*(2), Art. 20 (June), 28 paragraphs. Retrieved from http://www.qualitative-research.net/index.php/fqs/article/viewArticle/1089/2385

Mernissi, F. (1991). *Veil and the male elite: A feminist interpretation of women's rights in Islam*. New York, NY: Addison-Wesey.

Qutb/Kotb, S. (1970). *Social justice in Islam*. New York, NY: Octagon Books.

Ramadan, T. (2001). *Islam, the West and the challenges of modernity*. Leicester: The Islamic Foundation.

Said, E. W. (1978). *Orientalism*. London: Routledge & Kegan Paul.

Samuel, G. (2011). Islamic piety and masculinity. *Contemporary Islam, 5*, 309–322.

Schick, I. (1999). *The erotic margin: Sexuality and spatiality in alterist discourse*. London: Verso.

Schippers, M. (2007). Recovering the feminine Other: Masculinity, femininity, and gender hegemony. *Theory and Society, 36*, 85–102.

Stowasser, B. (1994). *Women in the Qur`an, traditions, and interpretations*. New York, NY: Oxford University Press.

Stowasser, B. (1998). Gender issues and contemporary Quran interpretation. In Y. Y. Haddad & J. Esposito (Eds.), *Islam, gender, and social change* (pp. 30–44). Oxford: Oxford University Press.

Taha, M. (1987). *The second message of Islam*. Syracuse, NY: Syracuse University Press.

Toch, H. (1998). Hypermasculinity and prison violence. In L. H. Bowker (Ed.), *Masculinities and violence* (Vol. 10, pp. 168–178). Thousand Oaks, CA: Sage.

Wadud, A. (1999). *Qur'an and woman: Rereading the sacred text from a woman's perspective*. New York, NY: Oxford University Press.

Zaman, M. R. (1996). Economic justice in islam, ideals and reality: The cases of Malaysia, Pakistan and Saudi Arabia. In N. H. Barazangi, M. R. Zaman, & O. Afzal (Eds.), *Islamic identity and the struggle for justice* (pp. 47–63). Gainsville: University Press of Florida.

JUDAISM, MASCULINITY AND FEMINISM

MICHAEL KIMMEL

In the late 1960s, I organized and participated in several large demonstrations against the war in Vietnam. Early on—it must have been 1967 or so—over 10,000 of us were marching down Fifth Avenue in New York urging the withdrawal of all U.S. troops. As we approached one corner, I noticed a small but vocal group of counter-demonstrators, waving American flags and shouting patriotic slogans, "Go back to Russia!" one yelled. Never being particularly shy, I tried to engage him. "It's my duty as an American to oppose policies I disagree with. This is patriotism!" I answered. "Drop dead, you commie Jew fag!" was his reply.

Although I tried not to show it, I was shaken by his accusation, perplexed and disturbed by the glib association of communism, Judaism, and homosexuality. "Only one out of three," I can say to myself now, "is not especially perceptive." But yet something disturbing remains about that linking of political, religious, and sexual orientations. What links them, I think, is a popular perception that each is not quite a man, that each is less than a man. And while recent developments may belie this simplistic formulation, there is, I believe, a kernel of truth to the epithet, a small piece I want to claim, not as vicious smear, but proudly. I believe that my Judaism did directly contribute to my activism against that terrible war, just as it currently provides the foundation for my participation in the struggle against sexism.

What I want to explore here are some of the ways in which my Jewishness has contributed to becoming an anti-sexist man, working to make this world a safe environment for women (and men) to fully express their humanness. Let me be clear that I speak from a cultural heritage of Eastern European Jewry, transmuted by three generations of life in the United States. I speak of the culture of Judaism's effect on me as an American Jew, not from either doctrinal considerations—we all know the theological contradictions of a biblical reverence for women, and prayers that thank God for not being born one—nor from an analysis of the politics of nation states. My perspective says nothing of Middle-Eastern machismo; I speak of Jewish culture in the diaspora, not of Israeli politics.

The historical experience of Jews has three elements that I believe have contributed to this participation in feminist politics. First, historically, the Jew is an *outsider*. Wherever the Jew has gone, he or she has been outside the seat of power, excluded from privilege. The Jew is the symbolic "other," not unlike the symbolic "otherness" of women, gays, racial and ethnic minorities, the elderly and the physically challenged. To be marginalized allows one to see the center more clearly than those who are in it, and presents grounds for alliances among marginal groups.

This essay was originally prepared as a lecture on "Changing Roles for the American Man" at the 92nd Street Y in November, 1983. I am grateful to Bob Brannon and Harry Brod for comments and criticisms of an earlier draft.

Michael S. Kimmel, "Judaism, Masculinity and Feminism" reprinted from *Changing Men,* Summer/ Fall, 1987. Copyright 1987. Reprinted by permission of the author. This essay was originally prepared as a lecture on "Changing Roles for the American Man."

But the American Jew, the former immigrant, is "other" in another way, one common to many ethnic immigrants to the United States. Jewish culture is, after all, seen as an ethnic culture, which allows it to be more oppressive and emotionally rich than the bland norm. Like other ethnic subgroups, Jews have been characterized as emotional, nurturing, caring. Jewish men hug and kiss, cry and laugh. A little too much. A little too loudly. Like ethnics.

Historically, the Jewish man has been seen as less than masculine, often as a direct outgrowth of this emotional "respond-ability." The historical consequences of centuries of laws against Jews, of anti-Semitic oppression, are a cultural identity and even a self-perception as "less than men," who are too weak, too fragile, too frightened to care for our own. The cruel irony of ethnic oppression is that our rich heritage is stolen from us, and then we are blamed for having no rich heritage. In this, again, the Jew shares this self-perception with other oppressed groups who, rendered virtually helpless by an infantilizing oppression, are further victimized by the accusation that they are, in fact, infants and require the beneficence of the oppressor. One example of this cultural self-hatred can be found in the comments of Freud's colleague and friend Weininger (a Jew) who argued that "the Jew is saturated with femininity. The most feminine Aryan is more masculine than the most manly Jew. The Jew lacks the good breeding that is based upon respect for one's own individuality as well as the individuality of others."

But, again, Jews are also "less than men" for a specific reason as well. The traditional emphasis on literacy in Jewish culture contributes in a very special way. In my family, at least, to be learned, literate, a rabbi, was the highest aspiration one could possibly have. In a culture characterized by love of learning, literacy may be a mark of dignity. But currently in the United States literacy is a cultural liability. Americans contrast egghead intellectuals, divorced from the real world, with men of action—instinctual, passionate, fierce, and masculine. Senator Albert Beveridge of Indiana counseled in his 1906 volume *Young Man and the World* (a turn of the century version of *Real Men Don't Eat Quiche*)

to "avoid books, in fact, avoid all artificial learning, for the forefathers put America on the right path by learning from completely natural experience." Family, church and synagogue, and schoolroom were cast as the enervating domains of women, sapping masculine vigor.

Now don't get me wrong. The Jewish emphasis on literacy, on mind over body, does not exempt Jewish men from sexist behavior. Far from it. While many Jewish men avoid the Scylla of a boisterous and physically harassing misogyny, we can often dash ourselves against the Charybdis of a male intellectual intimidation of others. "Men with the properly sanctioned educational credentials in our society," writes Harry Brod, "are trained to impose our opinions on others, whether asked for or not, with an air of supreme self-confidence and aggressive self-assurance." It's as if the world were only waiting for our word. In fact, Brod notes, "many of us have developed mannerisms that function to intimidate those customarily denied access to higher educational institutions, especially women." And yet, despite this, the Jewish emphasis on literacy has branded us, in the eyes of the world, less than "real" men.

Finally, the historical experience of Jews centers around, hinges upon our sense of morality, our ethical imperatives. The preservation of a moral code, the commandment to live ethically, is the primary responsibility of each Jew, male or female. Here, let me relate another personal story. Like many other Jews, I grew up with the words "Never Again" ringing in my ears, branded indelibly in my consciousness. For me they implied a certain moral responsibility to bear witness, to remember—to place my body, visibly, on the side of justice. This moral responsibility inspired my participation in the anti-war movement, and my active resistance of the draft *as a Jew*. I remember family dinners in front of the *CBS Evening News*, watching Walter Cronkite recite the daily tragedy of the war in Vietnam. "Never Again," I said to myself, crying myself to sleep after watching napalm fall on Vietnamese villagers. Isn't this the brutal terror we have sworn ourselves to preventing when we utter those two words? When I allowed myself to feel the pain of those people, there was no longer a choice; there was, instead, a moral imperative to speak out, to attempt to end that war as quickly as possible.

In the past few years, I've become aware of another war. I met and spoke with women who had been raped, raped by their lovers, husbands, and fathers, women who had been beaten by those husbands and lovers. Some were even Jewish women. All those same words—Never Again—flashed across my mind like a neon meteor lighting up the darkened consciousness. Hearing that pain and that anger prompted the same moral imperative. We Jews say "Never Again" to the systematic horror of the Holocaust, to the cruel war against the Vietnamese, to Central American death squads. And we must say it against this war waged against women in our society, against rape and battery.

So in a sense, I see my Judaism as reminding me every day of that moral responsibility, the *special* ethical imperative that my life, as a Jew, gives to me. Our history indicates how we have been excluded from power, but also, as men, we have been privileged by another power. Our Judaism impels us to stand against any power that is illegitimately constituted because we know only too well the consequences of that power. Our ethical vision demands equality and justice, and its achievement is our historical mission.

Note

1. Harry Brod, "Justice and a Male Feminist" in *The Jewish Newspaper* (Los Angeles) June 6, 1985, p. 6.

Masculinities
in the Media
and Popular Culture

Men are daily bombarded with images of masculinity—in magazines, television, movies, music, even the Internet. We see what men are supposed to look like, act like, be like. And social scientists are only now beginning to understand the enormous influence that the media have in shaping our ideas about what it means to be a man.

For one thing, it is clear that the media can create artificial standards against which boys as well as girls measure themselves. Just as idealized human female models can only approximate the exaggeratedly large breasts and exaggeratedly small waistline of Barbie, virtually no men can approach the physiques of the cartoon version of Tarzan or even G.I. Joe. The original G.I. Joe had the equivalent of 12.2-inch biceps when he was introduced in 1964. Ten years later, his biceps measured the equivalent of 15.2 inches. By 1994, he had 16.4-inch biceps, and today his biceps measure a simulated 26.8 inches—nearly 7 inches larger than Mark McGwire's 20-inch muscles. "Many modern figures display the physiques of advanced bodybuilders and some display levels of muscularity far exceeding the outer limits of actual human attainment," notes Dr. Harrison Pope, a Harvard psychiatrist.

No wonder boys and men so often feel like we fail the test of physical manhood. Media provide unrealistic images against which we measure ourselves. Both David

Nylund and Tristan Bridges and Kristen Barber look at the varieties of masculinities offered by the media. Media may offer images of idealized masculinity alongside a notion of idealized femininity—or, in the case of rap music, Ronald Weitzer and Charis Kubrin argue, a femininity that is hypersexualized only in relation to masculinity. And entire genres of media are offered to us as gendered, as Kathy Sanford and Leanna Madill suggest in their examination of video games as a "boy thing."

PART VIII DISCUSSION QUESTIONS

1. To what extent do "softer" approaches ensure the continued dominance of masculinities? To what extent do they show potential for a more gender egalitarian future?
2. The marketing of self-care products to women has routinely relied on undercutting women's self-confidence and body satisfaction while offering the solution to these "deficits" in the form of consumer products. How does "marketing manhood" as described by Barber and Bridges differ from this approach? Why do you think so?
3. How are masculinities negotiated in the media by both consumers and producers?
4. Authors Weitzer and Kubrin highlight socioeconomic forces, gender inequality, and record industry interests as central to explaining unfavorable representations of women in rap music. How might racism play a role?
5. Sanford and Madill highlight opportunities for resistance as an overarching narrative of video game play. Of course, these games are also conduits for the culture of hegemonic masculinity. Would games that mirror the opportunities for resistance but do not rely on gender stereotypes be as successful as the games cited by the authors? Why or why not?

Marketing Manhood in a "Post-Feminist" Age

KRISTEN BARBER AND TRISTAN BRIDGES

Isaiah Mustafa, shirtless, rises from a bubble bath on a white foam horse to spread the word: "Make Sure Your Man Smells Like a Man." This slogan appears at the bottom of the page, implying there is indeed such a thing as a "manly" scent. He wears foam cowboy boots, chaps, and gloves, as well as a foam hat and sheriff's badge. In his left hand, he displays a red bottle of Old Spice body wash. A woman, wrapped in only a towel, gazes at Mustafa as he whips his foam lasso in the air, sardonically engaging the iconic image of the American cowboy. With a subtle smirk that suggests a casual confidence, the meanings of Mustafa's gender display are diverse. Aimed at men and women alike, this advertisement identifies a potentially deficient man and offers a solution to shore up his masculinity. While the story of transformation through consumption is not new, the jocular exaggeration, wit, and satire seen here are unique features of a popular portrayal of men in advertising today. See figure 31.1 on the next page.

• • • Satire mocks while also revealing a supposed truth about some group, idea, thing, or behavior—here, who men are and who they can and should be. While Mustafa has achieved widespread recognition as the "Old Spice Guy," the satirical masculinity he helped to make famous is used to market an incredibly diverse array of products. Consider Kraft's "Let's Get Zesty" campaign for a line of salad dressings. Like Mustafa, actor Anderson Davis is presented as both a farce and a representative of a masculine ideal. Similarly, Yoplait features square-jawed, furrowed-brow actor Dominic Purcell in marketing its "fluffy," low-calorie Greek yogurt, see figure 31.2. When he produces a tiny spoon from his pocket, we see that men can maintain masculinity while enjoying a whipped, fruity treat.

All of these advertisements proceed from the assumption that masculinity is naturally at odds with anything even vaguely associated with women, like body wash, salad, and yogurt. Satirical masculinity produces a set of facetious cultural scripts that bridge this divide to create a new consumer base that "mans up" to purchase otherwise "feminine" products.

All of these advertisements present recognizable markers of what sociologist Raewyn Connell calls hegemonic—or culturally celebrated—masculinity, but they also poke fun at those very same markers. . . . For instance, in the Yoplait commercials, Purcell's size suggests strength and the ability to dominate others (consistent with his television roles in "Prison Break" and "Legends of Tomorrow"), and his deep voice thrums as he tells us in all seriousness: "It's like a little fluffy cloud in my mouth. Fluffy, fluffy cloud." Kraft's "Let's Get Zesty" uses the tagline, "The only thing better than dressing is undressing," playing on the advertising cliché that "sex sells"—no matter what you're selling. And Mustafa conjures images of intentionally over-the-top romance novel covers, see figures 31.3 and 31.4.

Figure 31.1 Foam Cowboy, Isaiah Mustafa, in an Old Spice advertisement.

Figure 31.2 A still of Dominic Purcell in Yoplait's "Hunger" television commercial for Yoplait Greek 100 yogurt.

These representations of masculinity are so distant from most men's everyday lives that they are laughable. But scholars who study humor have found that jokes allow for the perpetuation of sexism, as well as racism, homophobia, and classism.

It's worthwhile to ask whether these satirical representations of masculinity are indeed subversive—by making outdated cultural ideals comical—or whether they help to reproduce the very forms of inequality they seem to mock. By analyzing three popular advertising campaigns in the satirical masculinity genre, we connect a cultural phenomenon to the emerging theory of "hybrid masculinities," which considers shifting definitions of manhood in terms of their larger consequences for equality.

Satirical Masculinity and Hybridity

...[W]hat we think of as "manly," "macho," or "masculine" varies by society, subculture, and time.

But shifts in masculinity do follow a curious pattern: they are *reactive* rather than anticipatory. Masculinities scholar Michael Kimmel argues that anxiety about what masculinity actually is tends to *follow* transformations in femininity. Though the idea is counter-intuitive (we don't think of groups in power as being "pushed around" in this way), the historical record bears out Kimmel's point. When women enter into historically "masculine" arenas, like sports or the workplace, they shift the boundaries of femininity. And those are the moments when we get anxious about masculinity, claim that it is "in crisis," and find groups rallying around "solutions" to this suddenly pressing social issue.

...C. J. Pascoe and Tristan Bridges, who theorize hybrid masculinities, have surveyed the masculinities literature and argue that it shows White, straight, and well-to-do men sometimes adopt various elements of "other," more socially

Figure 31.3 Isiah Mustafa as a biker for the Old Spice "Smell Like a Man, Man" campaign.

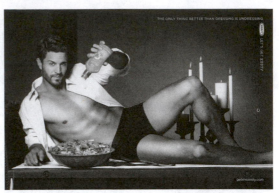

Figure 31.4 Anderson Davis in Kraft's "Let's Get Zesty" campaign.

marginalized masculinities (and sometimes femininities, too) into their own performances of masculinity. This behavior produces the impression that social change has occurred without any real shifts in privilege.

Inequalities that persist, adapt. The theory of hybrid masculinities suggests that adaption takes place via three interrelated processes. First, hybrid masculinities produce symbolic distance between men and hegemonic forms of masculinity. Michael J. Murphy, for example, shows that public service campaigns like "Real Men Don't Rape" or "My Strength is Not for Hurting" allow some men to position themselves as beyond reproach. Second, hybrid masculinities involve men "strategically borrowing" elements from disadvantaged groups, such as when White men adopt elements of African-American culture. Third, hybrid masculinities fortify boundaries between groups in ways that obscure the inequalities defining those boundaries.

So, when straight men play with "gay" culture, it can create the appearance that incredible change has occurred. But if structural inequalities between straight and queer men remain intact, playfulness accomplishes little more than expanding their gender repertoires via a kind of identity tourism.

As a heuristic device, the satirical masculinity in so much contemporary advertising aimed at men is a powerful illustration of hybrid masculinity. These ads show us one way that current forms of inequality persist even as popular and academic critiques of "toxic" masculinity gain attention.

In 2008, Old Spice began a drastic rebranding effort with its "Swagger" advertisements featuring football player Brian Urlacher and musician LL Cool J. The brand has long been associated with older men. . . .

As market research companies like Euromonitor International encourage cosmetic companies to appeal to young men and their wallets, though, we have seen a proliferation of commercials and print advertisements that engage satirical masculinity. . . .

Once-popular markers of adulthood such as marriage, children, and breadwinning jobs are less accessible to younger generations of men. In step, retail companies offer consumption as the new rite of passage to manhood. In the case of Old Spice, tackling the femininity of self-care and the association of its products with older men, the company's advertisements play with masculine stereotypes to widen its consumer base. . . . Old Spice facetiously

Figure 31.5 Kraft print advertisement for zesty Italian dressing.

Figure 31.6 Dominic Purcell eats "fluffy" Yoplait yogurt.

provides everyday men the potential to feel masculine. The material evidence of masculinity has shifted, from steady paychecks to sudsy products. . . .

Yet Mustafa's presentation of manhood is complicated. His cowboy is not *all* macho; it could even suggest a queer sensibility.

. . . [A]t the same time, the presence of a woman in the ads allows for the potential of dual advertising, a strategy originated by Calvin Klein to produce a more subtle resonance with gay men alongside a more overt pitch to straight men. This queerness creates a contradiction in masculinity, making it difficult to take seriously the hegemonic markers of power. In this symbolic murkiness, Pascoe and Bridges explain how hybrid masculinities make existing inequalities hard to identify. . . .

"Oh, hey ladies. Are you in the mood to do something special?" Actor Anderson Davis slowly sucks on a wooden spoon he's just used to toss a salad. "I sure am." The camera pans to a stick of butter that melts under his smoldering gaze. "You know, once you go Italian, you never go back." It's unclear if Davis is talking about himself or the sausages in the skillet. With a backdrop of the Tuscan countryside behind him, Davis steps over to a pot of boiling water. He lifts the lid: "Steamy." His tight white t-shirt clings to his chest, wet from the condensation. The idea is that this will be a romantic dinner and, drawing from larger cultural ideas that women are lucky if their husbands or boyfriends do the cooking, Davis is presented as the perfect man. . . .

But in the three-part series of Kraft ads starring Davis, the romantic man appears ridiculously cliché. It might be more accurate to call his performance of masculinity a caricature. With his faintly raised eyebrow, Kraft represents Davis as simultaneously—if awkwardly—celebrating and mocking domestic, hetero-romantic masculinity. This simultaneity illustrates change and continuity in relations between men and women—the audience is primed to see it as funny that a "manly-man" is enacting tropes about women's sexual desire (stoked by the fantasy of temporarily surrendering "their" domestic tasks).

In a print advertisement, Kraft depicts a naked Davis on a red and white–checkered picnic blanket, see figure 31.5. A corner of the blanket keeps him modest by covering his genitals, and a picnic basket overflows next to him. . . . The image plays on tropes about hetero-romantic masculinity, and especially on stereotypes about women's desires.

This campaign celebrates gender relationships and sexual practices that feminists have shown perpetuate gender inequality, but with a wink and a nod. They are the exception that proves the rule in that they revive heterosexist assumptions of masculine subjectivity that structure unequal relations between men and women. Again, the humor is in the presentation of women as sexual subjects rather than as the objects of desire.

General Mills, co-owner of Yoplait, declares that "Dominic Purcell is a Man of Yogurt." He is "noted for acting rugged and tough," the company's blog post states, but he can still tuck into a "smooth, creamy, and sometimes fluffy" treat, see figure 31.6.

Indeed, Purcell is built like a linebacker, and he doesn't smile in any of the Yoplait advertisements or television commercials. "You see this look on my face?" He asks the audience in one commercial, "It's not anger; it's hunger." And apparently, a cup of 100-calorie yogurt will take the edge off. He promises that as he eats it, "a look of satisfaction and contentment [will] blossom across my face." His deep, sober tone remains flat, as does his expression. "Yum. See?" That's the joke: that Purcell has only one mode: stoic, serious, possibly dangerous. Eating yogurt doesn't compromise it a bit.

Like both the Old Spice and Kraft campaigns, Yoplait is attempting to bridge a gender gap in consumption by acknowledging yogurt is culturally coded as "feminine" and potentially emasculating. . . .

Recall that satirical masculinity is used to sell men on products they presumably avoid for fear of what it might say about their gender and sexual identities. In response, all of these advertisements share a common feature: the intentionally excessive displays of masculinity. Through this, Yoplait's depiction of Purcell—like Kraft's use of Anderson and Old Spice's reliance upon Mustafa—appears to simultaneously celebrate and mock his masculinity. After commenting on the "fluffy cloud" quality of the yogurt, the lambo doors wing open on a silver sports car. By contrasting feminine yogurt with the phallic muscle car, this commercial appears to indicate some change, perhaps a softening of masculinity or a calling-out of unrealistic masculine types. But it also continues to celebrate elements of masculinity that feminist scholars argue are in dire need of change.

. . . These images offer a playful, ironic masculinity, and invite us to take pleasure in men who clearly embody idealized forms of masculinity while engaging in "feminine" consumption practices. But this joke really only works if the systems of power are both carefully concealed *and* reinforced. As illustrations of hybrid masculinity, these displays of masculinity underscore stereotypical gender and sexual differences—though in novel ways. The use of satire helps to obscure the full consequences of hybrid masculinities despite them being on full display. It is comical to see Purcell's big hands skillfully wield a tiny spoon with which to eat yogurt, but only because his association with masculine power remains intact.

These ads might also look like sexual objectification, and a great bit of popular discussion assumes this objectification affects men's self-esteem and relationships to their bodies. As gender scholar Susan Bordo argues in her book, *The Male Body*, "I never dreamed that 'equality' would move in the direction of men worrying more about their looks rather than women worrying less." But emergent research on hybrid masculinities finds that looks can be deceiving. This is because sexual objectification is a cultural process that disempowers women on a larger scale, affecting their abilities to be taken seriously in the workplace, for example, or setting the stage for sexual violence and slut-shaming. While displays of satirical masculinity are often sexual, they are not disempowering. These commercials do not wholly undermine the "feminine" nature of these products, nor do they challenge the masculinity of those men hired to sell them. And anyone who finds the joke offensive is implicitly chided for caring too much about something so superficial as an advertisement for body wash. After all, it's just a joke—right?

Recommended Resources

Susan M. Alexander. 2003. "Stylish Hard Bodies: Branded Masculinity in *Men's Health Magazine*," *Sociological Perspectives* 46(4): 535–554. An analysis of *Men's Health* magazine covers, stories, features, and advertisements examining the ways that consumption practices are framed as "masculine" throughout.

Bethan Benwell (ed.). 2003. *Masculinity and Men's Lifestyle Magazines*. Oxford, U.K.: Blackwell–Wiley. A collection of interdisciplinary essays on the emergence of men's lifestyle publications, including examinations of sports masculinities, American leisure, etc.

Hamilton Carroll. 2011. *Affirmative Reaction: New Formations of White Masculinity*. Durham, NC: Duke University Press. Examines the flexibility of contemporary representations of White masculinity across the popular cultural landscape, as well as how emergent iterations are related to durable forms of race, class, gender, and sexual inequality.

Kyle Green and Madison Van Oort. 2013. "'We Wear No Pants': Selling the Crisis of Masculinity in the 2010 Super Bowl Commercials," *Signs* 38(3): 695–719. Identifies a discourse of threatened masculinity in advertisements involving low patriarchal status, diminished confidence, failing bodies, and financial loss and uncertainty.

Michael A. Messner and Jeffrey Montez de Oca. 2005. "The Male Consumer as Loser: Beer and Liquor Ads in Mega Sports Media Events," *Signs* 30(3): 1879–1909. Considers tropes of masculinity used to sell beer and liquor to young men during Super Bowl commercials and in *Sports Illustrated* issues.

Transmitting Softer Masculinity

Sports Talk Radio and Masculinity

DAVID NYLUND

Introduction

Sports talk radio, which broadcasts sporting discussions, is a popular sport-media format with an almost exclusively male demographic. In addition to play-by-play coverage of local sports teams, most shows offer discussion and analysis of sport as part of their regular programming. These shows are generally characterized by an often-boisterous on-air style personality, and all-encompassing debate by both hosts and callers. Sports talk is available in both local and syndicated forms, and is carried in some form on both major North American satellite radio networks. In the United States, for example, most sports talk formatted radio stations air mostly syndicated programming, with ESPN and Radio Fox Sports Radio being the most popular.[1]

Sports Talk Radio Then

Sports radio stations, similar to political talk radio, mushroomed in the 1980s with the rise of late capitalism, the deregulation of the radio industry, corporate media consolidation, and niche marketing (Douglas, 2002). Ceding the radio airwaves to niche marketing and late capitalism has predictably generated sports radio programming that mirrors the content, style and success of talk radio hosts, such as Rush Limbaugh in the United States, who champion right wing policies (Smith, 2002).[2] According

to Goldberg (1998), Haag (1996), Mariscal (1999), and Nylund (2007), sports talk radio is just as hostile to feminists and gays as right wing political talk radio. These scholars suggest that sports radio has reproduced hegemonic masculinity, a dominant form of manhood predicated on competiveness, toughness, and the marginalization of women and gay men (Connell, 2000). In fact, according to Kevin Cook (1993: 20), sports talk radio, even more than political talk radio, feeds hegemonic masculinity as it is the only arena left for white men who have been "wounded by the indignities of feminism, affirmative action, and other groups' quest for social equality". In line with Cook's argument, Haag (1996) states:

> Sports talk show is a venue for the embattled White male seeking recreational repose; that it caters to this audience as surely as Rush Limbaugh articulates its discontents. Some sports talk stations define their listening audience explicitly as the Atlanta sports station [The FAN] manager states, "we make no pretensions about what we're doing here. The FAN is a guy's radio station. We're aiming at the men's bracket which is the hardest to reach."
>
> (p. 459)

. . . There is ample evidence that sports talk radio is an anti-democratic, sexist medium that reinforces

---

homophobia and male hegemony. However, my listening and analysis of sports radio programmes over the past ten years reveals some contradictions and fissures to hegemony; this includes the nationally syndicated *Jim Rome Show*. The host of the show, Jim Rome, historically known for his "macho" posturing and feminizing of athletes, has had many rich discussions on his show focusing on the discrimination against gay athletes. The following examples of the programme exemplify times when the show partially subverts hegemonic masculinity and homophobia. The first example relates to an editorial letter in the May 2003 issue of *Out* Magazine. In that issue, editor in chief, Brendan Lemon, stated that his boyfriend was a Major League baseball player. Lemon did not give names but hinted that the player was from an East Coast franchise. Rome and other conventional media programmes reacted quickly to the editorial. A media firestorm resulted in a rumour mill: players, fans, owners, and sports talk radio hosts swapped guesses and anxieties over the athlete's identity.

On May 18, 2003, Rome's monologue pondered these questions: What would happen if that person's identity became public? What would it mean for baseball, gays, and lesbians in sports in general, and for the man himself? Given that Lemon's boyfriend would be the first athlete in one of the "big four" major-league team sports (baseball, football, basketball, and hockey) to come out *during* his career, what effect would this have on the institution of sport? Rome decided to pose this question to one of his interview subjects, well-respected baseball veteran, Eric Davis.

> ROME: What would happen if a teammate of yours, or any baseball player, would come out of the closet and say, "I am gay"? What would the reaction be like? How badly would that go?
>
> ERIC: I think it would go real bad. I think people would jump to form an opinion because everybody has an opinion about gays already. But I think it would be a very difficult situation because with us showering with each other . . . being around each other as men. Now, you're in the shower with a guy who's

gay . . . looking at you . . . maybe making a pass. That's an uncomfortable situation. In society, they have never really accepted it. They want to come out. And if that's the cause fine but in sports, it would definitely raise some eyebrows . . . I don't think it should be thrown at 25 guys saying, "Yeah I am gay."
>
> [Rome changes the subject . . . no follow-up]

Rome asks a pointed question to Davis whose predictable homophobic response warrants more follow-up questions. Yet, Rome shifts the subject to something less problematic, letting Davis off the hook. After Rome ends the interview, he addresses Davis's comments in another monologue:

> That's [Eric Davis] a 17 year respected major league ballplayer. And I think that's a representative comment of a lot of these guys. . . . He is a very highly regarded guy. This is why I asked him the question. And he answered it very honestly. He would be concerned about having a gay teammate. . . . For instance, when he's showering. Personally, I don't agree with the take. It's my personal opinion. However, I posed the question to see what the reaction would be. And this is what I have been saying since this story broke. This is why it would not be a good thing. This is why the editor of that magazine clearly was wrong and has never been in a locker-room or clubhouse. That's why it hasn't happened. Eric Davis' reaction is what you would expect. Not everybody would feel that way, but a large majority would. It would make it nearly impossible for a gay player to come out.

Here, Rome is aware of the potential difficulties that would occur for an openly gay ballplayer. However, he articulates his opinion in the safety of his "expert" monologue, not in the presence of Eric Davis. He does not risk compromising his relationship with Davis by endorsing an unusually progressive stance in the presence of a famous ballplayer like Davis. But, when a listener calls immediately after the Davis interview, Rome responds differently:

> JOE: I never imagined my first take would be on gays but I had to call. Being gay, it matters to no

one but gays themselves. Why don't you guys, girls or gays ... whatever you guys are. Just do us a favor, do yourselves a favor and keep it to yourselves. I mean ... [Rome hangs up on the caller]

ROME: I think that's a very convenient response—"It's an issue only because you make it an issue." I don't agree with that frankly. It's an issue because they are often persecuted against, harassed, assaulted, or killed in some cases. That's why it is an issue. They are fired from jobs, ostracized. It's not only an issue because they are making it an issue. What you are saying is keep your mouth shut, keep it in the closet; you are not accepting them for whom they are and what they are. It's not an issue because they are making it an issue. It's an issue because of people saying things like, "keep your mouth shut ... we don't want you around ... we don't want to know you people exist". That's why it's an issue because of that treatment.

Rome's stance against homophobia demonstrates an appreciation of the injustices of homophobia and heterosexism, and positions him as avant-garde for the time. This position is worth mentioning, particularly in the context of a programme with an audience of mostly men steeped in traditional masculinity and for whom heterosexuality is the unquestioned norm. Rome's anti-homophobic stance represents the beginning of a fissure in hegemonic masculinity the way Anderson (2005) describes in his research on gay athletes of the time. It potentially fostered a new awareness in Rome's listeners and invited new voices into this important conversation about masculinity and sexuality, potentially spurring a rethinking of masculinity and sports. Cutting off the first time caller due to his homophobic comment could be viewed as a productive accountable manoeuvre, which is notable since straight men do not have a rich history of holding other straight men responsible for homophobic slurs.

Jim Rome's anti-homophobic stances became widely known earning him praise by many gay and lesbian activist organizations. Several openly gay ex-athletes were interviewed by Rome, including American football players Esera Tuaolo and David Kopay, and baseball player Billy Bean, all who "came out" once they retired from professional sports. These interviews were substantive and enlightening; it was clear that gay athletes felt supported and safe on Rome's show.

Sports Talk Radio Today

The forward-thinking views of Jim Rome have continued over the past decade, and have inspired other sports radio hosts to oppose homophobia. Several sports radio programmes, including the Rome show and ESPN's *Mike and Mike Show*, applauded the courage of Chief Operating Officer and president of the National Basketball Association (NBA) franchise, Phoenix Suns Rick Welts, for his recent revelation that he is gay. In response to homophobic insults by NBA stars Kobe Bryant and Joakim Noah (both athletes were fined by the NBA for their comments), Jim Rome said on his May 23, 2011 show:

> Speaking of rattled, never thought I'd see the Bulls [Chicago NBA franchise] come unglued the way they did. Miami's defensive pressure certainly had something to do with it but that doesn't explain all the offensive fouls, shot clock violations and their getting hooked by Heat players and in Joakim Noah's case, a fan. Noah was caught on tape yelling a gay slur at a fan in the first quarter. How does that guy not know better than that?! Joakim, did you not see the league ding Kobe Bryant $100 grand for a similar incident? Or that Sun's president Rick Welts come out of the closet recently? Or even more importantly those Public Service Announcements the NBA is running where Grant Hill and today's guest Jared Dudley drop manual buzzers on people for letting that type of ignorance fly. The league has made it pretty clear you and everyone else better keep that ignorance out of your mouth.

Homophobia is swiftly losing hegemonic status both in high school and university sports (Anderson, 2011) and in mainstream professional sports. Remarks that were once dismissed as just a kind of acceptable trash-talk ("you're gay") in sports are now being challenged by a growing number of professional athletes, including basketball player Grant Hill, who was part of a campaign by the NBA to take a stance against homophobia. On NPR, Hill (interviewed by NPR host Scott Simon) on the subject, said:

> SIMON: And why did you think this was so important to lend your voice to this issue [homophobia]?
>
> HILL: It's about words. You know, the most important thing is these words have meaning. And gay is not a bad word, but if you use it, you know, in a way that promotes negativity, then it is. Using gay to mean dumb or stupid: not cool. Not cool. Not in my house, not anywhere. It's not creative. It's offensive to gay people. And you're better than that.
>
> SIMON: Did you get any flak for it?
>
> HILL: Yeah, I think so. You know, I'd say you have a—you probably have three sort of groups of people, you know. You know, you have those that get it and understand it and appreciate it. You probably have a group of folks who took it to heart, you know. You know what? That makes a lot of sense, you know. Maybe I wasn't quite aware. I'll be more careful in the language and the words that I use. And then you have sort of, you know, I guess for lack of a better word, folks that are just going to be ignorant.
>
> SIMON: Charles Barkley—great player, for that matter, I think a very entertaining commentator, who's not known for pulling his punches—said that he had plenty of gay teammates in the NBA, and it was no big deal. Is that the case?
>
> HILL: I thought I heard, you know, that Charles had said, look, he probably had played with plenty of gay teammates. And, you know, I think the culture of male-dominated professional sports, that whole topic, you know, can be considered taboo. Our president, as you mentioned, Rick Welts, announced and came out last Sunday, the same day that our PSA aired for the first time. And for him, you know, I guess the pressure was such that he's been, you know, he's been hiding this for his entire life.

> SIMON: Has sports reached—is sports beginning to approach a tipping point on this subject? I mean, as you note, you have what Rick Welts said, Sean Avery, the hockey player, says he's in favour of gay marriage, and Will Sheridan, who played for Villanova, says, well, I was gay when I played. I'm gay, and everyone knew it.
>
> HILL: I don't know if it's reaching a tipping point, but I certainly think there's more discussion, there's more conversation about this subject matter than at any other time. And I think more and more, people are more comfortable with coming out and expressing themselves. But, you know, do I anticipate athletes coming out of the closet now left and right? I don't know. But I think it certainly is—you know, it's just a good start to be able to talk about it and have these discussions.

Further anti-heterosexist advancement occurred in 2011, when Jared Max, one of the best-known voices in New York sports radio and current ESPN New York 1050 morning host of "Maxed Out in the Morning", came out of the closet after talking about the other sports figures who have come out of the closet. On his July 2011 show he said:

> Are we ready to have our sports information delivered by someone who is gay? Well we are gonna find out. Because for the last 16 years, I've been living a free life among my close friends and family, and I've hidden behind what is a gargantuan sized secret here in the sports world. I am gay. Yeah. Jared Max. The sports guy who is one of the most familiar faces in New York sports isn't quite like the majority. And while you already knew I was a little different, this might help make sense of it. But more so, I'm taking this courageous jump into the unknown having no idea how I will be perceived.

Max received overwhelming support from his listeners, other sports radio hosts, athletes and ESPN.[3]

There is sufficient evidence to argue that homophobia is being confronted head-on in the traditionally masculinist world of sports talk radio and in the larger sports media world. For example, recent research is showing that the sports media is considerably less homophobic and less interested in reproducing orthodox (hegemonic) masculine discourse than before. One illustration of contemporary research is Kian and Anderson's (2009) content analysis of newsprint after professional basketball player John Amaechi came out. Kian and Anderson concluded that print media writers revealed little homophobia and recurrently called for more acceptance of gays athletes. Similarly, Anderson and Kian (2012) show that attitudes toward concussions and risk in the National Football League (the American professional football league referred to as the NFL) are also transforming; players are increasing valuing the elimination of head trauma, instead of playing at all costs. Not only is this change occurring among players, but it is also evident in sport media. These counter-hegemonic moments in sports radio are indicative of, and situated within, some of the recent advancements in gay rights in the larger American political context: same-sex marriage, don't ask don't tell, the passing of hate crimes legislation, and Barack Obama's recent support of marriage equality.

Sports Talk Radio and Transphobia

Now, a word of caution: while there is much to acknowledge about the progress made in the sports media, it is equally important to ask which athletes are allowed to become visible. What is their social location? How is their sexuality represented? Who continues to be marginalized and not benefiting from this recent headway? Virtually all the gay athletes who have been highlighted in sports talk radio are white gay men who define homosexuality as an essentialist identity and mimic some aspects of traditional masculinity. Scholar Lisa Duggan (2003) claims that much of the recent visibility of gays and lesbians is framed within a post-Stonewall, homonormative, identitarian private discourse. According to Duggan, homonormativity is an apolitical gay male identity anchored in domesticity and consumption. Gay homonormative representations, in sports radio or shows such as *Glee* (popular with youth and with several openly gay and lesbian characters on the show), are increasingly tolerated

within the dominant culture, while transgender persons are invisible or pathologised.

Some examples of the marginalization of athletes who transgress traditional gender norms included Jim Rome's ridiculing of former tennis star Martina Navratilova, referring to her as "Martin" due to her "mannishness".[4] Hence, sports talk radio both reflects and constitutes a homonormative, sexist, and transphobic discourse that benefits some, but not all sexual and gender minorities, particularly persons who resist assimilation into mainstream gay communities. This discourse is persuasively articulated by queer activist and writer Mattilda Bernstein Sycamore (2008):

> Even when the gay rights agenda does include real issues, it does it in a way that consistently prioritizes the most privileged while marginalizing everyone else. I'm using the term gay rights instead of the more popular term of the moment, GLBT rights, because GLBT usually means gay, with lesbian in parentheses, throw out the bisexuals, and put transgender on for a little window-dressing. A gay rights agenda fights for an end to discrimination in housing and employment, but not for the provision of housing or jobs; domestic partner health coverage but not universal health coverage. The gay rights agenda fights for tougher hate crimes legislation, instead of fighting racism, classism, and transphobia in the criminal justice system.
>
> (p. 2)

Conclusion

While there is a great deal of support that sports talk radio, similar to conservative talk radio reproduces sexism and homophobia, critical analysis indicates that this medium takes some surprising positions on gender and sexuality that contrast sharply with the prevailing discourse of conservative talk radio programmes. In particular, sports talk radio offers countervailing messages about gender and sexuality that intermittently disrupt hegemonic masculinity and homophobia. This reflects the changing culture of masculinity more broadly (Anderson, 2009, 2011, 2012).

Lastly, while these fractures of traditional masculinity offer hope and reflect (and may even shape on some small level) the advancement of gay rights, sports radio discourses are framed within the constraints of homonormativity. The real effects of homonormativity remind us as scholars and activists to problematize the gay rights movement by asking who is most benefiting from some of the recent progress (albeit limited and a long way to go) and who is disregarded. Sports talk radio discourse gives us an analytical prism to analyze and fight for the rights of gender non-conforming and transgender persons along with supporting the ongoing struggle for gay and lesbian rights.

Notes

1. Entertainment and Sports Programming Network, commonly known as ESPN, is an American global television and radio network focusing on sports-related programming including live and pre-taped event telecasts, sports talk shows, and other original programming.
2. Rush Limbaugh is an American radio talk show host and political commentator. His programme is the highest-rated talk show programme in the United States. Limbaugh is known for his championing of extreme right wing politics through a bombastic performance style. His popularity with a wide-ranging audience has allowed him to have a platform with conservative Republican politics influencing elected officials and public policy. Limbaugh is particularly known for his misogyny and critique of feminism popularizing the term "feminazi" referring to about two dozen feminists "to whom the most important thing in life is ensuring that as many abortions as possible occur."
3. I listen to the show on an almost daily basis. There is overwhelming support and I have never heard a homophobic comment from the callers.
4. Rome's comments about Martina Navratilova on June 2, 2005 (I was listening to the programme while driving in my car that day).

References

Anderson E 2012 Shifting masculinities in Anglo-American countries. *Masculinities and Social Change*, 1(1): 60–79.

Anderson E 2011 Updating the outcome: Gay athletes, straight teams, and coming out at the end of the decade. *Gender & Society*, 25(2): 250–268.

Anderson E 2009 *Inclusive masculinity: The changing nature of masculinities*. New York, NY: Routledge.

Anderson E 2005 *In the game: Gay athletes and the cult of masculinity*. Albany, NY: State University of New York Press.

Anderson E and Kian T 2012 Contesting violence, masculinity, and head trauma in the National Football League. *Men and Masculinities*, 15(2): 152–173.

Connell RW 2000 *The men and the boys*. Berkeley, CA: University of California Press.

Cook K 1993 Media. *Playboy, April Issue*, pp. 20–21.

Douglas SJ 2002 Letting the boys be boys: Talk radio, male hysteria, and political discourse in the 1980s. In: Hilmes M and Loviglio J (eds) *Radio reader: Essays in the cultural history of radio*. New York: Routledge, pp. 485–504

Duggan L 2003 *The twilight of equality: Neoliberalism, cultural politics, and the attack on democracy*. Boston, MA: Beacon Press.

Goldberg DT 1998 Call and response: Sports, talk radio, and the death of democracy. *Journal of Sport & Social Issues*, 22(2): 212–223.

Haag P 1996 The 50,000 watt sports bar: Talk radio and the ethic of the fan. *The South Atlantic Quarterly*, 95(2): 453–470.

Kian EM and Anderson E 2009 John Amaechi: Changing the way sport reporters examine gay athletes. *Journal of Homosexuality*, 56(7): 799–818.

Mariscal J 1999 Chicanos and Latinos in the jungle of sports talk radio, *Journal of Sport & Social Issues*, 23(1): 111–117.

Nylund D 2007 *Beer, babes, and balls: Sports talk radio and masculinity*. Albany, NY: SUNY Press.

Smith M 2002 The Jim Rome Show and negotiations of manhood: Surviving in "The Jungle". In: North American Society for the Sociology of Sport, Indianapolis, IN, May 2002.

Sycamore MB 2008 *That's revolting: Queer strategies to resist assimilation*. Berkeley: Soft Skull Press.

Misogyny in Rap Music

A Content Analysis of Prevalence and Meanings

RONALD WEITZER AND CHARIS E. KUBRIN

That's the way the game goes, gotta keep it strictly pimpin',
Gotta have my hustle tight, makin change off these women.
You know it's hard out here for a pimp,
When he tryin' to get this money for the rent.
"It's Hard Out Here For a Pimp"

Three 6 Mafia

The 2005 Academy Award for best original song in a feature film went to Three 6 Mafia's controversial "It's Hard Out Here For a Pimp" from the film *Hustle and Flow*. The song was performed at the Oscars, and immediately provoked a storm of criticism for glorifying the exploitation of women. This is only the most recent chapter in the mounting criticism directed at rap music's presentation of women. A few years earlier, rapper Eminem won a Grammy for his 2001 album, *The Marshall Mathers LP*—an album whose lyrics contained extreme hostility and violence toward women. Women's groups promptly condemned the award. More recently, the African American women's magazine *Essence* launched a campaign in 2005 against sexism in rap music. The magazine lamented the depiction of black women in rap and solicited feedback from readers on ways to challenge it.

Much of the criticism of rap music is impressionistic and based on a handful of anecdotes, rather than a systematic analysis. Exactly how prevalent are misogynistic themes in this music and what specific messages are conveyed to the listeners? The current study addresses this question through a content analysis of over 400 rap songs. We document five themes related to the portrayal of women in rap music and link them to the larger cultural and music industry norms and the local, neighborhood conditions that inspired this music.

Images of Women in Popular Music

Gender stereotypes are abundant in popular music, where women are often presented as inferior to men or are trivialized and marginalized (Tuchman 1978). Women are not portrayed monolithically, however (Butruille and Taylor 1987; Lay 2000; van Zoonen 1994), and lyrical depictions appear to have changed somewhat over time. It has been argued that the overall trend is one of "greater diversity, more complexity, and dramatically mixed messages about the individual female persona and women's roles in society" (Lee 1999:355). Despite this variegation, it remains uncommon for women to be presented as independent, intelligent, enterprising, or superior to men (Lee 1999). Derogatory images are far more common.

A body of research documents depictions of men and women in different genres. A content analysis of rock music videos found that a majority (57 percent) presented women in a "condescending" manner (e.g., unintelligent, sex object, victim) and a fifth placed them in a traditional sex role (e.g., subservient, nurturing, domestic roles), while 8 percent displayed male violence against women (Vincent, Davis, and Boruszkowski 1987). Only 14 percent presented women as fully equal to men. A more recent study of rock videos found that traditional sex role stereotypes continue to predominate: 57 percent of videos in which women were present depicted them in a "conventional" manner (passive, dependent on men, accenting physical appearance), while a third presented them as strong and independent (Alexander 1999).

Country music also casts women in subordinate roles. A study of 203 country music videos featuring male performers found that two-thirds devalued women (portraying them in a condescending manner or in traditional roles), while only 9 percent presented women as fully equal to men (Andsager and Roe 1999). Of the 80 videos by female artists, by contrast, half fit the fully equal category. Interestingly, country songs and videos do not feature violence against women or portray them as strippers and prostitutes, apparently because of strong industry norms against such images (Andsager and Roe 1999:81). In fact, one study found that country music advertisers pressure radio stations to screen out misogynistic songs in order to attract desired female listeners (Ryan and Peterson 1982).

Although rap music has been a topic of heated public debate for years, systematic content analyses are rare. One analysis of rap and heavy metal songs from 1985–1990 found that rap was more sexually explicit and graphic whereas heavy metal's allusions to sexual acts or to male domination were fairly subtle (Binder 1993), which is consistent with other studies of heavy metal songs and videos that have found that "blatant abuse of women is uncommon" in this genre (Walser 1993:117). Binder's comparative analysis was limited to only 20 songs which she deemed "controversial," and the time period examined preceded rap's ascendancy in the music field. In a unique study of Chicano rap songs from 1999–2002, McFarland (2003) identified two main themes: a critique of racial inequality and

injustice and an endorsement of male supremacy over women. Of the 263 songs that mentioned women, 37 percent depicted them "simply as objects of male desire and pleasure," while 4 percent justified violence against them. McFarland's sampling frame was based on songs he identified as popular in focus groups and on the Brown Pride website, rather than a more objective measure of popularity. Armstrong (2001) conducted a content analysis of 490 rap songs during 1987–1993. Lyrics featuring violence against women were found in 22 percent of the songs, and the violence perpetrated against women included assault, rape, and murder. Although his study makes a valuable contribution to the literature in its systematic focus on violence against women, it does not discuss other (nonviolent) depictions of women, provides little indication of coding procedures, and presents the lyrics in a brief and sketchy manner, decontextualized from larger song segments. Other content analyses of rap music (Kubrin 2005a, 2005b; Martinez 1997) do not examine the depiction of women or gender relations more broadly. The present paper addresses this issue.

Social Sources of Rap Lyrics

Most of the studies reviewed above did not attempt to *explain why* lyrics portray women as they do—an admittedly difficult task. Yet artists do not work in a vacuum. We suggest that rappers whose songs portray women negatively are influenced by three major social forces: larger gender relations, the music industry, and local neighborhood conditions. The most diffuse influence is the larger gender order, which includes the cultural valorization of a certain type of masculinity. *Hegemonic masculinity* has been defined as attitudes and practices that perpetuate heterosexual male domination over women. It involves "the currently most honored way of being a man, it requires all other men to position themselves in relation to it, and it ideologically legitimates the global subordination of women to men" (Connell and Messerschmidt 2005:832). For this type of masculinity, to be a "man" requires the acceptance of attitudes that objectify women, practices that subordinate them, and derogation of men who adopt an egalitarian orientation, equally affirmative of men and women and all sexual orientations (Connell 1987; Connell and Messerschmidt 2005; Donaldson 1993). Hegemonic masculinity exists alongside and in competition with what Connell calls "subordinated masculinities," and to remain normative, it requires ongoing reproduction via the mass media, the patriarchal family, and other socializing institutions. Media representations of men, for example, often glorify men's use of physical force, a daring demeanor, virility, and emotional distance (see Hanke 1998). Popular music is a case in point: As indicated by the studies reviewed above, only a minority of songs, across music genres, espouse egalitarian gender relations or alternative masculinities, whereas the majority can be viewed as texts on hegemonic masculinity. We argue that rap, like the other music genres, is part of this broader culture of gender relations, even as some of the music challenges the dominant culture (Lay 2000).[1]

Some argue that popular music over the past three decades is also part of a larger cultural resistance to feminism, an attempt to block progress toward gender equality and resuscitate male domination. As Lay (2000:239) argues, "Popular music can be read as a vehicle for heterosexual male concerns [over the advancement of women and gays] and, more importantly, for the recuperation of hegemonic masculinity." Stated differently, this music can be seen as part of a larger ideological process of persuading the population that heterosexual male supremacy is natural and normal. Rap is part of this backlash. Collins (2000:82, 144) considers rap to be one of the contemporary "controlling images" used to subordinate black women, and Oliver (2006:927) argues that rap's sexist lyrics "provide justifications for engaging in acts of violence against black women" (see also hooks 1994; Rhym 1997). But it may also be seen as an effort to control *all* women, since rap is consumed by youth from all racial and ethnic groups. Such images have real-world effects insofar as they contribute to gendered socialization and perpetuate gender inequality (Barongan and

Hall 1995; Johnson et al. 1995; Martino et al. 2006; Wester et al. 1997).

Rap artists are also influenced by pressures from elites in the music industry. To maximize sales, record industry moguls encourage provocative, edgy lyrics. Producers not only encourage artists to become "hardcore" but they also reject or marginalize artists who go against the grain. As a result of such practices, a directly proportional relationship has developed between rap music's explicitness and the sale of its records.

In response to corporate pressures, many rappers abandon political and social messages and focus instead on material wealth and sexual exploits (Powell 2000). In his documentary, "Hip-Hop: Beyond Beats and Rhymes," Byron Hurt (2007) asks one aspiring rapper why rap artists focus on violence and misogyny. The rapper freestyles a verse about whether he could have been a doctor, a father, or police officer. He then says, "That's nice, but nobody wanna hear that right now. They don't accept that shit." When Hurt asks, "Who is 'they,'" the rapper answers, "The industry. They usually don't give us deals when we speak righteously." Indeed, Kitwana (1994:23) finds that artists in search of securing record deals are often told their message is not hard enough, they are too clean cut, that "hardcore" is what is selling now, and that they should no longer engage in social commentary (see also Krims 2000:71). The consequence? According to Smith (1997:346), "Many of today's rappers make the ghetto visible in order to sell and to be sold."

The pressure for artists to rap about hardcore themes is perhaps most evident in gangsta rap.[2] A statement by Carmen Ashhurst-Watson, former President of Def Jam Records, is revealing:

The time when we switched to gangsta music was the same time that the majors [record companies] bought up all the [independent] labels. And I don't think that's a coincidence. At the time that we were able to get a bigger place in the record stores, and a bigger presence because of this major marketing capacity, the music became less and less conscious. (Ashhurst-Watson, quoted in Hurt 2007)

Her account is confirmed by recent research which documents that as rap increasingly became produced by major record labels, its content became more hardcore to encourage sales. In a longitudinal analysis of rap music production and lyrical content, Lena (2006:488) finds that "starting in 1988 the largest record corporations charted substantially more 'hardcore' rap songs than did independent labels. In the eight years between 1988 and 1995, majors charted up to five and a half times as many hardcore rap singles as all their independent competitors combined." She concludes that "major record labels produced the majority of puerile rap" during this later time period. This was in stark contrast to earlier periods of production where rap lyrics emphasized features of the local environment and hostility to corporate music production and values.

The bias fostered by record companies is recapitulated in the kind of rap music that gets the greatest airplay on radio stations. Hip-hop historian Kevin Powell points out that "in every city you go to in America . . . [rap stations are] playing the same 10–12 songs over and over again. So what it does is perpetuate the mindset that the only way you can be a man—a black man, a Latino man—is if you hard. To denigrate women. To denigrate homosexuals. To denigrate each other. To kill each other" (Kevin Powell, quoted in Hurt 2007). This privileging of hegemonic masculinity and negative depiction of women is driven by an interest in selling records (Rhym 1997). As long as this type of music continues to sell, "record labels will continue to put ethics and morality aside to release [violent or sexist rap]" (McAdams and Russell 1991:R-22).

Consumers play a key role in this process. Misogynistic representations of women and the more general marketing of "hood narratives" (Watkins 2001:389) occur, in part, in response to a perceived consumer demand for stereotypical representations of the ghetto, and specifically of young black men and women. Listeners of rap, many of whom are white youth, can vicariously experience the ghetto, a place symbolizing danger and deviance (Quinn 2005:85). As one white listener of rap music claims,

I've never been to a ghetto. I grew up in upper middle-class, basically white suburbia. . . . And to listen to [rap music] is a way of us to see . . . a completely different culture. It's something that most of us have never had the opportunity to experience. . . . And the stuff in the music, it appeals to our sense of learning about other cultures and wanting to know more about something that we'll never probably experience. (quoted in Hurt 2007)

Such cross-cultural learning may be quite biased. As Quinn (2005:91) argues, "with its provocative popcultural portrayals of the ghetto, there can be little doubt that gangsta rap helps to reinforce racial stereotypes held by many whites." Indeed, when Hurt asked the white listener quoted above whether the music reinforces stereotypes, she answered affirmatively. While explicit lyrics and misogynistic representations of women have made rap music highly marketable, they have also "reinvigorated popular beliefs about black deviance and social pathology" (Watkins 2001:389). In short, the production and lyrical content of rap music are inextricably linked; as such, music industry interests can be viewed as one important source of rap music lyrics.

Rap music also has local roots, which help shape the content of the lyrics. More so than other genres, rap is a "localized form of cultural expression" (Bennett 1999a:77; 1999b). Hip-hop and rap initially developed out of the lived experiences of youth in disadvantaged, black neighborhoods and was "incubated in the black community's house parties, public parks, housing projects, and local jams" (Powell 1991:245; Rose 1994a). And although the music industry's influence has become increasingly apparent, even today rap continues to be marketed as a cultural reflection of life on "the streets" of America's inner-cities. In fact, the music industry sends agents into these neighborhoods for the express purpose of gathering "street intelligence" on what is popular; they do this by visiting record stores, clubs, and parties (Negus 1999:502).

The degree to which a particular music genre, and particularly male artists within that genre, endorse male supremacy in their lyrics may be related to broader, societal opportunities for affirming hegemonic masculinity—opportunities that vary to some extent by racial and class background. Poor, marginalized black males have historically faced obstacles to asserting their masculinity, and they continue to be denied access to conventional institutional avenues through which masculinity may be established. According to Skeggs (1993), music historically served as a medium that provided black men with an alternative resource for asserting their masculinity.

This opportunity structure can be linked specifically to the conditions in disadvantaged neighborhoods. It has been argued that the content of rap music reflects, at least to some extent, gender relations among youth in many inner-city communities. Several ethnographic studies provide evidence of discord between men and women in disadvantaged, minority neighborhoods. The harsh conditions of the ghetto and barrio provide residents with few conventional sources of self-esteem (Bourgois 1995; Horowitz 1983; Liebow 1967), which can lead to unconventional means to win respect. Violence is one means of eliciting respect from others or punishing those who withhold it (Kubrin and Weitzer 2003), but men are also admired for economically and sexually exploiting women. Four decades ago, Liebow's (1967:140–144) ethnographic study of a low-income, black neighborhood described how important it was for men to be seen as "exploiters of women," even if they did not always treat women in this way. Recent research indicates that exploitation and degradation of young women is still a feature of some inner-city communities today and continues to shape gender relations (Miller and White 2003). Anderson's (1999) study of an African American community identified several dimensions of a distinctive neighborhood culture, what he calls the "code of the street." For many young men in such neighborhoods, the street code places a high value on sexual conquest, promiscuity, and the manipulation of women:

> Because of the implications sex has for their local social status and esteem, the young men are ready to be regaled with graphic tales of one another's sexual exploits. . . . Status goes to the winner, and sex is prized as a testament not of love but of

control over another human being. The goal of the sexual conquests is to make a fool of the young woman . . . [The male] incurs sanctions [from his peers] for allowing a girl to "rule" him or gains positive reinforcement for keeping her in line. . . . In many cases the more the young man seems to exploit the young woman, the higher is his regard within the peer group. (Anderson 1999:150, 153, 154)

A similar male street culture is documented in an ethnographic study of a Puerto Rican barrio in New York City (Bourgois 1995, 1996). Rooted in conditions of socioeconomic disadvantage which strip men of traditional sources of dignity, this street culture is characterized by a high level of male promiscuity, the "celebration of the gigolo image," the value of "being an economic parasite" on one's girlfriends, and justifications for violence against women (Bourgois 1995:276–295).

We do not argue that either neighborhood or industry forces, as just described, are necessarily direct causes of the lyrical content or images, but instead that these forces are an essential part of the *context* within which the messages contained in rap are best understood. Our study thus can be situated within the recent literature on gender relations, which recognizes the importance of multiple contexts in which gender roles and identities are reproduced (Connell and Messerschmidt 2005).

Research Methods

The current study focuses on a time period that has not been examined in previous research on this topic. All rap albums from 1992 through 2000 that attained platinum status (selling at least one million copies) were identified (N = 130). Sampling only platinum albums ensured that the music had reached a substantial segment of the population. To identify the sample, we obtained a list of all albums that went platinum between 1992 and 2000 from the Recording Industry Association of America (RIAA). The RIAA, which compiles, analyzes, and reports on the quantity and value of recorded music shipped into market channels, is considered the premier source for comprehensive market data on music trends in the U.S. We went through the list and used the Web site ARTISTdirect (http://www.artistdirect.com) to identify "rap" albums. ARTISTdirect is a comprehensive online network of resources that provides, among other things, detailed information about artists/groups. We typed in the name of each artist/group and the Web site classified the precise music genre.

Our analysis begins in 1992 because gangsta rap began to flourish around this time (Kelley 1996:147; Keyes 2002:104; Kitwana 2002:xiv; Krims 2000:83; Smith 1997:346; Watkins 2001:389).[3] Our interest in this starting point is related to the fact that misogyny and related themes (i.e., violence) are popularly thought to be more prevalent in gangsta rap than in rap generally. Yet these themes are not exclusive to gangsta rap, which is why we selected all rap albums rather than just gangsta albums. As noted by Krims (2000:87), rap albums typically mix genres and so songs that contain misogynistic lyrics would have been left out of the analysis had we only sampled gangsta rap albums.

The analysis ends in 2000 because that year marked a turning point in the industry's increasing commercialization and greater detachment from its neighborhood sources (Kitwana 1994:23; Krims 2000:71; Watkins 2001:382). This time frame thus captures a period when rap music more closely reflected grassroots values and local conditions on the street and was somewhat less commercialized than today, although the interests of record labels were important during this time period as well.

The 130 albums contained a total of 1,922 songs. Using SPSS, a simple random sample of 403 songs was drawn and then analyzed.[4] Each song was listened to twice in its entirety by the authors, while simultaneously reading the lyrics. The lyrics were obtained from *The Original Hip-Hop/Rap Lyrics Archive* (www.ohhla.com/all.html). Each line was coded to identify major misogynistic themes. *Misogyny* refers to lyrics that encourage, condone, or glorify the objectification, exploitation, or victimization of women. In cases of uncertainty regarding the meaning of a particular word or phrase, we consulted *The Rap Dictionary* (www.rapdict.org), a comprehensive online dictionary of rap terms.

During the coding, careful attention was paid to the context in which the lyrics were stated. This is especially important in rap, given that it is rooted in the Black oral tradition of signifying and other communicative practices (Smitherman 1997:4). Signifying is a way of speaking that involves ritual insult (commonly referred to as "playing the dozens") and double entendre (Lee 2005:83; see also Keyes 2002). With signifying, words have alternative meanings beyond their conventional practices and should not necessarily be taken literally. In our coding, we were careful to interpret the lyrics within their larger contexts. Finally, an independent researcher coded a random subset (16 percent of the sample songs) in order to assess inter-coder reliability. With respect to misogyny, agreement occurred in 73.4 percent [of] the songs, indicating fairly strong consensus.

Findings

Misogyny was present in 22 percent of the 403 songs (N = 90 songs, by 31 rappers).[5] This means that misogyny is much less pervasive in rap music than some critics believe, but is clearly a significant theme (Table 33.1). Female rappers accounted for only 5 of the 90 misogynistic songs, as well as an additional 8 songs (out of the remaining 313) that did not have misogynistic lyrics. The scarcity of female artists shows just how male-dominated rap was during this time period, especially at the platinum level (George 1998; Troka 2002: 82). We include a separate analysis of the 8 non-misogynistic songs by female artists for purposes of comparison to the messages contained in our main sample.

Table 33.1 Misogynistic Themes

Theme	Frequency in songs (%)*
Naming and Shaming	49
Sexual Objectification	67
Can't Trust 'Em	47
Legitimating Violence	18
Prostitutes and Pimps	20

*Frequency in songs identified as misogynistic, not within the larger sample of rap songs (where 22 percent of the songs were categorized as misogynistic).

Although misogynistic messages appear less frequently in rap than is commonly believed, significance is not simply a matter of frequency. Also important is the nature and intensity of the messages. Our content analysis identified five misogynistic themes that appear with some frequency: (1) derogatory naming and shaming of women, (2) sexual objectification of women, (3) distrust of women, (4) legitimation of violence against women, and (5) celebration of prostitution and pimping. Our presentation of findings identifies the frequency of each theme, substantive messages and subthemes in the lyrics, and the ways in which the lyrics reflect societal gender relations, record industry pressures, and neighborhood conditions in disadvantaged communities.

Naming and Shaming

A number of rap songs can be described as a full-fledged "status degradation ceremony" directed at women—a "ritual destruction of the person denounced" (Garfinkle 1956: 421). In these songs, it is typically women in general, rather than a specific person, who are shamed with derogatory names. This theme was present in half (49 percent) of the misogynistic songs.

Our analysis identified instances of naming-and-shaming but, as discussed earlier, we did not automatically assume that all conventionally "negative" labels were necessarily disparaging. For instance, in rap culture the terms "bitch" and "ho" are not necessarily intended to be derogatory, depending on the lyrical context (Keyes 2002; Kitwana 1994:25). Ice Cube talks about a "wholesome ho," and Too $hort refers to his "finest bitches" and a "top-notch bitch." While recognizing that some listeners consider such terms offensive in all usage, we coded conservatively by including in our naming-and-shaming category only lyrics that were unambiguously derogatory. For example, Eminem's song *Kill You* talks about "vile, venomous, volatile bitches." Other rappers condemn the slut, tramp, whore, hoochie, "lying-ass bitch," "shitty hoe," "prima donna bitch," and so forth. A favorite rap term is "chickenhead," which reduces a woman to a bobbing head giving oral sex. Status degradation was the sole theme of some songs, present in every

verse. Sweeping attacks are sometimes generalized, while other lyrics reveal particular rationales for degradation, such as women's failure to cooperate with men:

> We couldn't get no play from the ladies
> With seven niggas in a Nav [Navigator] is you crazy? . . .
> So we all said "fuck you bitch" and kept rolling.
> (Snoop Dogg, *DP Gangsta*)

Even rappers' female relatives are not immune from such attacks. Eminem says that "all bitches is hoes, even my stinkin' ass mom" (*Under the Influence*). Eminem's unbridled hostility toward all women, including relatives, is somewhat extreme but not unique in this music genre.[6]

The flipside of this naming process is found in lyrics that praise men who treat women poorly. In these lyrics, it is a badge of honor for men to verbally and physically abuse women, and men win respect from other men when they act like "players," "pimps," and exploiters of women—financially, sexually, and emotionally. This theme is reflected throughout the data, closely mirroring the neighborhood street code described by Anderson and others. The variety of disparaging labels for women is not paralleled for men, either in rap or in the larger culture. Insofar as rappers derogate other men, they tend to use feminized terms, such as bitch or pussy—a staple of hegemonic masculinity.

It is important to point out that these lyrics essentialize women by portraying them as inherently "Other" and different from men by nature. Many of the labels refer to women's anatomy or sexuality, and the lyrics endorse the age-old notion that "biology is destiny."

Some rappers report that verbal abuse of women is encouraged and rewarded by the music industry:

> Rappers like me always disrespectin' ladies,
> Wonder why it's like that, well so do I.
> But I just turn my back and then I go get high,
> 'Cause I get paid real good to talk bad about a bitch.
> And you bought it, so don't be mad I got rich.
> (Too $hort, *Thangs Change*)

In an interview, Brother Marquis from 2 Live Crew, echoed these sentiments: "I'm degrading [women] to try to get me some money. . . . And besides, you let me do that. You got pimps out here who are making you sell your body. Just let me talk about you for a little while . . . and make me a little money" (quoted in Collins 2000:143–144). By this logic, because women are already exploited by pimps, there is no harm in subjecting them to lyrical shaming. The larger point is that rap industry norms, more so than in other types of music, encourage artists to disparage women (Kitwana 1994:23; Krims 2000:71; Smith 1997:346).

Sexual Objectification

Sexual objectification of women was evident in 67 percent of our misogynistic songs. Sexual objectification refers to the idea that women are good only for sex. These lyrics mirror the street code's exhortation that men avoid commitment, marriage, and caring for children; instead, women are to be sexually used and then quickly discarded (Anderson 1999; Bourgois 1995; Liebow 1967; Miller and White 2003). N.W.A. captures this theme with a song titled "Findum, Fuckum, and Flee." Puff Daddy offers another example: "Call me Sean if you suck, call me gone when I nut. That's the end of us, get your friend to fuck" (Sean "Puffy" Combs, on Notorious B.I.G., *Notorious B.I.G.*). Consider also the following songs:

Bitches ain't shit but hoes and tricks

Lick on these nuts and suck the dick

Get's the fuck out after you're done

And I hops in my ride to make a quick run.
(Dr. Dre, *Bitches Ain't Shit*)

I'm only out to fuck a bitch, fuck tryin' to charm her.

I treat a fine ass bitch like dirt

No money in her purse, a fuck is all it's worth.

'Cause Short Dawg'll never cater to you hoes

And if you ain't fuckin', I say "later" to you hoes.
(Too $hort, *Coming Up $hort*)

High value is placed on having scores of sexual partners and even sharing them, another way in which women are de-individualized:

I meet a bitch, fuck a bitch

Next thing you know you fuckin' the bitch.
(Notorious B.I.G., *Friend of Mine*)

Anderson (1999) discusses the extreme peer pressure on young men in disadvantaged neighborhoods to have casual sex with women as a way of affirming their masculinity. This norm is a hallowed one in song lyrics:

I had niggas making bets like, did he fuck her yet?

Ask her did he touch her bra, when I say nah they say ahh

So tomorrow I use that pressure to undress her

But the more I caress her, more I feel like a molester.
(Mase, *I Need to Be*)

By the end of this stanza, peer pressure has resulted in sexual aggression.

Some rappers make it clear that they intend to put women "in their place" by demeaning strong and independent women: Redman boasts, "I turn an independent woman back into a hoochie" (*Keep On '99*) and Notorious B.I.G. raps, "I like 'em . . . educated, so I can bust off on they glasses" (*Big Booty Hoes*). Some of the lyrics in this thematic category, therefore, may be seen as resistance to women's growing autonomy, education, and independence—messages that cross-cut the other themes in this music as well. As indicated earlier, this backlash against women's liberation and reassertion of traditional masculinity can be found in other popular music genres as well.

Sexual objectification of women has a flip side in the sexual empowerment of men. Male sexual bravado and hypersexuality were present in 58 percent of the misogynistic songs. A common practice is bragging about how easy it is for "players" to get women to have sex: "Witness me holla at a hoochie, see how quick the game takes" (2Pac, *All 'Bout U*).

Men win respect from other men for a high number of sexual conquests without commitment. Although present throughout the culture, it appears to be especially prized in disadvantaged neighborhoods where men often lack other sources of dignity and self-esteem. In fact, there is a striking correspondence between the street code in inner-city communities and this music theme. Just as young men earn respect from their peers if they are viewed as having casual sex with many women (Anderson 1999; Bourgois 1995, 1996; Liebow 1967; Miller and White 2003), rappers likewise frequently brag about their sexual exploits, and are rewarded for doing so. A good example is rapper 50 Cent, who in the last several years has been frequently nominated for Grammy Awards for songs with precisely these themes (e.g., *Candy Shop* and *Magic Stick*). Both in rap songs and among neighborhood peers, bragging earns respect. Low sexual achievers and those who seek a long-term relationship with a woman are ridiculed and subordinated because they are less active practitioners of this (extremely utilitarian) version of hegemonic masculinity: "their games [are] seen as inferior, and their identities devalued" (Anderson 1999:151).

If having multiple sex partners earns respect, men also face an ongoing threat of sexual competition from other men. In other words, "Women provide heterosexual men with sexual validation, and men compete with each other for this" (Donaldson 1993:645). Men are thus instructed to use their sexual talents or material goods to steal other men's women:

> Say dog, what kinda nigga be on top of the world?
> Million dollar status got me on top of ya girl.
> (Hot Boys, *Fired Up*)

Men are also rewarded for demonstrating that they are sexually superior to other men:

> Get freaky, and do it wild
> On the floor, doggy style.
> While your bitch be crying "please don't stop"....
> I fuck her like I know you won't.
> If that's your bitch, homeboy you'd better keep her
> 'Cause she won't stay off my beeper.
> You can't fuck her and I appreciate it
> Even though I know you hate it.
> (Too $hort, *Step Daddy*)

Finally, sexual objectification is expressed in gangbanging. In these songs, several men have sex with one woman, whether consensually or not, and the woman is highly depersonalized. Some involve gangbangs with underage girls, while others describe sex with heavily intoxicated women:

> All on the grass [marijuana], every bitch
>   passed [out]
> A first not last, when we all hit the ass.
> Doin' tricks jacked up like a six
> One pussy, and thirteen dicks.
> (Westside Connection, *The Gangsta, the Killa, and the Dope Deala*)

> Kisha got did right yeah
> Fucked the whole Cash Money clique all in one night yeah.
> (Lil' Wayne, *Kisha*)

There is evidence that such gangbanging takes place in some disadvantaged minority neighborhoods. One study of black youth in north St. Louis, for example, reported that 40 percent of the young men interviewed admitted they had engaged in such behavior, which helped them gain status among their peers (Miller and White 2003:1219).

The sexual objectification of women and the hypersexuality of black men portrayed in these lyrics can be linked to larger stereotypes about black sexuality—stereotypes that date back to colonialism and slavery and that are still quite salient for consumers of rap music today (Skeggs 1993). Rappers exploit these stereotypes in their music.

Can't Trust 'Em

Suspicion of women is a significant theme in rap songs—a tension that is mirrored to some extent in the communities in which rap originated (Anderson 1999). Almost half (47 percent) of the misogynistic songs displayed deep distrust of women. There is both a diffuse sense of distrust (e.g., Dr. Dre's verse, "How could you trust a ho?", *Bitches Ain't Shit*) and several specific reasons to be suspicious of women, who are seen as prone to entrap, betray, exploit, or destroy men. First, it is claimed that teenage girls lie about their age:

> See nowadays man you got to know these bitches age
>
> 'Cause they ass be real fast when they be goin' through that phase.
>
> You fuck a girl that's young, and you gonna end up in the cage
> (Mase, *I Need to Be*)

Second, women stand accused of making false rape accusations in order to get a financial settlement:

> Don't take the pussy, if she fightin'
>
> 'Cause you saw what happened to Tupac and Mike Tyson.
>
> 'Specially if you large [famous], some hoes is trife [petty]
>
> Get you on a rape charge, have you servin' your life.
> (Nas, *Dr. Knockboot*)

Third, men are warned to be wary of the *femme fatale*—especially women who seek to set them up for robbery, assault, or murder. Ice Cube's song, *Don't Trust 'Em*, talks about a woman who lured a man to her home where there were four men who beat the man, stole his money, and killed him. The song ends, "I told you the bitch was a trap. Don't trust 'em." This scenario seems to be fairly common, judging from our data:

> You know they [women] might be the one to set me up
>
> Wanna get they little brother to wet [kill] me up. . . .
>
> Bitches be schemin', I kid ya not
>
> That's why I keep my windows locked and my Glock cocked.
> (Notorious B.I.G., *Friend of Mine*)

The *femme fatale* is iconic in popular culture, as illustrated in many films (e.g., *Double Indemnity, Fatal Attraction, Basic Instinct*), all of which feature a villainous woman who uses her beauty and sexuality to exploit or victimize innocent men. These women are presented as thoroughly evil and condemned for departing from their traditional gender role. Interestingly,

there is no equivalent label for men who act this way toward women. What is especially remarkable about rap's use of this icon is its claim that *all* young women are potential *femmes fatales*; the music sends a strong signal to men to be wary of women generally.

A fourth refrain is that women frequently lie to men in order to get pregnant. The value many young poor women place on having babies, as one of the few sources of dignity in their lives, is quite strong (Anderson 1999:162–166; Edin and Kefalas 2005). For many young men in these neighborhoods, a woman's pregnancy is viewed quite differently, something to be feared and denied: "To own up to a pregnancy is to go against the peer-group street ethic of hit and run" (Anderson 1999:156). Rappers express an identical concern. 2Pac asks, "Why plant seeds in a dirty bitch, waitin' to trick me? Not the life for me" (*Hell 4 a Hustler*). Paying child support is just one of the fears. Snoop Dog raps:

> I ain't lettin' nothin' leak cause if things leak, then I'm a get caught
>
> And I can't get caught cause you know how they do it about that child support.
>
> Shit, bitches is cold on a nigga who ain't got his game tight
>
> Getting 18.5 percent [child support payments] half your life.
> (Snoop Dogg, *Freestyle Conversation*)

Too $hort describes an even worse scenario after getting a woman pregnant:

> No more player, no Shorty the Pimp
>
> I get paid, divert a check and get 40 percent.
>
> All the homies talkin' bad, hair down, walkin' sad
>
> Got the broad livin' with me, baby sayin' "Dad!". . .
>
> I could try to mack again but the bitches won't want me
>
> 'Cause I'm all washed up, broke, fat, and funky.
>
> I lost everything that I worked to be
>
> Never thought I'd be a trick, payin' hoes to serve me.
> (Too $hort, *Coming Up Short*)

Young men who fall prey to such women are ridiculed by their peers (Anderson 1999). It is not only the material costs of fathering a child that is feared in these songs, but also fatherhood in general. This may be regarded as an extreme form of traditional masculinity, where the father is largely absent from his children's lives. As Donaldson (1993:650) states, "In hegemonic masculinity, fathers do not have the capacity or the skill or the need to care for children. . . . Nurturant and care-giving behavior is simply not manly." Our rap songs convey this message in no uncertain terms.

Even more common than the other subthemes in this category is our final one: The woman as gold digger only interested in men for their money:

> Watch the honeys check your style
>
> Worthless, when they worship what you purchase.
>
> They only see ice [diamonds], not me, under the surface
>
> What's the purpose?
> (The Lox, *I Wanna Thank You*)

> You must be used to all the finer things
>
> Infatuated by what money brings.
>
> It seems to me you hoes will never change
> (Scarface, *Fuck Faces*)

It is significant that the 2006 Grammy Award for Best Rap Solo Performance went to Kanye West's song, "Gold Digger," which complains about a woman who seduces a man to get his money. Such recognition can be interpreted as one way in which the music industry helps to perpetuate stereotyped images of women.

Several female rappers in our sample reinforce the idea of women as gold diggers interested solely in exploiting men (cf. Pough 2004). Missy Misdemeanor Elliott sings, "If you want me, where's my dough? Give me money, buy me clothes" (*All 'N My Grill*), and in another song:

> Hot boys
>
> Baby you got what I want.
>
> See 'cause y'all be drivin' Lexus jeeps
>
> And the Benz jeeps, and the Lincoln jeeps.
>
> Nothin' cheaper, got them Platinum Visa's
> (Missy Misdemeanor Elliott, *Hot Boys*)

As does Lil' Kim:

> I fuck with dudes with Member's Only jackets
>
> That sleep on brass beds, with money for a mattress.
>
> Everything I get is custom made
>
> Niggas wanna get laid; I gotta get paid.
> (Lil' Kim, *Custom Made*)

Men's fear of being exploited by women has a long history and is by no means unique to rap music. Yet, the gold digger fear is especially acute among men who are *nouveau riche* such as the newly successful rapper. They have achieved rapid upward mobility and celebrity status, and thus have precarious new wealth that can be lost. It may be less salient among poor men who have few assets to lose.

Legitimating Violence

Norms regarding appropriate conduct are ineffectual if not backed up with sanctions for those who disregard the norms. Violent punishment is one such sanction. Compared to the previous themes, condoning violence against women was less frequent but does appear in almost one-fifth (18 percent) of the misogynistic songs. Violence is portrayed in these songs, first of all, as the most appropriate response to women who act disrespectfully toward men, just as it is for men who disrespect other men (Anderson 1999; Kubrin 2005a; Kubrin and Weitzer 2003). Juvenile asks, "If she think you're jokin', is she goin' get a quick chokin'?" (*March Nigga Step*), and Dr. Dre tells us that "snobby-ass bitches get slapped out of spite" (*Ackrite*). Violence is seen as fitting for other "offenses" as well. Mase raps, "If she make my nuts itch [from an STD], I kill that slut bitch" (*I Need to Be*); N.W.A. has a song titled *To Kill a Hooker*, and Eminem tells listeners to "rape sluts" (*Who Knew*), prostitutes, and other women:

> Slut, you think I won't choke no whore
>
> 'Til the vocal cords don't work in her throat no more?!
>
> Shut up slut, you're causin' too much chaos
>
> Just bend over and take it like a slut, okay Ma?
> (Eminem, *Kill You*)

Several rappers threaten women with assault or rape if they refuse sex:

> Slap you with my paw, all across your jaw
>
> Break fool [act violent] on these bitches while I'm breakin' the law
>
> You come up in my room, look bitch you takin' it off.
> (Snoop Dogg, on Notorious B.I.G., *Dangerous MC's*)

These sorts of justifications for the use of violence are mirrored, to some extent, in disadvantaged communities, as borne out in some ethnographic research. For instance, Miller and White (2003:1237) found that both girls and boys in the inner city believed that male violence was appropriate when the girl seemed to have "forgotten her place." Examples of such misconduct include girls who "run their mouth," "act a fool," dress inappropriately, or drink too much. As in rap music, violence in these communities is portrayed as situationally appropriate. By contrast, girls' violence was defined by boys as "rooted in their greater emotionality," which is another example of how gender differences are naturalized (Miller and White 2003:1242).

A related subtheme is the positive value placed on sex that is aggressive and injurious to women. Rappers take pride in women being "drilled," "wrecked," and otherwise roughed up during intercourse. Men demonstrate their dominance over women by such representations of rough sex. This subtheme was also evident in rap during the preceding time period, as documented in Armstrong's (2001) study of songs produced in 1987–1993.

In the songs in this category, rappers (1) pride themselves on sex acts that appear to harm women, (2) justify other acts of violence, (3) warn women who challenge male domination that they will be assaulted, and (4) seem to invite male violence against women. There is a dual message here, one for women and one for men: Violence is portrayed as the most appropriate response to women who violate gendered etiquette or who don't "know their place" and men are encouraged to abide by this principle. The main purpose of such songs, therefore,

appears to be the *normalization of violence against women as a means of social control*. The music both espouses a set of gendered norms and advocates sanctions for those who violate these norms.

Women as Prostitutes, Men as Pimps

Pimp chic is a recent cultural innovation. It draws on pimp imagery and the language of pimping and prostitution, but has broader meaning. As Quinn (2000:116) observed, "The divergent articulations of the pimp as trope and type point to the versatility of this misogynist, street-heroic figure." To "pimp" something can mean to promote it or to accessorize it. MTV, for example, has a show called "Pimp My Ride," where old cars are spruced up with expensive gadgets to create the ultimate pimpmobile. The term pimp is often synonymous with "player," a man who excels at attracting women or glamorized hustlers who conspicuously display their riches. Here, "the pimp image is more central than his occupation" (Quinn 2000:124). The celebration of both pimp imagery and real pimps is pervasive in rap culture. Ice-T, Snoop Dogg, Jay-Z, and others claim to have been real-life pimps; at least one rapper (K-Luv the Pimp) has been arrested for pimping and pandering; a 2003 film called *Lil Pimp* starred a 9 year old boy as the film's hero; and a year after Nelly released his 2002 song and video, "Pimp Juice," he launched a new energy drink of the same name.

Although the mainstreaming of pimp chic is a fascinating cultural trend, we do not include it in this thematic category. Instead, we use the conventional, narrow definitions—namely, men who employ prostitutes. In coding, we were careful to distinguish references to prostitution and pimping, in the strict sense, from pimp chic. Women as prostitutes/men as pimps was a theme in 20 percent of the misogynistic songs.

Prostitutes are the quintessential figures of sexual objectification and exploitation, even if many of them see themselves as exploiting customers instead (Weitzer 2005). In rap, both prostitution and pimping are defined as legitimate economic pursuits and celebrated—themes which are almost non-existent in other music genres (Quinn 2000). The notion that women are only good for sex is epitomized in male discourse regarding prostitutes, and some rappers go to great lengths to present such women in one-dimensional, impersonal terms:

> Let's me and you lay in these hoes
>
> And show 'em what they pussy made fo'. . .
>
> Let's leave without payin' these hoes
>
> And show 'em what they pussy made fo'.
> (Scarface, *Use Them Ho's*)

Here women are reduced to their sex organs, and not even worth paying for their services.

Some artists describe the hardships faced by pimps, such as Ice-T's "Somebody's Gotta Do It, Pimpin' Ain't Easy!" and Three 6 Mafia's Academy Award–winning song, "It's Hard Out Here for a Pimp." Others revel in the multiple benefits of pimping:

> Around the world, getting money,
>
> I'm pimpin' hoes on Sunday.
>
> I'm the kind of nigga you'll work all night fo' . . .
>
> Wanna see how much pussy these hoes can sell.
>
> It's like hypnosis, I pimps your mother, I pimps yo sis'
>
> Hoes be nothin' but slaves for me, ready to go to their graves for me.
> (Too $hort, *Pimp Me*)

Pimping and prostitution are glorified:

> Nuthin' like pimpin' . . .
>
> I'll make the White House a hoe house, and all the pimps
>
> To just set up shops like they do in Vegas
>
> Legalize pimpin' for all the playas.
>
> Puttin' fine ass bitches in the streets and the hood
>
> Every year a nigga trade for a new Fleetwood [Cadillac].
> (Too $hort, *Ain't Nothing Like Pimpin'*)

And rappers ask listeners to give pimps the respect they deserve:

> This ho, that ho make me rich. . .
>
> I'm back in the game, getting' my dough
>
> And fuck any motherfucker that say it ain't so.
> (Snoop Dogg, *Buck 'Em*)

Quinn (2000:117, 135) argues that simply by drawing attention to pimps' exploitative practices and misogyny, these lyrics contain a "dissident" subtext that partially undermines such conduct even as it reinforces and condones it. This interpretation, of dual and perhaps contradictory messages, is a function of Quinn's broad definition of pimping to include both "players" and traditional pimps. In our sample of lyrics we found celebration, not critique, to be the norm with respect to the pimp–prostitute relationship.

Street prostitution is typically located in both disadvantaged and marginal/transitional neighborhoods. Residents of these areas face obstacles in finding work, and prostitution and pimping may be seen as preferable to dead-end, low-paying jobs. Insofar as rap music emerged out of conditions in these neighborhoods, we might expect the sex trade to be one theme, and indeed it is in one-fifth of our misogynistic songs. At the same time, neighborhood conditions do not exist in a vacuum but interact with external factors. Ice-T invokes legendary pimp Iceberg Slim's book, *Pimp: The Story of My Life*, as the inspiration for his lyrics: "Ghetto hustlers in my neighborhood would talk this nasty dialect rich with imagery of sex and humor. My buddies and I wanted to know where they picked it up, and they told us, 'You better get into some of the Iceberg stuff!'" (quoted in Quinn 2000:123). Several rappers also claim to have been influenced by the romanticization of the iconic pimps featured in the blaxploitation films of the 1970s (Quinn 2000). Snoop Dogg, for instance, states, "When I started seeing those movies in the '70s, like *The Mack* and *Superfly*, that helped me to more or less pick who I wanted to be in life, how I wanted to live my life, how I wanted to represent me" (quoted in Moody 2003). Those films not only painted pimps as role models for young black men but also purported to describe life in the ghetto—well illustrated in the 1999 documentary, *American Pimp*. Coming full circle, several famous pimps have appeared in rap videos. Rap's glorification of pimping is thus linked to both neighborhood conditions and a larger, pre-existing pimp culture (in films and books), which itself originated on the streets.

The Voices of Female Rappers

According to one analyst, "Rap provides a medium to mobilize feminist strategies of resistance, to give voice to the experience and concerns shared by young black women, or to explore and articulate various aspects of desire and pleasure" (Forman 1994:54). Did the lyrics of female rappers, during this time period, contain elements of an oppositional subculture directed at misogynistic male rap? Did they call hegemonic masculinity into question and reject the negative images and messages regarding women? Or were they silent or compliant with respect to male constructions of proper gender relations?

To determine whether female rappers objected to the negative portrayal of women in rap, we analyzed lyrics by female rappers that were not included in our original sample (because they did not contain misogynistic themes). Recall that only 13 of our 403 songs were by women; 8 of these 13 did not contain misogynistic lyrics. Analysis of these 8 songs reveals very little resistance to sexism during the time period under study. Only one song by Eve (*Love Is Blind*) directly challenges male mistreatment of women. In this song, Eve alternates between cursing a man who abused her girlfriend and questioning her girlfriend's decision to stay with this "snake motherfucker." In one stanza, she asks her friend:

> What kind of love from a nigga would black your eye?
>
> What kind of love from a nigga every night make you cry?
>
> What kind of love from a nigga make you wish he would die?
>
> And you stayed, what made you fall for him?
>
> That nigga had the power to make you crawl for him . . . .
>
> Smacked you down cause he said you was too tall for him, huh?
> (Eve, *Love Is Blind*)

This song stands alone in its rejection of violence towards women. This is not to suggest that female rappers accepted misogynistic lyrics; instead, the fact that they offered such little resistance

likely reflects industry norms at the time. During the 1990s, women were grossly underrepresented in rap generally, and gangsta rap in particular, and were channeled instead into hip-hop and R&B. For women to gain acceptance in this male-dominated industry, they had to conform to existing industry norms and required male sponsors, who often appeared on one of their songs or in their videos (Emerson 2002; Nelson 1998:184). For this reason, the most common theme in our sample of songs by female artists involves the entry-level claim to being a bona fide, skilled rapper. Like many male artists at the time (Kubrin 2005a), women demanded respect for their talents as rappers and would boast about this. In nearly all cases, bragging about one's skills on the microphone was the entire point of the song.

Apart from Eve's oppositional song, there was one remaining theme associated with gender relations—competition and fighting over men. In these songs, female rappers disparaged other women who they accused of trying to steal their men:

> Get your own stacks [money]
>
> Why you think these niggas pussy hungry?
>
> Cause you actin' triflin'
>
> Layin' up, takin' his money.
> (Eve, *Let's Talk About*)

In other scenarios, female rappers claimed ownership of their man even if he had sex with other women, usually because the former was the man's wife or longtime girlfriend:

> Shit, I got the ring bitch and his last name . . . .
>
> Any bitch could luck up and have a kid
>
> Any chick could fuck a nigga for spite
>
> But the nigga got to love you if he make you his wife
>
> Ughh, ya'll chicks is lonely, I'm ownin' that dick
>
> And on top of all this bullshit, I'm still his chick.
> (Foxy Brown, *It's Hard Being Wifee*)

Although our sample of female rappers is too small for definitive conclusions, most did not challenge the degradation of women by male artists at the time. Some female artists adopt the persona and status afforded them by men: Lil' Kim calls herself "Queen Bitch," Mia X is a "Boss Bitch" (Pough 2004), and others pride themselves on being gold diggers. But it is also important to remember that most songs by women neither accepted nor opposed such degradation. This pattern appears to have changed subsequent to the time period covered by our study. Currently female rappers more actively confront male domination and seek to empower women, although songs by female artists today still contain a contradictory mix of themes that both challenge and perpetuate misogynistic themes (Emerson 2002; Jennings 2004; Pough 2004:85–87; Troka 2002:83).

Conclusion

According to one review of popular music over the past century, the portrayal of women has increasingly shown "greater diversity, more complexity, and dramatically mixed messages about the individual female persona and women's roles in society" (Cooper 1999:355). Much rap music, at least rap produced by male artists, runs counter to this larger trend. Indeed, a segment of rap music naturalizes certain alleged characteristics of men and women and, in accordance with these imputed differences, seeks to restrict, rather than broaden, women's proper roles and resuscitate male domination. The messages are thus both essentialist and normative—portraying men and women as inherently different and unequal and espousing a set of conduct norms for each gender's proper behavior toward the other and sanctions for those who violate these norms.

Some analysts describe rap music as part of a larger reaction against the feminist movement, seeking to perpetuate women's inequality and re-empower men. As bell hooks (1994:6) argues, "Gangsta rap is part of the anti-feminist backlash that is the rage right now." The music contains a variety of "controlling images" directed at women (Collins 2000), and goes to great lengths to define strict gender roles, with women subordinate to men in several ways. In this sense rap speaks to larger gender relations by making universalistic claims and instructing all men on appropriate conduct toward women. But rap artists are not solely responsible for the content of their work. The entertainment industry plays an essential role, cultivating sexist lyrics and rewarding artists who produce them with huge sums of money, Grammy and Oscar awards, and spin-off products like Pimp Juice. In addition to this top-down dynamic, we have also pointed to a bottom-up process in which, as Negus (1999:490) argues, neighborhood "culture produces industry" as much as "industry produces culture." In other words, rap's messages have been incubated and resonate in communities where men have few opportunities for socioeconomic success and dignity and where respect is instead often earned by mistreating young women (Anderson 1999; Bourgois 1996; Liebow 1967) as well as other men (Kubrin and Weitzer 2003). As Connell and Messerschmidt (2005) point out, hegemonic masculinity is reinforced reciprocally at multiple levels—societal, community, and interactional.

It is important to emphasize that, like other music genres, rap is more varied in its content than is often recognized. For instance, this music has served as a consciousness-raising, politically progressive, liberating form of popular culture (Martinez 1997). Therefore, we want to emphasize that misogyny does not characterize rap music as a whole. This is an important finding in itself. A majority of songs in our sample do *not* degrade women, which we consider a major finding in itself. And there are rappers who actively challenge rap's misogynistic messages and endorse a more egalitarian form of masculinity. At the same time, a sizeable segment (more than one-fifth) of this genre does contain such messages, and our analysis indicates that these messages are rather extreme. While women are presented as subordinate to men in a majority of rock and country songs as noted earlier, rap stands out for the *intensity* and *graphic* nature of its lyrical objectification, exploitation, and victimization of women. Other genres, in the aggregate, make more subtle allusions to gender inequality or present more muted criticisms of women (Andsager and Roe 1999; Binder 1993; Cooper 1999; Rhym 1997; Ryan and Peterson 1982; Walser 1993). Furthermore, it is important to consider what themes are largely *absent* in rap lyrics. Rare are lyrics that describe women as independent, educated, professional, caring, and trustworthy. While the majority of songs in the original sample did not contain misogynistic lyrics, even these songs failed to present women in a favorable light. In other words, absence of misogyny does not equate with a positive representation of women.

Given its sources, we argue that changing the content of this music—specifically with respect to the portrayal of women—requires in part changing the conditions under which it is created, conditions that lie at the intersection of three important forces: socioeconomic disadvantage and associated gender relations in local communities, the material interests of the record industry, and the larger cultural objectification of women and associated norms of hegemonic masculinity.

Authors' Note

For their helpful comments on this paper, we are grateful to Ivy Ken, Michael Kimmel, Theresa Martinez, and the anonymous reviewers, and for research assistance we thank Ami Lynch.

Notes

1. It is important to recognize that rap is not monolithic. There are various themes in rap music, ranging from Afro-Centric community building to support for liberation struggles, to celebration of partying to problems of racism and drug dealing. See Kitwana (1994:32) and Krims (2000:55) for evidence of rap music's varied content.
2. Gangsta rap is a subgenre of rap music. It describes life in the ghetto, and has been controversial in part because it provides an insiders' view of crime, violence, and social conflict in the inner city (Kitwana 1994: 19; Krims 2000:70). More so than other rap genres, gangsta rap is noted for its violent and misogynistic lyrics, which depart from the rich political and social commentary that characterizes some other rap music (Kelley 1996:147).
3. We recognize that a few artists, such as NWA, produced gangsta rap songs before this time

period. However, gangsta rap gained ascendancy in the early 1990s.
4. Originally a random sample of one-third of the 1,922 songs was selected to be analyzed (N = 632). The findings are based on a final sample size of 403 because, during the course of coding, after song 350 we no longer encountered new themes. Nevertheless, we coded an additional 53 songs to ensure that we had reached saturation, which is standard practice in qualitative analysis (Glaser and Strauss 1967:111).
5. At first glance, it might appear that negative portrayals of women were less frequent in rap than in the other music genres reviewed earlier, based on the percentage differences. However, each study operationalized such depictions in somewhat different ways, so study findings cannot be directly compared. Similarly, our finding on rap music cannot be compared to Armstrong's (2001) study of earlier rap songs because he focused on expressions of violence against women whereas our measure of misogyny is more inclusive.
6. Eminem has marketed himself as a poor or working-class white youth, which gives him some "street credibility" among black rappers and record producers, and it has been argued that his misogynistic lyrics are intended to gain credibility as a rapper (Stephens 2005).

References

Alexander, Susan. 1999. The gender role paradox in youth culture: An analysis of women in music videos. *Michigan Sociological Review* 13:46–64.

Anderson, Elijah. 1999. *Code of the street: Decency, violence, and the moral life of the inner city.* New York: W.W. Norton.

Andsager, Julie, and Kimberly Roe. 1999. Country music video in country's year of the woman. *Journal of Communication* 49:69–82.

Armstrong, Gerald. 2001. Gangsta misogyny: A content analysis of the portrayals of violence against women in rap music, 1987–1993. *Journal of Criminal Justice and Popular Culture* 8:96–126.

Barongan, Christy, and Gordon Hall. 1995. The influence of misogynous rap music on sexual aggression against women. *Psychology of Women Quarterly* 19:195–207.

Bennett, Andy 1999a. Rappin' on the Tyne: White hip-hop culture in northeast England. *Sociological Review* 47:1–24.

_____. 1999b. Hip hop am Main: The localization of rap music and hip hop culture. *Media, Culture & Society* 21:77–91.

Binder, Amy. 1993. Media depictions of harm in heavy metal and rap music. *American Sociological Review* 58:753–767.

Bourgois, Philippe. 1995. *In search of respect: Selling crack in El Barrio.* New York: Cambridge University Press.

_____. 1996. In search of masculinity: Violence, respect, and sexuality among Puerto Rican crack dealers in East Harlem. *British Journal of Criminology* 36:412–427.

Butruille, Susan, and Anita Taylor. 1987. Women in American popular song. In *Communication, gender, and sex roles in diverse interactional contexts,* eds. L. Stewart and S. Ting-Toomey, 179–188. Norwood, NJ: Ablex.

Collins, Patricia Hill. 2000. *Black feminist thought.* 2nd Edn. New York: Routledge.

Connell, R. W. 1987. *Gender and power.* Cambridge: Polity.

Connell, R. W., and James Messerschmidt. 2005. Hegemonic masculinity: Rethinking the concept. *Gender & Society* 19:829–859.

Donaldson, Mike. 1993. What is hegemonic masculinity? *Theory and Society* 22:643–657.

Edin, Kathryn, and Maria Kefalas. 2005. *Promises I can keep: Why poor women put motherhood before marriage.* Berkeley: University of California Press.

Emerson, Rana. 2002. "Where my girls at?" Negotiating black womanhood in music videos. *Gender and Society* 16:115–135.

Forman, Murray. 1994. "Moving closer to an independent funk": Black feminist theory, standpoint, and women in rap. *Women's Studies* 23:35–55.

Garfinkle, Harold. 1956. Conditions of successful degradation ceremonies. *American Journal of Sociology* 61:420–424.

George, Nelson. 1998. *Hip hop America.* New York: Penguin Books.

Glaser, Barney, and Anselm Strauss. 1967. *The discovery of grounded theory.* Chicago: Aldine.

Hanke, Robert. 1998. Theorizing masculinity within the media. *Communication Theory* 8:183–203.

hooks, bell. 1994. Misogyny, gangsta rap, and the piano. *Z Magazine,* February.

Horowitz, Ruth. 1983. *Honor and the American dream: Culture and identity in a Chicano community.* New Brunswick, NJ: Rutgers University Press.

Hurt, Byron. 2007. *Hip hop: Beyond beats and rhymes.* Independent Lens series, PBS. First broadcast February 20th.

Jennings, Tom. 2004. Dancehall dreams. *Variant* 2 (Summer):9–13.

Johnson, James, Mike Adams, Leslie Ashburn, and William Reed. 1995. Differential gender effects of exposure to rap music on African American adolescents' acceptance of teen dating violence. *Sex Roles* 33:597–605.

Kelley, Robin. 1996. Kickin' reality, kickin' ballistics: Gangsta rap and postindustrial Los Angeles. In *Droppin science: critical essays on rap music and hip hop culture,* ed. W. Perkins, 117–158. Philadelphia: Temple University Press.

Keyes, Cheryl L. 2002. *Rap music and street consciousness.* Chicago: University of Chicago Press.

Kitwana, Bakari. 1994. *The rap on gangsta rap.* Chicago: Third World Press.

_____. 2002. *The hip hop generation: Young blacks and the crisis of African American culture.* New York: Basic Books.

Krims, Adam. 2000. *Rap music and the poetics of identity.* Cambridge: Cambridge University Press.

Kubrin, Charis E. 2005a. Gangstas, thugs, and hustlas: Identity and the code of the street in rap music. *Social Problems* 52:360–378.

_____. 2005b. I see death around the corner: Nihilism in rap music. *Sociological Perspectives* 48:433–459.

Kubrin, Charis E. and Ronald Weitzer. 2003. Retaliatory homicide: Concentrated disadvantage and neighborhood culture. *Social Problems* 50:157–180.

Lay, Frank. 2000. "Sometimes we wonder who the real men are": Masculinity and contemporary popular music. In *Subverting masculinity: Hegemonic and alternative versions of masculinity in contemporary culture,* ed. R. West and F. Lay, 227–246. Amsterdam: Rodopi.

Lee, Carol D. 2005. Intervention research based on current views of cognition and learning. In *Black education: A transformative research and action agenda for the new century,* ed. J. King, 73–114. Washington, D.C.: American Educational Research Association.

Lee, Cooper B. 1999. From Lady Day to Lady Di: Images of women in contemporary recordings, 1938–1998. *International Journal of Instructional Media* 26:353–358.

Lena, Jennifer C. 2006. Social context and musical content of rap music, 1979–1995. *Social Forces* 85:479–495.

Liebow, Elliot. 1967. *Tally's corner*. Boston: Little, Brown.

McAdams, Janine, and Deborah Russell. 1991. Rap breaking through to adult market. *Hollywood Reporter*, Sept. 19:4.

McFarland, Pancho. 2003. Challenging the contradictions of Chicanismo in Chicano rap music and male culture. *Race, Gender, and Class* 10: 92–107.

Martino, Steven, Rebecca Collins, Marc Elliott, Amy Strachman, David Kanouse, and Sandra Berry. 2006. Exposure to degrading versus nondegrading music lyrics and sexual behavior among youth. *Pediatrics* 118:430–441.

Martinez, Theresa A. 1997. Popular culture as oppositional culture: Rap as resistance. *Sociological Perspectives* 40:265–286.

Miller, Jody, and Norman White. 2003. Gender and adolescent relationship violence. *Criminology* 41:1207–1247.

Moody, Nekesa Mumbi. 2003. Pimps: The new gangstas of rap. *Associated Press*, July 21.

Negus, Keith. 1999. The music business and rap: Between the street and the executive suite. *Cultural Studies* 13:488–508.

Oliver, William. 2006. The streets: An alternative black male socialization institution. *Journal of Black Studies* 36:918–937.

Pough, Gwendolyn. 2004. *Check it while I wreck it: Black womanhood, hip-hop culture, and the public sphere*. Boston: Northeastern University Press.

Powell, Catherine T. 1991. Rap music: An education with a beat from the street. *Journal of Negro Education* 60:245–259.

Powell, Kevin. 2000. My culture at the crossroads: A rap devotee watches corporate control and apolitical times encroach on the music he has loved all his life. *Newsweek*, October 9:66.

Quinn, Eithne. 2000. "Who's the mack?" The performativity and politics of the pimp figure in gangsta rap. *Journal of American Studies* 34:115–136.

———. 2005. *Nuthin but a "G" thang: The culture and commerce of gangsta rap*. New York: Columbia University Press.

Rhym, Darren. 1997. "Here's for the bitches": An analysis of gangsta rap and misogyny." *Womanist Theory and Research* 2:1–14.

Rose, Tricia. 1994a. *Black noise: Rap music and black culture in contemporary America*. Hanover, NH: Wesleyan University Press.

Ryan, John W. and R. A. Peterson. 1982. The product image: The fate of creativity in country music songwriting. *Sage Annual Reviews of Communication Research* 10:11–32.

Skeggs, Beverley. 1993. Two minute brother: Contestation through gender, race, and sexuality. *Innovation: The European Journal of Social Sciences* 6:299–323.

Stephens, Vincent. 2005. Pop goes the rapper: A close reading of Eminem's genderphobia. *Popular Music* 24:21–36.

Smith, Christopher H. 1997. Method in the madness: Exploring the boundaries of identity in hip hop performativity. *Social Identities* 3:345–374.

Smitherman, Geneva. 1997. "The chain remain the same": Communicative practices in the hip hop nation. *Journal of Black Studies* 28:3–25.

Troka, Donna. 2002. "You heard my gun cock": Female agency and aggression in contemporary rap music. *African American Research Perspectives* 8:82–89.

Tuchman, Gaye. 1978. The symbolic annihilation of women by the mass media. In *Hearth and home: Images of women in the mass media*, eds. G. Tuchman, A. Daniels, and J. Benet, 3–38. New York: Oxford University Press.

van Zoonen, Liesbet. 1994. *Feminist media studies*. Thousand Oaks: Sage.

Vincent, Richard, Dennis Davis, and Lilly Boruszkowski. 1987. Sexism on MTV: The portrayal of women in rock videos. *Journalism Quarterly* 64:750–755.

Walser, Robert. 1993. *Running with the Devil: Power, gender, and madness in heavy metal music*. Hanover, NH: Wesleyan University Press.

Watkins, S. Craig. 2001. A nation of millions: Hip hop culture and the legacy of black nationalism. *The Communication Review* 4:373–398.

Weitzer, Ronald. 2005. New directions in research on prostitution. *Crime, Law, and Social Change* 43:211–235.

Wester, Stephen, Cynthia Crown, Gerald Quatman, and Martin Heesacker. 1997. The influence of sexually violent rap music on attitudes of men with little prior exposure. *Psychology of Women Quarterly* 21:497–508.

Resistance Through Video Game Play

It's a Boy Thing

KATHY SANFORD AND LEANNA MADILL

Youth, in particular boys, are finding many literacy activities, largely outside the realm of the school institution, that engage them and sustain long-term interest, e.g., video games (including computer and console systems). These games provide an interesting, engaging, dynamic, social space for many types of boys, both those who succeed at school literacy and those who struggle; they do not have to fit into any particular affinity group, they can engage without interference or sanction from adults, whenever they choose or when they have opportunities, and in ways that provide social capital for making connections with peers in real-time and virtual spaces. The lack of boys' success in formal schooling activities, so frequently reported in public press, can, we argue, be framed as resistance, both unconscious and conscious, against meaningless, mindless, boring schooling or workplace activities and assignments; instead, they engage in activities that provide them with active involvement and interest. Videogame play also serves as a form of resistance to stereotypical views of boys as a category who, by virtue of the fact that they are boys, has been categorized as unsuccessful learners—videogames are spaces where players can be successful in their endeavours.

Video Game Culture, Gender, and New and Critical Literacies

Video Game Culture

According to the Kaiser Family Foundation study *Kids, Media, and the New Millennium*, boys and girls differ in the amount of time engaged with media. Girls aged 8–18 spent less time per day than boys with the combination of media surveyed. Boys spent more time with TV, video games, and computers than did girls who spent more time with music media and print materials (as cited in Newkirk, 2002, p. 42). Rowan, Knobel, Bigum, and Lankshear (2002) report similar findings, claiming that "girls use the internet more than do the boys surveyed, but the girls use it more for educational purposes" (p. 131). The Canadian Teachers' Federation (2003), in *Kids Take on Media: Summary of Findings*, report that almost 60 per cent of boys in grades 3–6 play video or computer games almost every day, 38 per cent for boys in grade 10. For girls, 33 per cent of grade–3 girls play interactive games every day, but only 6 per cent of grade 10 girls (p. iv).

Boys and male youth are far more involved in videogames than are girls. By engaging in these activities that resist traditional literacy learning, video game players are keeping up with the changing technological world faster and more productively than schools are. Gee (2000) describes this changing world: "If our modern, global, high-tech, and science-driven world does anything, it certainly gives rise to new semiotic domains and transforms old ones at an even faster rate" (p. 19).

"Attempts to assess the effects of video games on young people have been extensive," report Alloway and Gilbert (1998), "and have come from a variety of research domains and methodologies" (p. 95). Although some studies (Alloway & Gilbert, 1998; Alvermann, 2002; Rowan, Knobel, Bigum, & Lankshear, 2002) have focused on connections between gender and videogame play, many have focused on these issues separately, addressing videogame play and learning (Gee, 2003), identity development through videogame play (Filiciak, 2003), the nature of computer games (Myers, 2003), the value of videogames (Newman, 2004), and gendered marketing strategies for videogames (Ray, 2004).

Although videogame culture is strongly male-focused and masculinist, developing aggressive themes and situations (Alloway & Gilbert, 1998), often children and youth are represented as a homogeneous group, ignoring issues of difference connected to gender (Kline, 2004) and differing impacts on diverse populations.

Gender and Masculinity

Gender as a social construct impacts learning both in and out of school, dictating what is and can be learned and what is out of bounds. Gender, and therefore masculinity, is not fixed in advance of social interaction, but is constructed in interaction, and masculinity must be understood as an aspect of large-scale social structures and processes (Connell, 1995, p. 39). From a post-structural perspective, there are multiple ways of being a male and creating/negotiating male subjectivity. These multiple and diverse positions open up the possibility of constituting subjectivity as multiple and contradictory (Davies, 1992): every individual male accesses, performs, and transforms multiple versions of masculinity in various contexts and at various times. There are multiple ways that masculinity

is performed; however hegemonic versions of masculinity are most highly valued, that is, performances of masculinity that embody "the currently accepted answer to the problem of the legitimacy of patriarchy, which guarantees (or is taken to guarantee) the dominant position of men and the subordination of women" (Connell, 1995, p. 77).

Family activities and values transfer into schooling practices where notions of masculinity (often linked to images of such things as strength, cleverness, winning, power, and status) are further developed and reinforced, creating powerful sites for gendered messages to be reinforced by teachers and young people themselves (Browne, 1995; Sanford, 2006). Hegemonic masculinity not only naturalizes masculine behaviours, but also male discipline areas, such as science, mathematics, mechanics, and technology—those areas seen to require rational, unemotional engagement.

Males and females develop attitudes towards science and machines differently, and at a very young age. As Ray (2004) notes, the concept of the computer as a male object is reinforced in children very early in their lives. Males, given machine-type toys, including computers, are encouraged to experiment with them; they are more likely to receive training (formal and informal) in using computers. One young participant in our study commented, "You've got to know how to make what go where and stuff. I learned some of that from a game manual, mostly just clicking around . . . that's how I learn that kind of thing, just trial and error." Males, like this participant, are socialized to engage with computers and video games.

New and Critical Literacies

In this article, we have discussed not only how males use videogames to create resistances, but also our concerns related to videogame play when viewed simply as another form of "text." We have raised questions about operational, cultural, and critical dimensions of learning. Based on a sociocultural perspective in examining new or alternative literacies comprehensively, we draw on Green's (1997) three-dimensional model that considers operational, cultural, and critical dimensions of literacy and learning. Operational literacy "includes but also goes beyond competence with the tools, procedures, and techniques involved in being able to handle the written language system proficiently. It includes being able to read and write/key in a range of contexts in an appropriate and adequate manner" (Lankshear & Knobel, 2003, p. 11). Cultural literacy "involves competence with the meaning system of a social practice; knowing how to make and grasp meanings appropriately within the practice . . . this means knowing what it is about given contexts of practice that makes for appropriateness or inappropriateness of particular ways of reading and writing" (Lankshear & Knobel, 2003, p. 11). Critical literacy addresses "awareness that all social practices, and thus all literacies, are socially constructed and 'selective': they include some representations and classifications—values, purposes, rules, standards, and perspectives—and exclude others" (Lankshear & Knobel, 2003, p. 11). We believe that as educators embrace videogames as a powerful learning tool (Gee, 2003), they must also find ways to raise critical questions relating to these texts and to disrupt unexamined hegemonic masculine attitudes related to power, status, and exclusivity.

Methodology

In this article, we examine video games as a domain that many boys and men choose to resist traditional school-based literacy, and examine how they use games to resist controlling societal forces and so-called feminized spaces such as home, daycare, and school. Given the considerable and growing involvement of boys with this alternative form of learning about literacy, technology, and the world, it is critical for both males and females that researchers and educators examine the implication of this male immersion into these new semiotic and technological domains.

In this study, we elucidate the complexity of the interplay between gender and videogame play, to better understand the nature of the learning done by male youth, and to consider the impact of this learning on them and on others in society.

We observed the youths (predominantly male) in this study as they engaged in the literacy practice of videogame play as a discursive tool. These observations provided a context in which we examined the performance of gender subjectivities through a range of alternative literacy practices (Gee, 1992; Street, 1984).

Participants and Data Collection

The informants for this study included two groups of participants/players. The first group, six young adolescent males attending a middle school in a small Canadian community, volunteered to participate in this study. Throughout the year, we observed them at school, both in classrooms and in less regulated spaces such as the hallways, out-of-doors, and in computer labs. We interviewed each participant twice throughout the year, where the discussion focused on his use of and interest in computers generally and game playing particularly. We transcribed the interviews, and used the first interview to shape the discussion of the second interview.

Our second group of participants, five young adult males, referred to us by acquaintances and selected for their interest in videogame play, were observed and videotaped in their home environments, playing videogames both independently and with a friend. We interviewed them in-depth two to three times over three months, where they discussed the nature of their videogame playing and reflected on the influences of videogame play on their lives. As with the first group, we transcribed the interviews, using the first interview to shape the focus of subsequent interviews. Both groups of participants, from the same geographical region, were predominantly from white, middle-class backgrounds. Our gender as two white females might have initially imposed barriers; however, the participants became very willing to share their ideas and expertise about videogames and helped us understand their specific references and to share their insider knowledge.

The interviews were analyzed and coded using NVivo text analysis software program. The data were coded into categories, mapped, searched, synthesized, and analyzed. We also conducted manual coding of themes to supplement the computer analysis which we shared with boys. To recognize themes of significance, we used critical discourse analysis to identify oppositions, recurrent key terms, and subjects spoken about by the participants and connected to the videogames identified by the participants.

Findings

A significant theme that we identified through the analysis was the participants' perception of resistance as they engaged in videogame play: resistance to institutional authority, hegemonic masculinity, and femininity. These themes often overlapped or were sometimes even contradictory as the participants talked about how and why they played. Some of the forms of resistance were consciously selected (resistance to societal rules and resistance to school) while others were not consciously selected, but seemed to us to be pushing back on some of the restrictions and taboos they faced in school and current Western society (versions of restrictive masculinity and at the same time all types of femininity).

Through discussions with the participants, we learned what games they played, the types of games available, and their operational critique of the games (Lankshear & Knobel, 2003). We observed and videotaped the young adult players as they engaged in a variety of games (e.g., NBA Live 2005; Grand Theft Auto: Vice City; Counter Strike). Surprisingly to us, the games discussed by the adolescents and the young adults were very similar. They identified a range of game types: role play games—RPG (Final Fantasy, Halo), First Person Shooter—FPS (Max Payne, Medal of Honour, James Bond), Strategy/Simulation (Sims), Real Time Strategy—RTS (Counterstrike), Multi-genre role play/First Person Shooter (Grand Theft Auto), sports games (NBA 2005; Triple Play 2001, NHL Hockey 2002), and Movie games (Harry Potter, Star Wars, Punisher, Man Hunt) as being games they chose to spend hours playing, with their friends or on their own. Boys and male youth are engaging in the same types of videogames as adults, even though the games are intended for mature adult players (Canadian Teachers' Federation study, 2003).

Sites of Resistance

We examined the role(s) that videogames play for males in challenging existing societal norms and expectations as they sought to define their masculine subjectivities in appropriate ways. Popular culture and media have historically been used as sites of resistance, whether through music, banners, graffiti, or alternative newspapers (Guzzetti & Gamboa, 2004) and this use of popular media continues today to resist constricting forms of education that stereotype, limit learning opportunities for segments of the population, and prevent meaningful learning for a rapidly increasingly global, technological, and digital world. Videogame players demonstrate many examples of resistance through challenges to rules and structures imposed by existing societal regulation and through challenges to restrictive identity formations and stereotypes.

Three significant areas of potential conflict and resistance include: institutional authority, hegemonic masculinity, and femininity. There are many ways in which students, particularly boys, overtly resist the hegemony of adult authority, and videogame play offers them a safe place to contest these power structures.

Resistance to Institutional Authority

Whether purposefully or unconsciously, youth engage in practices that serve to resist imposition of structures and rules currently prevailing in society. These rules are challenged in both private and social spaces. Even when speaking to us as researchers, the participants seemed more willing to share their expertise once it was clear that we were not negatively judging their videogame play. Players shared their frustrations and (either overtly or subtly) opposed authority within their cultural groups, ignoring and reshaping the rules. As they gained skills and confidence in playing games, they felt more able to resist traditional authority, relying on their fellow gamers for support and understanding—of the risks, the meaning, and the value. "I like lots of videogames" said one younger participant, "though there are some games that I had to defend that adults would think are stupid." They received immediate feedback not only from the game but also from their peers as they developed greater skill and confidence in playing the game.

The world of school, followed by the world of work, offers many routinized, dull tasks that do not offer the qualities reported by males as required for meaningful engagement, that is, personal interest, action, fun, purpose, or opportunities for success (Blair & Sanford, 2004; Smith & Wilhelm, 2002). Instead, they faced a world of ordinariness, lacking excitement or purpose. "I get bored quite a bit," one adolescent participant told us, "at school and at home. Then I usually go up and play on the computer." All the adult male participants explained that they used games to "zone out," to stop thinking or engaging with real people in their lives who have demands and remind them of their responsibilities. Videogames enabled players to create fantasy worlds for themselves where they were heroic, active, and respected.

Videogames also offer opportunities for players to learn information in alternate multi-modal ways through playing videogames, unlike traditional school learning that is most often linear and book based. Engaging in *Medal of Honor: Pacific Assault* allows youth to gain information about a significant historic event, but goes far beyond transmission of facts because adrenaline allows the players to feel the experience through sound and vibration, newer aspects of videogame play. Simulation games (Sim City, Speed Racing, Air Strike) enable players to learn about valued workplace and life skills, such as driving a car, flying a plane, or building a city. The immersion experiences that are promised, engaging players in the action, enabling them to feel the exhilaration and the fear, create a far more powerful and memorable learning experience than the reading of a textbook. One young adolescent participant reported, "I've learned tons about history, tons and tons, from *Civilization 3*. You just learn lots of stuff, and you don't really think about it." Not a far stretch, then for students to begin to challenge the material (both content and format) being presented in school, and to resist the linear, uni-dimensional approach to learning that is so often used in school.

Videogames provide many opportunities for players to explore alternatives to the reality of adult society and its patriarchal, imposed rules. These rules, or laws, create restrictive structures that adolescents yearn to resist. As one young adult commented, ". . . it's cool, you can just explore . . . you can fly with a jet pack, break into an airport, grab some pizza . . . you're not limited to what you can do." Through videogame play, they can try out resistant and dangerous choices and experience the consequences, all within the safety of game play. The opportunity to adopt an alternative persona and to experience characters' perceptions and actions, which are often inappropriate or illegal actions in the real world, and usually have no consequences, was a powerful enticement. One young adult participant commented,

> "You take street racing that's illegal and you take new cars and you soup them up and you make them look all flashy and crazy . . . and you race them on the street, swerving in and around other cars and things like that—it's slightly rebellious or whatever, but I'd like to see what that's like."

The players assume authority as the game character and thereby gives their individual consent for the actions and attitudes that they role play (Leonard, 2004). Playing games that transgress societal, family, and school rules and norms enables a freedom to experiment with and challenge existing restrictions that, while providing safety, are also limiting and dull. Trying on resistant thoughts and actions is highly appealing to our participants.

The technology of videogames allows players to cheat by downloading codes or finding glitches in the game. One participant explained that players use cheats[1] because "at the moment they're so angry or frustrated with the game that they just want to go ahead, or they wonder, Wow! It would be so great if I had that." By using cheats, and engaging in a community that understands the purpose of cheats and the importance of them, players can band together to resist traditional and mainstream rules as a community, using their social connections to succeed at their game play.

Many videogame story lines encourage players to resist society's expectations. From stealing cars to killing enemies or random people, the game allows players to play out scenarios that they would never actually do: "It's kinda fun to do because it's not something that you would do everyday, obviously." Videogames allow players to forego the rules of the real world and engage in a new fantasy frontier where they can be mavericks, able to ignore rules that others have to abide. When players state that the reason they play video games is to escape, they suggest that they are not having to think critically about what they play: "I definitely play it to get into the role and forget about other things" and "I just go and play it and space out" are answers from our adult participants as to why they play video games. This attitude allows them the right to ignore stereotypes, prejudices, or other usually conflicting messages that they would otherwise not be allowed to (or even want to) participate with. "It's like a feeling of power, but it's sadistic," one adult participant explained, "You really enjoy it, like killing someone, blasting them in the head . . . maybe it's cause you can't do it, it's such a forbidden thing, but like they make it so real and powerful, like in a game you can have the ability to smoke people continuously." Another participant commented, "I don't know why I enjoy it, I imagine myself living in Vice City [Grant Theft Auto] just doing missions and you can kill people and steal cars and just do bad stuff. You do all these things that you don't necessarily want to do, but it gives you so much power . . . ". To succeed the participants engaged in the rules of the game, even if the rules did not match socially constructed values or rules.

Resistance to Hegemonic Masculinity

Western society has responded to expanded and alternative gender positions with a rigid homophobic stance regarding masculinity. Young males today are faced with a fierce policing of traditional masculinity, and the rules of masculinity are enforced in many overt and subtle ways. Being a male who does not exhibit characteristics of physical strength, individuality, and machismo can find the

world dangerous and lonely space (Connell, 1995; Frank, Kehler, & Davison, 2003; Kehler, 2004; Martino & Pallotta-Chiarolli, 2001). Videogames provide players with spaces in which to experiment with identity: to safely resist traditional masculinities currently prevailing in society, or conversely, to demonstrate their heterosexual masculinity and resist connections to the feminine, and to challenge societal expectations of appropriateness regarding attitude, appearance, or behaviour. By adopting roles through which they can experiment with their identity formation, they can expand their sense of self and understand their world from new perspectives. One adult participant negotiated his identity as he described a game, "In *Halo*, I really like that it is shoot 'em up, not that I am a killer, but you know . . . I just like that it is go and shoot, shoot, and kill, kill, kill."

In another interview, an adult male participant was asked what characteristics of male video game characters he admired. He responded: "I'd like to have the big body, a six-pack not an 8 pack! . . . I'd like to be built; I don't want to be a drug dealer, king of the city." When he was asked, "What about saving the girl?" he answered, "That would be neat. . . . I've often had dreams about that, meeting a girl by doing something courageous, you know." Another adult participant commented on his desire to be a hockey player. "I didn't ever play hockey; I don't know the rules. But in the game I'm always trying to start a body check or start a fight . . . I like all the silly things like how the glass breaks when you do a body check."

Videogames provide a way to resist traditional hegemonic masculinities in a safe space, to play out alternative personas, such as personas of men of colour or of females. In reality, not all males are strong and macho (and may not want to be), but they may wish to try on the persona of a rugged heroic figure who rescues the weak from dangerous situations. By using online forums and Internet gameplay, subjectivities can be disguised and trans/reformed in myriad ways. One participant talked about a friend [whom] he described as a "very fairy tale type of person, similar to the *Everquest* type of thing. He's kind of creative, and likes imaginary types of stuff." This friend was able to engage in the videogame as a character who did not display traditional masculinity traits, yet in the context of the game it was safe for him to do so. However, his alternative masculine persona might not have been as safe to perform in reality.

As suggested earlier in this article, the media and the public have categorized boys as regularly experiencing failure in school, of underperforming, and of being less literate than girls. Videogames provide spaces where boys can dominate and create an alternative sense of success. They are finding many activities that engage them and sustain long-term interest; videogames provide an interesting, engaging, dynamic social space for many types of boys who do not have to fit into any particular category. Videogames also allow for the creation of additional social spaces where boys from various social groups (athletes, trades, academics, rebels) can belong, resisting imposed societal roles and positions. By creating fantasy personas for themselves, heroic powerful figures able to rescue innocent girls and garner the respect of their peers, they resist the traditionally stereotypical ways they are viewed in society. Additionally they develop skills that are valued in the workplace, giving them future social capital through which to be successful.

By connecting to communities, face-to-face or on-line communities, and engaging in extensive rounds of play, players gain skills in manual dexterity, ability to read multiple screens or texts simultaneously, and make quick, accurate decisions based on information provided. These operational literacies referred to earlier in this article (Lankshear & Knobel, 2003) teach the mostly male players how to use many functions of computers, to make repairs and adjustments to programs and glitches, to make accurate predictions, and to apply their knowledge to new situations—most importantly, they gain a confidence in their ability to use computers effectively, not just videogames, but many aspects of computers. This confidence enables them to resist traditional school literacies,

choosing instead modes of literacy that support the particular type of masculine persona they have selected for themselves, and make a commitment to that self-selected identity. As Gee (2003) comments, "Such a commitment requires that they are willing to see themselves in terms of a new identity, that is, to see themselves as the *kind of person* who can learn, use, and value the new semiotic domain" (p. 59, italics in original). And if they are successful, then they will be valued by and accepted in that affinity group.

Rejecting Femininity

One way that male game players use videogames as a form of resistance is to create a clearly non-female identity, that is, muscular, big, and dangerous-looking. Although it is interesting to try on different personas, even those of females, it is personally dangerous to associate oneself with the feminine. One young adult male participant explained how sometimes a friend of his might choose to be the princess in a Mario Bros. game and they would all tease him. "We started calling him princess." This adult participant is a football player in real life and he attempted to masculinize his interest in videogames; he comments,

> "I don't think many girls are too interested in playing a game of *Dead or Alive* and seeing another girl's scantily clad body bounce around like it is, that kind of stuff appeals to guys. It's on more of a primal level, just kinda like one-on-one combat. It really turns guys on for some reason."

He differentiates males from females in this sexual way, and includes himself in this masculine description; he is not sure why males are drawn to these primal interests but is not inclined to question his theory or his participation in this world.

A similar example of resistance within the role playing games is the type of avatars (game characters) that players select to become in the videogames. The selected character is often the strong, independent rebel, such as in *Max Payne*, all the *Grand Theft Auto* games, *Man Hunt*, and *Counter Strike*; one adult gamer described these characters as "not really dependent on anyone else, very like 'I am going to do this my way.'" The players' desire to shape their identity as rugged, independent, and strong precludes them from making choices of characters who seem weak, dependent, and feminine. This same participant talked about Max Payne as a character he admired. "He's kind of a dark and lonely character, very dark and devious, and he talks with kind of a low deep voice and he's very masculine and he usually gets with one woman in the storyline."

Although choice of creating videogame characters helps the players to experiment with diverse subjectivities, again the hegemonic masculinity model looms large in most of the games the participants report playing regularly. As they negotiate their sense of self through various videogame characters, we worry that they are reinforcing the binary that relegates females to subordinate positions and does not allow any space or opportunity for a critical reading of the gender positions offered in the games.

Discussion

There is no question in our minds that videogames encourage resistance to school values, parental authority, and societal expectations, and partly because of the perception of resistance are hence a major attraction for youth. Videogames are fun, and this is partly because they are perceived as dangerous, entering forbidden territory. There is no doubt that videogame players are developing an understanding of learning principles through playing games, as suggested by Gee (2003), in relation to text design, intertextuality, semiotics, transfer of knowledge, or probing and identifying multiple approaches. However, we are not convinced that, as Gee claims, there is significant learning about cultural models. We did not find evidence that learners were thinking consciously and reflectively about cultural models of the world, or that they were consciously reflecting on the values that make up their real or videogame worlds. The resistance that we have observed in one area of the players' lives did not necessarily lead to resistance of imposed

stereotypical and potentially harmful beliefs and attitudes. Resistance to hegemonic hypermasculinity in game play does not necessarily lead the players to challenge gender stereotypes, or present themselves to the world in alternative representations of masculinity. And although resistance to anything feminine enables male players to develop their own subjectivity, it does not cause them to be more aware of their privileged positions of power or to respect difference in any significant way. We are concerned that the resistances made possible by videogame play serves only to reify the traditional stereotypes and cement them firmly in place.

There is, perhaps, a place to encourage resistance on a more conscious and responsive level through videogame play. Is it possible that spaces for critical questioning can be identified and taken up in relation to the images, actions, attitudes, and values being presented at hyperdrive speeds throughout the duration of a videogame? As we began to see in our interviews with young adult males, there is a place for them to critically examine their motivation and attitudes as they engage in games. Critical questions, such as those posed by Rowan and colleagues (2002), can help to shape resistances that change the world, rather than merely playing with the world as it exists.

- Who and what are included? What groups of people are included or excluded? How do you know?
- What do those who are included get to do? What roles are taken by men/boys, women/girls? What evidence do you have?
- Which people and roles are valued and how is this communicated?
- Who has control? Who has access to power? Who exercises power? Who acts independently? Who initiates action?
- What are various people rewarded for and with?
- In what ways does the inclusion or exclusion reflect to your own life?
- What are the consequences of this relationship?
- What alternatives are there? (pp. 117–118)

These types of questions enable engagement with and purpose for resistance, encouraging videogame players to look beyond the superficial qualities of action, speed, and excitement to a consideration of more fundamental levels of meaning and value that includes issues of power, control, and difference.

Conclusion

Popular media has historically been used as sites of resistance, through underground newspapers, graffiti, and music. And it is being used today to resist constricting forms of education that stereotype, limit learning opportunities, and prevent meaningful learning for a rapidly and increasingly global, technological, and digital world. The speed at which literacies are being challenged and reshaped defies institutional support and knowledge from maintaining the pace. Children create connections when they learn: "Our experiences in the world build patterns in our mind, and then the mind shapes our experience of the world (and the actions we take in it), which, in turn, reshapes our mind" (Gee, 2003, p. 92). Gee acknowledges that the harmful side of patterned thinking can lead to prejudices or stereotypes. If videogames are a main area from which players gain knowledge about a certain type of person, setting, or event then knowledge is heavily influenced by the limitations, biases, and values found in the videogames. It is these potentially harmful effects that cause us to draw on Lankshear and Knobel's (2003) framework that includes a critical dimension of literacy and learning, and to recognize the need for further research into the effects of videogame playing in the long term, both for boys and for girls.

Through an examination of the opportunities for resistance to traditional authority and identity formation through videogame play, we can see the multiple types of literacy learning that are possible. Players are developing a wide range of useful operational knowledge that can be used as social capital in the workplace. As discussed previously, they are gaining a confidence in using new technologies, a belief that they can use and create programs

effectively; they are becoming accomplished at making speedy decisions and reactions, developing a new level of manual dexterity, and are able to read/process multiple pieces of information (text or screen) simultaneously.

However, as Gee (2003) points out, it is the potentially harmful effects of such opportunities for subversive and localized resistance as videogame play afford that also need to be interrogated. Educators and researchers need to be aware of the cultural and critical literacies that may or may not be addressed through the extensive videogame play that is currently in vogue with many boys and young men. Resistance to the videogame representations of gender, race, and sexual orientation are generally uni-dimensional and highly stereotypical; these can serve to reinforce societal prejudices that maintain hegemonic patriarchal power structures and understandings if the various types of resistance available to game players are not recognized and encouraged. More thought needs to be given to considerations of appropriateness related to specific contexts, indeed appropriateness of values and respect for diverse perspectives needs to be encouraged and supported.

In our observations of videogame play, we believe that the speed of decision making and action taking in videogames mitigates any reflective element of the game beyond how to win—during game play there is often little opportunity to consider alternative, more complex issues and decisions. There is opportunity to learn and experience historical events in multiple modes, but space and encouragement to reflect upon which of these perspectives holds more evidence of ethical and moral truth is also important.

Clearly evident in discussion with these videogame players is an element of critical literacy in relation to technical and technological qualities of videogames, in relation to the realism of visual components of the games, and in relation to comparisons with other modes of interaction. The participants are highly articulate about aspects of the game that function well, glitches in the games, and visual elements of the game. However, we are concerned about a lack of demonstrated critical thought in relation to alternate worldviews and perspectives on socio-cultural issues. As Lankshear and Knobel (2003) suggest,

> to participate effectively and productively in any literate practice, people must be socialized into it. But if individuals are socialized into a social practice without realizing that it is socially constructed and selective, and that it can be acted on and transformed, they cannot play an active role in changing it. (p. 11)

If players are not critically engaged in the literacies of videogames, they will not be able to understand the transformative and active production aspects of meaning making; rather they will be limited to existing in and engaging with literacies as they are created by others. There will be little room for players to consider the origins of the games, who creates the characters and the commercial aspects of the games, and the values that are subtly (or overtly) being perpetuated and encouraged.

Both educators and researchers need to consider whether the resistance to authority and to identity shaping enables future citizens to engage critically in the world, or whether their resistance is limited to small acts of adolescent defiance. Is the nature of their resistance limited itself to the individual or self-selected affinity group, or does their engagement in oppositional interactions engage the broader world? Do videogames desensitize players from moral and ethical responsibility for the world? Do videogames support concern for environmental and ecological realities that continue to consume the human and natural world or do they provide escapes from these global issues?

Further, how are schools developing the increased sophistication in operational literacies, but also creating opportunities for students to engage with cultural and critical literacies that are so necessary for the twenty-first century? How are schools understanding and addressing the knowledge capital that will be needed by our future generations for being successful in an increasingly technological and changing world? These are some

of the concerns that need to be taken up by educators and researchers as they attempt to gain deeper and broader understandings of the nature of video-game learning and the nature of resistance.

Note

1. Cheat is a code a player can enter into the game to make play easier.

References

Alloway, N., & Gilbert, P. (1998). Video game culture: Playing with masculinity, violence and pleasure. In S. Howard (Ed.), *Wired Up: Young people and the electronic media* (pp. 95–114). London, UK: UCL Press.

Alvermann, D. (Ed.). (2002). *Adolescents and literacies in a digital world.* New York: Peter Lang.

Blair, H. & Sanford, K. (2004). Morphing literacy: Boys reshaping their school-based literacy practices. *Language Arts*, 81(6), 452–460.

Browne, R. (1995). Schools and the construction of masculinity. In R. Browne & R. Fletcher (Eds.), *Boys in schools: Addressing the real issues* (pp. 224–233). Sydney, AU: Finch Publishing.

Canadian Teachers' Federation. (2003). *Kids take on media: Summary of finding.* Retrieved April 6, 2006, from www.ctf-fce.ca/en/projects/MERP/summaryfindings.pdf

Connell, R. W. (1995). *Masculinities.* Berkeley and Los Angeles, CA: University of California Press.

Davies, B. (1992). Women's subjectivity and feminist stories. In C. Ellis & M. Flaherty (Eds.), *Investigating subjectivity: Research on lived experience* (pp. 53–76). London, UK: Sage Publications.

Filiciak, M. (2003). Hyperidentities: Postmodern identity patterns in massively multiplayer online role-playing games. In M. Wolf & B. Perron (Eds.), *The videogame theory reader* (pp. 87–102). New York: Routledge.

Frank, B., Kehler, M. L. & Davison, K. (2003). A tangle of trouble: Boys, masculinity and schooling, future directions. *Educational Review*, 55(2), 119–133.

Gee, J. P. (1992). *The social mind: Language, ideology and social practice.* New York: Bergin & Harvey.

Gee, J. P. (2000). Teenagers in new times: A new literacy perspective. *Journal of Adolescent & Adult Literacy*, 43, 412–420.

Gee, J. P. (2003). *What video games have to teach us about learning and literacy*. New York: Palgrave Macmillan.

Green, B. (1997, May). Literacies and school learning in new times. Keynote address at the Literacies in Practice: Progress and Possibilities Conference, South Australian Department of Education and Children's Services and the Catholic Education office, Adelaide, Australia.

Guzzetti, B. J., & Gamboa, M. (2004). Zining: The unsanctioned literacy practice of adolescents. In C. Fairbanks, J. Worthy, B. Maloch, J. Hoffman & D. L. Schallert (Eds.), *53rd yearbook of the National Reading Conference* (pp. 208–217). Oak Creek, WI: National Reading Conference.

Kehler, M. (2004). "The Boys" interrupted: Images constructed, realities translated. *Education and Society*, 22(2), 83–99.

Kline, S. (2004, January). Technologies of the imaginary: Evaluating the promise of toys, television and video games for learning. Paper presented at the Sixth Australian and New Zealand Conference on the First Years, Tasmania.

Lankshear, C., & Knobel, M. (2003). *New literacies: Changing knowledge and classroom learning*. Buckingham, UK: Open University Press.

Leonard, D. (2004). Unsettling the military entertainment complex: Video games and a pedagogy of peace. *Studies in Media & Information Literacy Education*, 4(4). Retrieved September 25, 2005, from http://www.utpjournals.com/jour.ihtml?1p=simile/issue16/leonardl.html

Martino, W., & Pallotta-Chiarolli, M. (Eds.). (2001). *Boys' stuff: Boys talking about what matters*. Sydney, AU: Allen & Unwin.

Myers, D. (2003). *The nature of computer games: Play as semiosis*. New York: Peter Lang.

Newkirk, T. (2002). Foreword. In M. Smith & J. Wilhelm (Eds.), *Reading don't fix no Chevys: Literacy in the lives of young men* (pp. ix–xi). Portsmouth, NH: Heinemann.

Newman, J. (2004). *Videogames*. London, UK: Routledge.

Ray, S. G. (2004). *Gender inclusive game design: Expanding the market*. Hingham, MA: Charles River Media, Inc.

Rowan, L., Knobel, M., Bigum, C., Lankshear, C. (2002). *Boys, literacies and schooling*. Buckingham, UK: Open University Press.

Sanford, K. (2006). Gendered literacy experiences: The effects of expectation and opportunity for boys' and girls' learning. *Journal of Adult and Adolescent Literacy*, 49(4), 302–314.

Smith, M., & Wilhelm, J. (2002). *Reading don't fix no Chevys: Literacy in the lives of young men*. Portsmouth, NH: Heinemann.

Street, B. (1984). *Literacy in theory and practice*. New York: Cambridge University Press.

IX

Violence
and Masculinities

Nightly, we watch news reports of suicide bombings in the Middle East, terror-ist attacks on the United States, racist hate crimes, gay-bashing murders, or Colombian drug lords and their legions of gun-toting thugs. Do these reports ever mention that virtually every single one of these terrorists, suicide bombers, or racist gang members is male?

This fact is so obvious that it barely needs to be mentioned. Virtually all the violence in the world today is committed by men. Imagine, for a moment, if all that violence were perpetrated entirely by women. Would that not be *the* story?

Take a look at the numbers: Men constitute 99 percent of all persons arrested for rape, 88 percent of those arrested for murder, 92 percent of those arrested for robbery, 87 percent for aggravated assault, 85 percent of other assaults, 83 percent of all family violence, and 82 percent of disorderly conduct. Nearly 90 percent of all murder victims are killed by men.

From early childhood to old age, violence is the most obdurate, intractable behavioral gender difference. The National Academy of Sciences puts the case starkly: "The most consistent pattern with respect to gender is the extent to which male criminal participation in serious crimes at any age greatly exceeds that of females, regardless of source of data, crime type, level of involvement, or measure of participation." "Men are always and everywhere more likely than women to commit criminal acts," write criminologists Michael Gottfredson and Travis Hirschi.[1]

What can we, as a culture, do to understand, let alone prevent the casual equation of masculinity and violence? The articles in this part approach that equation in a variety of arenas. Michael Kaufman's alliterative description of men's violence offers a clever entry into a world that many of us would like to pretend is really about a few "bad" guys and most of us nonviolent "good" guys. CJ Pascoe and Jocelyn A. Hollander explore the associations between masculinity and rape, while Lise Gotell and Emily Dutton look at how specifically anti-feminist men's rights groups talk about rape. Finally, Tristan Bridges and Tara Leigh Tober examine the lethal equation of masculinity and mass shootings.

Note

1. National Academy of Sciences, cited in Michael Gottfredson and Travis Hirschi. *A General Theory of Crime* (Stanford: Stanford University Press, 1990), p. 145. See also Steven Barkan, "Why Do Men Commit Almost All Homicides and Assault?" in *Criminology: A Sociological Understanding* (Englewood: Prentice Hall, 1997); Lee Bowker, ed., *Masculinities and Violence* (Thousand Oaks, CA: Sage Publications, 1998).

PART IX DISCUSSION QUESTIONS

1. Following from Pascoe and Hollander's findings, how should anti-rape activists engage men who see themselves as "good guys"?
2. How does Gotell and Dutton's finding that antifeminist men feel targeted by regretful or vengeful women relate to Bridges and Tober's view of masculinities and mass shootings?
3. If patriarchy systematically advantages men and masculine traits, why does violence continue to be central to masculinities? Could masculinities maintain their dominance without violence? How?
4. What are some of the common themes evident in the seven P's of men's violence outlined by Michael Kaufman? How do these themes apply to some of the other readings in the text?

The Seven P's of Men's Violence

MICHAEL KAUFMAN

For a moment my eyes turned away from the workshop participants and out through the windows of the small conference room and towards the Himalayas, north of Kathmandu. I was there, leading a workshop, largely the outgrowth of remarkable work of UNICEF and UNIFEM which, a year earlier, had brought together women *and* men from throughout South Asia to discuss the problem of violence against women and girls and, most importantly, to work together to find solutions.[1]

As I turned back to the women and men in the group, it felt more familiar than different: women taking enormous chances—in some cases risking their lives—to fight the tide of violence against women and girls. Men who were just beginning to find their anti-patriarchal voices and to discover ways to work alongside women. And what pleasantly surprised me was the positive response to a series of ideas I presented about men's violence: until then, I wasn't entirely sure if they were mainly about the realities in North and South America and Europe—that is largely-Europeanized cultures—or whether they had a larger resonance.

Here, then, is the kernel of this analysis:

Patriarchal Power: The First "P"

Individual acts of violence by men occurs within what I have described as "the triad of men's violence." Men's violence against women does not occur in isolation but is linked to men's violence against other men and to the internalization of violence, that is, a man's violence against himself.[2]

Indeed male-dominated societies are not only based on a hierarchy of men over women but some men over other men. Violence or the threat of violence among men is a mechanism used from childhood to establish that pecking order. One result of this is that men "internalize" violence—or perhaps, the demands of patriarchal society encourage biological instincts that otherwise might be more relatively dormant or benign. The result is not only that boys and men learn to selectively use violence, but also, as we shall later see, redirect a range of emotions into rage, which sometimes takes the form of self-directed violence, as seen, for example, in substance abuse or self-destructive behaviour.

This triad of men's violence—each form of violence helping create the others—occurs within a nurturing environment of violence: the organization and demands of patriarchal or male dominant societies.

What gives violence its hold as a way of doing business, what has naturalized it as the *de facto* standard of human relations, is the way it has been articulated into our ideologies and social structures. Simply put, human groups create self-perpetuating forms of social organization and ideologies that explain, give meaning to, justify, and replenish these created realities.

Violence is also built into these ideologies and structures for the simpler reason that it has brought enormous benefits to particular groups: first and foremost, violence (or at least the threat of violence), has helped confer on men (as a group) a rich set of privileges and forms of power. If indeed

---

the original forms of social hierarchy and power are those based on sex, then this long ago formed a template for all the structured forms of power and privilege enjoyed by others as a result of social class or skin color, age, religion, sexual orientation, or physical abilities. In such a context, violence or its threat become a means to ensure the continued reaping of privileges and exercise of power. It is both a result and a means to an end.

The Sense of Entitlement to Privilege: The Second "P"

The individual experience of a man who commits violence may not revolve around his desire to maintain power. His conscious experience is not the key here. Rather, as feminist analysis has repeatedly pointed out, such violence is often the logical outcome of his sense of entitlement to certain privileges. If a man beats his wife for not having dinner on the table right on time, it is not only to make sure that it doesn't happen again, but is an indication of his sense of entitlement to be waited on. Or, say a man sexually assaults a woman on a date, it is about his sense of entitlement to his physical pleasure even if that pleasure is entirely one sided. In other words, as many women have pointed out, it is not only inequalities of power that lead to violence, but a conscious or often unconscious sense of entitlement to privilege.

The Third "P": Permission

Whatever the complex social and psychological causes of men's violence, it wouldn't continue if there weren't explicit or tacit permission in social customs, legal codes, law enforcement, and certain religious teachings. In many countries, laws against wife assault or sexual assault are lax or nonexistent; in many others laws are barely enforced; in still others they are absurd, such as those countries where a charge of rape can only be prosecuted if there are several male witnesses and where the testimony of the woman isn't taken into account.

Meanwhile, acts of men's violence and violent aggression (in this case, usually against other men) are celebrated in sport and cinema, in literature and warfare. Not only is violence permitted, it is glamorized and rewarded. The very historic roots of patriarchal societies is the use of violence as a key means of solving disputes and differences, whether among individuals, groups of men, or, later, between nations. I am often reminded of this permission when I hear of a man or women who fails to call the police when they hear a woman neighbour or child being beaten. It is deemed a "private" affair. Can you imagine someone seeing a store being robbed and declining to call the police because it is a private affair between the robber and the store owner?

The Fourth "P": The Paradox of Men's Power

It is my contention, however, that such things do not in themselves explain the widespread nature of men's violence, nor the connections between men's violence against women and the many forms of violence among men. Here we need to draw on the paradoxes of men's power or what I have called "men's contradictory experiences of power."[3]

The very ways that men have constructed our social and individual power is, paradoxically, the source of enormous fear, isolation, and pain for men ourselves. If power is constructed as a capacity to dominate and control, if the capacity to act in "powerful" ways requires the construction of a personal suit of armor and a fearful distance from others, if the very world of power and privilege removes us from the world of child-rearing and nurturance, then we are creating men whose own experience of power is fraught with crippling problems.

This is particularly so because the internalized expectations of masculinity are themselves impossible to satisfy or attain. This may well be a problem inherent in patriarchy, but it seems particularly true in an era and in cultures where rigid gender boundaries have been overthrown. Whether it is physical or financial accomplishment, or the suppression of a range of human emotions and needs, the imperatives of manhood (as opposed to the simple certainties of biological maleness), seem to require constant vigilance and work, especially for younger men.

The personal insecurities conferred by a failure to make the masculine grade, or simply, the threat of failure, is enough to propel many men, particularly when they are young, into a vortex of fear, isolation, anger, self-punishment, self-hatred, and aggression. Within such an emotional state, violence becomes a *compensatory mechanism*. It is a way of re-establishing the masculine equilibrium, of asserting to oneself and to others one's masculine credentials. This expression of violence usually includes a choice of a target who is physically weaker or more vulnerable. This may be a child, or a woman, or, it may be social groups, such as gay men, or a religious or social minority, or immigrants, who seem to pose an easy target for the insecurity and rage of individual men, especially since such groups often haven't received adequate protection under the law. (This compensatory mechanism is clearly indicated, for example, in that most "gay-bashing" is committed by groups of young men in a period of their life when they experience the greatest insecurity about making the masculine grade.)

What allows violence as an individual compensatory mechanism has been the widespread acceptance of violence as a means of solving differences and asserting power and control. What makes it possible are the power and privileges men have enjoyed, things encoded in beliefs, practices, social structures, and the law.

Men's violence, in its myriad of forms, is therefore the result both of men's power, the sense of entitlement to the privilege, the permission for certain forms of violence, and the fear (or reality) of not having power.

But there is even more.

The Fifth "P": The Psychic Armour of Manhood

Men's violence is also the result of a character structure that is typically based on emotional distance from others. As I and many others have suggested, the psychic structures of manhood are created in early child-rearing environments that are often typified by the absence of fathers and adult men—or, at least, by men's emotional distance. In this case, masculinity gets codified by absence and constructed at the level of fantasy. But even in patriarchal cultures where fathers are more present, masculinity is codified as a rejection of the mother and femininity, that is, a rejection of the qualities associated with care-giving and nurturance. As various feminist psychoanalysts have noted, this creates rigid ego barriers, or, in metaphorical terms, a strong suit of armor.

The result of this complex and particular process of psychological development is a dampened ability for empathy (to experience what others are feeling) and an inability to experience other people's needs and feelings as necessarily relating to one's own. Acts of violence against another person are, therefore, possible. How often do we hear a man say he "didn't really hurt" the woman he hit? Yes, he is making excuses, but part of the problem is that he truly may not experience the pain he is causing. How often do we hear a man say, "she wanted to have sex"? Again, he may be making an excuse, but it may well be a reflection of his diminished ability to read and understand the feelings of another.

Masculinity as a Psychic Pressure Cooker: The Sixth "P"

Many of our dominant forms of masculinity hinge on the internalization of a range of emotions and their redirection into anger. It is not simply that men's language of emotions is often muted or that our emotional antennae and capacity for empathy are somewhat stunted. It is also that a range of natural emotions have been ruled off limits and invalid. While this has a cultural specificity, it is rather typical for boys to learn from an early age to repress feelings of fear and pain. On the sports field we teach boys to ignore pain. At home we tell boys not to cry and act like men. Some cultures celebrate a stoic manhood. (And, I should stress, boys learn such things for survival: hence it is important we don't blame the individual boy or man for the origins of his current behaviours, even if, at the same time, we hold him responsible for his actions.)

Of course, as humans, we still experience events that cause an emotional response. But the usual mechanisms of emotional response, from actually experiencing an emotion to letting go of the feelings, are short-circuited to varying degrees among many men. But, again for many men, the one emotion that has some validation is anger. The result is that a range of emotions get channeled into anger. While such channeling is not unique to men (nor is it the case for all men), for some men, violent responses to fear, hurt, insecurity, pain, rejection, or belittlement are not uncommon.

This is particularly true where the feeling produced is one of not having power. Such a feeling only heightens masculine insecurities: if manhood [is] about power and control, not being powerful means you are not a man. Again, violence becomes a means to prove otherwise to yourself and others.

The Seventh "P": Past Experiences

This all combines with more blatant experiences for some men. Far too many men around the world grew up in households where their mother was beaten by their father. They grew up seeing violent behaviour towards women as the norm, as just the way life is lived. For some men this results in a revulsion towards violence, while in others it produces a learned response. In many cases it is both: men who use violence against women often feel deep self-loathing for themselves and their behaviour.

But the phrase "learned response" is almost too simplistic. Studies have shown that boys and girls who grow up witnessing violence are far more likely to be violent themselves. Such violence may be a way of getting attention; it may be a coping mechanism, a way of externalizing impossible-to-cope-with feelings. Such patterns of behaviour continue beyond childhood: most men who end up in programs for men who use violence either witnessed abuse against their mother or experienced abuse themselves.

The past experiences of many men also includes the violence they themselves have experienced. In many cultures, while boys may be half as likely to experience sexual abuse than girls, they are twice as likely to experience physical abuse. Again, this produces no one fixed outcome, and, again, such outcomes are not unique to boys. But in some cases these personal experiences instill deep patterns of confusion and frustration, where boys have learned that it is possible to hurt someone you love, where only outbursts of rage can get rid of deeply-imbedded feelings of pain.

And finally, there is the whole reign of petty violence among boys which, as a boy, doesn't seem petty at all. Boys in many cultures grow up with experiences of fighting, bullying, and brutalization. Sheer survival requires, for some, accepting and internalizing violence as a norm of behaviour.

Ending the Violence

This analysis, even presented in such a condensed form, suggests that challenging men's violence requires an articulated response that includes:

- Challenging and dismantling the structures of men's power and privilege, and ending the cultural and social permission for acts of violence. If this is where the violence starts, we can't end it without support by women and men for feminism and the social, political, legal, and cultural reforms and transformations that it suggests.
- The redefinition of masculinity or, really, the dismantling of the psychic and social structures of gender that bring with them such peril. The paradox of patriarchy is the pain, rage, frustration, isolation, and fear among that half of the species for whom relative power and privilege is given. We ignore all this to our peril. In order to successfully reach men, this work must be premised on compassion, love, and respect, combined with a clear challenge to negative masculine norms and their destructive outcomes. Pro-feminist men doing this work must speak to other men as our brothers, not as aliens who are not as enlightened or worthy as we are.

- Organizing and involving men to work in cooperation with women in reshaping the gender organization of society, in particular, our institutions and relations through which we raise children. This requires much more emphasis on the importance of men as nurturers and caregivers, fully involved in the raising of children in positive ways free of violence.
- Working with men who commit violence in a way that simultaneously challenges their patriarchal assumptions and privileges *and* reaches out to them with respect and compassion. We needn't be sympathetic to what they have done to be empathetic with them and feel horrified by the factors that have led a little boy to grow up to be a man who sometimes does terrible things. Through such respect, these men can actually find the space to challenge themselves and each other. Otherwise the attempt to reach them will only feed into their own insecurities as men for whom violence has been their traditional compensation.
- Explicit educational activities, such as the White Ribbon Campaign, that involve men and boys in challenging themselves and other men to end all forms of violence.[4] This is a positive challenge for men to speak out with our love and compassion for women, boys, girls, and other men.

Toronto, Canada
October 1999

Notes

1. This workshop was organized by Save the Children (UK). Travel funding was provided by Development Services International of Canada. Discussion of the 1998 Kathmandu workshop is found in Ruth Finney Hayward's book *Breaking the Earthenware Jar* (forthcoming 2000). Ruth was the woman who instigated the Kathmandu meetings.
2. Michael Kaufman, "The Construction of Masculinity and the Triad of Men's Violence," in M. Kaufman, ed. *Beyond Patriarchy: Essays by Men on Pleasure, Power and Change*, Toronto: Oxford University Press, 1985. Reprinted in English in Laura L. O'Toole and Jessica R. Schiffman, *Gender Violence* (New York: NY University Press, 1997) and excerpted in Michael S. Kimmel and Michael A. Messner, *Men's Lives* (New York: Macmillan, 1997); in German in BauSteineMänner, *Kritische Männerforschung* (Berlin: Arument Verlag, 1996); and in Spanish in *Hombres: Poder, Placer, y Cambio* (Santo Domingo: CIPAF, 1989.)
3. Michael Kaufman, *Cracking the Armour: Power, Pain and the Lives of Men* (Toronto: Viking Canada, 1993 and Penguin, 1994) and "Men, Feminism, and Men's Contradictory Experiences of Power," in Harry Brod and Michael Kaufman, eds., *Theorizing Masculinities* (Thousand Oaks, CA: Sage Publications, 1994), translated into Spanish as "Los hombres, el feminismo y las experiencias contradictorias del poder entre los hombres," in Luz G. Arango et al. eds., *Genero e identidad. Ensayos sobre lo feminino y lo masculino* (Bogota: Tercer Mundo, 1995) and in a revised form, as "Las experiences contradictorias del poder entre los hombres," in Teresa Valdes y Jose Olavarria, eds., *Masculinidad/es. Poder y crisis*, Ediciones de las Jujeres No. 23 (Santiago: Isis International and FLACSO-Chile, June 1997).
4. White Ribbon Campaign, 365 Bloor St. East, Suite 203, Toronto, Canada M4W 3L4 1-416-920-6684 FAX: 1-416-920-1678 info@whiteribbon.ca www.whiteribbon.com.

My thanks to those with whom I discussed a number of the ideas in this text: Jean Bernard, Ruth Finney Hayward, Dale Hurst, Michael Kimmel, my colleagues in the White Ribbon Campaign, and a woman at Woman's World '99 in Tromso, Norway, who didn't give her name but who, during a discussion period of an earlier version of this paper, suggested it was important to explicitly highlight "permission" as one of the "p's". An earlier version of this paper was published in a special issue of the magazine of the International Association for Studies of Men, v. 6, n. 2 (June 1999), www.ifi.uio.no/~eivindr/iasom).

Good Guys Don't Rape

Gender, Domination, and Mobilizing Rape

C. J. PASCOE AND JOCELYN A. HOLLANDER

When the University of Oregon Ducks football team defeated the Florida State University (FSU) Seminoles at the Rose Bowl in early 2015, the content of their post-game revelry may have surprised some viewers. In celebrating their victory, several Oregon players were filmed singing "No Means No!" to the tune of the "War Chant"[1] regularly sung by FSU fans. The song was presumably directed at a particular FSU player, quarterback Jameis Winston, who had been accused of (though not charged with or convicted of) raping a female student.

Some commentaries on this incident lauded it as a moment in which young men were collectively and publicly reprimanding another man accused of sexual violence by using a long-time feminist slogan: "no means no."[2] Certainly, on first read this appears to be *exactly* the sort of phenomenon antirape activists have been waiting for: normatively masculine men shaming other men for sexually assaulting women. It seemed to call into question assumptions about the central role of sexual assault in enforcing gender inequality.

We propose an alternate interpretation of this moment, however. What if the chanting football players were using the accusations against Winston not (or not only) to decry the practice of rape but to publicly shame their opponent in a way that specifically preserved or even enhanced their own gendered status as masculine? That is, perhaps they used the chant as an opportunity to celebrate their own dominance in two ways—over the losing team *and* over Winston himself. What if the point of the chant was not to make a statement about sexual assault but to position their opponent as a *failed man*—a man who needed to use force to secure sexual access to a woman's body? A *real* man, the chant implies, would be so sexually desirable as to render force unnecessary. A *real* man—like, presumably, the chanters themselves—would also be able to control his own sexual and violent urges such that they would not overwhelm him or others (Pascoe and Bridges 2015). . . .

We argue that both of these practices—participating in *and* publicly opposing sexual assault—may serve as resources that enable young men to solve the "identity dilemmas" (Wilkins 2009) posed by changing and conflicting expectations of gendered selves by drawing on cultural resources that affirm expectations of normative masculinity. Even though it may appear that some deployments of such resources support while other enactments challenge gender inequalities, Wilkins argues that both may actually achieve similar ends; that is, both may support meaning-making systems that invest in gendered inequalities (Wilkins 2009). We suggest that contemporary relationships

---

between masculinity and rape may be a concrete example of "hybrid masculinities," using new kinds of masculinity resources to "fortify existing social and symbolic boundaries in ways that often work to conceal systems of power and inequality in historically new ways" (Bridges and Pascoe 2014, 246). Thus, young men can simultaneously position themselves as "good guys" who don't rape while symbolically engaging with sexual assault to signal the dominance that is constitutive of Western masculinity at this historical moment.

We call this approach "mobilizing rape." Rape, in this sense, may be symbolically utilized in a variety of ways to reinforce the contemporary ordering of gender relations, a specific form of what Patricia Yancey Martin calls "mobilizing masculinity" (Martin 2001). While sexual assault has been defined as a situation in which "one or more persons impose a sexual interaction upon another unwilling person" (Cahill 2001, 15), through the concept of "mobilizing rape" we suggest that sexual assault is not simply an individual incident but a wide-ranging constellation of behaviors, attitudes, beliefs, and talk that work to produce and reproduce gendered dominance in everyday interaction. We conceive of mobilizing rape as a way of doing gender (Fenstermaker and West 2002; West and Zimmerman 1987): as an interactional accomplishment that includes not only engaging in activities legally defined as rape but also engaging in other forms of sexual assault and nonconsensual sexual interaction, talking about rape and sexual assault, making jokes about it, laughing at imagery about it, labeling oneself or others as rapists, blaming sexual assault survivors for their own victimization, or otherwise symbolically deploying the idea of rape. . . .

[A]s Raewyn Connell argues, gender inequality is sustained by men's dominance *over other men*, as well as men's dominance over women (Connell 1995). As such, we suggest that these hierarchical relations between men are in part constituted by processes of "mobilizing rape." These hierarchical relations can be established or supported by the rape of (other men's) women, by the rape, real or symbolic, of other men themselves—and, we

suggest, by claims of *not* raping. In other words, mobilizing sexual assault as a masculinity resource allows men to do the dominance work not only over women, but also over other men, that comprises masculinity at this historical moment, even as rape itself becomes increasingly framed as socially undesirable.

Rape Culture

Feminist scholars have pointed out that heterosexual relationships take place in the context of a "rape culture" (Buchwald, Fletcher, and Roth 1993) in which rape is normalized and sexual dominance is rendered "sexy" (Jeffreys 1998, 75). . . .

Precisely because "normal" heterosexual relationships take place in a "rape culture," the last 30 years have seen very public struggles over where, exactly, the border between rape and non-rape lies, ranging from controversies over Mary Koss's (1988) strategy of measuring rape behaviorally in the late 1980s, to the gradual criminalization of marital rape, to more recent debates over "incapacitated rape" (i.e., sex when one party is drunk, drugged, or otherwise unable to consent). Many of these struggles have eventually led to the acceptance of a broader understanding of rape. Nonetheless, there remains a wide zone of experience—between clear examples of bodily violation, on the one hand, and "enthusiastic consent" on the other—where the relationship of an experience to rape remains contested. For example, what if consent is achieved not through violence but coercion—for example, through explicit or implicit threats to the relationship or to one's job or children? What if consent is achieved through simple but relentless persistence? What if there is no active consent, but also no resistance? Because of this definitional blurriness, a range of behaviors that fall between the categories of rape and not-rape are available to enact male dominance while still allowing men to preserve their identity as non-rapists, and perhaps even allowing them to shame other men for being rapists. This definitional murkiness allows for the mobilization of rape as a symbol with no clear referent, such that men can engage in sexual assault and simultaneously distance themselves from it discursively in ways that not only reinforce dominance over women but, importantly, also over other men. Even active disavowals of rape may reaffirm normative understandings of masculinity as dominance over other men, thus rendering some moments of seeming resistance congruent with rape culture, rather than in opposition to it.

Mobilizing Rape

The depathologizing of rape that followed from conceptualizing rape as a culture, not (only) as a behavior, presents identity dilemmas for men. In a rape culture, sexual assault is not caused by a few deviant or depraved bad guys; "normal" men can be rapists, and rape is part of the very culture in which we live and forge romantic relationships. In a rape culture where rape is increasingly stigmatized and where any man is a potential rapist, how can a man distance himself from rape while still doing the dominance work demanded by cultural expectations of normative masculinity? Men are accountable to both these notions (Hollander 2013) and must find a way of navigating between them.

Jay, one of Pascoe's high school–aged respondents,[3] illustrates this dilemma. He angrily shared a story about how he had (according to him, wrongly) been charged and found guilty of sexual assault. One of his classmates accused him of rape, saying he "put a gun to her head and shit." Jay emphatically insisted that he was innocent, and that he was sentenced to wear an ankle bracelet under "house arrest" because she lied during the trial. While livid about being accused of rape, he later seemingly endorsed rape in conversations with his friends as they talked about a girl they agreed was "hella ugly" and "a bitch" but who "has titties." At the end of this conversation, Jay threatened to "take her out to the street races and leave her there. Leave her there so she can get raped." His friends responded with laughter. While Jay was angry at being found guilty of a rape he claimed he did not commit, he endorsed setting up a situation such that other men could inflict sexual violence on a young woman he found distasteful. In other words, Jay and his friends see sexual dominance over women as unproblematic, even if violating legal codes of rape is.

To be considered sufficiently masculine, one must demonstrate dominance over women and other men, but available avenues of sexual dominance are being redefined and curtailed. Mobilizing rape helps resolve this type of "masculinity dilemma" (Wilkins 2009). Consider the example with which we opened this paper: the post-game celebration during which victorious football players chanted "No means no!" at an opposing player accused of rape. In a context of growing opposition to sexual violence, rape can be used symbolically as a tool to emasculate other men. Rape, in this sense, is something that other, "bad," perhaps "less masculine" men do. Men can simultaneously draw upon discourses of rape to establish their masculinity and distance themselves from the actual practice of rape. Yet, who these "bad" men are is not neutral. As we discuss at greater length below, it is men of color who disproportionately bear the burden of being labeled as rapists.

This form of distancing is visible throughout the culture. A conversation with one of Pascoe's respondents is particularly illuminating in this regard. Chad, an extremely popular football player, described his sexual history as the following:

> When I was growin' up I started having sex in the 8th grade. . . . The majority of the girls in 8th and 9th grade were just stupid. We already knew what we were doing. They didn't know what they were doing you know? . . . Like say, comin' over to our house like past 12. What else do you do past 12? Say we had a bottle of alcohol or something. I'm not saying we forced it upon them. I'm sayin'. . . . (Pascoe 2007)

While the incident Chad describes—plying underage women with alcohol in order to have sex with them—is one that many would agree would constitute rape, he self-consciously distances himself from rape ("I'm not saying we forced it upon them"). Indeed, he went on to share that his friends, "Kevin Goldsmith and uh, Calvin Johnson, they got charged with rape," while claiming that, in contrast, he never had to force a girl to have sex: "I'll never (be in) that predicament, you know. I've never had [a] hard time, or had to you know, alter their thinking." The sort of sexual assault Kevin Goldsmith and Calvin Johnson participated in is something that *other, less masculine* guys do. By distancing himself from this practice, Chad confirms his own claim to masculine dominance—a claim that is stronger because he obtained sex without physical force.

. . . Some of Chad's religious peers used similar language in the service of refraining from, rather than engaging in, sex. As Sean said, "There will be some guys that they'll go up to a girl, you know? 'Hey, girl, come here.' And they will keep on bugging them. They'll try to grab and touch them and stuff like this. They're just letting all their, they're acting on emotions pretty much." Sean casts himself as more mature than other boys because of his sexual restraint, drawing on masculine discourses of self-control (Wilkins 2009) and maturity (Mora 2012). When asked if he felt less masculine because he planned not to have sex until he was married, another religious young man at River High said, "No. If anything, more. Because you can resist. You don't have to give in to it." Both these young men position themselves as *more* masculine, *more* in control than other young men *because* of their ability to control their bodily impulses. Their comments echo what both Amy Wilkins (2009) and Sarah Diefendorf (2015) have found in their research on young Christian men who abstain from sex: that this restraint was itself cast as a form of dominance over other men. Their self-control, in other words, trumps the lack of control exhibited by other, libido-driven young men.

Some organized anti-violence work can also be read through the lens of "mobilizing rape." The *My Strength Is Not for Hurting* campaign, for example, encourages men to use their (presumed) strength for good (Masters 2010; Murphy 2009)—not challenging the underlying assumption that men are strong and women are vulnerable (Hollander 2001). Men's not raping is thus a chivalrous choice, a courtesy extended to a subordinate rather than the respect due to an equal. At the Ohio State

University, the Rape Education and Prevention program posted signs near urinals that told men, "In your hands you hold the power to stop rape" (Gold and Villari 2000). In other words, the thing that presumably makes one a man, one's penis, also gives men the ability to end sexual violence against women. Additionally, participants in men's *Walk a Mile in Her Shoes* anti-violence marches, as Tristan Bridges' research demonstrates, mock femininity even while advocating an end to gendered violence (Bridges 2010). While opposing violence, these campaigns are founded on assumptions of men's greater strength and power and thus underscore the subordinate status of women. They "mobilize rape" by opposing rape in ways that work to reinforce, rather than challenge, underlying gender inequalities. . . .

Good Guys Don't Rape

Massive cultural changes have had to take place for members of a winning football team to publicly shame an accused rapist. While sexual assault remains widespread, being identified as a rapist has come to be seen, at least in some contexts, as unmasculine. However, this change coexists with the fact that dominance, especially sexual dominance, continues to be a central component of Western masculinity. As such, the changes surrounding rape need to be understood in the context of gender inequality that is perhaps more flexible, durable, and tenacious than is popularly assumed. Feminist theorists depathologized rape through the notion of rape culture, reconceptualizing it as something *any* man, not just pathological monsters, could commit. When men distance themselves from rape, they repathologize rape as something a *bad* man does, not something that informs all gendered relationships between men and women. This move depends on an understanding of rape as a narrowly defined category of behavior and experience. Rape, in this view, is a violent act of sexual intercourse committed by force and clearly resisted by the woman. The stereotype of the frightening stranger jumping out of a dark alley or from behind a car in a parking garage is perhaps the paradigmatic example of this kind of sexual assault (Estrich 1987); current assertions about a small group of serial rapists being responsible for sexual assaults on college campuses are a more subtle variant (Swartout et al. 2015). In other words, narrow definitions of rape allow for the mobilization of rape (and the label of rapist) such that it is seamlessly integrated into contemporary definitions of masculinity. With this constrained understanding of rape as background, everyday behaviors of sexual coercion and dominance (over men or women) can be framed as "not rape." . . .

Using the concept of "mobilizing rape" to think seriously about hierarchical relations between men moves theorizing about rape in two directions. First, it raises questions about *who* symbolizes the rapist in contemporary discussions about rape. When some men absolve themselves of the identity of rapist, who becomes the imagined rapist? Racism and sexual violence are deeply intertwined, as demonstrated by white men's sexual dominance over black women, as well as the representation of black men as the embodiment of sexual violence (Collins 2005; Davis 1983; McGuire 2011; Nagel 2000). As other scholars have argued, the specter of rape is largely transferred to poor men and men of color, symbolically purifying white, middle-class, or educated men of this sort of undesirable behavior (Collins 2005; Davis 1983; Hondagneu-Sotelo and Messner 1994; McGuire 2011; Messner 1993).

Second, the concept of mobilizing rape calls attention to actual or symbolic sexual domination of other men, phenomena often obscured by the heterosexual focus of research on sexual assault (Abdullah-Khan 2008; Lees 1997). Consider, for example, the wartime cartoons collected by folklorist Alan Dundes (1991) that depict multiple variations of Saddam Hussein being anally penetrated by a SCUD missile, which symbolically represented American military might at the time. These cartoons positioned a (male) America as militarily and culturally dominant through symbolizing male–male rape. Analyzing male–male rape indicates that "like the rape of women, sexual violence against men is thought to be an expression of power and control where sexuality is used as a weapon to

dominate, humiliate, and degrade" (Lundrigan and Mueller-Johnson 2013, 768). Being penetrated feminizes men, rendering them as less than masculine, perhaps as symbolic women, and rendering the perpetrator as dominant, that is, masculine.

The concept of mobilizing rape thus explores nuances of rape culture in which young men who might engage in sexualized dominance "play," such as punching a girl in the stomach "for fun," might also put down other young men who see fit to sexually assault young women. That is, the same young men can both engage in rape culture and attempt to distance themselves from it, all the while using rape as a "masculinity resource" in a way that undergirds gendered inequality by setting up hierarchical relations between men and women and men and men. As such, changing rape culture involves more than teaching men not to rape or rendering sexual dominance unsexy or unmasculine; it involves rethinking gendered dominance *intersectionally* such that attempts to combat sexual assault do not reinscribe gendered, raced, sexualized, and classed inequalities in more subtle ways. At first glance this may seem like a "damned if you do, damned if you don't" situation, where men reinforce gender inequality both by engaging in sexual assault and by *not* engaging in those same behaviors. We believe, however, that there are ways to oppose sexual assault that do not reinscribe gender inequality or dominate other men. A burgeoning body of literature on "allies" suggests ways that individuals may work for social justice while not investing in the current ordering of inequalities (see, for instance, Grzanka, Adler, and Blazer 2015; and Mathers, Sumerau, and Ueno 2015). Other violence prevention strategies, such as campaigns founded on mutual respect (e.g., Project Respect, http://vsac.ca/prevention/) or efforts to empower women through self-defense training (Hollander 2004), also resist sexual assault without relying on assumptions of men's physical superiority. When confronting issues of sexual assault, these approaches suggest that rather than simply making small adjustments in contemporary definitions of masculinity regarding *who* is dominated (for instance, women who can't help but be sexually drawn to a young man because of his virility or other young men who can't control their own bodily desires), we must think about what gendered messages are being deployed when condemning it. When we attend to the way in which we provide avenues to oppose rape, we must combat normative masculinity as a mode of domination, rather than relying on tactics that render opposing gendered sexual violence part of that very system of domination.

Notes

1. Both the chant and the "tomahawk chop" arm movements that accompany it are deeply racist imaginings of Seminole practices and culture.
2. See, for instance, http://www.bustle.com/articles/56478-oregon-football-players-chant-no-means-no-to-mock-jameis-winstons-rape-exoneration.
3. The names of Pascoe's respondents and school have been changed.

Authors' Note

The authors would like to thank Kemi Balogun, Tristan Bridges, Sarah Diefendorf, Aaron Gullickson, Patricia Gwartney, Jill Harrison, Matt Norton, Jianbinn Shao, and Jessica Vasquez-Tokos, the editorial team at *Gender & Society*, for their comments on earlier iterations of this article, as well as Andrea Herrera for her research assistance. Correspondence concerning this article should be directed to C. J. Pascoe, University of Oregon, 736 Prince Lucien Campbell, Eugene, OR 97403-1291; e-mail: cpascoe@uoregon.edu.

References

Abdullah-Khan, Noreen. 2008. *Male rape: The emergence of a social and legal issue*. London: Palgrave Macmillan.

Bridges, Tristan. 2010. Men just weren't made to do this: Performances of drag at "Walk a Mile in Her Shoes" marches. *Gender & Society*, 24 (1): 5–30.

Bridges, Tristan, and C. J. Pascoe. 2014. Hybrid masculinities: New directions in the sociology of men and masculinities. *Sociology Compass* 8 (3): 246–58.

Buchwald, Emilie, Pamela R. Fletcher, and Martha Roth. 1993. *No laughing matter: Sexual harassment in K–12 schools*. Minneapolis, MN: Milkweed Editions.

Cahill, Ann J. 2001. *Rethinking Rape*. Ithaca, NY: Cornell University Press.

Collins, Patricia Hill. 2005. *Black sexual politics: African Americans, gender, and the new racism*. New York: Routledge.

Connell, Raewyn. 1995. *Masculinities*. Berkeley: University of California Press.

Davis, Angela. 1983. *Women, race, & class*. New York: Vintage Books.

Diefendorf, Sarah. 2015. After the wedding night: Sexual abstinence and masculinities over the life course. *Gender & Society* 29 (5): 647–69.

Dundes, Alan. 1991. The mobile SCUD missile launcher and other Persian Gulf War lore: An American folk image of Saddam Hussein's Iraq. *Western Folklore* 50 (3): 303–22.

Estrich, Susan. 1987. *Real rape*. Cambridge, MA: Harvard University Press.

Fenstermaker, Sarah, and Candace West. 2002. *Doing gender, doing difference: Inequality, power, and institutional change*. New York: Routledge.

Gold, Jodi, and Susan Villari. 2000. *Just sex: Students rewrite the rules on sex, violence, activism, and equality*. Lanham, MD: Rowman & Littlefield.

Grzanka, Patrick R., Jake Adler, and Jennifer Blazer. 2015. Making up allies: The identity choreography of straight LGBT activism. *Sexuality Research and Social Policy* 12 (3): 1–17.

Hollander, Jocelyn A. 2001. Vulnerability and dangerousness: The construction of gender through conversation about violence. *Gender & Society* 15 (1): 83–109.

Hollander, Jocelyn A. 2004. "I can take care of myself": The impact of self-defense training on women's lives. *Violence Against Women* 10:205–35.

Hollander, Jocelyn A. 2013. "I demand more of people": Accountability, interaction, and gender change. *Gender & Society* 27 (1): 5–29.

Hondagneu-Sotelo, Pierrette, and Michael A. Messner. 1994. Gender displays and men's power: The "new man" and the Mexican immigrant man. In *Theorizing masculinities*, edited by Harry Brod and Michael Kaufman. New York: Sage.

Jeffreys, Sheila. 1998. *The idea of prostitution*. North Melbourne, Australia: Spinifex Press.

Koss, Mary P. 1988. Hidden rape: Incidence, prevalence, and descriptive characteristics of sexual aggression reported by a national sample of postsecondary students. In *Rape and sexual assault*, vol. 2, edited by A. W. Burgess. New York: Garland Publishing.

Lees, Sue. 1997. *Ruling passions: Sexual violence, reputation, and the law*. Buckingham, UK: Open University Press.

Lundrigan, Samantha, and Katrin Mueller-Johnson. 2013. Male stranger rape: A behavioral model of victim–offender interaction. *Criminal Justice and Behavior* 40 (7): 763–83.

Martin, Patricia Yancey. 2001. Mobilizing masculinities: Women's experiences of men at work. *Organization* 8 (4): 587–618.

Masters, Tatiana. 2010. "My strength is not for hurting": Men's anti-rape websites and their construction of masculinity and male sexuality. *Sexualities* 13 (1): 33–46.

Mathers, Lain A. B., J. Edward Sumerau, and Koji Ueno. 2015. "This isn't just another gay group": Privileging heterosexuality in a mixed-sexuality LGBTQ advocacy group. *Journal of Contemporary Ethnography* 44:306–34.

McGuire, Danielle L. 2011. *At the dark end of the street: Black women, rape, and resistance—A new history of the Civil Rights Movement from Rosa Parks to the rise of Black Power*. New York: Vintage.

Messner, Michael A. 1993. "Changing men" and feminist politics in the United States. *Theory and Society* 22 (5): 723–37.

Mora, Richard. 2012. "Do it for all your pubic hairs!" Latino boys, masculinity, and puberty. *Gender & Society* 26 (3): 433–60.

Murphy, Michael J. 2009. Can men stop rape? Visualizing gender in the "My Strength Is Not for Hurting" rape prevention campaign. *Men and Masculinities* 12 (1): 113–30.

Nagel, Joane. 2000. Ethnicity and sexuality. *Annual Review of Sociology* 26: 107–33.

Pascoe, C. J. 2007. *Dude, you're a fag: Masculinity and sexuality in high school*. Berkeley: University of California Press.

Pascoe, C. J., and Tristan Bridges. 2015. Bronies, anti-rape chants, and gendered change. *Manly Musings*, April 1. http://thesocietypages.org/girlwpen/category/manly-musings/.

Swartout, Kevin M., Mary P. Koss, Jacquelyn W. White, Martie P. Thompson, Antonia Abbey, and Alexandra L. Bellis. 2015. Trajectory analysis of the campus serial rapist assumption. *JAMA Pediatrics*. doi:10.1001/jamapediatrics.2015.0707.

West, Candace, and Don Zimmerman. 1987. Doing gender. *Gender & Society* 1 (2): 125–51.

Wilkins, Amy C. 2009. Masculinity dilemmas: Sexuality and intimacy talk among Christians and goths. *Signs: Journal of Women in Culture and Society* 34 (2): 343–68.

Mass Shootings and Masculinity

TRISTAN BRIDGES AND TARA LEIGH TOBER

On December 14, 2012, Adam Lanza—a white, twenty-year-old young man—shot and killed his mother, drove to Sandy Hook Elementary School in Newtown, Connecticut, and shot and killed twenty children and six members of the school staff. When first responders arrived on the scene, Lanza killed himself. Lanza's mass shooting has been identified as among the deadliest mass shootings at a school in the United States. Mass shootings are not common occurrences, yet when they do occur they affect everyone. The massacre at Sandy Hook was felt around the world, as international leaders sent their condolences and people from the Philippines to Egypt lit candles and expressed their collective grief online writing, "My heart is in Newtown" (Brown, 2012). In this way, mass shootings, like terrorist attacks, are significant in the cultural sense. They leave an indelible wound on our social fabric, evoking feelings of helplessness, fear, anger, and heartache.

Despite being rare, mass shootings like Sandy Hook happen more often in the United States than anywhere else in the world, and according to Follman et al. (2014), the rate of their occurrence has increased in recent years. The single most patterned fact associated with mass shooters is their gender—these acts are committed by men. A great deal end in a similarly tragic way when the shooters take their own lives, a fact that led sociologists Rachel Kalish and Michael Kimmel (2010) to refer to these incidents as "suicide by mass murder."

Many of those committing these crimes are heavily armed. They're not just carrying a gun; many carry enough to rival action films. In 1999, Eric Harris and Dylan Kleibold entered Columbine High School in Littleton, Colorado, with an arsenal many compared to lethal scenes in *The Matrix*. Pictures Seung-Hui Cho took of himself with the weapons he used when he committed a mass shooting on the Virginia Tech campus in 2007 were similar to action movie posters depicting the hero in a dynamic stance with guns drawn. James Eagan Holmes's assault on a movie theatre audience in Aurora, Colorado, in 2012 took place in a theatre showing *The Dark Knight*. Adam Lanza walked into Sandy Hook Elementary with a Bushmaster 223 caliber Remington semiautomatic rifle and killed twenty-seven people with that weapon. Beginning in 2010, this particular weapon was heavily marketed by Bushmaster, the manufacturer, using a "man card" campaign. For example, a full-page spread in *Maxim* magazine depicted a picture of the weapon at a dynamic angle with the caption: "CONSIDER YOUR MAN CARD REISSUED." . . .

Bushmaster's advertisement betrays the connection between violence and masculinity. As Michael Kimmel (2012) writes, "From an early age, boys learn that violence is not only an acceptable form of conflict resolution, but one that is admired." This connection between masculinity and violence is not inevitable and it is not the same everywhere. Mass shootings like the one Adam

Lanza committed are more common in the United States than anywhere else in the world. Although most American men will never commit this kind of violent act, they are all exposed to lessons early on about what it means to be a "real man" and what to do when your masculinity is questioned. The Bushmaster ad "works"—in the sense that audiences can quickly and easily interpret it—because viewers understand violence as culturally masculine. But what exactly does it mean to say that violence is culturally masculine? And how can we understand that a social problem like mass shootings is just as much about gender as it is about gun control?

Gun Control and Gun Culture

Mass shootings—which include school shootings[1]—are a social problem with more than one cause. Access to guns and to the type of weaponry often used in mass shootings are important pieces of this puzzle. Indeed, of the 143 guns possessed by the shooters in the past three decades, more than three-quarters were obtained legally (Follman et al., 2014). When we look at this issue from a global perspective, however, it becomes clear that guns are only part of the problem. Gun advocates often use the cases of Switzerland and Israel to argue that more guns do not necessarily lead to more gun violence (e.g., Klein, 2012). Military service is compulsory for Swiss men and nearly universal for Israelis. As a result, large numbers of the population have access to firearms. Yet, according to the United Nations Office on Drugs and Crime (2013), both nations have a homicide rate of less than 1 per 100,000, compared to 4 per 100,000 in the United States (Bureau of Justice Statistics, 2013). . . .

Canada is another example of a nation with relatively high rates of gun ownership and low rates of gun violence. According to the Small Arms Survey (2007), the United States has about 89 guns per 100 residents (ranked highest in the world), whereas Canada has about 31 (ranked twelfth highest). Yet rates of firearm homicide are dramatically lower in Canada—less than 1

per 100,000 people (Statistics Canada, 2014). Jennifer Carlson (2015) argues that the meanings surrounding guns are different in these two countries, suggesting that gun *culture* cannot be reduced to rates of gun *ownership*. One fact supporting this is the type of gun owned. Gun owners in Canada, for instance, are more likely to own long guns (generally used for hunting) as opposed to handguns (generally used for other purposes, such as target shooting and self-defense). A Congressional Research Service report states that as of 2009, the estimated total number of firearms available to civilians in the United States was 114 million handguns, 110 million rifles, and 86 million shotguns (Krouse, 2012). The report also notes that shotgun imports were decreasing in the United States, whereas handgun and rifle imports were increasing (Krouse, 2012). These facts suggest that Canada and the United States have dramatically different gun cultures (Carlson, 2015).

Although there is much debate concerning the relationship between gun control and mass shootings, the data show that perhaps the oft-cited National Rifle Association slogan—"Guns don't kill people, people kill people"—is accurate. The National Rifle Association relies on this when claiming that *people* and not *guns* are responsible for gun violence. It would be more accurate, however, if the slogan read: "Guns don't kill people, men with guns kill people." And it would be even more accurate if it read: "Guns don't kill people, men with guns kill people, and when lone gunmen shoot large numbers of people at random, your best bet is that they're doing it on U.S. soil." So, the social problem of mass shootings is not only about masculinity; it is about American masculinity. But what is the connection between mass shootings and men in the United States? . . .

Social scientific research on the topic points to two separate answers. One is a *social psychological explanation* drawing on research related to what social scientists call "social identity threat." The other is a *cultural explanation* that suggests boys and men are navigating gender identities on less certain terrain than their fathers and grandfathers.

Social Psychological Roots of Mass Shootings

The general idea behind what social scientists refer to as "social identity threat" is that when a person perceives an aspect of their identity they care about to be called into question, they respond by over-demonstrating qualities associated with that identity. In a famous essay on masculinity and homophobia, Michael Kimmel offers a classic example. He writes, "I have a standing bet with a friend that I can walk onto any playground in America where 6-year-old boys are happily playing and by asking one question, I can provoke a fight. That question is simple: 'Who's a sissy around here?'" (1994:131). Robb Willer et al. (2013) refer to this as the "masculinity overcompensation thesis." By forcing some boy's gender identity to be questioned, Kimmel assumes that he will demonstrate his masculinity in dramatic fashion—through violence. Kimmel's anecdote relies on an understanding of violence as a resource on which boys can rely to demonstrate their gender identity if and when it has been called into question. We might consider other methods by which the boy identified as the "sissy" might respond. But if we agree that violence is an available (and perhaps predictable) response, then we also must acknowledge that violence and masculinity are connected.

The research on this topic is primarily experimental, meaning research participants come into labs and receive stimuli, and their responses are weighed against others who received different stimuli. One way "masculinity threat" is studied is to bring men into a lab and have them take a survey they are told will measure how "masculine" or "feminine" they are. The feedback they receive is random—some are told they scored within the masculine range and others that they scored within the feminine range. And here is where the research *actually* begins. Men receiving feedback that they scored within the feminine range have had their masculinity experimentally "threatened." But do they respond differently from men whose masculinity has not been threatened? Research shows that they react by overdemonstrating masculinity in a variety of ways. . . .

There's nothing inherently "off" about the men involved in this research. They perceived that their masculinity was being questioned and responded by overcompensating. When we see how men respond to gender identity threats, it provides important information about what kinds of things qualify as masculine in the first place, and how men are likely to turn to those qualities when they are unable to demonstrate masculinity in other ways. Dominance over women is one means by which men respond. Homophobia and sexual prejudice is another. And although it would not be ethical to see whether threatened men are more likely to engage in physical violence toward others, Willer et al.'s (2013) finding that threatened men are more supportive of war suggests that supporting violent behavior is a patterned response as well.

James Messerschmidt's (1999) research with young boys builds on this idea. He refers to all of the things to which boys can turn to demonstrate their gender identities as "masculinity resources." Messerschmidt suggests that violence is a masculinity resource, but also that it is often *the* resource that boys turn to in a crisis. This is why Michael Kimmel (2013) argues that boys and young men involved in extremely violent behavior like school and mass shootings are perhaps best understood as "overconforming" to masculinity rather than as deviant. And the research on mass shooters aligns with these more general findings.

In an exhaustive review of news media articles surrounding random school shootings between 1982 and 2001, Kimmel and Mahler (2003) found that "nearly all had stories of being mercilessly and constantly teased, picked on, and threatened" (1445) and the most common method of teasing was "gay baiting." They found no evidence that any of the shooters identified as gay, but virtually all of them were called gay by their peers. Reuter-Rice (2008) suggests that gender-specific bullying (particularly homophobic bullying) among adolescent boys may be the primary characteristic we have for identifying the profile of boys and young men at risk of becoming school shooters. C. J. Pascoe's (2007) research on high school boys in California suggests that gender-specific homophobic bullying is an incredibly pervasive feature of the lives of boys and young men in high school and beyond, particularly among white boys. It is here, then, that we turn to the cultural explanation for mass shootings.

Cultural Roots of Mass Shootings

Certainly, boys and men are teased and gay baited and experience gender identity threat in other nations as well. So, why are American boys and young men responding with such extreme displays of violence? Why are mass shootings so much more common in the United States? To answer this question, we need a cultural explanation—we need an answer that explains the role that American culture plays in influencing boys and young men to turn to this particular sort of violent behavior at such higher rates than anywhere else in the world. Karen L. Tonso (2009) discusses the importance of context to the production of shooters. . . . This approach redirects attention from the individual characteristics of the shooters themselves and investigates the everyday sociocultural contexts in which violent masculinities are produced, reproduced, and even valorized (Tonso, 2009). Michael Kimmel (2013) suggests that the problem is associated with a group he refers to as "angry white men." When this group acts out, when they are violent, and when they kill, mental illness and gun access are often quick to be blamed. But these explanations focus on individuals rather than on the societies in which they live. As the *New York Times* editorial board noted in an article on school shootings, rates of "severe mental illness [are] roughly stable around the world . . . while gun violence varies" (Editorial Board, 2014). In other words, individual-level explanations are inadequate. By focusing on a few bad apples, we fail to examine the orchard.

. . . Kimmel's (2013) research on angry white men builds on Pascoe's work and suggests that feeling denied a position which they feel is rightfully theirs in social hierarchies is a key ingredient. . . . Although meritocracy is best understood as a myth in the United States, upward mobility remains a popular characterization of American society, "the land of opportunity." But opportunities for *some* were often made possible by systematically and structurally denying those opportunities to *others* throughout American history. From a historical perspective, white men have long been the recipients of this privilege. Social movements of various kinds, however, have slowly chipped away at these opportunities for white men. And although heterosexual white men today still benefit from racial, sexual, and gender inequality, they also work alongside women, gay men and lesbian women, and people of color in ways that were less true of previous generations. Men today must compete with women, people of color, and more because of the gradual erosion of privileges that have historically worked in their interests. And some of them are pissed off about it.

Kimmel suggests that one outcome of the move toward equal rights has been the production of *aggrieved entitlement* among a world-historically privileged group: straight, white men in the United States. Michael Kimmel explains it this way:

> The new American anger is more than defensive; it is reactionary. It seeks to restore, to retrieve, to reclaim something that is perceived to have been lost. Angry white men look to the past for their imagined and desired future. They believe that the system is stacked against them. Theirs is the anger of the entitled: we are entitled to those jobs, those positions of unchallenged dominance. And when we are told we are not going to get them, we get angry. (2013:21)

And in an essay on gender and mass shootings, Rachel Kalish and Michael Kimmel more explicitly connect aggrieved entitlement with these crimes. Aggrieved entitlement is a gendered sentiment—one that authorizes violence by entitling boys and men to exact revenge on others when they perceive their masculinity to have been threatened or otherwise inaccessible. But aggrieved entitlement does not always or only lead to mass shooting either. Much more commonly, Kimmel suggests that it is associated with negative opinions of women and racial minorities. This suggests, and Kimmel argues, that mass shootings are one (extremely violent) example of a much larger issue. . . .

Conclusion

Social psychological research demonstrates that many men understand violence as a method of compensating for a perceived threat to their masculinity. But, coupled with a gendered sense of "aggrieved entitlement," a cultural explanation allows us to explore why, in extreme circumstances, violence is so much more likely to take the form of mass shootings in the United States. Mass shootings are a social and cultural problem in the United States. Gun ownership and access are a part of this problem. But when we refocus our attention from the gun to the person wielding the gun and the gun culture within which that action is understood, it's hard to ignore gender. Mass shootings are enactments of masculinity. But they only "work" in this way if violence is culturally masculinized in the first place, such that men might turn to it as a resource when they are unable to demonstrate masculinity in other ways.

Note

1. We specify mass school shooters here because we are specifically referring to a subset of mass shooters—those who commit their acts of violence in a school setting. Familiar examples here include Columbine, Virginia Tech, and Sandy Hook Elementary. School shooters have been widely studied and profiled (e.g., Kimmel and Mahler, 2003; Newman et al., 2004).

References

Brown, Sarah. (2012, December 17). "World Reaction: 'My Heart Is in Newtown.'" *CNN*. Retrieved March 23, 2015. http://www.cnn.com/2012/12/17/world/irpt-sandy-hook-global-reaction/.

Bureau of Justice Statistics. 2013. *Firearm Violence, 1993–2011* [Data File]. Retrieved March 19, 2015. http://www.bjs.gov/content/pub/pdf/fv9311.pdf

Carlson, Jennifer. 2015. *Citizen-Protectors: The Everyday Politics of Guns in an Age of Decline*. New York: Oxford University Press.

Editorial Board, *New York Times*. (2014, Dec. 3). "Mental Illness and Guns at Newtown." Retrieved March 13, 2015. http://www.nytimes.com/2014/12/04/opinion/mental-illness-and-guns-at-newtown.html?_r=o/.

Follman, Mark, Gavin Aronson, and Deanna Pan. (2014, May 24). "A Guide to Mass Shootings in America." *Mother Jones*. Retrieved March 13, 2015. http://www.motherjones.com/politics/2012/07/mass-shootings-map/.

Kalish, Rachel, and Michael Kimmel. 2010. "Suicide by Mass Murder: Masculinity, Aggrieved Entitlement, and Rampage School Shootings." *Health Sociology Review* 19(4):451–464.

Kimmel, Michael. (2012, December 19). "Masculinity, Mental Illness and Guns: A Lethal Equation?" *CNN*. Retrieved March 18, 2015. http://www.cnn.com/2012/12/19/living/men-guns-violence/index.html/.

Kimmel, Michael S. 1994. "Masculinity as Homophobia." In *Theorizing Masculinities*, edited by Harry Brod and Michael Kaufman, 119–141. Thousand Oaks, CA: Sage.

Kimmel, Michael S. 2013. *Angry White Men: American Masculinity at the End of an Era*. New York: Nation Books.

Kimmel, Michael S., and Matthew Mahler. 2003. "Adolescent Masculinity, Homophobia, and Violence: Random School Shootings, 1982–2001." *American Behavioral Scientist* 46(1):1439–1458.

Klein, Ezra. (2012, December 14). Mythbusting: Israel and Switzerland Are Not Gun-Toting Utopias. *The Washington Post*. Retrieved March 13, 2015. http://www.washingtonpost.com/blogs/wonkblog/wp/2012/12/14/mythbusting-israel-and-switzerland-are-not-gun-toting-utopias/.

Krouse, William J. (2012, November 14). "Gun Control Legislation." *Federation of American Scientists*. Retrieved March 23, 2015. http://fas.org/sgp/crs/misc/RL32842.pdf/.

Messerschmidt, James W. 1999. *Nine Lives: Adolescent Masculinities, the Body, and Violence*. Boulder, CO: Westview Press.

Newman, Katherine S., Cybelle Fox, Wendy Roth, Jal Mehta, and David Harding. 2004. *Rampage: The Social Roots of School Shootings*. New York: Basic Books.

Pascoe, C. J. 2007. *Dude, You're a Fag: Masculinity and Sexuality in High School*. Berkeley, CA: University of California Press.

Reuter-Rice, Karin. 2008. "Male Adolescent Bullying and the School Shooter." *The Journal of Nursing* 24(6):350–359.

Tonso, Karen L. 2009. "Violent Masculinities as Tropes for School Shooters: The Montreal Massacre, the Columbine Attack, and Rethinking Schools." *American Behavioral Scientist* 52(9):1266–1285.

Small Arms Survey. 2007. *The Largest Civilian Firearms Arsenals for 178 Countries* [Data File]. Retrieved March 19, 2015. http://www.smallarmssurvey.org/fileadmin/docs/A-Year-book/2007/en/Small-Arms-Survey-2007-Chapter-02-annexe-4-EN.pdf/.

Statistics Canada. 2014. *Firearms and Violent Crime in Canada, 2012* [Data File]. Retrieved March 19, 2015. http://www.statcan.gc.ca/pub/85-002-x/2014001/article/11925-eng.htm#a1/.

United Nations Office on Drugs and Crime. 2013. Global Study on Homicide. Retrieved March 19, 2014, from http://www.unodc.org/documents/gsh/pdfs/2014_GLOBAL_HOMICIDE_BOOK_web.pdf/.

Willer, Rob, Christabel L. Rogalin, Bridget Conlon, and Michael T. Wojnowicz. 2013. "Overdoing Gender: A Test of the Masculine Overcompensation Thesis." *American Journal of Sociology* 118(4):980–1022.

Sexual Violence in the "Manosphere"

Antifeminist Men's Rights Discourses on Rape

LISE GOTELL AND EMILY DUTTON

Introduction

The problem of sexual assault has re-emerged as a politicized issue in the public sphere, with allegations against well-known media personalities, including Canadian radio host Jian Ghomeshi and American entertainer Bill Cosby, and publicized sexual assault scandals at several universities. In the midst of these stories gripping North America, there is strong evidence that feminist claims have made inroads into public discourse. Media coverage has begun to deploy feminist concepts like "rape culture" and there is growing outcry about institutional failures to respond (for example, Kingston 2015; Kohn 2015; Venton-Rublee 2014). At a time when feminists have again broken the silence around rape and sexual assault, there are also growing signs of a backlash. . . .

In this paper, we explore the role that antifeminist men's rights activism (MRA[1]) is playing in a contemporary backlash to feminist anti-rape activism. . . . Here we examine popular MRA websites to reveal a set of interrelated claims about sexual violence, including: that sexual violence, like domestic violence, is a gender-neutral problem; that feminists are responsible for erasing men's experiences of sexual assault; that false allegations of sexual assault against men are widespread; and that rape culture is a feminist-produced moral panic. . . . While these highly misogynist discourses are challenging sites for feminist research, we contend that it is important to engage as there is a real danger that MRA claims could come to define the popular conversation about sexual violence.

Situating Ourselves: "Don't Be THAT Guy/Girl"

We did not come to this research through scholarly interest. Instead, when MRAs sought to undermine a local anti-sexual violence campaign, this project found us. Edmonton has been home to an award-winning campaign against sexual assault, "Don't be THAT Guy." Labelled Sexual Assault Voices of Edmonton (SAVE, see http://www.savedmonton.com/) and comprised of a coalition that included the University of Alberta's Department of Women's and Gender Studies, this campaign used social marketing directed at men as a tool of sexual violence prevention. The edgy ads from SAVE's first campaign begin with the tagline "Just because . . . ("she isn't saying no"; "you helped her home"; "she's drunk"), and end with "doesn't mean . . . ("she's saying yes"; "you get to help yourself"; "she wants to f**k"). The ads challenge the social norm of male sexual entitlement and seek to delegitimize common excuses for sexual assault. Don't be THAT Guy intentionally

Lise Gotell and Emily Dutton, "Sexual Violence in the 'Manosphere': Antifeminist Men's Rights Discourses on Rape," *International Journal for Crime, Justice and Social Democracy*, 5(2):65–80. Copyright 2016 by the authors, reprinted by permission.

"Others" the rapist, who becomes THAT guy, that guy who you don't want to be. The campaign also seeks to raise awareness about Canada's strict legal standard for consent. Don't be THAT Guy disrupts rape myths by reminding its audience that the reality of sexual assault is not solely confined to having sex with someone who is saying no; sexual assault is legally defined as having sex with someone who is not saying yes.

In July 2013, Men's Rights Edmonton (MRE), a group closely affiliated with the well-known antifeminist website A Voice for Men (AVFM), created a copycat poster that distorted one of SAVE's original ads, see Figure 38.1. Entitled "Don't be THAT Girl," the poster plays on the myth that false allegations are widespread and states: "Just because you regret a one night stand, doesn't mean it wasn't consensual. Lying about sexual assault is a crime." Displayed around Edmonton and disseminated

Figure 38.1 Photo posted on Twitter by James Muir (https://twitter.com/ephraim_quin, accessed 16 September 2013).

online, the poster quickly spread throughout the "manosphere," the cyber-world of men's rights that, as Robert Menzies has argued, unveils "a truly remarkable gallery of antifeminist content" (Menzies 2007: 65). . . .

MRE's copycat campaign drew us in, politically and personally, though in different ways.

Lise Gotell:

As a spokeswoman for SAVE, my phone rang off the hook the day these posters went up. . . . I felt it was important to respond to misrepresentations disseminated by MRE's poster by emphasizing that false accusations are very rare (Lisak, Gardinier, Nicksa et al. 2010). Instead, high prevalence rates, under-reporting, high police un-founding rates, and low conviction rates cause what researchers in the field call a justice gap (Tempkin and Krahe 2008). . . .

. . . Following my public response to Don't be THAT Girl, MRE created a poster (Figure 38.2) and a blog post entitled "Lise Gotell, Bigot Extrodunaire [sic]" (MRE 2013a). Through these widely circulated attacks, I experienced firsthand the intimidation and harassment that are common tactics used by MRAs in efforts to silence and discredit feminist scholars and activists (Blais and Dupuis-Deri 2012).

Emily Dutton:

. . . The presence of these MRE posters made my progressive community and the University area feel unsafe. Quickly, a community response was created. Feminist organizers asked that folks rip down these hate-propagating posters and we held a series of community meetings to talk about the discomfort they created. We strategized about the best way to respond to MRE, as well as how to keep each other safe at rallies and lectures. In many ways, this paper is a way of continuing the dialogue started then.

Anti-Anti-Rape Backlash

In the past few years, counterclaims to anti-rape feminism have intensified, casting contemporary

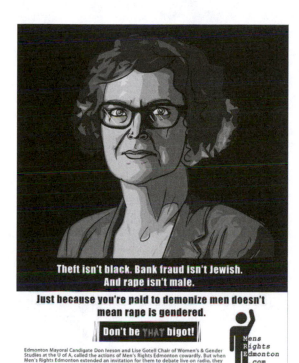

Figure 38.2 "Don't be THAT Bigot" poster (MRE 2013a).

feminism as a force of stultifying political correctness (Gotell 2015). This resistance shares much with earlier manifestations of what some have called the anti-anti-rape backlash (Bevaqua 2000: 181). In the 1990s, amidst law reform inroads as well as the first representative studies of sexual assault (Dragiewicz 2000), postfeminists Camille Paglia (1992) and Katie Roiphe (1994) pushed back against feminist research revealing the pervasiveness of sexual violence. They criticized a sexually correct form of feminism that they saw as convincing women to redefine bad sex as rape, in the process manufacturing a crisis. These polemical claims took the form of an ideological battle waged through the media and were eagerly taken up in a cultural context by those anxious to put to rest the troubling claims of anti-rape feminists.

We need to be mindful of the analytic problems with the metaphor of backlash. This concept presents an overly simplified view of both feminism and anti-feminism, obscuring historical, social and cultural complexities, and failing to capture intertwined periods of change and resistance (Chunn, Boyd and Lessard 2007: 6). Nevertheless, an analysis of backlash usefully draws our attention to intense periods of resistance to feminist successes (Gavey 2005: 64). . . .

The contemporary anti-anti-rape backlash consists of overlapping sites, both academic and popular. What weaves together these expressions is their shared dissemination of a caricatured depiction of anti-rape feminism as harmful. . . . Ignoring the complex feminist politics surrounding criminalization strategies, critics single out feminist law reform campaigns as having played a central role in consolidating punitive politics (Gotell 2015).

. . . In newspapers and on popular news websites, the concept "rape culture" has been identified as a feminist-produced moral panic (for example, Kitchens 2014). Statistical evidence of rape's pervasiveness has come under fire (for example, MacDonald 2014). Efforts to respond to sexual violence on university campuses have been condemned as abuses of due process that stigmatize innocent young men (MacDonald 2014). Media critiques blame "ideological" feminism for constructing men as rapists and for absolving women from taking reasonable steps (avoiding binge drinking, for example) to prevent rape.

These counter-claims respond to feminism's recent legal and cultural successes; specifically, to the consolidation of an affirmative consent standard in law, as well as to the growing cultural acceptance of prohibitions on victim-blaming. . . . In this context, it is increasingly clear that the injunction against blaming victims constitutes a radical challenge to the disciplinary messages of rape prevention, threatening to undo a set of rules that have constrained women's behavior, and unsettling responsibilizing codes that hold women accountable for the violence they experience. In response to this challenge, we are witnessing a move to reinstate gendered rules that cast women as safety-conscious victims-in-waiting, while leaving men's behaviours unscrutinized (Gotell 2010). As we illustrate, MRA claims about rape play a central part in this emergent backlash, positioning men as the scapegoated and silenced victims of anti-rape feminism.

Researching MRA Sites: To Engage or Not to Engage?

In this article we present our cyber-ethnographic and discourse analyses of sexual violence–related content posted on three MRA websites between mid-2013 and the end of 2014:[2] AVFM, the most visible North American antifeminist MRA website, which receives as many as 12,000 hits per day; the *Canadian Association for Equality* (CAFE), the website of the main Canadian MRA organization; and MRE, a website maintained by [a] local group that gained attention through its Don't be THAT Girl campaign. We also analyzed some of the videos posted on these sites, including *YouTube* videos produced by the popular female MRA Karen Straughan, who is associated with both MRE and AVFM, and who has spoken at CAFE-sponsored events. Together, websites such as these form a dense network of MRA content, through which articles that originate on "brother" sites are frequently reposted, with many of the same activists producing content across sites. . . .

Our experiences with MRE prompted us to become close observers of MRA web activity, monitoring websites, blogs and online discussions. . . . Like Molly Dragiewicz's (2008) examination of fathers' rights web discourses, our exploration of AVFM, CAFE and MRE was qualitative and purposive, closely interrogating constructions of sexual violence and of anti-rape feminism. The line between sexual violence and normative sexuality is socially constructed and a site of intensified struggle. . . . Our objective was to analyze MRA arguments in order to identify key themes, which form the basis for the sections of the paper which follow. . . .

As many activists have learned through participating in online or in-person debates, MRAs rely almost parasitically on feminist outrage. Scholarly attention can thus have the unintended consequence of amplifying their messages. In addition, serious engagement with the men's rights movement (MRM) reinforces a simplistic "us versus them" framework that leads to a number of strategic problems. . . . We can certainly understand the seduction of focusing on an external enemy at a time when feminist politics seems disunified and riven by internal conflict (with feminists divided around issues like sex work and prostitution, for example). Yet a rich theoretical and political pluralism has always marked feminism, and this needs to be understood as a source of strength. The desire for a unity that never was can result in the suppression of contestation within feminism, reinforcing an image of feminist politics as uniform and lending credence to the "feminazi" caricature propagated by MRAs and social conservatives.

Treating feminists and MRAs as two sides of a one-dimensional struggle also misdiagnoses resistance to feminism. . . . New norms of neoliberal governance encourage us to see ourselves as self-managing, degendered citizens, responsible for our own well-being. "Postfeminism," celebrating personal agency and promoting the view that feminism is passé, has become the dominant discourse on gender relations (McRobbie 2008). . . . Ignoring this broader context also ignores how MRA claims gain ground because of their resonance with neoliberal discourse, including an emphasis on gender-neutrality, formal equality and individual responsibility (Menzies 2007).

. . . Ultimately, we agree with Menzies that the analysis of MRA claims can deliver important lessons about the contemporary status of feminism (2007: 66). The escalation of MRA discourses on rape provides an indication of feminist success in reshaping social norms about sex and sexual violence. However, there is also a real danger that this highly visible MRA mobilization around sexual violence could foreshadow the erosion of feminist influence. . . . Undeniably, these antifeminist discourses can seem compelling, particularly since they redeploy progressive concepts like rights and equality, and play upon widespread anxieties about feminists having swung the pendulum too far.

Shifts in MRA Tactics and Discourse

Until recently, the MRM has been largely synonymous with fathers' rights activism (Boyd 2004; Boyd and Young 2002; Collier and Sheldon 2006; Menzies 2007). Throughout the 1980s, the 1990s and the early 2000s, MRM politics took a decidedly state-centered form, focused on feminism's perceived attack on fatherhood through family law. During this time, groups sought to shape law reform and policy discourse on child custody, access and support (Boyd and Young 2004). MRAs also contested feminist assertions about the gendered character of domestic violence and challenged anti-violence policies for being biased against men (Dragiewicz 2008, 2011). . . . Sidestepping structural understandings of inequality, the antifeminist MRM appropriated formal equality arguments, asserting men's equal right to parent and insisting on gender symmetry in domestic violence.

Fast forward to contemporary times, when MRA tactics have become decidedly virtual and focused on shifting attitudes through cyberactivism rather than by influencing law. Aside from the push for presumptive joint custody (for example, CAFE 2013), there is now relatively little MRA engagement in the realm of public policy. Interestingly, this anti-statism echoes developments in feminism, with third-wave feminism emphasizing grassroots direct action and cultural struggles, while turning away from engagement with the state and law (Snyder 2008). This mirroring of feminism lends support to the interpretation of the MRM as a reactionary "counter-movement." Yet the decline of state-focused strategies also needs to be understood in relation to the context of neoliberal governance. Given a political context in which gender and the gender equality agenda have been largely erased from political discourse (Gotell 2010), gender conflicts have increasingly moved outside formal politics. Cyberspace, in particular, has emerged as a new terrain of struggle. The Internet offers a decentralized mechanism for the dissemination of

MRA politics. Extremists and hate groups are increasingly embracing new media forums (such as websites, blogs and *YouTube* channels) as avenues to deliver their messages (Dunbar, Connelly, Jensen et al. 2014). In these spaces, MRAs are building virtual communities founded on malice against feminists and mobilizing men on the basis of a claimed identity as victims.

While fathers used to be constructed as the principal "victims" of feminism, MRA attention is increasingly shifting to young men and sexual politics. . . . [A]s Emily Matchar (2014: online) argued in a recent article in *The New Republic*, the MRM has shifted its attention to the issue of rape: "As the nation [United States] grapples with rape in increasingly public ways—Obama's January formation of a new task force to address rape on college campuses, the widespread publicity around the Steubenville and Maryville rape cases—the MRM is crying foul." As our analysis demonstrates, MRAs are crying foul through a number of interrelated assertions that emerged as themes in our analysis: that sexual violence is gender-neutral; that feminists are responsible for a cover-up of men's experiences of victimization; that feminists have created a climate where false allegations are rampant; and that rape culture is nothing more than a moral panic.

Sexual Violence as Gender-Neutral

There is an obvious parallel between MRA arguments about domestic violence and the thrust of newer claims about rape. . . . Grounding the antifeminist discourses examined by Dragiewicz is a set of misrepresentative empirical claims about women as perpetrators of domestic violence (2011: 88). MRA rhetoric on rape is likewise preoccupied with refuting statistics that demonstrate how sexual violence is gendered. MRAs contend that statistics distort reality, exaggerating women's victimization, while erasing the sexual violence experienced by men. . . .

Statistics are an ongoing focus of struggle because it is empirical research that brings feminist political claims about rape into [the] realm of scientific "fact" (Gavey 2005). As Nicola Gavey has argued, feminist empirical studies conducted in the 1980s and 1990s revolutionized the research on sexual violence by demonstrating that rape was not rare, that it coexisted with other forms of unwanted and coerced sex, and that most acts were committed by men known to their victims. These findings posed a serious challenge to normative heterosexuality by undermining the narrow view of "real rape" as violent stranger-rape and revealing how sexual violence is linked to everyday gender norms. The norms of male sexual activity and of female sexual submissiveness, which are still largely viewed as unremarkable within the commonsense logic of heteronormativity, form the "cultural scaffolding of rape" (Gavey 2005), gendered ideologies that enable and excuse sexual violence. . . . The significance of the methodological innovations pioneered by feminist researchers can be seen in their continued influence on approaches to measuring sexual violence used in government surveys (such as Canada's General Social Survey and the Center for Disease Control's National Intimate Partner and Sexual Violence Survey (NISVS)). Conducted using expanded methods, these studies have yielded considerably higher prevalence rates of sexual violence against women (Johnson 2012: 616). . . .

. . . MRAs contend that feminist empirical research is "junk science" that exaggerates a crime that is very rare. The repeated target of critique is the Sexual Experiences Survey (SES) conducted by Mary Koss, Christine Gidycz and Nadine Wisniewski (1987). Based on a random sample of 6,159 college women, the SES found that one in four women has experienced rape or attempted rape. According to Diana Davidson (2013), a former writer for AVFM, Koss should be added to the "Cunning Stunts of History" for producing an "imaginary epidemic." . . . MRAs insist that the SES exaggerates sexual violence because it operationalizes rape using multiple behaviorally specific questions, rather than by directly asking participants if they have been raped (for example, Davidson 2013; Straughan 2013). In short, MRAs assert that this methodology manufactures victims.

While feminist research is accused of constructing an "American rape machine" (Honey Badger Radio 2014), the statistics produced by this "machine" are used to bolster MRA claims about gender symmetry. American MRAs have seized on findings from the NISVS (Breiding, Smith, Basile et al. 2014) showing that, while women remain overwhelmingly the victims of rape, men and women have roughly equivalent 12-month rates of sexual coercion and unwanted sex (for example, Roe 2014). The behavioral methodology pioneered by Koss, Gidycz and Wisniewski (1987) (for example, asking if you have had unwanted sex "because someone gave you drugs or alcohol") is thus simultaneously spurned and embraced, used to underline men's victimization while rejected for supposedly inflating that of women (for example, Levental 2014). . . .

Although women and men can both be sexually aggressive, women disproportionately experience victimization, while men perpetrate the vast majority of sexual violence (for example, Johnson and Dawson 2011; Statistics Canada 2013). As the 2011 NISVS concludes, for example, "the burden of sexual violence . . . is not distributed evenly," with "women, in particular, impacted heavily during their lifetimes" (Breiding, Smith, Basile et al. 2014: online). MRAs distort this evidence, cherry-picking findings to reinforce their insistence on gender symmetry. The gender-neutral picture painted is one that depoliticizes and individualizes sexual violence, honing in on isolated acts abstracted from the power relations that define them. . . . As Dragiewicz has astutely observed, MRA tactics of minimization and denial mimic the justifications deployed by abusive men (2011: 65).

Men as Victims

Alongside assertions of gender symmetry, MRAs deploy the rhetoric of male victimization in order to contest anti-rape feminism's claims. SAVE's Don't be THAT Guy campaign became a lightning rod for MRA outrage. According to many articles and videos posted on the websites we researched, Don't Be THAT Guy is depicted as "misandry" (hatred of men) exemplified, constituting "hate speech" because it "targets a gender and all members of that gender as perpetrators of rape" (Straughan 2013). Straughan's widely viewed v-log "Don't Be that Lying Feminist" (2013) (86,298 hits) is posted on both MRE and AVFM. Straughan contends that feminist "ideologues" victimize men by "associating the behaviour of a small group with the group as a whole" (2013). "Don't be THAT Guy," she argues, is based on the erroneous assumption that "all men would rape if only you forget to remind them not to every 15 seconds" (Straughan 2013). Contrary to Straughan's depiction, this campaign's emphasis on men was not meant to construct all men as rapists, but instead to stigmatize perpetrators and to educate men about consent. SAVE was challenging the sexist thrust of prevention discourses that have long framed individual women as being primarily responsible for ending sexual violence through restricting their behaviour and mobility.

Seeking to deflect any male responsibility for sexual violence, MRAs construct men as the true victims of both women and feminism. . . . As Hannah Wallen argues in an article on AVFM, feminists are complicit in the erasure of men's victimization in order to "maintain [women's] monopoly on perceived victim status," which allows them to preserve a "government and corporate funding meal ticket" (2013). To pierce though what they present as being a feminist-enforced silence, MRA websites amplify stories of individual women perpetrators, while dismissing allegations against men, which are always represented as products of false accusations.

In addition to emphasizing literal victimization, the websites also position men as the victims of pervasive false allegations. David Lisak and his co-authors (2010) have concluded that the cumulative data soundly contradict the belief that false allegations are a common occurrence. Yet in typically hyperbolic tones, AVFM's Elam (2013) cites a discredited study by Eugene Kanin (1994) to argue that more than 50 per cent of police reports are fabrications. . . . "Ideological feminism" is blamed for creating a culture of believing victims, even at the cost of wrongful convictions (Straughan 2013).

Of course, these MRA claims fail to acknowledge the regularity with which police dismiss reports of sexual assault and the astronomical rates of attrition within the criminal justice system (Johnson 2012). Interestingly, in more recent activism, MRAs have begun to deploy progressive anti-racist rhetoric to bolster arguments about false accusations. Drawing on a longstanding history of racist rape allegations against black men, accusations against American entertainer Bill Cosby have been presented on AVFM as "high tech lynching" (Ali 2015). . . .

On the whole, and echoing Dragiewicz' (2008, 2011) observations about MRA domestic violence discourse, these arguments work to minimize men's responsibility for sexual violence. The claim to speak on behalf of powerless male victims lends moral status to the MRA claims, just as this rhetorical strategy serves to demonize feminists.

Rape Culture as Feminist-Inspired Moral Panic

. . . On the websites we examined, it was very often feMRAs—female men's rights activists—who were the strongest critics of rape culture, with activists like Straughan (2013), Fiamengo (2014) and Barbara Kay (2014a, 2014b) taking the lead in contesting feminist arguments. Women's voices can serve to legitimize claims that would likely be viewed as being clearly more offensive if put forward by men. And there is surely no shortage of highly offensive MRA writing on rape. As Warren Farrell, who is often represented as the "moderate" academic voice of the MRM, has written, "If a man ignoring a woman's verbal 'no' is committing date rape, then a woman who says 'no' with her verbal language but 'yes' with her body language is committing date fraud" (2000: 315). Elam (2010) is even more overt in insisting that women are asking for it:

> In that light, I have ideas about women who spend evenings in bars hustling men for drinks, playing on their sexual desires so they can get shitfaced on the beta dole; paying their bar tab with the pussy pass. . . . But are these women asking to get raped? In the most severe and emphatic terms possible

the answer is NO, THEY ARE NOT ASKING TO GET RAPED. They are freaking *begging* for it [emphasis in original].

. . . The assertion that rape culture is a feminist-inspired moral panic is a predominant theme within a broader backlash to anti-rape feminism (Gotell 2015). There are connections being forged between the MRM, and media manifestations of anti-anti-rape backlash. Right wing columnists writing in mainstream media venues, including Caroline Kitchens in *Time Magazine* (2014), Barbara Kay in *The National Post* (2014a) and Margaret Wente in *The Globe and Mail* (2013), have repeatedly made the argument that rape culture is feminist hysteria. . . .

. . . MRA rape culture critics typically begin by challenging statistical evidence of the pervasiveness of sexual violence (Byset 2014), instead depicting rape as being very rare (Kay 2014a, 2014b; Fiamengo 2014). The concept of rape culture underlines how sexual violence is normalized and excused. By contrast, MRAs insist that most men understand rape to be a horrific crime: "Feminists routinely deny, as a core article of faith, that rape is widely considered a heinous crime in North America" (Fiamengo 2014). Of course, the issue underlying this emphasis on rape as a widely condemned crime is not really whether people view rape as right or wrong. Instead, it is that rape is not seen as rape. Implicit in the MRA assertion that rape is both rare and horrific is an appeal to the idea of the narrow category of "real rape", thus making acquaintance sexual violence—which we know occurs far more frequently than violent stranger rape—disappear. . . .

. . . As if blind to evidence that women's allegations are so often discredited, Kay contends that "official sympathy for rape victims is creating a climate so overwhelmingly sympathetic to female victims of sexual abuse that the emerging cultural injustice is injustice to alleged perpetrators" (Kay 2014b). Fiamengo (2014) analyzes events at the University of Ottawa, including sexual assault allegations against members of the hockey team and online misogyny posted by student politicians; she

uses the unusually strong response by the University administration (or "slavish pro-feminism," in her terms) as evidence for the non-existence of rape culture. Men, she argues, "are browbeaten to wear the hair shirt of collective guilt as potential rapists." And, as a result of the "success of the feminist narrative," "the problems of men are ignored," and the "reality of male victimization" remains unacknowledged.

There have been too many recent reminders of rape culture's persistence: CNN's emphasis on the ruined football careers of the Steubenville rapists; circulated cellphone images that effectively celebrate rape; rape chants on university campuses; and male student leaders engaging in misogynous banter about raping their female colleagues. MRA challenges to the concept of rape culture are, in essence, attempting to erase the systemic character of sexual violence and to reconstitute an individualized framing that makes sexual assault into something women are responsible for preventing through sexual safekeeping. Many rape culture critics hone in on the necessity of responsible drinking, arguing that the best way for women to prevent sexual violence is to avoid getting drunk. As Kay (2014b) insists, for example, "it is fair comment to observe that those women students who do not drink to excess, who are prudent about the kind of parties they attend, and who are selective about their sexual partners in general will doubtless reduce their odds much further, down to statistically nugatory levels." According to Straughan (2013), feminist discourse on rape denies women's responsibility for rape prevention, "[t]reat[ing]] women as toddlers who can't be trusted to drink responsibly or plan ahead." . . . Hyper-vigilance, then, becomes promoted as a natural feminine state, a version of neoliberal (sexual) citizenship. By contrast, male sexual aggression is normalized. These reasserted sexual subject positions, with idealized masculine subjects consigned to the role of natural sexual aggressors and with idealized feminine subjects cast as re-action heroes, typifies the antifeminist backlash to anti-rape feminism.

Conclusion

Our analysis, though exploratory, suggests that sexual violence is emerging as a new focus of the MRM. MRA rhetoric on sexual violence works to contest a gendered analysis of rape and sexual assault, to accuse feminists of erasing the victimization of men, and to paint the feminist concept of rape culture as a moral panic. In many ways, these claims echo more familiar arguments about fathers' rights and domestic violence. Yet within MRA rhetoric on rape, it is young men, rather than fathers, who are being depicted as being feminism's principal victims. . . . The subject of MRA politics has shifted and is becoming less familial and more sexual. MRAs appear to be using the issue of rape to exploit young men's anxieties about shifting consent standards and changing sexual and gender norms.

As Matchar (2014) has warned, MRAs threaten to define the public conversation on sexual violence unless progressives, including feminists, start engaging with the issues they raise more comprehensively. Evidence that these misogynist discourses are moving into the mainstream lends urgency to this Matchar's warning. Last year, Rape Abuse and Incest National Network (RAINN), a prominent voice in the US public discourse on sexual violence, issued an influential critique of the concept of rape culture, arguing that blaming "culture" erases individual responsibility. While "rape culture" was never meant to excuse perpetrators, RAINN's critique ignores the role of systemic factors, most notably of sexism and of gendered sexual norms. Another recent indication of the mainstreaming of MRA politics was CAFE's attainment of charitable tax status, which in Canada requires an absence of political bias. . . .

. . . Academics concerned about the rise of antifeminist extremism need to explore both continuities and changes in strategies, including the shift towards young men and male sexual subjects as new emphases of MRA politics. Even though we are fully committed to retaining a gendered lens on sexual violence and to resisting the erasure of women's victimization, we suggest that it is important to grapple with men as victims. Feminist denial of the realities (though unequal) of men's victimization plays into the vilifying rhetoric of MRAs. It is necessary, we believe, to adopt a gender-inclusive view of victimization, while still maintaining a gendered analysis of sexual violence.

Notes

1. We use MRA as the acronym for both men's rights activism and men's rights activist.
2. In some cases we also refer to significant interventions that precede this.

References

Ali M (2015) The high tech lynching of William H. Cosby. *A Voice for Men*, 12 January. Available at http://www.avoiceformen.com/mens-rights/the-high-tech-lynching-of-william-h-cosby/ (accessed 5 January 2016).

Bevaqua M (2000) *Rape on the Public Agenda: Feminism and the Politics of Sexual Assault*. Boston: Northeastern University Press.

Blais M and Dupuis-Déri F (2012) Masculinism and the antifeminist countermovement. *Social Movement Studies: Journal of Social, Cultural and Political Protest* 11(1): 21–39. DOI: 10.1080/14742837.2012 .640532.

Boyd SB (2004) Demonizing mothers: Fathers' rights discourses in child custody law reform processes. *Journal for the Association of Research on Mothering* 6(1): 52–74.

Boyd SB and Young CFL (2002) Who influences family law reform? Discourses on motherhood and fatherhood in legislative reform debates in Canada. *Studies in Law, Politics and Society*, 26: 43–75.

Breiding MJ, Smith SG, Basile KC, Walters ML, Chen J and Merrick MT (2014) Prevalence and characteristics of sexual violence, stalking, and intimate partner violence victimization—National Intimate Partner and Sexual Violence Survey, United States, 2011. *Surveillance Summaries* 63(SS08): 1–18. Division of Violence Prevention, National Center for Injury Prevention and Control, Centers for Disease Control and Prevention. Available at http://www.cdc.gov/mmwr/preview/mmwrhtml/ ss6308a1.htm (accessed 17 May 2016).

Byset J (2014) The end of rape culture. *A Voice for Men*, 18 March. Available at http://www.avoiceformen.com/?s=The+end+of+Rape+Culture (accessed 5 January 2016).

Chunn DE, Boyd SB and Lessard H (2007) Feminism, law and social change: An overview. In Chunn DE, Boyd SB and Lessard H (eds) *Feminism, Law and Social Change: (Re)action and Resistance*: 1–28. Vancouver: University of British Columbia Press.

Collier R and Sheldon S (2006) Father's rights, fatherhood and law reform: International perspectives. In Collier R and Sheldon S (eds). *Fathers' Rights Activism and Law Reform in Comparative Perspective*: 1–26. Portland, Oregon: Hart Publishing.

Davidson D (2013) Cunning stunts of history: Mary Koss and rape culture. *A Voice for Men*, 9 November. Available at http://www.avoiceformen.com/feminism/cunning-stunts-of-history-mary-koss-and-rape-culture/ (accessed 5 January 2016).

Dragiewicz M (2000) Women's voices, women's words: Reading acquaintance rape discourse. In Frye M and Hoagland SL (eds) *Feminist Interpretations of Mary Daly*: 194–221. University Park, Pennsylvania: Pennsylvania State University Press.

Dragiewicz M (2008) Patriarchy reasserted: Fathers' rights and anti-VAWA activism. *Feminist Criminology* 3(2): 121–144. DOI: 10.1177/1557085108316731.

Dragiewicz M (2011) *Equality with a Vengeance: Men's Rights Groups, Battered Women, and Antifeminist Backlash*. Boston, Massachusetts: Northeastern University Press.

Dunbar NE, Connelly S, Jensen ML, Adam BJ, Rozzell B, Griffith JA and O'Hair HD (2014) Fear appeals, message processing cues, and credibility in the websites of violent, ideological, and nonideological groups. *Journal of Computer Mediated Communication* 19(4): 871–874. DOI: 10.1111/jcc4.12083.

Elam P (2010) Challenging the etiology of rape. *A Voice for Men*, 14 November. Available at http://www.avoiceformen.com/mens-rights/false-rape-culture/challenging-the-etiology-of-rape/ (accessed 5 January 2016).

Elam P (2013) AVFM Monday hangout: Cry rape, the plague of false allegations. *A Voice for Men*, 9 December. Available at http://www.avoiceformen.com/hangouts/AVFM-monday-hangout-cry-rape-the-plague-of-false-allegations/ (accessed 5 January 2016).

Farrell W (2000) *The Myth of Male Power*. Berkley, California: Simon and Schuster.

Fiamengo J (2014) Why call it rape culture? *A Voice for Men*, 9 April. Available at http://www.avoiceformen.com/feminism/feminist-lies-feminism/why-call-it-rape-culture/ (accessed 5 January 2016).

Gavey N (2005) *Just Sex? The Cultural Scaffolding of Rape*. London, United Kingdom: Routledge.

Gotell L (2010) Canadian sexual assault law: Neoliberalism and the erosion of feminist-inspired law reform. In McGlynn C and Munro V (eds) *Rethinking Rape Law: International and Comparative Perspectives*: 209–223. Milton Park, United Kingdom: Routledge.

Gotell L (2015) Reassessing the place of criminal law reform in the struggle against sexual violence: A critique of the critique of carceral feminism. In Anastasia Powell, Nicola Henry and Asher Flynn (eds) *Rape Justice Beyond Criminal Law*: 53–71. London, United Kingdom: Palgrave Macmillan.

Honey Badger Radio (2014) Mary Koss and the American rape machine. *A Voice for Men*, 13 February. Available at http://www.avoiceformen.com/allbulletins/honey-badger-radio-mary-koss-and-the-american-rape-machine (accessed 5 January 2016)

Johnson H (2012) Limits of a criminal justice response. In Sheehy E (ed.) *Sexual Assault in Canada: Law, Legal Practice and Women's Activism*: 613–634. Ottawa: University of Ottawa Press.

Johnson H and Dawson M (2011) *Violence against Women in Canada*. Don Mills, Ontario: Oxford University Press.

Kay B (2014a) Rape culture and the delusions of the feminist mind. *National Post*, 28 February. Available at http://news.nationalpost.com/2014/02/28/barbara-kay-rape-culture-and-the-delusions-of-the-feminist-mind/ (accessed 5 January 2016).

Kay B (2014b) Rape culture fanatics don't know what a culture is. *A Voice for Men*, 10 March. Available at http://www.avoiceformen.com/mens-rights/false-rape-culture/rape-culture-fanatics-dont-know-what-a-culture-is/ (accessed 5 January 2016).

Kanin EJ (1994) False rape allegations. *Archives of Sexual Behavior* 23(1): 81–92.

Kingston A (2015) Thank you, Margaret Wente, for exposing rape culture. *MacLean's*, 14 January.

Available at http://www.macleans.ca/society/thank-you-margaret-wente-for-exposing-rape-culture/ (accessed 5 January 2016).

Kitchens C (2014) It's time to end rape culture hysteria. *Time Magazine*, 20 March. Available at http://time.com/30545/its-time-to-end-rape-culture-hysteria/ (accessed 5 January 2016).

Kohn S (2015) Rape culture? It's too real. *CNN*, 24 March. Available at http://www.cnn.com/2015/03/24/opinions/kohn-rape-happens1/ (accessed 5 January 2016).

Koss MP, Gidycz CA and Wisniewski N (1987) The incidence and prevalence of sexual aggression in a national sample of higher education students. *Journal of Consulting and Clinical Psychology* 55(2): 162–170.

Levental Y (2014) An inquiry into the CDC's 1 in 5 rape figure. *A Voice for Men*, September 23. Available at http://www.avoiceformen.com/mens-rights/false-rape-culture/an-inquiry-into-the-cdcs-1-in-5-rape-figure/ (accessed 5 January 2016).

Lisak D, Gardinier L, Nicksa S and Cote AM (2010) False allegations of sexual assault: An analysis of ten years of reported cases. *Violence Against Women* 16(12): 1318–1334. DOI: 10.1177/1077801210387747.

MacDonald H (2014) This Obama administration's deserving victims. *National Review*, 8 May. Available http://www.nationalreview.com/article/377492/obama-administrations-deserving-victims-heather-mac-donald (accessed 5 January 2016).

Matchar E (2014) Men's rights activists are trying to redefine the meaning of rape. *The New Republic*, 26 February. Available at http://www.newrepublic.com/article/116768/latest-target-mens-rights-movement-definition-rape (accessed 5 January 2016).

McRobbie A (2008) *The Aftermath of Feminism*. London, United Kingdom: Sage.

Men's Rights Edmonton (MRE) (2013a) *Lise Gotell, Bigot Extrodunaire* [sic], 29 September. Available at http://www.mensrightsedmonton.com/lise-gotell-bigot-extrodunaire (accessed 5 January 2016).

Menzies R (2007) Virtual backlash: Representations of men's "rights" and feminist "wrongs" in cyberspace. In Chunn DE, Boyd SB and Lessard H (eds)

Feminism, Law and Social Change: (Re)action and Resistance: 65–97. Vancouver: University of British Columbia Press.

Paglia C (1992) *Sex, Art and American Culture*. New York: Random House.

Roe T (2014) NISVS released: Increased male violence and rape is still not rape. *A Voice for Men*, 14 September. Available at http://www.avoiceformen.com/misandry/nisvs-2011-released-increased-male-victimization-and-rape-is-still-not-rape (accessed 5 January 2016).

Roiphe K (1994) *The Morning After: Sex, Fear, and Feminism*. Boston, Massachusetts: Little Brown.

Snyder RC (2008) What is third-wave feminism? A new directions essay. *Signs: A Journal of Women and Culture* 34(1): 175–196. DOI: 10.1086/588436.

Statistics Canada (2013) *Measuring Violence Against Women: Statistical Trends* (Ottawa: Canadian Centre for Justice Statistics). Available at http://www.statcan.gc.ca/pub/85-002-x/2013001/article/11766-eng.htm (accessed 5 January 2016).

Straughan K (2013) Don't be that lying feminist. *Men's Rights Edmonton*, 15 July. Available at http://www.mensrightsedmonton.com/dont-be-that-lying-feminist-girl-writes-what (accessed 5 January 2016).

Tempkin J and Krahe B (2008) *Sexual Assault and the Justice Gap: A Question of Attitude*. Portland, Oregon: Hart Publishing.

Venton-Rublee J (2014) What is rape culture? Here is one example. *Globe and Mail*, 14 March. Available at http://www.theglobeandmail.com/news/national/education/whats-rape-culture-calling-it-as-it-is/article17463232 (accessed 5 January 2016).

Wallen H (2013) Feminists define rape to exclude male victims. *A Voice for Men*, 18 July. Available at http://www.avoiceformen.com/?s=%22feminists+Define+Rape+to+Exclude%22 (accessed 5 January 2016).

Wente M (2013) When booze culture and rape culture meet. *Globe and Mail*, 22 October. Available at http://www.theglobeandmail.com/globe-debate/rape-culture-and-booze-culture/article14968433 (accessed 5 January 2016).

Politics
of Masculinities

All of a sudden, it seems, masculinity has become "political"—both as men mobilize as men around political issues and as masculinities are directly implicated in some of the day's most pressing political issues. For example, Michael S. Kimmel describes the "aggrieved entitlement" among so many white men in America—a sense of righteous anger that propelled Donald Trump all the way to the White House. James W. Messerschmidt and Tristan Bridges look at Trump's masculinity itself in light of gender politics, while Tanya Golash-Boza and Pierrette Hondagneu-Sotelo note the consequences of these angry gendered politics on Latino men facing deportation.

Finally, Michael A. Messner looks at the way men have been mobilizing politically, examining the contrast between anti-feminist men's rights activists and men who support gender equality.

PART X DISCUSSION QUESTIONS

1. Kimmel argues that rage is manufactured by radio hosts to channel men's anger and generate listener loyalty. Where else in public discourse is this strategy evident? Why is this strategy less effective at generating support from women?

2. According to Golash-Boza and Hondagneu-Sotelo, how are gendered subjectivities (that are simultaneously raced and classed) shaped by macroeconomic forces? How do shifting perceptions of Latino men also change ideas about white men?

3. How do fluid masculinities flow from and reinforce patriarchal power? Can all men practice fluid masculinities? Why or why not?

Manufacturing Rage

The Cultural Construction of Aggrieved Entitlement

MICHAEL S. KIMMEL

"Tom," from Wichita, Kansas, has been waiting on hold, he tells us, for two hours and twenty minutes. An army veteran, he lost his job earlier this year. For months, he's been looking for work, sending out hundreds of résumés. A few interviews, no offers. What will happen to his family when his unemployment insurance runs out? "We're into the red zone," he explains. "We're cutting essentials: food, laundry, clothing, shoes." He's worried, he says, "scared to death." Repeatedly, he insists he is "not a whiner."

What he wants to know, he asks Rush Limbaugh on his nationally syndicated radio show, is what President Obama is doing to turn the economy around. Why was he spending all this energy on health care when people are out of work? What has the stimulus plan done to create jobs for people like him, with families to support? Fortunately, he says, his wife has a job that provides health care for the family. But if he doesn't find something soon, he's considering reenlisting. He lost his own father in Vietnam, he says, softly, and he's afraid that at forty-three, he might leave his own children fatherless. "My self-esteem is right now at its lowest that I've ever had it," Tom says. "I'm getting choked up."

"I know," replies Limbaugh empathetically. "I've been there." Limbaugh recounts his own history of unemployment. But then, he transforms Tom's experience. "I don't hear you as whining," says Rush. "I hear you as mad."

Wait a second. Did you hear Tom as mad? I'm no expert in auditory interpretation, but what I heard was anxiety, vulnerability, and more than just a slight tremor of fear. I heard someone asking for help. In a revealing analysis of Limbaugh's radio persona, antiviolence activist Jackson Katz carefully parses this particular exchange as emblematic—how the talk-show host transforms this plaintive emotional expression into something else. What starts as sadness, anxiety, grief, worry is carefully manipulated into political rage.[1]

Rush Limbaugh is a master at this translation of emotional vulnerability or insecurity into anger. All that he needs is that shared sense of aggrieved entitlement—that sense that "we," the rightful heirs of America's bounty, have had what is "rightfully ours" taken away from us by "them," faceless, feckless government bureaucrats, and given to "them," undeserving minorities, immigrants, women, gays, and their ilk. If your despair can be massaged into this Manichaean struggle between Us and Them, you, too, can be mobilized into the army of Angry White Men.

Limbaugh is one of hundreds of talk-show hosts on radio dials across the nation—indeed, the AM radio dial seems to have nothing but sports talk, Spanish-language stations, and vitriolic white men hosting radio shows. Talk radio is the most vibrant part of the radio dial—thirty-five hundred all-talk or all-news stations in the United States—up from about five hundred two decades ago.[2] According to the Pew Research Center for the People and the Press, while the majority of radio, newspaper, and magazine consumers are female (51 percent), Limbaugh (59 percent), Sean Hannity (57 percent), and Stephen Colbert (58 percent) skew most heavily toward men. (So, incidentally, does Rachel Maddow, at 52 percent.) Limbaugh's audiences skew slightly older, less educated (only 29 percent are college graduates, compared to 39 percent and 35 percent for liberals Colbert and Maddow, respectively). Their income tends to be squarely in the middle—30 percent make more than seventy-five thousand dollars, 37 percent between thirty and seventy-five thousand dollars, and 21 percent below thirty thousand dollars a year. Obviously, more than seven in ten identify as conservative.[3]

Visitors to Limbaugh's website tilt even more rightward. It's visited by 1.1 million people a month—more than 94 percent white and 85 percent male, most are between thirty-five and sixty-five, with the biggest bulge at forty-five to fifty-four. Most (54 percent) do not have kids. Two-thirds have incomes below one hundred thousand dollars a year, though two-thirds also have at least a college, if not a graduate, degree. (That's an index of downward mobility; their educational achievements haven't paid off in better jobs.)[4] This would make the typical Limbaugh fan (enough to view his website) a downwardly mobile white male, whose career never really panned out (college or grad school but only modest income) and whose family life didn't either (majority childless). That is a recipe for aggrieved entitlement. Everything was in place to partake of the American Dream, and it didn't quite work out. Just whose fault is that?

Sociologist Sarah Sobieraj and political scientist Jeffrey Berry call it "outrage media"—talk-radio, blog, and cable news designed "to provoke a visceral response from the audience, usually in the form of anger, fear, or moral righteousness through the use of overgeneralizations, sensationalism, misleading or patently inaccurate information, ad hominem attacks, and partial truths about opponents."[5] Sobieraj and Berry trace this development through the technological shifts from radio and TV to cable news, the blogosphere, and talk radio as the news vehicles of choices and to the incredible consolidation of media companies, so that only a handful of companies control virtually all of America's airwaves. (Women own about three of ten businesses in America but own only 6 percent of radio stations. Racial minorities own 18 percent of all businesses, but only 7.7 percent of radio stations. Clearly, white men are being squeezed out, right?)[6]

But it's also linked to the displacement of white men from every single position of power in the country. Talk radio is the last locker room, juiced not on steroids but on megahertz. It's the circled wagons keeping out the barbarian hordes, who may be just a millimeter away on that dial. It's the Alamo on AM frequency.

The rise of outrage media is coincident with the erosion of white male entitlement. Outrage media generally begins with Peter Finch in the film *Network* (1976), exhorting his audience to go to their windows and scream, "I'm mad as hell, and I'm not going to take it anymore!" Finch's impotent outburst provides a heroic riposte to a film about the steamroller of corporate takeovers, the ethically rudderless drive for ratings trumping all other criteria, including quality. Like the tabloid newspaper or local newscast—whose motto is "If it bleeds, it leads"—the motto of outrage radio is closer to "If he yells, it sells." . . .

You could hear that anger, the aggrieved entitlement, on election night 2012, as President Obama handily defeated Mitt Romney for president. Romney, the unfathomably wealthy corporate plutocrat, was unable to transform himself into a populist firebrand. Even though white men were the only demographic who went for Romney (although not decisively), it was too close in all those battleground states to offset the huge margins Obama racked up with African Americans, women, union workers, and Latinos.

The fact that white men are not a monolithic group—and that enough voted Democratic, especially in blue states—is, of course, an important empirical counterweight to the claims of many of the

Angry White Male choirmasters on talk radio and Fox News who say that they speak for all of "us."

But it hardly deters them. Do you recall the commentary on election night 2012? Rush Limbaugh said that he went to bed thinking "we'd lost the country." Bill O'Reilly quoted one of his listeners, mourning that "we have lost our American way of life." . . .

One has to feel a sense of proprietorship, of entitlement, to call it "our" country. That sense has led millions of Americans, male and female, white and nonwhite, to feel like stakeholders in the American system and motivated millions to lay down their lives for that way of life. It's prompted some of the most moving stories of sacrifice, the most heroic and touching moments of connectedness with neighbors and strangers during crises. But it has its costs. That sense of holding on to what's "ours" can be turned into something ugly, sowing division where unity should be. Just as religiosity can motivate the most self-sacrificing charity and loving devotion, it can also be expressed as sanctimonious self-righteousness, as if a privileged access to revealed truth grants permission to unspeakable cruelties.

It's not the depth of those collective feelings that is troubling—obviously, love of country can inspire us to great sacrifice; rather, it's their direction. When threatened, that sense of entitlement, of proprietorship, can be manipulated into an enraged protectionism, a sense that the threat to "us" is internal, those undeserving others who want to take for themselves what we have rightfully earned. "We" were willing to share, we might say, totally inverting the reality that "they" ask only for a seat at the table, not to overturn the table itself; "they" want it all for themselves. According to these angry white men, "they" not only want a seat, but now they got a guy sitting at the head of the table itself. . . .

Angry white men are genuinely floundering—confused and often demoralized, they experience that wide range of emotions. But their anger is often constructed from those emotional materials, given shape and directed at targets that serve other interests. Angry white men are angry, all right, but

their anger needs to be channeled toward some groups—and away from others.

Outrageous Radio

As an emotion, anger has a fairly short shelf life. It's a "hot" emotion, like sexual desire, not a cooler emotion like devotion to a loved one, or abiding love of country, or pride in one's child. Anger must be fed, its embers constantly stoked—either personally, by holding a grudge, or collectively, by having sustained the sense that you have been injured, wounded, and that those who did it must pay. Feeling like the wronged victim is a way to channel hurt into a self-fueling sense of outrage; a personal sense of injury becomes "politicized" as an illustration of a general theme.

The politicization of the countless injuries, hurts, and injustices is the job of the self-appointed pundits in the media. It is they who offer a political framework for the anguish that you might feel, suggest how it represents a larger pattern of victimization of "people like you," and then urge collective action to redress it. (The collective action can be simply tuning in to the same radio show every day, knowing that you are among friends and allies.)

As a result, Angry White Men are a *virtual* social movement. I don't mean that they are "virtually" a movement—as in "almost, but not quite." I mean that they organize virtually, that their social-movement organization is a virtual organization. They sit alone, listening to the radio, listening to Rush Limbaugh and Mike Savage and Sean Hannity. They meet online, in chat rooms and on websites, whether promoting antifeminist men's rights or the re-Aryanization of America. They troll cyberspace, the anti-PC police, ready to attack any blogger, columnist, or quasi liberal who dares to say something with which they disagree.

It is the task of the Angry White Male pundits in the media to act as the choirmasters of the Angry White Male chorus, to direct and redirect that rage, to orchestrate it so that the disparate howls of despair or anguish, the whimpers of pain, or the mumblings of confusion can sound unified. They are the conductors; they believe that we are their instruments. It's their job to take the anger that might, in fact, be quite legitimate and direct it elsewhere, onto other targets.

Say, for example, you are an autoworker, and you've seen your wages cut, your benefits dismantled, and your control over your hours steadily compromised. You may well be a bit miffed. But at whom? Left to your own devices—and conversations with your friends—you might conclude that it is the fault of rapacious corporate moguls, who line their pockets and pay themselves fat bonuses and who squeeze every drop they can from America's working man. You might even list to the Left and make common cause with others in similar situations and try to get the government to regulate the industry, raise wages, protect benefits, and institute national health care. You might even work with your union.

So, if I were to try to channel Rush Limbaugh or Mike Savage, my task would be to redirect that anger onto others, those even less fortunate than you. Perhaps the reason you are so unhappy is because of all those immigrants who are streaming into America, driving the costs of labor lower and threatening "American" jobs. Or perhaps it's because women— even, perhaps, your own wife—want to enter the labor force, and that's what is driving down labor costs, as corporations no longer need to pay men a "family" wage, since they no longer support a family. Your grievances are not with the corporations, but with those just *below* you. In other words, as Thomas Frank points out in *What's the Matter with Kansas?*, it's the task of the pundits to create "a French Revolution in reverse—one in which the sans-culottes pour down the streets demanding more power for the aristocracy."[7]

Limbaugh and Savage are only two of the hundreds of angry white men who have staked out an angry white male club on radio waves. I'll focus on them briefly here not because they are any worse than any of the others, but rather because they are so similar—in that masculinity is so central in their radio ratings. They're among the most popular: *The Savage Nation* is heard on 350 radio stations and reaches 8.25 million listeners each week,

ranking third behind only Rush Limbaugh and Sean Hannity. Limbaugh outpaces everyone else, heard on more than 600 stations, with a weekly audience of more than 20 million.[8] . . .

Angry White Men exhibit what French social theorist Georges Sorel called "ressentiment"—a personal sense of self that is defined always in relationship to some perceived injury and whose collective politics mixes hatred and envy of those who we believe have injured us. That "creative hatred," Sorel argues, is anathema to serious collective action because it is so easily manipulated; it is more likely to spawn sporadic spasmodic violent eruptions than a serious social movement.

This sense of self, grounded in victimhood, both hating and envying others, can be a brilliant strategy, generating an audience of consumers. And it's not only these angry white men. Indeed, Oprah Winfrey's early television success involved constructing her audience as victims. In the early 1990s, I entered a discussion to appear on her show following the publication of my book *Men Confront Pornography*. When I spoke to the producer, she suggested that I appear alongside several women whose "husbands or boyfriends had forced them to do degrading sexual things after they'd seen them in pornography." I said no, that my book was a serious effort to invite men to take on the political debate that was, at the time, roiling feminism. I proposed being on with a few men who took the issues seriously. We went back and forth, up the ladder of increasingly senior producers. Finally, the very seniormost producer of the show, the one who talks directly with Oprah, admitted she didn't understand how my idea would work or what was wrong with her idea. "I just don't see it," she said. "I don't see who the victim is. You can't have an Oprah show without a victim." . . .

Oprah's shows in her last years on the air were more inspirational—not necessarily a parade of victims, but more about people who had triumphed over adversity, who had fallen down seven times and gotten up eight. But the theme of viewers and victims resonates more now on talk radio. It's but a short hop from dichotomous viewers and victims to a more unified community of viewers as victims. The genius of Rush Limbaugh and the others is that they have appropriated a more commonly "feminine" trope of perpetual victimhood and successfully masculinized it. In fact, they claim, it's your very manhood that is constantly under threat! . . .

He defends white people against what Lothrop Stoddard and Madison Grant, early-twentieth-century racialists, called "the rising tide of color." Limbaugh's racism is as transparent as his nativism and sexism. Here's what he said after Obama was elected the first time: "It's Obama's America, is it not? Obama's America, white kids getting beat up on school buses now. You put your kids on a school bus, you expect safety, but in Obama's America, the white kids now get beat up with the black kids cheering, 'Yeah, right on, right on, right on,' and, of course, everybody says the white kid deserved it: he was born a racist; he's white."[9] . . .

Poor white people, the victims of government-sponsored racial discrimination. And poor men, victims of reverse sexism as well. For example, when Sandra Fluke, a graduate student at Georgetown, testified in support of requiring all institutions receiving federal funds to actually obey the law and provide contraception, Limbaugh launched into a vicious *ad feminam* attack against Fluke personally, calling her a slut and a whore for having so much sex, and demanded, as a taxpayer, that she provide high-quality videos of her sexual escapades. "If we are going to pay for your contraceptives and thus pay for you to have sex, we want something. We want you to post the videos online so we can all watch."

It's easy to understand the sense of entitlement that this sixth-generation upper-class heir to a Missouri family of lawyers and politicians might feel. And it's not so very hard to understand how so many of his white male listeners might identify with him, even if they're more recent arrivals, and they've always held jobs for which you shower after work, not before it.

What binds this bilious martinet to his listeners, though, is that they are men, at least the overwhelming majority of them, and their sense of entitlement comes from their deep-seated feeling

that they are the heirs to the American Dream that, as Woody Guthrie should have sung, this land was really made for them. Note that he assumes that his listeners are male—that "we" are entitled to see videos of Sandra Fluke or that it's a little white boy who is being harassed. "We" is white and male. Indeed, a cover story in *Newsweek* on talk radio called it "group therapy for mostly white males who feel politically challenged."[10]

Rarely, though, have commentators gone much further than noticing how these shows resonate with white men. . . . Nor do they see Limbaugh's rage as a particularly masculine rage, the "gender" of the pain he claims to channel into outrage. . . . In Limbaugh's case, right-wing racist and sexist politics is the conduit for the restoration of his manhood—and for the manhood of other fellow sufferers of aggrieved entitlement. Limbaugh offers a prescription for political Viagra, designed to get that blood flowing, reenergize a flagging sense of white American manhood.

But if the elite-born Limbaugh plays in the populist sandbox, Mike Savage is both the real deal and even more a poseur. . . .

Limbaugh is positively tame compared to Savage, who seems to believe that the higher the decibels of his denunciations, the more persuasive they will be. And like Limbaugh, he's interested in reversing the very multicultural trends that he represents. Like Limbaugh, he's immensely popular, and like Limbaugh, he engages in a conspiratorial Us-Them framing, in which "we" are the enlightened few and "they" are the dupes of the government-inspired hijacking of freedom. . . .

But ultimately, it all has to do with masculinity. Savage alternates between Limbaugh's conspiratorial outrage—can you believe what they are doing to us?—and chastising his audience for allowing this all to happen under their very noses. . . . Part of "the de-balling of America," "true red-blooded American types have been thrown out of the—out of the government."[11]

Part of this is women's fault, of course—feminist women who have become more masculine. Here's what he said on his show: "Particularly today, the women are not, you know, what they were thirty years ago. The women have become more like guys, thanks to the hags in the women's movement, and the white race is dying. . . . [T]hey've been encouraged to think like men, act like men, be like men. Consequently, they don't want to be women, and they don't want to be mothers."[12]

Were you to ask Limbaugh and Savage, and the others who aspire to their seats of influence, they'd likely tell you that they aren't really antiwomen but antifeminist. . . . Feminism comes under attack— after all, it was Limbaugh who popularized the term *feminazi*—phantasmagorically linking campaigns for wage equality, or safety from battery and rape, to the organized, methodical genocide in the Third Reich.

Now, why has this resonated? Because the defensiveness of white men is so narcissistic that any criticism of masculinity and male entitlement is seen as the effort to leverage the apparatus of the state in the service of the destruction of an entire biological sex. But these guys aren't really interested in women. They're interested in promoting the interests of white men.

In a particularly revealing rant, Savage links racism, sexism, and anti-immigrant nativism in his pitch to fellow angry white men:

Many of you have been hoodwinked into believing that we are a multicultural nation, which we are not. We're a nation of many races and many cultures, that is true, it has been true from the beginning, but in the past people would come over and become Americans. Now they come over, and they want you to become them. . . . We're going to have a revolution in this country if this keeps up. These people are pushing the wrong people around. . . . If they keep pushing us around and if we keep having these schmucks running for office, catering to the multicultural people who are destroying the culture in this country, guaranteed the people, the white male in particular . . . the one without connections, the one without money, has nothing to lose, and you haven't seen him yet. You haven't seen him explode in this country. And he's still the majority, by the way, in case you don't know it. He

is still the majority, and no one speaks for him, everyone craps on him . . . and he has no voice whatsoever. . . . And you're going to find out that if you keep pushing this country around, you'll find out that there's an ugly side to the white male.[13]

Outrage media is not, however, a one-way street. The audience is an active participant; together with the host, they produce the rage of the day and direct it toward the issues on which the free-floating rage will land. Each day offers no shortage of the horrors of what "they" are doing to "us"—"they" being government bureaucrats in thrall to the feminist cabal, implementing the gay agenda, illegals, and minorities guided by sinister Marxian forces. (They often come perilously close to denouncing their Zionist puppeteers of the International Jewish Conspiracy. Indeed, were it not for the convenience of stoking anti-Muslim sentiment since 9/11, we'd hear quite a bit more anti-Semitism from some of these hosts. Generally, the right wing loves Israel, but hates Jews.)

Angry White Male Radio is the New England town meeting of the twenty-first century. The participatory experience, with its steady stream of callers, ups the emotional ante. . . . Rush's followers call themselves "dittoheads," echoing every sentiment. "What Rush does on his shows is take frustration and rage and rearticulate and confirm them as ideology," writes Sherri Paris, after listening nonstop for several weeks. "Limbaugh's skill lies in weaving political alienation and anger into the illusion of common political ground." . . .

"I love it," says Jay, a twenty-six-year-old Nebraskan with obvious self-consciousness. . . . "I mean, all day long, all I get is multicultural this and diversity that. I love it because I can let off steam at how stupid the whole thing is. I can't stop it—there's no way. But I get all these other guys who remind me that it's not right, it's not fair, and the system's out of control. And I'm the one getting screwed!" . . .

You'd think that after nearly a half century of sustained critique of racial and gender bias in the media, of the most convincing empirical social and behavioral science research imaginable, of civil rights, women's, and gay and lesbian movements, white guys would have finally understood how bias works and would have accommodated themselves to a new, more egalitarian, more democratic, and more representative media. Or at least you'd think they'd be less vocal in their resistance. But as far as they're concerned, the world hasn't merely changed—it's been upended, turned upside down into its perverse mirror image. "It's completely crazy," says Matt. "The inmates are running the asylum. They're completely in power, and they get anything they want. And us regular, normal white guys—we're like nothing. We don't count for shit anymore."

Outrage media offers a case of what Frankfurt School philosopher Herbert Marcuse called "repressive desublimation." Although not exactly the catchiest of phrase makers, Marcuse was on to something that, as a refugee from Hitler's Germany, he found so scary: how the ability to sound off angrily, to express all your pent-up rage (the "desublimation" part), could actually serve the interests of those in power. Being able to rebel in these impotent ways actually enables the system to continue (hence, the "repressive" part). You think you're rebelling by listening to jazz, or punk rock, or even angry rap music, having a lot of sex, drinking and screaming your heads off about how the system is oppressing you. You find common cause with others who are doing the same thing: instant community. And, after desublimating, you go back to work, a docile, sated drone, willing to conform to what the "system" asks of you because the system also lets you blow off steam. . . .

Yet, ironically, the very medium that provides the false sense of community of Limbaugh's dittoheads can also be, simultaneously, isolating. "People tend to be less angry when they have to interact with each other," writes journalist and media commentator Joe Klein; they become afflicted with "Information Age disorder"—the "product of our tendency to stew alone, staring into computer screens at work, blobbing in front of the television at home." Perhaps we're not bowling alone, but fuming alone. Together.[14]

So American white men, still among the most privileged group of people on the face of the earth—if you discount hereditary aristocracies and sheikdoms—feel that they are the put-upon victims of a society that grows more equal every day. It's hard if you've been used to 100 percent of all the positions of power and privilege in the world to wake up one morning and find people like you in only 80 percent of those positions. Equality sucks if you've grown so accustomed to inequality that it feels normal.

Listen to the words of one leader, defending the rights of those disempowered white men: "Heaven help the God-fearing, law-abiding Caucasian middle class, Protestant or even worse evangelical Christian, Midwest or Southern or even worse rural, apparently straight or even worse admittedly [heterosexual], gun-owning or even worse NRA card-carrying average working stiff, or even worst of all, male working stiff. Because not only don't you count, you're a downright obstacle to social progress."[15] That leader was, incidentally, Charlton Heston, acting less like Moses and more like an angry Pharaoh, feeling powerless as he watches his slaves disappear.

These are not the voices of power but the voices of *entitlement* to power. The positions of authority, of power, have been stolen from them—handed over to undeserving "others" by a government bureaucracy that has utterly abandoned them. If listening to Guy Radio and watching Guy TV is about blowing off steam, this is what that steam smells like.

Far from fomenting a reactionary revolution, Limbaugh and his ilk are the Peter Finches of the twenty-first century, screaming about how they are mad as hell and not going to take it anymore—which is the very thing that enables them to take far more of it. . . .

Notes

1. Jackson Katz, "Rush Limbaugh and the Mobilization of White Male Anger in the Health Care Debate," *Huffington Post*, September 8, 2009, www.huffingtonpost.com/jackson-katz/rush-limbaugh-and-the-mob_b_279696.html.
2. Jeffrey Berry and Sarah Sobeiraj, "Understanding the Rise of Talk Radio," *PS: Political Science and Politics* 44, no. 4 (2011): 762.

3. Pew Research Center for the People and the Press, "In Changing News Landscape, Even Television Is Vulnerable," September 27, 2012, www.people-press.org/2012/09/27.

4. www.quantcast.com/rushlimbaugh.com#!demo.

5. Sarah Sobeiraj and Jeffrey Berry, "From Incivility to Outrage: Political Discourse in Blogs, Talk Radio, and Cable News," *Political Communication* 28 (2011): 19.

6. S. Derek Tucker, "Off the Dial: Female and Minority Radio Station Ownership in the United States," www.stopbigmedia.com/files/off_the_dial.pdf.

7. Thomas Frank, *What's the Matter with Kansas?* (New York: Henry Holt, 2005), 8.

8. www.washingtonpost.com/wp-dyn/content/article/2009/03/06/AR2009030603435.html.

9. http://mediamatters.org/mmtv/200909150017.

10. Sharri Paris, "In Bed with Rush Limbaugh," *Tikkun* 10, no. 2 (1995): 33.

11. Both quoted in Stephen J. Ducat, *The Wimp Factor* (Boston: Beacon Press, 2004), 45, 159.

12. *The Savage Nation*, August 4, 2009, my transcription from the recording.

13. *The Savage Nation*, August 20, 2009, http://mediamatters.org./mmtv/200908210049.

14. Joe Klein, "Stalking the Radical Middle," *Newsweek*, September 25, 1995, 32–36.

15. Citizens Project, 1998–1999, 3.

Forks in the Road of Men's Gender Politics

Men's Rights vs Feminist Allies

MICHAEL A. MESSNER

Introduction

For more than a century, men have responded to feminist movements in the US and in other western jurisdictions in varying ways, ranging from outright hostility, to sarcastic ridicule, to indifference, to grudging sympathy, to enthusiastic support (Kimmel 1987; Messner 1997). In this article I argue that large-scale social changes—those shaped by social movements, changing cultural beliefs, and shifts in political economy—create moments of historical gender formation that in turn shape, constrain and enable certain forms of men's gender politics. In particular, I trace the two most politically engaged tails of a continuum of gender politics—anti-feminist men's rights groups and pro-feminist men allies—with an eye to understanding how moments of historical gender formation shape men's gender politics. First, I draw from an earlier study that outlined the context that gave rise to opposing US men's movements in the 1970s and 1980s (Messner 1997), reiterating parts of that analysis that are relevant to thinking about the concurrent and mutually antagonistic rise of men's anti-feminism and men's pro-feminism. Second, I draw from a recent study of men anti-rape and anti-domestic violence activists in the US, to illuminate men's current engagements with feminism and gender politics (Messner, Greenberg and Peretz 2015).

The 1970s and the present moment generated possibilities for men's gender politics: forks in the road, as it were. The image of historical forks in the road implies choices for men's responses to feminism, but not an unlimited range of "free" choices. Rather, feminist challenges and shifts in the gender order confront men with a limited field of structured options: stop dead in your tracks, befuddled; attempt a U-turn and retreat toward an idealized past of male entitlement; turn right and join a backlash against feminism; or bend left and actively support feminism. Adapted from Omi and Winant's (1986) theory of racial formation, I introduce *historical gender formation*, a concept that provides a more nuanced view of the dynamics of gender politics than the dualistic image of a fork in the road. Central to the theory of racial formation is the idea that the grassroots racial justice movements of the 1950s through the 1970s wrested concessions from the state, altered the ways in which racial categories were defined, and created new foundations upon which subsequent racial tensions and politics arose. Similarly, the women's movements of the 1960s and 1970s wrested concessions from the state, challenged and partially transformed cultural values about sex and gender, and succeeded in bringing about substantial reforms in various social institutions. Thus, men's engagements with gender politics today take place in a very different context—one

Michael A Messner, "Forks in the Road of Men's Gender Politics: Men's Rights vs Feminist Allies," *International Journal for Crime, Justice and Social Democracy*, 5(2): 6–20. Copyright 2016 by the author. Reprinted by permission of the author.

partly transformed by feminism—than they did in the 1970s. I will demonstrate that the 1970s and the present are two moments of gender formation that create different limits and possibilities for men's engagements, both for and against feminism.

1970s Gender Formation: The Women's Movement and Men's Liberation

By the early 1970's, following several years of organizing, the women's liberation movement had exploded onto the social scene. In the United States, the most visible feminist activism took place "in the streets": small local consciousness-raising groups, grassroots groups linked by word-of-mouth and hand-printed newsletters, a sprouting of local rape-crisis centers and women's shelters run by volunteers in private homes or low-rent storefronts, all punctuated by mass public demonstrations for women's rights (Allen 1970; Stansell 2010). In other words, in relation to male-dominated institutions like the state, the economy, military, religion or medicine, feminism in the US was mostly on the outside looking in (with academia, where feminists gained an earlier foothold, a partial exception). The 1970s, then, was a time of deeply entrenched gender inequality across all institutions, against which a grassroots women's movement was organizing on many fronts, characteristically in alliance with gay rights and other social justice movements.

By the early 1970s a few US men—many of them veterans of the new left, anti-war and student movements—responded to the re-emergence of feminism in the 1960s by organizing men's consciousness-raising groups and networks, and asking a potentially subversive question: what does feminism have to do with us (Men's Consciousness-Raising Group 1971)? Some leaders promoted the idea of a "men's liberation movement" that would work symmetrically with the women's liberation movement to bring about progressive personal and social change (Farrell 1974; Nichols 1975). They reasoned that a men's liberation program that emphasized potential gains *for*

men might draw more interest than one that positioned men as oppressors whose only morally correct action was guilty self-flagellation. The language of sex roles, emerging at that time as the dominant discourse of liberal feminism—just one of multiple feminist positions that emerged in the wake of the 1960s rebirth of feminism—was an ideal means through which to package feminism for men in a way that lessened the guilt and maximized the potential gain that men might expect from "liberation" (Messner 1998). The "female sex role" had clearly oppressed women, men's liberationists argued, and "the male sex role" also harmed men. . . .

It did not take long before serious slippage began to occur with men's liberationists' attempts to navigate the tension between emphasizing men's privileges and the costs of masculinity. Less politically progressive leaders began to assert a false symmetry, viewing men and women as differently but equally oppressed by sex roles (Farrell 1974; Goldberg 1976). This assertion generated critical distrust from politically radical women, and vigorous debate from more politically radical men in the movement. By the mid-to-late 1970's, men's liberation had split directly along this fissure. On the one hand, men's rights organizations stressed the costs of narrow conceptions of masculinity to men, and either downplayed or angrily disputed feminist claims that patriarchy benefited men at women's expense. On the other hand, a profeminist (sometimes called "anti-sexist") men's movement emphasized the primary importance of joining with women to do away with men's institutionalized privileges. Patriarchy may *dehumanize* men, profeminists continued to insist, but the costs that men pay for adherence to narrow conceptions of masculinity are linked to the promise of patriarchal power and privilege.

In short, men's liberation had premised itself upon a liberal language of symmetrical sex roles, which contributed both to its promise as a movement and to its eventual demise. Following the fissuring of men's liberation, the men's rights movement continued to deploy a narrowly conservative language of sex roles. Now severed from its progressive roots, a more reactionary tendency within the men's rights movement unleashed overtly anti-feminist and sometimes outright misogynist discourse and actions (Baumli 1985). Meanwhile, the emergent profeminist men's movement largely rejected the language of sex roles, adopting instead a radical language of gender relations that facilitated an activist focus on ending men's institutional privileges and men's violence against women (Messner 1997, 1998).

By the mid-1970s the women's movement had altered the political context in ways that made a men's rights movement possible, if not inevitable. The men's rights movement was not simply a kneejerk backlash against feminism; it was a movement that co-opted the liberal feminist language of symmetrical sex roles and then turned this language back on itself. Men's liberationist-turned men's rights advocate Warren Farrell (1974), for instance, borrowed Betty Friedan's (1963) idea that a "feminine mystique" oppressed women, arguing that men were trapped in a "masculine mystique" that narrowly positioned them as breadwinners and protectors. In response to feminist criticisms of the effects on women of being constructed as "sex objects," Farrell posited an equally negative effect on men in being constructed as "success objects." Herb Goldberg's 1976 book *The Hazards of Being Male* asserted that male privilege is a "myth." Men actually have it worse than women, Goldberg argued, due to the fact that the male role is far more rigid than the female role, and because women have created a movement through which they can now transcend the limits of culturally-imposed femininity. Men's rights organizations broke from the men's liberation movement's gender symmetry and began to articulate a distinct discourse of overt and angry anti-feminist backlash. By the late 1970's and early 1980's, men's rights advocates were claiming that men are the true victims of prostitution, pornography, dating rituals, sexist media conventions, divorce settlements, false rape accusations, sexual harassment, and domestic violence (Baumli 1985). And in subsequent decades, the beating heart of the men's rights movement has been organizations that focus—largely through the Internet—on fighting

for fathers' rights, especially in legal cases involving divorce and child custody (Dragiewicz 2008; Menzies 2007).

Shifting Gender Formations

In the 1980s and into the 1990s the radical power of feminism fractured under a broadside of anti-feminist backlash (Faludi 1991), and fragmented internally from corrosive disputes among feminists around issues of race and class inequalities, and divisive schisms that centered on sex work and pornography (Echols 2002). Some key political efforts by US feminists such as the Equal Rights Amendment (ERA) had failed, and feminism was less visible as a mass movement. However in 1989 sociologist Verta Taylor argued that the US feminist movement had not disappeared; rather, this was a time of "movement abeyance," when activists in submerged networks continued to fight for equality, sustaining below-the-radar efforts that created the possibility for future political mobilizations. At the same time, in Canada, Australia and other jurisdictions where women's policy machineries were established, feminist networking and activism went "mainstream," as did states' commitment to gender mainstreaming globally (see Bacchi and Eveline 2003; Franzway, Court and Connell 1989).

But there was something more happening in the 1980s and 1990s US gender politics than "movement abeyance." Feminist momentum from the 1970s and networks of feminist activists combined with three substantial and interrelated social changes: the institutionalization and professionalization of feminism; the emergence of a widespread postfeminist cultural sensibility; and shifts in the political economy, including deindustrialization and the rise of a neoliberal state that slashes taxes for corporations and the rich, cuts public welfare and education, and celebrates individualism and the primacy of the market. These three changes created the current moment of gender formation that makes possible a range of men's engagements with gender politics, including men's rights organizing and profeminist men's activism that take substantially different forms than they did in the 1970s.

Professionally Institutionalized Feminism

The mass feminist movement was in decline in the 1980s and 1990s United States, but this was also a time of successful and highly visible feminist institutional reform, including the building of large feminist advocacy organizations like the National Organization for Women (NOW) and the National Abortion Rights Action League (NARAL), the institutionalization of women's and gender studies in universities, and the stabilization of myriad community and campus-based rape crisis and domestic violence centers (Martin 1990). Thus, as was occurring in Canada, Australia and elsewhere, feminists reformed police practices and legal responses to rape and domestic violence; workplaces incorporated sexual harassment trainings; and schools revised sexist curricula and expanded opportunities for girls' sports. These reforms were accompanied by the creation and expansion of professional sub-fields and occupational niches that focused on women's issues in social work, law and psychology. . . .

US feminists also managed to wrest significant concessions from the state, including the 1974 passage of Title IX (federal law related to gender equity in schools), and the 1994 *Violence Against Women Act*, which altered the landscape for feminist work against gender-based violence. Even given the fact that state support for women's issues in the US remained minimal, Kristen Bumiller (2013) argues that such "feminist collaboration with the state" threatens to water down, or even sever, the language and grassroots politics of feminism. Moreover, with the continuing decline of the welfare state and the concomitant expansion of neoliberalism, what Ruth Gilmore (2007) calls "the non-profit industrial complex" emerged as a sort of "shadow state" (Wolch 1990), funded by an exploding number of foundations, and advancing professionalized public health-oriented approaches to issues like violence against women.

The rise of professionally institutionalized feminism, in short, broadened and stabilized the field of feminist action, while simultaneously thinning its political depth, threatening even to make feminist language and analysis disappear altogether: university women's studies programs become "gender studies programs"; "violence against women" morphs to "gender-based violence"; and feminist organizations created by and for women become mixed-gender organizations whose historical roots are easily forgotten in the crush of day-to-day struggles to measure and document the effectiveness of service provisions, needed to win continued funding from foundations or the state (Messner, Greenberg and Peretz 2015). Professionally institutionalized feminism was also accompanied by a widespread shift in cultural values about gender: namely, the emergence of a postfeminist sensibility.

Postfeminism

As movement feminism receded from public view in the 1990s, a new and controversial "postfeminist" discourse emerged. Feminist scholars have explored and debated the claim that a whole generation of younger people express a postfeminist worldview. On the one side, drawing from public opinion data, sociologists Hall and Rodriguez (2003) found little support for claims of widespread adherence to postfeminism, which they defined as including antifeminist beliefs. But on the other side most scholars have drawn a distinction between postfeminism and opposition to feminism. Postfeminist narratives normally include an appreciation for feminist accomplishments, coupled with a belief that the work of feminism is in the past, and thus that feminist collective action is no longer necessary (Butler 2013). Sociologist Jo Reger (2012) argues that younger women and men for the most part agree with feminist positions on equal opportunities for women and men, but tend to experience feminism as both "everywhere and nowhere." The "everywhere" refers both to feminism's professional institutionalization and to the ways that liberal feminist values have permeated popular culture in much the same way that fluoride invisibly permeates public drinking water (in fact, Reger (2012) refers to today's youth as "generation fluoride"). However, feminism today is also experienced as "nowhere": young people do not see an in-the-streets mass feminist movement, nor do they see any reason for one. The continuing work of professional feminism is, to most young people, as invisible as the cavity-prevention work of fluoride in our public waters. . . .

This feminist optimism, however, faces an uphill struggle against the regressive tendencies built into a postfeminist sensibility that is coterminous with a larger political shift to neoliberal celebrations of individual market consumption choices as drivers for progress. And postfeminism is perfectly consistent with—indeed is shaped by and helps to naturalize—the eclipse of feminist language and politics within the professionalized non-profit industrial complex. Postfeminism also works in tandem with shifts in the political economy, including the nearly four-decade-long trend of deindustrialization that accompanied the ascendance of neoliberalism and that has disproportionately rendered poor and blue-collar young men redundant, a shift eventually referred to by some as "the decline of men."

Deindustrialization and "The Decline of Men"

. . . The economic restructuring that accelerated from the 1980s and 1990s had multiple and devastating effects; however, for my purposes here, I want to focus on how the neoliberalization of the economy was especially devastating for families headed by blue collar male wage earners. As women flowed into the labor market by the millions—as much out of necessity as for reasons sparked by ideals of feminist empowerment—the more educated ones poured into a growing field of professional occupations, while the greater mass of women filled an expanding array of low-paid pink collar and service sector jobs (Charles and Grusky 2004). While professional class men continued to fare reasonably well in this economic restructuring, blue collar and poor men—disproportionately men of color—faced an increasingly bleak field of economic opportunity (Wilson 1996). . . .

Men and Gender Politics Today

The three trends I have outlined—professionally institutionalized feminism, the emergent culture of postfeminism, and a post-industrial political economy characterized by deindustrialization and neoliberal state policies—together help to constitute the present moment of gender formation. Next, I will sketch how these three trends together make possible particular forms of men's antifeminist and profeminist actions.

Possibilities for Antifeminist Men's Rights Activism

By the 2000s, shifts in the political economy, combined with the increased visibility of women in higher education, popular culture and politics, and the growing public awareness of the institutionalization of women's rights, sparked journalistic and political hand-wringing about a supposed "war against boys" in public schools and a widespread "decline of males" in the public sphere (Sommers 2001; Tiger 2000). These escalating public concerns about boys and men created fertile ground for a resurgent men's rights movement.

But it is unlikely that we will see a widely popular or even marginally successful frontal attack on feminism from men's rights groups. This is in part because the same postfeminist sensibility that views feminism as a movement of the past is likely also to view aggressively anti-feminist men's rights activism as atavistically misogynistic. As values favoring public equality for women are increasingly institutionalized and defined not in a language of politicized feminism but more in a common sense language of equity and fairness, this shift also contracts the possibilities for anti-feminism. In a sense, I am suggesting that the institutional deck is stacked against overt anti-feminist backlash, be it frontal attacks on Title IX in schools, or men's rights groups' challenges to the state's (still minimal) support for women's shelters. While this outcome can and should be seen as feminist success, I am not arguing that it is time for a celebratory feminist victory lap. History, to be sure, has not ended. Dragiewicz's (2008, 2011) research on US men's rights groups' attempts to stop state funding of women's shelters shows how this moment of gender formation still includes openings for anti-feminist backlash, as does Girard's (2009) and Mann's (2012) research on similar efforts in Canada. However the story at the heart of this research also illustrates the legal limits of such backlash; after all, professional feminist legal activists defeated the anti-feminist actions analyzed by Dragiewicz, Girard and Mann. Today, contingent on the specifics of national political developments, institutionalized feminism continues to influence legal and other decision making, albeit in a context that is often marked by deep controversy (Brodie 2008). Arguably, institutionalized feminism in the US now occupies a legal high ground, notwithstanding one that is still sometimes contested.

Rather than overt anti-feminist backlash, I argue that what is more likely to gain traction today in the US is a "kinder, gentler" form of men's rights discourse and organizing, such as that now characterized by Warren Farrell, often considered the "godfather" of the men's rights movement. Farrell's analysis in the 1980s and early 1990s drifted from the liberal feminist symmetry of men's liberation to asserting in his book *The Myth of Male Power* (1993) that there are many ways in which men are victimized by women's less visible forms of power. . . .

Farrell's strategy is to raise sympathies for men, not to engage in anti-feminist polemics. In a postfeminist context, this more moderate men's rights discourse is likely to ring true as reasonable, as common sense. In this worldview, the women's movement succeeded in improving women's lives, and the logical flip-side is this: in the absence of a symmetrical men's movement to improve men's lives, men suffer harm. While anti-feminist vitriol continues to mark men's rights discourse on the Internet (Dragiewicz 2008, 2011), the emergent "moderate" voice of the men's rights movement does not directly attack feminism or disparage women. Rather, it maneuvers in the postfeminist interstices between the "everywhere" and the "nowhere" of feminism. The means to improve men's lives are articulated to the general public in a de-politicized and individualized "equality language" (Behre 2015) that resonates in a postfeminist and neoliberal context where present-day feminism

seems to be "nowhere." Meanwhile, leaders such as Farrell (2014) are apparently coming to realize that they need not rant to a men's rights audience that feminism is "everywhere," privileging women and holding men down. This is what these men already know; it is the fluoride in their ideological waters.

As a result, men's rights rhetoric that contains an *implicit anti-feminism* is likely to resonate with men who feel insecure or embattled. And I would speculate that moderate men's rights leaders' focus on individual choice and their implicit antifeminism resonates best with educated middle class white men who do not want to appear to be backwards misogynists. A central aspect of privileged men's gender strategies in recent years, after all, is to present one's self as an educated modern man who is supportive of gender equality. And this is achieved partly by projecting atavistic sexism on to less educated men, poor men, immigrant men and men of color (Dekeseredy, Shahid and Schwartz 2003; Hondagneu-Sotelo and Messner 1994).

In this context, is there a potential for less educated poor and working class men to constitute a sort of lumpen anti-feminist army for men's rights? After all, declining economic opportunities for working class men to achieve a traditional conception of the male breadwinner role, combined with the perception that the law favors mothers over fathers in divorce and custody settlements might seem to create a perfect storm for the creation of an army of angry working class fathers ready to join men's rights organizations (Kimmel 2013). Thus far, this has hardly been the case. Most leaders of the men's rights movement are not poor and working class men; rather, they are men with the educational and financial resources needed to form organizations, create websites or hire attorneys. But just as the multi-billionaire Koch brothers' well-financed right wing anti-statism appeals to many lower-middle class whites, the men's rights movement's anti-feminist backlash rhetoric could possibly appeal to men with less education and less resources, men who may have a powerful father hunger but feel that their "rights" have been denied them by controlling mothers, and especially by the state. . . .

. . . To date, there is very little evidence that masses of poor fathers are joining as foot soldiers in anti-feminist collective action. But if current industrial nations continue to lack the will to address the many ways in which a huge strata of young men are being treated as dispensable by the economy and the criminal justice system, it is possible that some of these men will find resonance with Internet-based anti-feminist men's rights discourse that blames women and the liberal state for men's woes.

Possibilities for Men's Profeminist Activism

The recent institutionalization and professionalization of feminism has included a modest expansion of opportunities for men professionals to work on gender issues in social work, academia, law and other fields. This expanding base of men's professional action in gender fields carries both promise and risk. Especially given the recent explosions of public awareness of sexual assault and domestic violence in academia, the military and men's sports, this moment of opportunity and risk is nowhere more apparent than within the array of professional fields that confront violence against women. In 2014, even the President of the United States—not usually a platform for feminist calls for action—called on men to take an active role in ending violence against women. . . .

In short, I suggest that while feminists continue to strategize vigilantly against eruptions of misogynist anti-feminist backlash, a less obvious but perhaps greater challenge springs from the ways in which the very conditions of historical gender formation that facilitate men's movement into professionalized "gender work" also threaten to eclipse feminism altogether. In particular, widespread ideologies of postfeminism, coupled with depoliticized and marketized anti-violence initiatives, threaten to further erase feminist women's organizational leadership as well as the feminist analysis that underlies anti-violence work. Today's anti-violence workers commonly refer to the "movement" not as an eruption of mass activism, but as a network of like-minded anti-violence professionals, and they talk of "politics" not

in terms of activism aimed to bring about structural transformations, but as strategies designed to keep their organizations funded (Messner, Greenberg and Peretz 2015). Much of the violence prevention curricula deployed in schools and communities today has jettisoned the feminist idea that violence against women springs from men's over-conformity with dominant conceptions of masculinity, instead deploying a pragmatic (and more individualistic) strategy of teaching boys and men to make "healthy choices"—a discourse that, not incidentally, is shaped so that it can be subjected to "metrics" that document program effectiveness in support of continuing requests for state or foundation funds.

What are the forces that potentially counter the depoliticization of anti-rape and anti-domestic violence work? One—though this is likely to be temporary—is the continued presence of older feminist women in the field, who mentor younger cohorts of professional women and men in ways that keep feminist analysis and goals at the center of the work. A second source of change, potentially more transformative, lies in the recent growth of diversity among men in the anti-violence field. As the field has expanded in the US, the opportunities for men to work in internships and paid jobs in rape and domestic violence prevention, state and foundation funders have increasingly targeted violence prevention efforts to communities of boys and men considered to be "at risk" due to poverty, crumbling schools, and high rates of gang violence and drug use. There is a widely held perception in the field today that boys of color from poor communities will be more open to learning from young men from their own communities, who look and talk more like they do. This in turn has created a demand for a more racially diverse influx of young men into violence prevention work. . . .

Men of color's movement into professionalized anti-violence work brings to the field not so much a background in academic intersectionality but, rather, an experience-based *organic intersectionality*, different in two ways from the experiences of most white middle-class men in the field. First, young men of color frequently begin with a commitment to addressing boys' vulnerabilities to various forms of violence—in the home, in the street, and from police. These young men often began working with boys around gang and substance abuse issues, in college internships and then paid jobs in non-profit organizations. In that work, they discovered the links between young men's vulnerabilities to multiple forms of violence with their experiences with rape and domestic violence. In short, it was through doing "race and class" work with young men that many of these anti-violence workers "discovered" gender. This in turn created the possibility for an analysis of violence that does not always start with gender as necessarily being foundational (as it so often does with white middle class men who enter the anti-violence field), instead developing into an intersectional understanding of violence, grounded organically in the everyday experiences of race, class, and gender as interlocking processes (Messner, Greenberg and Peretz 2015).

This organically intersectional analysis underlies a second difference between young men of color and white middle class men in the anti-violence field. Young men of color tend to view the now-standard curricula deployed in school- and community-based violence prevention efforts as flat, one-dimensional and thus inadequate. Instead, these young men are innovating and even departing from the standard curricula, developing approaches that draw, for instance, from "theatre of the oppressed," radical community education pedagogies that plumb the everyday life experiences of boys in order to "make it real." Men of color's emergent organically intersectional pedagogies frequently also circle back to academic feminist intersectionality, discovering there a ready resource for understanding connections between violence against women with other forms of "gender based violence"—like sexual abuse and homophobic bullying of boys and transgender youth—as well as with forms of violence that may not be so obviously (or at least primarily) *about* gender—such as gang violence or police violence.

The progressive potential of the rise of organic intersectionality in the anti-violence field is twofold.

First, it has direct appeal to young boys in poor communities because they can see their stake in working for change in their schools and communities. Second, it can re-infuse a powerful dose of radical social justice-oriented politics back into a professionalized anti-violence field that in recent years has seen a severe thinning of its politics, and a near-evaporation of its ability to address connections between gender-based violence with broader social justice issues like poverty, warfare, and cuts in public support for schools and families.

Conclusion

In this article I have argued that large-scale changes created by social movements and shifts in political economy generate moments of *historical gender formation* that in turn shape, constrain and enable certain forms of men's gender politics. The gender formation of the 1970s, constituted by a mass feminist movement operating for the most part outside of male-dominated institutions, created a context for the rise of an internally-contradictory men's liberation movement that soon split into an anti-feminist men's rights movement, and supportive pro-feminist men's organizations.

For feminism, and for men's activism around gender issues, the current moment of gender formation is constituted in part by three large shifts that accelerated in the 1980s and 1990s: the professional institutionalization of feminism; the rise of postfeminism; and neoliberal transformations in the political economy. . . . First, postfeminism and neoliberalism create a context conducive to a "kinder-gentler" moderate men's rights strategy that skirts analysis of structural inequalities in favor of a common-sense celebration of individual choice for women and men. This approach, if successful, will further erode feminist gains in public life, while affording already-privileged men a language through which they can position themselves not as atavistic backlashers, but as modern "new" men who are supportive of equal choices for women and men, unfettered by state policies.

Second, I have argued that the current moment of gender formation has expanded the possibilities for men's participation as allies with women in anti-violence work. While this is a welcome development for most feminists, on the one hand, the current professionalization of gender work in a context of postfeminism risks eclipsing the language and progressive possibilities of feminism, right at a time when men are moving into the field. On the other hand, the linkages of institutionalized anti-violence work with a growing public concern with "at-risk" boys and young men in poor schools and communities has drawn more young men of color into the field. In other words, the very social forces—neoliberalization of the economy, criminalization of poor young men of color—that some fear might form the basis for an army of angry anti-feminist men's rights activists, have also created the conditions for a movement of young men of color into the gender-based violence prevention field.

This influx of men of color into the anti-violence field has introduced a perhaps unexpected progressive counterforce against the ways in which professionalized anti-violence efforts under neoliberalism approach sexual assault or domestic violence as discrete, public health issues. Men of color's organically intersectional understandings of violence, coupled with resources from feminist social justice research, have led to the development of innovative strategies in the field that offer a progressive challenge to the depoliticizing drift of conventional professionalized and marketized anti-violence work. For the most part, this challenge emerges not in the language of a narrowly professionalized liberal feminism, but packaged instead in a broadened "social justice" framework within which feminist ideas about men's violence against women are a central thread in a broad intersectional framework that also addresses the institutionalized violences of racism, poverty, unemployment, declining schools, and the criminal justice system.

Does feminism risk being lost in the social justice configuration now emerging in the professionalized anti-violence field? Do women's concerns with sexual assault and domestic violence risk being subordinated once again to men's concerns about class and race issues? Yes. But the intersectional social justice framework also holds the promise of broadening feminism beyond the limits of the individualistic white professional class feminism so often criticized by feminist women of color. And here is where the continued importance and power of feminist professionals and institutions come into play: veteran feminists can keep alive the flame of a feminism that burns brightly precisely because its politics remain ignited by deep and multi-level commitments to justice efforts.

References

Allen P (1970) *Free Space: A Perspective on the Small Group in Women's Liberation*. New York: Times Change Press.

Bacchi C and Eveline J (2003) Mainstreaming and neoliberalism: A contested relationship. *Policy and Society: Journal of Public, Foreign and Global Policy* 22(2): 98–118. DOI: 10.1016/S1449-4035(03)70021-6.

Baumli F (ed.) (1985) *Men Freeing Men: Exploding the Myth of the Traditional Male*. Jersey City: New Atlantis Press.

Behre KA (2015) Digging beneath the equality language: The influence of the fathers' rights movement on intimate partner violence public policy debates and family law reform. *William & Mary Journal of Women and the Law* 21(3): 525–602.

Brodie J (2008) We are all equal now: Contemporary gender politics in Canada. *Feminist Theory* 9(2): 145–164. DOI: 10.1177/1464700108090408.

Bumiller K (2013) Feminist collaboration with the state in response to sexual violence: Lessons from the American experience. In Tripp AM, Marx Ferree M and Ewing C (eds) *Gender, Violence, and Human Security: Critical Feminist Perspectives*: 191–213. New York: New York University Press.

Butler J (2013) For white girls only? Postfeminism and the politics of inclusion. *Feminist Formations* 25(1): 35–58.

Charles M and Grusky DB (2004) *Occupational Ghettos: The Worldwide Segregation of Women and Men*. Stanford: Stanford University Press.

Dekeseredy W, Shahid A and Schwartz MD (2003) *Under Siege: Poverty and Crime in a Public Housing Community*. Lanham, Maryland: Lexington Books.

Dragiewicz M (2008) Patriarchy reasserted: Fathers' rights and anti-VAWA activism. *Feminist Criminology* 3(2): 121–144. DOI: 10.1177/1557085108316731.

Dragiewicz M (2011) *Equality with a Vengeance: Men's Rights Groups, Battered Women, and Antifeminist Backlash*. Boston: Northeastern University Press.

Echols A (1984 [2002]) The taming of the ID: Feminist sexual politics, 1968–1983. In Echols A (ed.) *Shaky Ground: The Sixties and its Aftershocks*: 108–128. New York: Columbia University Press.

Faludi S (1991) *Backlash: The Undeclared War against American women*. New York: Crown.

Farrell W (1974) *The Liberated Man*. New York: Random House.

Farrell W (1993) *The Myth of Male Power: Why Men are the Disposable Sex*. New York: Simon and Schuster.

Farrell W (2014) *International Conference on Men's Issues—Day 2 Excerpt—Warren Farrell*. Available at https://www.youtube.com/watch?v=V5PMS6VkJkY (accessed 10 November 2015).

Franzway S, Court D, and Connell RW 1989. *Staking a Claim: Feminism, Bureaucracy and the State*. Sydney: Allyn and Unwin.

Friedan B (1963) *The Feminine Mystique*. New York: Norton.

Gilmore RW (2007) In the shadow of the shadow state. In INCITE! Women of Color Against Violence (ed) *The Revolution Will Not be Funded: Beyond the Non-profit Industrial Complex*: 41–52. Cambridge, Massachusetts: South End Press.

Girard AL (2009) Backlash or equality? The influence of men's and women's rights discourses on domestic violence legislation in Ontario. *Violence against Women* 15(1): 5–23. DOI: 10.1177/1077801208328344.

Goldberg H (1976) *The Hazards of Being Male: Surviving the Myth of Masculine Privilege*. New York: Signet.

Hall EJ and Rodriguez MS (2003) The myth of postfeminism. *Gender & Society* 17(6): 878–902. DOI: 10.1177/0891243203257639.

Hondagneu-Sotelo P and Messner MA (1994) Gender displays and men's power: The "New Man" and the Mexican immigrant man. In Brod H and Kaufman M (eds) *Theorizing Masculinities*: 200–218. Sage Publications.

Kimmel MS (1987) Men's responses to feminism at the turn of the century. *Gender & Society* 1(3): 261–283.

Kimmel MS (2013) *Angry White Men: American Masculinity at the End of an Era*. New York: Nation Books.

Mann RM (2012) Invisibilizing violence against women. In Antony W and Samuelson L (eds) *Power and Resistance* (5th edn): 48–71. Halifax, Nova Scotia: Fernwood.

Martin PY (1990) Rethinking feminist organizations. *Gender & Society* 4(2): 182–206. DOI: 10.1177/089124390004002004.

Men's Consciousness-Raising Group (1971) *Unbecoming Men*. Washington, New Jersey: Times Change Press.

Menzies R (2007) Virtual backlash: Representations of men's "rights" and feminist "wrongs" in cyberspace. In Chunn DE, Boyd SB and Lessard H (eds) *Reaction and Resistance: Feminism, Law, and Social Change*: 65–97. Vancouver: UBC Press.

Messner MA (1997) *Politics of Masculinities: Men in Movements*. Lanham, Maryland: Altamira Press.

Messner MA (1998) The limits of "the male sex role": An analysis of the men's liberation and men's rights movements' discourse. *Gender & Society* 12(3): 255–276. DOI: 10.1177/0891243298012003002.

Messner MA, Greenberg MA and Peretz T (2015) *Some Men: Feminist Allies and the Movement to End Violence against Women*. New York: Oxford University Press.

Nichols J (1975) *Men's Liberation: A New Definition of Masculinity*. New York: Penguin.

Omi M and Winant H (1986) *Racial Formation in the United States: From the 1960s to the 1980s*. New York: Routledge and Kegan Paul Inc.

Reger J (2012) *Everywhere and Nowhere: Contemporary Feminism in the United States*. New York and Oxford: Oxford University Press.

Sommers CH (2001) *The War against Boys: How Misguided Feminism is Harming Our Young Men*. New York: Simon and Schuster.

Stansell C (2010) *The Feminist Promise: 1792 to the Present*. New York: Random House.

Taylor V (1989) Social movement continuity: The women's movement in abeyance. *American Sociological Review* 54(5): 761–775.

Tiger L (2000) *The Decline of Males: The First Look at an Unexpected New World for Men and Women*. New York: St Martin's Press.

Wilson WJ (1996) *When Work Disappears: The World of the New Urban Poor*. New York: Knopf.

Wolch J (1990) *The Shadow State: The Government and the Voluntary Sector in Transition*. New York: The Foundation Center.

Trump and the Politics of Fluid Masculinities

JAMES W. MESSERSCHMIDT AND TRISTAN BRIDGES

In the 1950s, a collection of sociologists and psychologists (which included, among others, Theodor Adorno) wrote *The Authoritarian Personality*. They were attempting to theorize the type of personality—a particular psychology—that gave rise to fascism in the 1930s. Among other things, they suggested that the "authoritarian personality" was characterized by a normative belief in absolute obedience to *their* authority in addition to the practical enactment of that belief through direct and indirect marginalization and suppression of "subordinates." While Adorno and his colleagues did not consider the gender of this personality, today gender scholars recognize authoritarianism as a particular form of masculinity, and current U.S. president Donald Trump might appear to be a prime illustration of a rigid and inflexible "authoritarian personality."

Yet Trump's masculinity avoids a direct comparison to this label precisely because of the fluidity he projects. Indeed, the "authoritarian personality" is overly fixed, immutable, and one dimensional as a psychoanalytical personality *type*. Sociologists understand identities as more flexible than this. Certain practices of Trump exemplify the fluctuations of masculinity that illustrate this distinction, and the transformations in his masculinity are highly contingent upon context. While this is a common political strategy, Trump's shifts are important as they enable him to construct a "dominating masculinity" that perpetuates diverse forms of social inequality. *Dominating masculinities* are those that involve commanding and controlling interactions to exercise power and control over people and events. These masculinities are most problematic when they also are *hegemonic* and work to legitimize unequal relations between women and men. Here are a few examples:

First, in his speeches and public statements prior to being elected, Trump bullied and subordinated "other" men by referring to them as "weak," "low energy," or as "losers," or implying they are "inept" or a "wimp." ("Othering" is a social process whereby certain people are viewed and/or treated as somehow fundamentally different and unequal.) For example, during several Republican presidential debates, Trump consistently labeled Marco Rubio as "little Marco," described Jeb Bush as "low energy Jeb," implied that John McCain was a "wimp" because he was captured and tortured during the Vietnam War, and suggested that contemporary military veterans battling PTSD are "inept" because they "can't handle" the "horror" they observed in combat. In contrast, Trump consistently referred to himself as, for example, strong, a fighter, and as the embodiment of success. In each case, Trump ascribes culturally-defined "inferior" subordinate gender qualities to his opponents while imbuing himself with culturally defined "superior" masculine qualities. This pairing signifies an unequal relationship between masculinities—one both dominating *and* hegemonic (Trump) and one subordinate (the "other" men).

A second example of Trump's fluid masculinity applies to the way he has depicted himself as *the*

James W. Messerschmidt and Tristan Bridges, "Trump and the Politics of Fluid Masculinities," DSA *Democratic Socialists of America*, posted on July 15, 2017. Reprinted by permission of the author.

heroic masculine *protector* of all Americans. This compassion may appear, at first blush, at odds with the hegemonic masculinity just discussed. For example, in his Republican Convention speech Trump argued that he alone can lead the country back to safety by protecting the American people through the deportation of "dangerous" and "illegal" Mexican and Muslim immigrants and by "sealing the border." In so doing, Trump implied that Americans are *unable* to defend themselves—a fact he used to justify his need to "join the political arena." Trump stated: "I will liberate our citizens from crime and terrorism and lawlessness" by "restoring law and order" throughout the country—"I will fight for you, I will win for you." Here Trump adopts a position as white masculine *protector* of Americans against men of color, instructing all US citizens to entrust their lives to him; in return, he offers safety. Trump depicts himself as aggressive, invulnerable, and able to protect while all remaining US citizens are depicted as dependent and uniquely vulnerable. Trump situates himself as analogous to the patriarchal masculine protector toward his wife and other members of the patriarchal household. But simultaneously, Trump presents himself as a compassionate, caring, and kind-hearted benevolent protector, and thereby constructs a hybrid hegemonic masculinity consisting of both masculine and feminine qualities.

Third, in the 2005 interaction between Trump and Billy Bush on the now infamous Access Hollywood tour bus, Trump presumes he is entitled to the bodies of women and (not surprisingly) admits committing sexual assault against women because, according to him, he has the right. He depicts women as collections of body parts and disregards their desires, needs, expressed preferences, and their consent. After the video was aired more women have come forward and accused Trump of sexual harassment and assault. Missed in discussions of this interaction is how that dialogue actually contradicts, and thus reveals, the myth of Trump's *protector* hegemonic masculinity. The interaction on the bus demonstrates that Trump is not a "protector" at all; he is a "predator."

Trump's many masculinities represent a collection of contradictions. Trump's heroic protector hegemonic masculinity should have been effectively unmasked, revealing a toxic *predatory* heteromasculinity. Discussions of this controversy, however, failed to articulate any sign of injury to his campaign because Trump was able to connect with a dominant discourse of masculinity often relied upon to explain all manner of men's (mis)behavior—it was "locker room talk," we were told. And the sad fact is, the news cycle moved on.

We argue that Trump has managed such contradictions by mobilizing, in certain contexts, what has elsewhere (and above) been identified as a *"dominating masculinity"* (see here, here and here)—involving commanding and controlling specific interactions and exercising power and control over people and events. This *dominating masculinity* has thus far centered on six critical features:

1) Trump operates in ways that cultivate domination over others he works with, in particular rewarding people based on their loyalty to him.
2) Trump's dominating masculinity serves the interests of corporations by cutting regulations, lowering corporate taxes, increasing military spending, and engaging in other neoliberal practices, such as attempting to strip away healthcare from 24 million people, defunding public schools, and making massive cuts to social programs that serve poor and working-class people, people of color, and the elderly.
3) Trump has relied on his dominating masculinity to serve his particular needs as president, such as refusing to release his tax returns and ruling through a functioning kleptocracy (using the office to serve his family's economic interests).
4) This masculinity is exemplified through the formulation of a dominating militaristic foreign policy (for example, U.S. airstrikes of civilians in Yemen, Iraq and Syria have increased dramatically under Trump; the MOAB bombing of Afghanistan; threats to North Korea) rather than engaging in serious forms of diplomacy. Trump has formed a global ultraconservative

"axis of evil"—whose defining characteristics are kleptocracy and dominating masculinity—with the likes of Putin (Russia), el-Sisi (Egypt), Erdogan (Turkey), Salman (Saudi Arabia), Duterte (Philippines) among others.

5) So too has this dominating masculinity had additional effects "at home" as Trump prioritizes domestically the repressive arm of the state through white supremacist policies such as rounding-up and deporting immigrants and refugees as well as his anti-Muslim rhetoric and attempted Muslim ban.

6) Trump's dominating masculinity attempts to control public discourse through his constant tweets that are aimed at discrediting and subordinating those who disagree with his policies.

Trump's masculinity is fluid, contradictory, situational, and it demonstrates the diverse and crisscrossing pillars of support that uphold inequalities worldwide. From different types of hegemonic masculinities, to a toxic predatory heteromasculinity, to his dominating masculinity, Trump's chameleonic display is part of the contemporary landscape of gender, class, race, age and sexuality relations and inequalities. Trump does not construct a consistent form of masculinity. Rather, he oscillates—at least from the evidence we have available to us. And in each case, his oscillations attempt to overcome the specter of femininity—the fear of being the unmasculine man—through the construction of particularized masculinities.

It is through these varying practices that Trump's masculinity is effective in bolstering specific forms and systems of inequality that have been targeted and publicly challenged in recent history. Durable forms of social inequality achieve resilience by becoming flexible. By virtue of their fluidity of expression and structure, they work to establish new pillars of ideological support, upholding social inequalities as "others" are challenged. As C. J. Pascoe has argued, a dominating masculinity is not unique to Trump or only his supporters; Trump's opponents rely on it as well (see also sociologist Kristen Barber's analysis of anti-Trump masculinity tactics). And it is for these reasons that recognizing Trump's fluidity of masculinity is more than mere academic observation; it is among the chief mechanisms through which contemporary forms of inequality—from the local to the global—are justified and persist today.

Latino Immigrant Men and the Deportation Crisis

A Gendered Racial Removal Program

TANYA GOLASH-BOZA AND PIERRETTE HONDAGNEU-SOTELO

Between 1997 and 2012, the US government carried out 4.2 million deportations. This figure amounts to more than twice the sum total of *every deportation* before 1997 (1.9 million people). Nearly all of these recent deportees have been Latino men, creating a crisis in Latino families and communities. We suggest this constitutes a *gendered racial removal program*, and argue that changes in immigration law, the War on Terror, the law enforcement racial profiling and criminalization of Latino men, and the male joblessness crisis in the United States have produced this deportation crisis. . . .

. . . We explain the legal and administrative mechanisms supporting this process, and we indicate how structural factors in the economy and the politics of race, criminalization and immigration have prompted these changes. Methodologically, we draw on secondary sources, surveys conducted in Mexico, the U.S. Department of Homeland Security (DHS) published statistics, and interviews with deportees conducted by the first author in Guatemala, the Dominican Republic, Brazil and Jamaica.[1] . . .

Gender and Immigration Control

Starting with the Page Law of 1875 and continuing through the mid-twentieth century with the Bracero Program (1942–1964), the United States actively recruited immigrant men from Asia and Latin America to fill expanding labor needs in the west, while only tenuously admitting Asian and Latina immigrant women into the nation. . . . Keeping the Asian and Latina women out or restricted in number was a strategy aimed at deterring the demographic reproduction and permanent settlement of Asian and Latino families and communities in the United States (Glenn, 1986; Chan, 1991; Hondagneu-Sotelo, 1994, 1995; Chavez, 2008). To be sure, men were deported in round-ups and incarcerated in prisons, detention centers and internment camps, but as recently as the fiscal crisis of the state in the 1990s, exclusionary policies such as California's Proposition 187 and the 1996 immigration and welfare reform acts targeted women (Hondagneu-Sotelo, 1995; Marchevsky and Theoharis, 2006; Chavez, 2008; Fujiwara, 2008; Park, 2011; Moloney, 2012).

We suggest that the current targeting of men for deportation signals a rupture with previous restrictionist immigration regime policies that had focused on excluding women (from reproduction) and including men for labor (production). Although no explicitly gendered legislation codifies this new turn, changes in administrative policies and practices have created a situation where the vast majority of deportees are working class men from Latin America and the Caribbean. We contend that the institutionalized criminalization

Tanya Golash-Bozaa and Pierrette Hondagneu-Sotelob, "Latino Immigrant Men and the Deportation Crisis: A Gendered Racial Removal Program," *Latino Studies* (11)3: 271–292. Copyright 2013 by Palgrave Macmillan UK Journals. Reprinted by permission of the publisher. Some notes and figures have been renumbered.

and surveillance of men of color in urban streets (Young, 1999; Zilberg, 2004; Wacquant, 2009; Ramirez and Flores, 2011; Rios, 2011)—heightened in the post-9/11 climate of Islamaphobia and male joblessness exacerbated by global financial crisis and economic restructuring—have created the context for this shift. This became evident in both practice and discourse, as police surveillance, detention and deportation targeted Latin American immigrant men (Dowling and Inda, 2012). A labor market that increasingly relies on service jobs and offers diminishing numbers of construction and manufacturing jobs deems these men disposable and redundant.

During the 1990s, political campaigns in the United States constructed the "immigrant danger" as a feminine reproductive threat (Hondagneu-Sotelo, 1995; Chavez, 2004, 2008; Gutierrez, 2008). . . . The safety net for immigrant women shrunk, the service sector jobs that traditionally employ women increased, and the perception of immigrant women as threats to the nation has become muted in recent years.

In this context, the gendered construction of immigrant danger has shifted. The new danger is masculine, one personified by terrorist men and "criminal aliens." The DHS, the cabinet department created after the September 11 attacks, which replaced the old Immigration and Naturalization Service (INS), has framed its efforts in a discourse of national security. Mass deportation emerged as a primary strategy for protecting the nation from the gendered and racial threats of criminal and fugitive aliens and terrorists.

Twenty-First Century Deportations: Gendered Racial Removal

. . . In 2011, the DHS deported 392,000 foreign nationals, and returned an additional 324,000 to their home countries without a removal order. At least since the early 1990s, Latino and Caribbean men have been the targets of deportation policy. . . . Between 1993 and 2011, deportations increased ninefold. This increase is due almost exclusively to increases in the numbers of Mexican and Central American deportees. There was a 10-fold increase in the number of Mexican deportees, and a 12-fold increase in the number of Central American deportees.In contrast, European and Asian deportations quadrupled, and African and Caribbean deportations doubled. By 2011, 97 per cent of deportees were from the Americas—only 5060 people were deported to Asia; 3131 to Europe; and 1602 to Africa (Table 41, *DHS Yearbook of Immigration Statistics*).

DHS has not released publically available data on the gender of deportees since 1997. . . . Between 1992 and 1995, only about 6 per cent of deportees were women. In 1996, the proportion rose to 12 per cent and increased to almost 16 per cent in 1997. This increase in the deportation of women in the mid-1990s happened at the same time that pundits constructed Latinas as breeders and drains on the welfare state.

More recent individual country studies show that the vast majority of deportees continue to be men, and that many have close ties to the United States. [For example,] Hagan *et al.* (2008) found that, in El Salvador, 95 per cent of deportees are men, three quarters were undocumented in the United States, nearly 79 per cent have family members in the United States, and their median stay in the United States had been 8 years. . . . In this article, we look at deportees more globally, and find similar trends—nearly all deportees are men, and many had strong ties to the United States before being deported. . . .

Mechanisms of the New Deportation Regime

Deportations have increased since the mid-1990s, facilitated by the passage of an arsenal of new laws, including the 1996 Illegal Immigration Reform and Immigrant Responsibility Act (IIRIRA), the 1996 Anti-terrorism and Effective Death Penalty Act (AEDPA) and the 2001 USA PATRIOT Act. As Hagan *et al.* (2008, 66) indicate, removals averaged about 20,000 annually from 1900 to 1990,[2] but began escalating in the 1990s. Deportations then ballooned to over 208,000 removals in 2005.

By 2012, that figure had nearly doubled to 409,849 removals.[3]

Scholars generally recognize the 1996 IIRIRA as the principal legislation facilitating the removal of hundreds of thousands of immigrants.... The 1996 legislation facilitated deportations by expanding the grounds on which non-citizens could be deported, eliminating most grounds for appeal, and implementing an expedited removal process.... [After a sharp increase starting in 1956 (Figure 42.1),] deportations leveled off, and even declined in 2002, only to rise precipitously with the creation of DHS and ICE in 2003.

The laws regarding deportation have not changed substantially since 1996. Instead, Congress has appropriated increasing amounts of money for immigration law enforcement, in line with DHS's annual budget requests. The Fiscal Year (FY) 2011 budget for DHS was $56 billion, 30 per cent of which was directed at immigration law enforcement through ICE and Customs and Border Patrol (CBP). Another 18 per cent of the total went to the US Coast Guard and 5 per cent to US Citizenship & Immigration Services—meaning over half of the DHS budget is directed at border security and immigration law enforcement (U.S. Department of Homeland Security (DHS), 2012). To put this $56 billion in perspective, the Department of Education FY 2011 budget was $77.8 billion, and the Department of Justice $29.2 billion.[4]...

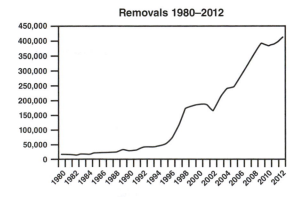

Figure 42.1 Removals: 1980–2012.
Note: Data for 1980–2011 from Table 39, DHS/OIS: http://www. dhs.gov/files/statistics/publications/YrBk10En.shtm, accessed 4 April 2013. Data for 2012 from: http://www.ice.gov/removal-statistics/, accessed 4 April 2013.

From Border to Interior Enforcement

The criminalization of immigrants constitutes a new form of legal violence in Latino communities, legally sanctioned social suffering resulting from the convergence of immigration law and criminal law (Menjivar and Abrego, 2012).... Mass deportation began with President Bush, but under the Obama administration, deportations have continued to rise, and the focus now centers on criminal aliens—non-US citizens who have been convicted of crimes.[5] During this same period, emphasis has shifted from border enforcement to interior enforcement. The ratio of returns to removals reflects this shift—as returns are primarily a border enforcement mechanism.[6] "Returns" occur when a Border Patrol agent denies entry, whereas a "removal" involves a non-citizen attending an immigration hearing or waiving the right to a hearing—as in an expedited removal. In 1996, there were 22 times as many returns as removals. This ratio has dropped continuously, and in 2011, for the first time since 1941, the United States removed more people than it returned [(Figure 42.2)]....

... Immigration law enforcement officers who work in two branches of the DHS carry out deportations: CBP and ICE. CBP is only authorized to work up to 100 air miles from the border; most interior enforcement falls to ICE.... In 2002, interior apprehensions accounted for 10 per cent of all DHS apprehensions. By 2011, that figure was nearly 50 per cent. Figure 42.3 displays these trends.

This shift towards interior enforcement has gendered implications—deported men leave behind women and children.... According to a 2012 ICE report, ICE removed 46,486 non-citizens who reported having at least one U.S. citizen child between 1 January and 30 June 2011 (US Department of Homeland Security, 2012). A previous report found that DHS deported about 100,000 legal permanent residents who had US citizen children in the 10 years spanning 1997 and 2007.[7] Since nearly all of these deportees are men, we can surmise that women left behind provide children with primary support and caregiving. Deportations also leave children orphaned and relegated to the foster care system.

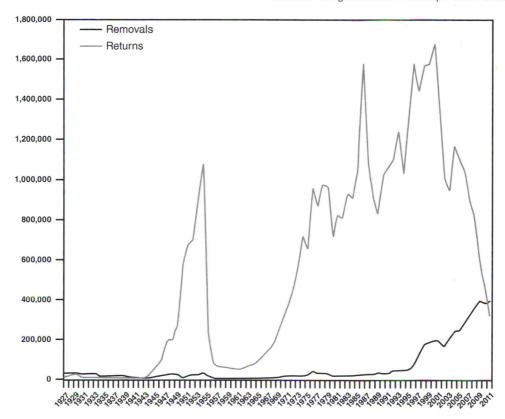

Figure 42.2 Removals and returns: 1927–2011.

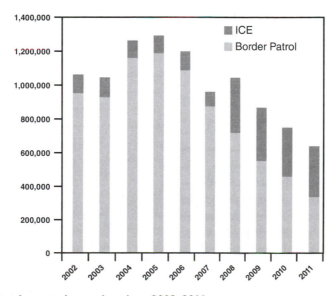

Figure 42.3 ICE and border patrol apprehensions 2002–2011.
Source: Table 35, DHS "Aliens Apprehended by Program and Border Patrol Section and Investigations Special Agent in Charge (SAC) Jurisdiction": FY 2002–2011.

How Interior Enforcement Works: Targeting Criminal Aliens

. . . As ICE lacks the power to patrol the streets of US cities and demand proof of US citizenship, and has only 20,000 employees overall, ICE depends on criminal law enforcement agencies to locate people eligible for deportation (Rosenblum and Kandel, 2012). . . . There are four programs designed to locate criminal aliens: The Criminal Alien Program (CAP), Secure Communities, 287(g) and the National Fugitive Operations Program (NFOP). Congress appropriated $690 million for the four programs in 2011—up from $23 million in 2004. This funding led to an increase in annual arrests through these programs from 11,000 to 289,000 during that time.[8] The shift towards criminal aliens has thus involved a discursive shift as well as large-scale funding of these initiatives.

287(g) came about through the IIRIRA, a complex, far-reaching, multi-faceted and draconian restrictionist legislation, prompted nationally by California's vote in favor of Proposition 187 (which proved un-Constitutional at the state level). Section 287(g) of the Immigration and Nationality Act allows ICE to enter cooperation agreements with state and local law enforcement, and even to deputize officers for immigration enforcement after 4-week training sessions from ICE. . . . These agreements enable police officers to enforce federal immigration laws even when stopping people for minor traffic violations. Since 2006, 287(g) officers have identified over 126,453 non-citizens eligible for deportation.

Much of the public controversy and scholarship centered on the 287(g) program has focused on racial profiling (Arnold, 2007; Lacayo, 2010; Coleman, 2012). A substantial body of research and legal cases concludes that police racially profile people who "drive while Brown" (or Black) (Johnson, 2003). . . . Latino immigrant men in public spaces are most likely to be targeted. Critics have pointed out that the vast majority (87 per cent) of jurisdictions that have implemented 287(g) programs have high immigrant growth rates, indicating that nativist fears drive these programs (Lacayo, 2010). . . . In

September 2012, the Justice Department released a report, subtitled, "Findings Show Pattern or Practice of Discriminatory Policing against Latinos." This report found that deputies in Alamance County, North Carolina, stopped Latinos at least four times as often as non-Latino drivers, consistently stopped Latinos at checkpoints, and arrested Latinos for minor traffic violations while issuing citations or warnings to non-Latinos for the same violations. . . .

Although scholars and policy analysts have argued that racial profiling is a concern in the 287(g) program, there has been less focus on another obvious fact—police officers are more likely to stop men than women (Lundman and Kaufman, 2003). . . . Although the 287(g) program deports few women, mounting evidence suggests that the program has pernicious effects on women. One example is domestic violence: a recent study found that only about half of all battered women report perpetrators to authorities. Immigrant women with stable status report at a rate of 43 per cent, and undocumented women at a rate of 19 per cent (Quereshi, 2010). Police cooperation with immigration authorities threatens to depress low reporting rates even further because women have good reason to fear deportation when the police cooperate with ICE.

. . . In 2008, 287(g) officers identified 33,831 foreign nationals who were eventually deported (Lacayo, 2010)—these arrests accounted for over a third of deportations from the interior of the United Sates. The majority of those detained under this program were apprehended for minor violations such as driving with a broken taillight (Lacayo, 2010). . . .

Walter,[9] a citizen of the Dominican Republic, exemplifies the trend of minor violations leading to deportation. Walter was deported after living in the United States for over a decade, and left two children behind. He was a legal permanent resident because of his marriage to a US citizen. Police officers stopped Walter for a traffic violation in 2004, and the immigration check on Walter's driver's license revealed an immigration hold. Walter had failed to mention on his application for legalization that he had unsuccessfully attempted to enter Puerto Rico when he was 15, and had been returned by the US Coast Guard. When DHS discovered this omission, they issued a Notice to Appear to Walter for immigration fraud. This Notice came up when the police officer ran Walter's license on the highway. . . . Walter's legal residency was rescinded owing to the charge of immigration fraud. . . . In 2008 the United States deported him to the Dominican Republic as a "criminal alien." . . .

ICE's stated mission is to find and deport "criminal aliens" like Walter (U.S. Department of Homeland Security, 2009). Who are these "criminal aliens?" According to ICE, 35.9 per cent of criminal deportees in FY 2008 were deported for drug offenses and 18.1 per cent for immigration offenses. Overall, less than 15 per cent were deported for violent crimes—7.7 per cent for assault, 3.2 per cent for robbery and 3 per cent for sexual assault (U.S. Department of Homeland Security, 2009). Very few of the deported "criminal aliens" present any real danger to society. Yet these deportations have damaging consequences for the family members left behind in the United States.

A DHS program called, without irony, "Secure Communities," also expands ICE's reach. This technological tool allows participating jails to submit arrestees' fingerprints not only to criminal databases, like those maintained by the FBI, but also to immigration databases maintained by ICE. . . . ICE launched this program in 2008, and as of September 2011, over 11 million fingerprint submissions allowed ICE to remove more than 142,000 people. Although Homeland Security claims Secure Communities will find deportees with criminal records, 26 per cent of people deported in FY 2011 through Secure Communities had no criminal convictions (only immigration violations) and 29 per cent were individuals convicted of level three crimes, which carry sentences of less than 1 year (Immigration Policy Center, 2011).

The case of Emerson, a Guatemalan teenager, illustrates how deportation works through Secure Communities. As a child, he came with his mother to the United States on a tourist visa and he never

legalized his status. After finishing high school, Emerson married a legal permanent resident of the United States and lived with her in Los Angeles. One day, Emerson's friend asked him for a ride across town. When his friend got out of the car, he allegedly tried to steal a car. Emerson left the scene, but police arrested him and charged him as an accomplice. The charges were dropped, but his arrest led to a police check on his immigration status. When they discovered he had overstayed his visa, he was deported. Emerson was never convicted of a crime, and he qualified to apply for legal permanent residency through his spouse, but he was deported before he could finish the legalization process. . . .

ICE reports and budgetary requests rely on these dehumanizing labels (for example, criminal, fugitive and illegal aliens) to argue that the removal of these non-citizens makes America safer. But over 80 per cent of all criminal deportees are deported for non-violent crimes (Immigration Policy Center, 2011). The term "fugitive aliens" sounds ominous, conjuring images of armed bank robbers, but it refers to people who were released from ICE custody and failed to report for their immigration hearings, and people who have been ordered deported yet have not left the country. The United States often hails itself as a nation of immigrants—indicating the positive association with the label "immigrant." In contrast, the labels "fugitive alien" and "criminal alien" point to a population the country would do well to expel. . . .

Consequences of the New Deportation Regime: Gendered Racial Removal

Despite its enormous budget, the DHS lacks the resources to find and deport the estimated 11 million undocumented migrants in the United States. Thus, immigration law enforcement must be selective. Overwhelming and conclusively, selective law enforcement has selected Latino and Black Caribbean working class men. Table 42.1 shows the top 10 receiving countries of deportees in 2010—these 10 countries accounted for 96 per cent of deportees in 2010.

Table 42.1 DHS OIS Table 38: Aliens Removed by Country of Nationality, FY 2010[a]

Mexico	282,003
Guatemala	29,378
Honduras	24,611
El Salvador	19,809
Dominican Republic	3309
Brazil	3190
Ecuador	2321
Colombia	2267
Nicaragua	1847
Jamaica	1475
All other countries	17,032
Total	387,242

[a]Immigration Enforcement Actions: 2010.

. . . In the 1990s, demographers Fix and Passel (1994) estimated that Asians and people of European background make up 24 per cent of undocumented immigrants in the United States. Yet popular opinion in the United States associates "Mexicanness" with illegality (Golash-Boza, 2012). Consequently, racial profiling targets Mexicans (or Latin Americans appearing to be Mexican) instead of immigrants of European or Asian backgrounds.

. . . During the Great Depression, the United States repatriated as many as half a million people of Mexican origin—some of them US-born, US citizens—to Mexico. . . . By 1940, the Mexican population in the United States had declined to about half of its size in 1930 (Gonzalez, 1983), resulting from what historian Mae Ngai (2004) has called a "racial removal program." . . . Figure 42.4 illustrates the enduring emphasis, as well as the emphasis on Caribbean nationals. As you can see in the placement of the darker shades, immigrants from Mexico, Central America and the Caribbean are disproportionately more likely than immigrants from the rest of the world to face deportation.

Although others have drawn attention to the racialized deportation crisis and the concentration of Latinos targeted (Lacayo, 2010; Coleman, 2012; Golash-Boza, 2012), we underscore that immigrant detainees and deportees are overwhelmingly male. In the Jamaican case, 96 per cent of criminal deportees are men (Headley *et al.*, 2005). A study of Dominican deportees by Brotherton and Barrios (2011) relied on a purposive sample that was 84 per cent male. The DHS does not make publicly available much of the data it collects on deportees. Thus, we do not have reliable universal data on the gender,

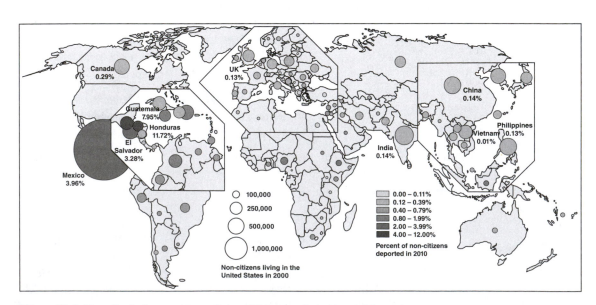

Figure 42.4 Map displaying number of non-citizens and number of deportees.

age or familial status of deportees. We have been able to piece together data from a variety of sources and can conclude that as many as 90 per cent, and at least 85 per cent, of deportees are men. For example, we know that, of the 32,000 immigrants in ICE custody on 25 January 2009, 91 per cent were male and 9 per cent were female (Kerwin and Lin, 2009)....

... The *Colegio de la Frontera Norte* (COLEF), the premier research institute on migration and borderlands in Mexico, has been collecting data on Mexicans who are sent back to Mexico since 2004—the EMIF Norte Study.[10] EMIF data collected during 2010 reflected that fully 89 per cent of Mexicans who were repatriated were men.[11]...

Consequences and Context

The Great Recession and Disappearing Men's Jobs

A gendered division of labor still prevails in the US economy, and beginning in 2007, the United States entered the worst economic crisis since the Great Depression, a crisis particularly marked by high rates of joblessness among men without college degrees, and among Black and Latino working class men. Globalization has now brought the United States three decades of deindustrialization, the erosion of union jobs and the manufacturing sector, and the normalization of off-shore production and consumer purchases of imports. In recent decades, Latino immigrant male labor has clustered in industries such as the construction and building trades, sectors that experienced extreme contraction due to the real estate bust during the recession. Signs of economic and employment recovery surfaced in 2012, but the big picture of predicted trends in employment growth suggest these traditionally male job sectors will not recover to pre-2007 levels. While no one can precisely predict long-term structural changes in the economy, indicators suggest concentrated job growth will continue in services....

The confluence of high unemployment and deportation among Latino immigrant men prompts us to ask: have Latino men and their jobs been declared disposable? We urge scholars, particularly labor economists and sociologists, to conduct sectoral and regional research to explore possible linkages between the current wave of deportations and local labor markets for Latino immigrant men. There are plenty of historical precedents of mass deportations following on the heels of major economic downturns (for example, the "Repatriation" programs of the 1930s, and Operation Wetback during the post-Korean War economic slump). The legal mechanisms for deportation have changed, but the outcomes seem eerily similar, with a key difference. Now, immigrant women's employment has expanded and they have been under-represented in deportation.

... In the current post-industrial economic context of globalization and high-tech, there is shrinking labor demand for men who lack higher education and advanced technology skill sets. Meanwhile, in the United States and in all post-industrial nations around the globe, demand for immigrant women in caregiving, cleaning and nursing sectors has increased. All indicators suggest that this labor demand will only continue to increase in relation to aging baby boomer populations.

The Impact on Latino Families and Communities

... Detention and deportation often remove critical sources of already meager male breadwinner income from Latino working families. Family members try to scrape together thousands of dollars in legal and immigration fees to avoid detention and deportation, and they may subsequently be unable to cover rent and other living expenses. Economic hardship pushes women who once relied on their partner's income into working two or three jobs, or generating informal sector income, and this results in a greater care squeeze for the very young and the infirm. ... In some instances, family members living in Mexico are now asked to send financial support, reversing a long-term historical trend of US migrants sending remittances back to their country. In the United States, many of the remaining families seek inadequate government-provided support....

Deportation also causes emotional and psychological trauma and family dissolution. It affects not only the deportees and their family members, but others in the community who, because they fear a similar fate, deter their health or protective services-seeking behavior. . . . Joanna Dreby's (2012) research based on interviews with 91 parents and 110 children in 80 households reveals that regardless of legal status, children in Mexican immigrant families now express fear and anxiety about potential family separations, leading her to suggest that children disproportionally shoulder the burden of deportation. . . .

In many instances, the deportation crisis deprives Latino families of face-to-face fatherhood. This return to institutionalized transnational fatherhood harkens back to the Bracero Program—a guest-worker program put into place after World War II—which separated families and caused despair and hardship for Mexican women, children and entire communities (Rosas, 2011). Now, the United States removes fathers back to their countries of origin while their spouses and children remain here, but the effects are similar.

The deportation crisis sometimes prompts the de facto deportation of US citizen children. More often the children stay in the United States, but their daily care may change: they might stay with one parent, or with relatives. Some of the children end up in foster care, and the "Shattered Families" report by the Applied Research Center conservatively estimates that "there are at least 5100 children currently living in foster care whose parents have been either detained[12] or deported" (Applied Research Center, 2011, 3). This raises a number of questions regarding family civil rights, and mental health trauma suffered by children and parents alike. . . . What are the short- and long-term consequences for Latino children and youth? And how do those effects reverberate in the deportation crisis' regional hotspots? How does the deportation regime era stunt the kind of optimism and outstanding second-generation achievements reported in studies such as the highly acclaimed book *Inheriting the City* (Kasinitz *et al.*, 2008)? . . .

Latino Studies and Immigration Studies

Latino immigrant communities in the United States have faced a siege of civil rights violations, and even if comprehensive immigration reform occurs, the repercussions of massive deportation remain and Latino Studies and immigration studies will need to contend with these. Scholars in Latino Studies who are considering topics as diverse as social movements, cultural and artistic life, and psychological well-being will need to contend with a decade and a half when deportations and forced removals swept through Latino communities. . . . Latino Studies scholars have made it clear that illegality is socially constructed, that illegality, deportability (De Genova, 2002) and policeability (Rosas, 2006) serve to control Latino labor and lives, and that "illegal" is a dehumanizing label. What about "criminal alien?" Many scholars and activists are willing to stand up for undocumented migrants and insist that they are not criminals, just hardworking folks who came to this country for a better life. However, there are fewer people who advocate for *organizing a social movement or legislative change to challenge the demonization of "criminal aliens."*

The deportation crisis also raises a number of new empirical questions for the study of international migration. . . . We normally think of forced migration as refugee movements responding to war, famine or natural disaster in faraway continents, but the United States now sponsors a major coerced migration that outstrips the dimensions of prior deportation regimes and that calls into question our taken-for-granted paradigms. The US deportees returning to Latin America constitute a new group of forced return migrants. How are they adapting to life in their home countries, and reshaping national culture and development trajectories? How does deportation affect the dynamics of immigrant incorporation and integration in the United States, and the life chances and trajectories of their family members? Immigration incorporation, assimilation and integration are important topics of study, especially now as the looming retirement of white baby boomers nears. While some scholars of international migration predict optimistic scenarios where the immigrant second generation will assume these vacated positions, the analysis must also grapple with the outcomes of the current gendered racial removal program. . . .

Looking Forward

As of this writing in June 2013, Congress is in the midst of an extended debate on immigration reform. President Obama has expressed a commitment to immigration reform, promising a path to citizenship to those on the right side of the law. Regardless of the outcome of this push towards comprehensive immigration reform, the interior enforcement and gendered racial removal of hundreds of thousands of Latino working class men will have enduring effects. . . . The first decade of the twenty-first century is already marked as a period when hundreds of thousands of Latino men were sent to their countries of birth while their children and partners struggled to remain in the United States. These children will grow up knowing that the US government is responsible for their father's exile, and this raises a number of questions for future notions of nation and belonging.

These findings point to the importance of more cross-disciplinary conversations between immigration scholars, Latino Studies scholars and scholars of criminal justice. The collateral consequences of mass deportation will be similar to those of mass incarceration. Latino Studies as a field provides a space for the development of these critical conversations.

Acknowledgement

The authors thank the anonymous reviewers, legal scholars Bill Ong Hing and Niels Frenzen, the *Latino Studies* editors Suzanne Oboler and Lourdes Torres, Helen Marrow for the Census data on non-citizens, and Sybil Adams for creating the map.

Notes

1. In 2009 and 2010, the first author conducted 150 semi-structured interviews with deportees in Jamaica, the Dominican Republic, Guatemala and Brazil, in addition to participant observation at airports where deportees arrive and interviews with government officials and NGOs in the four countries. Those interviews were part of a larger project focusing on the consequences of mass deportation.

2. The average number of "removals" between 1900 and 1990 was about 18,000. These figures did not include the hundreds of thousands of Mexicans who were repatriated in the 1930s, nor the million Mexicans who were returned during "Operation Wetback" in 1954. The reason for this is that, in the 1930s, hundreds of thousands of Mexicans departed "voluntarily" and thus were not recorded as removals. In 1954, the Border Patrol recorded 1 million "returns" as Operation Wetback was concentrated along border towns. See Lytle Hernandez (2010) for a discussion of Operation Wetback and Balderrama (1982) for a discussion of the mass repatriation of Mexicans and their children in the 1930s.

3. As of 1 April 1997, the government reclassified all exclusion and deportations procedures as "Removal proceedings," but in this paper we use the terms deportation and removal interchangeably. 2012 figure from: www.ice.gov/removal-statistics/.

4. FY 2011 Budget Summary and Background Information. Department of Education. www2.ed.gov/about/overview/budget/budget11/summary/11summary.pdf and FY 2011 Budget. Department of Justice. www.justice.gov/opa/pr/2010/February/10-ag-109.html, accessed 20 February 2012.

5. The Bush administration also conducted several highly visible immigration raids. These immigration raids generated more fear than actual immigration enforcement, as they accounted for a very small percentage of actual deportations—less than 1 per cent. See Golash-Boza (2012) for an analysis of these raids.

6. DHS defines returns in the following manner: "In some cases, apprehended aliens may be offered the opportunity to return to their home countries without being placed in

immigration proceedings. This procedure is common with non-criminal aliens who are apprehended at the border. Aliens agree that their entry was illegal, waive their right to a hearing, remain in custody and are returned under supervision. Return is also available for noncriminal aliens who are deemed inadmissible at ports of entry. In addition, some aliens apprehended within the United States agree to voluntarily depart and pay the expense of departing. These departures may be granted by an immigration judge or, in some circumstances, by a Detention and Removal Operations field office director. In certain instances, aliens who have agreed to a return may be legally admitted in the future without penalty." www.dhs.gov/xlibrary/assets/statistics/ publications/enforcement_ar_2009.pdf.

7. In the Child's Best Interest? The consequences of losing a lawful immigrant parent to deportation, www.law.berkeley.edu/files/Human_Rights_report.pdf p. 4, accessed 1 February 2013.

8. The Criminal Alien Program is the largest of the four programs. In FY 2011, ICE issued 212,744 charging documents for deportation through the CAP. In that same year, 78,246 people were removed through Secure Communities, a program where the FBI automatically sends the fingerprints of people arrested to DHS to check against its immigration databases. 287(g) allows state and local law enforcement agencies to act as immigration law enforcement agents within their jurisdictions. In 2010, 26,871 people were removed through 287(g). Only about 1500 were removed through NFOP. Much of the attention on Police/ICE cooperation has been on Secure Communities and 287(g), yet the vast majority of removals are occurring through the Criminal Alien Program (Rosenblum and Kandel, 2012).

9. "Walter" is a pseudonym. His story, like the other stories related in this article, comes from research the first author conducted with people who have been deported from the United States. The first author interviewed

150 deportees between May 2009 and August 2010 in Guatemala, the Dominican Republic, Brazil and Jamaica.

10. EMIF refers to the *Encuesta Sobre Migraciones en las Fronteras Norte y Sur de Mexico*.

11. La situación demográfica de México. Consejo Nacional de Población. http://www.conapo.gob.mx/publicaciones/sdm/sdm2011/SDM2011.pdf,p. 234, accessed 6 February 2012.

12. Detention refers to immigration detention—where immigrants await immigration hearings and deportation. Many more children are in foster care because their parents are in prison on criminal charges.

References

Applied Research Center. 2011. Shattered Families: The Perilous Intersection of Immigration Enforcement and the Child Welfare System, http://www.arc.org/shatteredfamilies, accessed 24 July 2013.

Arnold, C. 2007. Racial Profiling in Immigration Enforcement: State and Local Agreements to Enforce Federal Immigration Law. *Arizona Law Review* 49(1): 113–142.

Balderamma, F. 1982. *In Defense of La Raza: The Los Angeles Mexican Consulate and the Mexican Community 1929–1936*. Tucson, AZ: University of Arizona Press.

Brotherton, D. C. and L. Barrios. 2011. *Banished to the Homeland: Dominican Deportees and Their Stories of Exile*. New York: Columbia University Press.

Chan, S., ed. 1991. *Entry Denied: Exclusion and the Chinese Community in America 1882–1943*. Philadelphia, PA: Temple University Press.

Chavez, L. 2004. A Glass Half Empty: Latina Reproduction and Public Discourse. *Human Organization* 63(2): 173–188.

Chavez, L. 2008. *The Latino Threat: Constructing Immigrants, Citizens and the Nation*. Stanford, CA: Stanford University Press.

Coleman, M. 2012. The "Local" Migration State: The Site-specific Devolution of Immigration Enforcement in the U.S. South. *Law & Policy* 34(2): 159–190.

De Genova, N. 2002. Migrant "Illegality" and Deportability in Everyday Life. *Annual Review of Anthropology* 31: 419–447.

Dowling, J. A. and J. X. Inda. 2012. *Governing Immigration through Crime: A Reader*. Palo Alto, CA: Stanford University Press.

Dreby, J. 2012. The Burden of Deportation on Children in Mexican Immigrant Families. *Journal of Marriage and Family* 74(4): 829–845.

Fix, M. and J. S. Passel. 1994. Immigration and Immigrants: Setting the Record Straight. The Urban Institute Online at: http://www.urban.org/UploadedPDF/305184_immigration_immigrants.pdf, accessed 20 January 2012.

Fujiwara, L. 2008. *Mothers without Citizenship: Asian Immigrant Families and the Consequences of Welfare Reform*. Minneapolis, MN: University of Minnesota Press.

Glenn, E. N. 1986. *Issie, Nisei, Warbride*. Philadelphia, PA: Temple University Press.

Golash-Boza, T. 2012. *Immigration Nation: Raids, Detentions, and Deportations in Post-9/11 America*. Boulder, CO: Paradigm Publishers.

Gonzalez, R. M. 1983. Chicanas and Mexican Immigrant Families 1920–1940: Women's Subordination and Family Exploitation. In *Decades of Discontent: The Women's Movement 1920–1940*, eds. L. Scharf and J. M. Jensen, 59–83. Westport, CT: Greenwood Press.

Gutierrez, E. R. 2008. *Fertile Matters: The Politics of Mexican Origin Women's Reproduction*. Austin, TX: University of Texas Press.

Hagan, J., K. Eschbach and N. Rodriguez. 2008. U.S. Deportation Policy, Family Separation, and Circular Migration. *International Migration Review* 42(1): 64–88.

Headley, B., M. D. Gordon and A. MacIntosh. 2005. *Deported: Entry and Exit Findings. Jamaicans Returned Home from the U.S. between 1997 and 2003*. Kingston, Jamaica: Stephenson Litho Press.

Hernandez, K. L. 2010. *Migra! A History of the U.S. Border Patrol*. Berkeley, CA: University of California Press.

Hondagneu-Sotelo, P. 1994. *Gendered Transitions: Mexican Experiences of Immigration*. Berkeley, CA: University of California Press.

Hondagneu-Sotelo, P. 1995. Women and Children First: New Directions in Anti-immigrant Politics. *Socialist Review* 25(1): 169–190.

Immigration Policy Center. 2011. Secure Communities: A Fact Sheet. www.immigration policy.org/just-facts/secure-communities-fact-sheet, accessed 6 January 2012.

Johnson, K. 2003. The Case for African American and Latina/o Cooperation in Racial Profiling in Law Enforcement. *Florida Law Review* 55: 343–365.

Kasinitz, P., J. H. Mollenkopf, M. C. Waters and J. Holdaway. 2008. *Inheriting the City: The Children of Immigrants Come of Age*. Boston, MA: Harvard University Press.

Kerwin, D. and S. Y.-Y. Lin. 2009. Immigrant Detention: Can ICE Meet Its Legal Imperatives and Case Management Responsibilities? Migration Policy Institute. September. Online at: http://www.migrationpolicy.org/pubs/detentionreportSept1009.pdf, accessed 28 September 2012.

Lacayo, A. E. 2010. The Impact of Section 287(g) of the Immigration and Nationality Act on the Latino Community. National Council of La Raza. Online at: http://www.nclr.org/images/uploads/publications/287gReportFinal.pdf.

Lundman, R. J. and R. L. Kaufman. 2003. Driving while Black: Effects of Race, Ethnicity, and Gender on Citizen's Self-reports of Traffic Stops and Police Actions. *Criminology* 41(1): 195–220.

Marchevsky, A. and J. Theoharis. 2006. *Not Working: Latina Immigrants, Low-wage Jobs, and the Future of Welfare Reform*. New York: New York University Press.

Menjivar, C. and L. J. Abrego. 2012. Legal Violence: Immigration Law and the Lives of Central American Immigrants. *American Journal of Sociology* 115(5): 1380–1421.

Moloney, D. 2012. *National Insecurities: Immigrants and U.S. Deportation Policy since 1882*. Chapel Hill, NC: University of North Carolina Press.

Ngai, M. 2004. *Impossible Subjects: Illegal Aliens and the Making of Modern America*. Princeton, NJ: Princeton University Press.

Park, L. S. 2011. *Entitled to Nothing: The Struggle for Immigrant Health Care in the Age of Welfare Reform*. New York: New York University Press.

Quereshi, A. 2010. 287(g) and Women: The Family Values of Local Enforcement. *Wisconsin Journal of Law Gender and Society* 25(2): 261–300.

Ramirez, H. and E. Flores. 2011. Latino Masculinities in the Post-9/11 Era. In *Gender through the Prism of Difference*, eds. M. Baca Zinn, P. Hondagneu-Sotelo and M. A. Messner, 4th edn., 259–270. New York and Oxford: Oxford University Press.

Rios, V. 2011. *Punished: Policing the Lives of Black and Latino Boys*. New York: University Press.

Rosas, A. E. 2011. Breaking the Silence: Mexican Children and Women's Confrontation of Bracero Family Separation, 1942–1964. *Gender & History* 23(2): 382–400.

Rosas, G. 2006. The Managed Violences of the Borderlands: Treacherous Geographies, Policeability, and the Politics of Race. *Latino Studies* 4(4): 401–418.

Rosenblum, M. and W. Kandel. 2012. "Interior Immigration Enforcement: Programs Targeting Criminal Aliens" 20 December 2012 Congressional Research Service, http://www.fas.org/sgp/crs/homesec/R42057.pdf, accessed 1 January 2013.

U.S. Department of Homeland Security (DHS). 2012. FY 2011 Budget in Brief. Online at: http://www.dhs.gov/xlibrary/assets/budget_bib_fy2011.pdf, accessed 16 February 2012.

Wacquant, L. 2009. *Punishing the Poor: The Neoliberal Government of Social Insecurity*. Durham, NC: Duke University Press.

Young, J. 1999. *The Exclusive Society: Social Exclusion, Crime and Difference in Late Modernity*. London: Sage Publications.

Zilberg, E. 2004. Fools Banished from the Kingdom: Remapping Geographies of Gang Violence between the Americas (Los Angeles and San Salvador). *American Quarterly* 56(3): 759–779.

What Can Men Do?

Q: Why did you decide to record again?

A: Because this housewife would like to have a career for a bit! On October 9, I'll be 40, and Sean will be 5 and I can afford to say, "Daddy does something else as well." He's not accustomed to it—in five years I hardly picked up a guitar. Last Christmas our neighbors showed him "Yellow Submarine" and he came running in, saying, "Daddy, you were singing . . . Were you a Beatle?" I said, "Well—yes, right."

—John Lennon, interview for *Newsweek*, 1980

Are men changing? If so, in what directions? Can men change even more? In what ways should men be different? We posed many of these questions at the beginning of our exploration of men's lives, and we return to them here, in the last part of the book, to examine the directions men have taken to enlarge their roles, to expand the meaning of masculinity, to change the rules.

The articles in this part address the possibility and the direction of change for men: how shall we, as a society, understand masculinity in the modern world? Anjel Stough-Hunter and Julie Hart look at how anti-war veterans navigate norms of masculinity and military valor.

On the more personal side of the ledger, Erin Casey and Tyler Smith offer a sociological perspective on the moral and political efforts by men to support gender equality in moral and political terms, while Kelsey Kretschmer and Kristen Barber look at how men are attempting to mobilize as men to support feminist causes.

PART XI DISCUSSION QUESTIONS

1. Stough-Hunter and Hart demonstrate veterans' pacifist stances following the trauma of war. What is the role for trauma in challenging harmful consequences of masculinities? Is it necessary to precipitate a challenge against the violence and domination associated with hegemonic masculinity?

2. What are the prospects for social movements for healthier or freer masculinities that do not devolve into men's rights activism?

3. Casey and Smith provide a model for men's involvement in antiviolence activism. Is this model applicable to your institution? Why or why not?

4. How, if at all, can some of the more harmful aspects of hegemonic masculinity become jumping off points for men's solidarity with women and other men?

5. What are the roles for men in feminism? What are the roles of feminism for men? What, if any, are the limits of men's engagement with feminism?

"How Can I Not?" Men's Pathways to Involvement in Anti-Violence Against Women Work

ERIN CASEY AND TYLER SMITH

Engaging boys and men as antiviolence allies is an increasingly core element of efforts to end violence against women. In the past decades, men have become more of a presence in long-established domestic and sexual violence organizations and have created myriad men's organizing groups aimed at educating, engaging, and mobilizing other men to take an active stand against sexual and intimate partner violence. Based in the reality that the majority of perpetrators of violence are male (Tjaden & Thoennes, 1998), that risk for violence is connected to traditional notions of appropriate "masculinity," (Heise, 1998; Murnen. Wright, & Kaluzny, 2002), and that men are more likely to be influenced by other men (Earle, 1996; Flood, 2005), there is increasingly widespread agreement that the project of ending domestic and sexual violence requires male participation (Flood, 2005; DeKeseredy, Schwartz, & Alvi, 2000). Existing programs engage males in a continuum of involvement, ranging from raising men's awareness about violence against women to encouraging their active involvement in taking a stand against the abuse of women (being an "ally"). Examples include The Men's Program, a prevention intervention for men that has been shown to reduce rape-related attitudes and behaviors among some college students (Foubert, Newberry, & Tatum, 2007); Mentors in Violence Prevention (Katz, 1995); and Men Can Stop Rape's Men of Strength Clubs (Hawkins, 2005), ally-building programs considered "promising" prevention strategies (Barker, Ricardo, & Nascimento, 2007).

Still, knowledge building regarding men's antiviolence work is in its early stages. In particular, little data exist on the routes through which men initiate involvement in antiviolence efforts or come to define themselves as antiviolence "allies." In addition, although theorizing has developed regarding ally building in other social justice endeavors such as antiracism work, theoretical frameworks relative to men's antiviolence engagement are relatively new. Enhancing this knowledge and theory base holds promise for expanding outreach efforts to diverse men and for understanding how best to engage them. The purpose of this article, therefore, is to summarize research and theory regarding the process of initially engaging men, to present findings from a study of male allies about their involvement in antiviolence work and to evaluate the degree of congruence between these men's experiences and existing theoretical perspectives on ally development.

Models of Social Justice Ally Building

Engaging men as partners in efforts to end violence against women can be seen as parallel to "ally" development in other social justice arenas. Allies are typically defined as "members of dominant social groups (e.g., men, Whites, heterosexuals) who are working to end the system of oppression that gives them greater privilege and power based on their social-group membership" (Broido, 2000, p. 3). Significant model-building work describing the processes of ally building has occurred, particularly in relation to the development of antiracism allies. These models are likely instructive for enhancing theorizing and practice relevant for engaging men, particularly as many male allies may see their role as working to dismantle multiple forms of oppression (Funk, 2008) and because violence itself is inextricably linked with mechanisms of oppression (Sokoloff & Dupont, 2005).

Models of social justice ally formation are typically developmental in nature, noting the factors over time that collectively shape an individual's awareness of and commitment to rectifying social inequities. Across these models, critical elements of ally development include learning experiences regarding issues of racism and social inequity coupled with ongoing opportunities to process, discuss, and reflect on those experiences (Broido, 2000; Reason, Miller, & Scales, 2005) and opportunities to experience being a "minority" or to examine the parts of one's personal identity that are marginalized by "dominant" groups (Bishop, 2002; Reason et al., 2005). Specific invitations to participate in social justice work and modeling by respected peers or mentors is also important (Reason et al., 2005; Tatum, 1994). Finally, many models of social justice ally development highlight the central importance of developing self-awareness of personal sources of unearned social privilege in relation to other groups (Bishop, 2002; Reason et al., 2005; Tatum, 1994). Drawing on social identity theory, such as Helms' (1990) theory regarding White racial identity development, these models suggest that ally behavior is predicated on a "status" of identity development characterized by the acknowledgment of racism and other forms of social inequities, coupled with an awareness of how one's own privilege may be complicit in the marginalization of others. Taken together, these models highlight the multilayered nature of ally-promoting dynamics, which include intrapersonal factors (such as the ability to critically self-reflect), interpersonal factors (opportunities to engage with others across racial or gender "difference"), and environmental factors (concrete opportunities for involvement). These factors are likely highly applicable to male antiviolence ally development.

Theoretical Perspectives on Engaging Men as Allies

Although empirical models specific to male antiviolence ally formation have not been developed, researchers have proposed applying existing theoretical frameworks, such as cognitive behavioral theory and the Transtheoretical Model (TTM), to violence prevention and ally building efforts. For example, Crooks and colleagues (Crooks, Goodall, Hughes, Jaffe, & Baker, 2007) suggest that the cognitive behavioral principles of surfacing and reshaping an individual's core beliefs about an issue, identifying specific behaviors that build toward a desired behavior, and building opportunities to practice new behaviors could address common barriers to men's antiviolence involvement, such as ambivalence about the seriousness or relevance of the topic of violence against women and uncertainty about or lack of skill related to specific actions they can take.

Similarly, scholars argue that principles from the TTM are instructive in tailoring violence prevention and ally-building efforts (Banyard, Eckstein, & Moynihan, 2010; Berkowitz, 2002). A stages of change model, the TTM suggests that individuals occupy different statuses in terms of their readiness to engage in behavior change over time and that intervention strategies should be matched to an individual's current change stage (Prochaska, Redding, & Evers, 2002). Applying the model to a bystander-focused sexual assault prevention program, Banyard et al. (2010) found that participants' preintervention stage of awareness regarding sexual assault (ranging from denial of the problem to active involvement in prevention activities) was associated with the magnitude of the program's impact on the participants, with respondents in the "precontemplation" stage evidencing less change following the program. Although applied to a mixed-gender audience in this case, these findings suggest that the TTM can offer a helpful framework for thinking about differentially tailoring engagement efforts for men with different levels of awareness or concern for the issue of violence against women. This concept is echoed in previous conceptualizations of men's degree of engagement, such as Funk's (2006) "continuum of male attitudes toward sexism and sexist violence" (p. 78) that ranges from "overtly hostile" to "activist" in describing men's possible orientations to the issue of violence against women.

To date, however, the implementation of either cognitive behavioral or TTM principles in engaging male allies has not been expressly tested, nor do these models necessarily address the combination of internal or environmental precipitating factors that might motivate men to seek or avoid an opportunity to learn about the issue of violence against women in the first place.

Factors Associated with Men's Antiviolence Involvement

From the handful of studies that have explicitly examined factors associated with men's involvement in antiviolence or gender equity efforts, three themes are apparent. First, exposure to or personal experiences with issues of sexual or domestic violence appear to be a critical element (Coulter, 2003; Funk, 2008). Second, receiving support or encouragement from peers, role models, and specifically, female mentors is associated with initiation into antiviolence efforts (Coulter, 2003). This theme of peer support is echoed in findings that men's willingness to intervene in sexist peer behavior or a situation that may lead to violence against a woman is related to men's perceptions of their male peers' willingness to do the same (Fabiano, Perkins, Berkowitz, Linkenbach, & Stark, 2003; Stein, 2007). Finally, longer term dedication to antiviolence work is associated with employing a social justice analysis of violence that includes issues of racism and homophobia and that links violence against women to sexism (DeKeseredy et al., 2000; Funk, 2008).

Although these findings suggest that peers, mentors, and an awareness of violence or other social justice issues constitute a few of the possible important building blocks that support men's entrée into antiviolence involvement, little is known about the particular ways that these factors influence men. Other possible pathways in the probably complex process involved in deciding to join an antiviolence effort are also not yet elucidated. Furthermore, unlike more general models of social justice ally development, the degree to which social identity development and an awareness of male privilege are central to initial antiviolence ally formation is unknown. Although some approaches to engaging men in antiviolence work incorporate a focus on critically examining notions of masculinity, such as Men Can Stop Rape's focus on "re-storying" dominant narratives of manhood (www.mencanstoprape.org), the extent to which male antiviolence involvement is predicated on a critical awareness of male privilege remains unclear. As a whole, the specific factors influencing men's pathways to involvement have been identified by practitioners and current male allies as topics ripe for future research and investigation (e.g., Funk, 2008).

Summary and Purpose of the Study

In summary, although models of ally development have emerged from more general social justice arenas, the accuracy of these models in describing men's experiences of initiating antiviolence involvement is unknown. Furthermore, little data are available regarding the specific internal, interpersonal, and environmental factors that mutually facilitate men's antiviolence participation. Elucidating these gaps holds promise for more effectively reaching out to men and fostering their positive involvement in ending violence. To this end, this study examines qualitative data from interviews with 27 men who recently initiated membership or involvement in an anti-sexual or domestic violence effort. Specifically, this study aims to (a) describe the pathways through which these men became involved in antiviolence efforts, (b) build a conceptual model of participants' initiation into antiviolence work, and

(c) evaluate the degree of overlap between extant theorizing about social justice ally development and the participants' descriptions of their own experiences.

Method

Participant Recruitment

In accordance with procedures approved by the human subjects review committee, potential respondents were recruited in four ways. First, notices about the study were disseminated via several topic-relevant national email listserves, including the Prevention Institute's sexual violence prevention listserve and the Men Against Violence listserve on Yahoo. Permission to forward these notices to other relevant interest groups was included. Second, the first author attended relevant local community or agency meetings to announce and disseminate information about the study. Third, leaders of local men's antiviolence organizing groups were contacted and provided with information about the study. Finally, men who contacted the researcher regarding participation were invited to refer other potentially eligible men. Respondents contacted the researcher directly and were screened for eligibility. Participation eligibility criteria included initiating involvement in an antiviolence against women organization, event, or group within the past 2 years at the time of contacting the study and being a man 18 years or older. Consistent with the goals of the study, recent initiation into antiviolence work was included as an eligibility criterion to assess *current* factors and strategies associated with men's involvement; some data on factors associated with long-term antiviolence activism already exist (e.g., Funk, 2008). Eligible participants were then scheduled for a phone or in-person interview, depending on location.

Sample

A total of 43 men were screened for participation in the study. Fourteen described long-term antiviolence involvement and were therefore ineligible for participation. An additional two men did not return consent forms and therefore could not be interviewed. The final sample consisted of 27 men, aged 20 to 72. All but one identified as White; one man identified as Latino. This article, therefore, largely reflects the experiences of White men in coming to view the issue of violence as relevant to and actionable in their own lives. Of the 16 men whose length of participation or lack of consent form excluded them from the study, 5 identified as African American, 1 as Latino, and 10 as White. Participants from locations across the United States were recruited and represented all regions of the country. Length of involvement in antiviolence work at the time of the interview ranged from 1 to approximately 30 months.

Participants' involvement in antiviolence work generally fell into two categories: employment/volunteer work or involvement in a college campus-based organization. Of the 27 men, 10 (37%) were postcollege-aged men who worked or volunteered with a domestic and/or sexual violence–related program or government agency. These men's roles ranged from doing direct advocacy with survivors of violence to volunteering in a prevention education program for youth. Of these, 5 reported that part of their organizational role was to engage other men or boys around the issue of violence. Sixteen (59%) of the participants (aged 20–42) joined a campus-based antiviolence group or effort at the college or university in which they were enrolled. Typical activities in which these participants were engaged included facilitating educational presentations for other college students, organizing campus-wide antiviolence awareness events, or designing activities or events aimed at garnering additional male participation. Finally, one participant described his participation as being a part of a men's discussion group that had partnered in fundraising efforts with a local domestic violence agency.

Data Collection

Nine participants were interviewed in person and the remaining 18 were interviewed by phone. Interviews varied from 45 to approximately 90 min in length and were semistructured, with standardized general questions designed to elicit involvement narratives, followed by tailored follow-up questions to explore relevant issues in greater depth. Question topics included the nature of men's involvement; the factors precipitating their initiation into antiviolence work; their perceptions of effective and ineffective strategies for engaging other men; the impact of antiviolence involvement on their beliefs, attitudes, and behaviors; and their perceptions of the factors that sustain men's antiviolence efforts. For example, men were asked to describe what prompted them to become involved in their organization or event, followed by in-depth prompts to expand on any personal and/or environmental influences. All interviews were digitally recorded and transcribed.

Data Analysis

Data analysis was conducted using Grounded Theory techniques and principles (Strauss & Corbin, 1998). An inductive analysis strategy useful for building conceptual frameworks from data, Grounded Theory, emphasizes the development of conceptual categories derived through constant comparison of the dimensions of analytic concepts emerging from participants' data. Analysis was conducted by two researchers using the qualitative analytic software program ATLAS.ti. Coding was initially done separately by each researcher on several transcripts and then compared and negotiated until agreement was reached on categories in the data for the purposes of analyzing remaining transcripts. Coding proceeded in two phases. First, all transcripts were coded for general domains, with like domains pertaining to men's pathways to involvement grouped together. Second, close inductive coding on relevant domains was done using extensive memoing to uncover concepts within the data and relationships between those concepts. Particular attention was paid to the dimensions and qualities of the factors reported by participants as salient to their initiation into antiviolence involvement. Once saturation of concepts was reached, all transcripts were reread and compared for both confirming and disconfirming cases. When agreement between researchers was reached regarding

concepts and their theoretical relationships, trustworthiness was enhanced through the use of six member checks (Lincoln & Guba, 1985) and through third-party checks by two independent readers who evaluated the face validity of concepts and the data used to support them.

Results

Participants' descriptions of the specific factors related to their antiviolence involvement fell into three arenas. These arenas and the proposed relationships between them are summarized in Figure 43.1. First, all men but one had some sort of "sensitizing" or priming experience that raised their level of consciousness regarding issues of violence or gender inequity and seemed to lay the groundwork for being open to involvement when an opportunity arose. Second, all men had at least one tangible opportunity or entrée into an antiviolence group, volunteer opportunity, or job. Third, the meaning that participants had come to attach to the initial sensitizing and/or to the opportunity experience seemed to be a critical component of men's decision to devote time to antiviolence work. In other words, the impact of a sensitizing or opportunity experience or the particular ways men made sense of it, constituted the motivating factor that allowed men to take or seek an opportunity to get involved. Pathways of men's movement through these arenas are reflected in Figure 43.1 and described more fully below.

Sensitizing Experiences

Most men identified more than one previous experience that rendered the issue of violence against women more salient or visible. The sensitizing experience may have made the issue of violence more important or "real" and was the first influential involvement factor for 25 (92%) of the participants. One participant did not describe any sensitizing experiences, and a second participant encountered a sensitizing experience after his first involvement opportunity. The most common sensitizing experience was hearing a *disclosure of domestic or sexual violence* from a close female friend, family member, or girlfriend or witnessing violence in

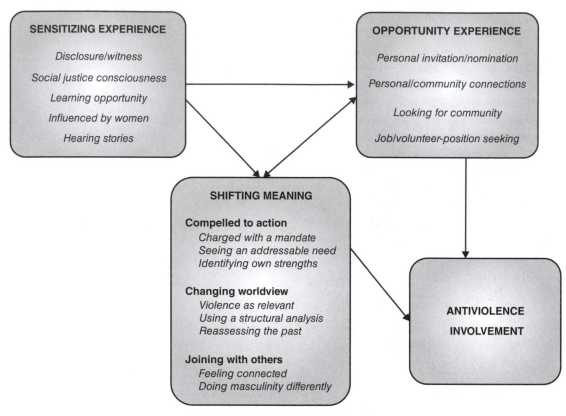

Figure 43.1 Conceptual model of men's pathways to antiviolence involvement.

childhood. Fifteen respondents (56%) reported exposure to violence or a disclosure of violence, and many of these participants described reevaluating the meaning of that exposure over time or as other sensitizing or opportunity incidents arose. Next, 8 respondents (30%) described a preexisting *social justice consciousness* or egalitarian value system as a factor in sensitizing them to issues of men's use of violence. This often stemmed from a respondent's own experiences of marginalization or from previous exposure to connected issues of racism, classism, and sexism. Another 8 respondents (30%) reported that they were exposed to a specific *learning opportunity* related to violence against women. For most of these men, this learning was a college-based prevention presentation on dating violence or sexual assault. Others were exposed to content through courses or lectures. Five

participants (18%) reported that *close relationships with influential women* (mostly mothers) made them more aware of threats to women's safety or fostered a feminist consciousness. Finally, 4 participants (15%) reported that they had been moved or troubled by a story or *stories of violence survivors* who were not personal acquaintances of the men. These stories emerged in a variety of contexts, including church, a work-related setting, and Take Back the Night marches.

Opportunity Experiences

Similar to their sensitizing experiences, many men encountered more than one tangible entrée into antiviolence involvement. Nine respondents (33%) were formally invited or nominated to become a part of an antiviolence group or event by an acquaintance, professor, or supervisor. Seven (26%)

of the participants were members of a friendship group or community in which others who were involved in antiviolence work encouraged the respondent to come to a meeting or communicated that participation was important, inspiring, or fun. Ten men (37%) reported that they were looking for a group, a "way to make a difference" or a community of similarly minded friends and that this active search precipitated involvement. Most of these men also knew someone involved in the group or effort that they ultimately joined. Finally, 5 participants (18%) initiated antiviolence work as the result of a job or volunteer position search. For 2 men, a formal involvement opportunity was the first influential factor precipitating their participation in some kind of antiviolence effort.

Shift in Meanings

As men discussed the nature and qualities of the experiences that led to their antiviolence involvement, they described specific meanings they had derived from these experiences. For 17 of the men, a meaning evolved over time from a sensitizing event, which then became a precipitate or motivating factor in seeking or accepting an opportunity to become active. For the remaining 10 participants, the meanings emerged following a tangible involvement opportunity, which often generated new reflection on earlier sensitizing experiences or exposure to additional sensitizing events. This new meaning making in turn precipitated accepting an offer to join an antiviolence effort or prompted the respondent to seek one. In both cases, the meaning that men attached to their sensitizing and opportunity experiences appeared to be a critical motivating factor in involvement. Three primary meanings surfaced, each with subthemes, and most men identified with more than one meaning. These are described more fully below.

Compelled to Action

This group of three subthemes was generally related to a sense of feeling obligated to take action or seeing a tangible opportunity for making a difference. Collectively, men who derived these meanings from their sensitizing or opportunity experiences felt that they no longer had a choice to do nothing, newly perceived doing nothing as contributing to the problem, or had a clear sense of how their own strengths could make a contribution to addressing violence.

Charged with a Mandate

The first of these sub-themes, "charged with a mandate," was reported by 9 participants (33%). These men reported a sense that their new knowledge or awareness of violence rendered them responsible for taking action. Several men felt that having this knowledge eliminated the option of being uninvolved or of not speaking up as long as women's safety was jeopardized. For example, the following respondent reflected on how his growing understanding of sexual violence led him to equate inaction with acquiescence and deepened his commitment to taking an active antiviolence stance:

> Instead of seeing isolated incidences of people that I knew who had been assaulted, [I] started looking at that as a systemic issue. And I think once I started doing that, it was like, okay, how can I not? . . . And I think I started putting that together . . . that it's a generalizable experience. Even people who haven't been assaulted experience some of this fear. I just knew what side of that I wanted to be on, and I knew that . . . not being active about it was being silent about it, and, therefore, in a sense condoning it. (MAV27)

Other men reported an increased awareness that simply not using violence in their own lives and being "decent" was not sufficient to reduce violence or to maintain the safety of women they care about. Describing the meaning he derived from a campuswide presentation, one participant stated,

> The thing that Jackson Katz was talking about is that, you could say, we're all good men here because we don't hit our girlfriends or wives, but he was saying, "Well, that's not good enough. You've got to be better men." And so that kind of inspired me. (MAV9)

Perceiving an Addressable Need

The second subtheme under the meaning "compelled to action," was "perceiving an addressable need," reported by 6 respondents (22%). The meaning is characterized by men's perception that violence against women is a problem that can be addressed or made tangibly better, perhaps more so than other social issues, as reflected in this respondent's statement, "I can't stop global warming tomorrow, and I can't stop poverty tomorrow, but tomorrow someone might not get hit" (MAV4). Other men got involved because they identified or were exposed to a specific need or to a contribution they could make. The following participant described the appeal of a full-time role in an antiviolence agency:

> I feel like I'm making a difference on a day-to-day basis by changing and/or having people listen to the story of the women. . . . Or the other day I got funded for a grant that I wrote. . . . And to get that notice in the mail saying we want to support what you're doing, you know those things are just huge for me. And I just feel like I'm making a difference every day. (MAV6)

Identifying Own Strengths

Finally, 5 respondents (18%) noted that the sensitizing or opportunity experience had the effect of highlighting or identifying a particular skill or quality in them that was needed. As a result, these participants felt that they had something specific to contribute, or felt trusted, honored, or recognized by encouragement to participate or by a disclosure from a survivor. Describing his reaction to a friend's disclosure of abuse one participant noted,

> I don't know if I knew the full power or the level of trust that's involved in telling someone else this, but I remember feeling really glad or good that she could trust me enough to say that . . . and that made me want to do that more. (MAV20)

On receiving a nomination to join an antiviolence education group, another participant learned about how his own skills could be tangibly useful,
which motivated him to pursue the involvement opportunity:

> I went through the interview process, you know I found out that the work they do was very presentation based, and I consider myself a very strong public speaker who's talking to a lot of male populations, or all male populations . . . and I thought that I could be a good, forceful speaker and really have a helpful role in trying to communicate with these populations. (MAV7)

Changing Worldview

As a result of processing their sensitizing or opportunity events, several respondents reported experiencing a deep shift in their thinking about their own experiences or behavior or in their level of comprehension of the ongoing vulnerability of women. This shift often served to connect the issue of violence much more closely to their own reality or priorities, or foster a previously absent emotional connection to the issue. Three subthemes also emerged in relation to the "changing worldview" meaning.

Violence as Relevant

First, 11 respondents (41%) reported a heightened awareness of the relevance of violence to their own lives, and particularly to lives of women they care about. Participants described feeling frightened, disturbed, or suddenly conscious of the multiple ways that violence against women manifests in their own communities. For many participants, disclosures of or learning opportunities about violence had the impact of splintering assumptions that violence is not a significant issue in circles close to them. For example, one participant described the magnitude of the impact of learning that his mother is a survivor of violence:

> To be completely honest, I really didn't think sexual assault was a very pertinent issue for me as a man until about my sophomore year. And, frankly, like probably until my sophomore year of college . . . I probably would have argued about the whole one in four statistic and other things like

that. Like I never thought sexual assault was a big problem on our University. And during a break I went home and found out through an argument that my mom and sister were having that my mom was actually a victim and survivor of sexual assault. And it really kind of turned my whole . . . my world over. (MAV12)

For many men, processing a sensitizing experience created a sudden awareness of ongoing vulnerability of people they love and generated an emotional connection to the issue of violence that was previously absent. This emotional connection in turn seemed to lay the groundwork for antiviolence involvement for these participants.

Employing a structural analysis was the second subtheme related to a changing worldview. Eight respondents (30%) reported that as they gained greater exposure to the issue of violence against women, they began to see it as connected with other social justice issues to which they were already committed. Linking sexual and domestic violence to social issues about which they had a preexisting concern, such as racism or homophobia, rendered the issue of violence against women more pressing or relevant. In making these connections, men felt that they could address larger issues of oppression by becoming involved in antiviolence efforts. For example, the following respondent employed an analysis in which he connected violence to two issues he cared deeply about, oppression and environmentalism, both of which he viewed as related to systems of domination and alienation:

And so when I work on the issue of sexualized violence, I'm conscious that I'm working specifically on the issue of sexualized violence, but I'm also conscious in that in working on that issue of sexualized violence, I'm also working on the general issue of violence itself and even more generally on that relationship between self and other, and if I can contribute toward undoing sexualized violence, then I see that as a contribution towards environmentalism, too. (MAV24)

For other respondents, employing a structural analysis was related to linking violence against women to other forms of oppression that they had experienced or witnessed in their own lives. Again, making this connection with personal experiences of marginalization rendered violence a more focal, "actionable" concern for these men:

I saw a lot of my friends growing up experience hate crimes and experience physical violence. . . . And so I guess I just . . . I was thinking about how I wanted to be as an ally to women in general. So I think that the way that I got involved in doing anti-violence work was through a lot of the anti-oppression work that I was doing when I was a youth. . . . I mean I started doing a lot of activism and stuff when I was 14, and you know I've been doing it pretty consistently since then. And so I think that my strong relationship to doing anti-oppression work really helped segue me into doing anti-violence work. (MAV 15)

In addition to the 8 respondents who identified a preexisting social justice consciousness or concern for social equality as a precipitating factor in their involvement, an additional 8 men spoke about how their antiviolence work has subsequently helped them form an analysis of violence that links it to social inequity in general, and patriarchal norms or "traditional" forms of masculinity in particular. These men explicitly made connections between violence against women and issues of sexism, male privilege, and race or sexuality-based oppression. In contrast, 8 men made no overt linkage between violence against women and broader issues of gender inequity or male privilege. Finally, 3 men could be characterized as beginning the process of examining how gender inequities are related to violence.

Reassessing the Past

Finally, 4 respondents (15%) spoke about how their sensitization or opportunity experiences led them to reevaluate past experiences or behavior. For these men, new learning about or new exposure to violence sparked additional reflection on past experiences, and perhaps viewing those experiences in a new way. The following 2 men spoke specifically about how their exposure to survivors of violence triggered a reassessment of past aggressive behavior that ultimately motivated antiviolence involvement.

> I guess I felt I sort of owed it to myself, if not society, and the universe to balance out who I used to be . . . so when this thing happened in high school, you know the accused . . . we literally kicked him out of our lives. And while I don't necessarily regret it. I do realize that is was ultimately probably not productive. And he probably went on to be a rapist or an abuser. He's probably more likely to turn out that way because of what we did. And so in a way it's like . . . sort of coming into my adulthood with this stuff, you know, I'm wanting to balance out the stupid, vigilante, adolescent emotions around this issue with adult proaction. (MAV3)

> My part in DV work is part of my redemption, a part of reconciliation with my violent past. Not guilt or shame, but redemption. (MAV31)

Reevaluating past responses to disclosure was also part of reassessment for two respondents. For these men, new learning about violence against women prompted uneasiness about the way they had handled past situations and motivated a desire to gain the knowledge and skills to provide support to survivors.

> In my senior year, the girl I was dating was actually sexually assaulted [by someone else], and there was a lot of gray in the sense that I didn't really recognize fully what had happened at the time. . . . I was really affected by that, and I felt very powerless. You know, I wasn't able to help her. I certainly blame myself a little bit for not realizing what had happened when it initially did. (MAV2)

Joining with Others

The third major meaning to emerge from men's sensitizing or opportunity experiences was a realization that antiviolence work was an opportunity to enact their own ideals with like-minded others or was a way of joining a compelling group that offered connection and support. Two subthemes are related to joining with others.

Feeling Connected

The first subtheme was described by 4 respondents (15%). Primarily through opportunity experiences, these men began to see antiviolence work as a way to build or enhance connection with others, particularly with other men. For these men, involvement was part of building community and a sense of mutual support. This is reflected in the following participant's description of his internal processing following his first exposure to a Take Back the Night event:

> Knowing that there was a community of people who cared and in caring, the community substantially contributed to the healing of individuals who were . . . being so vulnerable, and knowing that there was a community to work with and that we could support each other in this process because something as pernicious and insidious as sexual violence does not just affect individuals; it affects whole communities, and it's all of our burden to bear. And so knowing there was a community willing to stand in the face of that truth and stand together and then say no and then do the work to try and change some things . . . meant so much to me and made it worthwhile and continues to do so. (MAV13)

Doing Masculinity Differently

Another 5 participants described the appeal of realizing that they could work with other men in a way that was different from "traditional" approaches to masculinity or male friendship. These men expressed relief or excitement at the prospect of having close friendships with men in which they could express vulnerability, work collaboratively, and find broader ways of "being masculine" than masculine stereotypes might suggest. One participant noted,

> It was something about just sitting in a circle with a couple of guys and talking about, you know, how men dance compared to women, like how it's not okay to put your hands above your head when you dance or something [laughs]. Just things like that, that you would *never* talk about just walking

through campus or anything . . . and I thought that was really unique and really just honest, and it kind of lifts the weight off of your chest. Because I think a lot of the times, men walk around with this shield up, this . . . or we talk about the male stereotype *box* that we're always living in. Even if we don't want to, we're still put into that box, and that was the first time in my life where I didn't have that box around me. And I liked it. It was fun. (MAV30)

Discussion

Men's descriptions of the influences that precipitated their involvement in antiviolence work suggest that factors at multiple levels over the course of time coalesce into taking an active stand against violence. Specifically, initial sensitizing exposures to the issue of violence or to survivors, coupled with internal meanings that men attach to these experiences, and tangible involvement opportunities were critical to these men's pathways to engagement. Across these three arenas, four general commonalities characterizing men's antiviolence involvement surfaced. First, all participants described their initiation into active antiviolence participation as a *process* that unfolded over time and had multiple influences. Men's decision to take a stand against violence against women, attend an event or meeting, or join an antiviolence group was never constituted of or influenced by a single event or factor, but was rather precipitated by a combination of experiences and internal reflection that sparked or deepened men's interest in involvement. Second, respondents described specific ways in which the issue of violence against women had become personalized or emotion laden for them in some way. Their antiviolence involvement was predicated, in part, on discovering ways that violence was personally relevant to their own lives or those close to them or on making an empathic connection with the emotional consequences of violence. Third, the vast majority of participants became involved through or because of existing personal connections and social networks. Finally, many respondents made connections between their involvement and a sense of community: these participants felt that their

initiation into antiviolence efforts was supported by their own community or was part of an effort to find or build a sense of community for themselves. Collectively, these findings hold implications both for enhancing model development regarding antiviolence ally development and for the practice of engaging men in violence prevention endeavors. These are discussed in turn below.

Implications for Models of Ally Development

Men's descriptions of their experiences leading to antiviolence involvement evidence both areas of overlap and disconnect with the models of social justice ally development presented in the introduction to this article. Similar to the social justice ally models, antiviolence ally formation was a process that occurred over time, with factors at multiple levels (intrapersonal, interpersonal, and community) convening to influence involvement. Specifically, similar to models developed by Broido (2000) and Reason et al. (2005), men's pathways to involvement relied on initial exposure opportunities, engagement in reflection and meaning making over time, personal connections to the issue of violence against women, and tangible, clear invitations or opportunities to join an ally effort within their personal communities. These factors are likely important to retain and adapt in refining models of male antiviolence engagement. Future research could seek to more fully elucidate the mechanisms or intervention approaches that best foster the kinds of precipitating experiences, reflection, and meaning making described by both ally-development models and by men in this study.

A point of departure between models of social justice ally development and the experiences of men in this study is the degree to which male antiviolence allies engaged with their own social identities and male privilege as a precursor to involvement. Although approximately one third of the respondents described linking violence against women to structural justice issues as a meaning that fostered their involvement, this sometimes but not always took the form of interrogating their own social identities, ideas about "masculinity," or the role of male privilege in perpetuating woman abuse. About one third of men in the study made no explicit connection between violence against women and larger social inequities, such as sexism, even after a period of involvement. Although these men may have framed violence as problematic or people they love as in need of protection, there was an absence of exploration about the roles of gender and power in the perpetuation of woman abuse. Furthermore, only about 15% of the men in the study (those endorsing the "reassessing the past" meaning) explicitly described exploring the ways that their own past or current behavior might have reflected sexism as a step in their process of involvement. Unlike models of ally development more generally, therefore, the degree to which an awareness of gender-based social privilege is (or should be) a necessary prerequisite to antiviolence involvement remains a somewhat open question.

Several possible interpretations of the variance in men's engagement with issues of sexism exist. On a pragmatic level, interview probes may not have been specific enough to prompt all men to reflect on the ways that they engaged with the notion of male privilege as part of their involvement process. It may also be that the nature of many violence-related sensitizing or opportunity experiences (such as hearing a specific survivor's story, or receiving an invitation to attend an antiviolence event) do not contain explicit linkages between abuse and sexism, whereas sensitizing exposure experiences regarding racism or heterosexism likely contain, by their very nature, clear connections to notions of oppression and unearned social privilege.

It may also be that the relatively recent nature of participants' initiation into antiviolence work means that some are at the beginning stages of the process of employing a social justice analysis. The ongoing development of a critical awareness of gender inequity may be fostered by entrance into antiviolence work itself, as it was for about a third of men in this study. Practitioners have noted that initial awareness building and engagement efforts need to meet men "where they are" and that starting with conversations about male privilege may raise defensiveness

and deter preliminary participation from some men who have important contributions to make (e.g., Funk, 2006). At the same time, a lack of awareness of male privilege may create risk for recreating patterns of sexism within antiviolence work as more men become involved. Several practitioners have noted the need for men's antiviolence groups to continually consult with and be accountable to women and women's antiviolence networks to ensure that men's prevention efforts honor the considerable history of women's contributions to ending violence and do not replicate structures of inequity (Berkowitz, 2002; Funk, 2006). Although there is likely a middle ground of tailored engagement efforts for men that also gradually work toward a critical understanding of male privilege, the long-term effectiveness of ally efforts depend on tackling gender-based and other social inequities, as these ultimately buttress enduring violence. Further research is needed that examines the impact of involvement in antiviolence work over time on men's analysis of the roots of violence and how men's degree of engagement with issues of sexism and male privilege relates to their impact and effectiveness as "allies."

Principles from the Transtheoretical Model (TTM) may provide helpful strategies for moving men through the process from a lack of awareness about abuse, to engagement, to a more critical evaluation of sexism and its links to violence against women. Combining social justice ally models with processes identified by the TTM to support behavioral change may enhance both the accuracy and the interventive relevance of these models. For example. Prochaska et al. (2002) identify consciousness raising (increasing an understanding of the causes, impacts, and dynamics of a specific behavior) and environmental reevaluation (examining the impact of inaction or an unhealthy behavior on others) as typical processes associated with moving from denial of a problem to "contemplation," or a readiness to engage in new behaviors. Coupling these specific processes with initial factors in social justice ally development (such as sensitizing or exposure experiences) may increase the model's explanatory power and guide intervention development related to engaging men around deeper issues of sexism and violence.

Implications for Practice

As noted above, for most of the men in this study, the decision to become part of an antiviolence effort was influenced by multiple factors and occurred over time. Engaging men is a multifaceted process that likely demands repeated and diverse opportunities for exposure to the issue of violence against women as well as built-in mechanisms for men to discuss, reflect on, and make sense of the ways that violence is relevant to their worlds. Previously discussed applications of multiple, diverse strategies for men at different "stages" in their relationship to the issue of violence are needed, both to provide initial "sensitizing" experiences and the opportunities to create meaning from them. For example, large-scale community or educational events might be supported with a network of follow-up conversations, both formally and informally through peer groups, to allow for the kind of processing that could foster men's development as allies.

At the same time, although the men in this study were influenced by many different factors over time, a strong commonality among participants was the importance of personal connections and community in making linkages with concrete antiviolence opportunities. All but 5 participants located an opportunity for involvement through a friend or community member and 9 joined an antiviolence effort as the result of a formal personal invitation. This highlights the primacy of social networks as recruiting and engagement vehicles. Although many study participants were exposed to the topic of violence against women through educational presentations, community events, or college courses, these "learning opportunities" did not directly precipitate involvement on their own. Rather, encouragement and engagement from trusted peers or mentors constituted the tangible involvement opportunity that brought most of the men into antiviolence efforts. This echoes Broido (2000) and Reason et al. (2005) who found that the social justice allies in their studies did not actively seek action opportunities but initiated their social justice activities only after explicit invitations to do so. The project of engaging men and encouraging them to view themselves as allies is therefore perhaps best done individually through existing social networks and by admired peers and necessitates specific, personalized invitations to become a part of the work. Popular Opinion Leader (POL) approaches, which have previously been applied to HIV (Fernandez et al., 2003) and smoking prevention (Campbell et al., 2008), capitalize on the power of natural leaders in existing social networks and may be a relevant approach here. At the same time, engagement through social networks can build on "sensitizing experiences" that many men have likely already had and can foster the kind of meaning making from those experiences that supports antiviolence engagement.

Finally, this "meaning making" is likely central to men's process in coming to see themselves as antiviolence allies. Efforts to provide sensitizing experiences (such as learning opportunities or occasions to hear survivor stories) or to engage men through personal contact in their social networks may be bolstered by explicitly cultivating the kinds of meanings that men in this study came to attach to the issue of violence. These might include unambiguously issuing a charge of responsibility to addressing the issue, identifying specific needs and the ways that individual men's strengths and talents may contribute to ameliorating those needs, fostering connections with supportive groups or community, relaying the unacceptability and dangers of inaction, making explicit linkages between violence and other social issues men may care about, and highlighting the experiences of violence survivors in a way that helps men to interrogate their own underestimation of the degree to which sexual and domestic violence affect their communities and the people they love. Relaying information about the prevalence and impact of violence against women in general terms is likely insufficient to support men in seeing the issue as personally relevant; rather, helping men to form these deeper connections appears critical. Such efforts are reflected in existing men's engagement programs, such as A Call To Men (www.acalltomen.org), a national training organization dedicated to "galvanizing" men's antiviolence participation, and Men Can Stop Rape (www.mencanstoprape.org), which encourages young men to reframe and then act on "strength" in service of ending men's violence against women. Explicitly fostering several of these "meaning shifts" is likely an important element of any male antiviolence building effort.

Limitations

Study limitations should be noted. Perhaps most important, the sample of men in this study almost exclusively identified as White. Findings presented here, therefore, largely reflect White men's antiviolence ally development and the meanings and factors significant to their journey. A glaring gap in both the findings presented here and research about male antiviolence allies more generally is the experiences of men of color around antiviolence mobilization. Future research should examine both the unique factors that might influence the involvement of men of color as well as how racism affects men's relationships to ally movements and to taking a stand around issues of violence. A second limitation is the small, volunteer nature of the sample. Men in this sample self-selected to participate and therefore may represent a subgroup of male antiviolence allies who have particular interests or experiences relative to their work, which may not be more broadly generalizable. Future research with larger, more diverse samples is needed to evaluate the replicability of these findings. Finally, because this study focused only on men who have successfully been engaged in antiviolence work, it is not possible to contrast their stories with those of men who have had sensitizing or opportunity experiences but have not chosen to become involved or with those of men who have disengaged. Additional scholarship focusing on the discriminating factors separating male antiviolence allies from noninvolved men may shed additional light on how to design engagement strategies to maximize effective male participation.

Conclusion

Given that engaging and partnering with men is increasingly recognized as an important component of the formidable challenge of ending violence against women, it is critical to build on our understanding of the processes through which men incorporate antiviolence work into their own lives. This study suggests that, similar to existing models of social justice ally development, exposure to issues of violence, opportunities to critically reflect and make meaning from those exposures, and tangible invitations for involvement are some of the general interrelated factors that motivate men's antiviolence involvement over time. As the practice of engaging men and the models developed to describe it are refined over time, additional work is needed regarding the particular strategies that best foster the kinds of opportunities and meaning making associated with men's commitment to antiviolence efforts. This may be assisted by adapting elements of theoretical frameworks, such as the Transtheoretical Model, with models of ally formation to maximize the efficacy of efforts to broaden the range of men dedicated to ending violence in women's lives.

Authors' Note

The authors would like to thank the 27 men who volunteered their time to participate in this study, along with the many individuals who provided consultation throughout the process of the research, including Jonathan Grove, Taryn Lindhorst, Kevin Miller, Joshua O'Donnell, and Gayle Stringer.

References

Banyard, V. L., Eckstein, R. P., & Moynihan, M. M. (2010). Sexual violence prevention: The role of stages of change. *Journal of Interpersonal Violence, 25*, 111–135.

Barker, G., Ricardo, C., & Nascimento, M. (2007). *Engaging men and boys in changing gender-based inequity in health: Evidence from programme interventions.* Retrieved July 29, 2009, from www.who.int/gender/documents/Engaging_men_boys.pdf

Berkowitz, A. (2002). Fostering men's responsibility for preventing sexual assault. In P. A. Schewe (Ed.). *Preventing violence in relationships: Interventions across the life span* (pp. 163–196). Washington, DC: American Psychological Association.

Bishop, A. (2002). *Becoming an ally: Breaking the cycle of oppression in people* (2nd ed.). Halifax, Nova Scotia, Canada: Fernwood.

Broido, E. M. (2000). The development of social justice allies during college: A phenomenological investigation. *Journal of College Student Development, 41*, 3–18.

Campbell, R., Starkeya, F., Holliday, J., Audrey, S., Bloorc, M., Parry-Langdon et al. (2008). An informal school-based peer-led intervention for smoking prevention in adolescence (ASSIST): A cluster randomised trial, *Lancet, 371*, 1595–1602.

Coulter, R. P. (2003). Boys doing good: Young men and gender equity. *Educational Review. 55*, 135–145.

Crooks, C. V., Goodall, G. R., Hughes, R., Jaffe, P. G., & Baker, L. L. (2007). Engaging men and boys in preventing violence against women: Applying a cognitive-behavioral model. *Violence Against Women, 13*, 217–239.

DeKeseredy, W. S., Schwartz, M. D., & Alvi, S. (2000). The role of profeminist men in dealing with woman abuse on the Canadian college campus. *Violence Against Women, 6*, 918–935.

Earle, J. P. (1996). Acquaintance rape workshops: Their effectiveness in changing the attitudes of first-year college men. *NASPA Journal, 34*, 2–18.

Fabiano, P. M., Perkins, H. W., Berkowitz, A. D., Linkenbach, J., & Stark, C. (2003). Engaging men as social justice allies in ending violence against women: Evidence for a social norms approach. *Journal of American College Health, 52*, 105–112.

Fernandez, M. I., Bowen, G. S., Gay, C. L., Mattson, T. R., Bital, E., & Kelly, J. A. (2003). HIV, sex and social change: Applying ESID principles to HIV prevention research. *American Journal of Community Psychology, 32*, 333–344.

Flood, M. (2005). Changing men: Best practice in sexual violence education. *Women Against Violence, 18*, 26–36.

Foubert, J. D., Newberry, J. T., & Tatum, J. L. (2007). Behavior differences seven months later: Effects of a rape prevention program on first-year men who join fraternities. *NASPA Journal, 44*, 728–749.

Funk, R. (2006). *Reaching men: Strategies for preventing sexist attitudes, behaviors, and violence*. Indianapolis, IN: JIST.

Funk, R. (2008). Men's work: Men's voices and actions against sexism and violence. *Journal of Intervention and Prevention in the Community, 36*, 155–171.

Hawkins, S. R. (2005). *Evaluation findings: Men Can Stop Rape, Men of Strength Clubs 2004–2005.* Retrieved August 8, 2007, from www.mencanstoprape.org

Heise, L. L. (1998). Violence against women: An integrated, ecological framework. *Violence Against Women, 4*, 262–290.

Helms, J. E. (1990). Toward a model of White racial identity development. In J. E. Helms (Ed.), *Black and White racial identity: Theory, research and practice* (pp. 67–80). Westport, CT: Greenwood.

Katz, J. (1995). Reconstructing masculinity in the locker room: The Mentors in Violence Prevention Project. *Harvard Educational Review, 65*, 163–174.

Lincoln, Y. S., & Guba, E. G. (1985). *Naturalistic inquiry*. Newbury Park, CA: Sage.

Murnen, S. K., Wright, C., & Kaluzny, G. (2002). If "boys will be boys," then girls will be victims? A meta-analytic review of the research that relates masculine ideology to sexual aggression. *Sex Roles, 46*, 359–375.

Prochaska, J. O., Redding, C. A., & Evers, K. E. (2002). The Transtheoretical Model and stages of change. In K. Glanz, B. K. Rimer, & F. M. Lewis (Eds.), *Health behavior and health education: Theory, research and practice* (3rd ed., pp. 99–120). San Francisco, CA: Jossey-Bass.

Reason, R. D., Miller, E. A. R., & Scales, T. C. (2005). Toward a model of racial justice ally development. *Journal of College Student Behavior, 46*, 530–546.

Sokoloff, N. J., & Dupont, I. (2005). Domestic violence at the intersections of race, class and gender. *Violence Against Women, 11*, 38–64.

Stein, J. L. (2007) Peer educators and close friends as predictors of male college students' willingness to prevent rape. *Journal of College Student Development, 48*, 75–89.

Strauss, A., & Corbin, J. (1998). *Basics of qualitative research: Techniques and procedures for developing Grounded Theory*. Thousand Oaks, CA: Sage.

Tatum, B. (1994). Teaching White students about racism: The search for White allies and the restoration of hope. *Teachers College Record, 95*, 462–476.

Tjaden, P., & Thoennes, N. (1998). *Prevalence, incidence and consequences of violence against women: Findings from the National Violence Against Women Survey*. Washington, DC: National Institute of Justice and Centers for Disease Control.

Men at the March

Feminist Movement Boundaries and Men's Participation in Take Back the Night and SlutWalk

KELSY KRETSCHMER AND KRISTEN BARBER

Scholars and activists have long struggled with whether and how to incorporate men into feminist movements. Take Back the Night and SlutWalk marches are both feminist campaigns protesting sexual assaults on women and society's tendency to blame the victim. However, both campaigns tend to embrace different tactical and organizational strategies for managing men's participation. Born out of the North American women's movements of the 1960s and 1970s, Take Back the Night marches have frequently closed their boundaries completely or limited men's participation as a way to emphasize their claims for women's autonomy. In contrast, the more recent SlutWalk marches have decidedly open boundaries, allowing men to participate freely and to include their experiences as a central part of the event (SlutWalk Toronto 2014). These protest marches have spread globally and ignited popular discussions on women's rights to safety and sexual expression, becoming two of the most important and understudied forms of feminist collective action in recent decades. They highlight interrelated issues about how feminist movements have changed over time, the consequences of closed and open boundaries for movement messages, and how protest events are covered in the media.

In this article, we address two central questions: first, how have men been incorporated in or excluded from these feminist events over time; and second, how have these boundary decisions shaped the media coverage? By "boundaries," we mean the ways organizers explicitly or implicitly mark who counts as a movement insider, or "us," and who is a movement outsider, or "them" (Lamont and Molnár 2012). . . . Insiders and outsiders struggle over the movement boundaries of Take Back the Night and SlutWalk because the events attract media attention that can be leveraged to elevate some political perspectives over others in the public eye. Additionally, boundary disputes are attractive fodder for news reporters and editors because they add a dramatic angle for framing media stories about the events.

Our comparison of Take Back the Night and SlutWalk coverage offers two contributions to the social movements literature. While scholars have called attention to the ways American feminism has evolved over the last several decades (Reger 2012; Whittier 1995), less attention has been paid to the ways men have participated, how their participation has shifted over time, and the consequences feminist movements face for incorporating or excluding men (Bridges 2010; Messner, Greenberg, and Peretz 2015). Moreover, there has been little scholarly writing about how feminist events are covered in the media. . . . Taken together, a comparison of Take Back the Night and SlutWalk marches provides insight into how shifting movement boundaries have affected the organization of feminist protests and how these events are represented to a larger audience in newspaper coverage.

Men's Contested Place in Feminism

. . . Feminism has endured a long history of these boundary disputes, as movement actors struggle over men's place, as well as the role of women of color (Roth 2004), lesbians (Echols 1989), and transwomen (Connell 2012). Feminists in favor of expanding the boundaries to include men argue that men have a stake in creating a safer and more just world for women, and that without them, feminism settles for changing only half of society (Alilunas 2011). . . .

Activists aligned against men's inclusion, however, argue that the feminist movement should focus on women's experiences, knowledge, and understandings, with an emphasis on the structural disadvantages women face as a group (Messner 2011). . . .

Shifting Boundaries and Feminist Generations

Social movements are often long affairs, played out over decades or longer with each generation understanding their movement and its boundaries differently than those who came before and those who come later. Building on Karl Mannheim's ([1928] 1950) notion of political generations, scholars have argued that the feminist movement is best understood as successive generations "comprised of individuals . . . who join a social movement during a given wave of protest" (Reger 2012; Schneider 1988; Whittier 1997: 762). . . . Despite their differences, each generation reflects and responds to the claims and circumstances of previous generations, and

movements carry multiple, overlapping generations at any given time. Created by two distinct but interacting generations, with different understandings of men's role in the movement, and what their participation accomplishes, Take Back the Night and SlutWalk marches are prime cases to examine how shifting and contested boundaries affect the way feminist events are interpreted by the media.

Frequently referred to as the second-wave generation (Reger 2012), feminists of the 1960s, 1970s, and 1980s, varied tremendously in their ideologies and preferred tactics, but they shared a focus on women's common experiences of vulnerability to violence. This generation became active at a time when violence against women, and rape in particular, was not considered a serious problem (Bevacqua 2000). According to Ferree and Hess (2000: 103), "Rape was still treated as a joke, a sexual turn-on, and even as a sign of male accomplishment, but rarely as a physical assault, a psychological trauma for the victim or a major crime." In challenging the cultural and legal disregard for women's victimization, feminists who came of age in this era organized movement events in ways that emphasized women's collective vulnerability to men's domestic and sexual assault.

Feminists began organizing Take Back the Night marches on college campuses, downtown areas, local parks, and other areas where women are at risk of sexual assault. The marches have often taken the form of a nighttime vigil, with attendees carrying candles and chanting feminist and antiassault slogans. Many Take Back the Night organizers focused the event on women's experiences, but separatism from men was rarely absolute. . . . At the 1973 San Francisco event, for example, a small group of men trailed behind the large mass of marching women, encouraged by some women to join and rejected by others as "pricks in the parade" (Messner, Greenberg, and Peretz 2015: 27). . . .

For both pragmatic and ideological reasons, by the mid-1990s, younger feminists began pressing for expanded movement boundaries. . . . Pragmatically, feminists needed a broader movement base to withstand an increasingly hostile political and cultural climate dominated by the New Right, a conservative movement focused on pushing back feminist gains. The political environment forced younger activists to search out new allies, and, as a result, to reconsider the movement's boundaries. Unsurprisingly, this new generation proved more willing to accept men as legitimate members of the movement (Whittier 1995).

Ideologically, the third-wave generation was deeply influenced by the rise of transgender and queer politics in the 1990s and 2000s, which challenges the notion of a gender binary separating women from men (Connell 2012). . . . Third-wave activists declared their boundaries open to all kinds of feminists and all ways of expressing feminism, including differences in gender, race, class, sexual orientation, and sexual identity, among other characteristics (Bartky 1998; Hebert 2007; hooks 1998). . . . Rather than insisting on boundaries signifying women's common experiences of threat and violence from men, the third-wave generation constructs its movements as open, fragmented, and diverse, with multiple valid messages.

The emergence and development of SlutWalk marches reflect the increasing diversity in how feminists express their identity. In 2011, a Toronto police officer speaking to a group of college students told the women that if they wanted to be safe from sexual assault, then they should avoid "dressing like sluts." Many students angrily rejected the idea that women are responsible for their own victimization. On April 3, students of York University organized the first SlutWalk at Queen's Park in Toronto, with between 3,000 and 5,000 participants (O'Reilly 2012). On their website, the organizers explain, "We are tired of being oppressed by slut-shaming; of being judged by our sexuality and feeling unsafe as result. . . . No one should equate enjoying sex with attracting sexual assault" (SlutWalk Toronto 2014). They offer guidelines for "sibling marches" that explicitly include men as full and equal participants. In some cities, women and men wore the clothes they had been assaulted in, demonstrating that no particular style of clothing makes people vulnerable to rape (Carlton 2011). More frequently, SlutWalks consisted of women and men marching in provocative clothing and promoting a range of messages. Many of the marches paired pro-sex and antislut messages with messages about rape and victim blaming (Barber and Kretschmer 2013). . . .

Marches, Messages, and Media Coverage

Social movement actors almost always seek media attention as a way to validate the importance of their issues and to spread their messages (Gamson 2004), but they have little control over how they are covered or how well their messages are represented. . . . In courting media coverage, activists seek both "standing"—to be taken seriously in the coverage—and "demands"—being covered in ways that convey their frames and substantive messages (Gamson and Wolfsfeld 1993). . . . Evans (2015) argues that, in comparison to their moderate counterparts, radical groups can generate better coverage of their disruptive events because reporters and editors feel compelled by journalistic balancing norms to explain why they are controversial. These findings suggest that activists can leverage controversy around their event to achieve standing and demands in the media coverage of their events.

Given these dynamics, we expect that boundary disputes, like disputes over men's inclusion, matter for how protest events are covered and are likely a double-edged sword for feminist organizers. On one side, boundary conflicts at local movement events deliver precisely the kind of novelty and conflict preferred by journalists. Both the inclusion and exclusion of men provide journalists with a lens through which to view the event—either a surprising twist of men participating in a feminist march or a point of conflict when men fight to be recognized as a part of the events. In this way, the coverage of men threatens to overshadow the broader feminist message about women's safety and autonomy. On the other side, boundary disputes around men's participation might provide a critical opportunity for feminists to bolster their message in the resulting press coverage. Using the media bias for controversy, activists may be able to use men's exclusion to achieve both standing and demands in the resulting coverage. As our comparison of the newspaper coverage of SlutWalk and Take Back the Night marches demonstrates, not all organizers are equally able to do this.

Data and Methods

. . . We obtained newspaper accounts of the events by searching LexisNexis for the terms "Take Back the Night," "SlutWalk," and "Slut Walk." The sample was further narrowed to feature articles, announcements, editorials, and letters to the editor addressing a specific march, and by excluding articles about marches that happened outside of the United States or Canada, which have comparable gender politics and movement histories. We focus on articles in which a reporter, letter writer, or editor explicitly noted men's presence or absence, interviewed or quoted men at the marches, or discussed organizers' explicit decisions regarding men's participation at the events. Our analysis also includes articles that addressed other kinds of conflict occurring at the march, including generational and racial differences among activists. These parameters resulted in a total of 248 newspaper articles, with 72 published about SlutWalks between March 30, 2011 and January 17, 2013, and 176 articles published on Take Back the Night between May 24, 1980 and November 26, 2012.

Newspaper data allow us to evaluate several decades of feminist protest events by showing how men's involvement in the marches was framed over time and how the organization of the events shifted (Earl, Martin, McCarthy, and Soule 2004). Newspapers also include diverse kinds of information,

Table 44.1 Most Common Codes

Code	Take Back the Night	SlutWalk	Example
Defending men as not all rapists	12	0	"Or would it better suit march organizers' prejudicial agenda to believe all men are violent rapists deep down?" (Depasquale 1998).
Men explicitly excluded	38	0	"This march gives women the chance to walk the streets at night, unafraid, without male escort or permission" (Beads 1998).
Men explicitly included	40	15	"The men and women . . . were glad the two genders could finally march united in an effort to prevent violence against women" (Hewlett 2012).
Men included in limited and controlled ways	64	0	"[M]en are encouraged to take part in a program sponsored by the state Health Department" (Sutherlin 2002).
Men expressing feminist purpose of event	16	2	"'We need to hear . . . about what's making men and boys act in a certain way,' he said" (Paterson 2012).
Sympathetic family member/friend	12	6	"[Greg] Stevens told the crowd he joined the movement because his sister killed herself after being raped and hiding the fact out of shame" (Wiatrowski 2011).
Men as partiers and/ or dressed in costume or drag	0	13	"Dave Ferrier . . . wore a Superman outfit, with cape and microscopic bikini but no tights or shirt. He draped chains across his chest that held a bright green, plastic spike" (Hill 2011).
Men as victims	12	3	"He wanted to make it clear that men can be affected just as much as women. 'It does happen to men, too,' he said" (Rossetter 2011).

allowing us to evaluate multiple, distinct perspectives about the events (Mendes 2015). Of course there are also drawbacks to using data from newspaper reports. First, it forces us to rely on reporters' and editors' decisions about whether to cover marches, who to interview, and what to emphasize in their stories. If men were not mentioned in the newspaper coverage of an event, we cannot know if men were there or not, or how they participated. While this limits our analysis, the data offer a window into the consequences of inclusive and exclusive movement event coverage. Second, because Take Back the Night marches have occurred for decades and SlutWalks began much more recently, the time spread of newspaper accounts is uneven. Despite the imbalance, we include coverage from all of the years available on Take Back the Night in order to demonstrate the growing tensions reported in the coverage of these marches as the postfeminist generation began to press for greater inclusivity. . . .

Men at Take Back the Night and SlutWalk

. . . Specifically, we found reports of exclusive Take Back the Night marches, inclusive Take Back the Night marches, and Take Back the Night marches that allowed men some limited role in the event. SlutWalks, by comparison, were covered in the media as completely inclusive events with only one instance of organizers attempting to channel men's participation (see Table 44.1).

Exclusive Coverage

. . . Of the 176 articles on Take Back the Night marches that mention men, thirty-eight reported that leaders explicitly excluded men from participating in any part of the march or the accompanying events. The vast majority of these articles are clustered between the years 1991 and 1999. In fact, two of these articles reported on local marches that had previously included men but began restricting participation to women by 1992 (Todd 1992; Zacharias 1992). This clustering parallels the increased tension in those years between feminist generations around men's participation (Connell 1995;

Genz and Brabon 2009). While our data do not allow us to make claims about causality, it is clear that newspaper reporters and editors were growing sensitive to discussions about if and how men should participate in feminist movement events.

The coverage of Take Back the Night marches indicates that organizers faced criticism for the choice to exclude men, including threats of boycotts, charges that organizers labeled all men as violent, and arguments that the movement needed men's participation to be successful. . . . For example, in a letter to the *Providence Journal*, Kevin Farrell (1996), a student at Salve Regina University in Newport, Rhode Island, recounted his attempt to participate in the Providence Take Back the Night march when organizers asked him to leave. He wrote, "Women, in their struggle to end abusive relationships and educate others about domestic violence, forget that there are many good men out there who support them and want to help them. Let them not forget this so we can all work together to end this national tragedy" (Farrell 1996). Other men expressed a more hostile tone toward local marches after being excluded. Reporter Denise Davy (1992) of the *Hamilton Spectator* in Ontario, Canada, reported that a local radio host had accused Take Back the Night organizers of "drawing artificial gender battle lines," and warned, "When you exclude men or any group, you're provoking that group into some kind of backlash. . . . They're making men the enemy by excluding them." One particularly irate letter to the editor of the *Globe and Mail Toronto* argued that excluding men was going to cause men to become more violent toward women: "It's this elitist, condescending and untouchable attitude that breeds rapists" (Kennedy 1980).

Consistent with the literature on problems with men in feminism (Crowe 2011; Lingard and Douglas 1999), Take Back the Night organizers who excluded men had to defend themselves from charges that they were engaging in "reverse sexism" and victimizing men by excluding them. . . . Following a 1993 Take Back the Night event in Montreal, a female march participant complained that by excluding men, feminists had "overlook[ed] the many males who were abused as children, forced to hide their experiences like 'men,' and who cannot find help because of the lack of male support groups" (Bermingham 1993). Other reports included men and transwomen who protested that their exclusion from the event made their victimization invisible (Mohammad 2006). Based on the patterns of Take Back the Night coverage, organizers appear to have grown more sensitive and open to the claims of men and trans-women who have been victimized. . . . While the coverage of these marches included harsh criticism of the organizers, norms of balanced journalism meant that reporters and editors sought to include both sides of what had become a controversial issue (Gamson and Meyer 1996; Gitlin 1980). . . . For example, after criticism that the 1998 Take Back the Night march was discriminating against men, Tina Beads (1998), from the Vancouver Rape Relief and Women's Shelter, wrote to the *Vancouver Sun*, explaining, "We have always held this event as a women-only protest to make the point that all men are responsible for the violence done to women. This march gives women the chance to walk the streets at night, unafraid, without male escort or permission." Similarly, in a letter responding to an editorial in the *Calgary Herald* that had complained about men's exclusion, Take Back the Night marcher Melanie Burnell (1991) wrote,

> The women who march are asking men to listen to women for a change. So [the editor is] angry at being excluded and cannot accept the statement that "we want to show that women can act together and make a very powerful statement." Well, women have the right to be angry, too. And we have a lot to be angry about. For once, can a man not be supportive instead of trying to deny our right to find strength and love from each other?

Following a similar controversy at the local Take Back the Night march, activist Rose Simone explained in the Kitchener-Waterloo, Ontario newspaper, *The Record* (1991):

> Many men will say they are concerned about violence because it could happen "to my wife, or

daughter or sister." As genuine as this feeling is, the theme of these marches is that every woman—even a miniskirted prostitute getting into a man's car on the streets of Toronto—has an equal right to be free of violence. The notion that some women are more worthy than others—depending on what they wear, how they behave and where they walk—has been the basis of a lot of victim-blaming in our society.

. . . From this perspective, Take Back the Night organizers argue that when men participate because they want to protect particular women in their lives, they reduce the march's feminist structural critique to one of individual women. While Casey and Smith (2010) argue that men may benefit by participating in feminist movements by learning to connect individual experiences to structural sexism, exclusive Take Back the Night march organizers explicitly rejected this as a reason to include men.

. . . When reporters covered the controversy over men's exclusion, Take Back the Night leaders were able to gain attention for the event and articulate their message clearly and in their own words. . . . By keeping women's voices and experiences central to media coverage, denying these men's claims to the march became a second act of feminism.

Sometimes organizers announced an exclusive boundary but did not enforce it, and men marched as allies anyway. . . . At a 1992 march in Hamilton, Ontario, for example, organizers had asked men not to march, but a "handful" of male allies marched anyway. Marching with his female roommate, one man explained that while he "understood the reasons for excluding men, [he] didn't feel he deserved to be grouped with those who commit violence against women" (Todd 1992). While this sort of coverage shifted the focus to men's rights to be included in the march, reporters still asked march organizers to respond to the boundary breach. . . . In this way, when organizers erect boundaries, even when they are not enforced, this controversy provides a platform for organizers to reiterate their message.

Despite the benefits of exclusive boundaries, the newspaper coverage of Take Back the Night also indicates that this organizational strategy may be declining. Of the thirty-two total articles about Take Back the Night marches that explicitly excluded men, only six appeared between 2000 and 2012. Over the same time period, we found a sharp rise in reports about men's limited or complete inclusion in these events.

Limited Inclusion Coverage

While much of the earlier coverage of Take Back the Night focused on the conflict between organizers of exclusive marches and their critics in the community, later marches were able to generate standing and coverage of their messages by finding innovative ways to bring men inside movement boundaries while still barring them from the march. Articles describing this kind of limited participation for men are heavily clustered, with twenty-nine percent of them published in the 1990s and roughly 70 percent published between 2000 and 2012. In these events, men were invited to peripheral programs related to the march, including men-only discussion sessions about patriarchy or sexual violence or to provide support and services to marching women, such as childcare and refreshments. Newspaper coverage announced these opportunities in ways that affirmed women's centrality in the events, as in these examples: "Men who want to show support for women at the rally may participate in a separate event to be held near the women's rally site" (Penhale 1992), and "Men will have an opportunity to participate in the rally by lining State Street holding candles as the women march by" (*Capital Times* 1998). This kind of inclusion was the most frequent category of men's involvement in Take Back the Night marches. Again, we found no reports of SlutWalks where leaders limited or restricted men's participation in similar ways.

Men's limited inclusion carried its own distinct benefits for how the marches were covered in the newspaper. . . . Of the eighteen times that men were quoted in ways that clearly articulated a feminist purpose of the march, sixteen of them came from Take Back the Night events in which organizers prescribed men's roles. At a Take Back the Night march in Windsor, Ontario, during which organizers asked men to remain at the opening ceremony instead of joining the march, a male participant told the reporter, "This event is about women taking back the streets without being escorted. [Men] already have the privilege of walking safely. This is not our march tonight. . . . Men can be supportive . . . but step back in humility" (Hornsey 2003). Similarly, at a Take Back the Night march in Fredericton, New Brunswick, where men were allowed only at the beginning and end of the march, participant Bill Patrick told a reporter: "Sometimes in events like this, men show up but bring their sexism with them" (Hanley 2008). . . .

This method of including men allowed marchers to communicate messages about women's shared experiences and autonomy from men, while avoiding the negative backlash garnered by shutting men out completely. Allowing men to participate in limited ways also meant men had less opportunity in the coverage of the marches to complain that organizers were labeling them as violent or sexist, or to label feminists as man-haters (Pleasants 2011). The carefully controlled boundaries of these events also meant reporters had to explain why men were present but segregated. In this way, allowing men to participate in limited ways proved to be another effective way for organizers to gain positive coverage in the newspaper reports of the feminist protest events (Evans 2015). It also provided a way for activists to deal with increasing pressure to include men while maintaining the focus on women's experiences (Anderson, Kanner, and Elsayegh 2009; Digby 1998; Messner 2011).

Inclusive Coverage

In contrast with the more varied approaches to organizing Take Back the Night events, a defining feature of SlutWalks has been the open and inclusive boundaries for all participants and styles of participation. The event's creators explain on their website, "There is no prescription on what someone involved in SlutWalk needs to look like, be like, say, do, or identify as. . . . SlutWalk recognizes all gender expressions and identities as those that have been and can be negatively impacted. *All genders* are welcomed to SlutWalk" (SlutWalk Toronto 2014, emphasis in original). . . . Of the 72 articles that mention men's participation at SlutWalk, we found no reports of marches that blocked men from participating in any part of the event. . . . While we also found many reports of Take Back the Night marches allowing men to fully participate, its historical reputation as an event for women often shaped how men were discussed in the coverage.

Men as Allies

At both Take Back the Night and SlutWalk, reporters covered men who attended the protests to march in solidarity with important women in their lives. Eighteen of the 248 articles quoted or mentioned men who participated in order to honor specific women, with twelve reports coming from Take Back the Night marches and six coming from SlutWalks. . . . David Parra, for example, told reporter Sarah Mason at a 2009 Take Back the Night march at Washington State University, "I feel good about this. I was raised by a single mother and have a sister so I feel like I'm fighting for them, in a sense" (Mason 2009). At several SlutWalk events, male allies acted as leaders to honor women in their lives who had been hurt by sexual violence. In Tampa, Florida, for example, youth pastor Greg Stevens helped to organize a SlutWalk because, "his sister killed herself after being raped and hiding the fact out of shame. 'She knew people would label her a slut,' Stevens said" (Wiatrowski 2011). . . .

If SlutWalk organizers challenged this sort of participation from male allies, the newspaper accounts of the marches never reported it. As we demonstrate above, Take Back the Night coverage demonstrated a more complicated role for male allies participating in the march. But when organizers did not put boundaries around men's participation, male allies in Take Back the Night were covered in exactly the same ways as men in SlutWalks—as generally apolitical and motived by support for individual women.

Men as Victims

Both Take Back the Night and SlutWalk coverage contained men participating as victims of sexual or domestic violence. Across the marches, fifteen articles included men protesting their own experiences of sexual assault, with twelve coming from Take Back the Night marches and three coming from SlutWalks. . . .

. . . [T]here were significant differences in how the media covered their claims. For example, coverage of SlutWalks never reported that organizers challenged men's claims to equal victimhood. In these articles, reporters described or quoted the same number of male victims as female victims, giving the impression that men are victims of sexual violence at the same rate as women. In fact, one of the editorial articles covering a local Slut-Walk was devoted exclusively to male rape victims (Czernik 2011). In contrast, tension around victimhood status played out in the coverage of Take Back the Night marches even when the event being covered had explicitly included men. This coverage often included discussions of if and how men are victimized compared to women. In these articles, organizers often explain a shift in boundaries while contextualizing the march's historical focus solely on women's experiences.

. . . By the early 1990s, newspaper coverage began to include stories about Take Back the Night marches expanding to include men as equal victims of sexual and domestic violence, with 76 percent of these articles coming in 1994 or later, when calls for men's inclusion in feminism became louder. In Wilmington, North Carolina, organizers renamed their march, "Breaking the Silence," to communicate that sexual violence is "not only a women's issue." In a new effort to recognize the ways that Take Back the Night marches might be relevant to men, organizers told a reporter, ". . . men also are sexually assaulted. They also have to deal with girlfriends, sisters, or mothers who are victims" (*Wilmington Star-News* 1996). Similarly, the *Augusta Chronicle* noted that local organizers of a Take Back the Night march now refused to distinguish between assaults on women and men

(Steele 1996). Other Take Back the Night marches have expanded to include male and transgender assault victims as keynote speakers. By opening their events to men after years of exclusion, Take Back the Night organizers have proved sensitive to emerging claims about men and women's overlapping experiences of sexual violence (Walker 1995), and this increasing inclusivity was picked up in the coverage of the marches.

. . . While more inclusive boundaries likely encouraged greater media attention for men's victimhood, especially when Take Back the Night's theme was adjusted to include them, this choice also decenters women's experiences and voices, and shifts the core message about women's vulnerability to violence (Ashe 2007; Crowe 2011; Messner 1993). Abby Ulmer, a counselor at the Regina Women's Community Centre and Sexual Assault Line in Saskatchewan, for instance, struggled with balancing men's and women's experiences with sexual violence when she told a local reporter at a Take Back the Night march:

> Tonight is for anyone who has been a victim of violence. We know there's men who have been sexually assaulted and sexually abused as children, but a lot of times we talk about violence against women because when we're looking at issues of battering, sexual assault, childhood sexual abuse, still, the largest numbers are female . . . it's women who are often scared to walk at night, not men (Cowan 2003).

. . . In this way, many of the Take Back the Night marches that began including men lost the sharply focused original message about women's autonomy and safety and instead became general antiviolence protests.

Men as Co-Opters

The newspaper coverage of these protests included stories of men trying to co-opt the events for their own purposes, but the events' distinct boundaries meant that these efforts took very different forms. When men co-opted Take Back the Night marches, their efforts were often focused on communicating

that not all men were rapists (Snyder 2000). . . . In these cases, men used the march against women's experiences of assault to demonstrate their own innocence. The literature suggests this reflects men's interpretation of feminist messages as personal attacks rather than as engaging the larger structural problems that make men as a group more violent (Messner 2011).

In contrast, men's cooptation of SlutWalks more often took the form of revelry at the event. Of the 72 articles covering SlutWalks, fourteen of them specifically mentioned men attending in order to gawk at women, have a good time, or to dress in costumes. The *Ottawa Citizen* reported that both men and women attendees wore "corsets and fish-net stockings . . . leather, and sheer police costumes" before noting that some also arrived in jeans and t-shirts (Chen 2012). Across the coverage, male SlutWalk participants were reported in a wide range of costumes, including coming dressed in drag, as superheroes, or as TV characters (Hill 2011; MacLean 2011).

Reporters and editors sometimes celebrated the participation of gender nonconforming men and women, expressing explicit support for open feminist boundaries (*The Toronto Star* 2012). . . [Nonetheless], within feminist communities, the meaning of male drag is contested. While some say it is subversive and challenges constraining gender scripts around bodies and identities (Rupp, Taylor, and Shapiro 2010; Taylor, Rupp, and Gamson 2004), others claim drag is simply men reinforcing women's subordination through the caricaturing of heterosexualized femininity. In his study of "Walk a Mile in Her Shoes," an event in which men don high heel shoes for a mile long walk to raise awareness and money to combat violence against women, Bridges (2010) found that the participating men thought of the event as merely "for fun" and used dressing in drag to joke in ways that reinforced gender inequalities. Men's use of drag at SlutWalk appears similarly nonpolitical. . . . Reporters were eager to note men's use of costumes and drag, but these descriptions were rarely tied to any clear message about sexual violence or victim blaming.

Reporters at SlutWalks frequently focused on the men who did not appear committed to the feminist purposes of the event. Articles, editorials, and letters to the editor described men in attendance as wearing homemade t-shirts and carrying signs with slogans championing the sexual availability of women, including "I Love Sluts" (Turner 2011), "Trojan [condom] Field Tester," and "National Go Topless Day" (*Washington Times* 2011). These heteromasculine men sometimes explained to reporters that they attended the protest to physically touch women or to fraternize with "sluts" (Barber and Kretschmer 2013; Craig 2011). . . .

The coverage of men at SlutWalk marches often seemed to confirm activist concerns about men co-opting feminist movements in ways that undermine a feminist message (Ashe 2007; Digby 1998; Kahane 1998). Because reporters look for interesting angles in covering local events, men's presence at a feminist protest and their clothing choices became a central focus of SlutWalk coverage. When men participated, reporters more often covered participants' sex positivity and provocative clothing. . . . In this way, SlutWalk marches successfully attracted media attention. Yet while its organizers achieved standing, the feminist origins of the event were often buried in the coverage (Amenta et al. 2012; Gamson and Wolfsfeld 1993).

SlutWalks avoided negative community backlash by including men, but national reporters still used boundary disputes as a way to frame the events. In these cases, reporters focused on conflicts occurring among feminists, rather than between feminists and movement outsiders. Rebecca Traister (2011) of the *New York Times Magazine* argued that, in their effort to be broadly inclusive and to reappropriate the word "slut" for all women, SlutWalk organizers created an inhospitable environment for many women, including women of color, older women, and more conservative women (Black Women's Blueprint 2011; Hobson 2011). . . . While Traister named multiple groups of women who might feel excluded from SlutWalks, newspaper coverage focused exclusively on the divide between feminist generations, with representatives from both generations weighing in on the SlutWalk theme and the organizational style of the event (Howell 2011; Tillotson 2011; Valenti 2011; Wedlund 2011). . . .

Despite activist and scholarly concerns about SlutWalk's unintentional exclusion of women of color (Black Women's Blueprint 2011; Hobson 2011), we found no articles that mentioned a racialized boundary dispute. This is a puzzling finding, and we return to it in our conclusion. In sum, the media coverage of SlutWalks indicates that activists pay a particular cost when organizing with open boundaries. Reporters often focus on the varied styles of participation in ways that draw attention to the movement's sex-positive messaging, while de-emphasizing its antiassault message. Moreover, despite its open boundaries, some women feel uncomfortable and excluded anyway.

Conclusion

Questions about how men participate in Take Back the Night and SlutWalk protest events are at the heart of larger debates about movement boundaries. Our comparison of these understudied events demonstrates that boundary struggles can have unanticipated consequences for how activists and their events are covered in the media. We found that Take Back the Night's roots in 1970s feminism often made men's participation a complicated and controversial process, even when organizers included them. In contrast, SlutWalk's open ethos was reflected in the coverage of these marches, where there were virtually no reports of controversy over men's participation. . . .

Activists struggle to control their messages in media coverage, and this is especially true when they organize disruptive events, like protest marches (Amenta et al. 2012; Gamson and Wolfsfeld 1993; Sobieraj 2011). Consistent with this literature, we find that reporters of both SlutWalk and Take Back the Night focused on controversies and conflicts at the marches. Our data, however, provide an important insight for how some organizers are able to manage this media attention in ways that bring the focus back to their central demands.

Sharp event boundaries consistently garnered public condemnation from both men and women who disagreed with the decision to exclude men, but the controversy gave Take Back the Night organizers opportunities to rearticulate their reasoning and goals, giving them both standing and demands in the coverage.

Newer feminist generations frequently blur movement boundaries, emphasizing fluid sexual and gender identities, and creating space for men to participate in events like SlutWalk (Barber and Kretschmer 2013; Reger 2012; Snyder 2008; Walker 1992; 1995). While this approach gives men a stake in the movement, it also frees them to push their own movement frames and agendas. This freedom sometimes brought important recognition for men's and transwomen's experiences of violence and oppression, but it also allowed the SlutWalk message to broaden and depoliticize when reporters focused on the most flamboyant, celebratory, or heteromasculine participants. Responding to the increased pressure on feminists to lower movement boundaries, more Take Back the Night events have broadened to include men in unrestrained ways and have borne similar costs to SlutWalk, with broader messages and less focused demands. Other Take Back the Night organizers charted a middle course between these loaded choices by allowing men's limited participation. This strategy eased tensions by including supportive men without losing the potent message of women's only events in the newspaper coverage. . . .

. . . Building on our work, researchers should pay attention to where and why there are discrepancies between what organizers intend and what ultimately changes public perceptions of the movement and issues. We also believe that the racial boundaries of these events deserve greater attention. Given the amount of national media and scholarly attention dedicated to the racial differences around SlutWalk events (Black Women's Blueprint 2011; Hobson 2011; Reger 2015; Traister 2011), we find it puzzling that this discussion failed to show up in the local media accounts. . . . A direct racial analysis of both inclusive and exclusive boundaries in feminist protests could help us understand how these events are covered in the media and the consequences for *whose* sexual victimization receives public attention and protest. Our analysis suggests that, in addition to the boundaries that keep some actors out, there are also internal boundaries among activists sharing a movement that can affect the form and content of the movements' messages to the wider world.

References

Alilunas, Peter. 2011. "The (In)visible People in the Room: Men in Women's Studies." *Men and Masculinities* 14(2): 210–229.

Amenta, Edwin, Beth Gharrity Gardner, Amber Celina Tierney, Anaid Yerena, and Thomas Alan Elliott. 2012. "A Story-Centered Approach to the Newspaper Coverage of High-Profile SMOs." *Research in Social Movements, Conflicts and Change* 33: 83–107.

Anderson, Kristin J., Melinda Kanner, and Nisreen Elsayegh. 2009. "Are Feminists Man Haters? Feminists' and Nonfeminists' Attitudes toward Men." *Psychology of Women Quarterly* 33(2): 216–224.

Ashe, Fidelma. 2007. *The New Politics of Masculinity: Men, Power and Resistance*. London: Routledge.

Barber, Kristen, and Kelsy Kretschmer. 2013. "Walking Like a Man?" *Contexts* 12(40): 41–46.

Bartky, Sandra. 1998. "Foreword." In *Men Doing Feminism*, edited by Tom Digby. London: Routledge.

Beads, Tina. "March Gives Women a Chance to Walk Without Fear," *The Vancouver Sun*, September 26, 1998.

Bermingham, Clare. "Something Missing: Take Back the Night Should Include Men," *The Record*, October 21, 1993.

Bevacqua, Maria. 2000. *Rape on the Public Agenda: Feminism and the Politics of Sexual Assault*. Boston: Northeastern University Press.

Black Women's Blueprint. 2011. "An Open Letter from Black Women to the SlutWalk." (http://www.blackwomensblueprint.org/2011/09/23/an-open-letter-from-black-women-to-the-slutwalk/). Retrieved September 4, 2014.

Bridges, Tristan S. 2010. "Men Just Weren't Made to Do This: Performances of Drag at 'Walk a Mile in Her Shoes' Marches." *Gender & Society* 24(1): 5–30.

Burnell, Melanie. "Women Asking Men to Listen for a Change," *Calgary Herald*, October 12, 1991.

Capital Times. "Take Back the Night," September 28, 1998.

Carlton, Sue. "Support the Idea, if Not the Costumes," *Tampa Bay Times*, September 17, 2011.

Casey, Erin, and Tyler Smith. 2010. "'How Can I Not?': Men's Pathways to Involvement in Anti-Violence Against Women Work." *Violence Against Women* 16(8): 953–973.

Chen, Karen. "Targeting Abusers and Society; Slut-Walk Aims to Change Attitudes," *Ottawa Citizen*, August 20, 2012.

Connell, R. W. 1995. *Masculinities*. Berkeley: University of California Press.

———. 1997. "Men, Masculinities and Feminism." *Social Alternatives* 16(3): 7–10.

———. 2012. "Transsexual Women and Feminist Thought: Toward New Understanding and New Politics." *Signs* 37(4): 857–881.

Cowan, Pamela. "Stand Taken Against Violence," *The Leader-Post*, September 20, 2003.

Craig, Natalie. "A Rally to Find the Slut in Everyone," *Sunday Age*, May 29, 2011.

Crowe, Jonathon. 2011. "Men and Feminism: Some Challenges and a Partial Response." *Social Alternatives* 30(1): 49–53.

Czernik, Ann. "Why We Should Say We've All Had Enough . . . ," *Morning Star*, July 6, 2011.

Davy, Denise. "Critics Anger Organizers of March; Tonight's Walk Excludes Men," *Hamilton Spectator*, September 23, 1992.

Depasquale, Marie. "Feminism's Fundamental Value is Equality, Not Exclusion," *The Vancouver Sun*, September 25, 1998.

Digby, Tom. 1998. *Men Doing Feminism*. London: Routledge.

Earl, Jennifer, Andrew Martin, John D. McCarthy, and Sarah A. Soule. 2004. "The Use of Newspaper Data in the Study of Collective Action." *Annual Review of Sociology* 30: 65–80.

Evans, Erin M. 2015. "Bearing Witness: How Controversial Organizations Get the Media Coverage They Want." *Social Movement Studies* (pre-publication). Published 2016, 15(1): 41–59.

Farrell, Kevin J. "Let Men March, Too," *Providence Journal*, October 11, 1996.

Ferree, Myra Marx, and Beth Hess. 2000. *Controversy and Coalition: The New Feminist Movement Across Four Decades of Change*. New York: Routledge.

Gamson, William A. 2004. "Bystanders, Public Opinion, and the Media." Pp. 242–261 in *The Blackwell Companion to Social Movements*, edited by David A. Snow, Sarah A. Soule, and Hanspeter Kriesi. Malden, MA: Blackwell Publishing.

Gamson, William A., and David S. Meyer. 1996. "Framing Political Opportunity." Pp. 275–90 in *Comparative Perspectives on Social Movements: Political Opportunities, Mobilizing Structures, and Cultural Framings*, edited by Doug McAdam, John McCarthy, and Mayer Zald. Cambridge, UK: Cambridge University Press.

Gamson, William. A., and Gadi Wolfsfeld. 1993. Movements and Media as Interacting Systems. *Annals of the American Academy of Political and Social Science* 528: 114–125.

Genz, Stéphanie, and Benjamin A. Brabon. 2009. *Postfeminism: Cultural Texts and Theories*. Edinburgh: Edinburgh University Press.

Gitlin, Todd. 1980. *The Whole World is Watching: Mass Media in the Making and Unmaking of the New Left*. Berkeley, CA: University of California Press.

Hanley, Glenna. "Women Urged to Report all Sexual Violence," *The Daily Gleaner*, September 20, 2008.

Hebert, Laura A. 2007. "Taking 'Difference' Seriously: Feminism and the 'Man Question.'" *Journal of Gender Studies* 16(1): 31–45.

Hewlett, Jason. "Men Join Women in Protest over Violence," *Kamloops Daily News*, September 22, 2012.

Hill, Miriam. "At SlutWalk, Clothes Make the Woman—and a Point," *Philadelphia Inquirer*, August 7, 2011.

Hobson, Janell. 2011. *Should Black Women Oppose the SlutWalk?* (http://msmagazine.com/blog/2011/09/27/should-black-women-oppose-the-Slut Walk/). Retrieved March 12, 2014.

hooks, bell. 1998. "Men: Comrades in Struggle." Pp. 265 in *Feminism and Men: Reconstructing Gender Relations*, edited by Steven P. Schacht and Doris W. Ewing. New York: New York University Press.

Hornsey, Chris. "We're Still Fighting for Change," *Windsor Star*, October 20, 2003.

Howell, Sarah. "SlutWalk is like Gay Pride Parade," *The Calgary Herald*, July 28, 2011.

Ives, Millard K. "Crowd Rallies Against Domestic Violence," *Morning Star*, October 5, 2001.

Kahane, David J. 1998. "Male Feminism as Oxymoron." Pp. 213-236 in *Men Doing Feminism*, edited by Tom Digby. New York: Routledge.

Kennedy, Linn. "Rapists," *The Globe and Mail Toronto*, May 24, 1980.

Lamont, Michèle, and Virág Molnár. 2012. "The Study of Boundaries in the Social Sciences." *Annual Review of Sociology* 28: 167–195.

Lingard, Bob, and Peter Douglas. 1999. *Men Engaging Feminisms: Pro-Feminism, Backlashes and Schooling*. Buckingham, UK: Open University Press.

MacLean, Rory. "Walk Raises Awareness of Sexual Violence," *The Star Phoenix*, May 30, 2011.

Mannheim, Karl. [1928] 1952. "The Problem of Generations." Pp. 276–332 in *Essays on the Sociology of Knowledge*, edited by Paul Kecskemeti. London, UK: Routledge and Kegan Paul.

Mason, Sarah. "Rally for the Night: WSU Hosts 26th Annual March Against Violence," *Moscow-Pullman Daily News*, October 15, 2009.

Mendes, Kaitlynn D. 2015. *SlutWalk: Feminism, Activism and Media*. New York, NY: Palgrave Macmillan.

Messner, Michael A. 1993. "'Changing Men' and Feminist Politics in the United States." *Theory and Society* 22(5): 723–737.

———. 2011. "Review of *Men Speak Out: Views on Gender, Sex, and Power*, by Shira Tarrant (2008) and *Men and Feminism*, by Shira Tarrant (2009)." *Signs* 36(2): 487–490.

Messner, Michael A., Max A. Greenberg, and Tal Peretz. 2015. *Some Men: Feminist Allies in the Movement to End Violence Against Women*. New York, NY: Oxford University Press.

Mohammad, Susan. "450 Walk to Take Back the Night: Killing of Khatera Sadiqi Casts Shadow on Annual Protest," *Ottawa Citizen*, September 29, 2006.

O'Reilly, Andrea. 2012. "Slut Pride: A Tribute to SlutWalk Toronto." *Feminist Studies* 38(1): 245–50.

Paterson, David. "Malton Rally Calls for End to Sexual Violence," *The Mississaugua News*, September 29, 2012.

Penhale, Ed. "Tomorrow's March is for Women Only," *Seattle Post–Intelligencer*, May 8, 1992.

Pleasants, Robert K. 2011. "Men Learning Feminism: Protecting Privileges through Discourses of Resistance." *Men and Masculinities* 14(2): 230–50.

Reger, Jo. 2012. *Everywhere and Nowhere: U.S. Feminist Communities in the 21st Century*. New York, NY: Oxford University Press.

———. 2015. "The Story of a SlutWalk: Sexuality, Race, and Generational Divisions in Contemporary Feminist Activism." *Journal of Contemporary Ethnography* 44(1): 84–112.

Rossetter, Shelley. "No Excuse for Assault," *Tampa Bay Times*, September 18, 2011.

Roth, Benita. 2004. *Separate Roads to Feminism: Black, Chicana, and White: Feminist Movements in America's Second Wave*. New York, NY: Cambridge University Press.

Rupp, Leila J., Verta Taylor, and Eve Illana Shapiro. 2010. "Drag Queens and Drag Kings: The Difference Gender Makes." *Sexualities* 13(3): 275–294.

Schneider, Beth. 1988. "Political Generations in the Contemporary Women's Movement." *Sociological Inquiry* 58(1): 4–21

Simone, Rose. "Men Need their Own Anti-Violence Rallies," *The Record*, October 4, 1991.

SlutWalk Toronto. 2014. "Why." (http://www.SlutWalktoronto.com/ about/why). Retrieved March 14, 2014.

Snyder, Brady. "Marchers Take Back the Night," *Deseret News*, April 13, 2000.

Snyder, R Claire. 2008. "What is Third Wave Feminism? A New Directions Essay." *Signs* 34(1): 175–196.

Sobieraj, Sarah. 2011. *Soundbitten: The Perils of Media-Centered Political Activism*. New York: New York University Press.

Steele, Kathy. "March and Vigil Planned," *The Augusta Chronicle*, April 13, 1996.

Sutherlin, Michelle. "Events to Focus on Rape Awareness," *Daily Oklahoman*, November 6, 2002.

Taylor, Verta, Leila J. Rupp, and Joshua Gamson. 2004. "Performing Protest: Drag Shows as Tactical Repertoires of the Gay and Lesbian Movement." *Research in Social Movements, Conflict and Change* 25: 105–137.

Tillotson, Kristin. "Protest March Divides Feminists," *Star Tribune*, September 29, 2011.

Todd, Rosemary. "Women Divided on Barring Men; Marchers are United Against Violence," *Hamilton Spectator*, September 18, 1992.

Toronto Star. "Cheerfully Defusing the Hatred," May 26, 2012.

Traister, Rebecca. 2011. "Ladies, We Have a Problem: Sluts, Nuts and the Clumsiness of Reappropriation." *New York Times Magazine*, July 24, 9–10.

Turner, Janice. "SlutWalks are Treading on Dangerous Ground," *The Times (London)*, May 14, 2011.

Valenti, Jessica. "The New Feminists: As Slutty As We Want to be," *The Washington Post*, June 5, 2011.

Walker, Rebecca. 1992. "Becoming the Third Wave." *Ms. Magazine* January/February: 39–41.

———. 1995. *To Be Real: Telling the Truth and Changing the Face of Feminism*. New York, NY: Anchor Books

Washington Times. "Rape at the Washington Monument; Sightseeing Families Assaulted by R-rated Speeches," August 18, 2011.

Wedlund, Rachel. "SlutWalk March Draws All Types, A Few in Fishnets in Minneapolis," *Star Tribune*, September 30, 2011.

Whittier, Nancy. 1995. *Feminist Generations: The Persistence of the Radical Women's Movement*. Philadelphia: Temple University Press.

———. 1997. "Political Generations, Microcohorts, and the Transformation of Social Movements." *American Sociological Review* 62(5): 760–778.

Wiatrowski, Kevin. "SlutWalk Outs Sex-Assault Stigma," *Tampa Tribune*, September 18, 2011.

Wilmington Star-News. "Event to Target Sexual Violence," March 29, 1996.

Zacharias, Yvonne. "Women's Centre Leads the March; Concordia Group is Committed to Helping 'Build a Feminist Community,'" *The Gazette*, September 21, 1992.

Understanding Masculine Identity among Anti-War Veterans

ANJEL STOUGH-HUNTER AND JULIE HART

Introduction

There is a clear and strong connection between the military and masculinity in the USA, with the military as a key arena for the definition of hegemonic masculinity (Connell, 2005, p. 213). Joining the military provides ideological, symbolic, and material resources that aid men in aligning their identity to a hegemonic masculine ideal (Hinojosa, 2010). Leaving the military, regardless of one's position on war, to re-enter civilian life is challenging for many reasons. A key challenge is defining and verifying one's identity outside of the military organization, which may even lead to identity conflict (Smith & True, 2014). Adopting an anti-war position upon leaving has the potential to further complicate identity definition and verification. Given the strong connection between the military and masculinity, men who adopt an anti-war position may be particularly challenged in the renegotiation of their masculine identity upon re-entry to civilian life.

Informed by the Control Systems Approach of Identity Theory and hegemonic masculinity (Burke & Stets, 2009; Connell, 2005), this study examines masculine identity among a group of 26 veterans. We use male veterans, who due to their military experience, transformed from a pro-war to an anti-war identity. In assuming an antiwar identity, these veterans revised their meanings of masculinity for

themselves and with others. We ask: What happens to masculine identity when service members embrace an anti-war position? By exploring how veterans (re)-negotiate hegemonic masculinity from an anti-war position, this study augments the identity theory framework with the concept of hegemonic masculinity (Burke & Stets, 2009).

Masculinity and Identity Theory

Identity theory focuses on the importance of social interaction in the formation of one's self (Stryker, 1980). One's self is composed of multiple identities and corresponding identity standards (i.e. the meaning and criteria an individual associates with each of his or her identities). Individuals engage in a self-regulating cycle of identity verification through which they manage the maintenance and performance of their identities (Burke & Stets, 2009).

Several elements of identity theory are particularly important to this study. First, multiple identities are ordered in an identity hierarchy (Burke & Stets, 2009; Stryker, 1980). An individual's identities can be divided into three categories: person, role, and social or group. Person identities contain the unique attributes of an individual such as organized, intelligent, and caring. Role identities include positions one holds such as parent, teacher, or soldier. Social identities include the important groups one associates with such as Christian, US Military, and Republican (Burke & Stets, 2009). The higher an identity is in the hierarchy, the more influence it holds over other identities lower in the hierarchy and the more likely an individual is to strive to maintain that identity (Stets & Burke, 2000).

Second is the notion of internal regulation and verification of one's identity standards through a "feedback loop," which guides both immediate behavior and identity change (Burke & Stets, 2009). This feedback loop is the mechanism through which consistency between one's identity standard and both external and internal feedback is evaluated. As long as there is verification, both an identity and the behavior associated with an identity remain unchanged. However, when individuals experience a discrepancy between an identity standard and the "input" portion of the loop, they are motivated to reduce the emotional turmoil. The greater the discrepancy, the greater the emotional turmoil and the greater the attempt to reduce the disturbance. The individual can choose to change his or her behavior, identity or identity standard to reduce turmoil (Burke & Stets, 2009).

Gender is a role identity, which includes the self-meaning of being masculine or feminine, tied to the status of gender, which is a social structural position with associated expectations (Stets & Burke, 1996). Unlike some role identities which are unique to specific situations (e.g. "worker"), gender is a master identity. Master identities often operate across situations, groups, and other roles (Carter, 2014). As a high level master identity, gender identity helps set the standard of other lower level identities and changes relatively slowly (Burke & Stets, 2009).

Gender identity, similar to other identities, is constructed and maintained as individuals interact within various social contexts (Calasanti, 2004; Stets & Burke, 1996). Furthermore, gender identities can be fluid, multiple, and fragmented. At any moment, men and women are "doing gender," which is actively shaped and performed in their daily experiences and intersects with a number of other social positions (Butler, 1990; Christensen & Jensen, 2014; West & Zimmerman, 1987). As men and women verify their gender identity in a variety of social contexts, they must do so within a ranked, gendered social order. That said, identity theory does not explicitly discuss the existence of multiple masculinities that are rank ordered with society. It is to this gap that we add a discussion of hegemonic masculinity.

Hegemonic Masculinity

Hegemonic masculinity was introduced by Connell as a way to make sense of how gender inequality is legitimized (Christensen & Jensen, 2014; Messerschmidt, 2012). Hegemonic masculinity assumes that masculinity is not a single or fixed category that some men achieve, but rather there are multiple masculinities. These multiple masculinities are defined and ordered in relation to an idealized masculinity (i.e. hegemonic masculinity) (Connell & Messerschmidt, 2005). The construction of both masculinity and femininity occurs within a dualistic system in which a dominant masculinity is defined against the inferior feminized other, as well as inferior forms of masculinity (Connell, 2005). Thus, hegemonic masculinity is inherently relational and is maintained, in part, by confirming that difference (i.e. non-hegemonic masculinities and femininity) is inferior (Lusher & Robins, 2009, p. 391; Messerschmidt, 2012). . . . .

For the purpose of this study, we define hegemonic masculinity as the privileged masculinity that is set in opposition to "lesser" forms of masculinity and femininity within a particular time and place. Additionally, we consider that gender relations vary across multiple levels: local, regional, and global (Connell, 2002, p. 53; Lusher & Robins, 2009). The US military, as a male-dominated institution is one component of the US gendered social order at the regional level. However, the response of individual men to the military occurs at the local level both inside and outside the military, with gender performance and resistance occurring in the local setting (Hinojosa, 2010; Lusher & Robins, 2009). Anti-war veterans are an ideal population in which to examine the interplay of regional and local hegemonic masculinity and identity construction.

Military and Masculinity

. . . Military masculinity is one privileged form of masculinity in the USA and many Western societies, and thus a type of hegemonic masculinity. Military masculinity includes "a set of beliefs, practices and attributes that can enable individuals, men and women, to claim authority on the basis of affirmative relationships with the military or with military ideas" (Belkin, 2012, p. 3). A distinct benefit of joining the military for men is "access to resources of a hegemonic masculinity" (Hinojosa, 2010, p. 180). While there are multiple forms of military masculinity that also vary across time and place, several common descriptors of military masculinity exist including: being physical fit and powerful, mentally strong, unemotional, heterosexual, as well as endurance and loyalty (Barrett, 1996; Woodward, 2000).

. . . By applying the workings of hegemonic masculinities, militaries build cohesion with an "idealized" model of the military member contributing to a shared sense of pride and motivate particular behavior by "feminizing" un-desirable behavior (Belkin, 2012; Duncanson, 2015; Goldstein, 2001).

Anti-War and the (Re)negotiation of Masculine Identity

. . . Given the strong connection between masculinity and the military, veterans who adopt an anti-war identity present a challenge to understanding hegemonic masculinity. In adopting an anti-war identity, men may be forced to renegotiate the meanings of their gender identity or encounter situations in which their gender identity standard is not verified. If one's gender identity is non-traditional, the individual must adopt meanings that are consistent with the non-traditional identity standard across various situations (Burke & Stets, 2009). If a man perceives that he is being viewed as feminine, he is more likely to respond to a threat to his masculinity and may exaggerate his masculine behavior in an attempt to change others' perceptions (Kaufman &

Johnson, 2004; Willer, Rogalin, Conlon, & Wojnowicz, 2013). Similarly, men who are unable or refuse to enact a hegemonic masculinity may engage in a "compensatory" masculinity that compensates for their lower position (Collison, 1992; Connell, 2005; Ezzell, 2012).

It is important to note that higher status people have more influence in defining the identities of those around them and are less impacted by those with less status and influence (Burke & Stets, 2009; Cast, Stets, & Burke, 1999). Thus, we might anticipate that men with higher status and more power, based on other aspects of their social status, such as race and class, are less likely to have their masculinity questioned and may be better able to resist or protest hegemonic masculinity. Additionally, the degree to which masculine identity is "threatened" will vary based on social status, which in turn varies across situations (Coston & Kimmel, 2012).

This study integrates hegemonic masculinity and identity theory to examine how exit from an institution that upholds hegemonic masculinity influences masculine identity and identity change among anti-war veterans. We focus on how men position themselves within the gendered hierarchy in relation to both their past military experience and current anti-war position. Specifically we ask, what happens to masculinity when veterans come to embrace an anti-war identity?

Methodology

The data for this study are a subset of interviews with 114 veterans collected between 2005 and 2009 assessing catalysts of identity change from pro-war to anti-war. We identified participants from an announcement on the following organization's websites: Veterans for Peace www.veteransforpeace.org, Vietnam Veterans Against the War www.vvaw.org, and Iraq Veterans against the War www.ivaw.org. The announcements requested contact with veterans who had experienced a significant change in perspectives on war over the life course. In addition, we identified subjects with a snowball sample from members within the Mennonite Church USA, a Christian pacifist denomination. . . .

Measuring Anti-War Position

Being in the military does not mean that an individual is "pro-war." Furthermore, anti-war does not mean anti-military. For the purpose of this study, anti-war is defined as actively opposing a particular war due to its being unjust or unnecessary (a Just War position) or opposing the use of war as a response to violence or injustice in any situation (a Pacifist position). Veterans' identity change from pro-war to anti-war was measured using an 8-point scale with responses ranging from an indiscriminant pro-war perspective (1), to a Just War position (4–5), to a Pacifist position (6–8) (Appendix). The scale was designed in conjunction with a Christian Ethicist (Yoder, 1992). The researcher asked each veteran what they believed to be the appropriate use of war at age 18 and then today. Following these open-ended questions, the researcher asked each veteran what position on the 8-point scale they most identified with at age 18 and today. The researcher used this scale to determine the extent of identity change over time as related to issues of peace and war.

Reflexive Statement

Throughout the data collection and analysis processes, we were acutely aware of the potential for bias based on the relationship of the researchers to the research context and participants (Broom, Hand, & Tovey, 2009). Foley suggests that biases can be minimized through awareness of one's position and its potential impact on the research results throughout the research process (2002). We were particularly conscious of gender incongruence (female to male) and affiliation with an anti-war position (Pini, 2005). The interviews were conducted by the second author, a female progressive pacifist Christian. While the interviewer identified herself primarily as a university professor, elements of her identity were sometimes revealed during the interview to aid in building rapport and understanding.

   Both authors transcribed, coded, and analyzed the data. The first author identifies as a female and Christian, but is not part of the pacifist movement and does not take an overtly anti-war position. We believe this improved objectivity in the analysis by creating distance between the researcher and the researched. Additionally, the analysis involved a number of discussions concerning the impact of both the interviewer's pacifist position and the position of both researchers as females.

Analysis

We transcribed the interviews verbatim, and then analyzed the transcripts by manually sorting and coding the material. We each independently coded responses to the question, what does it mean to be a good man today using line-by-line emergent coding. We then, together, grouped the responses into emergent categories through an iterative process. This involved expanding categories, eliminating categories, and collapsing categories based on the similarities of each (Charmez, 2006). Through this emergent coding, several distinct patterns of masculinity emerged. Upon further examination, these patterns reflected varying types of masculinity. . . .

Findings

We begin by providing an overview of respondents' discussion of adopting an anti-war identity and how that relates to their understanding of masculinity. We find that as respondents adopt an anti-war identity, many also re-defined what it meant to be a man and that social activism played a key role in how many of the men renegotiated their masculine identity. We then further explore variations in descriptions of masculine identity and describe three types of masculinity among our respondents.

Anti-War Identity Change and Masculine Identity

We chose veterans for the study that self-identified as anti-war veterans with each participant experiencing a significant identity change in relation to his position on war. Some veterans align with a particular anti-war movement (i.e. Veterans for Peace) and some do not align with a movement at all. That said, all of the veterans in our study currently position themselves as a 4 or above on the anti-war scale used by the interviewer (Appendix). Additionally, respondents describe their anti-war position as different from their perspective at age 18, in which they rated themselves from 1 to 3 on the anti-war scale with the majority of veterans stating an indiscriminant pro-war perspective (a 1 on the scale) as their primary belief concerning the appropriate use of war prior to joining the military.

Respondents explained that the situations they experienced either in the military, during combat, during college or civilian life post war, or in religious settings, resulted in a significant change in their position on war. Their criteria for being just, fair, honest, and doing what is right, tightened over time and the meanings for how to meet these requirements changed dramatically from being pro-war with few restraints on US actions abroad to adopting either the strict criteria of Just War Theory or being pacifists and believing all war is wrong or unnecessary to address injustice. As 18 year olds, these veterans believed that US leaders were knowledgeable and fair and thus could be trusted to do the right thing in response to violence and injustice in the world. Finally, most veterans at age 18 believed it takes a strong military to guarantee peace and justice against "bad guys" around the world. Whether their heroes were their WWII fathers or John Wayne, images of strength and aggression in response to bad guys dominated their meanings of what it was to be fair and protective of others. For example, a 67-year-old former Air Force pilot and Chaplain describes military service in terms of wanting to do the right thing as both a Christian and a good man.

> I went into the Vietnam conflict because the church thought being a good Christian was doing what the community wanted you to do like be in Vietnam. Because I was a man, I had the responsibility to defend the community and to respond in places where there would be danger. As a man, I had been conditioned to fight and defend those who were less capable. I would never have chosen to be a soldier without that context . . . I was bold and courageous and was shot at and saw people blown up and I didn't back away. . . . When I realized my

actions had an impact on the lives of other people, it was important for me to not harm others. From that place, I began the transition of asking what is the practical way that that works itself out? So what choices do I need to make now? #53

In changing their position on war, many respondents were challenged to consider what it meant to be a good man. Identity theory would explain this as a disruption to the gender identity standard (Burke & Stets, 2009). An anti-war position and a masculine identity standard may conflict, especially if one's masculine identity standard aligns with a form of military masculinity that values aggression, dominance, and violence. If the two identities become salient simultaneously, creating identity verification for one may invoke a large discrepancy in the other. As illustrated in the above quote, many respondents explained that prior to adopting an anti-war position, they believed that a good man should serve his country during difficult times.

Thus, respondents' discussion of what makes a good man today often involved a reflection on their changing perspective on war and how that impacted their definition of masculinity. At times respondents positioned themselves against what they termed a stereotypical form of masculinity that was advanced within the military.

> . . . it [military masculinity] put all the emphasis on machismo and physical strength. . . . #35

Some described their definition of masculinity while in the military as an "old way of thinking" or a "wrong way of thinking."

> Uh, being a man, I think, uh, now for me recognizes that, uh, you know, there are differences in gender but they're; the differences I see now are less stereotypical, um, than they have been. Being a man still includes integrity, being honest, and those types of things, standing up when you need to stand up. It takes on a different method or form or expression in the sense that, um, I don't know how to describe this, it becomes, um, more gentle? . . . But it's, it's, I guess it has less machismo in it or something. #12

We further find that the activism of many of our respondents allowed them to verify their masculine identity and solidify their anti-war identity, thus providing congruence between these identities. Respondents were able to reconfigure a localized hegemonic masculinity by verifying traits such as courage, service to country, and responsibility through their activism. Traits emphasized in the military were redefined to align with the respondents' anti-war position. Activism becomes a way for men to continue to position themselves against an inferior other. The "inferior other" appears to be those that are less enlightened or those still buying into the traditional military masculinity.

> It challenged me every time I had to get up and say I was anti-war and anti-war very publicly. I constantly had to present myself as a person that umm, did this very archetypally masculine role but in order to say in so many ways that I was opposed to what that role was doing, I had to like manufacture this side of me that was still masculine. I didn't want to be perceived as someone who wasn't really deserving of that role. #35

> It takes courage to be antiwar, especially after 9/11. #23

> I think that, it takes more to be an advocate for peace than it does for war. War is the easier avenue than peace. It's so difficult. #52

Differing Types of Masculinity

In examining respondents' definition of masculinity at age 18 and now we found 3 distinct types of masculinity among our respondents: Feminist Masculinity, Responsible/ Accountable Masculinity, and Enlightened Male Masculinity. Here we present the masculinity scripts within these typologies, as well as patterns occurring within each type. . . .

Feminist Masculinity

The first type of masculinity, which we call "Feminist Masculinity,"[1] is characterized by clear language in opposition to what respondents identified as traditional masculinity or being strong, dominant, and alpha. These men described a good man as one who is able to embrace "feminine qualities" including nurturing, cultivating, and empowering others, while rejecting traditional masculine qualities such as aggression and dominance.

Among this group, the change in definition of a good man at age 18 and today was spoken of in terms of a conscious turn from a traditional definition of masculinity to one that embraces femininity.

> A man at age 18 was the opposite of being a woman, and masculinity was the opposite of femininity but today I have so many feminists that I'm working with who are so fucking strong that my idea today is totally different . . . being a man was being strong, not showing emotions, not crying, being willing to do the things that sissies wouldn't be able to do . . . being hard, a fighter, keeping your word . . . There wasn't anything more important to me growing up than being a man. Today, a man is . . . I'm a very sensitive person, I'm able to cry now. I'm able to cry in front of other people. I'm actually very good at expressing myself and my emotions just flow. . . . #111

> At age 18 a good man was an alpha male. #16

This veteran used the imagery of the chalice (cup) and blade to explain traditional masculinity and femininity. He explained he is striving to be more nurturing and like the chalice than the blade (referring to the book title *The Chalice and the Blade* by Riane Eisler).

> I feel like the male has the blade and I gravitate toward the chalice and I feel . . . I don't know if impotent is the word . . . I don't want to be an alpha male and I struggle with that . . . To be nurturing and to be facilitative and to empower people and to invest in people and . . . to make people feel like they are more than they ever could have been you know. #16

> . . . being secure enough that I don't need to be a male chauvinist or think I need to be in charge. #49

The masculinity scripts within this type, more so than the other two types, overtly challenge hegemonic masculinity. Men in this group were also aware of their privilege as white men.

> Being aware of the power and privilege that I hold and trying to help those that don't have the same privileges find their place in life and in our culture and society. Particularly paying attention to non-white cultures, women. So having more of a service approach, a more holistic approach to who I am. #7

> You can be present enough to understand the cultural idea of what a man is and that it's largely at odds with what is good for you and your family and society in general. #76

Nine out of the 26 respondents fit this masculine type and shared several characteristics. All of the men, except for one 49 year old, were part of the Baby Boomer generation. Five of the eight men in this type were pacifist Mennonite pastors. As such, their activism was a lifestyle activism rather than a traditional protest activism as is seen among other respondents. All of the men were married and all but one has children. Only two were ever divorced. While seven of the eight reported some form of conflictive relationships during childhood, often abusive, these men were more likely than other respondents to describe some kind of healing experience post abuse.

Given these commonalities, we see the clearest example of identity non-verification among the Feminist Type. The regional- or societal-level hegemonic masculinity is not verified in the feedback received from those with whom the Feminist Group most often interacts. This included spouses, progressive peace church congregations, and their fellow pastors. Rather, their version of masculinity is verified within these interactions and their relative status (well-educated professional, married, white) allows them to challenge hegemonic masculinity.

Recently, scholars argue that hegemonic masculinity has the potential to be "unraveled" with resulting forms of masculinity that legitimate gender equality, as opposed to inequality. For Duncanson (2015), this "unraveling" occurs as men construct their identities in terms of equality with others, rather than through relations of opposition or domination (p. 3). It appears that this group comes closest to "constructing their identities through recognition of similarity, respect, interdependence, empathy and equality with others" (Duncanson, 2015, p. 3). The masculinity described by men in this group may best represent what Messerschmidt terms "equality masculinities," which "legitimate an egalitarian relationship between men and women, between masculinity and femininity, and among men" (2012, p. 73).

Responsible/Accountable Masculinity

The second masculine type is what we term "Responsible/Accountable" masculinity. This type includes being strong, wise, and aware of one's relation to others. A key feature of these men's responses was an emphasis on the necessity of taking responsibility for your actions because actions have consequences.

Men in this group were more likely to discuss masculinity using characteristics that were part of their military training such as loyalty, responsibility, and accountability. Similarly, there was less change in how men described masculinity at age 18 and today.

> I think to feel like a man in my experience is to feel strong, like I'm a presence, to be acknowledged and to be a good man at 18 umm, I don't think it was a conscious topic for me. The word that comes to me right now is strength and to use strength wisely. That's kind of a cliché among military folk but to use strength to protect others. To be a male today is somewhat similar but it's expanded to include not just strength but to be a person that is responsible and acknowledge your role with others. #35

These masculine scripts appear to reflect what Niva (1998) identifies as a shift in the hegemonic masculinity of the military which occurred during the time of the 1991 Gulf War and embraces a "tough but tender" position. However, for these men, masculinity is intentionally disconnected from the activities of the military as an organization. Men in this group also appear to redefine and display their masculinity through their activism and often describe this activism in terms of responsibility to others.

[describing masculinity at age 18] "Sexual and warfare prowess." [Describing masculinity today] Today . . . I'm still trying to work that one out . . . . umm honest, firm and caring. I don't know, it's kind of hard. You can say the same thing about all of humanity . . . responsibility to the whole. #97

I think a good man is someone who is able to do whatever it takes to get the important things done whether that's putting food on their family's table or getting the job done when people are counting on you. I think being a man is not making excuses when you don't want to do it . . . you can find an excuse . . . if you really want to do it, you can get it done. I think being a man means really just keeping your word. If you say you are going to do something, do it. A lot of this would apply to all humans. But I think this makes me highly accountable and I think it means, while I don't necessarily think it means to be violent, I think it means to recognize that we have a lot of aggression and assertiveness and don't deny that. #103

Seven out of the 26 respondents fit this type of masculinity. This group of men were predominantly Generation Xers (5 out of 8), or young Baby Boomers. This group had the highest percentage of respondents who were never married, however, it also included more fathers with children at home than the other two groups. While their activism activity today ranges from low to high, all but one of the men in this group named activist as a primary identity today. Additionally, four of the men in this group would identify as conscientious objectors if asked to serve today. Compared to the other men in the study, men in this group occupied lower social status due to age, education, job, being disabled, or retired (Table 45.1).

Enlightened Male Masculinity

The third type is the least rigidly defined of the masculine typologies. The veterans describe their masculinity as being strong, caring, wise, supportive, loving, and listening. We call this group the "Enlightened Male" group because the descriptions of a good man were mostly "gender neutral" and might be used to more broadly define good human behavior. While some terms seem more closely aligned with a traditional feminine role, this group did not explicitly contrast these feminine characteristics against traditional masculinity. Unlike the Feminist Masculinity type, there is less resistance or protest language in this type. Change in masculinity from age 18 to today was described as movement toward becoming a better person.

Still, a good man goes to work . . . But there's more to life than what you do for work . . . I think I've gained some degree of wisdom. At least I know what I don't know. I'm not as idealistic but more patient than I once was. #52

Strong loving, leading still, the change is less macho—not that I was a macho kid but there is less emphasis on being a male and its more now about being human. That's something that I can see growing throughout my life. #134

Ten out of the 26 respondents fit this type of masculinity. Eight of the men in this group were Baby Boomers. All but two of the men in this group had a lower socioeconomic status than the men in the Feminist Group. Additionally, this group had the highest percentage of divorced respondents. Activism was a primary identity for 80% of men in this group. Six of the 10 in this type described experiences of trauma in war or childhood, with 8 experiencing combat while in the military. Additionally, only five expressed a religious identity, which is much lower than the feminist group.

Men in this group are more likely than the men in the Feminist Group to assume a Just War Position—opposing some wars but not all wars. The anti-war identity and masculine identity of being a "better human" are able to align. Additionally, men in this group are more likely to verify their masculinity from a position of subordination due to their lower social status positions relative to the men in the Feminist Masculinity group. Thus, this group may be less able to protest or resist hegemonic masculinity.

Table 45.1 Characteristics of Respondents by Masculine Type

	Total (n = 26)	Responsible/ Accountable (n = 7)	Enlightened Male (n = 10)	Feminist (n = 9)
Age				
20–39	7	5	2	0
40–59	9	1	2	6
60–86	10	1	6	3
Occupation				
Blue collar	10	4	5	1
White collar	16	3	5	8
Education				
High school	0	0	0	0
Some college	10	3	5	2
Undergraduate degree	9	4	4	1
Graduate degree	7	0	1	6
Marital status				
Married/never divorced	12	2	4	6
Divorced now remarried	9	1	5	3
Divorced now single	1	0	1	0
Single/never married	4	4	0	0
War served				
Vietnam	12	2	6	4
Iraq I	1	0	0	1
Iraq II	4	2	2	0
No war	9	3	2	4
Military branch				
Army	12	2	6	4
Navy	4	4	0	0
Airforce	5	0	2	3
Marines	5	1	2	2
# Career	4	0	2	2
# with combat experience	13	3	8	2
# with PTSD	5	1	3	1

Note: PTSD, Post Traumatic Stress Disorder.

Discussion and Conclusions

In examining men's understanding of masculinity, we found that the respondents had various ways of renegotiating the meaning of hegemonic masculinity and their own idiosyncratic position within the gendered hierarchy. Some men overtly protested and/or resisted hegemonic masculinity. Others, while rejecting specific wars or war all together, are still complicit in the hierarchy of masculinities, but no longer allow masculine military ideologies and icons to define their positions in the gendered social order. However, to some extent, all of the respondents make sense of their masculinity through their social activism related to peace and social justice and integrity of acting on their beliefs.

We identified three types of masculinity among our respondents. Ultimately, we found that variations in masculine identity were connected to variations in the men's social status. This aligns with current research in masculinity that argues masculinity is best understood by considering men's intersecting social statuses (Christensen & Jensen, 2014). Men in the Feminist Masculinity type were best able to challenge conventional, regional hegemonic masculinity and thus free themselves to embrace person identity standards such as nurturing, good listener, and empowering. This contrasts with men in the Responsible/Accountable and Enlightened masculinity type who are not challenging the regional hegemonic masculinity but simply embracing an idiosyncratic masculinity that corresponds more closely to their antiwar identity.

The age and birth cohort of our respondents may be important as research suggests that the contents of desired manhood may change over the lifespan as older men are less able to display aspects of hegemonic masculinity such as physical strength or sexual prowess (Calasanti, 2004). Similarly, an individual's age during periods of socio-cultural change and historical events, such as the second wave of the feminist movement, may influence his or her identification with masculine or feminine traits. Furthermore, the time when the men were in the military is also important as military masculinity has itself shifted over time (Duncanson, 2015).

While the Enlightened Male and Feminist typologies are similar in age and birth cohorts, the higher social statuses of the Feminist type as married, fathers and working professionals may explain their freedom to challenge hegemonic masculinity in comparison to the Enlightened Males. The Enlightened Males, as lower status men, still embrace aspects of the hegemonic masculinity and benefit from aligning themselves with the hegemonic ideal. They align themselves by constructing a narrative

in which they are "better" men now than before and "better" men than those serving in the military. . . .

The challenge of re-entering civilian life after exiting the military, as well as the persistent connection between the military and masculinity necessitates research on the negotiation of masculine identities. The results presented here suggest that understanding identity formation and change in this re-entry process must continue to acknowledge multiple-ranked masculinities. Future studies should examine how veterans negotiate their anti-war and masculine identities in various groups. In addition, fatherhood and religion played an important role in the lives of many of our participants. A closer examination of these variables is needed.

Acknowledgements

This work would not be possible without the willing participation of each of the veterans interviewed. We would also like to thank Dr Susan Alexander for her helpful feedback on this article.

Note

1. This term has been used in other research on masculinities (see, e.g., Hurtado & Sinha, 2008).

References

Barrett, F. (1996). The organizational construction of hegemonic masculinity: The case of the US Navy. *Gender, Work & Organization, 3*(3), 129–142.

Belkin, A. (2012). *Bring me men: Military masculinity and the benign façade of the American empire 1898 to 2001*. New York, NY: Columbia University Press.

Broom, A., Hand, K., & Tovey, P. (2009). The role of gender, environment and individual biography in shaping qualitative interview data. *International Journal of Social Research Methodology, 12*(1), 51–65.

Burke, P. J., & Stets, J. E. (2009). *Identity theory*. New York, NY: Oxford University Press.

Butler, J. (1990). *Gender trouble: Feminism and the subversion of gender*. New York: Routledge.

Calasanti, T. (2004). Feminist gerontology and old men. *Journal of Gerontology: Social Sciences, 59*(6), s305–s314.

Carter, M. J. (2014). Gender socialization and identity theory. *Social Sciences, 3*, 242–263.

Cast, A. D., Stets, J. E., & Burke, P. J. (1999). Does the self-conform to the views of others? *Social Psychology Quarterly, 62*(1), 68–82.

Charmez, K. (2006). *Constructing grounded theory.* London: Sage.

Christensen, A. D., & Jensen, S. Q. (2014). Combining hegemonic masculinity and intersectionality. *NORMA: International Journal for Masculinity Studies, 9*(1), 60–75.

Collison, D. (1992). Engineering humor: Masculinity, joking and conflict in shop-floor relations. In M. Kimmel & M. Messner (Eds.), *Men's lives* (pp. 232–246). New York, NY: Macmillan.

Connell, R. W. (2002). *Gender.* Cambridge, MA: Polity.

Connell, R. W. (2005). *Masculinities.* Oakland: University of California Press.

Connell, R. W., & Messerschmidt, J. W. (2005). Hegemonic masculinity: Rethinking the concept. *Gender & Society, 19*(6), 829–859.

Coston, B., & Kimmel, M. (2012). Seeing privilege where it isn't: Marginalized masculinities and the intersectionality of privilege. *Journal of Social Issues, 68*(1), 97–111.

Duncanson, C. (2015). Hegemonic masculinity and the possibility of change in gender relations. *Men and Masculinities, 18*(2), 231–248.

Ezzell, M. (2012). "I'm in Control" compensatory: Manhood in a therapeutic community. *Gender & Society, 26*(2), 190–215.

Foley, D. E. (2002). Critical ethnography: The reflexive turn. *International Journal of Qualitative Studies in Education, 15*(4), 469–490.

Goldstein, J. (2001). *War and gender, How gender shapes the War system and vice versa.* Cambridge, MA: Cambridge University Press.

Hinojosa, R. (2010). Doing hegemony: Military, men, and constructing a hegemonic masculinity. *The Journal of Men's Studies, 18*(2), 179–194.

Hurtado, A., & Sinha, M. (2008). More than men: Latino feminist masculinities and intersectionality. *Sex Roles, 59*(5–6), 337–349.

Kaufman, J. M., & Johnson, C. (2004). Stigmatized individuals and the process of identity. *The Sociological Quarterly, 45*(4), 807–833.

Lusher, D., & Robins, G. (2009). Hegemonic and other masculinities in local social contexts. *Men and Masculinities, 11*(4), 387–423.

Messerschmidt, J. W. (2012). Engendering gendered knowledge: Assessing academic appropriation of hegemonic masculinity. *Men and Masculinities, 15*, 56–76.

Niva, S. (1998). Tough and tender: New world order masculinity and the Gulf War. In M. Zalewski & J. Parpart (Eds.), *The man question in international relations* (pp. 109–128). Boulder, CO: Westview.

Pini, B. (2005). Interviewing men: Gender and the collection and interpretation of qualitative data. *Journal of Sociology, 41*(2), 201–216.

Smith, T., & True, G. (2014). Warring identities: Identity conflict and the mental distress of American veterans of the Wars in Iraq and Afghanistan. *Society and Mental Health, 4*(2), 147–161.

Stets, J., & Burke, P. (2000). Identity theory and social identity theory. *Social Psychology Quarterly, 63*, 224–237.

Stets, J. E., & Burke, P. J. (1996). Gender, control, and interaction. *Social Psychology Quarterly, 59*(3), 193–220.

Stryker, S. (1980) [2002]. *Symbolic interactionism: A social structural version.* Caldwell, NJ: Blackburn Press.

West, C., & Zimmerman, D. H. (1987). Doing gender. *Gender & Society, 1*(2), 125–151.

Willer, R., Rogalin, C., Conlon, B., & Wojnowicz, M. (2013). Overdoing gender: A test of the masculine overcompensation thesis. *American Journal of Sociology, 118*(4), 980–1022.

Woodward, R. (2000). Warrior heroes and little green men: Soldiers, military training, and the construction of rural masculinities. *Rural Sociology, 65*(4), 640–657.

Yoder, J. H. (1992). *Nevertheless: Varieties of religious pacifism.* Scottdale, PA: Herald Press.

Appendix

The Militarist/Pacifist Continuum Scale: **What did you believe about the appropriate use of war when you were 18 and what do you believe today? More than one response or a different response than those listed is fine.**

(1) It is appropriate for a nation to respond to an injustice anywhere in the world in any way it sees fit.

(2) War is appropriate only to defend one's national self-interest.

(3) War is appropriate if it meets the criteria of being a "Just Cause" to redress a wrong (this is a loose application of Just War Theory).

(4) War is only appropriate if it meets all eight Just War criteria. These include a just cause such as self-defense or to redress a wrong,

- waged by an authority determined to be legitimate, that is, a government,
- must be formally declared rather than covert,
- must be fought with intention to establish peace versus for resources,
- must be a last resort: all other options must be exhausted first,
- there must be a reasonable hope of success to redress the wrong,
- violence and suffering of the people must be proportional to the outcome that is possible, and

- the weapons used in war must discriminate between combatants and non-combatants.

(5) Christians or persons of conscience should never be involved in war but the use of war by the nation/state is sometimes necessary.

(6) Neither the Christian or person of conscience nor the nation/state should engage in war under any circumstances because it is contrary to the life and teaching of Jesus or another leader the person follows.

(7) Neither the Christian or person of conscience nor the nation/state should engage in war because all human life is sacred.

(8) I believe there are nonviolent means to resolve conflict peacefully w/o recourse to war or violence.

ABOUT THE CONTRIBUTORS

Eric Anderson is a professor and a leading authority on masculinities and sexualities research. He is the architect of inclusive masculinity theory and the author of seventeen books, including *21st Century Jocks, Out in Sport, The Monogamy Gap*, and *The Changing Dynamics of Bisexual Men's Lives*. www.ProfessorEricAnderson.com.

Kristen Barber is an associate professor of sociology and faculty affiliate in women, gender, and sexuality studies at Southern Illinois University, Carbondale. She is the author of the book *Styling Masculinity: Gender, Class, and Inequality in the Men's Grooming Industry* (Rutgers University Press).

Dana Berkowitz holds a PhD and is an associate professor of sociology and women's and gender studies at Louisiana State University. She is the author of *Botox Nation: Changing the Face of America* (New York University Press). Her scholarship has also appeared in high-impact journals such as *Journal of Marriage and Family, Qualitative Health Research, Journal of Contemporary Ethnography, Qualitative Sociology*, and *Symbolic Interaction*.

Tristan Bridges is an assistant professor of sociology at the University of California, Santa Barbara. He studies shifts in gender and sexual identity and inequality among men and, most recently, coedited the anthology *Exploring Masculinities: Identity, Inequality, Continuity, and Change* (Oxford University Press, 2016).

Jessica Schwartz Cameron received her PhD in social psychology from Stanford University and was a postdoctoral scholar and lecturer at the Haas School of Business at the University of California, Berkeley. She is currently working as a user experience researcher in Edinburgh, United Kingdom.

Daniel L. Carlson is an assistant professor of family, health, and policy at the University of Utah, where he studies the causes and consequences of change in couples' divisions of labor.

Erin Casey holds a PhD and MSW, and is an associate professor of social work and criminal justice at the University of Washington, Tacoma. She codirects the Mobilizing Men for Violence Prevention research collaboration and conducts research related to gender-based violence prevention.

Sapna Cheryan is an associate professor of psychology at the University of Washington. Her research interests include identity, stereotypes, and prejudice, and she has published numerous articles on these topics in journals such as *Psychological Science*, the *Journal of Personality & Social Psychology*, and *Psychological Bulletin*.

Marianne Cooper is a sociologist at the Clayman Institute for Gender Research at Stanford University. She is the author of the book *Cut Adrift: Families in Insecure Times*.

Bethany M. Coston is assistant professor of health and queer studies at Virginia Commonwealth University, and a sociologically trained activist scholar who has spent time in the Midwest and on the East Coast educating, protesting, and participating in research on the making of sexual identities, violence, health and wellness, and community-based organizing. She is a former predoctoral population health fellow with the National LGBT Health Education Center at Fenway Health and, currently, a Robert Wood Johnson Foundation New Connections scholar.

Angela Cowan is a postgraduate student in the Department of Sociology at the University of Newcastle. Her thesis topic is an investigation of the discursive world of young children. She is a trained primary schoolteacher and has worked as an observer on a number of psychiatric research projects.

Sarah Diefendorf is a PhD candidate at the University of Washington. Her research investigates moral debates and divides around gender and sexuality in the evangelical church.

Emily Dutton is a queer and feminist writer and activist who graduated from the University of Alberta women's and gender studies honors program in 2015. She is grateful to be a guest living and working on stolen indigenous lands in Treaty 6 and Métis Nation traditional territory.

Yen Le Espiritu is a distinguished professor of the Department of Ethnic Studies at the University of California, San Diego. She is also a founding member of the Critical Refugee Studies Collective.

Andrea Fitzroy holds an MS and is a doctoral candidate in sociology at Georgia State University with a specialization in gender and sexuality and a graduate certificate in gerontology. Her research interests include the broad spectrum of intimacy, from romantic relationships to intimate care partnerships among older adults.

Edward Flores is an associate professor in sociology at the University of California, Merced. He is the author of the forthcoming book *Prophetic Redemption* (New York University Press), as well as *God's Gangs* (New York University Press).

Tanya Golash-Boza is a professor of sociology at the University of California, Merced. She has published several books and dozens of articles and book chapters. Her latest book, *Deported: Immigrant Policing, Disposable Labor and Global Capitalism* (New York University Press, 2015), was awarded the Distinguished Contribution to Research Book Award from the Latino/a Studies Section of the American Sociological Association.

Lise Gotell is a professor of women's and gender studies at the University of Alberta. Her research focuses on Canadian sexual assault law and gender violence policies. She is the national chair of the Women's Legal Education and Action Fund, an advocacy with a thirty-two-year record of using equality rights activism to advance the rights of Canadian women and girls.

Chong-Suk Han is an associate professor of sociology at Middlebury College. His research focuses on the intersection of race, gender, and sexuality, particularly among gay Asian American men. His publications have appeared in several journals, including *Sexuality and Culture*, *Social Identities*, *AIDS Education and Prevention*, and *Contemporary Justice Review*, among others. In 2006, he was the recipient of the Martin Levine Dissertation Award from the Sexualities Section of the American Sociological Association.

Sarah Hanson has her master's in sociology from Northern Illinois University and is working on her doctorate at Georgia State University, with an emphasis on gender and sexuality. Her research varies in the gender and sexuality sphere, ranging from BDSM to division of labor in the household.

Julie Hart holds a PhD and is an associate professor of sociology at Ohio Dominican University. Her areas of expertise include peace and war and nonviolent social change.

Abdullah Hasan is a political science honors graduate from the University of Connecticut. His research interests include gender politics, national security, and constructions of male masculinities, especially in the Islamic context.

Jocelyn A. Hollander is a professor of sociology at the University of Oregon.

Pierrette Hondagneu-Sotelo is a professor of sociology at the University of Southern California. She is the author of several books on gender and immigration, and her most recent book is *Paradise Transplanted: Migration and the Making of California Gardens* (University of California Press, 2014).

Ellen Jordan in the early 1990s, along with two research assistants, began an observational project in the early 1900s in a number of schools and preschools to examine the interactions of young children with their teachers and one another, with an emphasis on gender. This resulted in the publication of five articles in academic journals between 1995 and 2002. She has since moved on to other topics, but digital transcriptions of the original observations are still available.

Zehra F. Kabasakal Arat is a professor of political science at the University of Connecticut. Her research explores theoretical and empirical questions pertaining to human rights in a global context, with an emphasis on women's rights.

Zach Katagiri lives in New York City and works for Columbia University. He lives with his wife Amanda and their eight-month-old son Alden. He hopes to instill in Alden what it means to be a kind and thoughtful man and knows the world needs empathic men more than ever before.

Michael Kaufman holds a PhD and is an educator and writer focused on engaging men and boys to promote gender equality and end violence against women. He has worked in forty-five countries, including extensively with the United Nations. He is the cofounder of the White Ribbon Campaign, the largest effort in the world of men working to end violence against women, and is the author or editor of seven books, including an award-winning novel. His articles and books have been translated into fourteen languages.

Michael Kehler is a research professor of masculinities studies in education at the Werklund School of Education, University of Calgary, Canada. His research addresses the intersections of masculinities, body image, health, boys' literacies, counterhegemonic practices, homophobia, and men as change agents. His work is published nationally and internationally in such journals as the *Canadian Journal of Education*, *McGill Journal of Education*, and the *International Journal of Men's Health*, as well as several coedited books including *Boys' Bodies: Speaking the Unspoken* (Peter Lang, 2010) and *The Problem with Boys' Education: Beyond the Backlash* (Routledge Publishing, 2009).

Allen Kim is an associate professor of sociology at International Christian University in Tokyo, Japan. His research interests include gender and globalization, gender inequality in Asia, work and entrepreneurship, and family and aging.

Michael Kimmel is a SUNY distinguished professor of sociology and gender studies at Stony Brook University. He is the founder and editor of the scholarly journal *Men and Masculinities*. He is the author of many books, including *Angry White Men*, *Manhood in America*, *The Gendered Society*, and the bestseller *Guyland*.

Paul Kivel is a social justice educator, activist, and author of *Men's Work*, *Boys Will Be Men*, *Helping Teens Stop Violence*, *Build Community and Stand for Justice*, and a new revised fourth edition of *Uprooting Racism*. www.paulkivel.com.

Neill Korobov is a professor and director of the PhD program in the Department of Psychology at the University of West Georgia. He uses a discursive approach to examine the ways that romantic couples pursue intimacy and conflict in their natural interactional contexts.

Kelsy Kretschmer is an assistant professor of sociology at Oregon State University, where she researches and teaches on social movements and organizations. Her current book, *Not NOW: Bureaucracy and Factionalism in the National Organization for Women*, is forthcoming from the University of Minnesota Press.

Charis E. Kubrin is a professor of criminology, law, and society at the University of California, Irvine. She has published widely on the intersection of music, culture, and social identity, particularly as it applies to hip-hop and youth in disadvantaged communities.

Leanna Madill received her PhD in education at the University of Victoria in 2011 and her Social Sciences and Humanities Research Council–funded dissertation is titled *Scripting Their Stories: Parents' Experiences with Their Adolescents and Video Games*. She now works with teens and parents in her private counseling practice, Life Dances Counselling.

Martha McCaughey is a professor of sociology and a faculty affiliate of the Gender, Women's, and Sexuality Studies Program at Appalachian State University. She is the author of a variety of books and articles on gender, violence, technology, and the body, including *The Caveman Mystique: Pop-Darwinism and the Debates over Sex, Violence, and Science*. She blogs at www.seejanefightback.com.

Amy D. McDowell is an assistant professor of sociology at the University of Mississippi. Her research focuses on the intersection of religion, culture, gender, and sexuality.

James W. Messerschmidt is a professor of sociology and chair of the Criminology Department at the University of Southern Maine. He has written widely on masculinities, and his most recent book is *Masculinities in the Making*.

Michael A. Messner is a professor of sociology and gender studies at the University of Southern California. He teaches and writes about gender and sport, gender-based violence, and war and peace.

Benoît Monin is the Bowen H. and Janice Arthur McCoy Professor of Ethics, Psychology, and Leadership at Stanford University, with appointments at the Graduate School of Business and in the Department of Psychology.

David Nylund holds an MSW and PhD, and is a professor of social work at California State University, Sacramento. He is the clinical director of the Gender Health Center, an agency that serves the transgender and queer communities.

C. J. Pascoe is an associate professor of sociology and the Nancy and David L. Petrone Faculty Scholar at the University of Oregon. With Tristan Bridges, she is the editor of *Exploring Masculinities: Identity, Inequality, Continuity and Change*.

David S. Pedulla is an assistant professor in the Department of Sociology at Stanford University. His research interests include race and gender stratification, labor markets, and economic and organizational sociology.

Jessica Pfaffendorf is an advanced PhD candidate in the School of Sociology at the University of Arizona. Her areas of interest include social psychology, inequality and stratification, gender, culture, and deviance.

Karen Pyke is a professor of sociology and distinguished teaching professor at the University of California, Riverside, and a visiting professor at St. George's University in Grenada, West Indies. As a critical race feminist theorist, Pyke's research on Asian Americans has contributed to an understanding of internalized racial oppression and intersectionality.

Hernan Ramirez is an assistant professor of sociology at Florida State University. His research focuses on Mexican immigrant entrepreneurship, immigrant social mobility, gender, and work.

Victoria Redel is the author of three books of poetry and five books of fiction, most recently the novel *Before Everything*.

Stefan Robinson holds a PhD in sociology, which he attained at the University of Winchester in the United Kingdom. He is currently working as a researcher in local government.

Don Sabo holds a PhD and is a professor of health policy at D'Youville College in Buffalo, New York. He has coauthored *Humanism in Sociology*, *Jock Sports & Male Identity*, and *Sport, Men and the Gender Order: Critical Feminist Perspectives*. His most recent books include *Sex, Violence and Power in Sports: Rethinking Masculinity* and *Men's Health & Illness: Gender, Power & the Body*. He has conducted many national surveys on gender issues in sport, is a trustee of the Women's Sports Foundation, and coauthored the 1997 Presidents' Council on Physical Fitness and Sports report "Physical Activity & Sport in the Lives of Girls."

Kathy Sanford is a professor in the Faculty of Education, Curriculum and Instruction at the University of Victoria, Canada. Her research interests include learning through video game play, gender, twenty-first-century learners, and digital electronic portfolios to support continuous learning for all students. Her work with video gamers spans over ten years of working with youth as collaborators and informants, enabling a deep understanding of ways in which gamers utilize their skills in diverse ways in their lives.

Kristen Schilt is an associate professor of sociology at the University of Chicago, where she serves as the faculty director for the Center for the Study of Gender and Sexuality. Her work focuses on the cultural processes that maintain gender and sexual inequalities.

Tyler Smith is a member of the Social Work and Care Coordination Team at the University of Washington–Medical Center and a disease intervention specialist for Public Health–Seattle & King County. In addition to medical systems and infectious disease research, his other areas of interest include health-care administration and relevant application of social work theory, intimate partner violence in same-gender relationships, and examining the experiences of LGBTQ youth within the child welfare system.

Gloria Steinem is a writer, lecturer, political activist, and feminist organizer. She travels nationally and internationally as an organizer and lecturer and is a frequent media spokeswoman on issues of equality.

Anjel Stough-Hunter is an assistant professor of sociology at Ohio Dominican University. Her research focuses on the importance of communities in our understanding of masculinity, health, and the environment.

Sarah Thébaud is an associate professor of sociology at the University of California, Santa Barbara. Her research identifies social psychological and institutional-level processes that contribute to gender inequalities in the workplace, in families, and in higher education.

Tara Leigh Tober is a sociologist at the University of California, Santa Barbara. She studies collective memory in post–World War II Ireland and is interested in sociological research on inequality.

Ann Travers is an associate professor of sociology at Simon Fraser University. She lives in Vancouver, British Columbia.

Ronald Weitzer is a professor of sociology at George Washington University. He has conducted research on police–community relations and sex work, among other things, and has an abiding interest in the relationship between the media and society.

Adam White is a lecturer in sport and physical education at the University of Bedfordshire. He researches the intersection of masculinities and young men's lives, with a particular focus on the role and function of contact sport in educational contexts.

Adia Harvey Wingfield is a professor of sociology at Washington University in St. Louis. Her research examines racial and gender inequality in professional workplaces, and she is the author of the award-winning book *No More Invisible Man: Race and Gender in Men's Work.*